P9-DBJ-931

ADDITIONAL COOKBOOKS AND DVD SETS AVAILABLE FROM THE PUBLISHER OF *COOK'S COUNTRY* INCLUDE:

The *Cook's Country* Cookbook
The *America's Test Kitchen* Family Baking Book
The *America's Test Kitchen* Family Cookbook
America's Best Lost Recipes
The Best of *America's Test Kitchen* 2009
The Best of *America's Test Kitchen* 2008
The Best of *America's Test Kitchen* 2007
Cook's Country 2007 Annual Edition
Cook's Country 2006 Annual Edition
Cook's Country 2005 Annual Edition

THE BEST RECIPE SERIES

The Best Slow and Easy Recipes
The Best Chicken Recipes
The Best International Recipe
The Best Make-Ahead Recipe
The Best 30-Minute Recipe
The Best Light Recipe
The *Cook's Illustrated* Guide to Grilling and Barbecue
Best American Side Dishes
Cover & Bake
The New Best Recipe
Steaks, Chops, Roasts, and Ribs
Baking Illustrated
Restaurant Favorites at Home
Perfect Vegetables
The Quick Recipe
Italian Classics
The Best American Classics
The Best Soups & Stews

THE *AMERICA'S TEST KITCHEN* SERIES

(companion cookbooks and DVD sets to our hit public television series)
America's Test Kitchen: The 2009 season companion cookbook
Behind the Scenes with *America's Test Kitchen:* 2008 season companion cookbook
Test Kitchen Favorites: 2007 season companion cookbook
Cooking at Home with *America's Test Kitchen:* 2006 season companion cookbook
America's Test Kitchen Live! 2005 season companion cookbook
Inside *America's Test Kitchen:* 2004 season companion cookbook
Here in *America's Test Kitchen:* 2003 season companion cookbook
The *America's Test Kitchen* Cookbook: 2002 season companion cookbook
The *America's Test Kitchen* 2008 season 4-DVD boxed set
The *America's Test Kitchen* 2007 season 4-DVD boxed set
The *America's Test Kitchen* 2006 season 4-DVD boxed set
The *America's Test Kitchen* 2005 season 4-DVD boxed set
The *America's Test Kitchen* 2004 season 4-DVD boxed set
The *America's Test Kitchen* 2003 season 4-DVD boxed set
The *America's Test Kitchen* 2002 season 4-DVD boxed set
The *America's Test Kitchen* 2001 season 2-DVD boxed set

ADDITIONAL BOOKS FROM THE EDITORS OF *COOK'S ILLUSTRATED* MAGAZINE INCLUDE:

The Cook's Bible
The *Cook's Illustrated* Complete Book of Pasta and Noodles
The Kitchen Detective
834 Kitchen Quick Tips
1993–2008 *Cook's Illustrated* Master Index
Cook's Illustrated Annual Editions from each year of publication (1993–2008)

To order any of our cookbooks listed above, give us a call at 800-611-0759 inside the U.S., or at 515-246-6911 if calling from outside the U.S.
You can order subscriptions, gift subscriptions, and any of our books by visiting our online store at www.cookscountry.com.

$35.00

Copyright 2008 © by The Editors of Cook's Country
All rights reserved, including the right of reproduction in whole or in part in any form.
Published by America's Test Kitchen, 17 Station Street, Brookline, MA 02445
ISBN-13: 978-1-933615-37-0   ISSN: 1552-1990

To get home delivery of *Cook's Country,* call 800-526-8447 inside the U.S., or 515-247-7571 if calling from outside the U.S., or subscribe online at www.cookscountry.com.

2008 Recipe Index

RC = Recipe card
IBC = Inside back cover

Cook's Country

FEBRUARY/MARCH 2008

Ultimate Garlic Roast Chicken
Secrets to Best Garlic Flavor

Chocolate Cake, Texas-Style!
Cake, Fudge, and Icing

Rating Spaghetti Sauces
Just Like Fresh-Cooked?

MAKE-AHEAD COFFEE CAKE
Easy Fridge-to-Oven Recipe

GARLICKY OVEN FRIES
No-Mess "Deep-Fried" Crunch

SOUTHERN CORN BREAD
Golden Crust, Bold Corn Flavor

BIG BEEF CHILI
Easier and Better

PORK POT ROAST
Easy Slow-Cooker Technique

CHICAGO ROAST BEEF
Spicy, Italian-Style Jus

COLD-OVEN POUND CAKE
Tender Crumb, Big Crust

BAKED STUFFED SHRIMP
Juicy Shrimp, Crisp Stuffing

TESTING PEPPER MILLS
Winner Grinds Competition!

$4.95 U.S./$6.95 CANADA

Our $1,000 Contest Winner!
Donna Bardocz of Howell, Mich., won first place in our muffin contest with a unique recipe that combines sweet and savory ingredients. See page 4 for **Grandma's Special Dutch Apple Cheese Muffins.**

0 74470 05251 7

Cook's Country

Dear Country Cook,

These days, the slow food movement is introducing many folks to the notion of eating locally as if this were a new idea. Books such as The 100-Mile Diet and Barbara Kingsolver's Animal, Vegetable, Miracle proffer pretty much the same advice. For anyone who grew up in the country, this notion seems about as original as promoting the joys of sitting by a warm fire in January.

My neighbor Tom used to ice fish every year, his portable plywood shack sitting behind the garage the other 10 months. Yes, he brought a good supply of hot chocolate laced with peppermint schnapps, plenty of tip-ups (fishing poles with flags that tip up when a fish is hooked), and, of course, more than his share of fishing stories about cars falling through the ice during spring thaw. Tom and our other Vermont neighbors have served us bear, moose, venison, woodchuck, squirrel, rabbit, and wild turkey, not to mention "locally sourced" goat cheese, watercress, and fiddlehead ferns.

None of this is revolutionary. Back in the 1950s and '60s when I worked on a small mountain farm, my neighbors rarely traveled beyond the town line, so it was no surprise that they ate locally. You had to wait until summer for any sort of berry, and the only "fresh" item on the table throughout the winter was milk from the one cow out back.

For many of us in America, however, locally grown food is no picnic. In fact, each winter our family still relies on four freezers stocked with local beef and pork, and our root cellar offers only apples, beets, Brussels sprouts, and potatoes. Let's be honest. There is something to be said for grapefruit in December.

Locally grown food? Sure. That is what our family eats most nights for dinner, but that doesn't mean we can't enjoy a crate of clementines at Christmas.

Christopher Kimball
Founder and Editor, Cook's Country Magazine

A fisherman and his catch on the frozen surface of a lake in Minnesota, 1955.
Photographer: Evans/Three Lions/Getty Images

FEBRUARY/MARCH 2008

Cook's Country

departments

in every issue

features

Founder and Editor Christopher Kimball
Editorial Director Jack Bishop
Executive Editor Amanda Agee
Deputy Editor Bridget Lancaster
Senior Editors Scott Kathan
Jeremy Sauer
Test Kitchen Director Erin McMurrer
Test Cooks Kelley Baker
Meredith Butcher
Greg Case
Cali Rich
Diane Unger
Assistant Test Cook Lynn Clark
Online Managing Editor Katherine Bell
Online Editor Kate Mason
Online Assistant Editor Leaya Lee
Copy Editor Will Gordon
Market Research Manager Melissa Baldino
Editorial Assistant Meredith Smith
Senior Kitchen Assistant Nadia Domeq
Kitchen Assistants Maria Elena Delgado
Ena Gudiel
David Lentini
Contributing Editor Eva Katz
Consulting Editor Guy Crosby

Design Director Amy Klee
Senior Designer, Magazines Julie Bozzo
Designers Tiffani Beckwith
Jay Layman
Erica Lee
Christine Vo
Staff Photographer Daniel J. van Ackere

Production Director Guy Rochford
Traffic & Projects Manager Alice Cummiskey
Production & Imaging Specialist Lauren Pettapiece
Color and Imaging Specialist Andrew Mannone

Vice President New Technology Craig Morrow
Systems Administrator S. Paddi McHugh
IT Development Manager Justin Greenough
Web Developer Doug Sisko
Support Technician Brandon Lynch

Chief Financial Officer Sharyn Chabot
Human Resources Manager Adele Shapiro
Controller Mandy Shito
Senior Accountant Aaron Goranson
Staff Accountant Connie Forbes
Office Manager Danielle Pezely
Receptionist Henrietta Murray

Vice President Marketing David Mack
Fulfillment & Circulation Manager Carrie Horan
Circulation Assistant Elizabeth Dayton
Direct Mail Director Adam Perry
Direct Mail Analyst Jenny Leong
Products Director Steven Browall
E-Commerce Marketing Manager Hugh Buchan
Partnership Marketing Manager Pamela Putprush
Marketing Copywriter David Goldberg
Customer Service Manager Jacqueline Valerio
Customer Service Representatives Julie Gardner
Jillian Nannicelli

Vice President Sales Demee Gambulos
Retail Sales & Marketing Manager Emily Logan
Retail Sales Associate Anthony King
Corporate Marketing Associate Bailey Vatalaro
Publicity Deborah Broide

ON THE COVER: PHOTOGRAPHY: StockFood/David Loftus. ILLUSTRATION: John Burgoyne.
IN THIS ISSUE: COLOR FOOD PHOTOGRAPHY: Keller + Keller. STYLING: Mary Jane Sawyer, Marie Piraino. ILLUSTRATION: Lisa Perrett.

Cook's Country magazine (ISSN 1552-1990), number 19, is published bimonthly by Boston Common Press Limited Partnership, 17 Station Street, Brookline, MA 02445. Copyright 2008 Boston Common Press Limited Partnership. Application to mail at periodical postage rates pending at Boston, Mass., and additional mailing offices. POSTMASTER: Send address changes to Cook's Country, P.O. Box 8382, Red Oak, IA 51591-1382. For subscription and gift subscription orders, subscription inquiries, or change-of-address notices, call 800-526-8447 in the U.S. or 515-247-7571 from outside the U.S., or write us at Cook's Country, P.O. Box 8382, Red Oak, IA 51591-1382.
PRINTED IN THE USA

Visit us at CooksCountry.com!
Go online for hundreds of recipes, food tastings, and up-to-date equipment reviews. You can get a behind-the-scenes look at our test kitchen, talk to our cooks and editors, enter recipe contests, and share recipes and cooking tips with the *Cook's Country* community.

READERS SHARE CLEVER TIPS FOR EVERYDAY COOKING CHALLENGES

Slip and Slide

I enjoy making individual desserts like mousses and puddings, but the problem I always run into is transporting the individual cups in and out of the refrigerator: I either have to grab them one at a time or watch them slide around when I use a tray or cookie sheet. I discovered that my large muffin tin works perfectly to hold the six 6-ounce cups I serve the dessert in. There's no more sliding around, and it's easy to bring them all to the table at once.

Lia Soscia, North Bellmore, N.Y.

Mix in Your Pitcher

On a busy day of cooking when clean bowls were in short supply, I found a new use for my plastic pitcher. When preparing a recipe that calls for dry ingredients to be mixed separately before being slowly incorporated into the wet ingredients, I combine the dry ingredients in the pitcher. This gives me more control over how much of the dry ingredients I add at a time and helps prevent spills.

Jessica Anderson
Galloway, Ohio

DOUBLE DUTY

Diced Avocado

When I need to cube a lot of avocados for a big batch of guacamole, I slice them in half and remove the pits. I then press the avocados into a grid-style cooling rack and slide the peel off, leaving perfect ½-inch cubes of avocado in no time.

Diane Conn
Sonora, Calif.

Easy Squeeze!

PEPPER PRESS

An easy way to finely chop jarred peppers is to place them in the hopper of your garlic press and squeeze. It's a quick way to add heat to your favorite dishes.

Stephanie Foust
Alhambra, Calif.

SMART COOKIE

If you don't have an unrimmed cookie sheet, just bake your cookies on a baking sheet turned upside down. Cookies will slide right off the bottom (now the top!) of the pan and onto a cooling rack.

John Davis
Cornelius, N.C.

NEW COUNTERTOP

I love to bake, but my kitchen is very short on counter space. To create another work surface, I bought a large (24- by 18-inch) piece of plexiglass at the lumber store for a few dollars. I set it over my sink and the adjoining counter, and it makes a nice space to knead and shape dough or to roll out and cut pie crust, biscuits, or cookies.

Liz Bierig
Mukilteo, Wash.

THUMBELINA

During the holidays, I make tons of thumbprint cookies. Because I make as many as 15 dozen, I wanted a quick way to make uniform indentations in the cookies and a fast way to fill them. Instead of carefully pressing my thumb into hundreds of cookies, I use a plastic thimble dipped in superfine sugar; the cookies look great, because each hole is exactly the same size and shape. To expedite filling the holes, I use a squeeze bottle filled with jam.

Susan Capaldo
West Warwick, R.I.

TASTY TREAT

When I bake cookies or brownies for my family, there are inevitably a few that break during the process. I put these bits and pieces into a plastic bag, freeze them, and use them for ice-cream topping.

Carla Kerper
Spring Valley, Calif.

KEEP YOUR DOUGH PUT

Whenever I roll out dough, I place it between two sheets of parchment paper to try to keep things tidy. But the paper always used to slip around my countertop, making it hard to roll the dough evenly. Now I place a silicone baking mat underneath the parchment paper. It holds the paper in place, so I can easily roll out my dough.

Kristen VanDamm
Cambridge, Mass.

DON'T FORGET THE BAG

While I love using cooking bags for my slow cooker, I frequently find that I only remember to use the bags after I have added the ingredients to the insert. My husband suggested storing the box of bags inside the cooker, and that simple idea solved the problem.

Sally Jackson
Via e-mail

QUICK TOASTED BREAD CRUMBS

If you don't have toasted bread crumbs on hand and don't want to tend to them in a skillet or wait for them in the oven, toast the bread in the toaster first and then pulse it a few times in the food processor.

Grier Hickman
Hong Kong

BAKING IDEA

When making individual rustic apple tarts, I arrange the apple slices in large custard cups and place the dough on top. Then I flip the cups over onto the baking sheet and pleat the dough. This prevents the tarts from losing their shape and the apples from spilling out.

Jack Graff
Palm Desert, Calif.

PRESLICED BUTTER

I keep a stick of butter sliced into tablespoon measurements in my fridge at all times. Whenever I need to add a tablespoon of butter to a pan or recipe, the butter is already cut and I don't have to dirty a knife or stop what I'm doing to cut the butter. It seems like such a basic thing, but it really saves time when cooking.

Amy Mills
Mahomet, Ill.

If you'd like to submit a tip, please e-mail us by visiting **CooksCountry. com/kitchenshortcuts** or send a letter to Kitchen Shortcuts, Cook's Country, P.O. Box 470739, Brookline, MA 02447. Include your name, address, and daytime phone number. If we publish your tip, you will receive a free one-year subscription to Cook's Country.

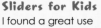

MORE FREEZER SPACE

For years we've maximized our freezer space by putting portions of soup, spaghetti sauce, stews, chili, or almost anything else into quart- or gallon-sized freezer bags and squeezing out as much air as possible. We freeze the bags piled flat on top of each other on a small tray until firm—that way, the frozen bags may be stacked vertically or horizontally in the freezer. We also weigh each bag before freezing so we know the portions are equal.

Suzie McGinn
Barrington, Ill.

ORGANIZE YOUR FRIDGE

I could never find items in my refrigerator door without pulling out jar after jar until I got the right one. Now I use a permanent marker to label each lid with the name of the item and the date it was opened. When I look down at the shelves of the door, all I have to do is read the jar tops.

Phyllis Maley
Colchester, Vt.

ICE-CREAM FRENCH TOAST

My favorite French toast recipe calls for soaking bread in a mixture of eggs, cream, sugar, and vanilla. I often don't have cream in the fridge—but I always have a pint or two of vanilla ice cream in the freezer, and I've found it makes a great substitution. Simply melt vanilla ice cream in the microwave and use it in place of the cream as well as the sugar and vanilla.

Sue Present
Silver Spring, Md.

CREATIVE THINKING

I used to make homemade cranberry sauce using the recipe on the bag, but that recipe is a little generic and bland. Now I add a whole cinnamon stick and whole cloves to the cooking sauce. To make it easier to remove the cloves at the end of cooking (and to add even more flavor), I cut a generous piece of orange peel and gently push the whole cloves through it. This method imparts the wonderful tang of citrus and spice without losing the cloves in the sauce.

Lorraine Bowyer
Summit, N.J.

UPRIGHT ALL THE TIME

Since small spice and honey jars won't always stay upright on standard wire pantry shelves, I bought inexpensive flexible cutting boards to place on each shelf, and now the bottles never tip over. A bonus: Drips and spills are easy to clean up.

Glenna Sullivan
Marietta, Ga.

NO STICK, NO MESS

I like the new flexible chopping boards, but sometimes they slip on the countertop. To prevent this, I place a disinfectant wipe underneath the board, which anchors it to the counter. And when I'm finished chopping and cutting, I already have a wipe to finish the cleanup!

Cathy King
Houston, Texas

KEEP IT COOL

Whether you are outside in the heat of summer or serving food in a warm living room, you can keep a serving platter chilled by placing it atop a frozen ice cream–maker insert. This way, deviled eggs, antipasti, fresh-cut fruit, and cold desserts stay fresher longer. To keep the insert clean and prevent trays from slipping, cover the insert with a thin napkin or towel.

Bill Bowersock Jr.
San Francisco, Calif.

Uncommon Usage

SCALE DOWN

I've always loved to cook fish, but I used to hate the messy hassle of removing the scales. I've recently found that a quick and easy way to scale fish is to use the nonblade edge of a swivel-headed vegetable peeler, which scrapes off the scales without cutting into the skin.

Linda Yamasaki
Via e-mail

Sliders for Kids

I found a great use for the heel of a loaf of bread: I use a 3-inch-round cookie cutter to make hamburger buns for my young daughter. She would never eat hamburgers at home, because the store-bought buns were too big for her to handle. Now she eats kid-sized burgers in buns she can easily hold.

Beth Rudolph Alexandria, Va.

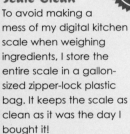

TIDY TIP

Keep Your Scale Clean

To avoid making a mess of my digital kitchen scale when weighing ingredients, I store the entire scale in a gallon-sized zipper-lock plastic bag. It keeps the scale as clean as it was the day I bought it!

Agnes Skinner
Portland, Ore.

Safety Smash

I don't like smashing garlic cloves (to get the skin off) with the side of my knife. I use a spatula, which works just as well as a knife—and I feel a lot safer doing it.

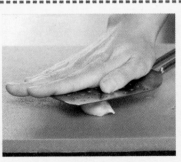

Karen Listick
Agoura Hills, Calif.

No More Dirty Dredges

Instead of using additional dishes when breading chicken or fish, I place my flour and bread crumbs on parchment paper.

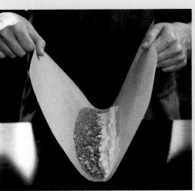

I can cut the paper to a size that allows enough room for easy breading of even the largest pieces. It is also a snap to clean up, as I pick the paper up and throw everything away.

Lynn Swanson
North Granby, Conn.

Top Muffins Use Inventive Ingredients to Beat the Competition

Our $1,000 Grand-Prize Winner!

Donna Bardocz
Howell, Mich.

Our winning recipe comes from an earlier era, when big department stores had restaurants where you could enjoy light fare while shopping. Donna explains, "I got this recipe from a friend who had worked at Dayton Hudson department store. The taste of these melt-in-your-mouth muffins is heavenly." Our tasters loved the combination of apples and cheddar cheese, and the cinnamon glaze is the crowning touch on this winning muffin.

Our four runners-up also won kudos for creativity. Two savory muffins (one a complete breakfast with sausage, the other a perfect companion to a bowl of chili) earned high marks from tasters. The unique combination of chocolate and apricot won another muffin a top spot. A healthy muffin loaded with oats and fruit (and with almost no fat) was another favorite.

GRANDMA'S SPECIAL DUTCH APPLE CHEESE MUFFINS MAKES 12 MUFFINS

Crisp, sweet-tart apples like Macoun, Jonagold, Cortland, and Empire work best here. You will need 2 to 3 apples for this recipe.

Muffins

- 2 cups all-purpose flour
- ½ cup sugar
- 1 tablespoon baking powder
- 1 teaspoon salt
- 8 tablespoons (1 stick) cold unsalted butter, cut into ½-inch pieces
- 8 ounces cheddar cheese, cut into ½-inch pieces
- 1 large egg
- ¾ cup whole milk
- 1 pound apples, peeled, halved, cored, and sliced crosswise into thin half-moons

Glaze

- ⅓ cup sugar
- 2 tablespoons water
- 2 tablespoons unsalted butter
- 1 tablespoon lemon juice
- ½ teaspoon ground cinnamon

1. For the muffins: Adjust oven rack to middle position and heat oven to 375 degrees. Grease and flour 12-cup muffin tin. Pulse flour, sugar, baking powder, salt, butter, and cheese in food processor until mixture resembles coarse meal; transfer to large bowl. Whisk egg and milk in measuring cup, then slowly stir into flour mixture until combined.

2. Spoon batter into prepared muffin tin. Arrange apple slices, cut-side down, on top of batter, pressing gently to adhere. Bake until edges of muffins are just golden, about 15 minutes.

3. For the glaze: While muffins are baking, heat sugar, water, butter, lemon juice, and cinnamon in saucepan over medium heat until butter is melted and sugar is dissolved, about 3 minutes. Once edges of muffins are just golden, brush muffins with glaze. Return to oven and bake until toothpick inserted into center comes out clean, about 10 minutes. Cool in tin for 5 minutes, then carefully transfer to rack. Cool 10 minutes longer. Serve. (Muffins can be kept in airtight container at room temperature for up to 2 days.)

Our grand-prize winner layers apple slices across a muffin flavored with cheddar cheese and brushed with a cinnamon glaze.

Barbara Estabrook
Rhinelander, Wis.

Joyce Hart
Prior Lake, Minn.

Laurie Balcom
Lynden, Wash.

Pamela Shank
Parkersburg, W.Va.

BLUEBERRY-PEAR-GINGER-OATMEAL MUFFINS
MAKES 12 MUFFINS

Barbara writes: "I have redone my original recipe many times in an attempt to make it as nutritious as possible." Frozen blueberries can be substituted for fresh.

Muffins
- 1¼ cups all-purpose flour
- 1¼ cups old-fashioned oats
- 2 teaspoons baking powder
- ½ teaspoon baking soda
- 1 teaspoon ground cinnamon
- ½ teaspoon ground ginger
- ½ teaspoon salt
- ¾ cup whole milk
- ¾ cup packed light brown sugar
- 1 large egg plus 2 egg whites
- 3 tablespoons vegetable oil
- ⅓ cup raisins, preferably golden
- 1 firm pear, peeled, cored, and chopped fine
- 1¼ cups fresh blueberries

Topping
- 2 tablespoons light brown sugar
- ⅛ teaspoon ground cinnamon
- ¼ cup sliced almonds

1. For the muffins: Adjust oven rack to middle position and heat oven to 375 degrees. Grease and flour 12-cup muffin tin. Combine flour, oats, baking powder, baking soda, cinnamon, ginger, and salt in large bowl. Whisk milk, sugar, egg, egg whites, and oil in another bowl until smooth. Stir milk mixture into flour mixture until combined, then fold in raisins, pear, and blueberries.

2. For the topping: Combine sugar and cinnamon in small bowl. Spoon batter into prepared muffin tin and sprinkle evenly with sugar mixture. Top with almonds and bake until toothpick inserted into center comes out clean, 20 to 25 minutes. Cool in tin for 5 minutes, then carefully transfer to rack. Cool 10 minutes longer. Serve. (Muffins can be kept in airtight container at room temperature for up to 2 days.)

CHOCO-APRICOT MUFFINS
MAKES 12 MUFFINS

Joyce writes: "I tried to re-create a muffin I remembered from a work potluck several years ago."

Muffins
- 2 cups all-purpose flour
- ⅓ cup granulated sugar
- ⅓ cup packed light brown sugar
- 2 teaspoons baking powder
- ½ teaspoon baking soda
- ½ teaspoon salt
- 1 cup sour cream
- 8 tablespoons unsalted butter, melted and cooled slightly
- 2 large eggs
- 1½ teaspoons vanilla extract
- ½ teaspoon almond extract
- 1 cup semisweet chocolate chips
- ¾ cup dried apricots, chopped
- ⅔ cup sliced almonds

Filling and Topping
- ¼ cup sugar
- ¼ teaspoon ground cinnamon
- ⅓ cup apricot preserves

1. For the muffins: Adjust oven rack to middle position and heat oven to 375 degrees. Grease and flour 12-cup muffin tin. Whisk flour, sugars, baking powder, baking soda, and salt in large bowl. Whisk sour cream, butter, eggs, and extracts in another bowl until smooth. Stir sour cream mixture into flour mixture until combined, then fold in chocolate chips, apricots, and almonds.

2. For the filling and topping: Combine sugar and cinnamon in small bowl. Spoon half of batter into prepared muffin tin, place dollop of preserves in center of batter, and top with remaining batter. Sprinkle with sugar mixture and bake until toothpick inserted into center comes out clean, 20 to 25 minutes. Cool in tin for 5 minutes, then carefully transfer to rack. Cool 10 minutes longer. Serve. (Muffins can be kept in airtight container at room temperature for up to 2 days.)

SOUTHWESTERN CHILI-CHEESE CORN MUFFINS
MAKES 12 MUFFINS

Laurie writes: "This recipe combines sweet, crunchy, and spicy all in one muffin."

Muffins
- 1 cup all-purpose flour
- 1 cup cornmeal
- ¼ cup packed light brown sugar
- 2 teaspoons baking powder
- ½ teaspoon baking soda
- 1 teaspoon chili powder
- ⅛ teaspoon cayenne pepper
- 1 teaspoon salt
- 1 cup sour cream
- 2 large eggs
- 4 tablespoons unsalted butter, melted and cooled slightly
- 1 cup frozen corn, thawed
- 3 scallions, sliced thin
- ½ red bell pepper, seeded and chopped fine

Filling
- 1 cup crumbled goat cheese, room temperature
- 1 jalapeño chile, seeded and minced
- ¼ red onion, minced

1. For the muffins: Adjust oven rack to middle position and heat oven to 425 degrees. Grease and flour 12-cup muffin tin. Combine flour, cornmeal, sugar, baking powder, baking soda, chili powder, cayenne, and salt in large bowl. Whisk sour cream, eggs, and butter in another bowl until smooth. Stir sour cream mixture into flour mixture until combined, then fold in corn, scallions, and bell pepper.

2. For the filling: Combine cheese, jalapeño, and onion in bowl. Spoon half of batter into prepared muffin tin, place dollop of cheese mixture in center of batter, and top with remaining batter. Bake until toothpick inserted into center comes out clean, 20 to 25 minutes. Cool in tin for 5 minutes, then carefully transfer to rack. Cool 10 minutes longer. Serve.

COUNTRY SAUSAGE AND CHEESE MUFFINS
MAKES 12 MUFFINS

Pamela writes: "These muffins make a meal on their own and travel well."

- 8 ounces bulk sausage meat
- 2 cups all-purpose flour
- 3 tablespoons sugar
- 2 teaspoons baking powder
- 1 teaspoon baking soda
- 1 teaspoon salt
- 6 tablespoons cold unsalted butter, cut into ½-inch pieces
- 8 ounces cheddar cheese, cut into ½-inch pieces
- ½ red bell pepper, seeded and chopped fine
- ½ red onion, chopped fine
- 1 large egg
- ¾ cup buttermilk

1. Adjust oven rack to middle position and heat oven to 375 degrees. Grease and flour 12-cup muffin tin. Cook sausage in nonstick skillet over medium heat, breaking up meat until no longer pink, about 5 minutes. Transfer to paper towel–lined plate and cool.

2. Pulse flour, sugar, baking powder, baking soda, salt, butter, cheese, bell pepper, onion, and cooled sausage in food processor until mixture resembles coarse meal; transfer to bowl. Whisk egg and buttermilk in measuring cup; stir into flour mixture until combined.

3. Spoon batter into prepared muffin tin and bake until toothpick inserted into center comes out clean, 20 to 25 minutes. Cool in tin for 5 minutes, then carefully transfer to rack. Cool 10 minutes longer. Serve.

We want your best holiday cookie recipes for an upcoming contest. Please submit entries by March 31, 2008. Send us your recipes by visiting **CooksCountry.com/emailus** or write to us at Recipe Contest, Cook's Country, P.O. Box 470739, Brookline, MA 02447. Include your name, address, and daytime phone number and tell us what makes your recipe special. The grand-prize winner will receive $1,000. All entries become the property of *Cook's Country.* Go to **CooksCountry.com** for more information on this and other contests.

Ask Cook's Country

WE'LL ANSWER ANY QUESTION YOU THROW AT US!

CHEESE, PLEASE

I hope you can settle an argument for me. My brother Dan says that Velveeta isn't real cheese, it's a cheese product. I say it's cheese. Who's right?

Jon Schafer
Buffalo, N.Y.

You're both partially right. Unlike other cheeses that are simply aged and sold, pasteurized process cheese goes a step further. One or more cheeses, such as colby or cheddar, are mixed with cream or milk fat and then heated with an emulsifier. The heating kills bacteria and increases the shelf life of the cheese, and the emulsifier promotes easy melting and a creamy texture. Since good bacteria provide cheese with much of its flavor, this process yields products with very little cheese flavor.

The U.S. Food and Drug Administration (FDA) regulates the labeling of pasteurized process cheese according to the percentages by weight of moisture and milk fat. The FDA assigns three labels to goods made with pasteurized process cheese (in descending order of actual cheese content): food, spread, and product. Pasteurized process cheese products, like Velveeta, are no more than 51 percent cheese.

CHEESE PRODUCT
Pasteurized process cheese products, like Velveeta, are made with cheese but contain other ingredients.

CREAM OF TARTAR

Recipes that call for whipping egg whites often add cream of tartar to the whites. What is it, and why is it added?

Bob Wen
Mesa, Ariz.

Cream of tartar, also known as potassium bitartrate, is a powdered byproduct of the winemaking process and, along with baking soda, is one of the two main ingredients in baking powder. Cream of tartar's acidic nature lowers the pH of egg whites, which encourages the eggs' proteins to unfold, thus creating more volume, greater stability, and a glossier appearance.

We compared whipped egg whites and cooked meringue (an egg white and sugar mixture) prepared with and without cream of tartar. For the whipped egg whites, the volume of the batch with cream of tartar was nearly double that of the batch without it. Both versions of the cooked meringue were similar right out of the oven, but after two days the meringue without cream of tartar had begun to separate and exude liquid (or "weep"), and the

meringue made with cream of tartar was fully stable. Since meringues are often used to top pies and frost cakes, adding the cream of tartar is a wise step.

TEARING UP

What's the best way to chop onions without messing up my eye makeup?

Carolyn Gibson
Via e-mail

Chopping onions ruptures their cells, allowing previously separated compounds and enzymes to commingle. This mixing creates a noxious gas that attacks the nerve endings in the eyes.

We found that the onion's temperature (frozen, refrigerated, or room temperature) and whether you breathe through your mouth or nose have no impact on tear production. We did discover that fresher onions cause less irritation than older ones.

NO MORE TEARS
Though old wives' tales abound, the only way to stay completely tear-free when chopping onions is to wear goggles.

We had moderate success keeping the tears at bay by chopping with a small fan blowing horizontally across the cutting board. Working beside a lit gas burner (to burn off the noxious gas) helped a bit, too. Testers who wore contact lenses fared slightly better than those who didn't. The only absolute way to avoid irritation is to create a physical barrier between your eyes and the fumes by wearing ski or swim goggles. Or pick up a pair of onion goggles sold just for this purpose.

GREAT GRAINS

My husband says that cornmeal, polenta, and grits are all the same thing. Are they?

Susie Hahn
Gordonsville, Va.

Raw polenta and cornmeal are exactly the same thing (although polenta often costs twice as much): dried corn that is ground into grains of varying coarseness. We prefer a medium grind (about the size of granulated sugar) of cornmeal for making prepared polenta (Italian-style cornmeal mush) and finely ground cornmeal for baked goods.

Grits are also dried corn, but they are ground more coarsely than cornmeal and the two should not be used interchangeably. In large-scale commercial production, grits are made from the same corn as cornmeal, but smaller boutique purveyors use different types of corn for each product: soft and starchy dent corn for grits and harder, grittier flint corn for cornmeal.

PICK A PAN

Many of your recipes call for a 13- by 9-inch baking pan. Should I use Pyrex or a metal pan?

Laura Flanders
Via e-mail

There are actually three basic pan choices—ovensafe glass (like Pyrex), nonstick metal, and regular metal. To test how these pans stack up against one another, we whipped up batches of yellow cake, brownies, and baked macaroni and cheese in each. The ovensafe glass and nonstick metal pans performed well across the board and can be used interchangeably with a few exceptions. The regular metal pans were quite shiny (the nonstick metal pans were dark) and didn't perform as well. That's because shiny surfaces reflect heat and don't brown as well as glass or dark nonstick surfaces.

Glass is sensitive to dramatic changes in temperature (especially if it is cracked), so it can't be used under the broiler and therefore doesn't work for casseroles that are broiled to crisp the top. And though its transparency is useful for monitoring browning, glass retains heat almost too well. Although all batches of brownies were cooked to the same internal temperature, those baked in the glass pan were noticeably drier once cooled, because they had continued to cook from the residual heat held by the pan.

In the test kitchen, we reserve nonstick pans for casseroles that go under the broiler or baked goods that cool completely in the pan. Otherwise, we generally use ovensafe glass.

BROILER-SAFE

HOLDS ITS HEAT
Both pans work well for just about any cooking task, but nonstick metal can go under the broiler and allows more temperature control than ovensafe glass.

To ask us a cooking question, visit **CooksCountry.com/ emailus.** You can also write to Ask Cook's Country, P.O. Box 470739, Brookline, MA 02447. See if you can stump us!

A 100-year-old recipe claims that starting in a cold oven yields a pound cake that is especially tall and boasts a crisp crust. Can this unlikely recipe really work?

Years ago, when my grandmother ran a small baked goods business out of her home, her most popular item was cold-oven pound cake. It had the buttery richness of a traditional pound cake, but instead of the typical dense texture, it was very light, with a tender yet sturdy crumb and a surprisingly crisp crust. What Grandma never told her customers was how easy it was to make: She beat eggs into the creamed butter and sugar, mixed in cream and flour, and poured the batter—absent chemical leavener—into a tube pan that went into a stone-cold oven. The cake magically emerged tall and golden about an hour later. Since her recipe was misplaced long ago, I set out to record my own version.

My hunt for the origin of this curious recipe took me back over a hundred years. At the turn of the 20th century, gas lighting was being phased out in favor of newer electric technology. Looking to replace lost revenue, gas companies set their sights on the oven business. One of their marketing gimmicks was to push easy and "thrifty" recipes, like cold-oven pound cake, that didn't require preheating. This cake became popular throughout the South and was later reported to be Elvis Presley's favorite pound cake.

I gathered several existing recipes and headed to the kitchen. While most of the cakes lacked the lift and tenderness of Grandma's, one contemporary recipe showed promise; it did, however, contain a nontraditional ingredient—baking powder. The addition of just ½ teaspoon of this leavener (less than half the amount used for standard pound cake) produced a consistently lofty, even rise. I was able to get away with using so little because baking powder is double-acting (it produces carbon dioxide bubbles—and thus rise—when mixed with liquid and then again in the heat of the oven), and putting the cake into a cold oven meant that the gluten did not set up as quickly, allowing the carbon dioxide more time to produce greater rise.

Though grand in stature, the cake was still too dense. To create a lighter crumb, I exchanged the heavy cream from the working recipe for leaner whole milk. This helped a little, but

swapping out all-purpose flour for cake flour yielded an even finer, more delicate crumb. Baking the cake on the lower-middle rack of an oven turned to 325 degrees ensured an evenly cooked cake with a crisp, golden crust that would have made Grandma proud.

–Cali Rich

COLD-OVEN POUND CAKE
SERVES 12

You'll need a 16-cup tube pan or angel food cake pan for this recipe; if not using a nonstick pan, make sure to thoroughly grease a traditional pan. In step 2, don't worry if the batter looks slightly separated.

- 3 cups cake flour
- ½ teaspoon baking powder
- 1 teaspoon salt
- 1 cup whole milk
- 2 teaspoons vanilla extract
- 20 tablespoons (2½ sticks) unsalted butter, softened
- 2½ cups sugar
- 6 large eggs

1. Adjust oven rack to lower-middle position. Grease and flour 16-cup tube pan. Combine flour, baking powder, and salt in bowl. Whisk milk and vanilla in measuring cup.

2. With electric mixer on medium speed, beat butter and sugar until fluffy, about 2 minutes. Beat in eggs, one at

a time, until combined. Reduce speed to low and add flour mixture in 3 additions, alternating with 2 additions of milk mixture. Mix on low until smooth, about 30 seconds. Use rubber spatula to give batter final stir.

3. Pour batter into prepared pan and smooth top. Place cake in cold oven. Adjust oven temperature to 325 degrees and bake, without opening oven door, until cake is golden brown and toothpick inserted in center comes out clean, 65 to 80 minutes.

4. Cool cake in pan for 15 minutes, then turn out onto rack. Cool completely, about 2 hours. Serve. (Cooled cake can be stored in airtight container at room temperature for up to 2 days.)

The distinguishing feature of this old-fashioned pound cake is its hearty, chewy, well-browned crust.

Why Pay for Preheating?

Gas ovens became widely available in the United States during the first decades of the 20th century. Because these ovens were more expensive than their wood- and coal-fired counterparts, gas companies had to get creative in marketing them. One popular tact was to develop and promote recipes started in a cold oven, with the hook that consumers could save money in their gas ovens by not paying for "needless" preheating.

COOKING WITH GAS
Cold-oven recipes were designed to save money.

A Cold Oven Really Makes a Difference

Curiosity led us to try baking our Cold-Oven Pound Cake in a preheated oven. The cake baked more quickly (no surprise), but it was squat and lacked the thick crust we'd come to expect. Evidently, the hot oven stopped the small amount of leavener in our recipe before its work was done. And it turns out the crust on our Cold-Oven Pound Cake is formed by moisture in the oven reacting with starch in the batter. A hot oven is drier than a cold oven (heat evaporates moisture), so there wasn't enough moisture in the preheated oven to form a nice, thick crust.

SQUAT CAKE
A preheated oven produces a squat, crustless cake with this recipe.

PERFECT CAKE
In contrast, a cold oven produces a high rise and a thick crust.

Beef shoulder is the classic choice for pot roast, but pork shoulder is just as nicely marbled and flavorful. So why does it make such a watery mess in the slow cooker?

A slow-cooker pot roast made with a pork shoulder roast—either a Boston butt or a picnic shoulder—makes perfect sense; after all, pork shoulder's fat content and marbling are similar to beef chuck's, meaning it requires the same low-and-slow cooking to become tender. To test this theory, I prepared the test kitchen's beef pot roast recipe using both cuts from the pork shoulder: I browned the meat, sautéed onions and garlic, added the braising liquid, and let the roasts simmer in the slow cooker until the meat was fall-apart tender.

The good news is that there was no difference between the Boston butt and the picnic shoulder. The bad news is that neither pot roast was very good. The pork roasts also released a lot of liquid, which made the sauce thin and watery. And the potent flavors in the sauce (red wine, beef broth, and canned tomatoes) overwhelmed the flavor of the pork.

I addressed the liquid problem first. Eliminating the broth altogether was a good first step, as the pork juices were plenty flavorful on their own. Using just ½ cup of red wine and draining the diced tomatoes also helped tighten things up, but the sauce was still a little too thin. Flour and cornstarch gave the sauce a pasty texture, but instant tapioca (a thickener the test kitchen likes for its neutral flavor and ease of use) produced just the right thick, glossy texture.

Draining the tomatoes and eliminating the broth had lightened the flavors of the sauce, but it was still a bit too strong. Switching from red to white wine was an improvement. Adding a splash of white wine vinegar at the end of cooking refreshed the wine flavor and added brightness and acidity. Thyme lent a soft herbal note.

Onions, garlic, and carrots were essential to the base flavor, and after trying plenty of other vegetables, my tasters arrived at a surprise favorite: parsnips, which contributed a welcome sweetness and heady perfume to the dish. The carrots and parsnips, however, were turning to tasteless mush after hours of cooking. Carefully arranging the ingredients in the slow-cooker insert was the solution—I layered the tomatoes and onions under the meat and arranged the carrots and parsnips on top, out of the liquid, where they cooked perfectly.

I'm still a big fan of beef pot roast, but it's nice to know there is an option for pot roast made with pork shoulder.

–Kelley Baker

SLOW-COOKER PORK POT ROAST SERVES 8

If you cannot find 2½- to 3-pound pork shoulder roasts, you can substitute one 6-pound pork shoulder roast. See page 31 for more information on preparing a larger roast for the slow cooker.

- 2 (2½- to 3-pound) boneless pork shoulder roasts, netting removed and tied according to photos at left
  Salt and pepper
- 2 tablespoons vegetable oil
- 2 onions, chopped
- 6 garlic cloves, minced
- 1 tablespoon tomato paste
- ½ cup white wine
- 3 tablespoons Minute tapioca
- 1 (28-ounce) can diced tomatoes, drained
- 2 teaspoons minced fresh thyme
- 1 pound carrots, peeled, halved lengthwise, and cut into 2-inch pieces
- 1 pound parsnips, peeled, halved lengthwise, and cut into 2-inch pieces
- 2 teaspoons white wine vinegar

1. Pat roasts dry with paper towels and season with salt and pepper. Heat 2 teaspoons oil in large skillet over medium-high heat until just smoking. Brown roasts all over, about 10 minutes. Transfer to slow cooker.

2. Add onions and additional 2 teaspoons oil to empty skillet and cook until browned, about 5 minutes. Add garlic and tomato paste and cook until fragrant, about 1 minute. Stir in wine and simmer, scraping up any browned bits with wooden spoon, until thickened, about 2 minutes. Stir in tapioca, tomatoes, and thyme; transfer to slow cooker.

3. Toss carrots, parsnips, ¼ teaspoon salt, ¼ teaspoon pepper, and remaining oil in bowl until vegetables are well coated. Scatter vegetable mixture over pork. Cover and cook on low until meat is tender, 9 to 10 hours (or cook on high 4 to 5 hours).

4. Transfer roasts to cutting board, tent with foil, and let rest 10 minutes. Remove twine from roasts and cut meat into ½-inch-thick slices; transfer to serving platter. Using slotted spoon, transfer carrots and parsnips to platter with pork. Stir vinegar into sauce and season with salt and pepper. Serve, passing sauce at table.

Kitchen Know-How
TWO ROASTS ARE BETTER THAN ONE

We like to use two smaller roasts for this recipe, because the meat cooks more quickly and the small roasts are easier to manage in the slow cooker—and to find in the supermarket. Most boneless pork shoulder roasts come bound in string netting, which is difficult to remove after cooking. We prefer to cut the netting off before cooking, trim the roasts, and then tie each one with cooking twine.

1. Remove the netting from the pork roasts. Open each roast and trim any excess fat.
2. Tie the roasts separately. To ensure even cooking, fold the smaller lobes under, then tie each roast with kitchen twine every 1½ inches around the circumference and once around the length.

The secret to not overcooking the carrots and parsnips is to layer them on top of the pork and above the liquid in the slow cooker.

Recipe Makeover BROCCOLI CHEDDAR SOUP

How do you make a low-fat version of a soup whose smooth texture and rich flavor are derived from cheddar cheese and heavy cream?

Using potent extra-sharp cheddar cheese allows us to use a smaller amount, helping to cut both the calories and the fat.

Good broccoli cheddar soup is a perfect balance of the earthy, vegetal flavor of broccoli and the richness of heavy cream and tangy cheddar cheese. Most recipes start by pureeing cooked broccoli florets and onions, then adding heavy cream, chicken broth, and plenty of cheese. But just because this soup starts with broccoli doesn't mean it's good for you: A typical version has 460 calories and 38 grams of fat per serving. I found plenty of low-fat recipes out there, most of which used reduced-fat dairy products (milk, yogurt, sour cream, and even cream cheese). I made a handful of them and was disappointed when they came out curdled, gloppy, and sour—and sorely lacking in both broccoli and cheddar flavors.

Incorporating the broccoli stems, which have just as much flavor as the florets, maximized flavor and increased the soup's bulk. For a subtle nuttiness that would complement the cheese, I added a few cloves of garlic to the sautéing broccoli and onions. But my tasters thought the pungency of the onions (I tried red, white, yellow, and sweet varieties) was masking the broccoli flavor, so I switched to milder leeks, which had the added benefit,

once pureed, of lending a silky texture to the soup.

But how to replace the heavy cream? I knew from my initial tests that most low-fat dairy products would curdle when the soup was heated. Then I remembered a test kitchen recipe for creamy macaroni and cheese that uses evaporated milk, which contains stabilizers that keep it from separating when cooked. Scanning the supermarket shelves, I found fat-free evaporated milk and decided to give it a try. Sure enough, it produced a perfectly rich and satiny soup.

You can't have broccoli cheddar soup without the cheddar, which lends a distinct flavor and creamy texture. Some recipes use as much as a full pound, but since the pureed leeks and evaporated milk were already providing silky creaminess, I needed only enough cheese to flavor the soup. By using extra-sharp cheddar instead of mild or sharp, I could get distinct cheese flavor from just 4 ounces. A little Dijon mustard provided extra tang and made the small amount of cheese taste more potent. With a few creative solutions, I had a lighter broccoli cheddar soup that was just as satisfying as the original.

–Meredith Butcher

And the Numbers...
All nutritional information is for one serving (about 1¼ cups of soup).

TRADITIONAL BROCCOLI CHEDDAR SOUP
CALORIES: **460**
FAT: **38g**
SATURATED FAT: **15g**

COOK'S COUNTRY LOW-FAT BROCCOLI CHEDDAR SOUP
CALORIES: **210**
FAT: **11g**
SATURATED FAT: **6g**

LOW-FAT BROCCOLI CHEDDAR SOUP SERVES 6

When pureeing the soup in step 2, work in batches and make sure to fill your blender no more than halfway with hot soup. Adding the cheese off heat prevents it from separating and becoming greasy.

- 1 tablespoon unsalted butter
- 2 leeks, white and light green parts only, halved lengthwise and sliced thin
- 1½ pounds broccoli, florets chopped, stems peeled and sliced thin
- 2 garlic cloves, minced
- 3 cups low-sodium chicken broth
- 1 cup water
- 1 tablespoon Dijon mustard
- ¾ cup fat-free evaporated milk
- 4 ounces extra-sharp cheddar cheese, shredded (about 1 cup)
  Salt and pepper

1. Melt butter in large pot over medium heat. Add leeks and broccoli stems and cook until just beginning to soften, about 8 minutes. Add garlic and cook until fragrant, about 1 minute. Stir in broth and water and bring to boil. Reduce heat to medium-low and simmer, covered, until stems are soft, about 8 minutes. Add broccoli florets, cover, and simmer until tender, about 5 minutes.

2. Transfer soup to blender and puree until completely smooth, about 30 seconds. Add mustard, milk, and cheese and puree until cheese is melted. Season with salt and pepper. Serve. (Soup can be refrigerated for up to 3 days. Reheat over medium-low heat; do not boil or cheese will separate.)

Soup Saver
For silky, rich texture, two ingredients were essential in this recipe makeover.

LEEKS
Leeks provided flavor, color, and silky consistency in the soup.

FAT-FREE EVAPORATED MILK
Using fat-free evaporated milk instead of cream gives this soup creamy texture without the extra fat.

Easy Chili con Carne

I was recently in Austin, Texas, and I sampled an amazing chili with big chunks of meat and no beans (I hate beans). Do you have an easy recipe for this style of chili? —Renée Carper, Boise, Idaho

Cooking the chili powder, meat, and vegetables in bacon fat helps build savory, smoky flavor in this streamlined chili.

Silky Sauce

Our chili gets silky texture and a hint of corn flavor from the addition of corn muffin mix.

THE SECRET INGREDIENT

What you're describing is chili con carne, a signature Tex-Mex stew that features large, tender chunks of beef, complex chile flavor and heat, a silky broth, and no beans. Years ago, the test kitchen developed an excellent chili con carne recipe that calls for toasting and grinding a variety of whole chiles. I wanted to create a simpler, authentic-tasting version using supermarket ingredients.

I prepared an assortment of streamlined recipes (avoiding those that called for ground beef), and I was disheartened by the results. Most of these recipes simply threw chili powder and beef (or chicken) broth over browned meat, and the results were predictably watery and bland. One had beef that was so tough it was literally inedible. I was going to have to start at the bottom—with the meat.

After some preliminary testing, I settled on using chuck; the test kitchen prefers this affordable cut for stews because its substantial marbling provides rich flavor and tender texture after prolonged cooking. I bought the meat as a roast and cut it into chunks myself to ensure all the pieces were of similar size and quality. To add a smoky meatiness to the chili, I browned the beef in bacon fat instead of plain oil.

Specialty dried chiles were out. Dumping in store-bought chili powder made for meek and dusty chili, but cooking the chili powder in the bacon fat brought out its complexity and richness. A little cumin, oregano, and garlic balanced out the flavors. I added fresh jalapeño for brightness and heat and minced chipotle (canned smoked jalapeño) for smoky, spicy depth. Surprisingly, my tasters preferred plain water to beef or chicken broth, as the broths muted the complex spice flavor. Although chili purists—especially in Texas—might disapprove, we found that modest amounts of onion and tomato were welcome additions.

The chili tasted great, but the texture wasn't thick and silky enough. Traditional recipes often call for stirring in corn flour (also known as masa harina) at the end of cooking to tighten the texture and add flavor, but I wanted to find a more readily available ingredient. Cornstarch thickened the chili but didn't add flavor. Cornmeal added flavor but lent a gritty texture. Softened and pureed corn tortillas tasted good but were a little grainy.

I scoured the grocery store shelves for another corn thickener before I finally saw it: corn muffin mix. I tossed a couple tablespoons into my chili and watched the mix seize and clump on the surface. Stirring the mix into some chili broth and cooking the mix-and-broth combination in the microwave produced a perfectly smooth and silky broth with plenty of fire and flavor in every bite. **–Cali Rich**

CHILI CON CARNE
SERVES 6 TO 8

If the bacon does not render a full 3 tablespoons of fat in step 1, supplement it with vegetable oil.

- 1 **(14.5-ounce) can diced tomatoes**
- 2 **teaspoons minced canned chipotle chile in adobo**
- 4 **slices bacon, chopped fine**
- 1 **(3½- to 4-pound) boneless beef chuck-eye roast, trimmed and cut into 1-inch pieces**
    Salt and pepper
- 1 **onion, chopped fine**
- 1 **jalapeño chile, seeded and chopped fine**
- 3 **tablespoons chili powder**
- 1½ **teaspoons ground cumin**
- ½ **teaspoon dried oregano**
- 4 **garlic cloves, minced**
- 4 **cups water**
- 1 **tablespoon brown sugar**
- 2 **tablespoons yellow corn muffin mix**

1. Process tomatoes and chipotle in food processor until smooth. Cook bacon in Dutch oven over medium heat until crisp, about 8 minutes. Transfer bacon to paper towel–lined plate and reserve 3 tablespoons bacon fat.

2. Pat beef dry with paper towels and season with salt and pepper. Heat 1 tablespoon reserved bacon fat in empty Dutch oven over medium-high heat until just smoking. Brown half of beef, about 8 minutes. Transfer to bowl and repeat with additional tablespoon bacon fat and remaining beef.

3. Add remaining bacon fat, onion, and jalapeño to empty Dutch oven and cook until softened, about 5 minutes. Stir in chili powder, cumin, oregano, and garlic and cook until fragrant, about 30 seconds. Stir in water, pureed tomato mixture, bacon, browned beef, and sugar and bring to boil. Reduce heat to low and simmer, covered, for 1 hour. Skim fat and continue to simmer uncovered until meat is tender, 30 to 45 minutes.

4. Ladle 1 cup chili liquid into medium bowl and stir in muffin mix; cover with plastic wrap. Microwave until mixture is thickened, about 1 minute. Slowly whisk mixture into chili and simmer until chili is slightly thickened, 5 to 10 minutes. Season with salt and pepper. Serve. (Chili can be refrigerated for up to 3 days.)

Southern-Style Skillet Corn Bread

Every skillet corn bread recipe I make turns out too tender, like a corn muffin, rather than crisp, like the corn bread I grew up on in Georgia. Any suggestions? –Polly Smith, Evansville, Ind.

As the lone Southern cook in a test kitchen full of New Englanders, I assumed the responsibility of introducing my coworkers to Southern-style corn bread. Unlike sweet and cakey Northern versions that are better suited to the dessert table, Southern corn bread contains neither sugar nor flour, making it savory enough to join the main course. I wanted to make a proper Southern corn bread with hearty corn flavor, a sturdy, moist crumb, and a dark brown crust that would win Northern allegiance.

Whereas Northern corn bread is cooked in a baking pan in a moderate oven, Southern skillet corn bread requires a little juggling—but the crisp crust is well worth the effort. The fat (oil, butter, bacon fat, or lard) is preheated in a cast-iron skillet and then combined with a mixture of cornmeal, buttermilk or milk, eggs, baking powder and baking soda, and salt. The batter is poured into the hot greased skillet and cooked in the oven until golden and crusty.

After whipping up a spread of existing recipes, I realized this wasn't going to be easy. One corn bread was flat as a pancake, another was drip-ping in grease, and most were sorely lacking in flavor. Since corn flavor is absolutely essential to good Southern-style skillet corn bread, I figured I'd work through flavor issues first and fix the texture later.

I moved forward using the least offensive recipe of the lot, which was made with flavorful whole-grain stone-ground cornmeal. Subsequent testing, however, exposed the stone-ground cornmeal as too gritty, even when I tried grinding it down further in a food processor. I made my next batch with widely available and finely ground Quaker cornmeal. The texture of this corn bread was certainly better, but now the corn flavor was very mild— not really a surprise, since the germ is removed from this cornmeal during processing. Hoping that toasting would intensify its flavor, I spread the finely ground cornmeal on a baking sheet and threw it into the oven. I couldn't believe what a difference a mere five minutes of toasting had made: The corn bread now had big corn flavor, with minimal grit.

Increasing the buttermilk, which my tasters preferred to milk, added a sharp tang that worked well with the corn. When it came to fat selection, my tasters rejected bacon drip-pings, shortening, and lard, saying that each had a distinct flavor that took away from the corn; a combination of butter (for flavor) and vegetable oil (which can withstand high heat without burning) worked much better. The flavor was now on track, but the texture was too crumbly.

One corn bread recipe I'd seen made a cornmeal mush by softening raw cornmeal with boiling water to moisten the bread's texture. Using the same principle, I mixed the hot toasted cornmeal with the buttermilk. The cornmeal soft-ened in just a few minutes; then I mixed the batter and put the skillet into the oven. Now *this* was the corn bread I remem-bered—crisp, slightly moist, cohesive and not crumbly, and with bold corn flavor. But would it win over my co-workers? I sliced up fat wedges and listened with satisfaction as each taster grudgingly admitted that when it comes to corn bread, the South just might be onto something. –Cali Rich

SOUTHERN-STYLE SKILLET CORN BREAD

SERVES 12

While any 10-inch ovensafe skillet will work here, our first choice (for both tradition and function) is a cast-iron skillet. Avoid coarsely ground cornmeal, as it will make the corn bread gritty.

- 2¼ **cups cornmeal**
- 2 **cups buttermilk**
- ¼ **cup vegetable oil**
- 4 **tablespoons unsalted butter, cut into pieces**
- 1 **teaspoon baking powder**
- 1 **teaspoon baking soda**
- ¾ **teaspoon salt**
- 2 **large eggs**

1. Adjust oven racks to lower-middle and middle posi-tions and heat oven to 450 degrees. Heat 10-inch oven-safe skillet on middle rack for 10 minutes. Bake cornmeal on rimmed baking sheet set on lower-middle rack until fragrant and color begins to deepen, about 5 minutes. Transfer hot cornmeal to large bowl and whisk in buttermilk; set aside.

2. Add oil to hot skillet and continue to bake until oil is just smoking, about 5 minutes. Remove skillet from oven and add butter, carefully swirling pan until butter is melted. Pour all but 1 tablespoon oil mixture into cornmeal mixture, leaving remaining fat in pan. Whisk baking powder, baking soda, salt, and eggs into cornmeal mixture.

3. Pour cornmeal mixture into hot skillet and bake until top begins to crack and sides are golden brown, 12 to 16 minutes. Let cool in pan 5 minutes, then turn out onto wire rack. Serve.

Dry-toasting the cornmeal before mixing the batter maximizes the corn flavor in this savory bread.

Secrets to SOUTHERN-STYLE CORN BREAD

Follow these steps to ensure bold corn flavor and the perfect texture, inside and out.

1. Toasting the cornmeal gives the bread richer corn flavor.

2. Combining the hot corn-meal and buttermilk softens the cornmeal, resulting in a tender, sturdy, slightly moist crumb.

3. A greased and thor-oughly heated pan creates a crisp crust.

Ultimate Garlic Roast Chicken

Whenever I try to flavor a roast chicken with garlic, I end up with burned, bitter garlic flavor. Can you help? –Jacob Beckett, Cleveland, Ohio

Kitchen Know-How
ROASTED GARLIC THREE WAYS

Getting great roasted garlic flavor into the chicken and pan sauce meant cooking halved garlic cloves in oil until their flavor had mellowed—and enhanced the oil. The mixture was then pureed (reserving some of the oil) to create a paste. Here's how we flavored the chicken and sauce with those elements.

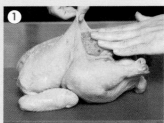

1. Use your hands to evenly distribute the garlic puree under the skin of the chicken. Be sure that the puree coats not only the breast meat but the thigh and leg meat as well.

2. For garlicky, crisp skin, rub the entire exterior of the chicken, front and back, with the reserved garlic oil.

3. Add the reserved garlic puree (along with chicken broth and white wine) to the roasting pan halfway through cooking; the mixture will cook down and serve as the foundation for the pan sauce.

Flavoring a roast chicken with garlic sounds easy, but while testing existing garlic chicken recipes I learned that the garlic flavor was either nonexistent or so strong the birds were inedible. Some recipes sprinkled powdered or granulated garlic over the chicken, but the garlic burned and turned bitter by the time the meat was done. Garlic butter rubbed under the skin tasted steamed and overly pungent. I wanted the sweet, nutty garlic flavor to be strong but not overpowering, with a pan sauce that would enhance the garlic in the chicken.

I started by using the test kitchen's method for roasting a whole chicken: breast-side down, elevated on a wire rack, at 375 degrees for 35 minutes, then breast-side up at 450 degrees for another 30 to 40 minutes. This ensures that the dark meat has more exposure to high heat, promoting even cooking and crispier skin.

The most promising recipe from my initial tests included instructions for roasted garlic, which was pureed and rubbed over the skin of the chicken during the last 15 minutes of cooking. This chicken exhibited pronounced but not overpowering garlic flavor. Roasted garlic was a good place to start, but roasting whole heads of garlic takes over an hour in the oven. Was there a faster way to roasted garlic flavor?

The test kitchen sometimes cooks garlic in oil to tame its bite and draw out its sweetness. Following this path, I cut garlic cloves in half (to speed their cooking), covered the garlic with olive oil, and cooked them over low heat for just 10 minutes then I pureed the softened cloves and olive oil to a smooth paste and carefully slid the paste under the skin of the breast, thighs, and legs (the paste burned on the exterior of the bird) and rubbed some reserved garlic-infused oil over the outside of the chicken to help crisp the skin. The resulting chicken had moist meat, crisp skin, and a nice garlic punch.

I needed 4 tablespoons of garlic puree to spread under the skin. This translated to a whopping 25 cloves!

In the test kitchen, we typically add water to the roasting pan to keep the drippings from scorching. I saw this as an opportunity to add more garlic puree and flavorful liquids (tasters liked chicken broth and white wine) that could cook down in the oven and form the foundation of a simple pan sauce. I was now making 8 tablespoons of garlic puree and needed 50 cloves of garlic. For cooks who can't imagine working with so much fresh garlic, I found that prepeeled garlic cloves were just fine in this recipe.

The pan sauce was perfumed with sweet garlic flavor, but the actual bits of garlic were pretty spent; I strained them out. A little cornstarch thickened the sauce, and butter and fresh tarragon added the finishing touches. I finally had a chicken and pan sauce with ultimate garlic flavor. –**Diane Unger**

GARLIC ROAST CHICKEN
SERVES 3 TO 4

You will need one 8-ounce jar of peeled garlic cloves or 3 to 4 whole heads of garlic (see page 31 for tips on peeling large amounts of garlic cloves).

- 50 garlic cloves, peeled and halved (see note)
- ¼ cup extra-virgin olive oil
- 1 (3½- to 4-pound) whole chicken
  Salt and pepper
- 1¾ cups low-sodium chicken broth
- ¾ cup white wine
- ½ cup plus 1 tablespoon water
- 1 teaspoon cornstarch

Our quick "roasted" garlic flavors the meat and serves as the base of the pan sauce we serve with this chicken.

- 2 tablespoons cold unsalted butter, cut into pieces
- 2 teaspoons finely chopped fresh tarragon

1. Adjust oven rack to lower-middle position and heat oven to 375 degrees. Combine garlic and oil in small saucepan. Cook, covered, over medium-low heat, stirring occasionally, until garlic is softened and straw-colored, 10 to 15 minutes. Reserve 1 tablespoon oil and transfer remaining garlic mixture to food processor; puree until smooth. Let cool.

2. Pat chicken dry inside and out with paper towels. Combine ¼ cup garlic puree, ¼ teaspoon salt, and ½ teaspoon pepper in small bowl. Tuck wings behind back, then, following photos 1 and 2 at left, spread garlic mixture under skin of chicken and rub reserved oil over outside of chicken. Tie legs together with kitchen twine. Season chicken with salt and pepper and arrange, breast-side down, on V-rack set inside roasting pan. Roast until just golden, about 35 minutes.

3. Remove chicken from oven and, using wad of paper towels, flip chicken breast-side up. Raise oven temperature to 450 degrees. Whisk broth, wine, ½ cup water, and remaining garlic puree in measuring cup, then pour into roasting pan. Return chicken to oven and roast until thigh meat registers 170 to 175 degrees, 30 to 40 minutes. Transfer chicken to cutting board and let rest 20 minutes.

4. Meanwhile, transfer pan juices and any accumulated chicken juices to saucepan; skim fat. Whisk remaining water and cornstarch in small bowl, then add to saucepan. Simmer until sauce is slightly thickened, about 2 minutes. Whisk in butter, then strain into serving bowl. Stir in tarragon and season with salt and pepper. Carve chicken and serve, passing sauce at table.

Baked Stuffed Shrimp

I've tried to make baked stuffed shrimp, but the recipes have been awful. I end up with undercooked, mushy stuffing and overcooked, rubbery shrimp. What am I doing wrong? –Martin Taylor, Augusta, Maine

Baked stuffed shrimp certainly sounds like a special occasion meal. Colossal shrimp are spread open, packed with a buttery stuffing, and baked until the stuffing is crisp and the shrimp are just cooked through. But after preparing several cookbook recipes, I realized that there are two big problems—mushy, bland stuffing and shrimp as chewy as rubber bands. I wanted crisp, flavorful stuffing and perfectly cooked shrimp without heading to a restaurant.

Most stuffing recipes simply stir melted butter and seasonings into bread or cracker crumbs. After sampling several recipes, my tasters preferred the sweeter flavor of fresh bread crumbs. More surprising was that they preferred mayonnaise to butter (which was too greasy) as a binder. Seasoned with mustard, lemon, garlic, cayenne pepper, and a splash of briny clam juice, the stuffing was now very flavorful. Toasting the bread crumbs before baking helped ensure a crispy baked stuffing.

After peeling, deveining, and butterflying the largest shrimp I could find (about 12 shrimp per pound), I divided the stuffing among the shrimp and popped them into a hot oven. Shrimp shrink and curl as they cook, and as a result the stuffing got forced out like a pilot in an ejector seat. To solve this problem, I turned the shrimp over and pressed the stuffing into them. Instead of pushing the stuffing out, this time the shrimp curled around to cradle it. But when I transferred the shrimp from the baking pan to the serving platter, the stuffing rolled right off. It was only when I accidentally cut clear through one shrimp in the prep stage that I found a way to keep the stuffing in place (see photos at right). As the shrimp contracted in the oven, the stuffing was sealed in place.

The cardinal rule of most shrimp recipes is to cook them quickly, otherwise they will overcook and become tough. I tried a range of temperatures from 350 to 475 degrees to crisp the stuffing and cook the shrimp; I was able to get the stuffing crisp, but I couldn't seem to avoid tough, rubbery shrimp—even with short cooking times. Thinking of how the test kitchen gently poaches shrimp for shrimp cocktail, I wondered what would happen if I broke the rule and baked the shrimp for a longer time at a lower temperature.

I arranged my shrimp on the pan and gave it a try. Sure enough, after a full 20 minutes at 275 degrees, the shrimp were moist and perfectly cooked—and they actually shrank less in the gentle heat. After a quick flash under the broiler to crisp up the stuffing, I finally had baked stuffed shrimp that were special enough for any occasion.

–Diane Unger

Visit us online!
For Baked Stuffed Shrimp with Crab and Baked Stuffed Shrimp with Sausage variations, visit CooksCountry.com and look for **Cook's Country Extras.**

We prefer colossal shrimp (about 12 per pound) here, but if you're using extra-large shrimp, start checking for doneness after 15 minutes.

BAKED STUFFED SHRIMP SERVES 4 TO 6

If you can't find clam juice, chicken stock will work in a pinch. Any sturdy rimmed baking sheet can be used in place of the broiler pan bottom.

- 4 slices hearty white sandwich bread, torn into pieces
- ½ cup mayonnaise
- ¼ cup bottled clam juice
- ¼ cup finely chopped fresh parsley
- 4 scallions, chopped fine
- 2 garlic cloves, minced
- 2 teaspoons grated zest and 1 tablespoon juice from 1 lemon
- 1 tablespoon Dijon mustard
- ⅛ teaspoon cayenne pepper Salt
- 1¼ pounds colossal shrimp, peeled and deveined

1. Adjust oven rack to upper-middle position and heat oven to 375 degrees. Pulse bread in food processor to coarse crumbs. Transfer crumbs to broiler pan bottom and bake until golden and dry, 8 to 10 minutes, stirring halfway through cooking time. Remove crumbs from oven and reduce temperature to 275 degrees.

2. Combine toasted bread crumbs, mayonnaise, clam juice, parsley, scallions, garlic, lemon zest and juice, mustard, cayenne, and ¼ teaspoon salt in large bowl.

3. Pat shrimp dry with paper towels and season with salt. Grease empty broiler pan bottom. Following photos 1 to 4 at right, butterfly and cut hole through center of each shrimp and arrange cut-side down on prepared pan. Divide bread crumb mixture among shrimp, pressing to adhere. Bake until shrimp are opaque, 20 to 25 minutes.

4. Remove shrimp from oven and heat broiler. Broil shrimp until crumbs are deep golden brown and crispy, 1 to 3 minutes. Serve.

Kitchen Know-How
PERFECT STUFFED SHRIMP

Cutting a hole clear through the center of each butterflied shrimp may seem like a mistake, but it actually gives the shrimp a way of holding on to the stuffing. The shrimp are butterflied on the convex side before being flipped over onto the pan.

1. Use a sharp paring knife to cut along (but not through) the vein line, then open up the shrimp like a book.

2. Using the tip of the paring knife, cut a 1-inch opening all the way through the center of the shrimp.

3. After the shrimp have been butterflied and the opening has been cut, flip the shrimp over onto the broiler pan so that they will curl around the stuffing.

4. Divide the stuffing among the shrimp, firmly pressing the stuffing into the opening and to the edges of the shrimp.

Chicago-Style Spicy Roast Beef

When I was growing up, my next-door neighbor's mom used to make a Sunday roast beef that was coated with a blend of dried Italian spices and served au jus, with a spicy, beefy broth on the side. Do you have a good recipe? –Robin Kendall, Fort Lauderdale, Fla.

1. Brown the meat before roasting to create a flavorful crust on the exterior. Transfer the roast to a rack in a roasting pan and begin work on the jus.

2. The browned bits left behind in the pan are the base for the jus. Cook onion, garlic, and seasonings in the empty skillet, then add the broths and water to help loosen the browned bits.

3. Pour the jus into the roasting pan below the elevated roast so it can catch flavorful drippings and cook down to the desired consistency while the meat cooks.

4. Apply a flavorful rub, mixed with oil to help it adhere, after browning to prevent the dried herbs from burning.

In Chicago, spicy Italian roast beef usually starts with an inexpensive rump roast, which is marinated overnight—most often in a blend of Italian spices, garlic, vinegar, and oil (or even bottled Italian dressing)—then oven-braised in beef broth. The roast is sliced thin and served with the spicy jus. The dish originated with street vendors outside the Union Stock Yards and was traditionally served as a sandwich (see page 15). For home cooks, it makes sense to serve this roast for dinner—and make sure to have enough leftovers for sandwiches the next day.

I tested several recipes and immediately identified two problems I wanted to fix—mushy meat with no crusty exterior, and a jus that was too salty but otherwise bland. To start, I had to choose an economical cut of meat. (You'd never use tenderloin or prime rib in this recipe.) My first test pitted blade and top sirloin roasts against the rump roast. The blade and rump roasts were pretty tough, especially in comparison to the meaty and tender top sirloin roast.

In the past, the test kitchen has found little benefit to marinating most cuts of meat. Highly acidic marinades tend to make meat mushy. A spice rub or herb paste provides just as much flavor and works in seconds—not hours. So for my next test, I skipped the overnight marinade and instead rubbed a top sirloin roast with a blend of dried oregano, basil, garlic powder, and red pepper flakes. The spice-rubbed roast tasted better than any roast I had marinated, but it was still too mushy. Roasting the meat in a pan filled with the jus was clearly the problem. Elevating the roast on a rack above the jus was a big improvement.

Serving this roast beef medium-rare ensures that it will be moist, and the spicy jus provides authentic Chicago flavor.

My roast still lacked the browned crust I consider the hallmark of a well-cooked roast. I tried browning the spice-coated roast in a skillet, but the smoke was intense and the rub tasted bitter and awful. Browning the meat in the skillet before rubbing it worked great—especially when I added a little oil to the spices so they'd adhere to the seared exterior of the meat. Once the roast was browned and coated with spices, a low oven temperature of 300 degrees helped the roast cook evenly and stay juicy inside.

With the roast settled, it was time to address the jus. No one liked the flat flavor of canned beef broth; a mix of chicken and beef broths tasted better. Adding some water to the broths helped tone down the salt (even the low-sodium broths preferred by the test kitchen have quite a bit), but the jus was still bland. Using the browned bits left in the skillet from searing the meat, I added onion and fresh garlic and toasted the dried spices to bring out their flavor. Once the base was established, I added the broths and water and then poured the jus into the roasting pan below the elevated meat so it could catch any drippings exuded during roasting. This way, there was no last-minute fuss. My jus was ready when the roast was done.

My Chicago-Style Italian Roast Beef has the perfect balance of spice, garlic, and herbs and sports a crusty, browned exterior. Enjoy it for Sunday dinner, but make sure to save leftovers for sandwiches.

–Lynn Clark

On the Side: Sautéed Broccoli Rabe

What's the secret to taming this leafy green's bitter edge?

Broccoli rabe is widely available in supermarkets, even in the dead of winter. And while the assertive, peppery flavor of this green (it's reminiscent of mustard greens or collards) is appealing, broccoli rabe can sometimes be downright bitter.

Rabe is made up of hearty stalks and more tender florets and leaves. To ensure that all components would cook properly, I knew I'd have to chop the rabe into small pieces and precook it before sautéing it with flavorful ingredients like garlic and roasted red peppers. Both steaming and microwaving produced decent texture, but they did nothing to temper the bitterness. Blanching (quickly cooking in salted boiling water) worked much better, as some of the bitterness had a chance to cook out. And after a quick spin in the sauté pan with the garlic and red peppers, the broccoli rabe was ready to serve. –Cali Rich

SAUTÉED BROCCOLI RABE WITH ROASTED RED PEPPERS SERVES 4

- 1 large bunch broccoli rabe (about 1 pound), trimmed and cut into 1-inch pieces
  Salt and pepper
- 3 tablespoons extra-virgin olive oil
- ¼ cup drained jarred roasted red peppers, chopped fine
- 2 garlic cloves, minced

1. Bring 4 quarts water to boil in Dutch oven. Add broccoli rabe and 1 tablespoon salt and cook until just tender, about 2 minutes. Drain thoroughly.

2. Heat 2 tablespoons oil in empty Dutch oven over medium-high heat until shimmering. Add drained broccoli rabe to pot and cook without stirring until lightly browned, about 2 minutes. Push broccoli rabe to side of pot and add another 1 teaspoon oil, red peppers, and garlic. Cook until fragrant, about 30 seconds, then stir into broccoli rabe. Season with salt and pepper, transfer to serving bowl, and drizzle with remaining oil. Serve. (Rabe can be refrigerated for up to 24 hours at the end of step 1.)

CHICAGO-STYLE ITALIAN ROAST BEEF

SERVES 6 TO 8

See page 30 for more information about buying a top sirloin roast. If your roast is larger than 4 pounds, you may need to increase the cooking time slightly in step 4. Save leftover meat and jus for sandwiches (below right).

- 4 teaspoons garlic powder
- 4 teaspoons dried basil
- 4 teaspoons dried oregano
- 1 tablespoon pepper
- 1 (4-pound) top sirloin roast, fat trimmed to ¼ inch thick
- 2 tablespoons vegetable oil
- 1 onion, chopped fine
- 3 garlic cloves, minced
- 1 tablespoon flour
- 2 cups low-sodium beef broth
- 2 cups low-sodium chicken broth
- 1½ cups water
- 1 teaspoon red pepper flakes
- 2 teaspoons salt

1. Adjust oven rack to lower-middle position and heat oven to 300 degrees. Combine garlic powder, basil, oregano, and pepper in small bowl.

2. Pat roast dry with paper towels. Heat 1 tablespoon oil in large skillet over medium-high heat until just smoking. Brown roast all over, about 10 minutes, then transfer to V-rack set inside roasting pan.

3. Add onion to fat in skillet and cook over medium heat until softened, about 5 minutes. Stir in garlic, flour, and 1 teaspoon spice mixture until fragrant, about 1 minute. Stir in broths and water, using wooden spoon to scrape up browned bits. Bring to boil, then pour into roasting pan.

4. Stir remaining oil, pepper flakes, and salt into remaining spice mixture. Rub mixture all over meat and roast until meat registers 125 degrees (for medium-rare), 75 to 90 minutes. Transfer roast to cutting board, tent with foil, and let rest 20 minutes.

5. Pour jus through fine-mesh strainer and keep warm. Slice roast crosswise against grain into ¼-inch-thick slices. Serve with jus.

What to Do with Leftovers:
Chicago-Style Italian Beef Sandwiches

For authentic Chicago-style sandwiches, the secret is in the spice.

Ask any Chicago transplants what they miss most about their home city and it's a good bet the list will include spicy Italian beef sandwiches. Unlike deep-dish pizza, this local favorite is almost impossible to find outside the Chicago city limits. Before I developed a recipe for this iconic sandwich, I had to go to the source and eat the real thing.

The ambience at Al's, a roadside sandwich stand on Taylor Street in Chicago's Little Italy (the neighborhood in which the sandwich is said to have been invented in the 1930s), wasn't much to speak of, but Al's Italian beef sandwich definitely was. The meat was seasoned with Italian spices (oregano, basil, garlic, and red pepper flakes), sliced thin, and bathed in a tangy, spicy jus before being piled high onto a jus-soaked roll and topped with a peppery giardiniera (a spicy relish of pickled vegetables). I was eager to get home to create my own recipe.

Back in the test kitchen, I got to work with the leftover beef and jus from our Chicago-Style Italian Roast Beef. I thinly sliced the leftover roast and heated the slices and the jus together to marry their flavors. I ladled the jus on a sub roll, loaded the beef on, and topped it with bottled giardiniera. But now the sandwich was too messy to pick up.

I gave the giardiniera a whirl in the food processor with a little mayonnaise, which added richness and brought the chopped vegetables together into a cohesive mixture. Adding a tablespoon of the seasoned brine from the giardiniera bottle gave the sandwiches a little extra bite. –Lynn Clark

CHICAGO-STYLE ITALIAN BEEF SANDWICHES SERVES 4

If you don't have enough leftover jus, visit CooksCountry.com for our Quick Jus recipe.

- 4 (6-inch) sub rolls, split partially open lengthwise
- 1 tablespoon vegetable oil
- 4 cups thinly sliced leftover roast beef
- 1½ cups leftover jus (see note)
- 1 (16-ounce) bottle giardiniera (page 31), drained, 1 tablespoon brine reserved
- 1 tablespoon mayonnaise
- ¼ teaspoon red pepper flakes

1. Adjust oven rack to upper-middle position and heat broiler. Brush interior of rolls with oil and arrange, oiled-side up, on baking sheet. Broil until golden brown, about 1 minute.

2. Combine beef, jus, and giardiniera brine in large skillet and simmer over medium heat until meat is no longer pink, about 6 minutes. Meanwhile, pulse giardiniera, mayonnaise, and red pepper flakes in food processor until finely chopped.

3. Arrange beef on toasted rolls, drizzle with jus, and top with giardiniera mixture. Serve.

I'm Looking for a Recipe

READERS HELP READERS FIND RECIPES

We've Got Mail

Scores of readers sent us recipes in response to the request for Apple Dapple Cake in our August/September 2007 issue. We really liked the recipe sent by Gloria Elkins (right). Go to **CooksCountry.com** and click **Looking for a Recipe** to find hundreds of recipes submitted by readers who responded to recipe requests in previous issues of *Cook's Country*.

APPLE DAPPLE CAKE Gloria Elkins Hendersonville, N.C.

SERVES 12

"My mother made this cake on the weekends and for camping trips when I was a child. I've been making the recipe myself for the past 35 years, and I especially like to serve it around the holidays for a crowd. It also freezes terrifically."

Cake		Glaze	
3	eggs	4	tablespoons unsalted butter
2	cups sugar	½	cup brown sugar
1⅓	cups vegetable oil	¼	cup milk
2	teaspoons vanilla extract		
3	cups all-purpose flour, sifted		**1. For the cake:** Adjust oven rack to middle position and
1	teaspoon baking soda		heat oven to 350 degrees. Beat eggs until light and fluffy.
1	teaspoon baking powder		Add sugar, oil, and vanilla and beat until combined. Beat in
1	teaspoon salt		flour, baking soda, baking powder, salt, and cinnamon. Add
1	teaspoon ground cinnamon		apples and walnuts. Pour into greased 16-cup tube pan
3	cups chopped Granny Smith		and bake until toothpick comes out clean, 60 to 75 minutes.
	apples (about 2 large)		Let cool 10 minutes, then invert onto serving plate.
1	cup chopped walnuts		**2. For the glaze:** Boil butter, brown sugar, and milk for
			1 minute. Pour glaze over warm cake and serve.

Forman's Piccalilli Relish

Piccalilli relish was a favorite of our family for many years. We discovered the Forman brand in the 1950s, but it has since disappeared from grocery store shelves. I know the main ingredients are green tomatoes, onions, brown sugar, and vinegar. I would love to have a recipe to make some for my family and friends. Thank you.

William McKenna Jr.
Secane, Pa.

Gilchrist Macaroons

I've been trying for years to get the recipe for the macaroon cookies that were sold at the old Gilchrist department store in Boston. They were moist and chewy on the inside, crunchy on the outside, and had a cherry on top. They are one of the most wonderful memories I have from my childhood visits to Boston with my mother, aunts, and cousins. I would be so appreciative if someone could find this wonderful old recipe. I have tried for years to make them on my own, but mine always come up short. I thank you in advance.

Elaine Glynn
Via e-mail

Pineapple Cheesecake

Help! Back in the mid-1970s, I had a wonderful pineapple cheesecake recipe that included a homemade crust. I remember that a sour cream concoction was poured on the top for the last 10 minutes of baking. I was in my teens then and gave the recipe to everyone I knew; however, no one seems to have kept track of it. I've been looking for the recipe for 30 years, so any help would be much appreciated.

Sandra Cox
Redford, Mich.

Apple Rice Cake

When I was a child, my grandmother made an apple rice cake with fresh apples, white rice, and lots of butter. The mixture was fried up in a skillet. She has since passed away, and no one remembers the recipe. I hope you can help!

Lynne Karniol
Boca Raton, Fla.

Dorothy Muriel's Golden Glow Cake

Whenever my brothers and sisters and I get together, the talk turns to the great things we ate growing up, like our favorite Golden Glow Cake from Dorothy Muriel's bakery. Unfortunately, the bakery has been out of business for several years, but I was wondering if any of the recipes survived, particularly one for Golden Glow. It was a light, golden-colored spice cake that was square in shape and topped with vanilla buttercream frosting and chopped walnuts. Any information would be really appreciated.

Winifred Pilla
Albuquerque, N.M.

Almond Tarts

I'm looking for a recipe for almond tarts. When I was growing up in St. Paul, Minn., there was a bakery on the east side of town that made little almond tarts about 3 or 4 inches in diameter. They had an almond pastry or shortbread tart shell that was filled with a rich, moist almond-cake filling and topped with white icing and a frosting flower. The bakery has been sold and no longer makes the little beauties my brother and I adored for over 40 years. Can anyone please help? I would be so grateful.

Julie McNeely
Lino Lakes, Minn.

Spanish Pudding

When I was young, my grandmother made a lovely vanilla-flavored dessert that she called Spanish Pudding. When the pudding was turned out onto a plate, it had formed two distinct layers. The top was an almost transparent gel and the lower layer was milky white. My grandmother has been gone many years now, and the recipe is lost. We just had a family reunion last fall and many of us remembered the pudding. I would love to be able to make it for the family. I certainly hope someone can help.

Susan MacFarland
Pine Beach, N.J.

Cherry Tootsie Fudge Cake

My mother is looking for a recipe from around 1945 that she thinks was called Cherry Tootsie Fudge Cake. This cake was made with a store-bought product called something like Tootsie Fudge Bits, and the recipe was printed on the package. I have looked everywhere for this recipe to no avail. My mother is almost 80, and I sure would love to surprise her on her birthday!

Antoinette McClement
Via e-mail

Elle's Pastry-Wrapped Pears

Elle magazine published a recipe for Elle Pears in the early 1990s. The pears were wrapped in strips of pastry and then cooked in a sauce. It was my family's favorite Christmas dessert for years, but I've since lost the recipe. I've contacted *Elle*, but they have not responded yet. I would really like to surprise my ill son with this recipe. Thank you for your help.

Janice James
Kirk, Colo.

Smoked Chicken Lasagna

Many years ago, probably in the 1980s, the *Chicago Tribune Magazine* printed the most delicious recipe for smoked chicken lasagna. I've lost the recipe, and the *Tribune* doesn't offer an archive of recipes. If one of your readers knows of this recipe and is willing to share, I would be most appreciative. It is a scrumptious alternative to traditional lasagna.

Lin Baer
Mesa, Ariz.

Stretch's Chicken Savoy

My favorite dish growing up in northern New Jersey was Stretch's Chicken Savoy from the Belmont Tavern in Bloomfield. The dish consisted of crispy chicken, onions, and button mushrooms and was finished with a vinegar sauce. I have searched in chicken cookbooks and online for a recipe, but I've come up empty every time. I hope maybe you can help.

Pauline Scarola
Via e-mail

Texas Hats

I lost a recipe for Texas Hats when my daughter took one of my cookbooks to college 25 years ago and misplaced it. It was a tasty hamburger concoction that was stir-fried, poured over crisp corn chips, and topped with shredded cheese. I can't seem to get the right proportions for the hamburger mixture.

Betsy Kerr
Placerville, Calif.

Are you looking for a special recipe? Or do you have a recipe a fellow *Cook's Country* reader is seeking? Post your requests and recipes by visiting **CooksCountry.com** and clicking on **Looking for a Recipe**. We'll share recipe requests and found recipes on CooksCountry.com and print as many as we can in the magazine. You may also write to us at Looking for a Recipe, Cook's Country, P.O. Box 470739, Brookline, MA 02447.

Find the Rooster!

A tiny version of this rooster has been hidden somewhere in the pages of this issue. If you find it, write to us with its location (plus your name and address) and you will be entered into a random drawing. The first correct entry drawn will receive a Unicorn Magnum Plus pepper mill (our test winner—see page 29), and the next five will each receive a complimentary one-year subscription to *Cook's Country*. To enter the contest, visit **CooksCountry.com/emailus** or write to us at Rooster, Cook's Country, P.O. Box 470739, Brookline, MA 02447. Entries are due by March 31, 2008.

Did you find the rooster in the December/January 2008 issue? It was hidden in the Ham and Bean Soup photo on page 10. Lorili Johnson of Newport, Wash., spotted it and won a KitchenAid Classic Plus Stand Mixer.

30-Minute Supper

SPICY PASTA BAKE WITH SAUSAGE

30-Minute Supper

BEEF AND VEGETABLE FAJITAS

30-Minute Supper

GARLIC SHRIMP WITH BASIL

30-Minute Supper

HEARTY CHICKEN, VEGETABLE, AND NOODLE SOUP

BEEF AND VEGETABLE FAJITAS SERVES 4

To warm the tortillas, stack them on a plate, wrap the plate with plastic, and microwave it on high power for about 1 minute. Serve with guacamole, shredded cheese, and/or sour cream.

- 1 flank steak (about 1½ pounds)
  Salt and pepper
- 2 tablespoons vegetable oil
- 4 tablespoons juice from 2–3 limes
- 1 red onion, halved and sliced thin
- 1 red bell pepper, seeded and sliced thin
- 1½ teaspoons chili powder
- 1 cup frozen corn
- 8 (6-inch) flour tortillas
- ½ cup chopped fresh cilantro

1. Pat steak dry with paper towels and season with salt and pepper. Heat 1 tablespoon oil in large skillet over medium-high heat until just smoking. Cook steak until well browned, about 5 minutes per side. Transfer to plate and drizzle with 2 tablespoons lime juice. Tent with foil and let rest 10 minutes.

2. Add remaining oil to empty skillet and heat until shimmering. Add onion, bell pepper, and chili powder and cook until softened, about 5 minutes. Stir in corn and remaining lime juice and cook until heated through, about 1 minute. Transfer to serving platter.

3. Slice steak thinly on the bias and against the grain. Transfer to platter with vegetable mixture. Serve with tortillas, passing cilantro at table.

SPICY PASTA BAKE WITH SAUSAGE SERVES 4

If you want a less-spicy dish or can't find Ro-Tel tomatoes, substitute 1¼ cups canned diced tomatoes. Andouille, linguica, or kielbasa sausage can be substituted for the chorizo.

- 1 pound chorizo sausage, halved lengthwise and sliced thin
- 1 onion, chopped fine
- 4 garlic cloves, minced
- 3 cups low-sodium chicken broth
- 1 (10-ounce) can Ro-Tel tomatoes (see note)
- ½ cup heavy cream
- 12 ounces penne pasta
  Salt and pepper
- 2 cups shredded pepper Jack cheese
- 4 scallions, sliced thin

1. Adjust oven rack to upper-middle position and heat broiler. Cook chorizo and onion in large oven-safe skillet over medium-high heat until lightly browned, about 8 minutes. Add garlic and cook until fragrant, about 30 seconds.

2. Stir in broth, tomatoes, cream, pasta, ½ teaspoon salt, and ½ teaspoon pepper and bring to boil. Cover pan and reduce heat to medium-low. Simmer, stirring frequently, until pasta is tender, about 15 minutes.

3. Off heat, uncover pan and stir in ½ cup cheese. Top with remaining cheese and broil until cheese is melted and spotty brown, about 3 minutes. Sprinkle with scallions. Serve.

HEARTY CHICKEN, VEGETABLE, AND NOODLE SOUP
SERVES 4

Light 'n Fluffy brand egg noodles are the test kitchen's favorite.

- 3 tablespoons unsalted butter
- 1 onion, chopped
- 1 celery rib, sliced thin
- 2 carrots, peeled and sliced into thin rounds
- 2 teaspoons minced fresh thyme
  Salt and pepper
- 8 cups low-sodium chicken broth
- 4 ounces egg noodles (about 2 cups)
- 1 rotisserie chicken, skin discarded, meat shredded
  into bite-sized pieces (about 3 cups)
- 1 cup frozen peas

1. Melt butter in Dutch oven over medium-high heat. Cook onion, celery, carrots, thyme, and ½ teaspoon salt until lightly browned, about 5 minutes. Stir in broth and simmer, covered, until vegetables are softened, 10 to 15 minutes.

2. Add noodles to pot and simmer, uncovered, until tender, about 5 minutes. Off heat, stir in chicken and peas until heated through, about 2 minutes. Season with salt and pepper. Serve.

GARLIC SHRIMP WITH BASIL SERVES 4

This garlicky dish can be served with crusty bread or over linguine or white rice.

- 1½ pounds extra-large shrimp, peeled and deveined
  Salt and pepper
- 2 tablespoons olive oil
- 10 garlic cloves, minced
- ¾ cup white wine
- 1 (14.5-ounce) can diced tomatoes
- ½ cup finely chopped fresh basil
- 4 tablespoons unsalted butter, cut into pieces
- 2 tablespoons capers, drained and minced
- 1 teaspoon lemon juice

1. Pat shrimp dry with paper towels and season with salt and pepper. Heat 1 tablespoon oil in large nonstick skillet over medium-high heat until just smoking. Add shrimp and cook until lightly browned, about 1 minute per side. Transfer to plate.

2. Add remaining oil, garlic, and ½ teaspoon pepper to empty skillet and cook until fragrant, about 30 seconds. Stir in wine and tomatoes and simmer until slightly thickened, about 5 minutes. Off heat, whisk in basil, butter, capers, and lemon juice. Add shrimp and any accumulated juices to skillet. Cover and let sit until shrimp are heated through, about 5 minutes. Season with salt and pepper. Serve.

STEAK TERIYAKI

CHEESY CHICKEN AND BROCCOLI BAKE

CHICKEN MILANESE

VEGETABLE FRIED RICE

CHEESY CHICKEN AND BROCCOLI BAKE SERVES 4

Serve over rice or egg noodles.

- 4 boneless, skinless chicken breasts (about 1½ pounds)
  Salt and pepper
- 4 tablespoons unsalted butter
- 1 onion, chopped fine
- ¼ cup all-purpose flour
- 1 cup low-sodium chicken broth
- ½ cup heavy cream
- ½ cup dry sherry
- 1½ pounds broccoli, florets chopped, stems peeled and sliced thin
- 1½ cups grated Parmesan cheese

1. Adjust oven rack to upper-middle position and heat broiler. Pat chicken dry with paper towels and season with salt and pepper. Melt 1 tablespoon butter in large nonstick skillet over medium-high heat. Cook chicken until golden brown, about 3 minutes per side. Transfer to plate.

2. Add remaining butter and onion to empty skillet and cook until onion is beginning to brown, about 2 minutes. Stir in flour and cook until golden, about 1 minute. Whisk in broth, cream, and sherry and simmer until thickened, about 3 minutes. Return chicken to skillet, reduce heat to low, and simmer, covered, until chicken is cooked through, about 15 minutes. Transfer chicken to broiler-safe baking dish.

3. Meanwhile, microwave broccoli on high power, covered, in large bowl until bright green and slightly softened, 2 to 4 minutes. Add broccoli and 1 cup cheese to skillet, stirring to combine. Season with salt and pepper and pour broccoli mixture over chicken. Sprinkle remaining cheese over top and broil until browned and bubbly, 2 to 4 minutes. Serve.

STEAK TERIYAKI SERVES 4

Sprinkle with toasted sesame seeds and serve with rice, if desired.

- ½ cup soy sauce
- ½ cup sugar
- 3 garlic cloves, minced
- 1 tablespoon grated fresh ginger
- ⅛ teaspoon red pepper flakes
- 2 tablespoons cider vinegar
- 2 teaspoons cornstarch
- 3 strip steaks (8–10 ounces each), about 1 inch thick
- 2 teaspoons vegetable oil
- 2 scallions, sliced thin

1. Whisk soy sauce, sugar, garlic, ginger, pepper flakes, vinegar, and cornstarch in bowl.

2. Pat steaks dry with paper towels. Heat oil in large nonstick skillet over medium-high heat until just smoking. Add steaks and cook until well browned, 3 to 5 minutes per side. Transfer to plate and tent with foil.

3. Wipe out skillet and add soy sauce mixture. Simmer over medium heat until sauce is thickened, about 2 minutes. Slice steak thinly against grain and transfer to platter. Pour sauce over steak and sprinkle with scallions. Serve.

VEGETABLE FRIED RICE SERVES 4

You can find coleslaw mix with the bagged lettuces at the supermarket. Four cups of leftover white rice can be substituted for the Uncle Ben's Ready Rice.

- 6 tablespoons soy sauce
- 2 tablespoons rice vinegar
- 1 tablespoon hot sauce
- 1 tablespoon grated fresh ginger
- 4 large eggs
- 4 teaspoons vegetable oil
- 10 scallions, white parts sliced thin, green parts cut into ½-inch pieces
- 4 cups bagged coleslaw mix (see note)
- 1 red bell pepper, seeded and chopped
- 2 (8.8-ounce) packages Uncle Ben's Original Long Grain Ready Rice

1. Whisk soy sauce, vinegar, hot sauce, and ginger in bowl. In another bowl, beat eggs with 2 tablespoons soy sauce mixture until combined.

2. Heat 2 teaspoons oil in large nonstick skillet over medium-high heat until just smoking. Add egg mixture to pan and cook, scrambling and breaking into small pieces, until just set, 1 to 2 minutes. Transfer to plate.

3. Heat remaining oil in empty skillet until just smoking. Cook scallion whites, coleslaw mix, and bell pepper until just beginning to soften, about 1 minute. Add rice and remaining soy sauce mixture and cook until liquid has evaporated and rice is heated through, 2 to 4 minutes. Stir in egg and scallion greens and cook, stirring constantly, until heated through, about 1 minute. Serve.

CHICKEN MILANESE SERVES 4

Serve these lemony cutlets over pasta, with a green salad, or as a sandwich.

- 5 slices hearty white sandwich bread, torn into pieces
- ¾ cup grated Parmesan cheese
- ¼ cup all-purpose flour
- 3 large eggs
- 2 garlic cloves, minced
- 1 teaspoon grated zest and 2 tablespoons juice from 1 lemon
- 6 thin-cut boneless, skinless chicken cutlets (about 1¼ pounds)
  Salt and pepper
- ½ cup vegetable oil

1. Adjust oven rack to middle position and heat oven to 200 degrees. Pulse bread and ¼ cup cheese in food processor until coarsely ground; transfer to shallow dish. Combine remaining cheese and flour in second shallow dish. Beat eggs with garlic and lemon zest in third shallow dish.

2. Pat chicken dry with paper towels and season with salt and pepper. One at a time, coat cutlets lightly with cheese-flour mixture, dip in egg mixture, and then dredge in bread crumbs, pressing to adhere.

3. Heat ¼ cup oil in large nonstick skillet over medium heat until just smoking. Fry half of cutlets until deep golden and crisp, about 2 minutes per side. Drain on paper towel–lined plate and transfer to oven to keep warm. Discard oil, wipe out skillet, and repeat with remaining oil and cutlets. Sprinkle cutlets with lemon juice. Serve.

Garlicky Oven Fries

What's the best way to make crunchy, deeply seasoned, garlicky oven fries?

Cooking fries in the oven not only minimizes mess, it also presents an opportunity to add a big garlic punch.

When a plate of French fries arrives at my table in a restaurant, I immediately pounce on the darkest morsels. Why? Because fries become darker when the sugar in the potato caramelizes and produces sweeter, more complex flavors. As an avowed garlic lover, I wanted to find a way to infuse dark, crunchy, homemade French fries with the nutty flavor of garlic.

Deep-frying at home is daunting and messy, so I turned to the test kitchen's recipe for making oven fries. Our method calls for oven-frying the cut potatoes on a well-oiled pan in a hot oven. For the first five minutes, the potatoes are cooked covered with foil to steam; then the foil is removed so the

exterior can crisp up and the interior can cook through.

I tossed raw potatoes with fresh minced garlic and then followed this procedure, but the garlic burned by the time the fries cooked. Garlic added halfway through the cooking didn't provide enough flavor, and garlic added at the end was too harsh. How was I going to get rich, nutty garlic flavor into these fries?

I went to the spice rack in search of alternatives to fresh garlic. I tried sprinkling garlic salt, dehydrated garlic, and garlic powder on the fries before cooking. Predictably, the garlic salt was too salty and lent little garlic flavor, and the dehydrated garlic had an unpleasant texture. But the garlic powder showed promise: Although it didn't

contribute enough fresh garlic flavor, it was at least making the potatoes subtly garlicky.

Looking to bump up the garlic flavor, I tried infusing the cooking oil with potent fresh garlic. I put a handful of minced garlic in a bowl, poured the oil on top, and heated it in the microwave to allow the garlic to perfume the oil. When I cooked the next batch in the infused oil, I was disappointed that the fries still didn't have the nutty, garlicky kick I was looking for.

But using the microwave to flavor the oil gave me an idea. Instead of covering the potatoes for the first part of baking, could I toss them with some of the infused oil and steam them in the microwave to achieve stronger garlic flavor (and get a jump-start on the cooking)? I placed the raw

cut potatoes in a bowl with some of the garlic oil, covered the bowl with plastic wrap, and microwaved them for five minutes. The potatoes emerged slightly softened and deeply enriched with garlic flavor. After tossing the spuds with garlic powder (and a little cornstarch for extra crunch) and baking them, the finished fries were as dark and crispy as deep-fried fries—with the added bonus of rich, nutty garlic flavor. –**Greg Case**

GARLICKY OVEN FRIES
SERVES 4

Be sure to use potatoes of a similar size and cut them into even wedges so all of the pieces cook at the same rate. Traditional-finish and nonstick baking sheets both work well for this recipe.

- 6 **garlic cloves, minced**
- 6 **tablespoons vegetable oil**
- 3 **russet potatoes (about 8 ounces each), scrubbed and each cut into 12 wedges**
- 2 **tablespoons cornstarch**
- 1½ **teaspoons salt**
- ¾ **teaspoon pepper**
- ½ **teaspoon garlic powder**

1. Adjust oven rack to lowest position and heat oven to 475 degrees. Combine garlic and oil in large bowl and microwave until garlic is fragrant, about 1 minute. Transfer 5 tablespoons oil (leaving garlic in bowl) to rimmed baking sheet, turning sheet to coat.

2. Add potatoes to bowl with remaining oil mixture and toss to coat. Wrap tightly with plastic wrap and microwave on high power until potatoes are translucent around edges, 3 to 6 minutes, shaking bowl to redistribute potatoes halfway through cooking.

3. Combine cornstarch, salt, pepper, and garlic powder in small bowl. Sprinkle over hot potatoes and toss to coat. Arrange potatoes in single layer on prepared baking sheet and bake, turning once, until deep golden brown and crisp, 30 to 40 minutes. Serve.

Kitchen Know-How
GETTING GREAT GARLIC FLAVOR

We use this three-step process to give our crunchy oven fries maximum garlic flavor.

1. Make a garlic-infused oil by microwaving minced garlic and oil until fragrant.

2. Pour 5 tablespoons of garlic oil onto baking sheet and reserve. Toss potato wedges with remaining garlic-oil mixture and microwave until just tender.

3. For a final layer of garlic flavor, toss the potato wedges with garlic powder (and cornstarch for extra crispness) before baking.

Getting to Know Tropical Fruits

The winter months bring a number of exotic fruits from tropical climates to supermarket shelves. Listed below are tasting notes for 12 of our favorites.

Mango
BIG PIT, BIG FLAVOR

Native to Southeast Asia, mangos have "sweet, floral, and silky-smooth" flesh that clings to a large, flat pit. To prepare a mango, trim one end flat, stand the fruit upright, and slice around the pit on either side. (Alternatively, mango splitters, which are similar to apple corers, cost about $10 and work very well.) Mangos are very fragrant when ripe; they will ripen at room temperature.

Carambola
STAR OF THE SHOW

This oblong, five-ribbed fruit is commonly called star fruit. Its crisp, yellowish-green skin is nearly translucent, and its "fragrant, juicy" flesh is dotted with seeds. Carambola's flavor is like a "diluted" combination of "plum, tangerine, and cucumber." Look for taut-skinned, fragrant fruits that yield to gentle pressure. Store at room temperature and slice and add to salads or desserts.

Guava
SWEET BUT SEEDY

The pebbly skin of this Brazilian fruit can be green or purple, and its soft flesh can range from stark white to bright pink. Guava's complex flavor is "honey-sweet and funky," with hints of "berry and pear" mixed with "gym socks." Fresh guavas are riddled with rock-hard seeds and are highly susceptible to fruit fly infestation: We recommend sticking with prepared guava juices or purees.

Pineapple
GO FOR THE GOLD

We prefer Costa Rican–grown pineapples (also labeled "extra-sweet" or "gold"), which are consistently "honey-sweet" in comparison to the "acidic" Hawaiian pineapples with greenish (not yellow) skin. Pineapples will not ripen further once picked, so be sure to purchase golden, fragrant fruit that gives slightly when pressed. Store unpeeled pineapples at room temperature.

Durian
SMELLS BAD, TASTES GOOD

Most westerners consider this Southeast Asian fruit an acquired taste. Once cut, it boasts a "powerfully sulfurous scent" similar to "very strong, very ripe cheese." Its flavor, however, is another matter; tasters liked the "eggnog" character and also praised the "puddinglike" texture. Ripe durian will be fragrant and give slightly when pressed. Use within a day or two of purchase.

Papaya
KING OF THE JUNGLE

Papayas come in a wide range of shapes, colors, and sizes (they can weigh up to 20 pounds!). Their "juicy, custard-smooth" flesh holds hundreds of edible, "peppery" seeds. Papaya is "very sweet" but "musky, like overripe cantaloupe." Ripe papaya is best eaten raw, but unripe papaya can be shredded and used in salads or cooked like a vegetable. Ripe papayas will yield to gentle pressure.

Coconut
SWEET AND EARTHY

To open a coconut, hold it over a bowl and strike it with the dull side of a chef's knife (or a hammer). The flesh is "dense and earthy," with a "vanilla-like finish." When choosing coconuts, give them a shake: They should be heavy and full of liquid. Store at room temperature for up to six months.

Passion Fruit
PULP PERFECT

A passion fruit is roughly the size of a lime and has a tough, leathery skin that wrinkles slightly when ripe. The interior is filled with a seedy, mustard-yellow, gelatinous pulp that is "intensely aromatic," with hints of "peach and raspberry." Passion fruit pulp is often strained to extract the juice. Passion fruit can be refrigerated for up to a week or frozen for up to a month.

Kiwi
FURRY EGG

Though native to China, this brown, egg-shaped fruit is so named because it was first commercially grown in New Zealand. Beneath its furry skin lies brilliant green or gold flesh studded with tiny, crunchy black seeds. Its flavor is "sweet-tart" and "berrylike," and it has a "firm but juicy" texture. Kiwis will ripen at room temperature and can be refrigerated for up to three weeks.

Plantain
COOKING BANANA

This large, starchy variety of banana is popular in Latin American, African, and Asian cuisines. Plantains mature from green to yellow to black. Though fully ripe plantains can be eaten out of hand, most plantains are cooked when they are still underripe. Their flavor is reminiscent of "squash and potato," and they have a "dense, spongy texture." Peel and fry, sauté, or boil.

Pitaya
SCALY AND SEEDY

Also called dragon fruit or strawberry pear, this member of the cactus family has scaly skin that ranges from yellow to purplish-green. The "tender, seedy" flesh can be creamy white to magenta. The fruit is "grainy like a watermelon," with notes of "strawberry" and "clay." To eat, cut in half and scoop out the flesh with a spoon. Pitayas will not ripen once picked, so buy only fragrant, slightly soft fruit.

Rambutan
HAIRY JELLYFISH

Although this Malaysian fruit looks intimidating, its purplish bristles are actually quite soft, and the skin is easily peeled by hand. The interior, which looks like "a jellyfish surrounding a large, woody pit," has a "delicate berry flavor," a "mild tartness," and a texture reminiscent of "gummy bears." Look for brightly colored, fragrant fruit with intact bristles. Peel and eat raw.

Make-Ahead Coffee Cake

Just once, I'd like to have homemade coffee cake with my morning coffee! By the time I assemble the ingredients, mix the batter, and bake the cake, it's nearly lunchtime. Any suggestions? –Tracey Reesce, Columbus, Ohio

Without the cook waking up two hours before the rest of the family, fresh homemade coffee cake isn't a feasible breakfast. Unless, that is, you consider a make-ahead option. I found several make-ahead coffee cake recipes in which the cake batter is mixed and poured into a pan the night before, topped with streusel, and kept overnight in the refrigerator. In the morning, all you have to do is throw the cold pan into the oven and let the smell of cinnamon-laced coffee cake rouse the rest of the house.

Unfortunately, the overnight stay in the refrigerator wreaks havoc on these cakes. Some recipes were dry, others squat and gummy, and a few over-domed, misshapen, and tainted by off-putting chemical flavors. When it came to the streusel, most of it was dull and floury.

It was no surprise that my tasters preferred the test kitchen's standard streusel (a mixture of softened butter, flour, pecans, cinnamon, and light brown and granulated sugars) to other contenders. However, a make-ahead recipe required a new cake batter. Nothing in the test kitchen's repertoire could withstand an overnight rest in the refrigerator.

The most promising recipe, which called for combining a mixture of melted butter, sugar, sour cream, and eggs with the dry ingredients (flour, baking powder, baking soda, cinnamon, and salt), tasted OK but didn't bake evenly in my 13- by 9-inch pan—by the time the middle was set, the edges were overdone and dry. A

switch to two 9-inch cake pans promoted even cooking, but the cake lacked height.

I tried adding more baking powder and soda, thinking maybe the overnight rest was negating their rising power, but using more leavener imparted an unappealing chemical flavor. Hoping to gain height with a different mixing method, I turned away from stirring in the melted butter and tried the standard creaming method, in which softened butter and sugar are beaten together until light and fluffy, then incorporating the wet and dry ingredients. Baked the next day, the resulting cake was definitely taller (as the beating had aerated the batter), but it was too light and delicate to support the streusel. Tucking half of the streusel inside the cake (between layers of batter) was a step in the right direction, but sometimes even a modest topping of streusel sank into the cake.

For my next test, I tried reverse creaming, a mixing method the test kitchen uses to create baked goods with especially solid structure. In reverse creaming, softened butter is mixed with the dry ingredients until crumbly before the wet ingredients are incorporated, and then the entire batter is beaten until fluffy and aerated. This technique worked wonders here, because less air is worked into the batter with reverse creaming, so there is less deflation. The sturdy batter held its loft in the refrigerator overnight and could now shoulder a thick coating of streusel.

Now I could simply wake up and, while still on my first cup of coffee, enjoy a freshly baked,

hot-out-of-the-oven coffee cake that was tender, fluffy, and packed with cinnamon streusel inside and out. **–Cali Rich**

MAKE-AHEAD COFFEE CAKE SERVES 12

This recipe produces two small coffee cakes, which can be baked on different days if desired (unbaked cakes can be frozen for up to 1 month). We omit the nuts from the streusel used inside the coffee cake, because the nuts give off steam when baked, which can make the cake soggy. If you don't have two 9-inch round pans, use two 8-inch square pans instead.

Streusel
- ⅔ cup packed light brown sugar
- ⅔ cup granulated sugar
- ⅔ cup all-purpose flour
- 1½ tablespoons ground cinnamon
- 8 tablespoons (1 stick) cold unsalted butter, cut into ½-inch pieces
- ½ cup chopped pecans

Cake
- 3½ cups all-purpose flour
- 1 cup packed light brown sugar
- 1 cup granulated sugar
- 2 teaspoons baking powder
- 1 teaspoon baking soda
- 1½ teaspoons ground cinnamon
- ½ teaspoon salt
- 12 tablespoons (1½ sticks) unsalted butter, softened
- 3 large eggs
- 1¾ cups sour cream

1. For the streusel: Pulse sugars, flour, cinnamon, and butter in food processor until mixture resembles coarse meal. Divide streusel in half. Stir pecans into one half and reserve separately.

2. For the cake: Grease two 9-inch cake pans. With electric mixer on medium-low speed, mix flour, sugars, baking powder, baking soda, cinnamon, and salt in large bowl. Beat in butter, 1 tablespoon at a time, until mixture is crumbly with pea-sized pieces,

1 to 2 minutes. Add eggs, one at a time, until combined. Add sour cream in 3 additions, scraping down bowl as necessary. Increase speed to medium-high and beat until batter is light and fluffy, about 2 minutes.

3. Divide half of batter between prepared pans. Sprinkle streusel without nuts evenly over each pan. Divide remaining batter evenly between pans and top with nutty streusel. Wrap pans with plastic wrap and refrigerate for up to 24 hours or freeze for up to 1 month.

4. When ready to serve: Adjust oven rack to middle position and heat oven to 350 degrees. Unwrap cakes and bake until golden brown and toothpick inserted in center comes out with a few dry crumbs attached, about 45 minutes (about 55 minutes if frozen). Cool at least 15 minutes. Serve.

The key to producing a batter that can sit overnight in the refrigerator and still bake up tall and light the next day is in the mixing method.

MAKE-AHEAD CHERRY-PISTACHIO COFFEE CAKE

Follow recipe for Make-Ahead Coffee Cake, replacing pecans with ½ cup chopped unsalted pistachios and adding ¾ cup chopped dried cherries to batter at end of step 2.

MAKE-AHEAD APPLE-WALNUT COFFEE CAKE

Follow recipe for Make-Ahead Coffee Cake, replacing pecans with ½ cup chopped walnuts. After filling prepared pans with second layer of batter in step 3, spread ⅓ cup apple butter over batter in each pan and top with nutty streusel.

Sheet Pan Pizza

Secrets to
TIDY SHEET PAN PIZZA

1. Sprinkling Parmesan over the dough before prebaking gives the sauce something to grab on to, which helps keep your toppings from sliding around.

2. After prebaking the dough with the Parmesan, spreading an even layer of tomato sauce on the dough and baking it for another 10 minutes helps evaporate excess moisture from the sauce, which keeps the pizza from becoming soggy.

Pizza Cutters

A pizza wheel is the most efficient way to cut even, clean slices of our sheet pan pizza. After testing a half-dozen models, our favorite is the OXO Good Grips 4-inch wheel ($11.95), which we liked for its nonslip handle, protective thumb guard, and angled neck, which makes cutting easier on the wrist.

REINVENTING THE WHEEL
OXO Good Grips

My family loves to make homemade sheet pan pizza, and everyone, including our 4-year-old son, Owen, pitches in to help. But we can never get the crust right—the bottom is always undercooked and soggy. How can we fix this problem? –The Bisal Family, via e-mail

A huge sheet pan pizza cooks through easily enough in the intense heat of a pizzeria oven, but cooking a thick-crust pizza loaded with toppings in a less-powerful home oven is another story. It's hard to get the middle of the pizza to cook through, and the generous toppings mean soggy crust is a real danger.

I started overhauling this recipe at the bottom. To fill a large baking sheet, I used a double batch of the test kitchen's pizza dough, a simple combination of flour, yeast, water, and olive oil. Using extra-virgin olive oil gave the dough more flavor (a must for a pizza in which the crust plays such an important role), and adding a thin layer of oil to the pan promoted better browning of the bottom crust.

The test kitchen's basic pizza sauce (crushed tomatoes, olive oil, garlic, salt, and pepper) was a good starting point, but for flavor big enough for this oversized pie, I upped the amount of garlic and added tomato paste and oregano. To help prevent sogginess, I found it necessary to simmer the sauce for at least half an hour to drive off excess moisture. I kept the cheese element simple with a mixture of lots of smooth-melting mozzarella and flavorful Parmesan.

All the individual components were in good shape, but when I baked the pizza, it turned into a soggy mess. I ran across several recipes that suggested prebaking the crust and then adding the toppings. Sure enough, prebaking kept the crust dry, but now the sauce and toppings had a bad habit of sliding onto my tasters' shoes: The sauce couldn't stick properly to the hardened prebaked crust. I wanted to avoid both soggy crust and saucy shoes, so I needed to devise a way to attach the sauce to the prebaked crust. I spread some of the Parmesan on the dough before it went into the oven; as I'd hoped, the melted cheese acted like a tread when I added the sauce 10 minutes later.

Although everything was now tasting good and staying put, I was still bothered by one part of my recipe—it took nearly 30 minutes to simmer the sauce to a thick consistency that wouldn't make the crust soggy. I wondered if I could evaporate some of the sauce's moisture with a second round of prebaking. Sure enough, baking the crust with just the sauce on top of the melted Parmesan thickened the sauce and intensified its tomato flavor. And after two rounds of prebaking, the pizza cooked very quickly when I finally added the cheese and other toppings.

–Meredith Butcher

SHEET PAN PIZZA
SERVES 12

After mixing in step 1, the dough will be very sticky. Be sure to coat your hands with flour before transferring the dough from the mixing bowl to the greased bowl.

Dough
- ½ cup extra-virgin olive oil
- 1¾ cups water, heated to 110 degrees
- 1 tablespoon sugar
- 5 cups all-purpose flour
- 2 envelopes (4½ teaspoons) rapid-rise or instant yeast
- 2 teaspoons salt

Sauce and Toppings
- 2 tablespoons extra-virgin olive oil
- 3 garlic cloves, minced
- 1½ teaspoons dried oregano
- ¼ teaspoon red pepper flakes
- 2 tablespoons tomato paste
- 1 (28-ounce) can crushed tomatoes
- 2 tablespoons chopped fresh basil
  Salt
- 1½ cups grated Parmesan cheese
- 3 cups shredded mozzarella cheese

1. For the dough: Adjust oven rack to lowest position and heat oven to 200 degrees. When oven reaches 200 degrees, turn off oven. Grease large bowl. Evenly coat 18- by 13-inch rimmed baking sheet with ¼ cup oil.

2. Combine water, sugar, and remaining oil in measuring cup. In bowl of standing mixer fitted with dough hook, mix flour, yeast, and salt on low speed until combined. Increase speed to medium-low and slowly add water mixture until dough is uniform in texture, about 3 minutes. Transfer dough to prepared bowl, cover with plastic, and place in warm oven. Let rise until doubled in size, about 30 minutes.

3. For the sauce and toppings: Heat 1 tablespoon oil in large saucepan over medium heat until shimmering. Cook garlic, oregano, and pepper flakes until fragrant, about 30 seconds. Stir in tomato paste and cook until just beginning to brown, about 2 minutes. Add tomatoes and simmer until reduced to 3 cups, about 10 minutes. Off heat, stir in basil and season with salt.

4. On lightly floured work surface, use rolling pin to roll dough into 16- by 12-inch rectangle. Transfer dough to prepared baking sheet and stretch dough to cover pan, pressing dough into corners. Brush dough with remaining oil and cover with plastic wrap. Set in warm spot (not oven) until slightly risen, about 20 minutes. Heat oven to 450 degrees.

5. Remove plastic wrap and, using fingers, make indentations all over dough. Sprinkle dough with 1 cup Parmesan and bake until cheese begins to melt, 7 to 10 minutes. Remove baking sheet from oven and spoon sauce over pizza, leaving 1-inch border. Bake until sauce

A pizza this big requires plenty of seasoning—and preventative measures to keep the crust from getting soggy.

is deep red and steaming, 7 to 10 minutes.

6. Sprinkle mozzarella and remaining Parmesan evenly over sauce and bake until cheese is golden brown, about 12 minutes. Remove pizza from oven and let rest 5 minutes. Serve.

MEAT AND CHEESE MANIA

- 1 **pound sweet Italian sausage, casings removed**
- 3½ **ounces thinly sliced deli pepperoni**
- 1 **additional cup shredded mozzarella cheese (4 cups total)**

Brown sausage in large nonstick skillet over medium heat, breaking up clumps, about 8 minutes. Transfer to paper towel–lined plate. Arrange pepperoni on separate paper towel–lined plate. Cover with 2 more paper towels and microwave for 1 minute. Let cool. Toss sausage, pepperoni, and mozzarella with cheeses in step 6 and proceed with recipe.

SOUTH PACIFIC

- 8 **ounces thinly sliced deli ham, cut into 2-inch pieces**
- 2 **(20-ounce) cans pineapple tidbits, drained**

Brown ham in large nonstick skillet over medium heat, about 8 minutes. Transfer to bowl. Cook pineapple in empty skillet until beginning to brown, about 8 minutes. Transfer to bowl with ham and let cool. Toss ham and pineapple with cheeses in step 6 and proceed with recipe.

VEGGIE DELIGHT

- 1 **tablespoon vegetable oil**
- 1 **onion, chopped**
- 1 **red bell pepper, seeded and chopped**
- 1 **green bell pepper, seeded and chopped**
- 10 **ounces white mushrooms, halved and sliced thin**

Heat oil in large skillet over medium-high heat until shimmering. Cook vegetables until browned, about 10 minutes. Let cool. Toss vegetables with cheeses in step 6 and proceed with recipe.

Skillet Supper: Penne with Sausage and Broccoli

Could we freshen the flavors of this often stodgy pasta dish—and make the cooking and cleanup easier, too?

broccoli on top, covered the skillet, and steamed the broccoli just until al dente. Fresh basil, a splash of balsamic vinegar, and Parmesan cheese added at the end of cooking rounded out the flavors of this new—and easy—take on an old favorite.

–Meredith Butcher

CREAMY SKILLET PENNE WITH BROCCOLI AND SAUSAGE

SERVES 4 TO 6

One large head of broccoli should yield about 8 ounces of florets. Alternatively, bags of cut broccoli florets are available in the produce section of most supermarkets, or you can package your own at supermarket salad bars.

- 1 **pound hot or sweet Italian sausage, casings removed**
- 1 **onion, chopped fine**
- 1 **red bell pepper, seeded and sliced thin**
- 8 **ounces penne (about 2½ cups)**
- 3 **garlic cloves, minced**
- ¼ **teaspoon red pepper flakes**
- 1 **cup white wine**
- 2 **cups low-sodium chicken broth**
- ½ **cup heavy cream**
- 8 **ounces broccoli florets, cut into 1-inch pieces (see note)**
- ½ **cup grated Parmesan cheese**
- 1 **tablespoon finely chopped fresh basil**
- 2 **teaspoons balsamic vinegar Salt and pepper**

Penne with sausage and broccoli in a rich cream sauce is an Italian-American classic. Unfortunately, the recipes I tried had some serious flaws: Greasy, gloppy sauces and overcooked broccoli were common problems. Worst of all, most recipes dirtied three pots to produce this basic weeknight dinner.

To save myself from boiling pasta in one pot, steaming broccoli in another, and making my cream sauce in a third, I wanted to cook everything in one skillet. An easy technique is to simmer pasta in the same liquid that will eventually become the sauce.

I started with the sausage. A full pound of Italian sausage for 8 ounces of pasta made for a hearty and meaty dish, but leaving it in the skillet as I added the other ingredients made the sauce too greasy.

Transferring the sausage to paper towels to drain removed most of the grease without compromising flavor.

Sautéed onion, red bell pepper, garlic, and pepper flakes bumped up the flavor. I also discovered that toasting the pasta with the vegetables (before adding liquid) enhanced its nutty flavor. Trying to simmer the pasta in cream was tricky because the cream was too thick to properly cook the pasta. After enduring much trial and many errors, my tasters preferred a lighter combination of just ½ cup of heavy cream, 2 cups of chicken broth, and 1 cup of white wine as a cooking liquid/sauce.

Broccoli added at the same time as the pasta turned mushy and army green in color. I didn't want to steam the broccoli separately, so I waited until the pasta was about halfway done, then nestled the

1. Cook sausage in large nonstick skillet over medium-high heat, breaking up pieces with wooden spoon, until no longer pink, about 5 minutes. Drain sausage on paper towel–lined plate.

2. Cook onion and bell pepper in sausage fat until softened, about 8 minutes. Add penne and cook, stirring often, until pasta is lightly toasted, about 3 minutes. Stir in garlic and pepper flakes until fragrant, about 30 seconds. Stir in wine, broth, and cream and bring to boil. Reduce heat to medium, cover, and simmer, stirring occasionally, until pasta begins to soften, about 8 minutes.

3. Arrange broccoli on top of pasta and continue to cook, covered, until broccoli is bright green and tender and pasta is al dente, about 8 minutes. Off heat, stir in Parmesan, basil, and vinegar. Season with salt and pepper. Serve.

Rediscovering Chicken Fricassee

Using a lot of mushrooms—and knowing how to handle them properly—gives this stew an earthy, meaty base flavor.

Growing up, I loved my mom's chicken fricassee. We always soaked up the creamy mushroom sauce with biscuits. Mom never wrote down her recipe, but I'd like to make this dish for my family. Can you help?

—Corey Muzylowski, Oakland, Calif.

Kitchen Know-How
PREPARING PORTOBELLO MUSHROOMS

The dark gills on the underside of the portobello mushroom caps caused the sauce of our fricassee to turn an unappealing brown color. Use a teaspoon to remove the gills before cooking the mushrooms for a more appealing color without a loss of mushroom flavor.

Chicken fricassee is an old-fashioned recipe that deserves a fresh look. Typically, a whole chicken is cut up, browned, braised in wine and broth, and then finished with heavy cream and lemon juice. Some recipes keep it as simple as that, while others add vegetables like pearl onions, carrots, celery, and mushrooms. I've always liked this dish with mushrooms, which lend meatiness and heft to the sauce.

While chicken fricassee has a solid premise and a long track record, the recipes I tried weren't very good. Cooking white and dark meat together in the same pot is a challenge because they cook at different rates, so the white meat was dried out before the dark meat came up to temperature. The sauces tended toward the thick and stodgy—in fact, many modern recipes replace the homemade sauce with canned cream of mushroom soup. I could see why this dish has fallen off the radar.

Early fricassee recipes relied on a whole bird, but modern supermarkets offer many more choices. After testing various combinations of white and dark meat, I settled on bone-in chicken breasts: The white meat cooked relatively quickly and evenly, and the bones added flavor to the sauce. By the time the chicken was finished cooking in the sauce, the skin was flabby and not terribly appealing. I addressed this problem by first browning the chicken, which rendered fat I could use to make my sauce, and then removing the chicken from the pot and discarding the skin—it had served its purpose.

I followed the test kitchen's basic braising method by sautéing onions and garlic with 12 ounces of sliced white mushrooms before adding 2 cups of chicken broth, a cup of white wine, and the browned and skinned chicken pieces. Twenty minutes later, I had perfectly cooked chicken nestled in a bland sauce studded with flavorless mushrooms. How could I get more flavor from the mushrooms?

The simplest fix was to add more. After making batches with several different varieties, I settled on adding an equal amount of meaty portobellos to the white mushrooms. To coax the best flavor and texture out of this big pile of mushrooms, I cooked them covered until they were soft and had released their liquid, then I uncovered them and let the liquid reduce and intensify. The sauce now had more mushroom flavor, but it wasn't quite there yet.

Replacing half the chicken broth with beef broth reinforced the meaty quality of the mushrooms. Many recipes finish the sauce with a cup of heavy cream, but my tasters thought all that cream was overwhelming the mushrooms. Cutting back to just ⅓ cup of cream gave the stew all the richness it needed and allowed the mushroom flavor to shine through. Finished with fresh parsley and lemon juice, this simple chicken fricassee is worth adding to any cook's repertoire.

–Diane Unger

CHICKEN AND MUSHROOM FRICASSEE
SERVES 4

Serve this creamy stewed chicken with white rice, egg noodles, biscuits, or crusty bread.

- 4 bone-in, skin-on split chicken breasts (about 3 pounds)
  Salt and pepper
- 2 teaspoons vegetable oil
- 2 onions, chopped fine
- 6 garlic cloves, minced
- 12 ounces white mushrooms, sliced thin
- 4 large portobello mushroom caps (about 12 ounces), gills removed (see photo at left), halved and sliced thin
- 1 tablespoon minced fresh thyme
- ¼ cup all-purpose flour
- 1 cup low-sodium chicken broth
- 1 cup low-sodium beef broth
- 1 cup white wine
- ⅓ cup heavy cream
- 4 teaspoons lemon juice
- 2 tablespoons chopped fresh parsley

1. Pat chicken dry with paper towels and season with salt and pepper. Heat oil in Dutch oven over medium-high heat until just smoking. Cook chicken, skin-side down, until deep golden brown, about 6 minutes. Flip and brown on second side, about 3 minutes. Transfer chicken to plate; remove and discard skin. Pour off all but 1 tablespoon fat from pot.

2. Cook onions in remaining fat until golden, about 5 minutes. Stir in garlic and cook until fragrant, about 30 seconds. Add mushrooms, thyme, and ¼ teaspoon salt. Reduce heat to medium and cook, covered, stirring occasionally, until mushrooms have released their juices, about 10 minutes. Uncover and cook until liquid evaporates and mushrooms begin to brown, about 7 minutes.

3. Stir in flour and cook until golden, about 1 minute. Slowly stir in broths and wine and bring to boil. Return chicken and any accumulated juices to pot. Reduce heat to low and simmer, covered, until meat registers 160 degrees, 20 to 30 minutes. Transfer chicken to serving platter and tent with foil.

4. Add cream to pot and simmer until sauce is thickened, about 15 minutes. Stir in lemon juice and parsley and season with salt and pepper. Pour sauce over chicken. Serve.

Sweet and Spicy Thick-Cut Pork Chops

I'd like to cook glazed thick-cut pork chops for my family more often, but I can't seem to keep the chops moist and juicy. And that's not even the worst part—my glaze is always watery. Can you help? –Richard Barry, Braintree, Mass.

The test kitchen's preferred method for cooking thick pork chops calls for browning the chops on the stovetop and then cooking them through in the oven. But with a glaze in the mix, the timing becomes tricky. Add the glaze ingredients too soon and they burn; add them too late and the glaze is a watery mess. After much trial and error, I realized that this recipe belongs on the stovetop, where you can easily monitor the chops and the glaze.

Too bad most of the stovetop-only recipes I tried yielded leathery chops that were very overcooked. Clearly, starting the chops over high heat (to create a flavorful browned crust) was the problem. Yes, the crust was nice and brown, but by the time the center of these thick chops finally came up to the desired temperature, much of the meat was dried-out and tough.

The test kitchen has addressed moisture loss in lean pork chops before; we have a recipe that slowly browns thin pork chops by starting them in a cold skillet and turning the heat to medium-low. The chops take longer to brown, but this technique maximizes the retention of juices. I was pleasantly surprised that this method worked with my thick-cut pork chops, which came out juicy and very tender. I then removed them from the pan and built my glaze, using a base of apple cider, brown sugar, and cider vinegar. My tasters wanted a bit more kick, so I enlivened the glaze with a little Dijon mustard and hot sauce.

Both the chops and the glaze tasted good, but their flavors weren't integrated—the glaze was more like a separate sauce. To bring the flavors together, I tried adding the glaze ingredients to the pan after I flipped the chops, which had the added benefit of keeping the exterior of the chops moist as they finished cooking in the liquid. I found that if I used just enough glaze to come halfway up the chops and covered the pan, the meat stayed juicy. Once the chops reached the proper internal temperature of 145 degrees, I let them rest on a plate for five minutes and simmered the glaze until it reached the ideal consistency. This gave me thick-cut pork chops that were both well cooked and nicely glazed.

–Meredith Butcher

SWEET AND SPICY THICK-CUT PORK CHOPS
SERVES 4

Frank's RedHot, the test kitchen's favorite hot sauce, is relatively mild; for a spicier glaze, substitute a hotter sauce.

- ⅓ cup apple cider
- ⅓ cup packed dark brown sugar
- ¼ cup cider vinegar
- 2 garlic cloves, minced
- 1 tablespoon Dijon mustard
- 1 tablespoon hot sauce (see note)
- ¼ teaspoon cornstarch
- 4 bone-in rib or center-cut pork chops, about 1½ inches thick
- 1 teaspoon vegetable oil
  Salt and pepper
- ½ teaspoon granulated sugar

1. Whisk cider, brown sugar, vinegar, garlic, mustard, hot sauce, and cornstarch in medium bowl. Pat chops dry with paper towels. Following photo 1 at right, cut 2 slits about 2 inches apart through fat on each chop. Rub chops with oil, season with salt and pepper, and sprinkle 1 side of each chop with granulated sugar.

2. Place chops, sugared-side down, in large nonstick skillet. Place skillet over medium-low heat and cook until chops are lightly browned, 10 to 12 minutes. Following photo 2, flip chops, add cider mixture, and cook, covered, until center of meat registers 145 degrees, 8 to 10 minutes. Transfer chops to platter. Increase heat to medium-high and cook, uncovered, until liquid is thick and syrupy, about 5 minutes.

3. Return chops to skillet and turn to coat with glaze. Transfer chops to platter and top with remaining glaze. Serve.

Starting these big chops in a cold pan and cooking them at a relatively low temperature helps keep them moist and juicy.

Secrets to GLAZING THICK-CUT PORK CHOPS

1. To keep the pork chops from curling and cooking unevenly, cut two slits about 2 inches apart through the exterior fat before placing the chops in a cold skillet.

2. When the chops have seared on the first side, flip them, add the glaze ingredients, cover the pan, and finish cooking.

3. When the chops reach an internal temperature of 145 degrees, remove them from the pan and simmer the glaze until thickened. The glaze is the proper consistency when a spatula dragged through it leaves a trail.

On the Side: Chinese-Style Rice

How do you make rice that sticks to your chopsticks and doesn't fall into your lap?

Chinese-style rice should be just soft enough to soak up savory sauces in dishes like General Tso's Chicken (see page 25) and just sticky enough to be easily eaten with chopsticks. While I was expecting to use starchy short-grain rice, my research revealed that this dish is typically made with regular long-grain rice. While the basic test kitchen recipe for long-grain rice yields separate fluffy grains, I found plenty of Chinese-style recipes that promised to turn the same rice into sticky clumps I could grab with my chopsticks.

Many of these recipes employ the absorption method, in which rice and water are brought to a boil, covered, and left on low heat to steam and absorb liquid. The test kitchen's ratio for perfect fluffy rice using this cooking method is 1½ cups water to 1 cup of long-grain rice. For my sticky rice, I tried using both more and less water; more made the rice mushy, and less prevented the rice from cooking through. I was going to have to find another cooking method.

I found a few recipes that call for letting the rice boil uncovered until the water in the pot drops below the level of the rice; then the heat is turned to low and the pot is covered to allow the rice to steam and absorb the remaining liquid. When I gave this a try, the initial uncovered rapid boil produced two interesting results. First, the boiling water agitated the rice, helping release its starch; when the water was fully absorbed, the released starch made the rice very sticky. Second, when the escaping steam formed tiny holes in the surface of the rice, I had a reliable visual cue that it was time to cover the pot and let the rice finish cooking over low heat. Now I had a recipe for perfectly cooked rice that would clump on my chopsticks every time. **–Kelley Baker**

CHINESE-STYLE STICKY RICE
SERVES 4 TO 6
Do not stir the rice as it cooks. The finished rice can stand off heat, covered, for up to 15 minutes.

- 2 cups long-grain white rice
- 3 cups water
- ½ teaspoon salt

1. Place rice in fine-mesh strainer set over bowl. Rinse under running water, swishing with hands until water runs clear. Drain thoroughly.

2. Bring rinsed rice, water, and salt to boil in saucepan over medium-high heat. Cook, uncovered, until water level drops below surface of rice and small holes form, about 5 minutes.

3. Reduce heat to low, cover, and cook until rice is tender and water is fully absorbed, about 15 minutes. Serve.

On the Side: Sesame Green Beans

Could we simplify the classic double-cooking method and still produce slightly browned, perfectly glazed green beans every time?

The best sesame green beans are tender-crisp and lightly glazed with a nutty sauce. Traditional recipes employ a double-cooking technique in which the beans are blanched and then deep-fried to achieve a lightly browned, blistered exterior before being glazed. I wanted to get the same results using just one pan.

The test kitchen's preferred method for cooking green beans sounded perfect: The beans are added to the skillet with a little oil and water and cooked covered to steam them. The lid is then removed so the water can evaporate, allowing the beans to be stir-fried in the oil until done. This gave me beans that were perfectly cooked, but they weren't properly blistered and browned. Straight stir-frying gave me good browning but didn't cook the beans through. The solution was a combination of the two techniques: stir-frying the beans in oil for a few minutes to start the browning process and then covering them to cook through. Since I wasn't adding any water, these beans developed a nicely browned and blistered exterior and a tender-crisp texture.

As for the sauce, most recipes rely on a simple combination of rice vinegar, soy sauce, sugar, and toasted sesame oil. But even when allowed to reduce, this mixture wasn't viscous enough to cling to the beans. To

remedy this, I replaced the sugar with honey and simmered the beans in just the honey and soy for a few minutes. Adding the vinegar and sesame oil off heat helped to preserve their flavors (sesame oil in particular loses flavor when heated too much) and gave the sauce the right light-yet-sticky consistency. Tasters wanted more sesame flavor, but more sesame oil made the dish greasy. The solution was adding toasted sesame seeds to the beans just before serving. **–Kelley Baker**

SESAME GREEN BEANS **SERVES 4**
Rice vinegar and toasted sesame oil can be found in the international section of most grocery stores.

- 2 teaspoons sesame seeds
- 1 tablespoon soy sauce
- 2 teaspoons honey
- 4 teaspoons vegetable oil
- 1 pound green beans, trimmed and cut into 2-inch pieces
- 2 teaspoons rice vinegar
- 2 teaspoons toasted sesame oil
- 3 scallions, sliced thin

1. Toast sesame seeds in large skillet over medium heat, stirring occasionally, until golden, about 5 minutes. Transfer to plate. Whisk soy sauce and honey in small bowl.

2. Heat oil in empty skillet over medium heat until shimmering. Cook beans until bright green, about 2 minutes. Reduce heat to medium-low and cook, covered, stirring occasionally, until beans are spotty brown and tender, about 10 minutes.

3. Uncover, stir in soy sauce mixture, and cook until beans are glazed, about 1 minute. Off heat, stir in vinegar, sesame oil, and scallions. Sprinkle with toasted sesame seeds. Serve.

General Tso's Chicken

This glazed fried chicken dish is great in restaurants, but homemade versions are typically gummy and bland. Could we find a way to give General Tso a four-star makeover?

There's a good reason General Tso's chicken, a Chinese restaurant staple named for an imposing 19th-century Hunan military officer, hardly resembles the fiery cuisine of that Chinese province—it was invented in New York City in the early 1970s. The appeal of this dish (which is also known as General Gau's, Cho's, and Tsang's) is easy to see: Boneless chicken pieces are marinated in soy sauce, battered, and deep-fried to a crispy brown before being coated with a sweet-hot sauce made with dried chiles, more soy, sugar, vinegar, hoisin sauce or tomato paste, garlic, and ginger.

I gathered several recipes and headed into the test kitchen to try to make a General Tso's chicken as good as my favorite Chinese restaurant's. My tasters and I were very disappointed with the results, as most of these recipes produced gummy, soggy chicken coated in a saccharine-sweet sauce.

I started on the ground floor, with the chicken. While many recipes use boneless thighs, in side-by-side tests my tasters preferred the milder white meat of boneless breasts. Marinating the chicken in soy sauce for 30 minutes added moisture and flavor, but the coating and frying were trickier. Most recipes call for the chicken to be dipped in egg whites, coated in cornstarch, and deep-fried. The resulting crust, though crispy when just out of the oil, was pale in color and quickly turned soft when sauced. Adding baking soda to the cornstarch helped the chicken brown better, and fortifying this mixture with flour kept the coating crisp, even when doused with sauce.

As for the sweet-and-spicy sauce, dried chiles were hard to find and had unpredictable levels of heat—some batches of sauce were searingly hot, others meek. Red pepper flakes were the perfect substitute, especially when I sautéed them with fresh garlic and ginger to round out their heat. My tasters never warmed to the tomato paste used in many recipes, but they loved sweet and spicy hoisin, a fermented bean sauce that's sometimes referred to as Chinese barbecue sauce. Soy sauce, white vinegar, and sugar enhanced the other flavors.

This sauce was so flavorful I wondered if it could double as a marinade in place of the traditional soy-only marinade. My tasters responded enthusiastically to the supercharged flavor of chicken marinated in the sweet and spicy sauce.

I thought my work was done, but then an astute colleague pointed out that the second batch of fried chicken (with 1½ pounds of chicken, my recipe required frying the meat in two batches) had a darker, crunchier crust than the first. I realized that when the first batch of chicken was passing through the cornstarch coating mixture, it was leaving traces of the marinade behind; those craggy pieces created extra crunch when they were picked up and fried on the second batch. Wanting to increase this effect, I added some marinade to the cornstarch mixture before I coated the first batch of chicken. The result was crunchy, flavorful coating on every piece.

With that signature sweet and spicy flavor infused into the chicken, coating, and sauce, this was a General Tso's Chicken worth saluting. **–Kelley Baker**

To build layers of flavor, our potent marinade is also used in the coating and as a base for the sauce.

GENERAL TSO'S CHICKEN SERVES 4

In step 4, the fried chicken pieces can be held in a 200-degree oven for up to 30 minutes before being added to the sauce (if held any longer, they will lose their crispness). If the sauce is too thick in step 5, whisk in 1 tablespoon of water before adding the crispy chicken.

Marinade and Sauce
- ½ cup hoisin sauce
- ¼ cup white vinegar
- 3 tablespoons soy sauce
- 3 tablespoons sugar
- 2 tablespoons cornstarch
- 1½ cups water
- 4 boneless, skinless chicken breasts (about 1½ pounds), cut into 1-inch pieces
- 1 tablespoon vegetable oil
- 4 garlic cloves, minced
- 2 tablespoons grated fresh ginger
- ½ teaspoon red pepper flakes

Coating and Frying
- 3 large egg whites
- 1½ cups cornstarch
- ½ cup all-purpose flour
- ½ teaspoon baking soda
- 4 cups vegetable oil

1. For the marinade and sauce: Whisk hoisin, vinegar, soy sauce, sugar, cornstarch, and water in bowl. Combine 6 tablespoons hoisin mixture and chicken in zipper-lock bag; refrigerate for 30 minutes.

2. Heat oil in large skillet over medium heat until shimmering. Cook garlic, ginger, and pepper flakes until fragrant, about 1 minute. Add 2 cups hoisin mixture and simmer, whisking constantly, until dark brown and thickened, about 2 minutes. Cover and keep sauce warm.

3. For coating and frying: Whisk egg whites in shallow dish until foamy. Combine cornstarch, flour, baking soda, and remaining hoisin mixture in second shallow dish until mixture resembles coarse meal. Remove chicken from marinade and pat dry with paper towels. Toss half of chicken with egg whites until well coated, then dredge chicken in cornstarch mixture, pressing to adhere. Transfer coated chicken to plate and repeat with remaining chicken.

4. Heat oil in Dutch oven over medium-high heat until oil registers 350 degrees. Fry half of chicken until golden brown, about 3 minutes, turning each piece halfway through cooking. Transfer chicken to paper towel–lined plate. Return oil to 350 degrees and repeat with remaining chicken.

5. To serve: Warm sauce over medium-low heat until simmering, about 1 minute. Add crispy chicken and toss to coat. Serve.

Texas Sheet Cake

My mom always used to make Texas sheet cake. I liked this huge cake, except it was just a little too sweet and lacking in the chocolate flavor department. I would like an update on this old family favorite. Any suggestions? –Rachael Rehm, Orem, Utah

Although this Texas specialty resembles frosted brownies, its signature fudgy texture is created when warm icing is spread over a hot cake.

Kitchen Know-How
TIMING IS EVERYTHING

The key to perfectly moist Texas sheet cake is to let the warm icing soak into the hot cake. As soon as the cake comes out of the oven, pour the warm icing over the cake and use a spatula to spread the icing to the edges of the cake. This creates the signature fudgy layer between the icing and the cake.

Texas sheet cake—the official state cake of Texas—is a huge, pecan-topped chocolate cake with three distinct layers of chocolaty goodness. A diverse range of textures is created when a sweet chocolate icing is poured over a cake that's still hot out of the oven; when the cake cools, you're left with an icing layer, a fudgy layer where the icing and hot cake have mixed together, and a bottom layer of moist cake. The cake is easy to make (no mixer is required) and great to take to potlucks and barbecues because, as its name implies, it's baked in a sheet pan and serves a crowd. But recipes I found all had one big problem: They didn't pack much chocolate wallop.

Most Texas sheet cake recipes start by blooming cocoa powder in water with margarine, oil, butter, vegetable shortening, or a combination thereof. The cocoa mixture is then combined with flour, sugar, baking soda, eggs, dairy (milk, buttermilk, or sour cream), and vanilla in a single bowl. I baked up cakes with different combinations of margarine, oil, butter, and shortening, and my tasters agreed that margarine imparted an unpleasant artificial flavor. The cake made with all butter tasted great, but the texture was too light and cakey. The cake made with a combination of butter (for flavor) and vegetable oil (to keep the cake moist) was the best overall, producing a cake with a dense, brownielike texture.

All of the recipes I found had a skimpy ¼ cup of cocoa, which accounted for the measly chocolate flavor. Doubling the amount of cocoa certainly helped, but adding 8 ounces of melted semisweet chocolate gave me the strong chocolate flavor my tasters were craving. The semisweet chocolate also contributed moisture and fat to the batter, which made for a fudgier cake. As for the dairy, tasters preferred rich, tangy sour cream over buttermilk or milk.

Standard recipes for the icing call for a stick of butter, milk, another ¼ cup of cocoa, and 4 cups of confectioners' sugar. My tasters deemed this formula too sweet, so I took the amount of sugar down to 3 cups and doubled the cocoa (as I had done in the cake) to ½ cup. To give the icing more body, I replaced the milk with heavy cream, and I added a tablespoon of corn syrup to give the frosting a lustrous finish.

Since my cake was already pretty moist, I was curious as to whether the icing absolutely had to be poured over the cake while it was hot. I baked up two sheet cakes, icing one directly out of the oven and icing the other after it had cooled. The results were clear—the cake iced while hot had that characteristic moist, gooey, fudgy layer under the frosting, while the other cake was an ordinary frosted cake. This sheet cake may come from Texas, but I think the rest of the country deserves to share its big chocolate flavor.

–Diane Unger

TEXAS SHEET CAKE

SERVES 24

Toast the pecans in a dry skillet over medium heat, shaking the pan occasionally, until golden and fragrant, about 5 minutes.

Cake
- 2 cups all-purpose flour
- 2 cups sugar
- ½ teaspoon baking soda
- ½ teaspoon salt
- 2 large eggs plus 2 yolks
- 2 teaspoons vanilla extract
- ¼ cup sour cream
- 8 ounces semisweet chocolate, chopped
- 4 tablespoons unsalted butter
- ¾ cup vegetable oil
- ¾ cup water
- ½ cup Dutch-processed cocoa powder

Chocolate Icing
- 8 tablespoons (1 stick) unsalted butter
- ½ cup heavy cream
- ½ cup Dutch-processed cocoa powder
- 1 tablespoon light corn syrup
- 3 cups confectioners' sugar
- 1 tablespoon vanilla extract
- 1 cup toasted pecans, chopped

1. For the cake: Adjust oven rack to middle position and heat oven to 350 degrees. Grease 18- by 13-inch rimmed baking sheet. Combine flour, sugar, baking soda, and salt in large bowl. Whisk eggs and yolks, vanilla, and sour cream in another bowl until smooth.

2. Heat chocolate, butter, oil, water, and cocoa in large saucepan over medium heat, stirring occasionally, until smooth, 3 to 5 minutes. Whisk chocolate mixture into flour mixture until incorporated. Whisk egg mixture into batter, then pour into prepared baking pan. Bake until toothpick inserted into center comes out clean, 18 to 20 minutes. Transfer to wire rack.

3. For the icing: About 5 minutes before cake is done, heat butter, cream, cocoa, and corn syrup in large saucepan over medium heat, stirring occasionally, until smooth. Off heat, whisk in confectioners' sugar and vanilla. Spread warm icing evenly over hot cake and sprinkle with pecans. Let cake cool to room temperature on wire rack, about 1 hour, then refrigerate until icing is set, about 1 hour longer. (Cake can be wrapped in plastic and refrigerated for up to 2 days. Bring to room temperature before serving.) Cut into 3-inch squares. Serve.

Slice-and-Bake Cookies

Most recipes for these simple cookies bake up bland and soft. What's the secret to flavorful, crisp icebox cookies?

Having slice-and-bake cookie dough in the refrigerator or freezer is great, because you can bake it off whenever the mood strikes. But because these simple cookies have so few basic ingredients (just butter, sugar, salt, egg, vanilla, and flour), imperfections are impossible to hide. With too much flour, the cookies are crisp but dry and bland; go overboard with butter, sugar, or egg and the cookies are rich but soft and misshapen. I set out to create a recipe that would combine both crispness and rich butter and vanilla flavor—in effect, shortbread shaped into a convenient slice-and-bake log.

Classic slice-and-bake cookie recipes start by creaming butter and sugar with an electric mixer until light and fluffy. Egg, vanilla, and flour are added to form a soft dough, which is rolled into a log, refrigerated, and kept ready to slice and bake. Easy enough, but I wasn't sure how to get more flavor into the cookies without changing their texture and character. I added as much butter as I could without making the cookies lose their crispy edge. Most recipes use a whole egg, but I found that using only the yolk made the cookies richer and firmer. I doubled the vanilla extract, but the flavor still lacked something. Confectioners' sugar made for dry, crumbly cookies, but replacing some of the granulated sugar with light brown sugar gave the cookies the richness and complexity I was after.

My cookies tasted great, but the texture wasn't quite right. The traditional creaming method uses an electric mixer to beat air into the butter and sugar. This is great if you want a light, delicate texture, but I was trying to create a dense shortbread texture. Mixing the stiff dough by hand was effective but not efficient—it took a lot of work. A better option was the food processor, which combined the ingredients in seconds without whipping in much air. Along with their rich, buttery vanilla flavor, my cookies finally had the shortbreadlike texture I wanted—and they were ready to bake whenever the craving hit.

–Greg Case

SLICE-AND-BAKE COOKIES

MAKES ABOUT 40 COOKIES

Be sure that the cookie dough is well chilled and firm so that it can be uniformly sliced.

- ⅓ cup granulated sugar
- 2 tablespoons light brown sugar
- ½ teaspoon salt
- 12 tablespoons (1½ sticks) unsalted butter, cut into pieces and softened
- 2 teaspoons vanilla extract
- 1 large egg yolk
- 1½ cups all-purpose flour

1. Process sugars and salt in food processor until no lumps of brown sugar remain, about 30 seconds. Add butter, vanilla, and yolk and process until smooth and creamy, about 20 seconds. Scrape down sides of workbowl, add flour, and pulse until dough forms.

2. Turn out dough onto lightly floured surface and roll into 10-inch log. Wrap tightly with plastic and refrigerate until firm, at least 2 hours or up to 3 days. (Dough can be wrapped in foil and frozen for up to 1 month.)

3. Adjust oven racks to upper- and lower-middle positions and heat oven to 350 degrees. Line 2 baking sheets with parchment paper. Slice chilled dough into ¼-inch rounds and place 1 inch apart on prepared baking sheets. Bake until edges are just golden, about 15 minutes, switching and rotating sheets halfway through baking. Let cool 10 minutes on sheets, then transfer to wire rack and cool completely. Repeat with remaining dough. (Cookies can be stored in airtight container at room temperature for up to 1 week.)

For the best crisp, shortbread texture, bypass the mixer in favor of the food processor.

Dressing Up Slice-and-Bake Cookies

Here are three simple variations on our basic recipe.

COCONUT-LIME COOKIES
In step 1, add 2 cups sweetened shredded coconut and 2 teaspoons grated lime zest to food processor along with sugars and salt.

WALNUT-BROWN SUGAR COOKIES
In step 1, add 2 more tablespoons brown sugar and 1 cup chopped walnuts to food processor along with sugars and salt.

ORANGE-POPPY SEED COOKIES
In step 1, add ¼ cup poppy seeds and 1 tablespoon grated orange zest to food processor along with sugars and salt.

Food Shopping

PASTA SAUCES: Seasoning Separates the Decent from the Awful

If you're going to buy pasta sauce (and Americans spend $1.7 billion a year on jarred sauces), you should know which one tastes best. To find out, we assembled a lineup of nine national brands of marinara (or basic tomato and basil) sauce and called our tasters to the table.

All of the sauces list reconstituted tomato puree (water and tomato paste) and tomatoes as their first two ingredients; we were surprised that the two sauces that list fresher diced tomatoes first (Barilla and Muir Glen) finished in the middle of the pack. If fresh tomato flavor wasn't our tasters' top consideration, was it texture? The sauces ranged from perfectly smooth to quite chunky. To measure the relative chunkiness of each sauce, we portioned an equal weight of each into a fine-mesh strainer, rinsed it under running water for 20 seconds, and then weighed the remains. Our tasters' favorite sauce, Bertolli, was the chunkiest, with 44 percent of its initial weight remaining after rinsing. But several other chunky sauces (Classico and Newman's Own) didn't score very high overall. So what drove our rankings?

Just as important as what our tasters did like—good tomato flavor and a chunky texture—was what they didn't like: overpowering dried herb flavor. Even a sauce with a chunky texture and fresh tomato flavor can be ruined by overseasoning with acrid, stale-tasting dried herbs (basil and oregano are the main offenders). While our lowest-rated sauce, Ragú Traditional, was actually bland and lacked seasoning, the rest of our lower-scoring sauces were downgraded for their harsh dried herb flavor; our top three sauces were more subtly seasoned, and compare favorably with homemade. The sauces are listed in order of preference. –Scott Kathan

Recommended

1. **BERTOLLI Tomato and Basil Sauce** $1.99 for 24 ounces
   Comments: This sauce had a "good balance of flavors" and "a nice chunky texture." Because it wasn't overseasoned with dried herbs, tasters thought this sauce tasted "the most like fresh-cooked tomatoes."

2. **FRANCESCO RINALDI Traditional Marinara** $1.69 for 24 ounces
   Comments: This brand's "mild sweetness and spice" helped to bring out its "tangy," "bright and tomatoey" qualities. Tasters appreciated its "thick" consistency and "good texture."

3. **PREGO Marinara Italian Sauce** $2.79 for 25 ounces
   Comments: Our tasters didn't love this sauce's "too smooth" texture, noting that it "looks like ketchup." But they were impressed that it "actually tastes like tomatoes" and "doesn't have that fake herb flavor."

4. **BARILLA Marinara Sauce** $1.99 for 24 ounces
   Comments: Tasters liked the "chunkiness" of this sample, but they complained that it was "candy-sweet" and overwhelmed by too much herb flavor. As one taster noted, "Tomato flavor is lost to oregano."

5. **NEWMAN'S OWN Marinara** $3.19 for 24 ounces
   Comments: This sauce was praised for being "spicy" and "peppery" without too many dried herb "distractions." "Good texture," said one taster of this "thick and pasty" sauce, "but not much tomato flavor."

6. **MUIR GLEN Organic Tomato Basil Pasta Sauce** $3.69 for 25.5 ounces
   Comments: Familiar refrains: "I like the chunky texture, but the dried basil is overwhelming" and "pleasantly chunky, but overpowering stale dried herb taste." Tomatoes "seemed more roasted" than other samples.

Recommended with Reservations

7. **EMERIL'S All Natural Italian Style Tomato & Basil Pasta Sauce** $4.99 for 25 ounces
   Comments: Astute tasters noted that this sauce "tastes artificial and sweet" and had a "funky aftertaste that tastes artificial"; it is the only sauce in our lineup that contains corn syrup.

Not Recommended

8. **CLASSICO Tomato & Basil Pasta Sauce** $2.59 for 26 ounces
   Comments: "Who can taste anything other than those terrible dried herbs?" bemoaned one wincing taster. "Major spice overload: I hardly detect tomato in here," said another.

9. **RAGÚ Old World Style Traditional Pasta Sauce** $1.59 for 26 ounces
   Comments: "What did you do with the SpaghettiO's that came with this?" asked one taster about this "thin and flat" sauce. One of the few samples that tasters thought "could use more spice."

Taste Test Chocolate

Pure chocolate comprises 55 percent cocoa butter (which provides creamy texture) and 45 percent cocoa solids (which provide chocolate flavor). Here are the chocolate products we stock in the test kitchen, including the brands that have won our taste tests, and how we use them.

Unsweetened/Baking Chocolate
Unsweetened chocolate is pure chocolate formed into bars; its texture can be a bit gritty. We use baking chocolate in cakes and brownies where smooth texture is not as important as big chocolate flavor.
★**TEST KITCHEN WINNER: Scharffen Berger Unsweetened Chocolate**

Cocoa Powder
Cocoa powder is powdered pure chocolate with most of the cocoa butter removed. Natural cocoa powder is very acidic; Dutched cocoa powder is chemically altered to be less acidic and is usually our first choice. Since cocoa powder has little fat, it is best used in recipes that contain a lot of butter or dairy. We typically bloom cocoa powder in hot liquid to release its full flavor.
★**TEST KITCHEN WINNER: Callebaut Dutch-Processed Cocoa Powder**

Semisweet/Bittersweet Chocolate
To be called by either name, a chocolate must contain at least 35 percent pure chocolate, but most contain between 50 percent and 70 percent; the rest is mainly sugar. Because they have a strong, complex flavor and melt well, we use these products for sauces, icings, and custards. Semisweet and bittersweet chips have less fat than bar versions of these chocolates (so they will hold their shape in cookies), but can be used in most recipes.
★**TEST KITCHEN WINNER: Ghirardelli Bittersweet Chocolate**

Milk Chocolate
Milk chocolate can contain as little as 10 percent pure chocolate, so its flavor is pretty meek. Sugar is the number one ingredient, and milk chocolate must contain at least 12 percent milk solids. Due to its lack of intensity, we do not use milk chocolate for cooking, although it is enjoyable eaten out of hand.
★**TEST KITCHEN WINNER: Dove Milk Chocolate**

White Chocolate
White chocolate is technically not chocolate at all because it contains no cocoa solids. Many white chips don't even contain cocoa butter; they use palm oil for a similarly creamy, fatty texture. Milk and vanilla are the main flavor components.
★**TEST KITCHEN WINNER: Callebaut White Chocolate**

Equipment Roundup

RATINGS
Good = ★★★
Fair = ★★
Poor = ★

PEPPER MILLS: Can New Models Withstand the Test Kitchen's Daily Grind?

When we tested pepper mills in 2001, we discovered two models, the Unicorn Magnum Plus and the East Hampton Industries PepperMate, that produced far more ground pepper than classic wooden, finial-topped pepper mills. We rounded up four promising newer models and one classic wooden mill and brought them into the test kitchen to see if they could compete with the Magnum Plus and the PepperMate.

A CLOSER LOOK: To test each mill's output, we had three testers grind medium-ground pepper at a steady rate for 30 seconds, then weighed and averaged the results. To gauge the uniformity of their grinds, we compared piles of pepper from each mill ground at fine, medium, and coarse settings.

QUANTITY AND QUALITY: We value output efficiency, as 2 tablespoons of freshly ground pepper can take 10 wrist-wrenching minutes with ineffective mills but only about a minute with an efficient mill. But the quality of a pepper mill's grind is just as important. We regularly use fine-, medium-, and coarse-ground pepper, and we want uniformity (pepper pieces of the same size) in each setting. And we want to be able to easily adjust the mill between settings.

A FINE GRIND: Uniformity of pepper ground at different settings is tied to the design and workmanship of the grinding mechanism: The best grinders have more and sharper teeth that fit together better than the teeth of inferior models. We particularly liked the William Bounds ProView and the PepperMate, both of which produced uniform grinds at all settings; this was most evident in the pristine powder of their finely ground pepper.

TWIST AND SHOUT: In the efficiency test, the Unicorn Magnum Plus again proved its mettle with a 30-second output (about 1 tablespoon) that was almost twice that of the runner-up—and it took less muscle to operate. Conversely, the Trudeau One Hand mill produced an average of only ⅓ teaspoon—nearly 10 times less than the Magnum Plus—in the same 30 seconds. Why? The Magnum Plus's grinding mechanism is not only well machined, it's also bigger than the others. The Magnum Plus and the PepperMate (still the top two mills for output) also have small, ergonomic cranks that make for wrist-friendly turning.

ADJUSTABILITY: While they weren't as efficient as the Magnum Plus, both the William Bounds and the Peugeot mills have adjustable rings that click into fixed settings—the William Bounds has settings for fine, medium, and coarse, and the Peugeot has six settings. The ease with which you can get to your desired grind setting is a real plus.

SUMMING UP: The Magnum Plus is still the best pepper mill on the market, and the PepperMate remains a solid choice. But if you value fast and easy adjustments between grind settings over extremely high output, the William Bounds and Peugeot are very good options. –Scott Kathan

Highly Recommended

UNICORN Magnum Plus
Price: $45 at unicornmills.com
Grind quality: ★★★
Grind quantity: ★★★
Adjustability: ★★

Comments: Our defending champ wins again for producing an abundance of perfectly ground pepper with minimal effort. "Prodigious," said one impressed tester. Its grind adjuster (attached to the grinding mechanism on the bottom of the mill) is easy to use, though it does not have fixed settings.

WILLIAM BOUNDS ProView Pepper Mill
Price: $39.95 at cooking.com
Grind quality: ★★★
Grind quantity: ★★
Adjustability: ★★★

Comments: Testers loved the "intuitive" grind adjustor with fixed settings and the window at the bottom of the hopper, which allows you to see when you need to refill. While this mill couldn't keep pace with the output of the Magnum Plus, it produced perfectly uniform pepper at the coarse, medium, and fine settings.

Recommended

PEUGEOT CHATEAUNEUF Adjustable Pepper Mill
Price: $80 at williams-sonoma.com
Grind quality: ★★
Grind quantity: ★★
Adjustability: ★★★

Comments: This mill produced a good volume of very uniform pepper at all six fixed settings, but our testers wanted the finely ground pepper to be finer and the coarsely ground to be coarser. At more than twice the price of most other models, it's a good thing this "straight shooter" mill felt "heavy and solid" and was easy to operate.

EAST HAMPTON INDUSTRIES PepperMate Ceramic Blade Pepper Mill (Model 723)
Price: $34.95 at cooking.com
Grind quality: ★★★
Grind quantity: ★★★
Adjustability: ★

Comments: This unique mill produces an ample quantity of perfectly ground pepper through a range of settings. Its side-twisting lever is "efficient" and minimizes fatigue. Its one drawback is the adjuster mechanism, which is awkwardly located inside the hopper. Testers especially liked the snap-on clear plastic reservoir that catches pepper as you grind.

Recommended with Reservations

VIC FIRTH Gourmet Sierra Cherry Pepper Mill
Price: $38.95 at cooking.com
Grind quality: ★★
Grind quantity: ★★
Adjustability: ★★

Comments: This model offers a few improvements to the basic finial-topped design: Its finial has fixed stops, which ensure that you won't lose your setting—and that the finial won't fall off when grinding. The directional guide points users to coarse or fine pepper. However, the hopper is small, and the coarse pepper was not very coarse.

OLDE THOMPSON WOOD Senator 8-Inch Pepper Mill
Price: $15.95 at cooking.com
Grind quality: ★★
Grind quantity: ★★★
Adjustability: ★

Comments: This is your classic, no-frills, finial-topped pepper mill—a design we've never loved, because, as one tester said, "It's hard to grind when you tighten [the finial], and it falls off when you loosen it." This mill's finely ground pepper was very nice, but the grind was not uniform at medium and coarse settings.

Not Recommended

TRUDEAU One Hand Pepper Mill
Price: $24.95 at cooking.com
Grind quality: ★★
Grind quantity: ★
Adjustability: ★★

Comments: This is not an efficient pepper mill. The one-hand action looked promising, but the mechanism was "physically tiring" and "annoying." It produced acceptably uniform pepper at fine and medium settings.

Are Electric Pepper Mills Any Good?

During research, we came across several electric models. The most promising of the bunch was the PepperMills Supreme 2000 ($39.95 at cooking.com). This mill has a big hopper, and with the touch of a button it produced more than 2 tablespoons of ground pepper in just 30 seconds, making it twice as efficient as any of the hand-operated mills tested. In addition, this mill has fixed grind settings (which we like) and a small spotlight that shines as you grind. However, testers complained about the "cheap" construction, which "feels like it might fall apart." Most important, this mill was incapable of producing finely ground pepper. –S.K.

SPEED ISN'T EVERYTHING

Notes from Our Test Kitchen

TIPS, TECHNIQUES, AND TOOLS FOR BETTER COOKING

Kitchen Creations
Cookie Glazes

We love the simplicity of our **Slice-and-Bake Cookies** (page 27), but a confectioners' sugar glaze is an easy way to dress them up. These flavored glazes can be applied to nearly any cookie or simple cake. Each glaze yields about ½ cup (enough to glaze about three dozen 2-inch cookies). If the glaze is too thick, thin it to the desired consistency with up to 1 tablespoon of water.

GINGER-LIME GLAZE

Whisk 1 tablespoon softened cream cheese, 1 teaspoon ground ginger, and 2 tablespoons lime juice in medium bowl until combined. Whisk in 1½ cups confectioners' sugar until smooth.

MALTED MILK GLAZE

Whisk 1 tablespoon softened cream cheese, 1 tablespoon malt powder, 1 teaspoon vanilla extract, and 2 tablespoons milk in medium bowl until combined. Whisk in 1½ cups confectioners' sugar until smooth.

CAPPUCCINO GLAZE

Whisk 1 tablespoon softened cream cheese, 1 tablespoon instant espresso powder, and 2 tablespoons milk in medium bowl until combined. Whisk in 1½ cups confectioners' sugar until smooth.

PEANUT BUTTER AND JELLY GLAZE

Whisk 1 tablespoon creamy peanut butter, 2 tablespoons strawberry jelly, and 1 tablespoon water in medium bowl until combined. Whisk in 1½ cups confectioners' sugar until smooth.

Inside the Test Kitchen
Filling an Angel Food Cake

The first slice into our Raspberry Coconut Cloud Cake (inside back cover) reveals a secret: a tunnel of raspberry-flavored cream filling. As impressive as this looks, the technique for filling the cake is actually quite easy.

1. Using a serrated knife, make a shallow vertical cut into one side of the cake as a guide for reassembly and then cut a 1-inch layer off the top of the cake.
2. Using a fork, hollow out the center of the cake, leaving a 1-inch border around the edges and bottom.
3. Spoon the filling into the tunnel, using a spatula to smooth the top. Arrange the top layer on the filled cake, using the precut notch to align the layers.

Buying a Muffin Tin

Larger price tags don't translate into better muffin tins. We've found that heavier, more expensive muffin tins don't perform any better than the lighter models you can buy at the supermarket for less than $10. The most important thing to look for is a dark coating, which will brown the muffin bottoms much better than will shiny metallic finishes. Another feature to look for is an inch or two of clearance from the perimeter of the muffin cups to the edge of the pan; this extra lip helps minimize mess.

Tip-Top Roast

When developing our recipe for **Chicago-Style Spicy Roast Beef** (page 14), we tested several different cuts before settling on a top sirloin roast, which is also called top sirloin butt, center-cut roast, or spoon roast. This roast has big, beefy flavor that can stand up to assertive seasonings, and it is more tender than rump roast, the traditional cut in this recipe.

TOP SIRLOIN ROAST
Big, beefy flavor—and relatively inexpensive

Shrimp Sizes

Shopping for shrimp, with their enigmatic descriptors—U/12, 51/60, 26/30, and so on—can be a bit intimidating. But don't worry; what looks like a random string of numbers is actually a basic code that relates to the size of the shrimp. Shrimp are sorted by size and given a number that corresponds to the amount of shrimp per pound. U/12, or colossal, shrimp (the size we call for in our recipe for **Baked Stuffed Shrimp** on page 13) contain under 12 shrimp per pound. A pound of shrimp bearing the designation 26/30 will contain between 26 and 30 shrimp. As the numbers go up, the size (and the price) of the shrimp goes down.

Prepeeled Garlic

Our recipe for **Ultimate Garlic Roast Chicken** (page 12) calls for a whopping 50 cloves of garlic. While cloves from a fresh head of garlic have the best flavor,

Kitchen Know-How STARCH MAKES IT STICKY

When developing the recipe for our **Chinese-Style Rice** (page 24), we found that rapidly boiling the rice for five minutes uncovered and then turning down the heat and covering the pot resulted in the sticky texture we desired. The stickiness is a result of the rapid boil, which agitates the grains and causes them to release excess starch into the cooking water. You know it's time to cover the pot when small holes (marking the escape route of the steam) appear in the surface of the rice.

1. Vigorously boil the rice until the water level in the pot drops below the rice and small holes have formed in the surface of the rice. This will take about five minutes.

2. Slide the lid in place and reduce the heat to low. Continue to cook the rice over very low heat until all the water has been absorbed and the rice is tender, about 15 minutes longer.

How to PREPARE LEEKS

To give our **Low-Fat Broccoli Cheddar Soup** (page 9) a silky, smooth texture and to enhance its flavor, we turned to leeks. A member of the onion family, leeks can grow to more than 2 feet in length. Their flavor is mildly oniony and earthy, and because they grow in sandy soil, they are often quite dirty. To prepare leeks for cooking, follow these simple steps.

1. Cut off the tough dark green portion of the leek and discard. Slice the remaining white and light green portion in half lengthwise.

2. Submerge halved leeks in cold water and agitate to remove any dirt. Once the leeks are clean, remove them from the water, pat them dry with paper towels, and chop them as desired.

Wild about Portobellos

To add a deep, earthy flavor to our **Chicken and Mushroom Fricassee** (page 22), we turned to portobello mushrooms. Their woodsy flavor and dense, meaty texture are prized in many dishes, but the dark gills on the underside of the cap can stain sauces and soups during cooking. To avoid this problem, we usually remove the dark gills before cooking them. We also prefer to buy just the portobello caps, as the stems are too tough to eat and must be discarded. Besides being recipe-ready, caps are often more economical, since whole portobellos are generally priced by the pound, which means you're paying for something you can't use.

Giardiniera Tasting

In Italy, giardiniera refers to pickled vegetables that are typically eaten as an antipasto. But here in the United States, it's most recognized as a combination of pickled cauliflower, carrots, celery, and sweet and hot peppers that is served alongside sandwiches or other lunch fare. On our trip to Chicago to research **Italian Beef Sandwiches** (page 15), we were impressed by that city's devotion to this spicy condiment. We tracked down three regional Chicago brands of jarred giardiniera (Scala's Hot, Dell'Alpe, and Il Primo) and tasted them against five national brands. While tasters were impressed by the "spicy complexity" and "pleasant bitterness" of Scala's Hot, we wanted a larger variety of

OUR FAVORITE GIARDINIERA

vegetables (the Chicago giardinieras are mostly peppers). Our favorite was the national brand Pastene, which was praised for its "sharp, vinegary tang" and variety of vegetables in the pickle.

Fat-Free Evaporated Milk

In our **Low-Fat Broccoli Cheddar Soup** (page 9), we call for fat-free evaporated milk, which is made by removing more than half the water found in milk to concentrate its flavor. The creaminess of fat-free evaporated milk makes it a perfect substitute for cream products—it adds body and silkiness that you can't get with regular fat-free milk. Note that evaporated milk is not the same thing as condensed milk, which is always sweetened and can't be used in savory recipes.

A Quick Idea
PEELING GARLIC MADE EASY

During weeks of testing recipes for **Garlicky Oven Fries** (page 17) and **Garlic Roast Chicken** (page 12), we wanted a quick way to peel a large amount of garlic cloves. While prepeeled garlic cloves (see page 30) were an acceptable substitute, here's the shortcut we came up with for peeling a lot of garlic. Break the heads of garlic into individual cloves and place them in a heavy-duty zipper-lock bag. Squeeze out most of the air, seal the bag, and gently pound the cloves with a rolling pin. Then just remove the peeled cloves from the bag, zip the bag back up (with the skins still inside), and discard.

GARLIC SHORTCUT
This is the quickest way to peel a lot of garlic cloves.

prepeeled cloves from the supermarket are a fine—and convenient—substitute. Look for packages of unblemished cloves and always store prepeeled cloves in the refrigerator, as they are more prone to spoilage than whole heads.

Toasted Sesame Oil

Toasted sesame oil gives our **Sesame Green Beans** (page 24) a deep, nutty sesame flavor. Made by pressing the natural oils from toasted sesame seeds, its color can range from golden amber to dark brown. Although toasted sesame oil is very potent and should be used sparingly, the flavor also fades quickly when exposed to heat; we prefer to add this oil to Asian-inspired dishes in the final moments of cooking or right before serving. Toasted sesame oil also works well in cold dishes, salad dressing, sauces, and marinades. Since this oil is highly perishable, it should be refrigerated after opening.

TOASTED SESAME OIL
Add at the end of cooking for the best flavor.

Chili Powder Primer

Authentic chili con carne recipes often call for toasting, cooling, and grinding a variety of dried whole chiles, which can be hard to come by in your average supermarket. For convenience, our

Chili con Carne recipe (page 10) uses jarred chili powder, which we toast to bloom its flavor. Chili powder is typically a blend of ground red chile peppers, cumin, oregano, garlic, and salt; sometimes cloves or allspice and/ or included. Watch out for chili powders labeled "pure," which are solely one kind of ground chile pepper (typically ancho and chipotle) with no added seasonings— they can be assertively hot and smoky. The test kitchen's favorite brand of chili powder, Spice Islands, was praised by our tasters for its "sweet," "smoky" flavor that was deemed "very potent."

THE SPICE IS RIGHT
Spice Islands is our favorite brand of chili powder.

Shoulder Subdivision

After testing every pork roast we could find for our **Slow-Cooker Pork Pot Roast** (page 8), we found that well-marbled shoulder cuts such as picnic shoulder and Boston butt held up best to the moist heat and long cooking time. We had no preference between the two cuts, although we did prefer to use two smaller boneless roasts in this recipe, because they cooked faster than one large cut. Most grocery stores carry the 2- to 3-pound boneless pork shoulder roasts (usually wrapped in netting) that we preferred; if you can only find a 5- to 6-pound roast, you can cut away the netting, open the roast up, and cut it into two equal pieces.

Gadgets & Gear Cast-Iron Skillets

We recommend using a 10-inch cast-iron skillet for our **Southern-Style Skillet Corn Bread** (page 11). In a recent testing of several brands, we preferred the Lodge Logic series of cast-iron pans. This preseasoned, no-frills line performed very well in all of our cooking tests (scrambled eggs, pan-seared steaks with a pan sauce, shallow-fried chicken, and yes, corn bread) and was virtually nonstick from the first use.

TEST KITCHEN FAVORITE
The Lodge Logic is the best pan for corn bread.

When Things Go Wrong in the Kitchen

READERS SHARE FUNNY STORIES ABOUT COOKING MISHAPS

MARBLE CHEESECAKE

A while back, I decided to make a marble cheesecake with my 9-year-old niece. We got all the ingredients ready and started mixing. A few moments later, my niece ran out of the room shouting that we had forgotten something. I checked the ingredients and was sure we had everything, and I couldn't possibly imagine that this little girl knew how to make a cheesecake. She came back into the kitchen holding a toy bag, and I asked her what she was doing. She said, "We forgot the most important ingredient. The marbles!"

Marie Delage Prospect, Ct.

COOKING WITH COLORS

As a new bride about 40 years ago, I decided to make a pot roast and brown gravy. I had made milk gravy before and thought I could make brown gravy by stirring the flour into the pan drippings before adding the milk, but it didn't get brown. I didn't know how to achieve the right color, but I did know that mixing blue, yellow, and red food coloring together makes brown, so I got out the bottles and went to work. I had the perfect color until the lid came off the red dropper. Needless to say, my husband was shocked when he saw the beautiful roast with the bright red gravy! The next day he bought me a cookbook.

Beverly Morefield Waco, Ky.

TAKE COVER

When I was first married, I didn't have much cooking experience. One day my husband brought home some bagged chestnuts, and I had no idea what to do with them. He told me they should be roasted in the oven. One snowy evening, I placed the chestnuts in a pan in the oven, sat down on the couch, and waited for them to bake and my husband to come home. Unfortunately, my husband neglected to tell me that chestnut shells need to be pierced before baking to prevent them from exploding. He came home to a terribly frightened wife cowering under the kitchen table, screaming to "Get down!" because we were being shot at!

Helen Fisher Paradise, Calif.

READING TOO CAREFULLY

Years ago, I decided to bake a cake for my husband. I figured that if I followed the directions precisely, with no deviations, the cake was certain to come out right. After successfully baking both cake layers, I was pleased with the way everything was going. The frosting directions read, "Simmer ingredients until they spin a thread." They didn't mention what color thread, but I decided on white since I wanted a white frosting. I grabbed my pot, threw in my ingredients—including 8 inches of thread—and stood at the stove waiting for the thread to start spinning. My neighbor came by and asked me what I was doing, and when I told her, she peeked in the pot and started laughing. I now know to not always take everything so literally, especially when it comes to cooking.

Marjorie B. Cross New London, N.H.

SURPRISE FILLING

My mom happened to be in town for Mother's Day while I was in college, and I wanted to make her a breakfast of sweet crêpes topped with some fresh strawberries from the farmers' market. I had made the batter several times before in the blender, which I found much easier than doing it by hand. I measured out all of the ingredients and used my tablespoon to give it a quick stir before hitting the "liquefy" button. When the pan was heated, I started to slowly pour in the batter. Soon after the batter hit the hot pan, I noticed a smell of burning plastic and some white lumps in the first crêpe. I went back to inspect the blender and found my plastic tablespoon measure had been chopped into tiny pieces! My mom teases me about it every Mother's Day.

Jessica Knight Los Angeles, Calif.

UP TO YOUR ELBOWS

My daughter has been helping me out in the kitchen since she was very young. As a preschooler, she would stand on a chair pulled up to the counter and beat eggs or sift flour with me. As she grew older, there was an awkward period when she was still too short to stand at the counter but a tad too tall to stand on a chair. One day, she was standing on top of a chair next to me as we assembled a massive pan of lasagna. We had gotten through the third level when I saw her reach forward to lay some noodles down. She lost her balance and was immediately up to her elbows in noodles, cheese, and sauce. I managed to scoop and scrape most of the lasagna off of her and salvaged enough to reassemble the pan. She was clearly upset, so I joked, "Well, no one can say you didn't throw yourself into this cooking project!" That made her smile.

Leon Lynn Milwaukee, Wis.

THREE-ALARM CRABS

While on a weekend trip to D.C., my fiancé bought a bushel of blue crabs to take back to Ohio. With a box of crabs, Old Bay seasoning, and instructions from the fishmonger to steam until done, we headed home for a feast. We didn't have any large pots, so we pulled out every small pot we owned, poured in some water, and added the crabs and Old Bay. The fishmonger didn't tell us how long to steam the crabs, and with their hard shells we figured it would take a very long time. Not until the fire department arrived did we realize one pot had boiled dry and the acrid Old Bay–seasoned smoke was being sucked out through the intake of our ventilation system. The inhabitants of the entire fourth floor were evacuated. We apologized profusely to our neighbors, then invited them all over for a feast!

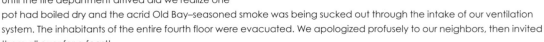

Stephanie Johnson Olympia, Wash.

Send us your funniest kitchen disaster stories. E-mail us by visiting **CooksCountry.com/kitchendisasters**. Or write to us at Kitchen Disasters, Cook's Country, P.O. Box 470739, Brookline, MA 02447. If we publish your story, you'll receive a complimentary one-year subscription to *Cook's Country.*

Raspberry Coconut Cloud Cake

Angel food cake makes an ethereal foil for an easy raspberry mousse filling made with whipped cream. More whipped cream and sweetened coconut are used to frost and decorate this light-as-air cake.

To make this cake, you will need:

- 1 teaspoon **unflavored gelatin**
- 2 tablespoons **raspberry liqueur**
- 4 cups **heavy cream, chilled**
- ¼ cup **confectioners' sugar**
- ¼ cup **seedless raspberry jam**
- 1 (10-inch) **angel food cake***
- 2 cups **sweetened shredded coconut**
- 1 cup **fresh raspberries**

For the frosting and filling: Combine gelatin and liqueur in large bowl. Let stand 5 minutes to soften gelatin. Bring ¼ cup cream to simmer in saucepan over medium heat, then whisk into gelatin mixture until no lumps remain; cool. Add sugar and remaining cream and, with electric mixer on medium-high speed, beat to stiff peaks, about 2 minutes. Transfer 2 cups whipped cream mixture to large bowl and fold in jam.

To assemble: Using serrated knife, cut 1-inch layer from top of cake. Using fork, hollow out center of cake, leaving 1-inch border on all sides (see photos on page 30). Spoon raspberry jam–whipped cream filling into hollowed-out cake and spread level. Return top layer to cake and transfer to serving platter. Frost top and sides of cake with remaining whipped cream mixture. Press coconut into sides of cake and sprinkle evenly over top. Refrigerate until filling and frosting are set, about 2 hours. (Cake can be refrigerated for up to 24 hours.) Garnish with raspberries. Serve.

*Go to **CooksCountry.com** for our Angel Food Cake recipe or use your own.
*If using a store-bought cake, be sure to purchase one that is 10 inches in diameter.

Recipe Index

RC = Recipe Card

Cook's Country

APRIL/MAY 2008

Better Fruit Salads
These Salads Dress Themselves

Make-Ahead Holiday Menu
The Cook Celebrates, Too

Herbed Roast Pork
Two Tenderloins Become One Flavorful Roast

RATING NONSTICK PANS
Inexpensive Skillet Cleans Up

LOW-FAT MEATLOAF
Forget Turkey. It's All Beef!

TASTING HOT SALSA
Which Brand Tastes Freshest?

BEST-EVER PORK CUTLETS
Secrets to Flavorful Breading

GRILLED BEEF TENDERLOIN
Perfect Roast Guaranteed

PANINI SANDWICHES
Skip the Press, Use a Pan

BERRY STREUSEL PIE
With Easy Press-in-Pan Crust

BAKED POTATO FANS
Crisp, Stuffed, and Crunchy!

PASTA AND BEAN SOUP
Big Flavor in 30 Minutes

BISCUITS & SAUSAGE GRAVY
Buttery Biscuits, Creamy Gravy

Our $1,000 Contest Winner!
Mary Van Driest of **Oostburg, Wis.,** won first place in our party appetizer contest with a twist on chips and salsa. See page 4 for her **Fruit Salsa with Cinnamon Tortilla Chips.**

$4.95 U.S./$6.95 CANADA

0 74470 05251 7

Cook's Country

Dear Country Cook,

Our neighbor, Jean, keeps hens (as we do) but she also has a rooster and that often means an early morning wake up call. Other wild noises that drift through our open bedroom window including the thumping of grouse in the spring (which sounds like an old tractor that can't quite get started), the hooting of bears, and the frenzied yapping of coyotes. On slow summer days one also hears the keening of red-tailed hawks and, once in a great while, the dense buzz made by a black column of swarming honeybees. I saw a swarm just three years ago as it moved across our lower pasture and floated up into the woods.

A friend of ours has two young girls, and one of them asked, while sitting down to a fried-chicken dinner, why they called what she was eating "chicken." She had no idea that her dinner was related to the bird. (After all, "beef" and "pork" are not the names of animals.)

The proud rooster in the photo below was photographed in 1922, the days when the farm and table were intimately acquainted, and when every child knew how the chicken came to be in the pot. A farm kitchen made a lot of sense—the growing, cooking, preserving, and eating were all connected. Even today, the country seems to hold more wisdom than the city. Kevin, another neighbor, has a saying about shoddy work, "There is never time to do it right but plenty of time to do it again!" When I asked the unlicensed deer hunters who always hunt behind the game warden's house why they chose to tempt fate they replied, "Well, this is the last place he'd look!" They have a point.

Simple food is just fine with all of us here at Cook's Country. We're proud of good home cooking. But most of all, we like to know where our food comes from, and that includes both the chicken and the egg.

Christopher Kimball
Founder and Editor, Cook's Country Magazine

Egg-Laying Contest Santa Cruz, California 1922.
Photographer: © Minnesota Historical Society/CORBIS

APRIL/MAY 2008

Cook's Country

(13)

(12)

(26)

features

10 Herbed Roast Pork
You can only pack so many herbs onto the exterior of a pork roast. For bolder herb flavor, we look inside the meat.

12 Baked Potato Fans
Despite their spectacular presentation, these crisp, fluffy, cheesy potatoes are surprisingly easy to make.

13 Spicy Grilled Beef Tenderloin
The grill is a great place to cook a whole tenderloin, especially if you coat the roast with a spicy rub.

14 Panini Sandwiches at Home
We've figured out how to make great pressed sandwiches without a fancy panini press.

15 Weeknight Pasta and Bean Soup
Could we pack long-simmered flavor into a quick and easy soup?

18 The Test Kitchen's Make-Ahead Holiday Menu
Our elegant menu makes it easy for the cook this year.

20 Chicken, Broccoli, and Ziti Casserole
We transform this Italian-American favorite into a casserole big enough to feed the whole family.

22 Better Pork Cutlets
Our technique for infusing flavor ensures that you'll never eat ho-hum pork cutlets again.

24 Biscuits and Sausage Gravy
Southern diners were once the sole provenance of this breakfast, but we set out to bring authentic biscuits and sausage gravy to home cooks everywhere.

25 Rethinking Fruit Salads
These four simple recipes will change the way you look at fruit salads.

26 Berry Streusel Pie
This pie has it all—a graham cracker crust, a flavorful (but not soupy) berry filling, and a crisp, buttery crumb topping.

27 Mississippi Mud Brownies
These moist, fudgy brownies are topped with marshmallow and more chocolate—what's not to like?

Founder and Editor Christopher Kimball
Editorial Director Jack Bishop
Executive Editor Amanda Agee
Deputy Editor Bridget Lancaster
Senior Editors Scott Kathan
Jeremy Sauer
Test Kitchen Director Erin McMurrer
Associate Editors Cali Rich
Diane Unger
Test Cooks Kelley Baker
Meredith Butcher
Greg Case
Assistant Test Cook Lynn Clark
Online Managing Editor Katherine Bell
Online Editor Kate Mason
Online Assistant Editor Leaya Lee
Copy Editor Will Gordon
Editorial Assistant Meredith Smith
Senior Kitchen Assistant Nadia Domeq
Kitchen Assistants Maria Elena Delgado
Ena Gudiel
David Lentini
TV Producer Melissa Baldino
Contributing Editor Eva Katz
Consulting Editor Guy Crosby

Design Director Amy Klee
Art Director, Magazines Julie Bozzo
Senior Designer Christine Vo
Designers Tiffani Beckwith
Jay Layman
Erica Lee
Staff Photographer Daniel J. van Ackere

Production Director Guy Rochford
Traffic & Projects Manager Alice Cummiskey
Production & Imaging Specialist Lauren Pettapiece
Color & Imaging Specialist Andrew Mannone

Vice President New Technology Craig Morrow
Systems Administrator S. Paddi McHugh
IT Business Analyst Doug Sisko
IT Support Technician Brandon Lynch

Chief Financial Officer Sharyn Chabot
Human Resources Director Adele Shapiro
Controller Mandy Shito
Senior Accountant Aaron Goranson
Staff Accountant Connie Forbes
Office Manager Danielle Pezely
Receptionist Henrietta Murray

Vice President Marketing David Mack
Fulfillment & Circulation Manager Carrie Horan
Circulation Assistant Elizabeth Dayton
Direct Mail Director Adam Perry
Direct Mail Analyst Jenny Leong
Products Director Steven Browall
E-Commerce Marketing Director Hugh Buchan
Partnership Marketing Manager Pamela Putprush
Marketing Copywriter David Goldberg
Customer Service Manager Jacqueline Valerio
Customer Service Representatives Julie Gardner
Jillian Nannicelli

Vice President Sales Demee Gambulos
Retail Sales & Marketing Manager Emily Logan
Retail Sales Associate Anthony King
Corporate Marketing Associate Bailey Vatalaro
Publicity Deborah Broide

ON THE COVER: PHOTOGRAPHY: Roulier/Turiot//photocuisine/CORBIS. ILLUSTRATION: John Burgoyne.
IN THIS ISSUE: COLOR FOOD PHOTOGRAPHY: Keller + Keller. STYLING: Mary Jane Sawyer, Marie Piraino. ILLUSTRATION: Lisa Perrett.

Cook's Country magazine (ISSN 1552-1990), number 20, is published bimonthly by Boston Common Press Limited Partnership, 17 Station Street, Brookline, MA 02445. Copyright 2008 Boston Common Press Limited Partnership. Periodicals postage paid at Boston, Mass., and additional mailing offices. POSTMASTER: Send address changes to Cook's Country, P.O. Box 8382, Red Oak, IA 51591-1382. For subscription and gift subscription orders, subscription inquiries, or change-of-address notices, call 800-526-8447 in the U.S. or 515-247-7571 from outside the U.S., or write us at Cook's Country, P.O. Box 8382, Red Oak, IA 51591-1382.
PRINTED IN THE USA

Visit us at CooksCountry.com!
Go online for hundreds of recipes, food tastings, and up-to-date equipment reviews. You can get a behind-the-scenes look at our test kitchen, talk to our cooks and editors, enter recipe contests, and share recipes and cooking tips with the *Cook's Country* community.

Kitchen Shortcuts

Grate Bread Crumbs

Since I don't have a food processor, I've come up with another way to make home-made bread crumbs. I freeze leftover hamburger and hot dog buns and then use my box grater to grate the bread into fine crumbs. They are perfect for mixing into meatloaf.

Lisa Bryant
Little Rock, Ark.

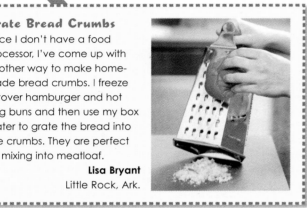

Quick Release

I love baking cakes but have always hated greasing cake pans. Since I don't like the sprays, instead I use an inexpensive paintbrush (which costs about half as much as a pastry brush) to paint the melted butter or shortening onto my pans. The cakes come out perfect every time.

Jana Marie Stankus
Greer, S.C.

Upright Storage

KEEP IT TIDY

I don't have a lot of drawer space for boxes of aluminum foil, plastic wrap, and parchment paper. I store the boxes upright in the slots of a cardboard six-pack bottle container. It fits nicely underneath the sink.

Courtney Schaeffer
Chicago, Ill.

Hardware Pie

FROM THE TOOL CHEST TO THE OVEN

I recently made a pie for my family, but when the pie crust was about to go into the oven to blind bake, I realized that I had lost my pie weights. To improvise, I grabbed a handful of nails, bolts, and screws and placed them on the foil in my pie dough. It worked so well that I don't care if I ever locate my pie weights.

Jennifer Chambers Los Angeles, Calif.

GET A GRIP

I use a shelf liner under waxed paper for grating. It keeps my flat grater or mandoline from sliding on the counter just as well as it steadies a cutting board.

Dee Dee Miles
Hamilton, N.J.

SPACE-SAVER

My kitchen is small, so I don't have a lot of counter space. To make a little extra room, I pull out the top drawer next to my oven and place a cutting board on top. That way I can put any food I am about to cook on top of it.

Elvira Chang
Jamaica Plain, Mass.

FROZEN MASHED POTATOES

We love mashed potatoes, but since there are only two of us, we always have leftovers. After the meal, I cool the leftovers and put them into a gallon-sized zipper-lock freezer bag, which I flatten to about half an inch thick. The next time I want mashed potatoes, I just take the potatoes out of the bag, break off as much as I need, put the bag back in the freezer, and heat the potatoes up in the microwave. It's a great way for a small family or single person to enjoy mashed potatoes any time!

Pat Burden
Yale, Mich.

NEATER SPRAYING

I used to avoid greasing pans with cooking spray, because it got all over everything no matter how much I tried to confine it. I finally started grabbing a plastic grocery bag and spraying the pans inside the bag.

Margaret Thibert
Fort Worth, Texas

UNDER PRESSURE

When my pressure canner broke in the middle of a canning project, I needed to use an old-fashioned water bath to seal the jars. My regular metal tongs wouldn't securely grip the wet jars, so I wrapped rubber bands around each end of the tongs, which worked great.

Sharon Friedner
Amherst, Mass.

COOL UNDER PRESSURE

Before I roll out my pie dough, I freeze a large cookie sheet. I then flip the frozen cookie sheet over, place parchment paper down, and roll out my dough. The frozen sheet keeps the dough cold, so I don't have to refrigerate the crust for as long before baking.

Susan Sims
Orem, Utah

CAST-IRON CONVENIENCE

I never seem to have enough pie plates for holiday baking. One time, in a pinch, I used a heavy cast-iron skillet to bake a pumpkin pie; the crust crisped up beautifully and didn't get soggy in the refrigerator. Now I always bake my pumpkin pie in that skillet.

Jane Bourgoin
Lakewood, Colo.

SWEET TIP

I like to sweeten drinks with honey, which doesn't dissolve easily in cold liquid. I found that if I put some honey in a small bowl, add a bit of water, microwave it, and stir, the honey thins out a little and can then dissolve easily into my iced teas.

Victoria Scott
Santa Fe, N.M.

STEM REMOVER

When mushroom stems are pried out by hand to make stuffed mushrooms, the mushrooms often break. I discovered that I can use my small tomato corer to easily scoop the stem out without breaking the mushroom.

Valerie Gardner
Chubbuck, Idaho

If you'd like to submit a tip, please e-mail us by visiting **CooksCountry. com/kitchenshortcuts** or send a letter to Kitchen Shortcuts, Cook's Country, P.O. Box 470739, Brookline, MA 02447. Include your name, address, and phone number. If we publish your tip, you will receive a free one-year subscription to *Cook's Country*.

SPLASH GUARD

For salad dressing made in a blender, many recipes call for the oil to be drizzled in slowly through the removable cap on the lid while the blender is running. Even when you do this very slowly and carefully, the dressing can still splash out of the blender. I eliminated the problem by resting a funnel in the opening and pouring the oil through the funnel.

Eunice Ranch
Parkville, Md.

MASON JAR STORAGE

I use Mason jars instead of plastic containers for all my food storage. They are inexpensive, durable, and dishwasher-safe. Plus the seal on the jar is much tighter than with plastic containers, so food tends to stay fresh for a little longer. Leftover pasta sauce is particularly well suited to this storage method, as it is so easy to recognize in the fridge when in a Mason jar.

Michi Sakurai
Pasadena, Calif.

A NEW WAY TO MAKE LEMONADE

Instead of mashing sliced lemons by hand when making old-fashioned lemonade, I add the lemon slices and sugar to my stand mixer—fitted with the paddle attachment—and set the mixer on low. The lemons and sugar are muddled within minutes.

Heather Lindquist
San Diego, Calif.

NICELY WHIPPED

I don't have room in my freezer for my mixing bowl. So whenever I need to whip some cream, I fill my mixing bowl with ice cubes and wait about 10 minutes. Once the bowl is chilled, I empty the cubes, wipe the bowl dry, and start whipping. Within minutes, I have perfectly whipped cream.

Amy Parker
Cypress, Texas

FILL 'ER UP

I like to make individual fruit tarts, but adding the pastry cream can be a messy job, and I usually end up spilling some on the crust. Now I use my bulb baster to add just the right amount of pastry cream. No more spills or mess.

Jennifer Marchand
Rockland, Mass.

BUNDLE UP

When making chicken soup, I tie the ingredients together in cheesecloth bundles before tossing them into the pot. I make four bundles: one for the chicken, one for the vegetables I'll discard after cooking, one for the vegetables that stay in the soup, and one for the herbs. After the broth has cooked and cooled, I just remove the bundles. I'm left with a completely clear broth and easy access to the chicken and vegetables.

Andrea Widburg
Corte Madera, Calif.

FREEZE YOUR SPICES

To keep my spices fresher for longer, I buy the larger containers and store them in the door of my freezer, where I can easily read the labels.

Virginia Czarnecki
Buffalo, N.Y.

TREAD LIGHTLY

I don't have a lot of room in my kitchen to store pots and pans, so I have to stack them. To protect my nonstick pans, I went to the dollar store and purchased some rolls of rubber rug mats. They cut easily and do a great job of protecting the surface of the pans. They're inexpensive, too.

Carleen Whitney
Cleveland, Ohio

COOKING GENTLY

I am notorious for breaking my eggs when I put them in the pan for hard-cooked eggs. Now I use my pasta server to gently lower the eggs into the water—it's much easier and helps prevent cracked shells.

Mary Ash
Ridgecrest, Calif.

MICROWAVE YOUR VEGGIES

For a quick way to make steamed broccoli or cauliflower, just put the vegetables in a microwavable zipper-lock bag with two or three ice cubes. Microwave for a minute or so and you'll have a quick side dish.

Henrietta Braatz
Eden Prarie, Minn.

Protect Your Books

I cut a zipper-lock bag in half and drape it over the open pages of my cookbook. I pin the plastic-covered sheet in place with two clothespins at the top. That way, my book stays open to where I need it, and I don't have to worry about ruining the pages with dripped or splashed food.

Emily Evans
Olathe, Kan.

Stick and Release

NEAT TIP

Every once in a while, one of my blueberry muffins will stick no matter how well I grease the pan. For those stubborn muffins, I use my curved grapefruit knife to gently dislodge the stuck part. No muffin is lost!

Erin McGrath
San Diego, Calif.

For More Than Cheese

I use my cheese plane to peel the skin off cucumbers and also to slice them. It works well as a peeler and is a great way to get thin, even slices for salads and sandwiches.

Monique Gawryk
Chicago, Ill.

Not Just for Aches & Pains

HEATING HELPER

When I'm baking and forget to pull the butter and eggs out of the refrigerator in time for them to come to room temperature, I set my heating pad on low and wrap the butter in a towel before slipping both the butter and the eggs inside the heating pad. The towel prevents the butter from getting too soft too quickly, and the eggs and butter are warmed in no time.

Diane Kuszewski
Damascus, Md.

Lemon Ricer

EASY SQUEEZE

I don't have a juicer, so when I need to squeeze a lot of lemons at one time, I pull out my potato ricer. I cut the lemons in half, place them in the ricer, and squeeze the handles together. The juice drips down, and the ricer catches the seeds.

Tina Henley
La Jolla, Calif.

Recipe Contest PARTY APPETIZERS

Winning Recipes Put New Spins on Classic Party Snacks

Our $1,000 Grand-Prize Winner!

Mary Van Driest
Oostburg, Wis.

No matter how good they are, even the best recipes need a little shaking up from time to time. The winners of this recipe contest put a premium on creativity by giving us inventive—but still crowd-pleasing—updates on classic party foods: chips and salsa, chicken wings, spinach dip, cheese balls, and deviled eggs.

Our grand-prize winner took the leap from savory to sweet with her rethinking of chips and dip as a sweet starter. Mary says, "This recipe has appeal in the warm weather because of the fruit, but it's also nice to serve during the holidays, because it's very festive. I also like the fact that once it's served, no attention is required." Our tasters loved how the cinnamon-sugar tortilla chips complement the vibrant mixture of chopped fruit.

FRUIT SALSA WITH CINNAMON TORTILLA CHIPS SERVES 12

Once cool, the chips can be stored at room temperature in an airtight container for 4 days; the salsa is best served immediately.

Fruit Salsa
- 2 tablespoons apple jelly
- 2 tablespoons light brown sugar
- ¼ cup orange juice
- 1 jalapeño chile, seeded and minced
- 2 Granny Smith apples, peeled, cored, and chopped fine
- 1 pint strawberries, hulled and chopped fine
- 3 kiwis, peeled and chopped fine

Cinnamon Chips
- 2 tablespoons granulated sugar
- 1 tablespoon ground cinnamon
- 12 (6-inch) flour tortillas

1. For the fruit salsa: Whisk jelly, sugar, orange juice, and jalapeño in large bowl. Add apples, strawberries, and kiwis and toss to coat.

2. For the cinnamon chips: Adjust oven racks to upper-middle and lower-middle positions and heat oven to 350 degrees. Combine sugar and cinnamon in bowl. Lightly coat tortillas on both sides with cooking spray and cut each into 6 wedges. Arrange tortillas in single layer on 2 baking sheets and sprinkle sugar mixture evenly over top of tortillas. Bake until golden and crisp, 10 to 15 minutes, switching and rotating sheets halfway through baking time. Serve with salsa.

This recipe transforms ordinary flour tortillas into cinnamon-sugar tortilla chips for dipping.

Sheryl Little
Sherwood, Ark.

Barbara Lanke
Pittsburgh, Pa.

Angelia Filer
Dickenson, Texas

Dianne Miller
Arnold, Md.

CURRIED HONEY-MUSTARD WINGS SERVES 12

Sheryl writes: "My best friend and her husband are beekeepers, and I am fortunate to get fresh, pure honey from them all the time. I like to incorporate their wonderful honey into my cooking."

- ¼ cup honey
- ¼ cup yellow mustard
- ¼ cup mango chutney, such as Major Grey's
- 1 tablespoon grated fresh ginger
- 2 garlic cloves, minced
- 1 teaspoon curry powder
- ½ teaspoon cayenne pepper Salt
- 3 pounds whole chicken wings, halved at joint and wingtips removed
- 2 tablespoons toasted sesame seeds

1. Adjust oven rack to middle position and heat oven to 475 degrees. Process honey, mustard, chutney, ginger, garlic, curry powder, cayenne, and ½ teaspoon salt in food processor until smooth; transfer to large bowl.

2. Lightly coat slotted broiler pan top with cooking spray and arrange over foil-lined broiler pan bottom. Transfer to oven and heat until just smoking, about 5 minutes. Pat chicken dry with paper towels and season with salt. Arrange in single layer on heated broiler pan top and roast until golden brown, 35 to 45 minutes, rotating pan and flipping chicken halfway through cooking.

3. Remove chicken from oven and transfer to bowl with honey mixture. Toss to coat, then return chicken to broiler pan. Continue to cook until well browned, about 5 minutes. Sprinkle with sesame seeds. Serve.

PESTO CHEESE BALL SERVES 12

Barbara writes: "This recipe is a family favorite served when we watch the Pittsburgh Steelers football games with family and friends. When the Steelers win, we're sure it's because of the lucky dip." Pecorino Romano is a hard sheep's-milk cheese with a strong, tangy flavor. If you cannot find it, Parmesan can be substituted. Toast the nuts in a dry skillet over medium heat, shaking the pan occasionally, until golden and fragrant, about 5 minutes.

- 1 cup lightly packed fresh basil
- 1 cup lightly packed baby spinach
- ½ cup grated Pecorino Romano cheese
- 2 garlic cloves, minced
- 2 tablespoons olive oil
- 2 (8-ounce) packages cream cheese, softened
- 8 ounces goat cheese, softened
- ½ cup chopped toasted walnuts
- ½ cup sun-dried tomatoes packed in oil, rinsed, patted dry, and chopped fine

1. Line 1-quart bowl with plastic wrap, leaving 4-inch overhang. Process basil, spinach, Pecorino, garlic, and oil in food processor until smooth. Stir cream cheese and goat cheese together in separate bowl until combined.

2. Spread one-third of cheese mixture on bottom of prepared bowl. Spread half of basil mixture evenly over cheese. Sprinkle with half of walnuts and half of tomatoes. Repeat with half of remaining cheese mixture and remaining basil mixture, walnuts, and tomatoes. Top with remaining cheese mixture. Fold plastic wrap over cheese ball and refrigerate until firm, at least 4 hours or up to 24 hours. Let sit at room temperature for 1 hour before serving.

MEXICAN SPINACH DIP SERVES 12

Angelia writes: "This recipe was given to me by a neighbor with toddler-age twins. This was one of the kids' favorite recipes. I knew if a toddler liked it, it had to be good!" If you can't find Ro-Tel tomatoes, substitute one 14.5-ounce can of diced tomatoes and one 4-ounce can of chopped green chiles. Serve with tortilla chips.

- 1 (8-ounce) package cream cheese, softened
- ⅓ cup sour cream
- 1 jalapeño chile, seeded and chopped fine
- 2 (10-ounce) cans Ro-Tel tomatoes, drained
- ½ small onion, chopped fine
- 1 (10-ounce) box frozen spinach, thawed and squeezed dry
- 3 cups shredded sharp cheddar cheese
- 1 teaspoon salt
- ½ teaspoon chili powder
- ½ teaspoon ground cumin

Adjust oven rack to middle position and heat oven to 350 degrees. Grease 8-inch-square baking dish. With wooden spoon or rubber spatula, combine cream cheese, sour cream, and jalapeño in large bowl. Fold in tomatoes, onion, spinach, cheddar, salt, chili powder, and cumin until well combined. Scrape into baking dish and bake until bubbling at edges and top is golden brown, about 30 minutes. Serve. (Dip can be assembled and refrigerated for 24 hours prior to baking.)

CRABBY DEVILED EGGS SERVES 12

Dianne writes: "My mother always made deviled eggs at Easter to use up the dozens of eggs we colored for our baskets. I thought I had outgrown this dish until I inherited my grandmother's deviled egg plate. When we moved to the Chesapeake Bay last year, I added crabmeat and Old Bay seasoning in honor of my new home. The crowds remain pleased!" Be sure to use brined horseradish (instead of creamy) in this recipe.

- 12 large eggs
- ¼ cup mayonnaise
- 1 tablespoon prepared horseradish
- 2 teaspoons Dijon mustard
- ¼ teaspoon salt
- ½ teaspoon Old Bay seasoning, plus additional for sprinkling
- 8 ounces crabmeat, picked over for shells

1. Bring eggs and enough water to cover by 1 inch to boil in large saucepan over high heat. Remove pan from heat, cover, and let stand 10 minutes. Drain and transfer eggs to large bowl filled with ice water. Let cool 5 minutes.

2. Peel eggs and halve lengthwise. Transfer yolks to large bowl and set whites aside. Mash yolks, mayonnaise, horseradish, mustard, salt, and Old Bay with potato masher until smooth. Fold in crabmeat, then spoon filling into egg whites. Sprinkle with additional Old Bay. Serve. (Eggs can be refrigerated for 12 hours before serving.)

We want your best holiday cookie recipes for an upcoming contest. Please submit entries by May 31, 2008. Send us your recipes by visiting **CooksCountry.com** or write to us at Recipe Contest, *Cook's Country*, P.O. Box 470739, Brookline, MA 02447. Include your name, address, and daytime phone number and tell us what makes your recipe special. The grand-prize winner will receive $1,000. All entries become the property of *Cook's Country.* Go to **CooksCountry.com** for more information on this and other contests.

Ask Cook's Country

WE'LL ANSWER ANY QUESTION YOU THROW AT US!

LEMON SUBSTITUTION

If I don't have fresh lemon zest, can I substitute lemon extract?

Margaret Lux
Ostrander, Ohio

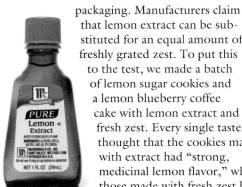

LEMON EXTRACT
Not worthy of a starring role, but acceptable as a supporting player

Lemon extract is an oil derived from lemon peel; the oil is mixed with alcohol and water before packaging. Manufacturers claim that lemon extract can be substituted for an equal amount of freshly grated zest. To put this to the test, we made a batch of lemon sugar cookies and a lemon blueberry coffee cake with lemon extract and fresh zest. Every single taster thought that the cookies made with extract had "strong, medicinal lemon flavor," while those made with fresh zest had "mellow yet refined" lemon flavor. When it came to the coffee cake, however, most tasters didn't notice any difference in lemon flavor between the two samples. So when preparing baked goods that showcase lemon as the main flavor, stick with fresh zest. But for baked goods in which lemon is used for background flavor, substituting extract in a pinch is fine.

BAKING POWDER SHELF LIFE

What's the best way to store baking powder? Does it go bad?

Robert S. Hoff
Gaithersburg, Md.

Baking powder is a chemical leavener that produces carbon dioxide (the gas that gives baked goods their lift) when mixed with liquid. It is made of baking soda, acid salt (such as cream of tartar), and cornstarch, which helps prevent the other two active ingredients from reacting with moisture in the air. Baking powder will lose its ability to produce carbon dioxide over time; most producers claim that it will last about one year once opened if stored properly in a dry, cool place.

To put this to the test, we opened new cans of baking powder at monthly intervals over the course of a year. After 12 months, we gathered the opened cans and began our testing by adding 1 teaspoon of powder to ½ cup of warm water—a common test to see if baking powder is still effective. All of the powders (even the one that had been opened for a year) made the water bubble and thus passed this test.

But we were skeptical that these powders all had equal leavening ability, so we whipped up a batch

of biscuits with each—and saw a big difference. The rise began to decrease with the 6-month-old powder and continued to decline to half the height of fresh at the 10-month mark. So instead of relying on the bubbling water test, we recommend writing the date you open your baking powder right on the can and discarding open baking powder after six months.

PROOF OF POWDER FATIGUE
Biscuits made with 6-month-old baking powder (left) showed some signs of a reduced rise, but were acceptable. Biscuits made with 10-month-old powder (right) did not rise properly.

ALL ABOUT ALLSPICE

What is allspice, and can I mix together spices in my cabinet to make a quick substitution?

Amie Merritt
Washington, D.C.

Allspice is a pea-sized berry from the evergreen pimento tree that grows in tropical climates, such as Jamaica's. While allspice is often included in savory Caribbean seasonings, such as jerk, it's better known in the United States as a baking spice. It is most commonly sold ground and tastes like a blend of cinnamon, nutmeg, and cloves; while numerous sources provide recipes for making allspice from these

ALLSPICE BERRIES
Allspice is an actual spice, not a spice blend.

spices, we didn't find a mixture that captured its unique "woodsy, sugary, dried fruit" flavor. Allspice definitely deserves its own place in the spice rack.

STORING MUSHROOMS

What's the best way to keep mushrooms fresh?

Martha Lane Camp
Wilson, N.C.

Mushrooms' delicate exteriors bruise easily and can rapidly go from taut to shriveled in the refrigerator. To determine the best way to store mushrooms, we purchased dozens of packages of white button mushrooms, opened the packages, and tested the following storage methods: covering the original box in plastic wrap, covering the original box with a damp paper towel, wrapping the mushrooms in aluminum foil, storing them in a paper bag, storing them in a

paper bag with air holes cut in it (to allow moisture to escape), storing them in an airtight zipper-lock bag, and simply leaving them uncovered.

Five days later, we checked on the mushrooms and found that those left in their original box and covered with plastic were in the best shape; this makes sense, as this method most closely mimics the entirety of the original packaging. These mushrooms had minimal discoloration and were still plump and tender to the touch. The mushrooms stored in the paper bag and in the foil were slightly brown but were acceptable. As for the failures, the ones stored in the perforated bag were discolored and soggy, the ones left uncovered were dehydrated, the ones covered with the damp paper towel were slimy, and the mushrooms that had been trapped in the zipper-lock bag were the worst of the lot: black and soggy. Don't open a mushroom package until you are ready to use it, but if you don't use the entire package at once, simply cover the box with plastic wrap. If you buy loose mushrooms, store them in a paper bag or wrapped in foil.

RATING THE BURN

Every time I make my jalapeño salsa, the fiery kick is different. Is there a way to tell the mild jalapeños from the spicy ones?

Clay Havard
Fairhope, Ala.

Many cooks claim that the smaller the chile, the bigger the burn. To see if this was true, we gathered a dozen jalapeños of varying size and started sampling. A flood of tears later, we learned that there was no correlation between the size of the jalapeño and its heat level.

Not willing to take the pain in vain, we chose a more quantitative approach and sent a handful of similarly sized jalapeños to a lab to test their levels of capsaicin, the chemical compound responsible for their heat. Shockingly, some peppers had as much as 10 times the kick as seemingly identical peppers. Unfortunately, the only way to gauge a pepper's burn is to try a small piece. If you want to preserve the flavor of the chile but lose some of the heat, cut away the white ribs and seeds (we like to wear gloves when handling any hot chile), which is where the capsaicin is located; the flesh of a jalapeño has just a fraction of the heat of the interior.

IT'S IN THE PREP, NOT THE PICKING
While it's impossible to visually determine the heat level of a jalapeño, removing the fiery ribs and seeds lessens the burn.

To ask us a cooking question, visit **CooksCountry.com/emailus.** You can also write to Ask Cook's Country, P.O. Box 470739, Brookline, MA 02447. See if you can stump us!

Lost Recipes SHAKER LEMON PIE

This simple recipe mixes lemon slices—peel and all—with sugar and eggs to form a custardy filling. But unless you macerate the lemon slices for 24 hours, the pie turns out bitter. Could we speed up this recipe for modern times?

The sliced, unpeeled lemons break down to create a bright-tasting, slightly chewy lemon custard.

Shakers were renowned for their ingenuity, attention to detail, and thrift. These qualities, famously evident in the austerity and simple grace of their architecture, furniture, and handcrafts, also influenced their food. Shaker lemon pie is a fine example: Instead of using only the juice and/or zest of lemons, the Shakers used the entire fruit. To make the bitter pith and rind palatable, they sliced whole lemons thinly and macerated the slices with sugar to mellow them. The sugared lemons were then combined with eggs and baked into a double-crust pie. As if by magic, the spartan ingredients were transformed into a brightly flavored pie filling that eliminated the anxiety of making a fussy stovetop custard. This I had to try.

Nearly every recipe I found gave the same directions: Macerate three thinly sliced lemons with 1¾ cups of sugar, add four beaten eggs, pour the filling into an unbaked crust, top it with a second crust, and bake the pie until golden. The only difference in the recipes was the macerating time: Some called for only two hours, while others demanded a full 24. A pie using the former timing was bitter and medicinal, as the sugar didn't have adequate time to draw the bitterness out of the lemon's pith. The 24-hour maceration produced a lemon pie with bright, sweet lemon flavor—but I was determined to find a faster way.

One modern recipe suggested quickly boiling the whole lemons before slicing them. Since the bitter pith wasn't exposed to the boiling water, this did nothing to temper its harsh flavor, but the idea inspired me to try boiling the sliced lemons. After quickly boiling the slices, I drained them, stirred in the sugar and the eggs, and poured the filling straight into the pie shell. Some bitterness remained, but there was marked improvement. Increasing the cooking time to several minutes took away all bitterness but also diluted the fresh lemon flavor. The solution was to squeeze the sliced lemons and reserve the brightly flavored juice before simmering the slices; I then added the juice back in with the sugar and eggs. I finally had bright—not bitter—lemon flavor without any macerating time.

I was almost ready to finalize the recipe, but I couldn't help noticing that each time I made the pie the texture of the filling was slightly different. Since the pie spent a generous 40 minutes in the oven, the heat-sensitive eggs were occasionally curdling. Similar egg-rich custard pies avoid this problem by adding a thickener to stabilize the eggs. Flour made the filling unappealingly pasty, but a tablespoon of cornstarch ensured a smooth filling every time.

This was a pie worthy of the highest praise, with bold lemon flavor, silky texture, and an efficiently Shaker-like preparation time of just about an hour.

—Cali Rich

SHAKER LEMON PIE SERVES 8

See page 30 for tips on slicing the lemons thinly. You will need 6 tablespoons of lemon juice for this recipe. Have an extra lemon on hand in case the 3 sliced lemons do not yield enough juice. Visit CooksCountry.com for our double-crust pie dough recipe or use one 15-ounce box of Pillsbury Ready to Roll Pie Crust.

- 1 double-crust pie dough (see note)
- 3 large lemons, sliced thin and seeded (see note)
- 1¾ cups sugar
- ⅛ teaspoon salt
- 1 tablespoon cornstarch
- 4 large eggs
- 1 tablespoon heavy cream

1. Adjust oven rack to lowest position and heat oven to 425 degrees. Line 9-inch pie plate with 1 dough round and refrigerate for 30 minutes.

2. Squeeze lemon slices in fine-mesh strainer set over bowl; reserve juice (you should have 6 tablespoons). Bring drained slices and 2 cups water to boil in saucepan, then reduce heat to medium-low and simmer until slices are softened, about 5 minutes. Drain well and discard liquid. Combine softened lemon slices, sugar, salt, and ¼ cup reserved lemon juice in bowl; stir until sugar dissolves.

3. Whisk cornstarch and remaining lemon juice in large bowl. Whisk eggs into cornstarch mixture, then slowly stir in lemon slice mixture until combined. Pour into chilled pie shell. Brush edges of dough with 1 teaspoon cream and top with remaining dough round. Seal, crimp edges, and brush top of dough with remaining cream. Using paring knife, cut 4 vents in top of dough.

4. Bake until light golden, about 20 minutes, then decrease oven temperature to 375 degrees and continue to bake until golden brown, 20 to 25 minutes. Cool on wire rack for at least 1 hour. Serve. (Pie can be wrapped in plastic and refrigerated for 2 days.)

Kitchen Know-How
BUILDING BOLD, NOT BITTER, LEMON FLAVOR

Using sliced whole lemons, pith and all, can produce an overwhelmingly bitter filling. We found a few tricks to create bright lemon flavor while tempering the bitterness of the pith.

1. Squeeze the seeded lemon slices and reserve the juice for the filling.
2. Simmer the slices to mellow the bitterness of the pith and then add them to the filling with the uncooked juice.

The American Table:
Shaker Cooking

The Shakers' food was never ornate and was always healthy and hearty enough to support their industrious, hard-working lifestyle. Shakers scrubbed—rather than peeled—their vegetables (and, in the case of Shaker Lemon Pie, their citrus fruit) to minimize waste. They were also pioneers in using exact measurements in cooking at a time when many recipes called for a "dash," "glob," or "handful" of something.

Most chicken noodle soups from the slow cooker are watery graves for tough, stringy chicken. What's the secret to a potent broth and tender meat?

Making rich, meaty chicken noodle soup in the slow cooker requires handling the light and dark meat differently.

Test Kitchen Secret
PROTECTING CHICKEN BREASTS

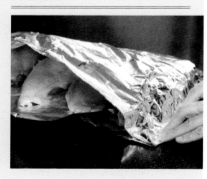

Wrapping the chicken breasts in a foil pack insulates the delicate white meat, helping keep it moist and tender. To make the foil pack, place the chicken on one side of a large piece of heavy-duty aluminum foil. Fold the foil over, shaping it into a packet that will fit into your slow cooker, then crimp to seal the edges.

Almost every slow-cooker cookbook features a recipe for chicken noodle soup, and why not? It seems like you should be able to dump chicken parts, vegetables, and water into a slow cooker and come back half a day later to find that time and low heat have worked together to render a rich broth and tender meat.

The reality, however, is disappointing. I made a handful of recipes, and they were all watery, bland, and lacking in chicken flavor. To make matters worse, the meat was tough and flavorless. These recipes were fundamentally flawed: It takes a lot of chicken parts to make enough homemade broth for a good soup, and most of my sample recipes relied on too little chicken. In addition, since there's no evaporation in a covered slow cooker, the broth never has a chance to reduce and intensify in flavor. I was going to have to build this recipe from the ground up.

With a goal of soup with rich chicken flavor, tender vegetables, and succulent meat, I started by browning bone-in chicken thighs and breasts on the stovetop (I would take the meat off the bone at the end of cooking). The test kitchen often discards chicken skin after browning, but I found that the broth needed the skin's rich flavor—I could ditch the skin later in the process, before shredding the meat and adding it back to the soup. Then I browned carrots, celery, onions, and garlic and added them to the slow cooker. For a rich, full-bodied base, I used low-sodium chicken broth in place of the water favored in many slow-cooker soup recipes. Thyme, bay leaves, and crushed red pepper flakes rounded out the seasoning for my very flavorful broth.

The next issue was the texture of the chicken. I knew from my initial tests that the eight to 10 hours suggested in many recipes was too long for delicate chicken meat, even on the low setting. Halving the cooking time gave me perfectly cooked chicken thighs—and breast meat that was still grossly overdone. Then I discovered that if I skipped browning the chicken breasts (which accelerated the cooking process) and wrapped them in foil to insulate them from the heat, the breasts cooked perfectly in the same amount of time as the thighs. It was a bit more work than just dumping the breasts in at the beginning, but well worth it for such tender, juicy meat.

–Diane Unger

SLOW-COOKER CHICKEN NOODLE SOUP SERVES 8 TO 10

You will need a 6-quart slow cooker for this recipe. Do not cook this soup on high power or the chicken will be too tough. Three 32-ounce cartons of chicken broth will yield 12 cups.

- 6 bone-in, skin-on chicken thighs (about 3 pounds)
  Salt and pepper
- 1 tablespoon unsalted butter
- 6 carrots, peeled and sliced into ½-inch rounds
- 4 celery ribs, sliced
- 2 onions, chopped
- 4 garlic cloves, minced
- 1 teaspoon dried thyme
- ¼ teaspoon red pepper flakes
- 12 cups low-sodium chicken broth
- 2 bay leaves
- 4 bone-in, skin-on split chicken breasts (about 3 pounds)
- 2 cups cooked egg noodles
- 1 cup frozen peas, thawed
- 2 tablespoons minced fresh parsley

1. Pat chicken thighs dry with paper towels and season with salt and pepper. Melt butter in Dutch oven over medium-high heat. Add chicken thighs, skin-side down, and cook until skin is deep golden brown, about 8 minutes. Transfer to slow cooker.

2. Pour off all but 1 tablespoon fat from pot. Cook carrots, celery, and onions until softened, about 5 minutes. Stir in garlic, thyme, and pepper flakes and cook until fragrant, about 30 seconds. Add 1 cup broth to pot and scrape up any browned bits with wooden spoon. Transfer vegetable mixture, bay leaves, and remaining broth to slow cooker.

3. Season chicken breasts with salt and pepper and wrap in foil according to photo at left. Place foil packet in slow cooker. Cover and cook on low until breasts are cooked through and thighs are tender, 4 to 4½ hours.

4. Remove foil packet from slow cooker. Carefully open foil and transfer chicken breasts to plate. Remove chicken thighs from slow cooker and transfer to plate. When cool enough to handle, shred meat into bite-sized pieces, discarding skin, bones, and excess fat.

5. Stir shredded chicken, cooked noodles, peas, and parsley into slow cooker. Cover and cook until heated through, about 5 minutes. Discard bay leaves. Serve.

Recipe Makeover MEATLOAF

With the average slice weighing in at over 700 calories, meatloaf is a prime candidate for a recipe makeover. The challenge arises if you want to keep the meat 100 percent beef—and keep the meatloaf 100 percent edible.

As its core ingredients include fatty ground beef, eggs, milk, and bread (or crackers), it shouldn't come as a surprise that a typical slice of meatloaf is laden with calories and fat. Most low-fat recipes start by using healthier, leaner meats like chicken or turkey, but I wanted to make a tender, flavorful low-fat meatloaf with beef as the only meat.

I rounded up a slew of low-fat recipes, most of which included terrifying (for meatloaf) ingredients like rolled oats, egg substitutes, coleslaw(!), and frozen hash browns, and headed into the kitchen to see if any had promise. The wretched flavors and grainy, chewy textures of these failed recipes didn't make me any friends in the test kitchen that day. An improvised recipe using lean ground beef, skim milk, egg whites, and reduced-calorie bread wasn't any better. Was this recipe makeover destined for failure?

I started with the cooking method. Most recipes cook meatloaf in a loaf pan, but the test kitchen prefers to use an aluminum foil–covered wire rack. The rack keeps the meat from steaming, thus allowing a better crust to form, and the foil makes it easier to move the meatloaf when it's done. Poking some holes in the foil helps the fat drain off, making this setup perfect for my makeover.

I knew that I couldn't use 80 percent lean ground beef here—it was just too fatty. Working with 90 percent lean ground beef reduced the fat grams by half, but tasters felt the meatloaf had a dry and grainy texture. I decided to keep the leaner 90 percent beef and look for other ingredients to add moisture back into the meatloaf.

The test kitchen's standard meatloaf uses saltines for structure, but these low-fat crackers dried out the loaf's texture even more, so I returned to the more traditional ingredient: bread. Using a single whole egg (many recipes use two or three) as a binder helped hold the loaf together and added richness. Instead of using milk, I found that tomato juice provided moisture and a boost of tangy flavor. We often use soy sauce to help emphasize meaty flavor in beef dishes, and it worked like a charm here, providing flavor and moisture with minimal added fat and calories. Garlic and thyme

rounded out the flavors.

The meatloaf was better, but still too dry. Recalling that our recipe for Low-Fat Meaty Lasagna cuts the ground beef with "meaty" mushrooms, I wondered if mushrooms would work here. They did. Sautéing the mushrooms first was necessary to rid them of excess moisture, and a quick spin in the food processor broke them down so that they could "disappear" into the meatloaf.

Since I had reduced the fat and calories so much already, I didn't have to sacrifice the ketchup and brown sugar glaze, which caramelized after a few minutes under the broiler.

–Meredith Butcher

LOW-FAT MEATLOAF SERVES 6
The test kitchen's favorite hot sauce is Frank's RedHot.

Meatloaf
1	teaspoon vegetable oil
1	onion, chopped fine
	Salt and pepper
10	ounces cremini or white mushrooms, sliced thin
3	garlic cloves, minced
1	teaspoon minced fresh thyme
¼	cup tomato juice
1	slice hearty white sandwich bread, torn into pieces
1½	pounds 90 percent lean ground beef
1	large egg
1	tablespoon soy sauce
1	tablespoon Dijon mustard
2	tablespoons finely chopped fresh parsley

Glaze
⅓	cup ketchup
3	tablespoons cider vinegar
1	teaspoon hot sauce (see note)
2	tablespoons light brown sugar

1. For the meatloaf: Adjust oven rack to middle position and heat oven to 375 degrees. Following photo 1 at right, set wire rack inside rimmed baking sheet and arrange 8- by 6-inch piece of aluminum foil in center of rack. Using skewer, poke holes in foil at ½-inch intervals.

2. Heat oil in large nonstick skillet over medium heat until shimmering. Cook onion and ¼ teaspoon salt until softened, about 8 minutes. Add

mushrooms and cook until they release their liquid, about 5 minutes. Increase heat to medium-high and cook until liquid has evaporated, about 5 minutes. Add garlic and thyme and cook until fragrant, about 30 seconds. Stir in tomato juice and cook until thickened, about 1 minute. Let mixture cool 5 minutes, then transfer mixture to food processor, add bread, and process until smooth. Add beef to food processor and pulse to combine.

3. Whisk egg, soy sauce, mustard, parsley, ¼ teaspoon salt, and ½ teaspoon pepper in large bowl. Add beef mixture and mix with hands until evenly combined. Using hands, shape mixture into loaf covering entirety of prepared foil. Bake until meatloaf registers 160 degrees, about 1 hour. Remove meatloaf from oven and heat broiler.

4. For the glaze: Combine ketchup, vinegar, hot sauce, and sugar in small saucepan. Simmer over medium heat until thick and syrupy, about 5 minutes. Spread glaze over meatloaf and broil until glaze begins to bubble, about 3 minutes. Let rest 10 minutes. Serve.

And the Numbers...
All nutritional information is for one serving (about 1½-inch slice) of meatloaf.

TRADITIONAL MEATLOAF
CALORIES: 740
FAT: 43g
SATURATED FAT: 17g

COOK'S COUNTRY LOW-FAT MEATLOAF
CALORIES: 280
FAT: 13g
SATURATED FAT: 5g

Kitchen Know-How
A BETTER WAY TO COOK MEATLOAF

Allowing meatloaf to steam in its own juices in a loaf pan makes for a greasy mess—and minimal crust. Here is our solution for optimal drainage and a crustier meatloaf.

1. Set a wire rack inside a rimmed baking sheet and top with an 8- by 6-inch rectangle of aluminum foil. Using a skewer, poke holes in the foil about ½ inch apart to allow the fat to drain away.

2. Shape mixture into loaf covering entirety of prepared foil.

Unlike most low-fat meatloaf recipes, ours features all beef and tastes as good as full-fat versions.

Herbed Roast Pork Tenderloin

I recently tried making a roasted, herbed pork tenderloin, but the recipe was a disaster. The meat never took on any flavor, and the herbs just dried out and tasted like burnt grass.

–Rebecca Co, Northern, N.J.

Kitchen Know-How
TURNING TWO TENDERLOINS INTO ONE ROAST

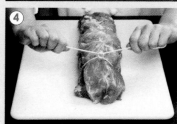

1. Butterfly the tenderloins by laying them flat on a cutting board and slicing down the middle of each. Leave about ¼ inch of meat intact, then open like a book.

2. Spread interior of each tenderloin with butter mixture.

3. Arrange tenderloins so that thick and thin ends are opposite one another, then overlap tenderloins halfway. Fold to interlock cut sides of tenderloins.

4. Tie folded tenderloins securely with butchers' twine at 1½-inch intervals.

Recipes abound for herb-flavored pork tenderloin, employing techniques such as crusting, marinating, and stuffing the pork with sundry combinations of herbs. Like Rebecca, I also had poor luck with herb crusts—the herbs came close to combusting on the outside of the meat. Marinating in an herb-infused oil took a long time, and the herb payout was minimal. Stuffing was the most promising method, and since a single tenderloin only feeds about three people, I decided to proceed using two tenderloins so that the dish would be more substantial.

I butterflied the roasts and rubbed the inside of each with a simple herb paste of parsley and olive oil. I rolled them back up, tied them for even cooking, and roasted them side by side in a 450-degree oven. The herbs stayed bright green but had a dull flavor, and the roasts weren't browning much on the outside. I had a lot of work to do, and I decided to start with the stuffing.

After trying several herbs alone and in combination, I discovered that soft herbs like parsley, basil, and tarragon (which have a high moisture content) all tasted washed-out, because they were steaming inside the meat. When I turned to heartier (and drier) fresh herbs, my tasters rejected rosemary as being too potent, but they liked a combination of fragrant thyme and sage. Mustard, garlic, and lemon juice and zest added more bold flavors. The final step was replacing the olive oil with rich butter; tasters liked the herb butter so much that I made extra to brush on the finished roasts.

In an attempt to promote browning, I coated the exterior of the roasts with a rub of sugar, salt, and pepper (a little olive oil helped the rub adhere), but these 1½ pound roasts weren't in the oven long enough for the sugar to caramelize by the time the interior had cooked through. Browning the roasts in a skillet and then transferring them to the oven was the only reliable way to create a good crust without overcooking the meat—but I wanted a good crust with less work.

It was then that I remembered seeing two pork tenderloins tied together into one big roast at the butcher shop. Since this double-wide tenderloin would take longer to cook, I hoped it would give the sugar-rubbed exterior a chance to brown in the oven. After butterflying and rubbing the roasts, I overlapped them by a couple of inches and folded them up lengthwise into a cylinder. I tied the double roast and cooked it in a 450-degree oven, flipping it once to ensure even cooking. When the supersized tenderloin came out of the oven, my efforts were rewarded with a nicely browned roast that, when sliced, revealed a juicy spiral of herb-infused meat.

–Kelley Baker

HERBED ROAST PORK TENDERLOIN SERVES 4 TO 6

Pork tenderloins can vary greatly in weight; try to find 2 large roasts for this recipe. We prefer to remove the tough silver skin with a paring knife before butterflying (see photo 1 on page 22). Save leftover meat for Hoppel Poppel (right).

3 tablespoons unsalted butter, softened
2 tablespoons coarse-grain mustard
1 teaspoon grated zest and 1 teaspoon juice from 1 lemon
1 garlic clove, minced

By folding two herb-coated pork tenderloins together, we create a larger mass of meat that can stay in the oven long enough to obtain a nicely browned crust.

1 tablespoon minced fresh sage
1 tablespoon minced fresh thyme
 Salt and pepper
1 teaspoon sugar
2 pork tenderloins (about 3 pounds total)
1 tablespoon olive oil

1. Adjust oven rack to middle position and heat oven to 450 degrees. Using fork, beat butter, mustard, lemon zest and juice, garlic, herbs, ¼ teaspoon salt, and ¼ teaspoon pepper in bowl until combined. Reserve 3 tablespoons butter mixture. Combine sugar, ¼ teaspoon salt, and ¼ teaspoon pepper in small bowl.

2. Pat tenderloins dry with paper towels and, following photos 1 to 4 at left, butterfly tenderloins, spread interior evenly with herb-butter mixture, interlock tenderloins, and tie securely with kitchen twine at 1½-inch intervals. Rub pork with oil and sprinkle sugar mixture evenly over exterior.

3. Roast meat on rimmed baking sheet until exterior is golden brown and meat registers 140 degrees, about 35 minutes, flipping pork halfway through cooking. Transfer to cutting board and brush top of pork with reserved herb-butter mixture. Tent with foil and let rest 10 minutes. Remove kitchen twine. Slice and serve.

What to Do with Leftovers: *Hoppel Poppel*

A popular breakfast in the Midwest, this hearty meat and potato scramble can be a big disappointment if the eggs are rubbery, the potatoes pale, and the vegetables soggy.

Hoppel poppel may sound nonsensical, but morning regulars at Midwestern establishments like Benji's Deli in Milwaukee, Wis., and the Ronneburg in Amana, Iowa, take this breakfast concoction seriously. The dish has German origins (the name loosely translates to "hodgepodge") and takes a decidedly kitchen-sink approach to ingredients: crisp, browned potatoes; sautéed onions, bell peppers, and mushrooms; salami, German sausage, or leftover meat (preferably pork); and parsley, all bound together by soft-set scrambled eggs and plenty of melted cheese. A hearty one-skillet breakfast, the ease with which hoppel poppel comes together also makes it an appealing weeknight supper.

Most recipes I found used leftover potatoes, meat, and vegetables—all staples in diners, but not at home. I'd have to start with raw potatoes and vegetables. Restaurants make this dish to order, but at home you'd want to make it for at least four people. And a dozen eggs stirred into a pan already brimming with ingredients cooked unevenly: They were rubbery in some spots and runny in others. The only logical thing to do was separate the filling from the eggs.

I started by sautéing onion, red bell pepper (which was preferred over green for its sweetness), and mushrooms until soft. Unfortunately, no matter how I handled the mushrooms—even when I precooked them—they ended up spongy, so I decided to leave them out of the mix. I then added the potatoes to the skillet, but the moisture from the other vegetables created steam that prevented them from browning. The solution was to cook the onion and pepper first, remove them from the skillet, and then cook the potatoes. Now the spuds were getting a nice dark crust, but it was taking 20 minutes. On a lark, I tried replacing the diced potatoes with frozen diced hash browns, which are precooked; the hash browns not only tasted good but also were ready in a fraction of the time.

The meat component here was easy, as I was using 2 cups of diced leftover pork tenderloin (page 10) and chunks of deli salami—all I had to do was add them to the pan as the potatoes finished cooking so that they could brown up and heat through. As for the eggs, since scrambling the eggs in a full skillet had already proven cumbersome, I tried emptying the skillet a second time and giving the eggs some space to scramble. Folding everything back in was still a challenge, because the skillet was so full.

Taking a cue from the test kitchen's frittata recipe, I went back to adding the eggs on top of the sautéed potatoes and meat and then finishing the dish under the broiler. The result was an evenly set, sliceable egg pie that was easy to manage. My Hoppel Poppel may not look like classic Midwestern versions, but it tastes just as good. **–Kelley Baker**

HOPPEL POPPEL SERVES 6 TO 8

Be sure to use diced, not shredded, hash browns for this recipe (you do not need to thaw them). Chopped cooked bratwurst can be substituted for the pork.

- 12 large eggs
- 3 tablespoons half-and-half
  Salt and pepper
- 4 tablespoons unsalted butter
- 1 onion, chopped
- 1 red bell pepper, seeded and chopped
- 2 garlic cloves, minced
- 2 cups frozen diced hash brown potatoes
- 2 cups leftover meat from Herbed Roast Pork Tenderloin (page 10), cut into ½-inch pieces
- 3 ounces thick-cut deli salami, cut into ½-inch pieces
- 2 cups shredded sharp cheddar cheese
- 2 tablespoons minced fresh parsley

1. Adjust oven rack to upper-middle position and heat broiler. Whisk eggs, half-and-half, ½ teaspoon salt, and ½ teaspoon pepper in large bowl.

2. Melt 2 tablespoons butter in large ovensafe nonstick skillet over medium heat. Cook onion and pepper until softened, about 5 minutes. Add garlic and cook until fragrant, about 30 seconds; transfer onion mixture to plate. Melt remaining butter in skillet, then add potatoes, ¼ teaspoon salt, and ¼ teaspoon pepper and cook until golden brown, 5 to 7 minutes. Add pork and salami and cook until browned, about 3 minutes.

3. Whisk onion mixture, cheese, and parsley into eggs. Add egg mixture to skillet and cook, using rubber spatula to stir and scrape bottom of skillet, until large curds form but eggs are still wet, about 2 minutes. Shake skillet to distribute eggs evenly and cook, without stirring, until bottom is set, about 30 seconds.

4. Broil until surface is spotty brown, 3 to 4 minutes. Transfer to wire rack and let rest 5 minutes. Slide onto platter and cut into wedges. Serve.

On the Side: *Peas and Carrots*

Fresh vegetables and a flavor boost improve this classic combo.

Frozen peas and carrots are a bland cliché. But there's nothing inherently wrong with this combination if you start with fresh vegetables. Given that fresh English peas rarely show up in supermarkets, I decided to start this marriage over with a new partner—sugar snap peas.

To ensure crunch and bright color, I found it best to quickly blanch the sugar snap peas in salted water. After some trial and error, I figured out that the sliced carrots could be cooked in the same pot if given a one-minute head start.

Simmering the vegetables yielded the right texture, but their sweet flavor was being diluted. Adding a couple of tablespoons of sugar to the water, as is sometimes necessary to help corn along, was a step in the right direction. To finish the vegetables, I returned them to the empty pot with a little butter. I added lemon juice, lemon zest, and garlic for kick and a drizzle of honey to coat the vegetables in a light glaze.

–Kelley Baker

GLAZED SUGAR SNAP PEAS AND CARROTS SERVES 4

If desired, the blanched vegetables can be shocked in a bowl of ice water, then drained, dried, and refrigerated in a zipper-lock bag for 3 days. When ready to serve, proceed with step 2.

- 2 tablespoons sugar
  Salt and pepper
- 2 medium carrots, peeled and sliced into thin rounds
- 1 pound sugar snap peas, stems snapped off and strings removed
- 1 tablespoon unsalted butter
- 1 garlic clove, minced
- ½ teaspoon grated zest and 1 teaspoon juice from 1 lemon
- 1 tablespoon honey

1. Bring 6 cups water to boil in large pot. Add sugar, 1 teaspoon salt, and carrots and cook for 1 minute. Add peas and cook until vegetables are nearly tender, about 2 minutes longer. Drain vegetables and transfer to paper towels.

2. Melt butter in empty pot over medium-high heat. Add vegetables and cook until just tender, about 2 minutes. Stir in garlic and cook until fragrant, about 30 seconds. Off heat, stir in zest, juice, and honey to coat. Season with salt and pepper. Serve.

Baked Potato Fans

This stunning potato dish delivers a fluffy interior, a crisp exterior, and a cheesy bread crumb topping—if you can get the potatoes cooked right.

Test Kitchen Technique
PREPPING BAKED POTATO FANS

These potatoes may look difficult to make, but we found a few simple, no-fuss tricks to ensure perfect potato fans every time.

1. Trim ¼-inch slices from the bottom and ends of each potato to allow them to sit flat and to give the slices extra room to fan out during baking.
2. Chopsticks provide a foolproof guide for slicing the potato petals without cutting all the way through the potato.
3. Gently flex fans open while rinsing under cold running water; this rids the potatoes of excess starch that can impede fanning.

Baked potato fans were popularized as Hasselback potatoes, the namesake dish of the restaurant at the Hasselbacken hotel in Stockholm, Sweden. American recipes stay true to the original concept by combining the fluffy interior of a baked potato with the crisp, golden exterior of an oven fry—all with that distinctive, fanned-out presentation.

The fanning is accomplished by slicing almost all the way through a whole potato crosswise along its length at ¼-inch intervals, leaving the bottom of the potato intact and allowing the slices to gently fan open like an accordion as the potato bakes. The skin crisps while the fans create openings into which seasonings, cheese, and bread crumbs can be sprinkled before a final pass in the oven. This dish sounded fit for company, but I was glad I tried out a few recipes before I put them on my dinner table: These potatoes were harder to manipulate than I expected.

Most recipes would have you believe that baked potato fans can be made with any type of potato. I learned that was definitely not the case after trying waxy red potatoes, which dried out in the oven, and Yukon Golds, which were better but still too dry. The russet, or Idaho, potato was the right choice here, as its starchy flesh translated into a fluffy texture when baked.

Working with the russets, I cut ¼-inch crosswise slices down the length of each potato, trying to leave the bottom intact to hold the slices together. This was hard to do if the bottom of the

potato wasn't almost perfectly flat. Following the lead of one astute recipe, I sliced the bottom from each potato, which gave me a flat surface to work with, and placed a chopstick on either side to prevent my knife from slicing all the way through. I brushed the potatoes with oil and baked them. But after all that work, they barely fanned out. The slices were stuck together. The skin had also developed a leathery texture by the time the inside was cooked through.

I tackled the sticky fans first. Excess starch exposed to the oven heat was creating a tacky seal and causing the fans to stick together. I found that taking the time to rinse the potatoes of that surface starch after they were sliced prevented them from sticking together. Even better, taking a slice off each end of the potato gave the remaining slices more room to fan out as they baked, allowing even more heat to penetrate and crisp their surfaces.

I was pleased that my potatoes now looked like little accordions; it was time to fix the tough, overcooked exteriors. Rather than relying entirely on the dry and sometimes punishing heat of the oven, I precooked the potatoes in the microwave and then moved them to the oven to finish cooking through and crisp up their skins. Brushing the potatoes with oil before baking helped crisp their skins further.

Most recipes sprinkle the potatoes with a topping of grated cheese, bread crumbs, and seasonings during the last few minutes of baking. Cheddar cheese was too

greasy, but a combination of Parmesan (for nutty flavor) and Monterey Jack (because it melts well) was perfect. Store-bought bread crumbs were too sandy, but homemade crumbs stayed moist in the oven, especially with a little melted butter added. Fresh garlic didn't have enough time to cook and mellow, but garlic powder (mixed with some sweet paprika) worked nicely. As a final step, I broiled the potatoes to make the topping irresistibly crunchy.

–Kelley Baker

For perfectly cooked fans, we precook the cut potatoes in the microwave before baking and then crisp up the topping under the broiler.

CRISPY BAKED POTATO FANS SERVES 4

To ensure that the potatoes fan out evenly, look for uniformly shaped potatoes.

Bread Crumb Topping

- 1 slice hearty white sandwich bread, torn into pieces
- 4 tablespoons unsalted butter, melted
- ½ cup shredded Monterey Jack cheese
- ¼ cup grated Parmesan cheese
- 1 teaspoon paprika
- ½ teaspoon garlic powder
  Salt and pepper

Potato Fans

4 russet potatoes, scrubbed
2 tablespoons extra-virgin olive oil
Salt and pepper

1. For the bread crumb topping: Adjust oven rack to middle position and heat oven to 200 degrees. Pulse bread in food processor until coarsely ground. Bake bread crumbs on rimmed baking sheet until dry, about 20 minutes. Let cool 5 minutes, then combine crumbs, butter, cheeses, paprika, garlic powder, ¼ teaspoon salt, and ¼ teaspoon pepper in large bowl. (Bread crumb topping can be refrigerated in zipper-lock bag for 2 days.)

2. For the potato fans: Heat oven to 450 degrees. Following photos 1 to 3 at left, cut ¼ inch from bottom and ends of potatoes, then slice potatoes crosswise at ¼-inch intervals, leaving ¼ inch of potato intact. Gently rinse potatoes under running water, let drain, and transfer, sliced-side down, to plate. Microwave until slightly soft to the touch, 6 to 12 minutes, flipping potatoes halfway through cooking.

3. Arrange potatoes, sliced-side up, on foil-lined baking sheet. Brush potatoes all over with oil and season with salt and pepper. Bake until skin is crisp and potatoes are beginning to brown, 25 to 30 minutes. Remove potatoes from oven and heat broiler.

4. Carefully top potatoes with stuffing mixture, pressing gently to adhere. Broil until bread crumbs are deep golden brown, about 3 minutes. Serve.

BLUE CHEESE AND BACON BAKED POTATO FANS

In step 1, substitute ⅓ cup crumbled blue cheese for the Monterey Jack. In step 4, sprinkle 4 slices bacon, cooked until crisp and then crumbled, over the potatoes just prior to serving.

Spicy Grilled Beef Tenderloin

Roasted whole beef tenderloin with horseradish cream is my holiday standby. Do you have a similar recipe for the grill?
–Annie Hamnett, Charleston, S.C.

When the test kitchen roasts a whole beef tenderloin in the oven, we concentrate on adding texture and flavor to this tender and relatively mild-tasting cut. Grilling a tenderloin makes a lot of sense, as a good sear from a hot grill provides both crusty texture and smoky flavor. But could I introduce the pleasant burn of horseradish, a traditional flavor accompaniment to tenderloin, on the grill?

The test kitchen's method for grilling a whole tenderloin is to first sear the meat over a hot fire and then move it to a cooler part of the grill to finish cooking. I decided to start my testing by creating a horseradish crust on the surface of the meat.

Bottled horseradish comes in two varieties: creamy and brined. The creamy version is very mild, so in search of a big spicy kick, I rubbed a full 8-ounce jar of the more potent brined horseradish over the exterior of the roast. Unfortunately, the horseradish slipped off the meat almost as soon as I put the roast on the grill. Draining the horseradish helped it adhere better at first, but when I turned the roast, the crust stuck to the grate. I tried applying the horseradish crust after searing, but even the small amount that stayed put lost its punch and pungency by the time the meat cooked through. Lesson learned: A horseradish crust was not going to cut it.

My secondary plan was to rub spices into the meat to create a fiery crust that would complement a horseradish serving sauce. The nasal heat of dry mustard, combined with the burn of cayenne and plenty of black pepper, created a pleas-antly spicy and flavorful crust.

Next, I concentrated on making a pungent horseradish sauce to serve with the grill-roasted tenderloin. I mixed brined horseradish with oil, sour cream, cayenne, and lemon juice to create a creamy horseradish vinaigrette that lent a decidedly cool and spicy kick to the charred, boldly flavored beef. –Cali Rich

SPICY GRILLED BEEF TENDERLOIN WITH HORSERADISH SAUCE

SERVES 12 TO 16

Buy brined—not creamy—horseradish for this recipe. See page 30 for information on trimming a beef tenderloin.

4 teaspoons pepper
1 tablespoon dry mustard
1 tablespoon salt
1½ teaspoons cayenne pepper
6 tablespoons olive oil
1 whole beef tenderloin (5 to 6 pounds), trimmed, patted dry, and tied according to photos at right
½ cup prepared horseradish (see note)
½ cup sour cream
1 tablespoon lemon juice
1 garlic clove, minced
1 tablespoon finely chopped fresh chives

1. Combine pepper, mustard, salt, and cayenne in medium bowl; reserve 1 teaspoon spice mixture. Add 2 tablespoons oil to bowl with remaining spice mixture and stir to combine. Rub oil mixture all over tenderloin. Let stand at room temperature 1 hour.

2. Heat all burners on high for 15 minutes, then leave primary burner on high and turn other burner(s) off. (For charcoal grill, light 100 coals; when covered with fine gray ash, spread coals over half of grill. Heat covered, with lid vent open completely, for 5 minutes.) Scrape and oil cooking grate. Arrange tenderloin on hot side of grill and cook, covered, until well browned on all sides, 8 to 12 minutes. Slide meat to cool side of grill and cook, covered, until meat registers 125 to 130 degrees (for medium-rare), 20 to 25 minutes. Transfer to cutting board, tent with foil, and let rest 15 minutes.

3. Meanwhile, combine horseradish, sour cream, lemon juice, garlic, and reserved spice mixture in bowl. Slowly whisk in remaining oil and add chives. Slice beef and serve, passing horseradish sauce at table.

Kitchen Know-How
TUCK, TIE, THEN RUB

Follow these easy steps for flavorful and evenly cooked spicy grilled beef tenderloin.

1. To promote even cooking, tuck tail of tenderloin under and tie roast with kitchen twine every 1½ inches.
2. Rub entire tenderloin thoroughly with spice paste before grill-roasting.

A boldly spiced crust is the perfect complement to the creamy burn of our horseradish vinaigrette.

Panini Sandwiches at Home

Could we find a way to make these grilled Italian sandwiches without a panini press or an indoor grill?

Three Keys to Perfect Homemade Panini

In lieu of a $100 panini press, here's how to make panini that look and taste authentic. If you don't have a grill pan, use a preheated nonstick pan instead; you'll miss out on the grill marks, but the panini will still be as crisp as any made in a press.

GOOD GRILL PAN
To give the panini their characteristic grill marks, use a large nonstick grill pan, such as the Simply Calphalon Nonstick 13-Inch Round Grill Pan ($39.95), which won our testing of eight leading grill pans.

HEAVY DUTCH OVEN
For a perfectly crisp exterior and gooey interior, weight the panini with a Dutch oven (wrapped in aluminum foil for easy cleanup).

STURDY BREAD
A rustic 8-inch loaf (often called a boule) with a crusty exterior and substantial, slightly chewy crumb works best here.

When it comes to sandwiches, I think the Italians have it right. They load meat, cheese, and flavorful condiments between slices of crusty bread and then compact the sandwich in a heated, ridged press. The pressing accomplishes two things: First, the fillings melt together and become neater to eat; and second, the bread crisps and acquires the signature grill marks from the ridges of the hot metal.

But what if you don't have a press or an indoor grill? The test kitchen has had success in the past by using a heavy Dutch oven to press Cuban sandwiches cooked in a nonstick skillet. That method worked great with the panini, but tasters missed the ridged grill marks. The solution was to use a nonstick grill pan, which has raised ridges, to cook the sandwiches.

Now that I'd found my method, I could concentrate on the ingredients, starting with the bread. Softer breads, such as sandwich bread, flattened into an undesirable crackerlike thickness. A hearty peasant loaf from the supermarket bakery worked best—it compressed and toasted perfectly under the weight of the Dutch oven.

After a great deal of trial and error with the fillings, I learned that 4 ounces of meat and 3 ounces of cheese were the right amounts for one sandwich; this ratio gave the sandwiches just enough cheese to melt around the filling without becoming messy. Thick, flavorful condiments like spicy mustard,

Visit us online!
For a free Portobello, Mozzarella, and Fresh Basil Panini recipe, visit **CooksCountry.com** and look for **Cook's Country Extras.**

flavored mayonnaise, and olive relish helped bump up the flavor inside the sandwich. I was surprised to find that brushing the outside of the bread with butter or oil—as you would in making grilled cheese—wasn't working here; it was just making the bread greasy. It was best to press these sandwiches without any fat for the proper crispy, toasted texture. **–Diane Unger**

HAM, CHEDDAR, AND GRILLED ONION PANINI
SERVES 4
Grey Poupon Country Dijon is our favorite brand of coarse-grain mustard (see page 30).

- ½ cup coarse-grain mustard
- 2 tablespoons prepared horseradish, drained
- 2 teaspoons honey
- ¼ teaspoon cayenne pepper
- 1 large red onion, halved and sliced ½ inch thick
- 1 tablespoon extra-virgin olive oil
  Salt and pepper
- 8 slices thick-cut crusty bread
- ¾ pound thinly sliced deli sharp cheddar cheese
- 1 pound thinly sliced deli ham

1. Whisk mustard, horseradish, honey, and cayenne in small bowl. In separate bowl, toss onion, oil, ¼ teaspoon salt, and ¼ teaspoon pepper. Heat large nonstick grill pan over medium heat for 1 minute. Arrange onion in single layer on pan and weight with Dutch oven. Cook, stirring occasionally, until onion is browned, 8 to 10 minutes. Transfer to paper towel–lined plate and wipe out pan.

2. Spread mustard mixture evenly on 1 side of each slice of bread. Layer half of cheese on 4 slices bread, then top with ham, onion, and remaining cheese. Arrange remaining bread, mustard-side down, over cheese.

We use heat—and the weight of a Dutch oven—to transform flavorful ingredients into cohesive sandwich fillings.

3. Heat grill pan over medium heat for 1 minute. Place 2 sandwiches in pan and weight with Dutch oven. Cook sandwiches until golden brown and cheese is melted, 4 to 6 minutes per side. Transfer to wire rack and repeat with remaining sandwiches. Serve.

SPICY TURKEY, RED PEPPER, AND PEPPER JACK CHEESE PANINI
SERVES 4
For a spicier sandwich, increase the jalapeño or hot sauce.

- ½ cup mayonnaise
- ¼ cup minced fresh cilantro
- 1 jalapeño chile, seeded and minced
- 1 tablespoon hot sauce
- 2 red bell peppers, seeded, halved, and sliced ½ inch thick
- 1 tablespoon extra-virgin olive oil
  Salt and pepper
- 8 slices thick-cut crusty bread
- ¾ pound thinly sliced deli pepper Jack cheese
- 1 pound thinly sliced deli turkey breast

1. Whisk mayonnaise, cilantro, jalapeño, and hot sauce in small bowl. In separate bowl, toss peppers, oil, ¼ teaspoon salt, and ½ teaspoon pepper. Heat large nonstick grill pan over medium heat for 1 minute. Arrange peppers in single layer on pan and weight with Dutch oven. Cook, stirring occasionally, until peppers are browned, 8 to 10 minutes. Transfer to paper towel–lined plate and wipe out pan.

2. Spread mayonnaise mixture evenly on 1 side of each slice of bread. Layer half of cheese on 4 slices bread, then top with turkey, peppers, and remaining cheese. Arrange remaining bread, mayonnaise-side down, over cheese.

3. Heat grill pan over medium heat for 1 minute. Place 2 sandwiches in pan and weight with Dutch oven. Cook sandwiches until golden brown and cheese is melted, 4 to 6 minutes per side. Transfer to wire rack and repeat with remaining sandwiches. Serve.

SALAMI, CAPICOLA, AND PROVOLONE PANINI SERVES 4

The tangy flavor of sharp provolone works best here.

- ¾ cup sun-dried tomatoes packed in oil, drained, 1 tablespoon oil reserved
- ½ cup pimento-stuffed green olives
- ½ cup pitted kalamata olives
- ¼ cup chopped fresh basil
- 2 tablespoons red wine vinegar
- 1 teaspoon dried oregano
- 8 slices thick-cut crusty bread
- ¾ pound thinly sliced deli provolone
- ½ pound thinly sliced deli salami
- ½ pound thinly sliced deli hot capicola

1. Pulse tomatoes, reserved oil, olives, basil, vinegar, and oregano in food processor until finely chopped.

2. Spread tomato mixture evenly on 1 side of each slice of bread. Layer half of cheese on 4 slices bread, then top with salami, capicola, and remaining cheese. Arrange remaining bread, tomato-side down, over cheese.

3. Heat grill pan over medium heat for 1 minute. Place 2 sandwiches in pan and weight with Dutch oven. Cook sandwiches until golden brown and cheese is melted, 4 to 6 minutes per side. Transfer to wire rack and repeat with remaining sandwiches. Serve.

Weeknight Pasta and Bean Soup

I often order a hearty pasta and bean soup for lunch at my favorite Italian restaurant. It has chunks of meat and makes a great meal. I'd like to try making this soup on my own, but I don't have much time to cook. Can you help?

–Josh Tinker, Providence, R.I.

Cooking the pasta separately, and adding it to the soup at the end of cooking, prevents the pasta from absorbing too much liquid and becoming bloated.

Traditional pasta and bean soups start by cooking dried beans for hours in either water or broth (sometimes with a meaty bone) to create a rich, flavorful base to which vegetables, meat, and pasta are added. It's hard to go wrong with this approach. Fast recipes, however, rely on canned beans and store-bought broth. I tried several of these and found that this approach rarely succeeds. Some quick soups were dull, bland, and watery; others were greasy, with rubbery ground beef; and one was so overloaded with vegetables and tomatoes that it would have made a fine minestrone—but it was an awful pasta and bean soup.

Because I was going to try to use canned beans and store-bought broth, I knew I'd have to get a lot of flavor out of the meat and vegetables. Starting the soup with pancetta (cured Italian bacon) resulted in a broth that was a little gamy, and the pancetta didn't provide much to chew on. Regular bacon proved too smoky for this soup, and ground beef was bland and greasy. Hot Italian sausage was perfect—it was hearty and fully seasoned. I removed the meat from the casings, crumbled it, and browned it to start my soup.

For the vegetable component, I sautéed onions, carrots, celery, garlic, and rosemary in oil and sausage drippings; next, I added the beans, fresh tomatoes, and broth, followed by the pasta. My tasters thought this soup was too vegetal, so I tried a batch without the carrots and celery and was pleasantly surprised by the clean and sweet flavor of the soup. A small can of diced tomatoes turned out to be better—and less effort—than fresh tomatoes, as their juices added a bright flavor.

In traditional, long-cooked recipes, the dried beans slowly break down and thicken the broth; dumping canned beans into my broth resulted in a soup that was too thin. To create more body, I tried pureeing everything before adding the pasta, but this made the soup too thick and starchy. I found a happy compromise by pureeing half the beans with a portion of the broth before cooking. This gave the soup a hearty, creamy texture that was still studded with whole beans and pieces of meat and vegetables—and I didn't have to go through the hassle of pureeing hot soup in a blender. Best of all, this satisfying soup was ready to enjoy in under an hour. –Eva Katz

PASTA AND BEAN SOUP
SERVES 6 TO 8

If you cannot find hot Italian sausage, use the sweet variety and add ¼ teaspoon red pepper flakes to the soup along with the garlic and rosemary in step 2. Serve with extra Parmesan cheese and a drizzle of extra-virgin olive oil, if desired.

- 2 (16-ounce) cans cannellini beans, drained and rinsed
- 4 cups low-sodium chicken broth
- 8 ounces hot Italian sausage (about 2 links), casings removed (see note)
- 2 tablespoons extra-virgin olive oil
- 2 onions, chopped fine
- 4 garlic cloves, minced
- 1 teaspoon finely chopped fresh rosemary
- 1 (14.5-ounce) can diced tomatoes
  Salt and pepper
- 1 cup ditalini or other small pasta shape
- ½ cup finely chopped fresh basil
- 1 cup grated Parmesan cheese

1. Puree half of beans and 2 cups broth in food processor or blender until smooth; set aside. Cook sausage in large pot over medium-high heat, breaking up pieces with wooden spoon, until no longer pink, about 5 minutes.

Drain sausage on paper towel–lined plate.

2. Add oil and onions to fat in pot and cook until softened, about 10 minutes. Add garlic and rosemary and cook until fragrant, about 30 seconds. Add tomatoes, remaining whole beans, remaining broth, pureed bean mixture, cooked sausage, 1 teaspoon salt, and ½ teaspoon pepper. Bring to boil, then reduce heat to low and simmer until tomatoes and onions are very soft, about 15 minutes.

3. About 10 minutes before soup is done, bring 2 quarts water to boil in large saucepan. Add 1 teaspoon salt and pasta and cook until al dente. Drain pasta, then add to soup. Stir in basil and Parmesan and season with salt and pepper. Serve.

Make Ahead: Soup can be refrigerated for 3 days, but do not add pasta. Store pasta and soup in separate containers and combine just prior to serving.

I'm Looking for a Recipe

READERS HELP READERS FIND RECIPES

We've Got Mail

Dozens of readers sent us recipes in response to the request for Graham Cracker Cake in our August/September 2007 issue. We really liked the recipe sent by Mary Partak (right). Go to **CooksCountry.com** and click **Looking for a Recipe** to find hundreds of recipes submitted by readers who responded to other recipe requests in previous issues of *Cook's Country*.

GRAHAM CRACKER CAKE Mary Partak Campbell, Calif.

SERVES 8 TO 10

"My mother baked this family favorite about once a month throughout my childhood. She made it the old-fashioned way by using a rolling pin to crush the graham crackers." The graham crackers add lightly sweetened hearty flavor to this fluffy cake. For best results, process the crackers in a food processor until fine. This cake goes well with vanilla frosting. See CooksCountry.com for our Quick Vanilla Frosting recipe.

¼	cup all-purpose flour
1½	teaspoons baking powder
	Salt
17	graham crackers, crushed into fine crumbs (about 2¼ cups)
¼	cup vegetable shortening
4	tablespoons unsalted butter, softened
1	cup sugar
3	large eggs, separated
1	teaspoon vanilla extract
¾	cup milk

1. Combine flour, baking powder, pinch of salt, and graham cracker crumbs. Cream shortening and butter. Beat in sugar gradually. Beat in yolks and vanilla until fluffy. Add flour mixture and milk alternately. Beat egg whites to nearly stiff peaks, then fold into batter.

2. Pour into 2 greased 8-inch cake pans and bake at 350 degrees, 20 to 25 minutes. Cool and frost with vanilla frosting.

Apple Pizza

My grandmother used to make a great dessert she called apple pizza. It had a sweet, light crust covered in an apple pie–type filling and a light glaze topping. I've searched everywhere for the recipe, to no avail. Can you help me find this recipe? I think my grandmother got it from a newspaper some 30 years ago.

Catherine Schaumberg
Via e-mail

Sausage Cake

In the late 1960s, my mother owned and operated a restaurant that served fried chicken, hamburgers, and such. One of her cooks made a sausage cake, and she generously passed the recipe on to me, but I've since lost it. As I remember it, the sausage fat was the only shortening in the cake. I would love to have this recipe again. I will always remember how delicious it was, though with a name like "sausage cake" you wouldn't think so.

Martha Pegues
Cheraw, S.C.

Fingerlings

During the early 1950s, my aunt, a 4-H leader in Helena, Mont., used to make bar cookies she called fingerlings. They resembled brownies made with molasses, buttermilk, dates, raisins, nuts, and spices. I've been trying unsuccessfully for years to duplicate the rich fudginess of her recipe. My attempts have either been too cakey or tasted too much like gingerbread. Can anyone help me find a recipe for this very moist, brownielike molasses bar cookie?

Morreen Hansen
Mercer Island, Wash.

Liège Waffles

Our daughter tasted Liège waffles as a street food in Brussels. She says the outside was crusty, the interior was soft, and the center was crystalline sugar. They are made with yeast and something called pearl sugar. Can you help us find a recipe?

Fran Jennings
Madison, Conn.

Toasted Marshmallow Ice Cream

I recently had some delicious homemade toasted marshmallow ice cream at a restaurant in town. It was light tan in color and had slightly melted mini marshmallows mixed in. The ice cream had a wonderful toasted marshmallow flavor and would have been great in a s'mores sundae with graham crackers and hot fudge. Can anyone help?

June Shen-Epstein
Freeville, N.Y.

Coney Island Meat Sauce

A recipe that I've been looking for is Coney Island meat sauce. The original Nick's Coney Island restaurant in Portland, Ore., had the best, but they have gone out of business. I would love to have this recipe for my grandkids.

Roger Haldeman
Vancouver, Wash.

Elias Cole's Coconut Custard Pie

I'm looking for a recipe for the spongelike meringue piled high atop the coconut custard pie at Elias Cole's Restaurant in Colesville, N.J. It is definitely unique, extremely delicious, and obviously a well-guarded secret.

Lois Andrews
Washington, N.J.

Artichoke Relish

My friend's grandmother used to make a great Jerusalem artichoke and red pepper relish. We would eat it with our pepper Jack grilled cheese sandwiches. Unfortunately, the recipe is now lost, and we haven't been very successful in finding a decent replacement. Do you have any recipes for this Southern relish?

Liz Levy
Via e-mail

Chocolate Fried Pie

My grandmother made the most delicious chocolate fried pies. She is now gone and none of her children know how to make them! I do remember that they were made with Hershey's cocoa. If anyone can find this recipe, it will make my whole family so happy!

Dawn Morgan
Dallas, Texas

Chocolate Wisconsin Cake

Almost two decades ago, I lost this recipe while moving. I remember it came out of a magazine such as *Woman's Day*, *Family Circle*, or *Better Homes and Gardens*. The recipe was put together in three stages: A mixture was cooked on the stove, the cooked mixture was added to a cake batter, and then a frosting was made. Please help, because now there are three generations in the family who love to bake.

Angie Carusillo
Anaheim Hills, Calif.

Pineapple One, Two, Three, Four Cake

Sixty or 70 years ago, my mother baked a delicious, moist cake with crushed pineapple between the layers. It was called One, Two, Three, Four Cake, since it was made with 1 cup of butter, 2 cups of sugar, 3 cups of flour, and 4 eggs. Unfortunately, that's all I remember of the recipe. Can any of your readers help me find the complete recipe?

Bob Reimann
Cazenovia, N.Y.

Pig 'n Whistle's Racetrack Coffee Cake

The Pig 'n Whistle in Hollywood has been famous for years for their bakery goods and dining. They used to have a most delectable item called racetrack coffee cake. It was shaped in a circle with an open center and had raisins, almonds, and cinnamon in it. Does anyone have a recipe for this coffee cake?

Shirley Schusler
Sun Lakes, Ariz.

Emma Rannings's German Cookies

My mother used to make a delicious cookie recipe given to her by her friend Emma Rannings. The bottom layer was a sugar cookie dough that was pressed into a pan and baked. Jelly was then spread over the cookie layer and topped with meringue, and it was then baked until golden and sliced into small bars for serving. I really wish I could find this recipe again.

Margery Patten
Owings, Md.

> **Are you looking for a special recipe?** Or do you have a recipe a fellow *Cook's Country* reader is seeking? Post your requests and recipes by visiting **CooksCountry.com** and clicking on **Looking for a Recipe**. We'll share recipe requests and found recipes on CooksCountry.com and print as many as we can in the magazine. You may also write to us at Looking for a Recipe, Cook's Country, P.O. Box 470739, Brookline, MA 02447.

Find the Rooster!

A tiny version of this rooster has been hidden somewhere in the pages of this issue. If you find it, write to us with its location (plus your name and address) and you will be entered into a random drawing. The first correct entry drawn will receive a WearEver Premium Hard Anodized 12-Inch Nonstick Skillet (our test winner—see page 29), and the next five will each receive a complimentary one-year subscription to *Cook's Country*. To enter the contest, visit **CooksCountry.com/emailus** or write to us at Rooster, Cook's Country, P.O. Box 470739, Brookline, MA 02447. Entries are due by May 31, 2008.

Did you find the rooster in the October/November 2007 issue? It was hidden in the animal crackers photo on page 27. Jessie McGaffin of Nevada, Iowa, spotted it and won a KitchenAid Classic Plus Stand Mixer.

30-Minute Supper

SKILLET CHICKEN WITH CHILE AND LIME

30-Minute Supper

STIR-FRIED BEEF WITH GREEN BEANS
AND WATER CHESTNUTS

30-Minute Supper

PASTA WITH LEMONY CHICKEN AND ASPARAGUS

30-Minute Supper

CREAMY CHICKEN AND BISCUIT BAKE

STIR-FRIED BEEF WITH GREEN BEANS AND WATER CHESTNUTS SERVES 4

To prepare the flank steak, slice the meat with the grain into 3 long strips, then cut each strip across the grain into ⅛-inch-thick slices.

- ⅓ cup oyster sauce
- ⅓ cup low-sodium beef broth
- 2 teaspoons rice vinegar
- ½ teaspoon red pepper flakes
- 2 tablespoons vegetable oil
- 1 flank steak (about 1½ pounds), cut into thin slices (see note)
- 1 pound green beans, trimmed and cut into 2-inch pieces
- 2 (8-ounce) cans sliced water chestnuts, drained
- 8 garlic cloves, minced
- 2 tablespoons grated fresh ginger

1. Whisk oyster sauce, broth, vinegar, and pepper flakes in bowl. Heat 2 teaspoons oil in large nonstick skillet over high heat until just smoking. Cook half of steak until browned, about 1 minute per side. Transfer to bowl and repeat with additional 2 teaspoons oil and remaining steak.

2. Heat remaining 2 teaspoons oil in empty skillet until just smoking. Cook beans and water chestnuts, covered, stirring occasionally, until beans are bright green and just tender, about 3 minutes. Add garlic and ginger and cook until fragrant, about 30 seconds. Return steak and any accumulated juices to pan. Add oyster sauce mixture and cook until thickened, about 1 minute. Serve.

SKILLET CHICKEN WITH CHILE AND LIME SERVES 4

Ro-Tel tomatoes are a brand of diced tomatoes seasoned with spicy green chiles. If you can't find them, use 1¼ cups of plain diced tomatoes and an additional jalapeño.

- 4 boneless, skinless chicken breasts (about 1½ pounds)
  Salt and pepper
- 6 tablespoons unsalted butter
- 1 jalapeño chile, seeded and chopped fine
- 4 garlic cloves, minced
- 1 (10-ounce) can Ro-Tel tomatoes (see note)
- ½ cup low-sodium chicken broth
- 1 tablespoon grated zest and 2 tablespoons juice from 2 limes
- ¼ cup finely chopped fresh cilantro

1. Pat chicken dry with paper towels and season with salt and pepper. Melt 2 tablespoons butter in large nonstick skillet over medium-high heat. Cook chicken until golden, about 3 minutes per side. Transfer to plate.

2. Add jalapeño and garlic to skillet and cook until fragrant, about 30 seconds. Stir in tomatoes and broth and bring to boil. Return chicken and any accumulated juices to skillet and simmer, covered, over medium heat until chicken is cooked through, about 10 minutes.

3. Transfer chicken to serving platter and tent with foil. Simmer sauce, uncovered, until slightly thickened, about 5 minutes. Off heat, stir in remaining butter, lime zest and juice, and cilantro. Season with salt and pepper. Pour sauce over chicken. Serve.

CREAMY CHICKEN AND BISCUIT BAKE SERVES 4

Boursin cheese comes in multiple flavors; the Garlic & Fine Herbs variety works best here.

- 1 rotisserie chicken, skin discarded, meat shredded into bite-sized pieces (about 3 cups)
- 2 (5.2-ounce) packages Boursin cheese, crumbled (see note)
- 1¼ cups heavy cream
- 1¼ cups low-sodium chicken broth
  Salt and pepper
- 4 scallions, sliced thin
- 1 cup frozen peas and carrots, thawed
- 2 cups all-purpose flour
- 2 teaspoons baking powder
- 1 cup shredded sharp cheddar cheese

1. Adjust oven rack to middle position and heat oven to 450 degrees. Heat chicken, Boursin, ¼ cup cream, ¾ cup broth, ½ teaspoon salt, 1 teaspoon pepper, scallions, and vegetables in large pot over medium heat, stirring often, until cheese is melted and mixture is heated through, about 5 minutes. Transfer to greased 13- by 9-inch baking dish.

2. Meanwhile, combine flour, baking powder, cheddar, remaining cream, remaining broth, 1 teaspoon salt, and ½ teaspoon pepper in bowl. Space heaping tablespoons of batter about ½ inch apart over chicken mixture (you will have about 16 small biscuits). Bake until biscuits are golden brown and filling is bubbling, about 20 minutes. Serve.

PASTA WITH LEMONY CHICKEN AND ASPARAGUS SERVES 4

The ruffled nooks and crannies of campanelle pasta (also called bellflowers) work great here, but penne is an acceptable substitute.

- 4 boneless, skinless chicken breasts (about 1½ pounds), cut crosswise into ¼-inch-thick slices
  Salt and pepper
- 4 tablespoons unsalted butter
- 1 pound asparagus, trimmed and cut into 1-inch pieces
- 8 garlic cloves, minced
- ½ pound campanelle (see note)
- ¼ cup juice from 2 lemons
- 1 cup grated Parmesan cheese
- ¼ cup chopped fresh parsley

1. Bring 4 quarts water to boil in large pot. Pat chicken dry with paper towels and season with salt and pepper. Melt 1 tablespoon butter in large nonstick skillet over medium heat. Cook half of chicken until golden, 1 to 2 minutes per side. Transfer to bowl. Repeat with additional 1 tablespoon butter and remaining chicken.

2. Add additional 1 tablespoon butter and asparagus to empty skillet and cook until asparagus is just tender, about 5 minutes. Add garlic and cook until fragrant, about 30 seconds. Transfer to bowl with chicken and cover to keep warm.

3. Add 1 tablespoon salt and pasta to boiling water and cook until al dente. Reserve ½ cup cooking water. Drain pasta and return to pot. Add remaining butter, chicken, asparagus, lemon juice, cheese, and parsley to pot and toss to combine, adding reserved pasta water as needed. Season with salt and pepper. Serve.

PORK CHOPS WITH ROASTED RED PEPPER CREAM

GRILLED HONEY MUSTARD CHICKEN

SKILLET MACARONI AND CHEESE

PAN-SEARED BEEF TENDERLOIN
WITH PORT WINE SAUCE

GRILLED HONEY MUSTARD CHICKEN SERVES 4

Toast the almonds in a dry skillet over medium heat, shaking occasionally, until golden, about 5 minutes. This recipe can also be made in a grill pan over high heat.

- ¾ cup Dijon mustard
- 2 tablespoons honey
- ¼ teaspoon cayenne pepper
- ¼ cup sour cream
- 2 teaspoons chopped fresh tarragon
- 4 boneless, skinless chicken breasts (about 1½ pounds), pounded ½ inch thick
  Salt and pepper
- ¼ cup sliced almonds, toasted (see note)

1. Combine mustard, honey, and cayenne in bowl. Transfer ½ cup mustard mixture to separate bowl and stir in sour cream and tarragon; set aside.

2. Pat chicken dry with paper towels and season with salt and pepper. Grill over hot fire until cooked through, 2 to 4 minutes per side. Transfer chicken to platter, brush with remaining mustard mixture, and sprinkle with almonds. Serve, passing sour cream mixture separately.

PORK CHOPS WITH ROASTED RED PEPPER CREAM
SERVES 4

Our favorite brand of jarred roasted red peppers is Divina.

- 4 bone-in rib or center-cut pork chops, about 1 inch thick
  Salt and pepper
- 1 tablespoon vegetable oil
- ½ onion, sliced thin
- 6 garlic cloves, minced
- ¾ cup low-sodium chicken broth
- ¾ cup heavy cream
- 1 (12-ounce) jar roasted red peppers, drained and chopped (see note)
- 2 teaspoons light brown sugar
- ¼ cup chopped fresh basil

1. Pat chops dry with paper towels and season with salt and pepper. Heat oil in large skillet over medium-high heat until just smoking. Add chops and cook until well browned and meat registers 145 degrees, about 5 minutes per side. Transfer to serving platter and tent with foil.

2. Add onion to empty skillet and cook until softened, about 5 minutes. Add garlic and cook until fragrant, about 30 seconds. Stir in broth, cream, roasted peppers, and sugar and simmer, scraping up any browned bits with wooden spoon, until sauce is slightly thickened, about 5 minutes. Off heat, add any accumulated pork juices back to pan and stir in basil. Season with salt and pepper. Spoon sauce over chops. Serve.

PAN-SEARED BEEF TENDERLOIN WITH PORT WINE SAUCE SERVES 4

While tawny and vintage port will work in this recipe, we prefer to use the sweeter and typically less expensive ruby port.

- 4 center-cut tenderloin steaks, about 1 inch thick
  Salt and pepper
- 2 tablespoons vegetable oil
- 2 shallots, minced
- 2 teaspoons tomato paste
- ¾ cup ruby port (see note)
- ½ cup low-sodium chicken broth
- 1 teaspoon minced fresh thyme
- 2 teaspoons balsamic vinegar
- 3 tablespoons unsalted butter

1. Pat steaks dry with paper towels and season with salt and pepper. Heat 1 tablespoon oil in large skillet over medium-high heat until just smoking. Cook steaks until well browned and meat registers 125 degrees for medium-rare, 3 to 5 minutes per side. Transfer to platter and tent with foil.

2. Add remaining tablespoon oil and shallots to empty skillet and cook until softened, about 2 minutes. Stir in tomato paste and cook until beginning to brown, about 1 minute. Stir in port, broth, and thyme and simmer, scraping up any browned bits with wooden spoon, until sauce is slightly thickened, about 5 minutes. Off heat, whisk in vinegar, butter, and any accumulated steak juices. Season with salt and pepper. Pour sauce over steaks. Serve.

SKILLET MACARONI AND CHEESE SERVES 4

We prefer homemade bread crumbs. To make them, pulse 2 slices of hearty white sandwich bread in a food processor until coarsely ground.

- 2 tablespoons unsalted butter
- 2 cups fresh bread crumbs (see note)
  Salt and pepper
- 3¾ cups water, plus more as needed
- 1 (12-ounce) can evaporated milk
- 3 cups elbow macaroni
- 1 teaspoon cornstarch
- 2 teaspoons hot sauce
- 3 cups shredded sharp cheddar cheese
- 2 cups shredded Monterey Jack cheese

1. Melt butter in large nonstick skillet over medium-high heat. Add bread crumbs, ¼ teaspoon salt, and ¼ teaspoon pepper and cook, stirring frequently, until deep golden brown, about 5 minutes. Transfer to bowl and wipe out skillet.

2. Bring water, 1¼ cups evaporated milk, and ½ teaspoon salt to simmer in skillet over medium-high heat. Add macaroni and cook, stirring often, until macaroni is al dente, 8 to 10 minutes.

3. Whisk remaining evaporated milk, cornstarch, and hot sauce in small bowl, then stir into skillet. Simmer until slightly thickened, about 1 minute. Off heat, stir in cheeses, one handful at a time, adding water as needed to adjust consistency. Sprinkle with toasted bread crumbs. Serve.

Recipe Revival:
Chicken Marengo

This hearty stew has a colorful history that dates back to Napoleon. Over time this baroque recipe—the original calls for crayfish and truffles—has become simpler but blander. Could we bring back bold flavors without extra effort?

Many recipes have murky histories, and none more so than chicken Marengo. Legend has it that this stew was invented by Napoleon's chef, a man named Dunand, after a victory over the Austrians near the Italian town of Marengo in 1800. As the story goes, the supply wagons were trailing behind, so Dunand and his minions had to scavenge the countryside for ingredients to cook for their hungry and demanding leader. A stew was supposedly made with chicken (cut up with a saber), tomatoes, brandy from Napoleon's flask, olives, mushrooms, truffles, crayfish, cilantro, bread scraps, and fried eggs. Napoleon loved the dish so much that he demanded it after every ensuing victory.

Food historians take issue with this tale for several reasons: Some claim Dunand wasn't employed by the French army in 1800; others say some ingredients would not have been available in the region. What is indisputable, however, is that chicken Marengo went on to become a widely popular recipe throughout Europe and America. Recipes for chicken Marengo appeared in American cookbooks as early as 1886 and were featured in the 1887 edition of *Miss Parloa's Kitchen Companion*. (There were actually two recipes; one was fairly plain, and the second included fried eggs and triangles of toast.) By the time the recipe appeared in the *Joy of Cooking*, the truffles, crayfish, and fried eggs were long gone and the focus was on the big flavors in the sauce—tomato, brandy, and olive.

As it was to so many older recipes, the post–World War II era was unkind to chicken Marengo. The sauce was downgraded to canned cream of mushroom soup mixed with canned cream of tomato soup. Chicken Marengo began as a rustic yet noble dish designed to satisfy the hunger of a victorious soldier. I wanted to bring this recipe back to its roots.

In the test kitchen, we know that most good stews and braises start with browning the meat to establish a base of flavor. My tasters had a preference for white meat in this recipe, but boneless, skinless breasts didn't brown well and turned rubbery when stewed. Instead, I used skin-on, bone-in breasts: The bones added flavor to the stew, and the skin browned well and contributed flavor of its own.

After browning the chicken, I removed it from the pot to start building the sauce. I sautéed mushrooms, onion, and garlic, then added tomato paste and canned crushed tomatoes. Tasters didn't think the crushed tomatoes were adding enough flavor, so I switched to fresher-tasting canned diced tomatoes, which I quickly buzzed in the food processor to begin the breaking-down process (large chunks were unappealing in this sauce). My tasters wanted a strong hit of brandy; I eventually settled on ½ cup as the right amount for the sauce. We especially liked briny kalamata olives here, and chopping the olives and adding them at the outset allowed their flavor to permeate the sauce.

Since I wasn't removing the chicken skin, I knew I'd have to take measures to prevent it from becoming chewy during the stewing process. First, I made sure to have only enough sauce in the pot to come halfway up the chicken breasts. To keep the skin crisp and the meat moist, I nestled the browned chicken into the sauce skin-side up, then placed the pot, uncovered, in a 450-degree oven for about 30 minutes to cook the chicken through and let the sauce reduce and intensify. This gave me a hearty, full-flavored Chicken Marengo ready to conquer the modern dinner table. **–Diane Unger**

CHICKEN MARENGO
SERVES 4

Since canned crushed tomatoes are often packed in a stale-tasting tomato sauce, we prefer to use drained diced tomatoes in this recipe. The tomatoes can be roughly chopped by hand or pulsed 3 or 4 times in a food processor.

- 4 **bone-in, skin-on split chicken breasts (about 3 pounds)**
  Salt and pepper
- 1 **tablespoon extra-virgin olive oil**
- 1 **onion, chopped fine**
- 4 **garlic cloves, minced**
- 10 **ounces cremini or white mushrooms, sliced thin**
- 2 **teaspoons minced fresh thyme**
- 2 **tablespoons tomato paste**
- 1 **(28-ounce) can diced tomatoes, drained and roughly chopped (see note)**
- ¾ **cup low-sodium chicken broth**
- ½ **cup brandy**
- ¼ **cup pitted kalamata olives, chopped fine**
- ¼ **teaspoon red pepper flakes**
- 3 **tablespoons unsalted butter**

1. Adjust oven rack to middle position and heat oven to 450 degrees. Pat chicken dry with paper towels and season with salt and pepper. Heat oil in Dutch oven over medium-high heat until just smoking. Cook chicken, skin-side down, until deep golden brown, about 5 minutes. Flip and brown on second side, about 2 minutes. Transfer to plate.

2. Reduce heat to medium. Add onion to fat in pan and cook until softened, about 5 minutes. Stir in garlic and cook until fragrant, about 30 seconds. Add mushrooms, thyme, and ¼ teaspoon salt. Cover and cook, stirring occasionally, until mushrooms have released their juices, about 10 minutes. Stir in tomato paste and cook until thickened, about 2 minutes.

3. Stir in tomatoes, broth, brandy, olives, and pepper flakes and bring to boil. Add chicken pieces, skin-side up, along with any accumulated juices. Transfer pot to oven and cook, uncovered, until chicken registers 160 degrees, about 30 minutes. Transfer chicken to serving platter. Stir butter into sauce and season with salt and pepper. Pour sauce around chicken. Serve.

Our recipe forgoes the canned soup base and instead builds flavor with rich ingredients like olives, brandy, and mushrooms.

Kalamata Olives

Although kalamata olives are often packed in olive oil in their native Greece, on American soil we almost always find them swimming in a vinegary brine. We prefer the fresher kalamatas from the refrigerator section of the supermarket, as the jarred, shelf-stable ones are bland and mushy in comparison. If you can't find kalamatas in the refrigerator section of your market, look for them at the salad bar.

KALAMATA OLIVES

Test Kitchen's Make-Ahead Holiday Menu

Each of these recipes has a make-ahead component that allows the cook to celebrate with guests and not be tied to the stove all day.

LEMON ASPARAGUS SALAD

SERVES 8

The asparagus can be blanched and the dressing can be prepared in advance, but don't combine the 2 elements in this salad until serving time.

- 2 pounds asparagus, trimmed
  Salt and pepper
- ¼ cup juice from 2 lemons
- 1 tablespoon Dijon mustard
- 1 tablespoon honey
- 1 garlic clove, minced
- ¾ cup extra-virgin olive oil
- 1 tablespoon finely chopped fresh chives

1. Bring 4 quarts water to boil in large pot. Add asparagus and 1 tablespoon salt and cook until just tender, 2 to 4 minutes. Drain and immediately transfer to bowl of ice water. When completely cool, drain and pat dry with paper towels.

2. Combine lemon juice, mustard, honey, garlic, ½ teaspoon salt, and ¼ teaspoon pepper in bowl. Slowly whisk in oil to emulsify. Stir in chives. Arrange asparagus on platter and drizzle with vinaigrette. Serve.

Make Ahead: The blanched asparagus can be refrigerated in a large zipper-lock bag for 24 hours. The vinaigrette can be prepared (with exception of the chives) and refrigerated for 3 days. The chives should be chopped and added to the vinaigrette just prior to serving.

MAPLE ROAST TURKEY BREAST **SERVES 8**

If using a frozen turkey breast, thaw it in the refrigerator for 24 hours.

- 4 tablespoons unsalted butter, softened
- ¾ teaspoon salt
- ¼ teaspoon pepper
- ¼ cup maple syrup
- 1 tablespoon Dijon mustard
- 1 whole bone-in, skin-on turkey breast (about 6 pounds; see box below)

1. Adjust oven rack to lower-middle position and heat oven to 425 degrees. Mix butter, salt, and pepper in small bowl. Combine maple syrup and mustard in another small bowl.

2. Carefully separate turkey skin from meat. Rub butter mixture under skin. Arrange turkey breast-side up on greased V-rack set inside large roasting pan. Pour 2 cups water into bottom of pan and roast until turkey is golden, about 30 minutes.

3. Decrease oven temperature to 325 degrees. Roast until turkey is deep golden brown, about 1 hour. Begin basting turkey with maple mixture every 15 minutes until skin is glossy and meat registers 160 degrees, 15 to 30 minutes. Transfer turkey to cutting board and let rest 20 minutes. Carve and serve.

Make Ahead: After the turkey is rubbed with seasoned butter in step 2, it can be covered and refrigerated for 24 hours.

Turkey Breast: Some Birds Are Best Brined

Most turkey breasts weigh between 6 and 7 pounds and will serve eight. Sold frozen year-round, as well as fresh during the holidays, turkey breasts come in a few varieties: natural (untreated), self-basting (injected with a brine solution), and kosher (salted and rinsed during the koshering process). Although any of these options will work in our recipe for Maple Roast Turkey Breast, if using a natural turkey breast, you may want to explore brining the bird in a saltwater solution to season the meat and help keep it moist. (Self-basting and kosher birds will be plenty moist and should not be brined.)

Here's how to brine a natural turkey breast: Dissolve ½ cup of table salt in 4 quarts of cold water in a large container. Submerge the turkey breast in the brine, cover it with plastic wrap, and refrigerate it for 3 to 6 hours. (Do not brine the turkey breast any longer or it will be too salty.) Rinse the turkey breast under cold water and dry it thoroughly with paper towels before cooking.

GLAZED PEARL ONIONS WITH GRAPES AND TOASTED ALMONDS **SERVES 8**

To toast the almonds, heat them in a dry skillet over medium heat, stirring frequently, until golden and fragrant, about 5 minutes. The frozen onions do not need to be thawed prior to cooking.

- 2 tablespoons unsalted butter
- 2 pounds frozen pearl onions
- 1 cup low-sodium chicken broth
- 2 tablespoons brown sugar
- 3 tablespoons red wine vinegar
- 1½ teaspoons minced fresh rosemary
- ½ cup red grapes, halved
- ⅓ cup sliced almonds, toasted
  Salt and pepper

1. Melt butter in large skillet over medium-high heat. Add onions and cook until light brown, about 10 minutes. Stir in broth, sugar, 2 tablespoons vinegar, and rosemary; bring to boil. Reduce heat to medium-low and simmer, covered, until onions are tender, 12 to 14 minutes.

2. Remove lid and increase heat to medium-high. Cook until liquid is reduced to glazelike consistency, about 5 minutes. Off heat, stir in grapes, almonds, and remaining vinegar. Season with salt and pepper. Serve.

Make Ahead: After the onions have been simmered in step 1, they can be covered and refrigerated for 24 hours. When ready to serve, combine chilled onions and ¼ cup additional chicken broth in large skillet. Cook, covered, over medium-high heat until heated through, about 5 minutes. Uncover and proceed with step 2.

BACON SCALLOPED POTATOES **SERVES 8**

Other mild, semisoft cheeses, such as gouda or fontina, may be substituted for the cheddar in this recipe. Fresh chives can be used in place of the parsley.

- 8 slices bacon, chopped fine
- 1 onion, chopped fine
- 2 garlic cloves, minced
- 2½ teaspoons salt
- ¼ teaspoon cayenne pepper
- 5 pounds russet potatoes, peeled and sliced thin
- 3 cups half-and-half
- ¼ teaspoon baking soda
- 2 cups shredded cheddar cheese
- 3 tablespoons chopped fresh parsley

1. Adjust oven rack to middle position and heat oven to 425 degrees. Cook bacon in Dutch oven over medium heat until crisp, about 8 minutes. Transfer bacon to paper towel–lined plate and pour off all but 1 tablespoon fat. Cook onion in bacon fat until softened, about 5 minutes. Add garlic, salt, and cayenne and cook until fragrant, about 30 seconds. Stir in potatoes, half-and-half, and baking soda and bring to simmer. Reduce heat to medium-low, cover, and cook, stirring occasionally, until potatoes are almost tender, about 15 minutes.

2. Off heat, stir in cheese, cooked bacon, and parsley and transfer mixture to 13- by 9-inch baking dish. Bake until sauce is bubbling around edges and top is golden brown, about 15 minutes. Cool 10 minutes before serving.

Make Ahead: After the potato mixture has been transferred to a baking dish in step 2, the dish can be wrapped in foil and refrigerated for 24 hours. When ready to serve, bake until bubbling, 30 to 35 minutes. Remove foil and continue baking until top is golden brown, about 15 minutes.

Chicken, Broccoli, and Ziti Casserole

Our enhanced béchamel packs plenty of flavor, without the heavy richness of the traditional cream sauce.

I often make pasta casseroles for my son's Little League teammates because one dish can feed a crowd. I've tried some casserole versions of ziti with chicken and broccoli, but they never quite live up to the original. Can you help? –Megan Burke, Scottsdale, Ariz.

All About Asiago

Asiago is a cow's-milk cheese made in the mountains of northern Italy. Although Asiago is produced in both fresh and aged forms, it's likely you will find only the aged version in your supermarket's cheese case. Aged Asiago is made with partially skimmed milk and aged for three months to a year. Its nutty, slightly assertive flavor is often described as a cross between cheddar and Parmesan, and its firm texture is perfect for grating on pasta, soups, or salads.

Chicken, broccoli, and ziti tossed in a creamy sauce is such a crowd-pleaser that it makes sense to turn it into a crowd-feeding casserole. Adding a blanket of crunchy bread crumbs should make it that much better, but the recipes I tried for this casserole came out of the oven a mess. The pasta was limp, the chicken was dry and tough, and the broccoli was gray and waterlogged. Even worse, the once-silky sauce became stodgy and bland. I wanted my version of this dish to have it all: moist chicken, crisp-tender broccoli, and firm ziti served in a cheesy sauce that stayed creamy even after baking.

I started with the unifying element of the dish: the sauce. Some recipes use a reduced cream sauce, which tasted great but made this casserole so rich that my tasters couldn't finish a small portion. Other recipes use a béchamel sauce (made by cooking butter, flour, and milk until thickened), which had a creamy consistency when baked and wasn't too rich. I boosted the flavor by sautéing onion, lots of garlic (six minced cloves), and red pepper flakes in the butter before I added the flour and milk, and by replacing some of the milk with savory chicken broth. Parmesan is the traditional cheese in this dish, but it wasn't adding enough flavor—even in large quantities. Asiago has a sharper, more pungent flavor that stayed strong even when baked.

I quickly found that strips of boneless, skinless chicken breast needed to be precooked before going into the casserole to prevent the other ingredients from overcooking by the time the chicken was done. Browned chicken tasted great, but it became tough and dried-out in the oven. Poaching the chicken in the sauce flavored the meat and kept it moist.

Keeping the pasta from overcooking in the oven took more than just draining it when still slightly underdone. I had to undercook the pasta and then rinse it with cold water to completely stop the carryover cooking. The best option for precooking the broccoli turned out to be the microwave.

Adding minced garlic and more Asiago to the fresh bread crumbs created a topping that was as flavorful as the casserole itself. –Lynn Clark

CHICKEN, BROCCOLI, AND ZITI CASSEROLE
SERVES 8
Add more red pepper flakes for a spicier casserole.

- 4 slices hearty white sandwich bread, torn into pieces
- 8 garlic cloves, minced
- 2½ cups grated Asiago cheese
- 5 tablespoons unsalted butter, 2 tablespoons melted
  Salt and pepper
- 1 pound ziti
- 1 onion, chopped fine
- ¼ teaspoon red pepper flakes
- ¼ cup all-purpose flour
- ½ cup white wine
- 3 cups whole milk
- 2 cups low-sodium chicken broth
- 4 boneless, skinless chicken breasts (about 1½ pounds), cut crosswise into ¼-inch slices
- 12 ounces broccoli florets, cut into 1-inch pieces

1. Pulse bread, 2 minced garlic cloves, ½ cup Asiago, and melted butter in food processor until coarsely ground. Set aside.

2. Adjust oven rack to middle position and heat oven to 400 degrees. Bring 4 quarts water to boil in large pot. Add 1 tablespoon salt and ziti to boiling water and cook until nearly al dente. Drain in colander and rinse under cold water until cool.

3. Melt remaining butter in empty pot over medium heat. Cook onion until softened, about 5 minutes. Add remaining garlic and pepper flakes and cook until fragrant, about 30 seconds. Stir in flour and cook until golden, about 1 minute. Slowly whisk in wine and cook until liquid is almost evaporated, about 1 minute. Slowly whisk in milk and broth and bring to boil. Add chicken and simmer until no longer pink, about 5 minutes. Off heat, stir in remaining cheese until melted.

4. Microwave broccoli, covered, in large bowl until bright green and nearly tender, 2 to 4 minutes. Stir cooked broccoli and drained ziti into pot and season with salt and pepper. Transfer to 13- by 9-inch baking dish. Sprinkle with bread crumb mixture and bake until sauce is bubbling around edges and topping is golden brown, 20 to 25 minutes. Cool 5 minutes. Serve. (Casserole can be assembled, minus bread crumbs, 24 hours in advance. Bring to room temperature before adding bread crumbs and baking.)

Getting to Know Cruciferous Vegetables

Everyone knows this family of vegetables is good for you. Here's how we cook and serve them so they taste good, too.

Broccoli
CRUCIFEROUS KING
However you choose to cook broccoli, give the heartier (but equally flavorful) peeled stems a minute or two head start before adding the tender florets. Look for broccoli with dark green, tightly packed florets and stems that are firm and not shriveled or dried-out.

Cauliflower
COOKED IS BETTER
Although the dense, pebbled crown (or curd) of this vegetable is often served raw, the "chalky" texture and "bland" flavor of cauliflower are improved with cooking. Steam, boil, or roast florets to bring out their "subtle, earthy sweetness" and "firm, crunchy texture." Overcooked cauliflower may develop an unpleasantly sulfurous smell.

Colored Cauliflower
PRETTY, HEALTHY
There is more to these vegetables than just aesthetics: The orange variety has roughly 25 times more vitamin A than traditional cauliflower and tastes a bit "like winter squash." Purple cauliflower is high in antioxidants and has a "slightly bitter" flavor. Both varieties can be substituted for regular cauliflower in any application.

Broccoflower
A GREAT MIX
Broccoflower is a trademarked hybrid of broccoli and cauliflower that was developed in Holland. While the tightly packed curd is similar in texture to cauliflower, the flavor skews more toward broccoli, with a "mild wheatiness" and subtle "touch of sweetness." Substitute for cauliflower in any application.

Romanesca
FRACTAL FLORETS
The delicate, intricately spiraled florets of this vegetable—which is sold as Romanesca cauliflower, broccoli, or cabbage—make it instantly recognizable. Its flavor combines "green beans and cauliflower," with an "aftertaste of fresh corn." Sprinkle steamed florets with lemon juice or sauté them in olive oil and finish with minced garlic.

Broccolini
HYBRID BROCCOLI
Broccolini is a hybrid of Chinese kale and broccoli. Broccolini is typically sold in bunches like asparagus, and it can be prepared similarly. Its flavor is "slightly mineral" and "sweet, like a cross between spinach and asparagus." Discard the bottom inch of the stems and steam, boil, sauté, or drizzle with olive oil and grill.

Radish
WHITE HEAT
The root of a plant in the mustard family, radishes can be red, green, black, or white on the exterior, and their flesh ranges from deep pink to stark white. The most common variety is the Cherry Belle, a round, red radish with "crisp and refreshing" white flesh. Refrigerate in a zipper-lock bag. Eat raw, sauté, or pickle.

Brussels Sprout
MICROCABBAGE
Brussels sprouts, which grow in clusters on long stalks, are so named because they originated in Belgium. Smaller sprouts are "tender and sweet," but those larger than an inch across can be "bitter," with a "rotten egg" aroma. Trim the stem ends and remove any discolored leaves. We prefer Brussels sprouts when braised in a flavorful liquid (stock, cream, or cider) or tossed with olive oil and roasted.

Bok Choy
CHINESE CABBAGE
Also called Chinese white cabbage, bok choy looks like a wide-stalked version of Swiss chard. Its "tender, spinachy" leaves and "crisp" stalks are common ingredients in stir-fries; for the best texture, add the crisp white stalks first and the tender leaves toward the end of cooking. Look for deep green leaves devoid of yellowing. Wrap bok choy in damp paper towels before refrigerating.

Horseradish
PACKS A PUNCH
When peeled and grated, this large (about a foot in length) brown root emits a noxious gas that can irritate the sinuses. The flavor of horseradish is "astringent," with a "biting, nasal heat." When exposed to air or heat, horseradish quickly loses its characteristic pungency, mellowing to a "bland, earthy sweetness." Peel away the fibrous skin and shred the white flesh on a box grater.

Kohlrabi
GARLICKY AND EARTHY
This vegetable is sometimes referred to as a cabbage turnip. Look for firm kohlrabi bulbs that are no wider than 3 inches. Though most often sold without their leaves, the greens have an "earthy, mineral quality" when quickly sautéed, while the bulbs are "slightly bitter" and have a "garlicky kick." The bulb should be peeled and sliced prior to being steamed, boiled, or stir-fried.

Daikon
GIANT RADISH
This Asian radish can grow to well over a foot in length. Unlike other varieties of radish, daikon has a slight sweetness and is only mildly spicy. Its texture is similar to a "water chestnut" and its flavor is "mild and milky to start," with a "peppery finish." We prefer daikon thinly sliced and eaten raw or quickly stir-fried. Wrap daikon in damp paper towels before refrigerating.

Better Pork Cutlets

What's the best method for infusing breaded pork cutlets with big flavor?

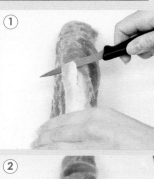

1. Use a paring knife to remove silver skin and extraneous fat from the tenderloin.
2. Cut the tenderloin into four equal pieces.
3. Arrange the pieces of tenderloin cut-side up on a cutting board and pound into ½-inch-thick cutlets.

The appeal of tender, crispy, golden brown breaded pork cutlets is easy to see—and taste—but there are only so many times you can eat them plain or in a sandwich. I wanted to find a way to dress up these pan-fried cutlets with interesting flavors.

The test kitchen's method for breading cutlets calls for dredging the pork first in flour, then in beaten eggs, and finally in bread crumbs to create a classic bound breading. Prepounded cutlets from the supermarket prepared this way were awful—the cutlets were ragged, tough, and uneven in thickness, which meant they cooked unevenly when pan-fried. Instead, I bought boneless thin-cut pork chops and pounded them to a uniform thickness; these cutlets cooked evenly, but they were a little tough and bland. Tasters much preferred the tender, flavorful cutlets made by pounding slices of pork tenderloin to an even thickness.

It took only one test to confirm why we typically don't like store-bought bread crumbs—they were sandy, dry, and lacking in flavor (even the seasoned varieties). Making homemade bread crumbs from white sandwich bread and then toasting them in the oven gave the breading a fresh taste and crunch.

Now I could focus on punching up the flavors. Taking each element of the bound breading in sequence, I first tried adding dried and fresh herbs to the flour, but the herb flavor was barely detectable. Herbs added to the beaten egg didn't adhere well enough to help. I tried using fresh herbs in the bread crumbs, but it took so much to add flavor that it wasn't practical. The concentrated nature of dried herbs worked much better to flavor the bread crumbs, especially when used in conjunction with other potent flavors, like cheese and lemon zest.

Searching for one more layer of seasoning, I turned to the vegetable oil I was using to pan-fry the cutlets. I experimented with infusing the oil with big flavors like black pepper, garlic, more lemon zest, and fresh herbs before frying the cutlets, and discovered that this method imparted a lot of flavor. It was also a fast way to add seasoning, as I could start the ingredients in cold oil, then add the cutlets as soon as the oil was hot. With so many potential flavor combinations, my crispy pork cutlets will never be bland again.

–Meredith Butcher

CRISPY PARMESAN-PEPPER PORK CUTLETS
SERVES 4
Shred the Parmesan on the large holes of a box grater.

- 3 **slices hearty white sandwich bread, torn into pieces**
- 1 **cup shredded Parmesan cheese (see note)**
- 5 **teaspoons pepper**
- ½ **cup all-purpose flour**
- 2 **large eggs**
- 1 **pork tenderloin (about 1 pound), trimmed, cut into 4 pieces, and pounded ½ inch thick (see photos at left)**
  Salt
- 1 **cup vegetable oil**

1. Adjust oven rack to middle position and heat oven to 200 degrees. Pulse bread in food processor until coarsely ground. Bake bread crumbs on rimmed baking sheet until dry, about 20 minutes. Transfer crumbs to shallow dish and stir in Parmesan and 1 teaspoon pepper. Spread flour in second shallow dish. Beat eggs in third shallow dish.

2. Pat pork dry with paper towels and season with salt.

For the boldest-tasting cutlets, we flavor the cooking oil with potent ingredients like black pepper, fresh thyme and sage, garlic, and lemon zest.

One cutlet at a time, coat lightly with flour, dip in egg, and dredge in bread crumb mixture, pressing to adhere.

3. Heat ½ cup oil and additional 2 teaspoons pepper in large nonstick skillet over medium heat until shimmering. Fry 2 cutlets until deep golden and crisp, about 2 minutes per side. Drain on paper towel–lined plate and transfer to oven to keep warm. Discard oil, wipe out skillet, and repeat with remaining oil, pepper, and cutlets. Serve.

CRISPY LEMON-THYME PORK CUTLETS
In step 1, omit Parmesan and pepper and add ½ teaspoon dried thyme and 2 teaspoons grated lemon zest to bread crumbs. In step 3, omit pepper and add 2 sprigs fresh thyme and 2 teaspoons grated lemon zest to each batch of oil.

CRISPY GARLIC-OREGANO PORK CUTLETS
In step 1, omit Parmesan and pepper and add ½ teaspoon dried oregano to bread crumbs. In step 3, omit pepper and add 3 peeled and smashed garlic cloves and 1 tablespoon minced fresh oregano to each batch of oil.

CRISPY BACON-SAGE PORK CUTLETS
Cook 3 slices finely chopped bacon in large nonstick skillet until crisp, about 8 minutes. Remove bacon with slotted spoon and pour bacon fat into separate bowl. (Wipe out skillet and use in step 3.) In step 1, omit Parmesan and pepper and add bacon and ½ teaspoon dried sage to bread crumbs. In step 3, omit pepper and add half of reserved bacon fat and 1 tablespoon minced fresh sage to each batch of oil.

On the Side: Greek Salad

Despite its laundry list of flavorful ingredients, this pizza parlor classic is often lackluster. Could we find a way to breathe new life into it?

With chunks of tangy feta cheese, salty black olives, and an assertive red wine vinaigrette, Greek salad is not meant to be timid. But most Greek salads are just that, featuring pale lettuce, watery tomatoes and cucumbers, and a sad pool of dressing at the bottom of the bowl. The canned olives taste flat, and the feta is typically elusive. I was determined to bring the boldness back to this mistreated salad.

Replacing bland ingredients with more flavorful ones and controlling the water exuded by the vegetables were the obvious first steps. I lost the tired iceberg lettuce and used heartier romaine instead. Canned black olives were banished in favor of brighter kalamatas. Seeding the cucumbers and using fleshy cherry tomatoes (instead of beefsteak or Roma) meant there was less liquid to dilute the dressing. Raw onion was the one ingredient that tasters found too strong. Several recipes suggested marinating the sliced onion in the dressing; sure enough, 20 minutes tamed its harshness.

But the dressing—olive oil, red wine vinegar, garlic, and dried oregano—still pooled at the bottom of the bowl. To create a creamier dressing with better cling, I added an ingredient popular in Greek cuisine: yogurt. For a final hit of still bolder flavor, I blended extra cheese into the dressing to ensure that every bite carried a tangy taste of feta. **–Lynn Clark**

GREEK SALAD SERVES 4 TO 6

We prefer the richness of whole-milk yogurt, but low-fat and nonfat plain yogurt are acceptable substitutes.

- 1¼ cups crumbled feta cheese
- 3 tablespoons plain whole-milk yogurt
- 1 teaspoon dried oregano
- 1 garlic clove, minced
- 3 tablespoons red wine vinegar
- 6 tablespoons extra-virgin olive oil
- ½ red onion, sliced thin
- 1 cucumber, peeled, halved lengthwise, seeded, and sliced thin
- 1 pint cherry tomatoes, halved
- ¾ cup pitted kalamata olives
- 2 romaine hearts, torn into bite-sized pieces (about 8 cups)
  Salt and pepper

1. Process ½ cup feta, yogurt, oregano, garlic, vinegar, and oil in blender until smooth, about 30 seconds. Combine dressing and onion in large bowl and let sit 20 minutes.

2. Add remaining feta, cucumber, tomatoes, olives, and romaine to bowl with dressing mixture and toss to combine. Season with salt and pepper. Serve.

On the Side: Creamed Spinach with Parmesan and Prosciutto

Most creamed spinach is bland and pasty. Could we reinvigorate this staple side dish?

Creamed spinach is a classic steakhouse side dish of chopped fresh spinach in a rich, cheesy cream sauce. Unfortunately, most recipes produce gray, stringy spinach in a stodgy, heavy sauce.

Typical renditions start by cooking melted butter and flour to form a pasty roux; cream and cheese are whisked in until smooth, and then chopped cooked spinach is added. To build a deeper flavor base, I sautéed onion and garlic in butter before stirring in the flour. Using whole milk instead of cream lightened the sauce and allowed more of the spinach flavor to shine through.

I wanted to cook the spinach directly in the sauce, but it gave off too much moisture. The large volume of spinach I was using ruled out the microwave as a pre-cooking method. Instead, I decided to quickly sauté the spinach in a large Dutch oven before building the cream sauce. To prevent it from watering down my sauce, I drained and pressed the spinach to remove as much moisture as possible, then finely chopped it to avoid the stringiness that plagues most recipes. For an Italian flair, I added chopped prosciutto, fresh sage, a pinch of nutmeg, and Parmesan cheese. **–Diane Unger**

CREAMED SPINACH WITH PARMESAN AND PROSCIUTTO SERVES 4 TO 6

While three 9-ounce boxes of frozen leaf spinach (defrosted and squeezed dry) may be substituted for the fresh, avoid baby spinach — it becomes slimy once cooked. Be sure to press as much liquid as possible from the spinach in step 1.

- 4 tablespoons unsalted butter
- 8 thin slices prosciutto, chopped fine
- 2 (10-ounce) bags curly-leaf spinach, stemmed and torn into bite-sized pieces
- 1 small onion, chopped fine
- 2 teaspoons minced fresh sage
- 4 garlic cloves, minced
- ⅛ teaspoon ground nutmeg
- 2 tablespoons all-purpose flour
- 1¾ cups whole milk
- ¾ cup grated Parmesan cheese
  Salt and pepper

1. Melt 1 tablespoon butter in large Dutch oven over medium heat. Cook half of prosciutto until lightly browned and crisp, about 5 minutes; transfer to paper towel–lined plate. Add spinach to pot in handfuls, stirring to allow each batch to wilt slightly before adding next. Continue to cook until spinach is uniformly wilted and glossy, about 1 minute. Transfer spinach to colander set over bowl and press with wooden spoon to release extra liquid.

2. Wipe out Dutch oven and melt remaining butter over medium heat. Add onion, remaining prosciutto, and sage and cook until onion is softened, about 5 minutes. Stir in garlic and nutmeg and cook until fragrant, about 30 seconds. Stir in flour and cook until golden, about 1 minute. Whisk in milk and simmer, stirring constantly, until thickened, about 3 minutes.

3. Return spinach to pot and stir until heated through, about 1 minute. Off heat, stir in ½ cup Parmesan and season with salt and pepper. Transfer to serving bowl, sprinkle with remaining Parmesan, and top with crispy prosciutto. Serve.

Biscuits and Sausage Gravy

Hearty buttermilk biscuits topped with creamy, spicy sausage gravy are a Southern breakfast tradition. So why do so many recipes feature hockey-puck biscuits soaked with pasty, flavorless sauce?

I got my first taste of biscuits and gravy at a busy diner just off the Blue Ridge Parkway in North Carolina. Having been raised far north of the Mason-Dixon line, I was surprised to see "Biscuits and Gravy" on the breakfast menu, as gravy to me was the concentrated brown sauce I ladled onto my Thanksgiving turkey. I took a flier and ordered it; minutes later, a bowl was plunked down in front of me. In it sat a huge, tangy biscuit smothered in a sausage-studded white cream gravy. After one bite, I knew that this was my new favorite breakfast.

Since then I've eaten my share of biscuits and gravy, but none as good as that first serving. Wanting to create my own version, I started by digging up some biscuit recipes. Identifying the right biscuit for the job—flaky, crumbly, or fluffy—was as simple as baking up a batch of each. Flaky breakfast biscuits might be great with butter and jam, but they didn't properly soak up the gravy. Crumbly cream biscuits were too rich and dense for a gravy with similar characteristics. Fluffy buttermilk biscuits, however, provided a substantial tang that complemented the gravy, and they were sturdy enough to absorb some gravy without turning to mush.

I wanted big biscuits—biscuits and gravy is not a dainty meal—so I upped the flour from the standard 2 cups to 3 cups, which allowed me to bake off eight big, 3-inch biscuits. To ensure a sturdy, tender texture and buttery flavor, I used a 2-to-1 ratio of butter to shortening—the butter provided the flavor and the shortening made the biscuits tender. I found that briefly kneading the dough

yielded biscuits with better structure. I also increased the baking powder and baking soda to provide maximum lift in the oven. Now I had sturdy, tender, and buttery biscuits that were perfect for the meaty gravy.

Traditional Southern cream gravy recipes cook a pound of bulk pork sausage and then sprinkle it with flour, which combines with the sausage fat to form a thickening roux. Dairy is added (my tasters much preferred milk to half-and-half and cream, which were too heavy), and the gravy is brought to a simmer. One recurring problem was the quantity of flour: Too little flour and the gravy was watery, but too much and it was pasty. I arrived at ¼ cup of flour to 3 cups of milk for a perfect, creamy texture. Bumping up the amount of sausage to 1½ pounds ensured plenty of meat in every bite.

With all these rich ingredients, the gravy was a little bland. I discovered that I could augment the sausage's flavor by adding ground fennel and sage, both seasonings typically found in pork sausage. And a generous dose of black pepper gave the gravy some serious heat. **–Kelley Baker**

Kitchen Know-How
STAMP BUT DON'T TWIST

Twisting the cutter when stamping out biscuits pinches the dough, resulting in an uneven rise. Using a well-floured cutter and pressing down with equal pressure on both sides of the cutter (and not twisting) ensures that the biscuits will rise evenly.

TWISTED

STAMPED

While this gravy might not look appealing to the uninitiated, its spicy, meaty flavor quickly converts the hungry.

BISCUITS AND SAUSAGE GRAVY SERVES 8

If you don't have buttermilk on hand, whisk 1 tablespoon of lemon juice into 1¼ cups of milk and let it stand until slightly thickened, about 10 minutes.

Biscuits
- 3 cups all-purpose flour
- 1 tablespoon sugar
- 1 tablespoon baking powder
- ½ teaspoon baking soda
- 1 teaspoon salt
- 8 tablespoons (1 stick) unsalted butter, cut into ½-inch pieces and chilled
- 4 tablespoons vegetable shortening, cut into ½-inch pieces and chilled
- 1¼ cups buttermilk (see note)

Sausage Gravy
- ¼ cup all-purpose flour
- 1 teaspoon ground fennel
- 1 teaspoon ground sage
- 1½ teaspoons pepper
- 1½ pounds bulk pork sausage
- 3 cups whole milk
  Salt

1. For the biscuits: Adjust oven rack to middle position and heat oven to 450 degrees. Line baking sheet with parchment paper. Pulse flour, sugar, baking powder, baking soda, salt, butter, and shortening in food processor until mixture resembles coarse meal. Transfer to large bowl. Stir in buttermilk until combined.

2. On lightly floured surface, knead dough until smooth, 8 to 10 kneads. Pat dough into 9-inch circle, about ¾ inch thick. Using 3-inch biscuit cutter dipped in flour, cut out rounds of dough and arrange on prepared baking sheet. Gather remaining dough, pat into ¾-inch-thick circle, and cut out remaining biscuits. (You should have 8 biscuits in total.)

3. Bake until biscuits begin to rise, about 5 minutes, then rotate pan and reduce oven temperature to 400 degrees. Bake until golden brown, 12 to 15 minutes, then transfer to wire rack and let cool.

4. For the sausage gravy: Combine flour, fennel, sage, and pepper in small bowl. Cook sausage in large nonstick skillet over medium heat, breaking up meat with wooden spoon, until no longer pink, about 8 minutes. Sprinkle flour mixture over sausage and cook, stirring constantly, until flour has been absorbed, about 1 minute. Slowly stir in milk and simmer until sauce has thickened, about 5 minutes. Season with salt. Serve over split biscuits. (Biscuits can be stored in zipper-lock bag for 2 days.)

Rethinking Fruit Salads

A sugar syrup is the best way to sweeten and moisten a bowl of cut fruit, but can a quick fruit syrup do more?

In my mind, a bowl of chopped fruit isn't elevated to fruit salad status until it's dressed with a sugar syrup. Sugar syrups, also called simple syrups, can be made in various concentrations, but the most common ratio is 2 parts water to 1 part sugar; the mixture is cooked over low heat to dissolve the sugar, then chilled for use in cocktails, desserts, and, yes, fruit salads. A moderate amount of simple syrup sweetens and moistens cut fruit, but I saw it as something more—a way to add big flavor to an otherwise plain fruit salad.

A classic way to infuse simple syrup with flavor is to add potent seasonings like vanilla, ginger, mint, or even jalapeños as the syrup cooks. Incorporating these ingredients did perk things up a bit, but I wanted even more flavor.

My cutting board was getting messy with juice and pulp as I chopped my way through pounds of fruit, and I wondered if there was a way to incorporate this juice into my simple syrup. I tried mashing some of the juicier fruits (watermelon, peaches, and cantaloupe) with a splash of citrus in the syrups as they cooked. After straining and cooling the syrups, I poured them over my cut fruit and was amazed at how much flavor they added. These fruit salads are still simple, but no longer plain.

–Meredith Butcher

PEACH, MANGO, AND BANANA SALAD

SERVES 4 TO 6

Avoid overly ripe bananas; they will break down and make the salad stodgy.

- 3 ripe peaches, pitted and chopped
- 2 tablespoons lime juice
- 2 tablespoons water
- 2 tablespoons brown sugar
- ¼ teaspoon vanilla extract
- 2 mangos, peeled, pitted, and chopped
- 2 bananas, peeled and sliced into ½-inch rounds

1. Combine ¼ cup chopped peaches, lime juice, water, sugar, and vanilla in saucepan and mash with potato masher until peaches break down. Bring to simmer over medium heat and cook until sugar dissolves, about 2 minutes. Cool to room temperature and then strain, reserving juices.

2. Toss mangos, bananas, remaining peaches, and reserved fruit juice in large bowl. Let sit 5 minutes. Serve.

WATERMELON, KIWI, AND STRAWBERRY SALAD

SERVES 4 TO 6

Seedless watermelon works best for this recipe. You will need about a quarter of a large watermelon.

- 3¼ cups chopped watermelon
- 2 tablespoons water
- 2 tablespoons honey
- 1 teaspoon red wine vinegar
- 1 teaspoon grated fresh ginger
- 2 ripe kiwis, peeled, halved lengthwise, and sliced thin
- 1 quart strawberries, hulled and quartered

1. Combine ¼ cup chopped watermelon, water, honey, vinegar, and ginger in saucepan and mash with potato masher until watermelon breaks down. Bring to simmer over medium heat and cook until honey dissolves, about 2 minutes. Cool to room temperature and then strain, reserving juices.

2. Toss kiwis, strawberries, remaining watermelon, and reserved fruit juice in large bowl. Let sit 5 minutes. Serve.

SPICY CANTALOUPE, PLUM, AND GRAPE SALAD

SERVES 4 TO 6

To ensure ripeness, choose a cantaloupe that is fragrant and gives slightly when the stem end is pressed.

- 3¼ cups chopped cantaloupe
- 2 tablespoons orange juice
- 2 tablespoons water
- 2 tablespoons sugar
- 1 small jalapeño chile, seeded and chopped fine
- 2 plums, pitted and chopped
- 2 cups green seedless grapes, halved

1. Combine ¼ cup chopped cantaloupe, orange juice, water, sugar, and jalapeño in saucepan and mash with potato masher until cantaloupe breaks down. Bring to simmer over medium heat and cook until sugar dissolves, about 2 minutes. Cool to room temperature and then strain, reserving juices.

2. Toss plums, grapes, remaining cantaloupe, and reserved fruit juice in large bowl. Let sit 5 minutes. Serve.

HONEYDEW, RASPBERRY, AND NECTARINE SALAD

SERVES 4 TO 6

To prevent the raspberries from breaking down, toss the salad gently in step 2.

- 3¼ cups chopped honeydew melon
- 2 tablespoons lemon juice
- 2 tablespoons water
- 2 tablespoons sugar
- 4 tablespoons finely chopped fresh mint
- 2 nectarines, pitted and chopped
- 1 pint fresh raspberries

1. Combine ¼ cup chopped honeydew, lemon juice, water, sugar, and 2 tablespoons mint in saucepan and mash with potato masher until honeydew breaks down. Bring to simmer over medium heat and cook until sugar dissolves, about 2 minutes. Cool to room temperature and then strain, reserving juices.

2. Toss nectarines, raspberries, remaining honeydew, remaining mint, and reserved fruit juice in large bowl. Let sit 5 minutes. Serve.

Test Kitchen Tip
BOOSTING FRUIT FLAVOR

Many fruit salad recipes toss the cut fruit with a simple syrup made with water and sugar. Infusing the syrup with spices and herbs is common. We took this idea one step further and mashed some of the fruit into the syrup (and lost some of the water in the process) for an extra flavor boost.

Use these fruit combinations as a guide to creating your own fruit salad recipes.

Mixed Berry Streusel Pie

My homemade berry pies look great, but when I cut into them they are always too juicy, so the crust is soggy and the streusel topping turns to mush. How can I best control the moisture of the filling while keeping fresh berry flavor? –Lureen Cathey, McCleary, Wash.

See photos on page 30

How to
MAKE A SLICEABLE PIE

Most of our initial tests left us with runny, loose berry fillings that were better served in a soup bowl than on a plate. Here's how we tightened things up.

1. For intense berry flavor without too much liquid, cook a portion of the berries with sugar and lemon zest in a saucepan until syrupy. When the mixture is thick enough, it will be bubbling and a spatula will leave a trail when dragged through the mixture.
2. To further tighten the filling, toss the cooked berry mixture with the remaining fresh berries and tapioca.

All those fresh berries guarantee a pie with great flavor, but their juices can make for a sodden crust and streusel. I wanted to create a pie with intense berry flavor that would slice neatly and have a crisp crust and crunchy streusel topping. Most important, I wanted it to be as easy as possible.

To keep things simple, I started with the test kitchen's press-in-the-pan No-Fear Pie Crust, which relies on cream cheese to make the dough easy to handle. The texture was ideal, but I was disappointed that my tasters said they wanted a more flavorful crust to accent the sweet berry filling. I tried our recipe for a graham cracker crust, which tasted great but was too sandy and loose to handle the moist berry filling. Thinking that flour and finely ground cracker crumbs aren't totally dissimilar, I made a hybrid dough by replacing some of the flour in our No-Fear recipe with graham cracker crumbs. This dough had the best of both worlds: rich graham flavor and sufficient sturdiness.

A little lemon zest added brightness to my mixed berry and sugar filling, but it was still too watery to slice neatly. Cooking the berries before adding them to the pie thickened the filling nicely, but it compromised their fresh flavor—the cooked filling tasted like jam. Cooking just a portion of the berries gave me a thicker filling with nice depth of flavor, but I still couldn't coax tidy slices from the pie. I needed to thicken the berry juices.

In search of a neutral-tasting thickener that wouldn't make the filling too rubbery or stodgy, I did a side-by-side test of pectin, flour, cornstarch, and tapioca. Tasters preferred the pie made with tapioca for its ability to thicken the filling without calling attention to itself. I could now cut perfect slices from the pie, so all that was left was the crowning streusel.

The raw pie dough already contained the butter and flour-crumb mixture that form the base of streusel. I made a batch of my pie dough as usual and reserved enough to pat in the pan for my crust. I then fortified the remaining dough mixture with oats for texture and brown sugar for sweetness, filled the pie, and sprinkled the streusel on top. It baked up sweet, crunchy, and buttery. Finally, all the elements were in place for a perfect slice of pie. **–Greg Case**

MIXED BERRY STREUSEL PIE SERVES 8 TO 10

While any combination of strawberries, blackberries, blueberries, and raspberries will work here, we recommend using no more than 2 cups of strawberries, which tend to be watery. If your berries aren't sweet enough, you can add an extra ¼ cup of sugar to the filling in step 3.

Crust and Streusel
- 1½ cups all-purpose flour
- 9 graham crackers, broken into rough pieces
- ½ teaspoon salt
- 12 tablespoons (1½ sticks) unsalted butter, cut into ½-inch pieces and softened
- 2 ounces cream cheese, cut into ½-inch pieces
- 1 teaspoon vanilla extract
- ½ cup old-fashioned oats
- ½ cup packed light brown sugar

Filling
- 6 cups mixed fresh berries (see note)
- ¾ cup granulated sugar
- ½ teaspoon grated lemon zest
- 3 tablespoons Minute tapioca

1. For the crust and streusel: Grease 9-inch pie plate. Process flour, graham crackers, and salt in food processor until finely ground. Add butter, cream cheese, and vanilla and pulse until dough forms. Remove 2 cups dough from food processor (leaving remaining dough in bowl of food processor) and turn out onto lightly floured surface. Flatten dough into 6-inch disk and transfer to prepared pie plate. Press dough evenly into pie plate and flute edges (see photos on page 30). Cover dough with plastic and refrigerate until firm, at least 1 hour or up to 24 hours.

2. Add oats and brown sugar to food processor with remaining dough and pulse until mixture resembles coarse meal. Transfer to bowl and use fingers to pinch topping into peanut-sized clumps; cover and refrigerate streusel.

3. For the filling: Adjust oven rack to lowest position and heat oven to 350 degrees. Cook 2 cups berries in saucepan over medium-high heat until juicy, about 3 minutes. Stir in sugar and lemon zest and simmer until thickened, about 5 minutes. Let cool 5 minutes, then gently toss cooked berry mixture, remaining berries, and tapioca in large bowl until combined.

4. Transfer berry mixture to chilled crust. Scatter oat mixture evenly over pie. Bake pie on rimmed baking sheet until fruit is bubbling around edges and streusel is browned and crisp, 45 to 55 minutes. Cool on rack 30 minutes, then refrigerate until set, at least 2 hours or up to 24 hours. Serve.

We streamline the kitchen work for this pie by using the same base mixture for both the crust and the streusel.

Mississippi Mud Brownies

I love the idea of topping brownies with marshmallows and chocolate frosting, but the recipes I've tried are so sweet they make my teeth ache. Is there any way to make this recipe less sugary but still delicious?

–Colleen Preble, Roanoke, Va.

To maximize the chocolate flavor in these moist brownies, we added cocoa powder to the brownie base and kept the amount of sugar in check.

Mississippi mud might not sound like something you'd like to eat, but Mississippi mud brownies definitely are. These moist, fudgy brownies are related to Mississippi mud pie and Mississippi mud cake—desserts that can be defined in countless ways but share one trait: dense gooeyness that approximates the texture of the silt that settles in the Mississippi River delta. The brownie variation is topped with mini marshmallows when the base is set but still quite moist, briefly returned to the oven, and then covered with chocolate frosting when the confection has cooled.

I prepared several existing recipes, but they were more like candy than brownies—and their chocolate flavor was lost under the marshmallows (which turned chewy in the oven) and cloying frosting (which is generally spread much too thick). All these great ingredients were not living up to their potential.

I started with the most promising brownie recipe from my initial testing, which had a decent fudgy texture, thanks to plenty of butter and sugar, but little chocolate flavor. Most mud brownie recipes call for unsweetened chocolate, and adding more helped, but the flavor was still a little flat. I tried introducing chocolate in a couple of other forms: syrup and cocoa powder. The chocolate syrup did add flavor, but it made the brownies too sticky and messy. Cocoa powder lent deeper chocolate flavor and

had no adverse effect on the brownie's texture.

The mini marshmallows caused problems by turning hard and chewy after a stint in the oven. An easy solution was to swap the mini marshmallows out for marshmallow créme. A thin layer of marshmallow créme evenly coated the brownies and kept the sugar quotient in check.

My tasters thought the thick blanket of chocolate frosting was overkill. A colleague suggested that since the brownie layer was so chocolaty, the frosting could now be minimized to just a melted drizzle. I melted a few chocolate chips and added a little oil to keep the chocolate flowing from the spoon I waved back and forth over my brownies. With just a small quantity of chocolate, I was able to create a polished finish to these brownies, which were now decadent but not over-the-top. –Greg Case

MISSISSIPPI MUD BROWNIES MAKES 24

Be careful not to overbake these brownies; they should be moist and fudgy.

Brownies

- 6 ounces unsweetened chocolate, chopped
- 16 tablespoons (2 sticks) unsalted butter
- 1½ cups all-purpose flour
- ⅓ cup Dutch-processed cocoa powder
- ½ teaspoon salt
- 3 cups sugar
- 5 large eggs
- ¾ cup chopped pecans

Topping

- ¾ cup marshmallow créme (see page 31)
- ¼ cup semisweet chocolate chips
- 2 teaspoons vegetable oil

1. For the brownies: Adjust oven rack to middle position and heat oven to 325 degrees. Line 13- by 9-inch baking dish with aluminum foil, allowing excess to overhang edges. Spray foil with cooking spray.

2. Melt chocolate and butter in large heatproof bowl set over medium saucepan filled with ½ inch of barely simmering water (don't let bowl touch water), stirring occasionally, until smooth, 5 to 7 minutes; cool slightly. Combine flour, cocoa, and salt in bowl. Whisk sugar and eggs in separate bowl, then whisk in melted chocolate mixture. Stir flour mixture into

chocolate mixture until no streaks of flour remain. Fold in pecans and scrape batter evenly into prepared pan. Bake until toothpick inserted in center comes out with a few wet crumbs attached, about 35 minutes. Transfer to wire rack.

3. For the topping: Spoon marshmallow créme over hot brownies and let sit until softened, about 1 minute. Meanwhile, microwave chocolate chips and oil in small bowl until smooth, 30 to 60 seconds. Following photos at right, spread marshmallow créme evenly over brownies and then drizzle with chocolate. Cool brownies in pan for at least 2 hours. Using foil overhang, lift brownies from pan and cut into 2-inch squares. Serve. (Brownies can be stored in airtight container at room temperature for 2 days.)

How to MAKE MISSISSIPPI MUD BROWNIES

1. Use a spatula to spread the marshmallow créme evenly over the hot brownies.
2. Drizzle the melted chocolate from a spoon to create a decorative pattern.

Food Shopping

JARRED HOT SALSAS: Are Hot Salsas Better Than Mild?

We don't like jarred salsa. Yes, we know it's now America's favorite condiment, but previous taste tests have been disappointing. Almost no jarred salsas have reached "recommended" status, and none have come close to the allure of homemade fresh salsa. But our prior taste tests have focused on mild and medium varieties. Might jarred hot salsas be more interesting than their timid cousins?

To find out, we sampled nine national brands and were surprised that most tasters didn't need to quell the burn with cold milk or water as they nibbled. Only the Pace, Frontera Habanero, and Green Mountain Gringo salsas were considered sufficiently hot, and none were excessively incendiary.

These hot salsas *were* livelier and better than the mild salsas we've tasted in the past, with eight of the nine receiving passing grades. But even the best—Pace, Frontera, and Newman's Own—were merely good, not great, and didn't approach the quality of fresh salsa. Why? Good salsa relies on the interplay of fresh vegetable flavors and textures. Jarred salsas have the freshness and crispness cooked out of them.

Our first- and third-place salsas, Pace and Newman's Own, respectively, came closest to replicating the fresh flavors and colors of homemade salsa, in part because they had high percentages of tomatoes and vegetables: The test kitchen measured both at around 60 percent solid matter by weight. (By comparison, lowest-rated Chi-Chi's contains just 45 percent solids.) Second-place Frontera Habanero contains an average amount of solids (51 percent) but uses roasted tomatoes to produce a fiery salsa that our tasters appreciated for its complexity.

Our advice: If you're going to buy jarred salsa, go for the hot stuff. The brands we tasted are listed below in order of preference. **–Scott Kathan**

Recommended

1. PACE Hot Chunky Salsa, $2.49 for 16 ounces
Most tasters were impressed by this spicy salsa's "bright tomato and chile" and "vegetal" flavors, as well as its "chunky," "crunchy" texture. There is a "quick hit of tomato flavor, then fire" from the big burn.

2. FRONTERA Hot Habanero Salsa with Roasted Tomatoes and Cilantro, $4.69 for 16 ounces
The roasted tomatoes in this brand were clearly identifiable: "Smoky and complex, yet still has fresh zing," said one taster. "Exciting to eat," said another. This was also the hottest salsa in our tasting.

3. NEWMAN'S OWN All Natural Chunky Hot Salsa, $2.79 for 16 ounces
This salsa is seasoned with plenty of garlic, cilantro, and black pepper. One taster made note of an "herby flavor I like, but that isn't typical for salsa." "Could be hotter" was a common comment.

4. HERDEZ Hot Salsa Casera, $3.49 for 16 ounces
This salsa was the saltiest of the lot—and tasters noticed, saying, "Less of a cooked taste, but too salty." With the shortest ingredient list in our lineup, several tasters praised this brand as "fresh-tasting" and "clean and crisp."

Recommended with Reservations

5. TOSTITOS Hot Chunky Salsa, $2.99 for 15.5 ounces
This "basic and inoffensive," "ordinary" salsa had average scores for heat level, flavor, and texture.

6. OLD EL PASO Thick n'Chunky Hot Salsa, $2.79 for 16 ounces
Many tasters commented on the "cloyingly sweet" nature of this salsa. The "strong tomato flavor" comes from the wealth of tomato chunks—this salsa had more solids (65 percent) than any other in our test.

7. EMERIL'S Kicked Up Chunky Hot Salsa, $3.79 for 16 ounces
"Another bland, tomatoey salsa" that was "not very interesting" but had "decent flavor." "Not hot enough," said one uninspired taster; "tastes like canned tomato puree," said another.

8. GREEN MOUNTAIN GRINGO Hot Salsa, $3.79 for 16 ounces
This brand received some very high marks but also some dreadfully low ones. One thing is not debatable—it has a "fierce," "lingering" heat. The only brand to include tomatillos, which might have polarized tasters.

Not Recommended

9. CHI-CHI'S Hot Fiesta Salsa, $2.79 for 16 ounces
"I wouldn't dip into this twice," said one wincing taster. Many detected "soapy," "musty," "funky," "sour," or "bitter" flavors. "Just all-around bad," and thin, too—this salsa had the lowest solid content of the brands tasted. "Tastes stale, but if you had beer and chips you might not notice," cracked another.

Taste Test Thickeners

We regularly use dry thickeners to adjust the consistency of soups, sauces, pie fillings, and more. Here are the thickeners we stock in the test kitchen, along with notes on how we use them.

Cornstarch

Cornstarch is a common thickener for puddings, sauces, and soups. We also frequently incorporate cornstarch into the breading of fried foods to enhance crispness. When using it to thicken liquids, we first mix the cornstarch with cold or room-temperature water (or some of the liquid to be thickened) to form a slurry. If you skip this step, cornstarch will clump. Cornstarch loses its thickening ability with prolonged exposure to heat.

Flour

When flour is cooked in fat, it forms a roux—the base of many sauces, stews, and gravies. It is important to let the flour cook in the fat—with continual stirring—for a minute or two to eliminate the raw flour flavor. If the roux is cooked until the flour actually browns, the flour adds flavor to dishes (such as gumbo) but loses some thickening power. In any case, liquids added to the roux must be stirred in gradually for smooth incorporation and maximum thickening power.

Gelatin

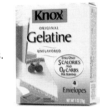

Gelatin is a pure protein commonly derived from cows or pigs. To maximize its jelling power, powdered gelatin is typically allowed to swell (or "bloom") in a small amount of cold liquid for five to 10 minutes before being used. Gelatin is often called on to thicken refrigerator pies and fruit desserts and is the basis for Jell-O products.

Tapioca

Tapioca is a starch extracted from cassava, a tropical root vegetable also known as manioc and yuca. In the test kitchen, we use neutral-flavored tapioca to thicken soups, stews, sauces, and desserts; it does not have to be mixed into a slurry before use. Tapioca can be problematic in lattice-topped pies, as granules can harden and become tough. Quick or Minute tapioca is finely ground and works faster than flakes or pearls.

Pectin

This carbohydrate occurs naturally in various fruits and vegetables (but is most commonly harvested from apples and citrus) and is a standard thickener for jams, jellies, and preserves. Pectin must be used in conjunction with sugar and an acid (usually lemon juice) to reach its full thickening power, and thus is mostly used in jams and jellies.

Equipment Roundup

RATINGS
Good = ★★★
Fair = ★★
Poor = ★

12-INCH NONSTICK SKILLETS: Can You Buy a Good Pan for Under $60?

We've always recommended buying inexpensive nonstick skillets, because with regular use the nonstick coating inevitably scratches, chips off, or becomes ineffective. Why spend big bucks on a pan that will only last a year or two? Since our testing of inexpensive 12-inch nonstick skillets in 2006, several new pans have come on the market. We rounded up 8 models priced under $60 and pitted them against our gold standard, the $135 nonstick skillet from All-Clad, to see how they measure up.

INTO THE FIRE: We sautéed onions and carrots, cooked thin fillets of sole, made omelets, and fried eggs (with no added fat) in each pan. We found that they all did an acceptable job cooking and releasing these foods. There were noticeable differences in sauté speed, but most home cooks know if their cookware runs a bit fast or slow and adjust accordingly; we did not factor sauté speed into our scoring.

REAL SIZE: Each skillet measures 12 inches from lip-to-lip, but we found plenty of differences in the usable cooking space. The actual flat cooking surface ranged from 9 inches (in four pans) to 10½ inches (for the T-Fal pan), which can make all the difference when you need room to sear an extra pork chop or piece of chicken. Volume capacity ranged from the WearEver pan's shade below 13 cups to the Circulon's 19-plus cups. Unless the pans were too heavy for some users (like the KitchenAid and Farberware models), we think bigger is better. Testers also preferred pans with flared sides (which made maneuvering food easier).

GET A GRIP: Our testers preferred handles made entirely of metal, which are securely riveted to the pan and can withstand higher temperatures in the oven. The Farberware, Rachael Ray, and Circulon handles consist of metal and heat-resistant silicone, but their heat resistance is limited to 400 degrees (per manufacturers' recommendations). A skillet handle should also be comfortable, sturdy, and balanced, and it should stay cool during cooking. Finally, all testers disliked the helper handles on the Cuisinart and KitchenAid skillets, which made the pans cumbersome to use on a stove filled with other pots and pans.

STAYING POWER: To gauge durability, we cooked 12-egg frittatas while doing several things that manufacturers specifically forbid in each pan: broiling, cutting with a sharp knife, removing the slices with a metal pie server, and washing with an abrasive metal scrubber. Two pans, the Circulon and WearEver, made it through these tests with only minimal scratching, while the Cuisinart, Rachael Ray, and T-Fal pans were quite beat up.

SUMMING UP: The $135 All-Clad is still the best pan out there, but some of the cheaper pans performed nearly as well. You can buy four of the solid WearEver pans (and get change back) for the cost of the All-Clad. The larger Circulon pan is a good choice for the strong-armed cook. **–Scott Kathan**

Recommended

WEAREVER Premium Hard Anodized 12-Inch Nonstick Skillet
$28.03 at amazon.com
Weight: 2.35 pounds
Cooking Surface: 9 inches
Capacity: 12.8 cups
Handle: ★★★
Durability: ★★★

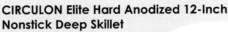

Comments: This light pan was a breeze to maneuver and sautéed at a rapid pace. Testers "liked the feel" of the "comfortable" handle, which stayed cool on the stovetop. We wish the cooking surface and capacity were a tad larger.

CIRCULON Elite Hard Anodized 12-Inch Nonstick Deep Skillet
$59.95 at cooking.com
Weight: 2.95 pounds
Cooking Surface: 9.5 inches
Capacity: 19.2 cups
Handle: ★★
Durability: ★★★

Comments: This "heavy" pan aced the durability test; the signature raised concentric ridges really do seem to improve longevity. One tester was especially impressed by the huge volume: "You could make stock in this." A few testers were put off by its straight sides, which made manipulating food a little tricky.

CALPHALON Simply Calphalon Nonstick 12-Inch Skillet
$54.95 at cooking.com
Weight: 2.85 pounds
Cooking Surface: 9 inches
Capacity: 13.8 cups
Handle: ★★
Durability: ★★★

Comments: This pan performed well, thanks in part to its light weight and the even, gentle slope of the sides. The "nicely angled" handle stayed cool, but many testers disliked the "awkward" molded ridge on the grip. This pan has a relatively small capacity.

CUISINART Chef's Classic Non-Stick Hard Anodized 12-Inch Skillet
$49.95 at cuisinart.com
Weight: 3.15 pounds
Cooking Surface: 9.5 inches
Capacity: 15 cups
Handle: ★★
Durability: ★

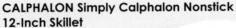

Comments: This heavy pan cooked well, and testers liked the nicely flared lip and overall shape. The handle stayed cool in the kitchen but was considered to be "too thin" for a perfect grip, and the helper handle was deemed "completely unnecessary."

Recommended (continued)

FARBERWARE Millennium Soft Touch Stainless 12-Inch Nonstick Skillet
$39.99 at cooking.com
Weight: 3.95 pounds
Cooking Surface: 10 inches
Capacity: 14.9 cups
Handle: ★★
Durability: ★★

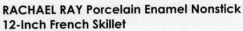

Comments: This "nicely shaped" pan felt "very sturdy" and sautéed very slowly. Some testers praised this pan as "heavy and big," but others thought it too "awkward," "too heavy," and "not well balanced." The handle was comfortable but "not balanced perfectly."

Recommended with Reservations

KITCHENAID Gourmet Distinctions Stainless Steel 12-Inch Nonstick Skillet
$49.95 at cooking.com
Weight: 4.40 pounds
Cooking Surface: 9 inches
Capacity: 14.2 cups
Handle: ★★
Durability: ★★

Comments: As the heaviest pan in our lineup, this drew mixed reviews. Some testers called it "beastly" and "ridiculously" heavy, but a few praised its "hefty" construction. The helper handle just "got in the way." A few testers felt the "cooking surface seems small for such a heavy pan."

RACHAEL RAY Porcelain Enamel Nonstick 12-Inch French Skillet
$29.95 at cooking.com
Weight: 2.15 pounds
Cooking Surface: 9 inches
Capacity: 14.4 cups
Handle: ★★
Durability: ★

Comments: This "wok-like" pan has a "comfortable" metal-and-silicone handle—but the exposed metal closest to the pan got dangerously hot. The cooking surface became significantly scratched up during our abuse tests; even before that, a few testers were asking, "Will it last?"

Not Recommended

T-FAL SOLANO Hard Enamel 12-Inch Sauté Pan
$24.99 at target.com
Weight: 2.40 pounds
Cooking Surface: 10.5 inches
Capacity: 14.6 cups
Handle: ★
Durability: ★

Comments: "Bad ergonomics" and "handles awkwardly" were typical complaints from testers. We liked the large cooking surface, but this pan finished at the bottom of all our other criteria, and its screw-on plastic handle loosened considerably during testing.

Notes from Our Test Kitchen

TIPS, TECHNIQUES, AND TOOLS FOR BETTER COOKING

Kitchen Creations
Quick Chutneys

These chutneys are great with the **Maple Roast Turkey Breast** (page 18).

MANGO-PEACH CHUTNEY

Heat 1 tablespoon vegetable oil in large nonstick skillet over medium-high heat. Cook 2 large mangos, peeled and chopped, until lightly browned, about 5 minutes. Add 1 tablespoon grated fresh ginger and cook 30 seconds. Stir in ½ cup rice vinegar and ½ cup peach preserves and simmer until thickened, about 5 minutes. Stir in ¼ cup minced fresh cilantro and cool to room temperature.

PEAR-WALNUT CHUTNEY

Heat 1 tablespoon vegetable oil in large nonstick skillet over medium-high heat. Cook 3 firm pears, peeled, cored, and chopped, until lightly browned, about 5 minutes. Add 1 minced shallot and cook 30 seconds. Stir in ½ cup red wine vinegar and ½ cup cherry preserves and simmer until thickened, about 5 minutes. Stir in ¼ cup toasted and chopped walnuts and cool to room temperature.

SPICED APPLE-ONION CHUTNEY

Heat 1 tablespoon vegetable oil in large nonstick skillet over medium-high heat. Cook 3 Granny Smith apples, peeled, cored, and chopped, until lightly browned, about 5 minutes. Add ½ cup finely chopped red onion and cook 2 minutes. Stir in ½ cup cider vinegar and ½ cup apple jelly and simmer until thickened, about 5 minutes. Stir in ½ teaspoon ground cinnamon and ¼ teaspoon ground nutmeg and cool to room temperature.

Inside the Test Kitchen
NO FUSS PRESS-IN CRUST

The secrets to a perfect press-in pie crust are distributing the dough properly in the pie plate and creating an attractive fluted edge. Here's how we do it.

1. Use the heel of your hand to press the dough evenly over the bottom and up the sides of the pie plate.
2. Press your thumb between the opposite thumb and forefinger to create a fluted edge.

The Slice Is Right

While developing our recipe for **Shaker Lemon Pie** (page 7), we found that using a knife to evenly cut the lemons into paper-thin slices was a difficult and time-consuming task. We had better results with a mandoline (or V-slicer), which produced perfectly thin slices in no time at all. If you don't have a mandoline, we did find another piece of kitchen equipment that will make the process easier—the freezer. Popping the lemons into the freezer for about 30 minutes firms them up for better hand-slicing, which is best accomplished with a serrated knife.

Sugar Snap Peas

Sugar snap peas are a recent addition to supermarkets, dating back only about 30 years. A cross between shell (aka English) peas and snow peas, this sweet variety has a crisp, edible pod that houses small, juicy peas. Prepare sugar snap peas by snapping off the stem and removing the fibrous string that runs down the length of the pod. Snap peas make a great addition to crudités platters and can also be steamed, blanched, or sautéed very quickly to retain their crunch and bright green color.

Grainy Dijon Mustard

Dijon mustard is made around the world. Although it always starts with brown or black mustard seeds (rather than white or pale yellow), there is some variation among recipes, especially the degree to which the raw seeds are milled. Smooth Dijon consists of very finely milled seeds, and grainy mustards often contain completely unmilled seeds. We use grainy Dijon to add bright flavor and help bind the filling in our **Herbed Roast Pork Tenderloin** (page 10). In our tasting of 11 leading brands of grainy Dijon, Grey Poupon Country Dijon (made in Pennsylvania) came out on top. Tasters appreciated its "pleasantly grainy" texture and "spicy bite."

SPICY BITE
The test kitchen's favorite grainy mustard

How to TRIM BEEF TENDERLOIN

Trimmed (or peeled) beef tenderloins are sold with the outer layer of fat and silver skin already removed. Although trimmed tenderloins are convenient and can save the cook about 20 minutes of trimming time, at roughly $25 per pound, compared with about $14 per pound for untrimmed roasts (which often sell for as little as $9 per pound at warehouse clubs), we prefer to do the work ourselves.

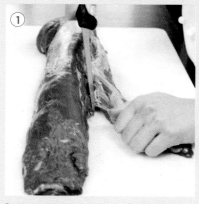

1. Discard the fatty strip (or chain) that runs along the length of the tenderloin.

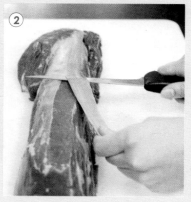

2. Remove the sinewy silver skin (and any other large pieces of fat) by inserting the tip of the knife under it and slicing outward at a slight angle.

Oyster-Flavored Sauce

Our recipe card for **Stir-Fried Beef with Green Beans and Water Chestnuts** uses bottled oyster-flavored sauce, a staple in Chinese cooking. This salty, boldly flavored sauce is made by cooking oysters in water until a white broth is extracted. Then the opaque broth is reduced and caramelized into a thick, dark brown sauce that can be added to savory dishes like steamed vegetables and stir-fries (a little goes a long way, so use it sparingly). The test kitchen favors Lee Kum Kee Premium Oyster Flavored Sauce, which is as rich in history as it is in flavor—the company's founder, Lee Kam Sheung, invented oyster-flavored sauce in 1888.

SALTY KICK
The test kitchen's favorite oyster-flavored sauce

Graham Crackers

The crust of our **Mixed Berry Streusel Pie** (page 26) is a hybrid of a press-in-the-pan crust and a graham cracker crumb crust. It bakes up tender and flaky, with an earthy-sweet graham flavor. But what kind of cracker makes the best crust? After experimenting with the three leading brands, we discovered subtle but distinct differences among them and found that these differences carried over into the crusts made with each kind of cracker. Our favorite was Nabisco Original Graham Crackers: Tasters liked their hardy molasses flavor. The two other brands tested (Nabisco Honey Maid and Keebler Graham Crackers) use honey and yielded crusts that were slightly too sweet.

NABISCO ORIGINAL
The deep flavor of molasses makes these graham crackers the test kitchen's favorite.

How to PIT OLIVES

Kalamata olives, an important ingredient in our **Greek Salad** (page 23), can usually be found pitted in your supermarket's deli department or at the salad bar. If you can't find pitted olives (or if you prefer to buy olives with pits, which are cheaper), here's a quick way to do the work yourself.

Place the olive on the work surface and hold the flat edge of a knife over the olive. Press the blade firmly with your hand to loosen the olive meat from the pit, then remove the pit with your fingers.

Two Ways to Toast Nuts

The process of toasting nuts helps deepen their flavor and enhance their crunchy texture. But what's the best way to toast them? If a recipe calls for a cup or less of nuts (like our recipe for **Glazed Pearl Onions with Grapes and Toasted Almonds**, on page 18), we stick to the stovetop and toast the nuts in a dry skillet set over medium heat until they are golden and fragrant, about 5 minutes. If you're going to toast more than a cup of nuts, we suggest using the oven. Place the nuts in a single layer on a rimmed baking sheet and bake on the middle rack in a 350-degree oven until golden and fragrant, about 10 minutes.

Bulk Pork Sausage

Our recipe for **Biscuits and Sausage Gravy** (page 24) uses bulk pork sausage, which is packaged in a large roll that allows the cook to shape and form the meat as needed. Bulk meat typically contains added fat, salt, and seasoning, all of which help preserve the meat and contribute to tender, flavorful cooked pork sausage. Look for packaged bulk pork sausage in the meat case or the freezer aisle. In a side-by-side comparison, our tasters preferred the "meaty" texture of Jones All Natural bulk sausage to Jimmy Dean.

NATURAL BULK SAUSAGE
More versatile than links

Marshmallow Fluff

When testing marshmallow créme toppings for our **Mississippi Mud Brownies** (page 27), we found that any brand of marshmallow créme will work just fine. For much of our recipe testing we used Marshmallow Fluff, an iconic marshmallow créme (and integral ingredient in the Fluffernutter sandwich) hailing from Lynn, Mass. This regional product is thicker than most other marshmallow crémes, but it still worked great as a topping for these decidedly Southern brownies.

Making the Grade

Pure maple syrup is a key ingredient in our **Maple Roast Turkey Breast** (page 18). In the test kitchen, we prefer grade B maple syrup for its "rich, complex maple flavor." Fancy or grade AA syrup is lighter in color (and usually more expensive), but it doesn't have the rich flavor of the darker grade B. Grade C syrup is so potent and molasses-y that the maple flavor can be lost.

Cooking with Brandy

While many recipes for **Chicken Marengo** (page 17) call for white wine or sherry, we vastly preferred the dish when it was spiked with brandy. Brandy is a generic name for a spirit distilled from wine made from grapes or other fruits. Most brandies fall into one of three categories: grape brandies (such as "plain" brandy—the best choice for Chicken Marengo—and cognac), pomace brandy (such as Italian grappa and French marc, which are made from the pulp left over from the winemaking process), and fruit brandies (such as Calvados, which is made from apples). Like wine, brandies are available in a wide price range; for an inherently flavorful dish like Chicken Marengo, there's no need to use a fine cognac. Any type of inexpensive grape-based brandy will do.

Capicola

One of the star ingredients in our **Salami, Capicola, and Provolone Panini** (page 15) is capicola (sometimes spelled capocolla or capicolla), an aged Italian cold cut made from spiced pork shoulder. Depending on where it is produced in Italy, authentic capicola can be seasoned with paprika, fennel, spicy red pepper flakes, juniper berries, or even wood smoke. Most domestic capicola is heavily seasoned with black pepper. Look for capicola in the deli of your supermarket or specialty food store.

Drying Frozen Spinach

Frozen spinach is a convenient option for our **Creamed Spinach with Parmesan and Prosciutto** (page 23) recipe. If using frozen spinach, it is important to defrost it (either overnight in the refrigerator or in the microwave according to package instructions) and squeeze out excess moisture before cooking. In the test kitchen, we do this by wringing out the thawed spinach in clean kitchen towels until dry.

Feta cheese is an important ingredient in our **Greek Salad** (page 23). Within the European Union, only cheese made in Greece from a mixture of sheep's and goat's milk can be legally called feta, but most of the feta in American supermarkets is made from pasteurized cow's milk that has been curdled, shaped into blocks, sliced (feta is Greek for "slice"), and steeped in a brine. Feta can range from soft to semihard and has a tangy, salty flavor. Feta dries out quickly when removed from its brine, so always store feta in the brine it is packed in (we do not recommend buying precrumbled "dry" feta).

FETA CHEESE
Buy and store in its liquid.

Gadgets & Gear
Meat Pounders

Whether you call them paillards, scaloppini, or cutlets, the basic concept is the same: Take big pieces of meat and pound them out to an even thickness for quicker cooking. While any heavy, blunt object is capable of doing the dirty work (a small skillet does a decent job in a pinch), kitchen stores stock a bounty of pounders designed specifically for meat. Our favorite, the Norpro Meat Pounder ($23.99), packs 26 ounces of walloping power into an ergonomic design, producing perfectly thin cutlets for our **Crispy Breaded Pork Cutlets** (page 22), with a minimum of arm fatigue.

NORPRO MEAT POUNDER
Our favorite pounder

When Things Go Wrong in the Kitchen

READERS SHARE FUNNY STORIES ABOUT COOKING MISHAPS

CARROT CAKE HARD CANDY

One year on my birthday, my children surprised me with my favorite treat, a carrot cake. I was delighted! But when I tried to cut the cake, I got through only about an inch of the fluffy frosting before the knife stopped dead. A sawing 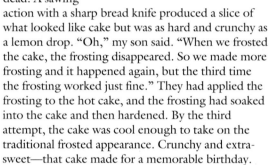 action with a sharp bread knife produced a slice of what looked like cake but was as hard and crunchy as a lemon drop. "Oh," my son said. "When we frosted the cake, the frosting disappeared. So we made more frosting and it happened again, but the third time the frosting worked just fine." They had applied the frosting to the hot cake, and the frosting had soaked into the cake and then hardened. By the third attempt, the cake was cool enough to take on the traditional frosted appearance. Crunchy and extra-sweet—that cake made for a memorable birthday.

Kathleen Bennett Annapolis, Md.

BOUILLON MISTAKE

To help me learn how to cook, my mother gave me the responsibility of cooking the family dinner once a week. One night, I tried a baked spaghetti recipe that called for 1 cup of beef bouillon. I diligently crushed beef bouillon cubes until I had a full cup. When the dish was complete, I had a salty disaster that nothing could fix, but I did learn the very important difference between powdered and reconstituted beef bouillon.

Diana Lee Baraboo, Wis.

BEAR-Y TASTY

Years ago, I would experiment with different recipes when my mother was out at her bridge game. Things would often go terribly wrong—one time, I had to throw out chocolate chip cookies because I had forgotten to add the flour and the cookies just melted into a mess. To hide the evidence and keep myself out of trouble, I ran behind our house and scraped the dough into the woods. Many of my recipes met this fate. I never told my parents, but everyone else in the house knew what I was doing. Some 25 years later, we were all reminiscing and my dad mentioned how he could never figure out what caused so many bears to come to our yard all the time. Well, my sisters, brother, and I started laughing hysterically because we all knew why! My sister blurted out that I had been feeding the bears my kitchen disasters for years!

Valerie Powery Slidell, La.

IT CAN'T BE BUTTER

When I was about 10 years old, I joined the local 4-H club. One of our assigned projects was to bake a simple yellow layer cake and then enter it in a competition at the county fair. I made three practice cakes and was pleased with my progress. When I went to make my final cake, I couldn't find any more butter, so I asked my older sister what I should use instead. She told me to just use the shortening in the can on top of the stove. I baked the cake and proudly carried it to the judges' table. After the competition was over, my high hopes were dashed when I saw the judges had left a white ribbon and a note on my cake asking what I had used to produce its "very strange taste." I went home and took a look at the can of "shortening" on the stove, at which time I discovered I had used a can of hardened leftover bacon grease!

Jean Becker Fort Wayne, Ind.

LEG UP

Years ago, I decided to fry some chicken to take to work for lunch. I fried up the whole package of chicken and headed to the office. A co-worker stopped by my desk to say hello during lunch and saw how very frustrated I was after multiple attempts to eat my fried chicken leg. I told him that I could not understand why the leg was so chewy. He burst out laughing and said, "That's the chicken neck, not the leg!" I thought it was just a funny-looking leg. My co-worker took me out to eat that day for fear that I would starve on my cooking!

Diane Sisk Dunn, N.C.

SAVE THE PRIME RIB

My family and I went to my niece's house for a holiday dinner. Since the niece didn't cook, my husband agreed to make his specialty, prime rib, for all 24 guests. We knew her kitchen was poorly stocked, so we brought everything— knives, salt and pepper, pans, utensils, etc.— with us. As it is somewhat disorienting to cook in someone else's kitchen, my husband was a bit harried as he prepared the meat and made sure the oven was the right temperature. While this was going on, everyone was in the kitchen talking and distracting him. The meat cooked perfectly, and my husband set it on the counter to rest. He started searching for the carving utensils that he swore he brought with him. We looked everywhere before finding them in the pan, under the meat, all nicely roasted! Two knives, a fork, and a vegetable peeler lost their lives that night, all for the sake of a prime rib.

Cheryl Hansen-Mannhalter Via e-mail

CHILI ROCKS

While I was in college, my girlfriend wanted to learn to cook, and I volunteered to be the guinea pig. The first meal she cooked was chili, and when I took a bite, I nearly broke my tooth. While she watched waiting for my response, I took a second bite with the same result. Putting my spoon down, I kindly asked, "So, how did you make this?" After she described the steps she went through, I asked her, "How long did you soak the dried kidney beans for?" She responded, "What do you mean 'soak'?"

Patrick Andrus Annandale, Va.

Send us your funniest kitchen disaster stories. E-mail us by visiting **CooksCountry.com/kitchendisasters**. Or write to us at Kitchen Disasters, Cook's Country, P.O. Box 470739, Brookline, MA 02447. If we publish your story, you'll receive a complimentary one-year subscription to *Cook's Country*.

The Great American Cake
Lane Cake

Emma Rylander Lane of Clayton, Ala., first published the cake recipe that bears her name in 1898, after it had won the blue ribbon at a county fair in Columbus, Ga. Her cake became nationally famous when it was featured in Harper Lee's 1960 novel, *To Kill a Mockingbird*.

To make this cake, you will need:

1¼ cups pecans, toasted and chopped
1 cup sweetened shredded coconut
1 (13-ounce) jar cherry preserves
1 tablespoon bourbon
2 large egg whites
⅔ cup sugar
4 teaspoons water
½ teaspoon cream of tartar
½ teaspoon vanilla extract
3 (8-inch) white cake rounds*

For the filling: Pulse 1 cup pecans, coconut, 1 cup preserves, and bourbon in food processor until coarsely ground.

For the frosting: Combine egg whites, sugar, water, and cream of tartar in large heat-resistant bowl set over medium saucepan filled with ½ inch of barely simmering water (don't let bowl touch water). With hand-held mixer on medium-high speed, beat egg white mixture to stiff peaks, about 4 minutes; remove bowl from heat, add vanilla, and beat egg white mixture until very thick and stiff and cooled to room temperature, about 4 minutes.

To assemble: Spread half of filling on bottom cake layer. Repeat with second cake layer and remaining filling. Top with final cake layer. Spread frosting on sides of cake, leaving top plain. Spread remaining preserves in thin layer over top of cake and decorate with remaining chopped nuts.

* Go to **CooksCountry.com** for our white cake recipe or use your own.

Recipe Index

RC = Recipe Card

Cook's Country

JUNE/JULY 2008

South Carolina Pulled Pork
Easy Grill-to-Oven Method

Best Blueberry Crumble
Juicy Berries, Crunchy Topping

Drunken Steak
Rum Marinade Boosts Flavor

TASTING DIJON
Which Brand Cuts the Mustard?

GREEN BEAN SALAD
Cool, Creamy, and Easy

CREOLE FRIED CHICKEN
Extra-Crisp, Extra-Spicy

SMOKEHOUSE BURGERS
Big Smoke, Big Flavor

ICEBOX OREO CHEESECAKE
Our Secret? White Chocolate!

SWEET POTATO FRIES
Cornstarch Keeps Them Crisp

GLAZED GRILLED CHICKEN
V-Rack Controls Flare-Ups

STICKY BBQ RIBS
Just Use Cola—Lots of It!

STOVETOP GRIDDLES
Which Models Take the Heat?

$4.95 U.S./$6.95 CANADA

Our $1,000 Contest Winner!
Gilda Lester of **Wilmington, N.C.,** won first place in our summer pasta sauce contest with a recipe full of vegetables from her garden. See page 4 for her **Garden of Eden Pasta Sauce.**

Cook's Country

Dear Country Cook,

Not too many years ago, a local farmer, Charlie Bentley, hooked up his team to an old wooden planter, filled it with corn, and planted the lower pasture down below the Haggerty place. I took a few photos since I had never seen one of these machines outside of the farm museum at the annual Washington County Fair. Charlie has his own "museum" in a small room off his kitchen, and he gave me a tour once. The walls are hung with turkey bells, bread kneaders, hand-held potato planters, blue ribbons from the horse draws up in Wells, and plenty of items that I didn't recognize. Our own barn, on the other side of town, holds ice saws, old gut snowshoes, a special chair used for skinning animals, whiffletrees, and ox yokes. (The woman in the photo is using an old-fashioned row weeder. It actually works; I've used one.)

You can look back at the past and conclude that life was rather primitive, but all these implements were once state-of-the-art. The same thing is true about the kitchen. Many of the items I grew up with—ice crushers, citrus squeezers, pie lifters, coconut graters, and the Top-Off screw top opener—are now mysterious antiques. Modern life emphasizes the timesaver over the timeless. Who among us would consider cooking over a wood or coal stove these days? I do now and then, not just because it is fun or an exercise in historical discovery, but also because the old stoves were, in fact, practical.

Country living and country cooking are, in part, about separating the trendy from the classic, knowing what works and sticking with it. Pot roast and mashed potatoes are still with us for good reason. In this magazine, as in all our endeavors, we try to sort out the useful from the useless, the temporary from the eternal. Nothing is out-of-date if it still works.

Christopher Kimball
Founder and Editor, Cook's Country Magazine

Woman Pushing a Harrow Between Rows of Plants in Vegetable Garden, 1940
Photographer: H. Armstrong Roberts/Stringer

JUNE/JULY 2008

Cook's Country

features

Founder and Editor Christopher Kimball
Editorial Director Jack Bishop
Executive Editor Amanda Agee
Deputy Editor Bridget Lancaster
Senior Editors Scott Kathan
Jeremy Sauer
Test Kitchen Director Erin McMurrer
Associate Editors Cali Rich
Diane Unger
Test Cooks Kelley Baker
Meredith Butcher
Greg Case
Assistant Test Cook Lynn Clark
Assistant Test Kitchen Director Matthew Herron

Online Editor Kate Mason
Online Assistant Editor Leaya Lee
Editorial Assistant Meredith Smith
Senior Kitchen Assistant Nadia Domeq
Kitchen Assistants Maria Elena Delgado
Ena Gudiel
Ben Peskin
TV Producer Melissa Baldino
Contributing Editor Eva Katz
Consulting Editor Guy Crosby

Design Director Amy Klee
Art Director, Magazines Julie Bozzo
Senior Designer Christine Vo
Designers Tiffani Beckwith
Jay Layman
Erica Lee
Staff Photographer Daniel J. van Ackere

Production Director Guy Rochford
Traffic & Projects Manager Alice Cummiskey
Production & Imaging Specialist Lauren Pettapiece
Color & Imaging Specialist Andrew Mannone

Vice President New Technology Craig Morrow
Systems Administrator S. Paddi McHugh
IT Business Analyst Doug Sisko
Web Production Coordinator Evan Davis
IT Support Technician Brandon Lynch

Chief Financial Officer Sharyn Chabot
Human Resources Director Adele Shapiro
Controller Mandy Shito
Senior Accountant Aaron Goranson
Staff Accountant Connie Forbes
Accounts Payable Specialist Steven Kasha
Office Manager Danielle Pezely
Receptionist Henrietta Murray

Vice President Marketing David Mack
Fulfillment & Circulation Manager Carrie Horan
Circulation Assistant Elizabeth Dayton
Partnership Marketing Manager Pamela Putprush
Direct Mail Director Adam Perry
Direct Mail Analyst Jenny Leong
Marketing Database Analyst Ariel Gilbert-Knight
Products Director Steven Browall
Product Promotions Director Randi Lawrence
E-Commerce Marketing Director Hugh Buchan
Associate Marketing Manager Laurel Zeidman
Marketing Copywriter David Goldberg
Customer Service Manager Jacqueline Valerio
Customer Service Representatives Julie Gardner
Jillian Nannicelli

Vice President Sales Demee Gambulos
Retail Sales & Marketing Manager Emily Logan
Retail Sales Associate Anthony King
Corporate Marketing Associate Bailey Vatalaro
Publicity Deborah Broide

ON THE COVER PHOTOGRAPHY: Michael Paul, StockFood Munich/Stockfood. ILLUSTRATION: John Burgoyne.
IN THIS ISSUE COLOR FOOD PHOTOGRAPHY: Keller + Keller. STYLING: Mary Jane Sawyer, Marie Piraino. ILLUSTRATION: Lisa Perrett.

Cook's Country magazine (ISSN 1552-1990), number 21, is published bimonthly by Boston Common Press Limited Partnership, 17 Station Street, Brookline, MA 02445. Copyright 2008 Boston Common Press Limited Partnership. Periodicals postage paid at Boston, Mass., and additional mailing offices. POSTMASTER: Send address changes to Cook's Country, P.O. Box 8382, Red Oak, IA 51591-1382. For subscription and gift subscription orders, subscription inquiries, or change-of-address notices, call 800-526-8447 in the U.S. or 515-247-7571 from outside the U.S., or write us at Cook's Country, P.O. Box 8382, Red Oak, IA 51591-1382.
PRINTED IN THE USA

Visit us at www.CooksCountry.com!
Go online for hundreds of recipes, food tastings, and up-to-date equipment reviews. You can get a behind-the-scenes look at our test kitchen, talk to our cooks and editors, enter recipe contests, and share recipes and cooking tips with the *Cook's Country* community.

Kitchen Shortcuts

READERS SHARE CLEVER TIPS FOR EVERYDAY COOKING CHALLENGES

Homemade Vacuum Seal

Whenever I store food items in a plastic bag, I close the mouth of the bag around a drinking straw, suck the air out through the straw, and then withdraw the straw as I finish closing the bag. This trick helps to preserve the food and works like an expensive vacuum-sealing system without the cost.

Barbara Anne Dugger
Knoxville, Tenn.

Pop Out

Recently I found myself in need of my Pyrex baking dish, but it was in the freezer with a casserole in it. So, the next time I made a casserole, I lined the dish with aluminum foil before starting the assembly. When completed, I put the whole thing in the freezer for several hours, removed the frozen casserole from the baking dish and rewrapped it, and put it back into the freezer without the dish. When the time came to bake it, I simply removed the foil and put the casserole into the original dish to thaw. This not only gave me the use of the baking dish during the time the casserole was in the freezer, it also freed up space in the freezer.

SMART TIP!

Joan Vogan
Sugar Land, Texas

Thread 'Em & Forget 'Em

I often throw big barbecues, so when I know I'm going to be grilling several dozen hot dogs in one afternoon, I thread an entire package (eight hot dogs) onto two skewers. I can flip all the hot dogs at once instead of fiddling around with each with my tongs. You can do the same thing to toast the buns.

Courtney Johnson
St. Paul, Minn.

A Sticky Situation

SQUASH HANDS

I recently made a pot of butternut squash soup, and I peeled the raw squash with a vegetable peeler. Anyone who has done this knows that you end up with an orange-tinted coating on your hands from handling the squash. I tried soap and water, a scrubby pad, rubbing alcohol, nail polish remover, etc., but nothing worked to get rid of that orange color. Later in the evening, I was using Scotch tape and realized that the adhesive on the tape easily pulled off the squash residue. I quickly got a roll of packing tape and removed the residue from my poor squash hands.

Laura Burger Charlottesville, Va.

SAFE TRAVELS

While making pumpkin pie, I sometimes spill some of the liquid as I'm carrying the filled pie to the oven. I solved this problem by mixing all the wet ingredients in my blender. Then I pour the liquid into the empty pie shell while it sits on the oven rack. This makes the whole enterprise a lot less messy.

Carol Dudley
Harrold, S.D.

COLOR COORDINATOR

I bought an artist's color chart at a craft store to use for when I want my icing to be a specific color, such as mauve or peach. The chart helps me figure out just how much of the primary colors of food coloring to mix together to get the exact shade I want.

Debra Layne
St. Joseph, Mich.

RECYCLED KERNELS

For flavorful corn bread, I save the unpopped kernels from my popcorn and grind them in a coffee grinder until they are medium-fine in texture. I use them to replace the same amount of plain cornmeal in my corn bread recipe, then mix and bake as usual. The ground kernels give my corn bread a stronger corn flavor.

F. North Ross
Rochester, Ill.

KEEP YOUR FOOD WARM

Whenever I use my gas grill to prepare meat and vegetables for dinner, the vegetables always get done first and turn cold on the serving platter while I wait for the meat to finish. To remedy this, I keep a metal bowl on top of my grill lid, where it heats up during cooking. Once the vegetables are done, I transfer them to the warm bowl and put it back on top of the grill lid. The grill keeps the bowl heated, which keeps my vegetables warm until serving time.

Greg Hockert
Melbourne, Fla.

HOT DOG BUNS FOR BURGERS

Hot dogs and hot dog buns are typically packaged in different quantities (I usually end up with extra buns). When I'm planning to grill burgers and dogs, I grind up an extra bun in the food processor and mix it with a little milk to make a panade for the burgers, which helps to keep them moist. It saves me from using a piece of sandwich bread in the panade, and the extra buns don't go to waste.

Lindsey Thomas
Brooklyn, N.Y.

SANDWICHES FOR A CROWD

I go to a lot of summer picnics with family and friends every year. Instead of wrapping individual sandwiches for everyone (our picnics sometimes have 20 or more people), I build a large sandwich on a whole baguette or ciabatta loaf, wrap it tightly in plastic, and place the supersized sandwich in the bottom of my cooler. Piling sodas and other snacks on top of the sandwich compresses it, making it easier to cut and serve. Plus, the flavors from the sandwich seep into the bread, giving it a great taste.

Allison Montgomery
Duluth, Minn.

NO MORE GUESSING

I found an easy trick for recipes that call for reducing a sauce by half. I take a chopstick and put a rubber band around it (you will have to wrap it a few times). Then I stand the chopstick straight up in the liquid that needs to be reduced, and roll the rubber band down to the surface of the liquid. This marker can be used during the reduction process to gauge how much the sauce has reduced.

David Smith
Murray, Utah

If you'd like to submit a tip, please e-mail us by visiting CooksCountry.com/kitchenshortcuts, or send a letter to Kitchen Shortcuts, Cook's Country, P.O. Box 470739, Brookline, MA 02447. Include your name, address, and phone number. If we publish your tip, you will receive a free one-year subscription to *Cook's Country*.

ANCHOR YOUR RECIPE CARDS

I always knock over the recipe-card holder that holds the card high off my countertop. To solve this problem, I started using a floral arrangement anchor, which has lots of wires that poke up vertically from a heavy base. The recipe card sits securely between the wires and is only an inch up from the countertop, so I don't knock it over!

Lori Cottle
Jerome, Idaho

EASY GREASING

I've found a good tip for when a recipe calls for oil and the baking pan needs to be greased: After measuring and adding the oil to the recipe, I use a sandwich bag to wipe the inside of the measuring cup. I then use this residual oil to grease the pan.

Melissa Jones
Via e-mail

MINIMIZING WASHING

When roasting a chicken, I've found that doing so in my Dutch oven is really handy. It holds a 3- to 4-pound bird perfectly, and the pan's high edges minimize splatter during roasting. After I've removed the cooked chicken to my cutting board, I can make a pan sauce in the Dutch oven from all the drippings. Then, after dinner, I throw the chicken carcass right back into the "dirty" pan to make a stock for soup. This way I roast, make the sauce, and make stock in one pot!

Henry Barton
Cody, Wyo.

QUICKER PICKER UPPER

I used to find myself using my salad spinner several times to get a head of lettuce dry. To reduce the time you spend spinning, rinse your lettuce as you normally would and place it in your spinner. Tear a paper towel in half and place it inside the spinner with the lettuce. When you spin, the towel will absorb the excess water that is unable to make its way to the outside of the spinner.

Bettina Mullin
Pacifica, Calif.

BUTTERY MAPLE SYRUP

We keep our real maple syrup in the refrigerator to prevent spoilage, but cold syrup on pancakes is not very pleasant. So after the pancakes are made, I melt some butter in the hot pan, add the cold maple syrup, and let it boil for 20 or 30 seconds, stirring with a silicone spatula, before pouring it over the waiting pancakes. An added advantage is that the thick sauce sticks to the pancakes and does not run off onto the plate as fast as regular maple syrup.

Bob Johnson
Coupeville, Wash.

NO MORE STICKING

If you need to measure shortening in a recipe that also calls for an egg, break the egg into the measuring cup that you'll use for the shortening. Swirl the egg around and then empty the measuring cup. When you pack the shortening into the measuring cup, the shortening will slide right out—no more scraping to get every last bit.

Shirley Ryle
Big Spring, Texas

SOFTENING BUTTER IN A HURRY

Whenever I need to soften cold butter quickly, rather than use my microwave (which inevitably results in some melted butter), I cut the butter into pieces and place them in a small zipper-lock bag. Then I squeeze out the excess air and seal it tight. Using the warmth from my hands, I knead the butter until soft.

Jillian Pearson
Las Cruces, N.M.

MESH STRAINER

Rather than throwing away the fine-mesh bags used to package shallots or heads of garlic, I found another use for them. I cut the bags into squares so that whenever I need to squeeze lemons for juice, I can cover each lemon half with a cut square and squeeze away. The mesh cover prevents seeds from falling into the bowl of juice.

Sally Howard
Lansing, Mich.

FAIR SHARE

When making lunch for my husband and me, sometimes a whole sandwich is too much for me, but not enough for him. I've solved this lunchtime dilemma by making two identical sandwiches and cutting them both "off center." I take the two smaller pieces and my husband gets the two larger ones. We both end up happy, with the right amount of food!

Fay Abrahamsson
Killingworth, Conn.

Cool Your Cookies

PLAN AHEAD, MOM

My kids love homemade cookies, so when I bake I place two or three cookies into small zipper-lock bags and pop them into the freezer. Then when I make the kids' lunches for school, I take the bags out and put them in their lunchboxes. This helps to keep their lunches cool, and the cookies thaw just in time for lunch!

Lisa Ashton Aston, Pa.

Easy as Pie

I used to get annoyed when I rolled out a pie dough top that was uneven and too small. To solve this problem, I take a piece of parchment paper and trace the large lip of the pie pan with a marker. Then I measure 2 inches from the outside of that circle and roughly draw another circle around it, flip the parchment paper over, dust it with flour, and roll out the dough. The larger circle is a good guide for the size (and shape) I should aim for when rolling out the dough.

Tom Smith Via e-mail

Carrying Case

During the summer, my kids and I eat outside almost every day. I used to pull bottles of condiments from my refrigerator several times in the course of a summer day (and with only two hands, I dropped many bottles). Now I keep a small roasting pan with all the condiments in the refrigerator, so I can just pull out the pan and have everything organized and easy to carry.

Norma Dudley
Conway, N.H.

Makeshift Cooler

When I have to transport ice cream or serve it outside, I take the insert for my ice cream maker out of the freezer. Round containers of ice cream fit inside it perfectly. The insert keeps the ice cream frozen long enough to take to a friend's summer party

Sara Morey
Bellevue, Wash.

COOL TRICK!

Lids Off to You

Whenever I steam vegetables, I find the steamer basket gets hot and is difficult to maneuver out of the pot. Instead, I remove the vegetables by simply scooping them onto the lid, which has a handle I can grip from below. I can then easily transfer the vegetables to a serving dish or divide them among plates.

Buffy Arden
Holyoke, Mass.

Garden Vegetables Take Center Stage in Prize-Winning Sauce

Our $1,000 Grand-Prize Winner!

Gilda Lester
Wilmington, N.C.

The summer garden is the inspiration for our grand-prize winner: "All the vegetables in this sauce grow in my garden," Gilda proudly explains. Our tasters loved the unusual additions of cucumber, scallions, and ground cumin in this fresh tomato and mozzarella sauce. It is important to allow this no-cook sauce to sit at room temperature for an hour so the vegetables can soften slightly and the flavors can marry.

The recipes from our four runners-up are also creative interpretations of classic dishes. Traditional pesto receives an update with Southwestern flavors; a garden-fresh tomato sauce gets spiced up with three varieties of pepper; shrimp scampi is reinvented with a Thai twist; and clams casino moves from the appetizer table to a main course. Congratulations to all of our winners!

GARDEN OF EDEN SAUCE
MAKES ENOUGH TO SAUCE 1 POUND OF PASTA
This fresh, chunky sauce matches nicely with short pastas, such as penne, campanelle, and farfalle.

- 2 large tomatoes, cored and chopped
- 1 yellow or orange bell pepper, seeded and chopped
- 1 medium cucumber, peeled, seeded, and chopped
- 8 ounces fresh mozzarella cheese, cut into ½-inch chunks
- 2 scallions, sliced thin
- ½ cup chopped fresh basil
- 1 teaspoon salt
- ⅓ cup extra-virgin olive oil
- 2 tablespoons red wine vinegar
- 1 garlic clove, minced
- ½ teaspoon ground cumin
- ½ teaspoon dried oregano

1. Combine tomatoes, bell pepper, cucumber, cheese, scallions, basil, and salt in large bowl. Whisk oil, vinegar, garlic, cumin, and oregano in small bowl. Pour oil mixture over tomato mixture and toss to coat. Cover and let stand at room temperature 1 hour.

2. Toss tomato mixture with cooked pasta and reserved pasta cooking water, if necessary (see "Cooking Pasta 101" below). Serve.

Gilda recommends sprinkling the finished dish with freshly grated Parmesan cheese and toasted pine nuts before serving.

Cooking Pasta 101

1. Always use 4 quarts water and 1 tablespoon salt for every pound of pasta.

2. To prevent overcooking, don't rely on the cooking instructions on the pasta box; you may need to shave several minutes off the recommended cooking time for perfectly al dente pasta.

3. Use a liquid measuring cup to retrieve ½ cup of pasta water from the pot just before draining. If your sauced pasta is too dry, this water can be added to achieve the desired consistency.

Sherri McCluskey
Manchester, N.H.

Elaine Fry
St. Charles, Mo.

Marcy Kaiser
Maple Glen, Pa.

Heather Tuccio
Highlands Ranch, Colo.

TRIPLE-CHILE TOMATO SAUCE
MAKES ENOUGH TO SAUCE 1 POUND OF PASTA

Sherri says: "With four very hungry teenagers, I'm always looking for something quick and easy to make. This fresh, flavorful (and spicy!) sauce hits the spot." Although serrano chiles resemble slender jalapeños, they are significantly hotter. If you can't find serranos, jalapeños may be substituted (and you may wish to add an extra chile). Jars of sliced banana peppers can be found in the condiment aisle of most supermarkets, near the pickles. Short pastas, such as penne, fusilli, and campanelle, are best with this slightly chunky sauce.

- ¼ cup extra-virgin olive oil
- 3 jalapeño chiles, seeded and chopped fine
- 3 serrano chiles, seeded and chopped fine (see note)
- 4 garlic cloves, minced
- 6 large tomatoes (about 3 pounds), cored, seeded, and chopped
- 3 tablespoons finely chopped jarred banana peppers, plus 2 tablespoons banana pepper brine (see note)
  Salt and pepper

1. Heat oil in large skillet over medium heat until shimmering. Add chiles and cook until softened, about 3 minutes. Add garlic and cook until fragrant, about 30 seconds. Add tomatoes and simmer, stirring occasionally, until juices are nearly evaporated, about 20 minutes. Off heat, stir in banana peppers and brine and season with salt and pepper.

2. Toss sauce with cooked pasta and reserved pasta cooking water, if necessary (see "Cooking Pasta 101" on page 4). Serve.

THAI SHRIMP SCAMPI SAUCE
MAKES ENOUGH TO SAUCE 1 POUND OF PASTA

Elaine says: "After a trip to Thailand three years ago, I came up with this recipe as a way to re-create some of the dishes that we enjoyed there. You can change it up by using chicken, fish, or scallops instead of shrimp." Red curry paste and chili-garlic sauce are available in the international section of most supermarkets. Light coconut milk can be used, but we prefer the creamy richness of full-fat coconut milk in this recipe. Thin strand pastas, such as vermicelli and capellini, match well with this sauce.

- 1 tablespoon vegetable oil
- 3 garlic cloves, minced
- 2 teaspoons red curry paste (see note)
- 1 (14-ounce) can coconut milk (see note)
- 1 cup low-sodium chicken broth
- 2 tablespoons chili-garlic sauce (see note)
- 1 pound large shrimp, peeled and deveined
- ¼ cup finely chopped fresh cilantro
- 2 tablespoons grated zest and 3 tablespoons juice from 3 limes

1. Heat oil in large skillet over medium-high heat until shimmering. Add garlic and red curry paste and cook until fragrant, about 30 seconds. Whisk in coconut milk, broth, and chili-garlic sauce and cook until slightly thickened, about 15 minutes. Reduce heat to medium, add shrimp, and simmer, covered, until shrimp are just cooked through, about 3 minutes. Off heat, stir in cilantro, lime zest, and lime juice.

2. Toss sauce with cooked pasta and reserved pasta cooking water, if necessary (see "Cooking Pasta 101" on page 4). Serve.

CLAMS CASINO SAUCE
MAKES ENOUGH TO SAUCE 1 POUND OF PASTA

Marcy says: "This recipe is a twist on the classic seafood favorite, and it comes together in a jiffy." Strand pastas, such as linguine or spaghetti, work best here.

- 8 slices bacon, chopped
- 1 small onion, chopped fine
- 2 red bell peppers, seeded and chopped fine
- 4 garlic cloves, minced
- ½ cup white wine
- 1 (8-ounce) bottle clam juice
- 3 (6.5-ounce) cans chopped clams, drained
- 2 tablespoons chopped fresh parsley
- 1 tablespoon chopped fresh oregano
- 3 tablespoons unsalted butter
  Salt and pepper
- 1 cup toasted bread crumbs (see page 30)

1. Cook bacon in large skillet over medium heat until crisp, about 8 minutes. Transfer to paper towel–lined plate. Pour off all but 1 tablespoon bacon fat. Cook onion and peppers in bacon fat until softened, about 5 minutes. Stir in garlic and cook until fragrant, about 30 seconds. Add wine and simmer, scraping up any browned bits, until reduced by half, about 3 minutes. Stir in clam juice and bring to boil. Simmer until slightly thickened, about 6 minutes. Stir in clams and cook until heated through, about 2 minutes. Off heat, whisk in parsley, oregano, and butter. Season with salt and pepper.

2. Toss sauce with cooked pasta and reserved pasta cooking water, if necessary (see "Cooking Pasta 101" on page 4). Sprinkle with bread crumbs and crisp bacon. Serve.

GREEN CHILE-CILANTRO PESTO SAUCE
MAKES ENOUGH TO SAUCE 1 POUND OF PASTA

Heather says: "My family loves green chiles, and since I've always made a mean basil pesto, one day I decided to spice up my pesto a bit. This recipe was an instant favorite." We prefer the heat of canned hot green chiles, but medium or mild chiles will also work here. Toast the pine nuts in a dry skillet over medium heat, shaking often, until lightly browned, about 3 minutes. This pesto works with both strand pastas and tubular shapes.

- 2 cups lightly packed fresh cilantro
- 1½ cups grated Parmesan cheese
- 4 (4-ounce) cans chopped green chiles (see note)
- 1 jalapeño chile, seeded and chopped fine
- ¼ cup toasted pine nuts (see note)
- 2 garlic cloves, peeled
- ½ cup olive oil
  Salt and pepper

1. Puree cilantro, cheese, green chiles, jalapeño, pine nuts, and garlic in food processor until smooth, scraping down sides as necessary. With processor running, add oil in steady stream until emulsified. Season with salt and pepper.

2. Toss pesto with cooked pasta and reserved pasta cooking water, if necessary (see "Cooking Pasta 101" on page 4). Serve.

We want your best holiday cookie recipes for an upcoming contest. Please submit entries by July 31, 2008. Send us your recipes by visiting **CooksCountry.com/emailus** or write to us at Recipe Contest, Cook's Country, P.O. Box 470739, Brookline, MA 02447. Include your name, address, and daytime phone number and tell us what makes your recipe special. The grand-prize winner will receive $1,000. All entries become the property of *Cook's Country*. Go to **CooksCountry.com** for more information on this and other contests.

Ask Cook's Country

WE'LL ANSWER ANY QUESTION YOU THROW AT US!

REUSING OIL

I hate to throw away frying oil after using it just once. Can it be reused?

Trudy Gorman Woodstock, Ga.

We fried up several batches of french fries, donuts, chicken, and fish, reusing the oil each time, and found that the oil used to fry the potatoes or donuts could be reused if strained—but only two or three times before the oil contributed chemical flavors to the food. In contrast, no amount of straining rid the oil used to fry fish or chicken of distracting flavors. Our conclusion: Oil used to fry starchy foods can be reused, but oil used to fry proteins should be discarded.

To recycle oil that has been used to fry starchy foods, cool the oil completely and then slowly strain it through cheesecloth or a coffee filter into a sealable receptacle (such as the bottle it came in). The straining removes food particles that could flavor the oil or burn during the next use. The strained oil should last several months in a cool, dark place. If your recycled oil starts to smell rancid, throw it out and use fresh oil.

SAVE THAT OIL
Oil used to fry starchy foods can be reused up to three times if properly cooled, strained, and stored.

INSTANT COFFEE VERSUS ESPRESSO

Can instant coffee and instant espresso be used interchangeably in recipes?

Theresa Tardella Dingmans Ferry, Pa.

Many recipes call for instant coffee or the more concentrated instant espresso to be added to chocolate desserts; besides lending coffee flavor, these products help to accentuate chocolate flavor. Instant coffee is made by freeze-drying liquid brewed coffee, while instant espresso is typically just dark-roasted coffee beans that are very finely ground.

We made batches of mocha icing, devil's food cupcakes, and tiramisù with equal amounts of each product to see how they compared. Even the most discerning tasters didn't notice a difference between the two in the tiramisù, but a few tasters did think the cupcakes made with the

CREATED EQUAL?
Both products do a fine job of accentuating chocolate flavor in desserts, but when a recipe requires a big coffee punch, use the instant espresso.

instant espresso were slightly more "rich and chocolaty" than those made with the instant coffee; the coffee version, however, was perfectly acceptable. The major disparity between the two showed up in the mocha icing—the one preparation we tested that relied on the instant products for pronounced coffee flavor. The instant coffee version was flat and bitter, but the espresso icing had a rich, "deep, roasted" coffee flavor. We found that you can use either instant coffee or instant espresso to bring out chocolate flavor in desserts, but when a recipe requires a pronounced coffee flavor, stick to the instant espresso.

FREEZING ZEST

Can lemon zest be frozen for later use?

Joe Cacka Canby, Ore.

To see how lemon zest would fare in the freezer, we grated fresh zest from a dozen lemons and froze it in a zipper-lock freezer bag. After one month, we whipped up batches of lemon sugar cookies and lemony pasta with the frozen and fresh zest. While a few tasters noticed a slightly "brighter" flavor in the cookies and pasta made with fresh zest, they agreed that the convenience of freezing was worth the minimal decline in flavor. Also, we found that premeasuring and bundling teaspoons of zest in plastic wrap before placing the zest in a freezer bag provides extra protection from freezer burn, as well as easy access to conveniently premeasured portions. Lime and orange zest froze equally well.

CLEANING CUTTING BOARDS

Whenever I chop potent ingredients like onions on my plastic cutting board, I can't get the smell off the board until it's been run through a dishwasher. Is there a quicker way to clean a stinky plastic cutting board?

Sara Shaddix California, Md.

In a perfect world, every kitchen would be stocked with several cutting boards, each used for a specific task (one for onions and garlic, one for fruit, and so forth), but in many kitchens one board is used for everything. Our research uncovered several methods that claimed to rid cutting boards of strong odors, so we headed into the test kitchen to see if they really worked. The cleaning lineup included a diluted bleach solution, a paste of 1 tablespoon baking soda and 1 teaspoon water, white vinegar, lemon juice, and mouthwash (yes, we'll try anything).

After chopping a half-dozen onions and smearing plenty of cut garlic on five plastic cutting boards, we cleared the boards of debris, applied each cleaning solution, and let the boards sit for 5 minutes. We then washed each with the same amount of hot

water and dish soap and dried them thoroughly. We then sliced apples on the "clean" boards to see which cleaning product, if any, eradicated the persistent onion and garlic flavors. The best performance went to the baking soda paste, which left an odor-free board and "pristine-tasting" apples. The bleach solution and vinegar boards also produced acceptable apples (with only the slightest hint of allium odor), while the lemon juice left a "slight oniony aroma and flavor." The worst was the mouthwash board, on which apples not only tasted oniony and garlicky but also predictably "minty."

FOOLPROOF PHYLLO

I love phyllo-based recipes, but every time I try to use frozen phyllo it tears and dries out. Can you help?

LeAnn Skrzynski Kanab, Utah

Tissue-thin phyllo dough lends its crisp, flaky, and delicate texture to dishes like strudel and baklava, but it can go from soft and pliable to brittle in minutes if left exposed to air. Since phyllo is most commonly sold frozen in sheets, our first challenge was to pinpoint the best technique for defrosting it. We compared room-temperature, refrigerator, and microwave defrosting methods and found that an overnight thaw in the refrigerator, coupled with a 30-minute room-temperature rest on the counter before using, produced the least amount of tearing.

Many recipes recommend covering the thawed dough with a damp towel, but we found that method made the top sheet soggy and difficult to work with. We prefer to sandwich the dough between sheets of parchment paper and then cover it with a damp towel to keep the phyllo just moist enough to be properly pliable.

Once phyllo is ready to work with, most sources call for frequently brushing the dough with butter to prevent it from drying out, but too much butter results in oversaturated sheets that tear easily. Using a spray bottle with a 3-to-1 ratio of melted butter to vegetable oil (to keep the butter fluid), mist the dough just enough to keep it from becoming brittle and to reduce tearing. As for cutting the phyllo, we found that scissors are far easier to use than a knife.

TEST KITCHEN FAVORITE
Athens Phyllo is available nationwide and is consistently easy to use.

To ask us a cooking question, visit **CooksCountry.com/emailus.** You can also write to Ask Cook's Country, P.O. Box 470739, Brookline, MA 02447. See if you can stump us!

These once-popular cinnamon-sugar cookies are now mostly forgotten—maybe because the dough is so hard to work with. Could we resurrect these crisp cookies, but make them easy?

Plenty of butter and sugar make these old-fashioned cookies especially crisp.

Thin, crisp, buttery, and dusted with a "sandy" coating of cinnamon sugar, sand tarts were once one of America's favorite cookies. I found recipes in the *Presbyterian Cook Book* and *Buckeye Cookery*, both from the 1870s, and in *Fannie Farmer Original 1896 Boston Cooking-School Cook Book*. It is believed that these cookies were brought to American shores by German immigrants in the 19th century, and they became especially popular in Maryland, Pennsylvania, and Ohio.

Twentieth-century recipes aimed for flat, crisp cookies dusted with cinnamon sugar and decorated with a ring of sliced almonds (which makes the cookies look a bit like sand dollars). Almost every recipe I uncovered gave similar instructions: cream copious amounts of butter and sugar, add two whole eggs and flour, refrigerate the dough to make it more workable, then roll it ultra-thin, stamp out the cookies, adorn them with cinnamon sugar and almonds, and bake until crisp. But when I prepared these recipes, I began to see why this cookie has fallen out of favor. Even when chilled overnight, the rich, sticky dough was almost impossible to roll out to the desired thickness without tearing.

Considering other shaping options, I tried a trick the test kitchen often employs for sugar cookies—rolling the dough into balls, rolling the balls in a potent cinnamon-sugar mixture, and then flattening them with the bottom of a measuring cup before baking. This method was easy and worked great, provided I coated the bottom of the measuring cup with cooking spray to minimize sticking.

But the cookies were doming, and I wanted them to be flat and crisp. Eliminating one of the egg whites reduced the doming slightly, but not enough. Turning to my mixing method, I realized I was beating a lot of air into the dough as I creamed the butter and sugar—air that was giving the cookies extra height. Switching from a stand mixer to a food processor helped minimize air in the dough, but my real breakthrough happened when I switched the order in which I added ingredients to the processor. Cutting the butter into the sugar and flour (a technique known as reverse creaming) incorporated almost no air and finally produced the flat, crisp cookies I was after. In the end, a modern appliance helped make this recipe relevant for a new generation of American bakers. **–Cali Rich**

SAND TARTS
MAKES ABOUT 3 DOZEN COOKIES
Both sliced natural almonds and blanched slices work well here.

- 2 cups all-purpose flour
- 1¾ cups sugar
- ¾ teaspoon salt
- 16 tablespoons (2 sticks) unsalted butter, softened
- 1 large egg plus 1 egg yolk
- 1½ teaspoons ground cinnamon
- ¼ cup sliced almonds (see note)

1. Adjust oven racks to upper-middle and lower-middle positions and heat oven to 350 degrees. Line two baking sheets with parchment paper. Process flour, 1½ cups sugar, and salt in food processor until combined. Add butter, 1 tablespoon at a time, and pulse until just incorporated. Add egg and yolk and pulse until soft dough forms.

2. Wrap dough in plastic wrap and flatten into 1-inch-thick disk. Transfer to freezer until firm, about 15 minutes. Combine cinnamon and remaining sugar in small bowl. Break disk of chilled dough into two pieces and return one piece to freezer. Working with floured hands, take 1½ tablespoons chilled dough and roll into 1½-inch ball, and then roll in cinnamon-sugar mixture to coat. Place balls 3 inches apart on prepared baking sheets. Press balls into 2½-inch disks with greased measuring cup, sprinkle with cinnamon sugar, and garnish with almonds.

3. Bake cookies until edges are lightly browned, 10 to 12 minutes, switching and rotating sheets halfway through baking. Let cool 5 minutes on sheets, then transfer to wire rack and cool completely. Repeat rolling, shaping, and garnishing process with remaining dough and bake as directed. Serve. (Cookies can be stored in airtight container at room temperature for 3 days.)

How to
SHAPE A SAND TART
Rolling and cutting out this soft, butter-rich dough can be frustratingly messy. Pressing the individual balls of dough into thin cookies works much better. Here's how we do it.

1. Roll each 1½-inch ball of dough in cinnamon sugar.
2. Spray the bottom of a measuring cup with cooking spray, then use it to press each ball into a 2½-inch disk.
3. Sprinkle each cookie with more cinnamon sugar before decorating with sliced almonds and baking.

The big flavors of ham, bacon, and chiles perfectly complement the creamy, rich black beans in this satisfying chili.

Kitchen Know-How
TWO TYPES OF BEANS ARE BETTER THAN ONE

For the right combination of creamy whole beans and a thick, rich chili, we stirred a mashed can of black beans into a base of slow-cooked dried black beans.

CANNED BEANS
We take advantage of canned beans' soft texture by mashing one can's worth and adding it to thicken the chili at the end of cooking.

DRIED BEANS
Perfectly cooked dried beans become full flavored and creamy in our hearty black bean chili.

Black beans go into the slow cooker with an army of flavorful ingredients. So why is the result so often a dull, muddied mess?

Packed with bold ingredients like garlic, chiles, tomatoes, ham hocks, and plenty of chili powder, Latin-inspired black bean chili should explode on the palate. Slow-cooker recipes vary in their choice of dried versus canned beans, but all the recipes I tried had three things in common: a muddied gray color, improperly cooked (either too hard or too soft) beans, and a distinct lack of flavor. Was a slow-cooker black bean chili with creamy, tender beans, a fresh appearance, and big flavor even possible?

I knew that if I was going to build assertive flavor, I'd have to get the cooking going before the ingredients hit the slow cooker. I began by sautéing chopped onion, bell pepper, garlic, and jalapeños in a Dutch oven to build a savory, spicy base for the chili. Starting this sauté with bacon fat, rather than the usual oil, helped amplify the meaty richness of the chili. The test kitchen likes to sauté spices to intensify their flavor, so when the vegetables were tender I added ¼ cup of chili powder, plus cumin and oregano, and let the spices bloom in the hot pan. Tasters preferred the brighter flavor and chunky texture of canned diced tomatoes to sauce or puree.

Ham hocks traditionally add flavor to the broth and a few shreds of meat to the chili, but my tasters wanted enough meat to chew on. After testing several kinds of pork, we opted for the salty richness a small smoked ham lent to the chili as it cooked; removing the ham at the end of cooking and chopping it provided plenty of meat.

Canned beans were much too soft and yielded a mushy chili, but dried beans added to the cooker at the outset were still too hard by the time the chili was done. Soaking the beans overnight helped them cook faster, but I wanted a quicker way. I tried a shortcut by boiling the beans for five minutes and then letting them sit off heat for an hour. This helped jump-start the cooking, but I discovered an even simpler solution—simmering the beans right in the Dutch oven with the sautéed vegetables for 15 minutes before transferring the contents to the slow cooker. A full 10 cups of liquid was essential to evenly cook the 1½ pounds of beans I was using, and my tasters preferred the clean flavor of a combination of water and chicken stock.

To thicken this brothy chili (slow cookers don't allow for much evaporation), I tried mashing some of the cooked beans right in the slow cooker; this was messy and gave the chili a muddy look again. Remembering the mushy canned beans from my initial testing, I mashed the contents of one can and stirred it into the finished chili to thicken it. For a fresher, more appealing texture and appearance, I also found it better to add the tomatoes and half the sautéed vegetables at the very end of cooking. This black bean chili was worth the wait. **–Bridget Lancaster**

SLOW-COOKER BLACK BEAN CHILI SERVES 6 TO 8

We prefer the sweetness of red bell peppers here, but any bell pepper will work. Small boneless hams are available in the meat case at most supermarkets. The aluminum foil in step 2 helps keep all the beans under the surface of the liquid, where they cook evenly. We like to serve this chili with sour cream, shredded Monterey Jack cheese, and fresh cilantro.

8	slices bacon, chopped
2	onions, chopped fine
2	red bell peppers, seeded and chopped (see note)
2	jalapeño chiles, seeded and chopped fine
¼	cup chili powder
2	tablespoons ground cumin
2	tablespoons dried oregano
5	garlic cloves, minced
6	cups water
4	cups low-sodium chicken broth
	Salt
1½	pounds dried black beans, rinsed and picked over
1	(1- to 1½-pound) boneless ham (see note)
1	(28-ounce) can diced tomatoes
1	(16-ounce) can black beans, drained and rinsed
3	tablespoons juice from 2 limes

1. Cook bacon in Dutch oven over medium heat until crisp, about 8 minutes. Transfer bacon to paper towel–lined plate. Cook onions, peppers, and jalapeños in bacon fat until softened, about 8 minutes. Transfer half of sautéed vegetables to medium bowl, wrap with plastic, and reserve in refrigerator. Add chili powder, cumin, and oregano to pot with remaining vegetables and cook until deeply fragrant, about 2 minutes. Add garlic and cook until fragrant, about 30 seconds. Stir in water, broth, 2 teaspoons salt, dried beans, ham, and crisp bacon. Bring to boil and let simmer 15 minutes.

2. Transfer bean mixture to slow cooker and arrange piece of aluminum foil on surface of liquid. Cover and cook on low until beans are tender, 7 to 9 hours (or cook on high 4 to 6 hours).

3. Remove lid, discard foil, and transfer ham to cutting board. Stir tomatoes into slow cooker, cover, and cook on high until tomatoes soften, about 20 minutes. Meanwhile, transfer canned beans to bowl and mash with potato masher until rough paste forms. Chop (or shred) ham into bite-sized pieces. Stir mashed beans, ham, lime juice, and refrigerated vegetables into slow cooker. Cook, covered, until heated through, about 5 minutes. Season with salt. Serve.

Recipe Makeover LEMON POUND CAKE

How do you cut the fat and preserve lemon pound cake's trademark buttery richness and moist, super-fine crumb? We tried everything from diet lemon soda to low-fat pudding mix to find out.

And the Numbers...
All nutritional information is for one serving (one 1-inch slice).

TRADITIONAL LEMON POUND CAKE
CALORIES: **500**
FAT: 28g
SATURATED FAT: 16g

COOK'S COUNTRY LOW-FAT LEMON POUND CAKE
CALORIES: **310**
FAT: 11g
SATURATED FAT: 6g

The best lemon pound cakes are dense and moist, with a rich, buttery flavor complemented by a refreshing hit of lemon. But how do you create a low-fat version of a recipe in which each slice of cake typically weighs in at 500 calories and 28 grams of fat? Determined to find out, I rounded up a dozen recipes for low-fat lemon pound cake and headed into the test kitchen to bake them off.

Tasters were not impressed with these "healthy" lemon pound cakes. Recipes that used unconventional ingredients such as diet lemon-lime soda, nonfat lemon yogurt, and low-fat lemon pudding all baked up gummy and dense, with artificial lemon flavor. A few recipes tried to cheat the nutritional numbers by halving both the ingredients and the size of the cake—an unacceptable tack in our book. I wanted a full-sized low-fat lemon pound cake that delivered the richness and bright lemon flavor of the real thing.

Weeks of testing variables in dozens of pound cakes led to two fundamental discoveries. First, as long as the pound cakes were moist, dense, and packed with fresh, clean lemon flavor, my tasters didn't mind a dramatic reduction in butter. Second, and perhaps more obvious, nothing produces clean, bright lemon flavor as well as fresh lemon juice and zest. The rest of my recipe development was mostly about tweaking ratios in our favorite full-fat lemon pound cake, seeing where I could make cuts and where I couldn't.

Our full-fat recipe calls for a whopping 16 tablespoons of butter. After much trial and error, I found that just 6 tablespoons of butter delivered sufficient flavor, but the cake was a little tough and became unpalatably dry after a few hours. Replacing the full-fat sour cream in our original recipe with low-fat sour cream worked so well that I could use a bit more sour cream, which improved the texture of the cake, but not enough.

Trading some of the butter for vegetable oil made the cake a little moister, but the oil also made the cake denser and less domed. I found that substituting a single tablespoon of shortening for a tablespoon of the butter not only made the cake much more tender and moist but also helped with the structure, making a cake that domed nicely and held its shape.

I couldn't eliminate the eggs entirely (egg substitutes baked up dry and cottony), but using three, instead of the customary five, gave my cake plenty of structure and richness. Reducing the flour by ¼ cup sacrificed a tiny bit of height but helped keep this lower-fat cake moist. The sugar remained constant at a full cup—any less and the cake wasn't sweet enough, and artificial sweeteners contributed off-flavors.

Since I had cut so many calories, I was even able to add a very thin layer of frosty lemon glaze for a final blast of fresh citrus flavor. **–Meredith Butcher**

LOW-FAT LEMON POUND CAKE
SERVES 8
This recipe was developed in the test kitchen's favorite loaf pan, the Williams-Sonoma Nonstick Goldtouch Loaf Pan ($19), which measures 8½ by 4½ inches; the cake may not dome properly if baked in a larger pan.

Cake
- 1½ cups all-purpose flour
- ½ teaspoon baking powder
- ¼ teaspoon salt
- ⅓ cup low-fat sour cream
- 1½ tablespoons grated zest and 1½ tablespoons juice from 2 lemons
- ½ teaspoon vanilla extract
- 1 cup granulated sugar
- 5 tablespoons unsalted butter, softened
- 1 tablespoon vegetable shortening
- 3 large eggs, at room temperature, beaten

Glaze
- 2 tablespoons confectioners' sugar
- 1 teaspoon lemon juice

1. For the cake: Adjust oven rack to middle position and heat oven to 300 degrees. Grease and flour 8½- by 4½-inch loaf pan. Combine flour, baking powder, and salt in bowl. Whisk sour cream, lemon juice, and vanilla in second bowl.

2. Stir granulated sugar and lemon zest in large bowl until zest is evenly distributed. With electric mixer on medium-high speed, beat butter, shortening, and sugar mixture until light and fluffy, about 2 minutes. Add eggs in three additions and mix until combined (mixture will begin to look curdled). Reduce speed to low and add flour mixture in three additions, alternating with two additions of sour cream mixture. Mix on low until smooth, about 30 seconds. Use rubber spatula to give batter final stir.

3. Scrape batter into prepared pan and smooth top. Tap pan against counter several times. Bake until cake is golden brown and toothpick inserted in center comes out with a few crumbs attached, 60 to 70 minutes. Cool cake in pan for 10 minutes, then turn out onto rack. Cool completely, about 2 hours.

4. For the glaze: Whisk confectioners' sugar and lemon juice in bowl until smooth. Brush glaze over cake. Let glaze set for 10 minutes before serving. (Cake can be wrapped tightly in plastic and stored at room temperature for 5 days.)

This tender cake becomes moister when it sits on the counter, tightly wrapped in plastic, for a day or two.

Shopping SOUR CREAM

Supermarkets typically stock three alternatives to full-fat sour cream: low-fat, light, and reduced-fat varieties. We found that the leanest of the three—low-fat sour cream—worked perfectly well to add moisture and tang to our Low-Fat Lemon Pound Cake.

LOW-FAT SOUR CREAM
Contains only 2 grams of fat per serving.

South Carolina Pulled Pork

Slathering a tangy mustard-based sauce on barbecued pork is a good start, but this regional specialty demands more than just a last-minute dose of bold flavors.

Secrets to
SMOKY, MUSTARDY PULLED PORK

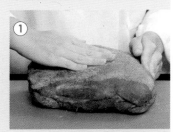

1. Rubbing the pork shoulder with a spice mixture that's heavy on the dry mustard ensures a mustardy crust.
2. Slow-cooking the pork with a packet of smoking wood chips gives the meat plenty of smoke flavor.
3. Brushing the pork with the mustardy barbecue sauce before it goes into the oven produces a second hit of mustard flavor.
4. Tossing the shredded pork with the remaining sauce gives the meat a final layer of mustard flavor.

Throughout America's barbecue belt, pit masters balance the meaty richness of pulled pork by dressing it with all manner of barbecue sauces. On a recent trip to South Carolina—to Columbia and Charleston, to be exact—I discovered a mustard-based sauce I'd never tried before. Nicknamed Carolina gold, this sauce originated in the state's Midlands area, with historians at the South Carolina Barbecue Association attributing it to the mustard-loving German immigrants who settled there in the 1700s. This savory, tangy barbecue was so good I ate it for lunch, mid-afternoon snack, and dinner for two days running on my trip.

I was determined to re-create this barbecue in the test kitchen. After years of testing, we've perfected an easy cooking technique in which boneless pork shoulder is rubbed with dry spices (to help it develop a flavorful crust) before being slow-smoked on the grill for a few hours. Once the pork has taken on plenty of smoke, it's wrapped in foil and allowed to gently steam to tenderness in the convenience of a low oven before being shredded and sauced.

There was one issue to address before I figured out how to re-create the sauce—the spice rub. Since Carolina gold is largely about mustard, I wanted to see if I could use the rub to jump-start the mustard flavor. To a basic mixture of sugar, salt, pepper, paprika, and cayenne I added a tablespoon of dry mustard. Tasters approved, but wanted more mustard. It took a full 3 tablespoons to get a solid mustard punch from the rub, which cooked into a rich,

spicy crust on the grill.

Most authentic South Carolina sauces use regular yellow mustard, but I wanted to see if another kind of mustard might work better. Tasters found the German, English, Dijon, and powdered mustards too overpowering. Spicy brown mustard was deemed "murky tasting," while honey mustard introduced an unwelcome extra sweetener to the mix. Yellow mustard was the clear favorite, with tasters praising its bright, assertive tang.

For the other sauce ingredients, tasters preferred rich brown sugar to white sugar, honey, or molasses. White vinegar lent an uncomplicated sharpness that augmented the tang of the mustard. While most barbecue sauces are built on a foundation of onions and garlic, I was surprised that tasters thought their distinct flavors competed with the mustard, and preferred the sauce without them. A little savory Worcestershire and hot sauce rounded out the flavors of the sauce, which tasters

preferred uncooked to preserve its brash flavors.

The sauce was such a success that I wondered if I could get additional mileage from it. I increased the proportions to yield a little extra, which I then spread on the meat before putting it into the oven. The spicy, smoky crust was good to begin with, but now it was even thicker, tangier, and more deeply flavored. This barbecued pulled pork really struck gold—Carolina gold!

–Adam Ried

Our pulled pork is flavored with a no-cook mustard sauce and piled high on hamburger buns.

SOUTH CAROLINA PULLED PORK SERVES 8

Pork shoulder—usually labeled pork butt or Boston butt—comes both boneless (usually wrapped in netting) or on the bone. The boneless roast is easier to handle, but either one can be used in this recipe. If your roast weighs more than 5 pounds, plan on an extra 30 to 60 minutes of oven time. The cooked meat can be shredded or chopped.

Spice Rub and Pork

- 3 tablespoons dry mustard
- 1½ tablespoons light brown sugar
- 2 tablespoons salt
- 2 teaspoons pepper
- 2 teaspoons paprika
- ¼ teaspoon cayenne pepper
- 1 (4- to 5-pound) boneless pork shoulder roast (see note)
- 4 cups wood chips, soaked for 15 minutes

Mustard Barbecue Sauce

- ½ cup yellow mustard
- ½ cup packed light brown sugar
- ¼ cup white vinegar
- 2 tablespoons Worcestershire sauce
- 1 tablespoon hot sauce
- 1 teaspoon salt
- 1 teaspoon pepper

1. For the spice rub and pork: Combine dry mustard, brown sugar, salt, pepper, paprika, and cayenne, breaking up any lumps. Dry pork with paper towels and rub all over with spice mixture. (Roast can be wrapped tightly in plastic and refrigerated for 24 hours.)

2. Seal wood chips in foil packet and cut vent holes in top. Open bottom vent on grill. Light 50 coals; when covered with fine gray ash, pour in pile on one side of grill. Arrange foil packet directly on coals. Set cooking grate in place and heat, covered, with lid vent open halfway until wood chips begin to smoke heavily, about 5 minutes. (For gas grill, place foil packet directly on primary burner. Heat all burners on high, covered, until wood chips begin to smoke heavily, about 15 minutes. Leave primary burner on high and shut other burner[s] off.) Scrape and oil cooking grate. Place pork on cool side of grill and barbecue, covered, until exterior of pork has a rosy crust, about 2 hours.

3. For the mustard barbecue sauce and to finish: Adjust oven rack to lower-middle position and heat oven to 325 degrees. Whisk mustard, brown sugar, vinegar, Worcestershire, hot sauce, salt, and pepper in bowl until smooth. Transfer pork to roasting pan and brush ½ cup sauce over meat. Cover roasting pan tightly with foil and bake until fork inserted into pork can be removed with no resistance, 2 to 3 hours. Remove from oven and rest, still wrapped in foil, for 30 minutes. Unwrap pork and, when cool enough to handle, pull meat into thin shreds, discarding fat, if desired. Toss pork with remaining sauce. Serve.

The American Table:
The Barbecue Sauces of the Carolinas

The most austere of the Carolina barbecue sauces is found in eastern North Carolina, where shredded or chopped whole hog is typically dressed with a pungent sauce of vinegar, sugar, and black pepper. Central and western North Carolina barbecue sauces introduce the tomato, often in the form of ketchup, to this basic sauce. And when you travel down to South Carolina, you'll find barbecue sauces (like the one in this recipe) based on yellow mustard. They're all delicious with pork barbecue.

On the Side: Apple-Cabbage Slaw

What are the secrets to tender cabbage, crunchy apples, and the sweet and spicy dressing that brings them together in this Southern barbecue side dish?

wasn't clinging to the cabbage and apples.

A few recipes that I'd found in my research heated the dressing and poured it—still hot—over the slaw. I tried this and was pleased to discover that the cabbage and apples more readily absorbed a hot dressing—especially if the slaw was allowed to sit for an hour before serving. Piled on top of a pulled pork sandwich or standing on its own, this tangy slaw will be a fresh new addition to any summer barbecue.

–Meredith Butcher

TANGY APPLE-CABBAGE SLAW SERVES 6 TO 8

In step 1, the salted, rinsed, and dried cabbage can be refrigerated in a zipper-lock bag for up to 24 hours. To prep the apples, cut the cored apples into ¼-inch-thick planks, then stack the planks and cut them into thin matchsticks.

- 1 medium head green cabbage, cored and chopped fine
- 2 teaspoons salt
- 2 Granny Smith apples, cored and cut into thin matchsticks (see note)
- 2 scallions, sliced thin
- 6 tablespoons vegetable oil
- ½ cup cider vinegar
- ½ cup sugar
- 1 tablespoon Dijon mustard
- ¼ teaspoon red pepper flakes

In most parts of the country, "coleslaw" means one thing: shredded cabbage dressed with mayonnaise. But south of the Mason-Dixon line, you'll find lighter, brighter slaws enlivened by dressing made with oil and vinegar. One such Southern slaw features chopped cabbage studded with refreshing bits of apple. The sweet, tangy, and spicy flavors of the dressing make this slaw the perfect accompaniment to barbecue. But as early test recipes revealed, this simple side dish can go awry, especially if the apples are mushy, the cabbage is chewy, and the dressing just pools up at the bottom of the bowl.

I started by chopping a single head of green cabbage, which gave me a sturdier foundation than preshredded coleslaw mix. Since cabbage is a relatively watery vegetable, the test kitchen typically salts cut cabbage to draw out excess moisture before dressing it;

this prevents the moisture from releasing into the dressing later, thus diluting it.

I tested several varieties of apple, but most were mushy and bland when dressed. The one exception was Granny Smith, which tasters loved for its sturdy crunch and tart bite. Grating the apples negated their crunch, but cutting them into matchsticks meant they could be easily mixed with the cabbage while retaining their crispness.

The classic dressing calls for sugar, white vinegar, vegetable oil, and various seasonings. I tried swapping out the granulated sugar for more flavorful brown sugar, maple syrup, and honey, but in the end nothing beat the clean sweetness of regular sugar. Cider vinegar contributed a fruity flavor lacking in the traditional white vinegar. Red pepper flakes, chopped scallions, and mustard added some punch. The dressing tasted pretty good, but it

1. Toss cabbage and salt in colander set over medium bowl. Let stand until wilted, about 1 hour. Rinse cabbage under cold water, drain, dry well with paper towels, and transfer to large bowl. Add apples and scallions and toss to combine.

2. Bring oil, vinegar, sugar, mustard, and pepper flakes to boil in saucepan over medium heat. Pour over cabbage mixture and toss to coat. Cover with plastic and refrigerate at least 1 hour or up to 1 day. Serve.

Drunken Steak

At a recent barbecue, I was served steak with a sweet, deep caramelized flavor and a bold kick that was hard to identify. I was told it was "drunken steak." Was someone pulling my leg?

–Donald White, Sun Valley, Idaho

Secrets to PERFECT DRUNKEN STEAK

Here are three important techniques to ensure boldly flavored steak every time.

1. Using a sharp knife, lightly score both sides of the steak at 1½-inch intervals. This allows the marinade to flavor the meat more deeply.
2. The marinade's sugar content (from the alcohol and the brown sugar) encourages a crust to form on the steak when it's grilled.
3. Patting the steak dry before cooking further facilitates the formation of the crust.

I too was skeptical when I started researching drunken steak, but I quickly discovered that it's a popular preparation at some restaurants and with backyard barbecuers. The idea is to get the steaks "drunk" in a potent marinade of bold ingredients—typically soy sauce, Worcestershire, garlic, and, of course, liquor—before grilling. Aside from the lively kick of the liquor, the sugar in the alcohol is supposed to help create a thick, caramelized crust on the steaks. I grilled up several recipes and loved the great crust on the steaks, but the flavor was all over the place. Some steaks were barely "drunk" at all, while others had us picking a designated driver. Was there a happy medium?

Contrary to popular belief, the test kitchen has found that marinades don't actually tenderize meat, but they do add flavor. Steaks can be divided into two categories: tight-grained (like sirloin and strip) and loose-grained (like flank, flap meat, and skirt). Side-by-side tests determined that loose-grained steaks are able to absorb more marinade, and thus more flavor, than their tight-grained brethren. I chose flank steak, the most readily available loose-grained steak, for this recipe.

The first thing I discovered about working with liquor in this recipe is that strongly flavored varieties, like dark rum and brandy, were heavy and overpowering. Tasters preferred the cleaner flavors of light rum and tequila. Using light rum in my working recipe, I found that soy sauce was a must in the marinade, not just for intense flavor but also because its salt content helps to keep meat moist during cooking. Worcestershire sauce, on the other hand, was rejected by tasters for being too "steak sauce-y." Garlic, ginger, and a little brown sugar rounded out the flavors.

The steak was much improved, but tasters still wanted more flavor inside the meat. Marinating it longer than four hours caused the alcohol in the marinade to "cook" the steak, turning the meat an unappetizing gray color. Pricking the steak with a fork before marinating helped to carry flavor into the meat, but it also turned the interior that awful gray color. I found a compromise by scoring the surface of the meat; these shallow slashes allowed the marinade to penetrate a short distance into the steak without compromising the interior color or texture.

Although the steak was nicely seasoned and sported a robust charred crust, the flavor of the marinade was being dulled a little during cooking. To refresh the flavor of the marinade—and leave no doubt that this steak was indeed "drunken"—I drizzled a little reserved marinade over the rested and sliced cooked steak just before serving. We're not pulling your leg—this "drunken" steak is one of the best steaks we've ever eaten.

–Lynn Clark

DRUNKEN STEAK
SERVES 4

Other thin steaks with a loose grain, such as skirt or steak tips, can be substituted for the flank steak. Avoid dark or spiced rum here—its intense flavor will overwhelm the steak. If using a gas grill, grill the steak covered for maximum heat output.

- 1 cup light rum
- ½ cup soy sauce
- 1 tablespoon dark brown sugar
- 1 tablespoon grated fresh ginger
- 1 garlic clove, minced
- 1 scallion, minced
- 1 flank steak (about 1½ pounds), scored according to photo 1 at left

1. Whisk rum, soy sauce, sugar, ginger, and garlic in bowl until sugar dissolves. Transfer ¼ cup rum mixture to small bowl and stir in scallion; set aside. Place remaining marinade and steak in gallon-size zipper-lock bag. Press air out of bag, seal, and refrigerate for at least 1 hour or up to 4 hours.

2. Remove steak from bag, pat dry with paper towels, and discard marinade. Grill steak over hot fire until well browned and cooked to desired doneness, 4 to 7 minutes per side.

3. Transfer steak to cutting board, tent with foil, and let rest 5 minutes. Slice thinly on bias and against grain. Drizzle with reserved rum mixture. Serve.

MARGARITA-STYLE DRUNKEN STEAK

In step 1, whisk ¾ cup tequila, ¼ cup triple sec, 1 tablespoon granulated sugar, ½ teaspoon ground cumin, and ¼ teaspoon cayenne pepper in bowl until sugar dissolves. Transfer ¼ cup tequila mixture to small bowl and stir in 1 tablespoon finely chopped fresh cilantro; set aside. Place remaining marinade and steak in gallon-size zipper-lock bag. Press air out of bag, seal, and refrigerate for at least 1 hour or up to 4 hours. Proceed with recipe as directed.

Pouring reserved marinade over the sliced steak provides a lively finishing kick of flavor.

Brightening Up Wilted Spinach Salad

A bacon dressing tastes great, but is there a fresher approach to this typically rich, heavy salad?

A classic wilted spinach salad starts with a warm dressing of bacon fat, red wine vinegar, and mustard, which is tossed with sturdy curly spinach, crumbled bacon, red onion, and hard-cooked egg until the spinach has wilted. While this recipe is tried and true, it's also pretty hearty fare. I wanted to create a quartet of lighter wilted spinach salads better suited to warm weather.

The first things to go were the bacon and the bacon fat. I built these salads on a base of fruity extra-virgin olive oil instead. For brighter flavor, I lost the sharp vinegar in favor of fresh citrus juices. The citrus was such a hit that I tried adding grated zest to the dressings; tasters loved the flavor, but not the texture of the little bits of zest. Since I was already heating the oil to make the dressing, I realized that adding strips of zest to the hot oil was the perfect way to infuse the dressing with more citrus flavor. Then I could pull the pan off-heat, remove the strips of zest, pour in the citrus juice, and add the spinach to wilt in the hot dressing.

I wanted to add bulk to these salads, but not so much as to weigh down the spinach. Chopped fresh fruit and vegetables (apples, radishes, mangos, avocados, and strawberries) were a good place to start, but they didn't add quite enough substance. Soft crumbled cheeses—feta, blue, and goat—beefed up the salads without bogging them down,

especially when I quickly froze the cheeses to prevent them from melting in the heat of the dressing. A handful of crunchy nuts added a welcome textural contrast to each of these refreshing summer salads.

–Cali Rich

LEMON, FETA, AND PISTACHIO SPINACH SALAD SERVES 4 TO 6

We recommend unsalted pistachios in this salad.

- ⅓ **cup crumbled feta cheese**
- ¼ **cup extra-virgin olive oil**
- 1 **(3-inch) strip zest and 1½ tablespoons juice from 1 lemon**
- 1 **shallot, minced**
- 2 **teaspoons sugar**
- 1 **(10-ounce) bag curly-leaf spinach, stemmed and torn into bite-sized pieces**
- 6 **radishes, sliced thin**
- ¼ **cup chopped toasted pistachios (see note)**
  Salt and pepper

1. Place cheese on plate and freeze until slightly firm, about 15 minutes.
2. Heat oil, zest, shallot, and sugar in Dutch oven over medium-low heat until shallot is softened, about 5 minutes. Remove pot from heat, discard zest, stir in lemon juice, and add spinach; cover, allowing spinach to steam until just beginning to wilt, about 30 seconds.
3. Transfer steamed spinach and hot dressing to large bowl. Add radishes, pistachios, and cheese and toss to combine. Season with salt and pepper. Serve.

Test Kitchen Tip SELECTING SPINACH

We found that tender flat-leaf and baby spinach become soft and mushy when tossed with hot dressing. The heartier curly-leaf variety, wilted until just tender, can stand up to the heat just fine.

CURLY SPINACH
Wilted winner

Each of these lively salads is built on a foundation of citrus juice, a creamy element, and toasted nuts.

ORANGE, BLUE CHEESE, AND PECAN SPINACH SALAD SERVES 4 TO 6

A sweet red apple, such as Gala, works best here.

- ⅓ **cup crumbled blue cheese**
- ¼ **cup extra-virgin olive oil**
- 1 **(3-inch) strip zest and 1 tablespoon juice from 1 orange**
- 1 **shallot, minced**
- 2 **teaspoons sugar**
- 1 **teaspoon white vinegar**
- 1 **(10-ounce) bag curly-leaf spinach, stemmed and torn into bite-sized pieces**
- ½ **apple, cored and chopped (see note)**
- ¼ **cup chopped toasted pecans**
  Salt and pepper

1. Place cheese on plate and freeze until slightly firm, about 15 minutes.
2. Heat oil, zest, shallot, and sugar in Dutch oven over medium-low heat until shallot is softened, about 5 minutes. Remove pot from heat, discard zest, stir in vinegar and orange juice, and add spinach; cover, allowing spinach to steam until just beginning to wilt, about 30 seconds.
3. Transfer steamed spinach and hot dressing to large bowl. Add apple, pecans, and cheese and toss to combine. Season with salt and pepper. Serve.

STRAWBERRY, GOAT CHEESE, AND ALMOND SPINACH SALAD SERVES 4 TO 6

We recommend slightly sweet Ruby Red grapefruit for this salad.

- ⅓ **cup crumbled goat cheese**
- ¼ **cup extra-virgin olive oil**
- 1 **(3-inch) strip zest and 1½ tablespoons juice from 1 grapefruit (see note)**
- 1 **shallot, minced**
- 2 **teaspoons sugar**
- 1 **(10-ounce) bag curly-leaf spinach, stemmed and torn into bite-sized pieces**
- 6 **strawberries, hulled and sliced thin**
- ¼ **cup toasted sliced almonds**
  Salt and pepper

1. Place cheese on plate and freeze until slightly firm, about 15 minutes.
2. Heat oil, zest, shallot, and sugar in Dutch oven over medium-low heat until shallot is softened, about 5 minutes. Remove pot from heat, discard zest, stir in grapefruit juice, and add spinach; cover, allowing spinach to steam until just beginning to wilt, about 30 seconds.
3. Transfer steamed spinach and hot dressing to large bowl. Add strawberries, almonds, and cheese and toss to combine. Season with salt and pepper. Serve.

MANGO, AVOCADO, AND PEANUT SPINACH SALAD SERVES 4 TO 6

When perfectly ripe, an avocado will give slightly to gentle pressure.

- ¼ **cup extra-virgin olive oil**
- 1 **(3-inch) strip zest and 1½ tablespoons juice from 1 lime**
- 1 **shallot, minced**
- 2 **teaspoons sugar**
- 1 **(10-ounce) bag curly-leaf spinach, stemmed and torn into bite-sized pieces**
- ½ **large mango, pitted, peeled, and chopped**
- ½ **ripe avocado, pitted, skinned, and chopped**
- ¼ **cup chopped salted roasted peanuts**
- 1 **tablespoon finely chopped fresh cilantro**
  Salt and pepper

1. Heat oil, zest, shallot, and sugar in Dutch oven over medium-low heat until shallot is softened, about 5 minutes. Remove pot from heat, discard zest, stir in lime juice, and add spinach; cover, allowing spinach to steam until just beginning to wilt, about 30 seconds.
2. Transfer steamed spinach and hot dressing to large bowl. Add mango, avocado, peanuts, and cilantro and toss to combine. Season with salt and pepper. Serve.

Creole Fried Chicken

I love the crisp, spicy fried chicken I've tasted in New Orleans. I've tried to make it at home, but the store-bought Creole seasoning makes the coating too salty, and no flavor gets inside the meat. –Rebecca Dyess Roper, via e-mail

Secrets to
BOLDLY FLAVORED
CREOLE FRIED CHICKEN

1. Soaking the chicken in a brine of salt, sugar, Worcestershire, Tabasco, and garlic powder seasons the chicken down to the bone.
2. After brining, a sprinkling of homemade Creole seasoning adds flavor without the dusty saltiness of packaged spice blends.
3. The homemade Creole seasoning lends a potent punch to the chicken's flour coating.
4. For a peppery finish, sprinkle the hot chicken with more of the homemade Creole seasoning when it comes out of the oil.

Creole fried chicken should be deeply seasoned with the complex, lively heat of black, white, and cayenne pepper. The crust should be crisp and well seasoned, the meat juicy and bursting with flavor.

Most of the recipes for this style of fried chicken are variations on basic Southern fried chicken: The chicken is dipped in buttermilk, dredged in flour, and fried. Creole flavor is introduced by adding store-bought Creole seasoning to the flour. But supermarket Creole seasoning typically tastes of dusty, stale paprika and is far too salty. I made my own Creole seasoning based on its three traditional ground peppers: three parts black, two parts cayenne, and one part white. Garlic and onion powders, dried oregano, and celery salt rounded out my homemade mixture, which had more flavor and kick than packaged varieties.

I added my Creole seasoning to the flour and fried up a batch of chicken. Although it was an improvement on the recipes I'd tried, this chicken didn't have enough flavor to earn the Creole tag. I turned to brining, a method in which raw meat is soaked in salted and seasoned water to add flavor and moisture. Most of the flavors in my Creole seasoning didn't carry through in the brine, so I decided to experiment with other ways to flavor it. After some trial and error, I settled on a brine made with water, salt, sugar, garlic powder, Worcestershire sauce (for "meaty" background flavor), and Tabasco sauce (for heat).

Moving on to the frying, I found that the chicken pieces actually sat on the bottom of the pan (which is hotter than the oil) when shallow-frying; this caused the spices in the flour to burn and turn bitter, necessitating a switch to deep-frying (in which the chicken bobs in a deeper pool of oil) for the best-tasting crust. My tasters determined that any sort of egg or dairy—including buttermilk—in the coating muted the spice flavor, so I simply moved the chicken directly from the brine to the seasoned flour. But the quick dip in seasoned flour wasn't giving me the substantially crisp crust I was seeking.

As I stood over a batch of floured chicken waiting for the oil to heat up, I noticed that after about 10 minutes, the flour coating became wet and doughy. On a lark, I rolled these chicken pieces in the seasoned flour again and carefully lowered them into the oil. The extra coating rewarded me with the crisp, substantial, craggy crust I had hoped for.

One of the hallmarks of Creole cooking is its layering of flavors, and though my chicken was now much better than the recipes I'd started with, it still lacked depth. Instead of just using my homemade Creole seasoning in the flour, I decided to try sprinkling it on the raw chicken, and then also on the cooked chicken when it was just out of the oil (the hot crust would readily absorb flavors). My tasters were pleasantly surprised at how many layers of flavor this simple three-step approach brought to the dish. –Diane Unger

With its richly seasoned meat and crispy exterior, this fried chicken is anything but timid.

CREOLE FRIED CHICKEN
SERVES 4 TO 6

To ensure even cooking, breasts should be halved crosswise and leg quarters separated into thighs and drumsticks. We prefer the brash flavor of Louisiana's own Tabasco sauce in this recipe, but any hot sauce will work. In step 1, do not soak the chicken longer than 8 hours, or it will be too salty.

Seasoned Brine
- 1 quart water
- ¼ cup sugar
- 3 tablespoons Worcestershire sauce
- 3 tablespoons Tabasco sauce
- 2 tablespoons salt
- 1 tablespoon garlic powder
- 4 pounds bone-in, skin-on chicken pieces (see note)

Three Peppers of Creole Cooking

We tested several brands of packaged Creole seasoning and found they were too salty and tasted of stale herbs. We had much better results by making our own Creole seasoning based on the three peppers of Creole cuisine, each of which lends a distinctive spicy bite.

BLACK PEPPER   **WHITE PEPPER**   **CAYENNE PEPPER**

Creole Coating

- 1 tablespoon black pepper
- 1 tablespoon dried oregano
- 1 tablespoon garlic powder
- 2 teaspoons onion powder
- 2 teaspoons cayenne pepper
- 1 teaspoon white pepper
- 1 teaspoon celery salt
- 2 cups all-purpose flour
- 3 quarts peanut oil or vegetable shortening

1. For the seasoned brine: Whisk water, sugar, Worcestershire, Tabasco, salt, and garlic powder in large bowl until sugar and salt dissolve. Add chicken and refrigerate, covered, for 1 hour or up to 8 hours.

2. For the Creole coating: Combine black pepper, oregano, garlic powder, onion powder, cayenne, white pepper, and celery salt in large bowl; reserve 4 tablespoons spice mixture. Add flour to bowl with remaining spice mixture and stir to combine.

3. Remove chicken from refrigerator and pour off brine. Sprinkle chicken with 3 tablespoons reserved spice mixture and toss to coat. Working in batches of two, dredge chicken pieces in flour mixture. Shake excess flour from chicken and transfer to wire rack. (Do not discard flour mixture.)

4. Adjust oven rack to middle position and heat oven to 200 degrees. Heat oil in large Dutch oven over medium-high heat to 375 degrees. Return chicken pieces to flour mixture and turn to coat. Fry half of chicken, adjusting burner as necessary to maintain oil temperature between 300 and 325 degrees, until deep golden brown and white meat registers 160 degrees (or dark meat registers 175 degrees), 10 to 12 minutes. Transfer chicken to clean wire rack set over baking sheet and place in oven. Bring oil back to 375 degrees and repeat with remaining chicken. Sprinkle crisp chicken with remaining tablespoon spice mixture. Serve.

Ranch Potato Salad

Bottled ranch dressing sounds like a quick way to dress up potato salad, but many versions are surprisingly dull and bland.

With its tangy, creamy base and big hits of garlic, dill, and cilantro, it's easy to see why cooks employ ranch dressing for dishes other than green salad. Perhaps the most popular of these dishes is ranch potato salad, in which a bottle of the creamy dressing is poured over boiled potatoes.

I wasn't surprised that my tasters rejected recipes calling for just bottled salad dressing and boiled potatoes. Bottled ranch dressing is too sweet and bland. To make this recipe worthwhile, I'd have to whip up a quick ranch dressing myself. Potatoes generally require a heavy hand with seasonings, and this dish was no exception. My homemade dressing would have to pack a real wallop.

But before I worked on the dressing, I wanted to settle on the best potato for the job. After sampling salads made from Idaho, Yukon Gold, and red-skinned potatoes, tasters preferred the firmness of the red potatoes. I found that peeling the potatoes allowed them to absorb more dressing.

Most recipes for home-made ranch dressing start with a base of buttermilk and mayonnaise, and that's where I began. I doubled the amount of cilantro used in most recipes and found that fresh garlic and scallions added welcome bite. The dill proved to be a little trickier—too little fresh dill and my tasters didn't know it was there, but too much made the dressing taste overpow-eringly grassy. The solution was to use dried dill; just ⅛ teaspoon lent the perfect amount of dill flavor. Dijon mustard and vinegar provided acidity and bite, and for a sweet counterpoint I added chopped roasted red peppers.

This dressing tasted great on the spoon, but tossing it with hot boiled potatoes cooked the buttermilk and mayo into a decidedly unappealing slimy texture. Tossing the dressing with cooled potatoes resulted in a salad that still tasted a little flat because the dressing wasn't permeating the spuds. To better season the potatoes, I pulled the Dijon and some of the vinegar out of the dressing and tossed them with the hot potatoes. After the seasoned potatoes cooled, I mixed them with the flavorful dressing. Even tasters who claimed not to like ranch dressing came back for seconds of this potato salad. **–Diane Unger**

RANCH POTATO SALAD
SERVES 6 TO 8

We prefer white wine vinegar here, but white and cider vinegars are acceptable substitutes.

- 3 pounds red potatoes, peeled and cut into ¾-inch chunks
  Salt
- ¾ cup mayonnaise
- ½ cup buttermilk
- ¼ cup white wine vinegar
- ¼ cup drained jarred roasted red peppers, chopped fine
- 3 tablespoons finely chopped fresh cilantro
- 3 scallions, chopped fine
- 1 garlic clove, minced
- ⅛ teaspoon dried dill
- 2 teaspoons pepper
- 2 tablespoons Dijon mustard

1. Bring potatoes, 1 tablespoon salt, and enough water to cover by 1 inch to boil in large pot over high heat. Reduce heat to medium and simmer until potatoes are just tender, about 10 minutes. While potatoes simmer, whisk mayonnaise, buttermilk, 2 tablespoons vinegar, red peppers, cilantro, scallions, garlic, dill, 1 teaspoon salt, and pepper in large bowl.

2. Drain potatoes, then spread in even layer on rimmed baking sheet. Whisk mustard and remaining vinegar in small bowl. Drizzle mustard mixture over hot potatoes and toss until evenly coated. Refrigerate until cooled, about 30 minutes.

3. Transfer cooled potatoes to bowl with mayonnaise mixture and toss to combine. Cover and refrigerate until well chilled, about 30 minutes. Serve. (Salad can be refrigerated in airtight container for 2 days.)

Garlic, dill, and cilantro—a potent trio—are the signature seasonings of ranch dressing.

The American Table:
Hidden Valley Ranch Dressing

The original ranch dressing first became popular at the Hidden Valley Guest Ranch near Santa Barbara, Calif., in the late 1950s. It began as a dried herb mixture that Steve Henson, the ranch's owner, combined with mayonnaise and buttermilk to make a creamy, tangy dressing for the ranch's house salad. It was so well received that guests clamored for bottles of the dressing to take home with them. Recognizing the potential of his concoction, Henson began marketing the mix in small packets, and the rest is culinary history. The little packets are still around, but the dressing really took off in 1983 when manufacturers figured out how to bottle this creamy dressing in a shelf-stable format.

I'm Looking for a Recipe

READERS HELP READERS FIND RECIPES

We've Got Mail

Dozens of readers sent us recipes in response to the request for Aggression Cookies in our December/January 2008 issue. We really liked the recipe sent by Susan Hammond (right). Go to **CooksCountry.com** and click on **Looking for a Recipe** to find hundreds of recipes submitted by readers who responded to other recipe requests in previous issues of *Cook's Country*.

AGGRESSION COOKIES   Susan Hammond Cambridge, Mass.

MAKES 4 DOZEN

"Aggression Cookies are great to make with small children because all the ingredients are safe to eat raw. I first made this recipe as a college student around 1980. Since that time, I've also made variations with raisins and peanut butter." Either light or dark brown sugar will work in this recipe.

3	cups old-fashioned oats	Dump all ingredients into a large bowl. Mash it! Knead it! Pound it! The longer and harder you mix it, the better it tastes. Roll dough into small balls about the size of whole walnuts. Space dough balls about 3 inches apart on a parchment-lined cookie sheet and bake at 350 degrees until edges brown, 10 to 12 minutes. Repeat with remaining dough.
1½	cups packed brown sugar	
1½	cups all-purpose flour	
24	tablespoons (3 sticks) unsalted butter, softened	
1½	teaspoons baking powder	

Orange Chocolate-Chip Pound Cake

I've lost my favorite recipe! It was an orange-iced chocolate-chip pound cake that was made with shredded chocolate in the batter. Just after baking, the cake was poked with a cake tester and coated with an icing of orange juice and confectioners' sugar. Once the icing soaked in, several more coatings were poured on until the orange flavor permeated the cake. Oh, it was so good! If anyone has this recipe, I'd love to have a copy. Thanks ever so much.

Julie Reiner
Via e-mail

Hinkley Bakery Molasses Cookies

My grandmother was the cookie baker at Hinkley Bakery in Jackson, Mich., in the 1940s. Two kinds of cookies were sold there, one of which was a mild and soft molasses cookie that had a pecan half in the center. I have tried several recipes and, maybe it is me, but they are either too molasses-y or too hard. My grandmother is no longer with us, but I hope the recipe hasn't gone on to the great recipe heaven with her.

Sandra DiMascio
Akron, Ohio

Ginger Creams

My grandmother used to make Ginger Creams, which were basically a dense gingerbread with a delicious frosting made in a skillet using butter, powdered sugar, and walnuts. I can't remember the other ingredients or the method, and no one else in my family recalls this fabulous dessert.

Donna Green
Via e-mail

Stouffer's Sherry Chiffon Pie

About 30 years ago, my mom and I went to Stouffer's Restaurant in Pittsburgh and had a piece of sherry chiffon pie. It was delightful. Does anyone have the recipe? I have been looking for it for years.

Deb Swartz
Pasadena, Calif.

French Fort Salad Dressing

I lost a salad dressing recipe called French Fort that was similar to Russian dressing. It included ketchup, vinegar, and dry mustard, but I can't remember the rest. Can anyone help?

Barb Elich
Via e-mail

Lemon Sponge Pie

My mother used to make a dessert called Lemon Sponge Pie. She would blind-bake a crust, pour in a lemony batter, and return it to the oven to finish baking. The completed pie had a unique cakelike texture on top.

Ann Gillespie
Via e-mail

Raisin Pie

Raisin pie used to be commonly available in Iowa. It is a simple two-crust pie with a raisin filling. While sour cream raisin pie has gained popularity, I think plain raisin pie is much better. I've tried to make it a couple of times, but it never seems to come out right. I think part of the magic involves letting the filling soak into the bottom crust a little, but this is difficult if you precook and prethicken the filling, both of which seem necessary to me. Does anyone have a recipe?

Rex Newman
Brooklyn Center, Minn.

Chicken Madrid

We were served a dish called Chicken Madrid at the home of my husband's co-worker in 1967. (I remember the year because it was his first Air Force assignment.) I didn't think to ask for the recipe then and wish I had. Over the years, I've looked for it in many cookbooks and searched online, with no luck.

Carol Self
Beavercreek, Ohio

Praline Muffins

My mother-in-law used to make praline muffins in a large cast-iron muffin pan. I know that she used brown sugar, butter, cream, pecans, and probably a little flour. The muffins were squat and had a moist, sticky bottom. I don't know if you have ever heard of this recipe, but I would love to have one similar to hers.

Rachel Williams
Via e-mail

Health Bread

My mom used to make a recipe she called Health Bread. I remember that it contained wheat germ, blackstrap molasses, and brewer's yeast, but I can't remember the rest. It was dark, dense, and incredibly delicious. Has anyone heard of this recipe?

Conni Tobin
Kansas City, Mo.

Nutty Star Pockets

I'm looking for a cookie recipe that came from the German mother of a dear friend of mine. You make sugar cookie dough, roll it out, and then cut it using a star-shaped cookie cutter. After mixing chopped nuts, such as pecans or walnuts, with butter and brown sugar, a teaspoon of this nut mixture is placed in the center of each star. Next, the arms of the star are pulled around the nut mixture and pinched together at the ends, making an exposed pocket. The cookies were absolutely delicious, but I lost the recipe some 30 years ago and have never found another that compares. Ring any bells with anyone?

Viviane McKay
Hazelwood, Mo.

No-Good Cake

When I was about 8 years old, I remember my mom baking an unfrosted dark chocolate cake in a 13- by 9-inch pan that she ironically called No-Good Cake. My brother loved to put a piece of it in an old metal cup, cover it with milk, and eat it with a spoon. I never got the recipe from my mother and haven't been able to find a recipe with this name.

Connie Johnson
Ames, Iowa

Lyndon Johnson's BBQ Sauce

I'm looking for a wonderful BBQ "mop sauce" that President Johnson's cook used on BBQ beef. I got this recipe from a magazine in 1972. Everyone loved the sauce, but I lost the recipe during the move to my new home.

Jon Roper
Via e-mail

Sunshine Cake

One of my Grandma Rudd's many achievements was sunshine cake. It had the sponge-like texture of an angel food cake, but it was bright yellow due to the many egg yolks (instead of egg whites) in the recipe. I have searched frantically through her old cookbooks but I've never found it. Can you help?

Ginni Davis
Simi Valley, Calif.

> Are you looking for a **special recipe?** Or do you have a recipe a fellow *Cook's Country* reader is seeking? Post your requests and recipes by visiting **CooksCountry.com** and clicking on **Looking for a Recipe.** We'll share recipe requests and found recipes on CooksCountry.com and print as many as we can in the magazine. You may also write to us at Looking for a Recipe, Cook's Country, P.O. Box 470739, Brookline, MA 02447.

Find the Rooster!

A tiny version of this rooster has been hidden somewhere in the pages of this issue. If you find it, write to us with its location (plus your name and address) and you will be entered into a random drawing. The first correct entry drawn will receive an Anolon Advanced Double Burner Griddle (our test winner—see page 29), and the next five will each receive a complimentary one-year subscription to *Cook's Country.* To enter the contest, visit **CooksCountry.com/emailus**, or write to us at Rooster, Cook's Country, P.O. Box 470739, Brookline, MA 02447. Entries are due July 31, 2008.

Did you find the rooster in the February/March 2008 issue? It was hidden in the Penne with Sausage and Broccoli photo on page 21. Cheryl Bardaville of St. Louis, Mo., spotted it and won a Unicorn Magnum Plus Pepper Mill.

STEAK HOAGIES WITH MUSHROOMS,
ONIONS, AND PEPPERS

CHOPPED COBB SALAD

GRILLED CHICKEN WITH PANZANELLA SALAD

CHIPOTLE-GRILLED PORK TACOS

CHOPPED COBB SALAD SERVES 4

Go to CooksCountry.com for our quick and foolproof recipe for hard-cooked eggs.

- 1 cup crumbled blue cheese
- ¼ cup extra-virgin olive oil
- 2 tablespoons red wine vinegar
  Salt and pepper
- 8 slices bacon, chopped
- 2 boneless, skinless chicken breasts (about 12 ounces), cut into ½-inch pieces
- 3 romaine hearts, chopped
- 1 pint cherry tomatoes, halved
- 2 ripe avocados, pitted, skinned, and chopped
- 3 hard-cooked large eggs, peeled and quartered

1. Process ½ cup cheese, oil, vinegar, ¼ teaspoon salt, and ½ teaspoon pepper in food processor until well combined.

2. Cook bacon in large nonstick skillet over medium-high heat until crisp, about 5 minutes. Transfer bacon to paper towel–lined plate and pour off all but 1 tablespoon fat from skillet. Pat chicken dry with paper towels and season with salt and pepper. Cook chicken in bacon fat until golden brown and cooked through, 2 to 4 minutes. Transfer to plate and let cool 5 minutes.

3. Combine lettuce, tomatoes, remaining cheese, cooled chicken, and dressing in large bowl. Top salad with crisp bacon, avocados, and eggs. Serve.

STEAK HOAGIES WITH MUSHROOMS, ONIONS, AND PEPPERS SERVES 4

Sliced mozzarella or American cheese from the deli counter can be substituted for the provolone. To make cleanup easier, line the rimmed baking sheet with foil in step 3.

- 2 strip steaks, about 1 inch thick
  Salt and pepper
- 2 tablespoons olive oil
- 1 onion, sliced thin
- 1 red bell pepper, seeded and sliced thin
- 8 ounces white mushrooms, sliced thin
- 1 tablespoon steak sauce (such as A.1.)
- ½ teaspoon dried oregano
- 4 (6-inch) sub rolls, slit partially open lengthwise
- 6 ounces thinly sliced deli provolone cheese

1. Adjust oven rack to upper-middle position and heat oven to 450 degrees. Pat steak dry with paper towels and season with salt and pepper. Heat 1 tablespoon oil in large skillet over medium-high heat until just smoking. Cook steaks until well browned, 3 to 5 minutes per side. Transfer to plate and let rest 5 minutes, then slice thin against the grain.

2. Meanwhile, add remaining oil, onion, bell pepper, mushrooms, and ½ teaspoon salt to empty skillet and cook until vegetables are softened and golden brown, 8 to 10 minutes. Off heat, stir in steak sauce, oregano, and sliced steak until well combined.

3. Divide steak mixture among rolls and top with cheese. Arrange sandwiches on rimmed baking sheet and bake until cheese is melted and rolls are golden brown around edges, about 5 minutes. Serve.

CHIPOTLE-GRILLED PORK TACOS SERVES 4

Halving the tenderloins lengthwise creates more surface area for the wet rub to develop into a flavorful crust. Serve these tacos with shredded cheese and lime wedges, if desired.

- ¼ cup mayonnaise
- 1 (8-ounce) can pineapple chunks in juice, drained and chopped, ¼ cup juice reserved
- 3 tablespoons minced fresh cilantro
- 3 garlic cloves, minced
- 1½ tablespoons minced canned chipotle chiles in adobo
- 1 (8-ounce) bag coleslaw mix
- 3 scallions, sliced thin
  Salt
- 2 pork tenderloins (1½ to 2 pounds total), sliced in half lengthwise
- 12 corn tortillas

1. Whisk mayonnaise, pineapple juice, cilantro, garlic, and chipotle in large bowl; reserve ¼ cup mayonnaise mixture. Add pineapple chunks, coleslaw mix, scallions, and ½ teaspoon salt to bowl with remaining mayonnaise mixture and toss to combine.

2. Pat pork dry with paper towels and season with salt. Rub with reserved mayonnaise mixture and grill over hot fire until browned all over and meat registers 145 degrees, about 6 minutes. Transfer to cutting board, tent with foil, and let rest 5 minutes.

3. Grill tortillas over hot fire until lightly charred, about 15 seconds per side. Slice pork thin, arrange on tortillas, and top with coleslaw. Serve.

GRILLED CHICKEN WITH PANZANELLA SALAD SERVES 4

Any variety of ripe summer tomato can be used here.

- 5 tablespoons extra-virgin olive oil
- 4 garlic cloves, minced
- 1 red onion, sliced into ¼-inch rounds
- 4 (1-inch-thick) slices Italian bread
- 4 boneless, skinless chicken breasts (about 1½ pounds)
  Salt and pepper
- 3 ripe tomatoes, cored and chopped
- ½ cup chopped fresh basil
- 3 tablespoons red wine vinegar

1. Combine oil and garlic in bowl and microwave until bubbling and fragrant, about 1 minute. Brush onion slices with 1 tablespoon oil mixture and grill over hot fire until lightly charred, about 2 minutes per side. Transfer to large bowl. Brush bread with 1 tablespoon oil mixture and grill over hot fire until crisp and golden, about 1 minute per side. Transfer to cutting board.

2. Pat chicken dry with paper towels. Brush chicken with 1 tablespoon oil mixture and season with salt and pepper. Grill over hot fire until browned and cooked through, about 5 minutes per side. Transfer to plate and tent with foil.

3. Add tomatoes, basil, vinegar, and remaining oil mixture to bowl with grilled onions and toss to combine. Cut bread into ¾-inch chunks, then fold into tomato mixture. Transfer chicken and tomato salad to individual plates. Serve.

PASTA WITH ARUGULA, FRESH HERBS,
OLIVE OIL, AND GARLIC

CRISPY CHICKEN SALAD WRAPS

SAUTÉED LEMON CHICKEN STRIPS

QUICK CORN CHOWDER WITH BACON

CRISPY CHICKEN SALAD WRAPS SERVES 4

To prevent the wraps from unrolling during cooking, be sure to start them seam-side down in step 3.

- ⅓ cup mayonnaise
- ⅓ cup chopped fresh cilantro
- 3 scallions, sliced thin
- 2 celery ribs, chopped fine
- 2 tablespoons sour cream
- 2 teaspoons hot sauce
- 1 rotisserie chicken, skin discarded, meat shredded into bite-sized pieces (about 3 cups)
  Salt and pepper
- 2 cups shredded sharp cheddar cheese
- 4 (12-inch) flour tortillas

1. Whisk mayonnaise, cilantro, scallions, celery, sour cream, and hot sauce in large bowl. Add chicken and toss to combine. Season with salt and pepper.

2. Sprinkle cheese over tortillas, leaving ½-inch border around edges, then arrange chicken salad in center of tortilla. Roll stuffed tortillas, spray all over with cooking spray, and sprinkle with salt and pepper.

3. Heat large nonstick skillet over medium heat for 1 minute. Arrange 2 wraps, seam-side down, in pan and cook until golden brown and crisp, about 1 minute per side. Transfer to plate and repeat with remaining wraps. Serve.

PASTA WITH ARUGULA, FRESH HERBS, OLIVE OIL, AND GARLIC SERVES 4

Bagged baby arugula can be found in the produce section of most supermarkets. If you cannot find arugula, baby spinach is an acceptable substitute. Use campanelle, fusilli, or penne in this dish.

- ¼ cup extra-virgin olive oil
- 7 garlic cloves, minced
- ¼ teaspoon red pepper flakes
- 2 tablespoons lemon juice
  Salt and pepper
- 1 pound pasta (see note)
- 2 cups lightly packed baby arugula
- ½ cup lightly packed fresh parsley
- ½ cup lightly packed fresh basil
- 1 cup grated Parmesan cheese

1. Bring 4 quarts water to boil in large pot. Heat oil, garlic, and pepper flakes in large nonstick skillet over medium-low heat until garlic is just golden, about 3 minutes. Off heat, stir in lemon juice; cover and keep warm.

2. Add 1 tablespoon salt and pasta to boiling water and cook until al dente. Reserve ½ cup cooking water, drain pasta, and return to pot. Add warm oil mixture, arugula, parsley, basil, cheese, and reserved cooking water and toss until greens are just wilted. Season with salt and pepper. Serve.

QUICK CORN CHOWDER WITH BACON SERVES 4

Frozen corn can be quickly defrosted in a bowl in the microwave. If using fresh corn, you'll need about 1 dozen medium ears; use a chef's knife to cut the kernels off the husked and silked ears.

- 8 cups (about 2 pounds) frozen corn kernels, thawed (see note)
- 3 cups low-sodium chicken broth
- 6 slices bacon, chopped fine
- 1 onion, chopped fine
- 2 pounds russet potatoes, peeled and cut into ½-inch chunks
- ½ cup heavy cream
- 1 teaspoon minced fresh thyme
- ⅛ teaspoon cayenne pepper
  Salt and pepper

1. Puree 4 cups corn and 2 cups broth in blender or food processor until smooth. Cook bacon in large pot over medium-high heat until crisp, about 5 minutes; transfer to paper towel–lined plate. Reduce heat to medium and cook onion and potatoes in bacon fat until onion is softened, about 5 minutes.

2. Whisk in pureed corn mixture, cream, thyme, cayenne, and remaining broth and simmer until potatoes are tender, about 15 minutes. Stir in remaining corn and cook until corn is heated through, about 2 minutes. Season with salt and pepper. Sprinkle with crisp bacon. Serve.

SAUTÉED LEMON CHICKEN STRIPS SERVES 4

You can make your own chicken tenderloins by slicing boneless, skinless breasts lengthwise into ¾-inch strips. Serve over egg noodles or rice pilaf.

- 1½ pounds chicken tenderloins (see note)
  Salt and pepper
- 2 tablespoons vegetable oil
- 3 tablespoons unsalted butter
- 3 garlic cloves, minced
- 2 tablespoons drained capers, minced
- 1 tablespoon flour
- 1 cup low-sodium chicken broth
- ⅓ cup juice from 2 lemons
- 2 tablespoons minced fresh parsley

1. Pat chicken dry with paper towels and season with salt and pepper. Heat 1 tablespoon oil in large nonstick skillet over medium-high heat until just smoking. Cook half of chicken until golden brown and cooked through, about 2 minutes per side. Transfer to platter and tent with foil; repeat with remaining oil and chicken.

2. Add 1 tablespoon butter, garlic, and capers to empty skillet and cook until fragrant, about 30 seconds. Stir in flour and cook until beginning to brown, about 30 seconds. Stir in broth and lemon juice and simmer, scraping up any browned bits, until slightly thickened, about 3 minutes. Off heat, whisk in parsley and remaining butter. Stir in browned chicken along with any accumulated juices and season with salt and pepper. Serve.

Icebox Oreo Cheesecake

Last summer, I made a no-bake Oreo cheesecake for my family—what a disaster! The texture was bouncy, and the color was gray. Is there any way to make this dessert as good as a baked cheesecake?

–Kay Taylor, South Windsor, Conn.

The idea of a no-bake Oreo cheesecake is especially appealing in the summer months because there's no hot oven and no messy water bath (which most baked cheesecakes require). The method for this cake is simple: Thicken heavy cream with gelatin, mix it with sweetened cream cheese and ground Oreos, pour the mixture into a crust, and chill until set. These gelatin-based cheesecakes are easy to prepare, but their texture is never quite as creamy as that of an egg-thickened baked cheesecake's. I set out to make an icebox Oreo cheesecake that would rival the best baked cheesecake for flavor and texture.

My quest for great icebox Oreo cheesecake began with preparing several existing recipes for this popular dessert. I was disheartened to find that all of these cheesecakes were either too springy from gelatin overload or so runny that they wouldn't slice properly. And if the Oreos weren't dispersed as an unappealing gray powder, they remained distractingly chunky.

For big Oreo flavor, I started by grinding some cookies and mixing them with melted butter to make an easy press-in, no-bake crust for my springform pan. I thought I could finesse the amount of gelatin in standard recipes to get the creamy-textured filling I was after, but I was wrong. After countless tests, my tasters determined that cakes made with gelatin were never going to have the dense, velvety texture that comes from the eggs in baked versions. Was there a way to incorporate eggs into my icebox cheesecake?

Thinking an eggy pudding might work, I cooked a mixture of egg yolks, milk, and cornstarch, combined it with sweetened cream cheese, poured the filling over my Oreo crust, and put the pie in the refrigerator. This pie tasted pretty good and held together well, but the cornstarch had given it a slippery, glossy texture. Replacing the cornstarch with flour gave the cake stability without the slippery texture.

But it still didn't exhibit the creamy density of baked cheesecake. I tried adding sour cream and ricotta cheese, but neither was dense enough to help create that baked texture. A colleague suggested that melted white chocolate might help make the cheesecake denser while adding a pleasant sweetness. I gave it a shot by stirring chopped white chocolate into my hot pudding before cooling the pudding and combining it with the cream cheese. When set, the white chocolate firmed up the filling, and the resulting texture (and flavor) was very close to baked cheesecake.

I was almost there, but my tasters were clamoring for more Oreo flavor. Working to avoid the ugly gray cheesecake of my earlier tests, I broke a dozen cookies into large pieces and added them to the cheesecake in distinct layers. With the flavorful crust, the clean look of the layered filling, and the smooth, velvety texture created by the pudding and white chocolate, I had an icebox Oreo cheesecake that rivaled the best baked versions. **–Greg Case**

ICEBOX OREO CHEESECAKE SERVES 12

You can substitute 1⅓ cups of white chips for the 8 ounces of chopped white chocolate.

Oreo Cookie Crust

- 30 Oreo cookies, broken into rough pieces
- 7 tablespoons unsalted butter, softened

Cheesecake Filling

- 1 cup whole milk
- 4 large egg yolks
- ¼ cup all-purpose flour
- 8 ounces white chocolate, chopped (see note)
- 2 pounds cream cheese, cut into 1-inch chunks and softened
- ⅓ cup confectioners' sugar
- 2 teaspoons vanilla extract
- ⅛ teaspoon salt
- 12 Oreo cookies, broken into rough pieces

1. For the Oreo cookie crust: Process cookies and butter in food processor until finely ground. Following photos on page 30, press cookie mixture evenly into bottom and sides of 9-inch springform pan. Refrigerate until set, at least 1 hour or up to 2 days.

2. For the cheesecake filling: Heat ¾ cup milk in medium saucepan over medium heat until simmering. Meanwhile, whisk yolks, flour, and remaining milk in large bowl until smooth. Slowly whisk hot milk into yolk mixture. Return mixture to saucepan and cook over medium heat, whisking constantly, until very thick and glossy, 1 to 2 minutes. Off heat, whisk in white chocolate until melted. Transfer pudding to bowl, press plastic wrap directly on surface, and refrigerate until cold and set, at least 1 hour or up to 2 days.

3. With electric mixer on medium-high speed, beat cream cheese, sugar, vanilla, and salt until light and fluffy, about 2 minutes. Reduce speed to medium-low and mix in chilled pudding until just combined, about 30 seconds. Pour one-quarter of cream cheese mixture evenly into prepared pan and sprinkle one-third of cookies over surface. Repeat process twice, then top with remaining filling. Refrigerate until set, at least 6 hours. Remove sides of pan. Serve. (Cheesecake can be wrapped in plastic and refrigerated for up to 3 days.)

Layering the cheesecake filling with cookie pieces prevents the gray, muddied appearance that makes many recipes look unappealing.

Secret Ingredient

White chocolate dramatically tightens the texture of our cheesecake while adding sweetness.

NET WT 3.5 OZ (100 g)

WHITE CHOCOLATE

Smokehouse Burgers

The best burger I ever had was at a smokehouse restaurant in Texas. It was a huge burger with a charred, spicy crust and a hint of smoky flavor all the way through. How can I make a burger like this in my own backyard? –Ronald D. Parsons, Kingston, Mass.

Kitchen Know-How
WRAPPING WOOD CHIPS IN FOIL

To get wood chips to slowly produce aromatic smoke, soak them in water for 15 minutes and then spread the soaked, drained chips in the center of a 15- by 12-inch piece of heavy-duty aluminum foil. Fold the foil to seal the edges of the packet, then cut several slits to allow smoke to escape.

Smokehouses constantly feed their cooking fires with hardwood logs, permeating the grill (as well as the restaurant and its patrons) with the unmistakable aroma of wood smoke. Burgers cooked in these covered grill-smokers have no choice but to pick up great flavor. To make them even more appealing, most smokehouse burgers are very big, very juicy, and highly seasoned with spices.

The test kitchen's method for cooking with smoke on a standard gas or charcoal grill is to make a fire with a hotter side and a cooler side, wrap soaked hardwood chips in a foil packet (see photo at left), and set the packet directly over the fire until it starts to smoke. Then the meat—typically a large cut like a pork shoulder or rack of ribs—is set on the cooler side of the grill and cooked (with the lid on) for several hours.

Using this setup, I wrapped soaked hickory chips in foil and tossed the packet on the fire until it started smoking. Since burgers need a good crusty sear, I knew that "low and slow" wasn't going to work here, so I placed my patties over the hotter part of grill, put on the lid to trap the smoke, and cooked them for about 6 minutes per side. These burgers were overwhelmingly smoky, reminding my tasters of the inside of a chimney. To temper the harshness of the smoke flavor, I tried slowing down the process by searing the burgers for only 4 minutes per side on the hotter, smokier side of the grill, and then letting them finish cooking on the cooler, less smoky side. These burgers had the mellow, smoky flavor I was after, but my tasters wanted more assertive seasoning both inside and out.

Simply adding salt and pepper to the ground meat didn't cut it. I tried stirring all sorts of ingredients into my burger mixture, including Worcestershire sauce, ketchup, mustard, dried herbs, and even soy sauce, before it hit me: Why not add barbecue sauce to these "barbecued" burgers? Sure enough, just 3 tablespoons of bottled barbecue sauce seasoned the meat perfectly, carrying that slightly sweet, smoky flavor all the way through the burgers.

Good smokehouses typically use "secret" spice rubs to flavor large cuts of meat before the lengthy smoking process. Would a spice rub help round out the flavors in my quick-cooking burgers? Trial and error helped me eliminate spices (like paprika and dry mustard) that tasted harsh when seared onto the surface of the meat, leaving me with a simple rub of salt, pepper, garlic powder, and onion powder. I now had burgers with a subtle smoky flavor as well as a potent spice rub to seal the deal.

–Diane Unger

SMOKEHOUSE BURGERS
SERVES 4

Bull's-Eye is our preferred brand of barbecue sauce, but feel free to substitute your favorite. Making large burgers enables the meat to absorb more smoke and seasoning; these big burgers fit better on bulkie or kaiser rolls than on standard hamburger buns. Toasting the rolls on the grill adds even more smoke flavor.

- **2 pounds 85 percent lean ground beef, broken into small pieces**
- **3 tablespoons barbecue sauce**
  Salt and pepper
- **2 teaspoons onion powder**
- **2 teaspoons garlic powder**
- **2 cups wood chips, soaked for 15 minutes**

1. Gently knead beef, barbecue sauce, ½ teaspoon salt, and 1 teaspoon pepper in large bowl until well incorporated. Shape meat mixture into four 1-inch-thick patties. Combine onion powder, garlic powder, ½ teaspoon salt, and 1 teaspoon pepper in small bowl; sprinkle spice mixture evenly over both sides of patties.

2. Seal wood chips in foil packet, cut vent holes in top, and place packet directly on primary burner. Heat all burners on high, covered, until wood chips begin to smoke heavily, about 15 minutes. Leave primary burner on high and shut other burner(s) off. (For charcoal grill, light 100 coals; when covered with fine gray ash, spread over half of grill. Place foil packet directly on coals. Set cooking grate in place and heat, covered, with lid vent completely open, until wood chips begin to smoke heavily, about 5 minutes.) Scrape and oil cooking grate.

3. Arrange burgers on hotter side of grill but not directly over foil packet. (If working on small gas grill, see "Smokehouse, Not Smoke Out" box at left.) Grill burgers, covered, until well browned, about 4 minutes per side. Move burgers to cooler side of grill and continue to cook, covered, to desired doneness, 3 to 5 minutes longer. Transfer to plate, tent with foil, and let rest 5 minutes. Serve.

For traditional barbecue flavor, we mix barbecue sauce into the meat, cover the patties with a spice rub, and smoke the burgers over soaked hardwood chips.

Smokehouse, Not Smoke Out

In step 3, grilling the burgers directly over the smoking packet of wood chips can result in a harsh smoke flavor. On most grills, you can simply position the burgers and packet away from each other. But on small gas grills, where there isn't enough room for four burgers above the primary burner but slightly removed from the foil packet, we suggest turning all burners to high and searing the burgers over high heat away from the chips for the first stage of cooking. Once the burgers are well browned, simply turn off the burner below the burgers while they finish cooking via indirect heat.

Crispy Sweet Potato Fries

Most sweet potatoes turn soggy seconds after emerging from the hot oil. To stay crisp, sweet potatoes need to be treated differently from regular potatoes.

Until recently, I've been a french fry purist and never understood the appeal of trendier sweet potato fries. That changed about a year ago when a friend invited me to lunch at her neighborhood pub. Upon sitting down, she ordered her favorite "hot and sweets," and minutes later a basket arrived, piled high with orange fries tossed in a seasoned salt. The combination of the sweet, creamy interior and spicy crust was irresistible. And while my previous encounters with sweet potato fries had ended in soggy disappointment, these were really crisp.

Sweet potatoes obviously have more sugar than regular potatoes, but they also have more moisture, which creates steam—the enemy of crispness. What was the secret to those memorable pub fries?

To create my own recipe, I began with the classic french fry method, wherein the potatoes are first fried in 325-degree oil to gently cook them through without browning. The fries are then removed from the pot and rested for 10 minutes; during this rest, the natural starches in the potato form a thin film on the fries. When the potatoes are fried again at a more aggressive 375 degrees, the starchy coating browns and turns into a crisp, crunchy exterior. Sweet potato fries prepared this way emerged from the oil slightly crisp, but turned soggy by the time I could serve them.

Hoping to rid the sweet potatoes of excess water, I tried dehydrating them for up to an hour in a low-temperature oven before frying. This step only worked to toughen the fries and added no crispness. Instead of trying to remove moisture, what about adding a coating that would crisp during frying and stand up to the potatoes' moisture-rich interior?

Most of the coatings I tried yielded a greasy, thick exterior that masked the sweet potato flavor and looked odd. A tempura-style batter with water, egg, and cornstarch was a step in the right direction, but the coating was still too thick and flaked off easily. Wanting something lighter and less easily detected, I omitted the egg and replaced the water with club soda. The bubbles in the carbonated water kept the cornstarch from clumping and helped to create a starchy coating similar to what forms on french fries between frying sessions. What about the finished fries? They were crisp, and no one could detect any taste other than sweet potato. Even more important, the crust stayed unbelievably crisp for up to 15 minutes while I rounded up tasters.

I had one last test. Did I need to stick with double-frying—the standard method for making regular fries—or did my cornstarch coating make this step unnecessary? I was pleasantly surprised to find that there was no benefit to double-frying here. When combined with my cornstarch coating, a straightforward single fry at 375 degrees produced perfectly cooked, crisp fries.

I wanted to create a spicy salt to accentuate the sweetness of the potatoes. After a little trial and error, I concocted a mixture of chili powder, garlic powder, cayenne, and salt that had my tasters battling for every last fry. –Cali Rich

CRISPY SWEET POTATO FRIES SERVES 4

To prevent the sweet potatoes from turning brown, do not cut them until ready to use. In step 2, place a layer of paper towels under the wire rack to collect any drippings; alternatively, place the wire rack over the sink. The sweet potatoes are fried in two batches to prevent overcrowding the pot, which can lead to a reduction in oil temperature and uneven cooking.

- ½ teaspoon chili powder
- ½ teaspoon garlic powder
- ½ teaspoon cayenne pepper
- 1 teaspoon salt
- 2 quarts peanut or vegetable oil
- 1 cup cornstarch
- ¾ cup club soda, chilled
- 2 pounds sweet potatoes, peeled and cut into ½- by ¼-inch lengths (see photos at right)

1. Adjust oven rack to middle position and heat oven to 200 degrees. Combine chili powder, garlic powder, cayenne, and salt in large bowl.

2. Heat oil in large Dutch oven over high heat to 375 degrees. While oil is heating, whisk cornstarch and club soda in medium bowl. Working in small batches, dip sweet potatoes in cornstarch mixture, allowing excess to drip back into bowl, and transfer to wire rack.

3. When oil is ready, fry half of sweet potatoes, stirring occasionally, until golden brown and crisp, about 6 to 8 minutes. Drain fries on paper towel–lined baking sheet and transfer to oven. Return oil to 375 degrees and repeat with remaining fries. Transfer crisp fries to bowl with spice mixture and toss to coat. Serve.

Make Ahead: In step 2, the coated sweet potatoes can be frozen on a wire rack set over a rimmed baking sheet until just set, about 15 minutes, then transferred to a zipper-lock bag and kept frozen for up to 1 month. When ready to serve, proceed with step 3 (the fries might take a minute or two more to become golden brown and crisp).

These spicy fries feature a sweet, creamy interior and an exterior that stays crisp down to the last bite.

How to CUT SWEET POTATO FRIES EVENLY

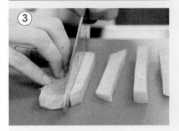

1. To stabilize sweet potatoes for slicing, cut a ¼-inch piece from one side of each sweet potato so that it sits flat.
2. Cut the sweet potatoes into ½-inch-thick planks.
3. Cut each plank into ¼-inch-thick fries.

Keys to Better Batter

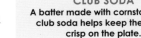

CORNSTARCH AND CLUB SODA
A batter made with cornstarch and club soda helps keep these fries crisp on the plate.

Cola-Barbecued Ribs

I recently tried a recipe for cola-marinated barbecued ribs, but the outside burned and there was barely any cola flavor. Is there a better recipe for these ribs? —Sean Flynn, Tucson, Ariz.

The Cola Taste Test

To see if it really made a difference what type of cola we used in the sauce for our Cola-Barbecued Ribs, we picked up all of the nationally available brands—Coke, Pepsi, Rally, and RC (as well as diet colas)—and put them to the test. After tasting barbecue sauce made with each cola, the winner was clear: Tasters preferred Coke for its "balanced sweetness" and "warm, vanilla" flavor. Rally and RC both fared well in this tasting, but tasters found Pepsi to be "flat" and "one-dimensional." Diet sodas were not acceptable in this barbecue sauce.

OUR FAVORITE COLA

Secrets to BIG COLA FLAVOR

The key to adding rich cola flavor to our homemade barbecue sauce was to dramatically reduce the soda before building the sauce.

BEFORE
We start with a full quart of cola.

AFTER
For the boldest flavor, the quart of cola is reduced down to a single cup.

Cola ribs are becoming increasingly popular with backyard and even competition barbecuers. The premise for this dish is simple: pork ribs (usually baby backs) are marinated for a few hours in cola, slow-grilled until tender, and finished with a barbecue sauce flavored with more cola. The sweet, spicy flavor of cola is supposed to lend complexity to the meat and sauce. I eagerly rounded up a handful of recipes and headed outside to fire up the grills. What a disappointment! Like our reader Sean, I found that the sugary cola burned on the outside of the ribs (even with indirect heat), and the cola flavor was minimal.

I decided to skip the marinade and add cola flavor in other ways. I started with the test kitchen's method for cooking ribs on the grill. I covered the ribs with a spice rub, smoked them with indirect heat on the grill, and then finished them wrapped in foil in the oven so they would become tender without further browning on the exterior.

Next, instead of using traditional barbecue rub spices like cumin and garlic powder, I wondered if I could identify ingredients that would mimic cola flavor. Through sampling various brands of cola, my tasters determined that cola flavor consists of caramel, vanilla, and warm spices such as cinnamon and cloves. A spice rub of cinnamon, cloves, salt, and pepper wasn't complex enough; potent Chinese five-spice powder (a mixture of cinnamon, cloves, fennel seed, star anise, and spicy Sichuan peppercorns) perfectly married the warm flavors of cola with traditional barbecue heat.

The secret to harnessing cola flavor is to tame the soda's sweetness and augment its base flavors with similar spices.

Simply adding cola to bottled barbecue sauce was a nonstarter. Instead I made an easy homemade sauce by mixing ketchup, mustard, vinegar, and a cup of cola with minced onion. Tasters liked the flavor of the onion but not the texture, so I pureed raw onion with a little water and added this "onion juice" to the mix. A little savory, salty Worcestershire sauce rounded out the flavors.

This sauce tasted good, but it was still lacking the essence of cola. I kept increasing the amount of soda, all the way up to 4 cups, but the sauce got too thin and the flavor was still wan. Cooking down the sauce never produced the clean, concentrated cola flavor I needed. Brainstorming ways to get elemental cola flavor, I thought of the cola syrup used in fountain drinks. Since I couldn't get my hands on the actual syrup, I decided to make my own. I poured 2 cups of cola into a saucepan and reduced it by half, which was an improvement, but not as good as when I reduced a full quart of soda down to 1 cup. This created a sauce redolent of caramel and vanilla, and a little vanilla extract intensified the effect even more.

To bring the sauce and ribs together, I brushed a bit of sauce on the ribs before they finished in the oven. Safe from the flame of the grill, the sauce melted into the smoky ribs and carried the distinctive caramel cola flavor right to the bone.

–Adam Ried

COLA-BARBECUED RIBS
SERVES 4
Use a paring knife to loosen the membrane on the back of the ribs, grasp with a paper towel, and peel off in one piece. Chinese five-spice powder is available in the spice aisle of most supermarkets.

Spice Rub and Ribs
- 2½ tablespoons light brown sugar
- 1½ tablespoons paprika
- 1½ tablespoons pepper
- 2 teaspoons salt
- 1 teaspoon Chinese five-spice powder
- 2 racks baby back ribs (about 1½ pounds each), membrane removed (see note)
- 2 cups wood chips, soaked for 15 minutes

Cola-Barbecue Sauce
- 4 cups cola
- ½ onion, cut into large chunks
- ¼ cup water
- 1¼ cups ketchup
- 1 tablespoon red wine vinegar
- 2 teaspoons yellow mustard
- 1½ teaspoons Worcestershire sauce
- ¼ teaspoon vanilla extract

1. For the spice rub and ribs: Combine sugar, paprika, pepper, salt, and five-spice powder, breaking up any lumps. Reserve 2 tablespoons

for sauce. Dry ribs with paper towels and rub all over with remaining spice mixture. (Ribs can be wrapped tightly in plastic and refrigerated for 24 hours.)

2. Seal wood chips in foil packet and cut vent holes in top (see Kitchen Know-How, page 18). Open bottom vent on grill. Light 100 coals; when covered with fine gray ash, pour in pile on one side of grill. Arrange foil packet directly on coals. Set cooking grate in place and heat, covered, with lid vent open halfway, until wood chips begin to smoke heavily, about 5 minutes. (For gas grill, place foil packet directly on primary burner. Heat all burners on high, covered, until wood chips begin to smoke heavily, about 15 minutes. Leave primary burner on high and shut other burner[s] off.) Scrape and oil cooking grate. Arrange ribs on cool side of grill and barbecue, covered, flipping and rotating racks once, until ribs are deep red and smoky, about 2 hours.

3. For the sauce: While ribs are barbecuing, bring cola to boil in large saucepan. Reduce heat to medium and simmer until liquid is reduced to 1 cup, about 40 minutes. Meanwhile, process onion and water in food processor until finely ground. Transfer mixture to fine-mesh strainer set over bowl and press on solids to collect as much liquid as possible; discard solids. Whisk ¼ cup onion juice, ketchup, vinegar, mustard, Worcestershire, and reserved spice mixture into pot with reduced cola. Simmer until slightly thickened, about 10 minutes. Off heat, stir in vanilla.

4. Adjust oven rack to middle position and heat oven to 250 degrees. Brush ribs liberally with sauce and wrap tightly with foil. Arrange foil-wrapped ribs on rimmed baking sheet and bake until ribs are completely tender, about 2 hours. Transfer ribs (still in foil) to cutting board and let rest 15 minutes. Unwrap ribs and serve, passing remaining sauce at table.

Cool and Creamy Green Bean Salad

Replacing potatoes with green beans sounds like a winning recipe for a light summer salad. So why are most creamy green bean salads mushy and bland?

The best creamy green bean salads combine crisp-tender beans with bits of sweet red onion, all coated with a bright and creamy mayonnaise-based dressing. But most of the recipes I tried just boiled the beans, let them cool, and dumped on the mayo. The results were bland, limp beans smothered in an unappealingly thick dressing.

I wanted a creamy dressing that would flavor, but not overpower, the beans. Most recipes use mayo as the sole creamy component, but I found that alone it is too heavy and rich. I tried combining the mayonnaise with sour cream and yogurt to brighten its flavor. The sour cream was still too heavy, but yogurt provided creamy texture and a welcome tang. A little salt, sugar, and white vinegar helped balance out the dressing.

Many of the test kitchen's recipes for potato salad dress

the hot potatoes with potent ingredients (like vinegar and mustard) and wait until they cool before adding the mayonnaise; the hot potatoes soak up flavors and become seasoned throughout. But that technique didn't work with green beans, because the carryover cooking made it too hard to get the perfect crisp-tender texture (which you don't need for potatoes), leaving the beans mushy and limp.

To achieve that perfect crisp-tender texture, I boiled the beans for just a few minutes and then removed them to a bowl of ice water to immediately stop the cooking and lock in their texture and color. Unfortunately, the dressed beans were bland, because the dressing wasn't absorbed.

Wondering if I could cook the beans and season them at the same time, I added some of the noncreamy dressing ingredients to the cooking water. A little

salt and sugar paid immediate dividends, but the white vinegar was hard to detect. I increased the amount of vinegar from a tablespoon to a whole cup, which allowed the beans to soak up considerable seasoning while they cooked.

Finally, tasters liked red onion in this salad but thought its flavor was overpowering and its texture too crunchy. Briefly blanching the sliced onion with the beans solved both problems.

–Lynn Clark

COOL AND CREAMY GREEN BEAN SALAD
SERVES 8
We prefer the richness of whole-milk yogurt, but low-fat yogurt is acceptable here. Yellow wax beans may be substituted for all or some of the green beans.

- 1 cup plus 2 teaspoons white vinegar
- 1 tablespoon sugar
  Salt and pepper
- 2 pounds green beans, stem ends trimmed
- ½ small red onion, sliced thin
- ½ cup mayonnaise
- ¼ cup plain whole-milk yogurt
- 1 tablespoon extra-virgin olive oil
- 1 garlic clove, minced

1. Fill large bowl with ice water. Bring 4 quarts water and 1 cup vinegar to boil in large pot over high heat. Add sugar, 1 tablespoon salt, and beans and cook until beans are just tender, about 3 minutes. Add onion to pot and cook until just softened, about 30 seconds. Drain vegetables in colander and immediately transfer to ice water. Once beans and onion are cool, drain again and dry thoroughly with paper towels. (Cooked vegetables can be refrigerated in zipper-lock bag for 24 hours.)

2. Whisk mayonnaise, yogurt, oil, garlic, and remaining vinegar in large bowl. Add chilled beans and onions and toss until well coated. Season with salt and pepper. Serve. (Salad can be refrigerated in airtight container for 2 days.)

Garden Minestrone

A good minestrone captures the fleeting flavors of summer vegetables in a bowl. But as with so many soups, this one can turn stodgy and bland if you don't treat the vegetables right.

How to
PUT THE GARDEN INTO MINESTRONE

Many minestrone recipes settle for overcooked vegetables and dull broth. Here's how to pack your soup with garden-fresh flavor.

1. To preserve the delicate texture of summer squash while maximizing its sweet flavor, brown the seeded squash (with plenty of garlic) at the onset of cooking, remove it from the pot, and then add it back to the soup just prior to serving.

2. To add body to the soup without making it too heavy, make a fresh "tomato paste" by cooking half of the seeded tomatoes until they begin to brown.

3. To add a bright herbal flavor and leafy texture, stir in freshly chopped basil just before serving.

Minestrone, literally "big soup" in Italian, is a broth- and tomato-based soup packed with vegetables, beans, herbs, and usually a starch (either pasta or rice). In some regions of Italy, minestrone is garnished with a potent dollop of pesto. There is no definitive recipe, because Italian cooks typically use whatever vegetables and leftovers they have on hand, and those ingredients vary widely from region to region. I wanted to create a lighter, livelier minestrone that could showcase a windfall of summer vegetables.

I began building flavor by sautéing onions and carrots (a must in almost every recipe) in olive oil. For fresher flavor, I skipped the traditional canned tomatoes and used chopped fresh tomatoes instead. My tasters preferred the mild flavor of chicken broth as a base, rather than heavier beef broth or flavorless water. I added garlic, green beans, canned beans, summer squash, and pasta and let the soup cook until everything was tender.

This soup was lighter, all right—so light it didn't taste like much. For bolder tomato flavor, I cooked some of the tomatoes—seeded to concentrate their flavor more quickly—with the onions and carrots until they broke down and began to resemble a fresher, sweeter tomato paste. A little white wine added a bright note of acidity, and fresh thyme lent a welcome herbal quality. When I added the chicken broth and more raw tomatoes (for another layer of garden-fresh flavor), my soup base was much improved, and I could focus on fine-tuning the rest of the ingredients.

Aside from the washed-out flavors, my tasters had complained about the slimy texture of the summer squash (both yellow squash and zucchini) in my initial test. To correct the texture of the squash, I removed its watery seeds and browned the squash—with lots of garlic—right in the pot before starting the soup; I set this mixture aside so that I could add it back at the end of cooking, thus preserving its texture.

Many minestrone recipes call for hearty greens like cabbage, collard greens, or kale. For a lighter, more summery feel, I tried fresh spinach, but its mild flavor faded quickly. Since some recipes offer a pesto garnish, I wondered if fresh basil leaves could serve double duty as an herb and a "vegetable." Tasters loved the bold herbal flavor and vegetal texture a full four cups of roughly chopped basil added. To further lighten the soup, I eliminated heavy starches such as pasta and rice altogether. Instead, I relied solely on the creamy texture and delicate flavor of small white navy beans to add a subtle heartiness to the soup. Now this was a minestrone that tasted like summer.

–Kelley Baker

GARDEN MINESTRONE
SERVES 6 TO 8

Zucchini can be substituted for half or all of the summer squash; see page 31 for information on seeding these types of squash. If desired, serve minestrone with grated Parmesan cheese and a splash of extra-virgin olive oil.

- ¼ cup extra-virgin olive oil
- 3 medium summer squash, seeded and chopped (see note)
- 6 garlic cloves, minced
- 1 onion, chopped fine
- 1 carrot, peeled and chopped
- 6 medium tomatoes, cored, seeded, and chopped
- Salt and pepper
- ½ cup white wine
- 8 ounces green beans, trimmed and cut into 1-inch pieces
- 2 (16-ounce) cans navy beans, drained and rinsed
- 2 teaspoons minced fresh thyme
- 8 cups low-sodium chicken broth
- 4 cups loosely packed basil leaves, bruised (see Bruising Is Best, right) and chopped rough

1. Heat 2 tablespoons oil in large Dutch oven over medium-high heat until shimmering. Cook squash until golden and just tender, about 5 minutes. Add half of garlic and cook until fragrant, about 30 seconds. Transfer to plate and tent with foil.

2. Add remaining oil, onion, and carrot to empty Dutch oven and cook until onion is golden, about 8 minutes. Add half of tomatoes, ½ teaspoon salt, and ½ teaspoon pepper and cook, stirring occasionally, until juices have evaporated and tomatoes begin to brown, 5 to 7 minutes. Add remaining garlic and cook until fragrant, about 30 seconds. Add wine and simmer, scraping up any browned bits, until slightly thickened, about 2 minutes. Add green beans, navy beans, thyme, broth, and remaining tomatoes and bring to boil. Reduce heat to medium-low and simmer until green beans are tender, about 15 minutes.

3. Stir in reserved squash and basil and simmer until heated through, about 1 minute. Season with salt and pepper. Serve.

Make Ahead: The soup can be prepared through step 2 and then refrigerated for 2 days, with the squash reserved separately. When ready to serve, bring the soup to a simmer over medium heat and proceed with step 3.

> ### Bruising Is Best
> To release the basil's flavorful oils, we bruise the leaves and add them to the pot just before serving this soup. Place the basil leaves in a zipper-lock bag or between two sheets of plastic wrap. Gently pound the basil with a rolling pin or meat mallet.

Instead of topping this minestrone with a dollop of pesto, we integrate plenty of garlic and basil into the soup.

Getting to Know Fresh Beans and Peas

Fresh beans and peas, also known as legumes, can be divided into two categories: those with edible pods and those from which only the seeds (the beans and peas) are eaten. Here are our tasting notes and serving suggestions for 12 varieties.

Haricots Verts
FANCY AND FRENCH

These beans, sometimes called French filet beans, are smaller, slimmer, and more delicate cousins of American string beans. They have a "light, crunchy texture" and a flavor that is "sweet and not at all bitter." Look for dark green, slender beans with taut skin and intact stems. Remove stem ends and serve raw, blanched, or steamed.

Fava Beans
MEDITERRANEAN FAVORITE

Also called broad or horse beans, favas grow in large, fuzzy pods that hold three to six large beans. Each bean is covered with a thin, tough skin that should be loosened by quickly blanching and then peeling by hand. While young fava beans are "tender and sweet," larger beans can be "woody and sulfurous." Favas can be gently sautéed in butter, cooked and pureed into dips, or ground into falafel.

Sugar Snap Peas
HALF-AND-HALF

These are a hybrid of English peas and snow peas, and they combine the best of both worlds—crisp, edible pods stuffed with plump, sweet peas. Properly cooked, sugar snaps are "crunchy and juicy," with a "delicate sweetness," but if even slightly overcooked they become wrinkled, mushy, and bland. Snap off the stem end and remove the string before eating raw, stir-frying, or quickly boiling and then tossing with butter or olive oil.

String Beans
AMERICAN STAPLE

Also known as pole, snap, or just green beans, these large, hearty, edible-pod beans are a garden favorite. Although their long shelf life makes them ideal for the supermarket, these "slightly bitter" beans can become "tough and fibrous" as they age. Despite their name, most string beans have been bred to not have a string. Older, thicker beans are best braised or roasted, and thinner beans should be blanched or steamed.

Yellow Wax Beans
PALE AND MILD

These are green beans that have been bred to display a pale yellow color. Their name comes from the slightly waxy appearance and feel of their skin. Their flavor is similar to that of standard green beans, though our tasters found them to be "slightly more mild," with a "sweeter finish." Wax beans can be substituted for green beans in any dish.

Snow Peas
FLAT AND CRUNCHY

These edible-pod peas are recognizable for their flat, almost translucent pods. Their flavor is "mildly vegetal and sweet," but the real appeal is their crunchy texture (which disappears with even slight overcooking). To check freshness, pick up a snow pea and try to bend it until it breaks—fresh peas will snap cleanly, but older peas will bend rather than break. Snap off the stem end and remove the string before eating raw or quickly stir-frying.

English Peas
FROZEN IS BETTER

Freshly picked peas are "as sweet as candy," but within hours they begin to turn "starchy and stale." Because it is difficult to buy freshly picked peas, we recommend using the bagged frozen variety, which are picked, blanched, and quick-frozen at the height of their sweetness. Peas are best quickly steamed, boiled, or sautéed in butter.

Flat Runner Beans
LONG AND FLAT

Also known as Kentucky wonder beans, these long, flat beans are sometimes grown for their brilliant flowering blossoms. The young pods are edible, but as they mature they become very fibrous and only the beans should be eaten. Runner beans are "meaty and dense," with a "grassy" flavor "reminiscent of broccoli." Runner beans can grow to 10 inches in length, but smaller beans are more tender and sweet. Boil or steam whole beans, or cut into lengths and stir-fry.

Purple Wax Beans
PURPLE PRETENDER

Once these beans are cooked, they lose their namesake color and turn a deep, muddy green. Tasters felt that these beans, which are rare and relatively expensive, were "slightly tough," with an "unpleasantly bitter" and "wheaty" aftertaste. We do not recommend purchasing these beans.

Dragon Tongue Beans
A BIT OF BITE

Though not often found in grocery stores, these string beans' violet streaks make them a farmers market favorite. They have an "herbal, peppery" flavor balanced by a "fruity" aftertaste. Boil or steam these beans, but be aware that cooking will cause the brightly colored beans to fade to light beige. Dragon tongue beans are best eaten within a day or two of being picked, as the pods will quickly dry out and become tough and fibrous.

Soybeans
NUTTY AND DENSE

Often referred to by their Japanese moniker, edamame, protein-rich soybeans are "savory and nutty," with a "firm, dense texture." The thin, fuzzy, and fibrous shell is inedible. Immature soybeans (either fresh or frozen) are typically boiled in their pods, then salted and eaten out of hand. Frozen shelled beans can be cooked and served like shelled peas. Mature soybeans are used to make products like tofu and soy sauce.

Long Beans
A BEAN OF MANY NAMES

These thin beans can grow to nearly three feet in length and have a list of names almost as long: yard-long beans, asparagus beans, snake beans, and so on. They are deep green, more pliable than string beans, and pack a "mellow earthiness" to go along with their "meaty, slightly chewy" texture. Cut into lengths, long beans are a traditional choice in Chinese stir-fries, but they can also be blanched or steamed just like a typical green bean.

Glazed Grill-Roasted Chicken

I am both enticed and intimidated by the prospect of glazing a grill-roasted chicken. It sounds delicious, but I have a hard enough time with flare-ups and charring when grilling an unglazed bird. Do you have a recipe?

–Clark Louis, Chicago, Ill.

Secrets to
PERFECTLY GLAZED GRILL-ROASTED CHICKEN

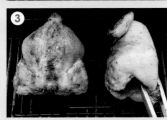
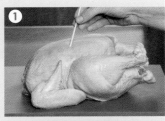

1. Prick the chicken skin all over with a skewer to allow the fat an escape route.
2. Place chickens breast-side up and head-to-tail on the V-rack. Make sure they are well balanced on the rack.
3. To evenly brown and render the skin before glazing, grill chickens about 30 minutes per side, rotating the V-rack 180 degrees after 15 minutes. When flipping the chickens, be sure to rotate them as well to promote even browning.
4. Once the chickens have reached 155 degrees in the thickest part of the thigh, begin glazing, flipping, and rotating every 5 minutes until they are cooked through.

A smoky grill-roasted chicken finished with a sweet, sticky glaze certainly sounds appealing. But anyone who has grill-roasted a whole bird knows that there are plenty of problems lurking. There's the issue of getting both white and dark meat to cook evenly. With too little heat, the chicken can fail to brown. With too much, the skin can burn before the meat is cooked through—and to compound the problem, a sweet glaze has the potential to create flare-ups.

The most common recipes for grill-roasted chicken call for slow cooking with indirect heat, and that's where I started. I set up the grill with the heat on one side. Working with two chickens (to feed six people), I patted the birds dry, seasoned them with salt and pepper, and set them on the cooler side of the grill to cook. But the absence of direct heat meant that the chickens didn't brown well, and the glaze (I was using a simple honey-mustard glaze, and adding it only at the end of cooking) didn't caramelize properly. When I tried finishing the chickens by glazing them directly over the heat, flare-ups resulted in flaming chickens.

It was time to take a look at the cooking method. How could I get some direct heat on these birds without burning them? I recalled seeing fancy grills with rotisseries that elevate the meat above the fire, thus allowing you to grill over direct heat without the risk of flare-ups. I didn't want to call for a rotisserie here, but was there another way to elevate the chickens for a similar effect? When we roast chickens in the test kitchen's ovens, we typically use a V-rack to lift the bird out of the juices. Would a V-rack work on the grill? Now that the chicken would be a safe distance from the flame, I pricked the skin all over to give the rendering fat an escape route and added some sugar to my seasoning rub to help the rendered skin crisp and brown. I arranged the seasoned chickens breast-side up on the rack directly over low heat, a safe distance from the fire. Flipping the birds halfway through cooking ensured that the white and dark meat cooked evenly. This method gave me nicely bronzed birds that were begging for a flavorful glaze.

After trying several sweet glazes, I concluded that since thinner glazes ran off like water (and caused more flare-ups), the glaze had to have a viscous texture to adhere when brushed on the skin. Also, the glaze had to be concentrated in flavor to be detectable on the finished chicken. Precooking the glaze made for great improvement in both thickening the mixture and concentrating the flavor, especially when I started with already thick and intensely flavored bases such as brown sugar, honey, and molasses.

On the grill, glazing the chickens too soon slowed their cooking to a crawl (repeated opening of the lid let too much heat escape). I found it was best to wait until the chickens reached 155 degrees before beginning the glazing process. For a substantial coating, I brushed the chickens with the glaze and turned the birds at least three times during their final minutes on the grill. The only question I had left to answer was "leg or wing?"

–**Kelley Baker**

Cooking two chickens is no more work than cooking one, so you can feed more people without working harder.

GLAZED GRILL-ROASTED CHICKEN SERVES 6 TO 8

To prevent flare-ups, be sure that your grill is clean and the chickens are trimmed of any excess fat before cooking.

- 2 (3½- to 4-pound) whole chickens
- 1 tablespoon sugar
- 1 tablespoon salt
- 1 teaspoon pepper
- 1 recipe glaze (see page 25)

1. Spray V-rack with cooking spray. Pat chickens dry with paper towels and prick skin all over with skewer or paring knife. Combine sugar, salt, and pepper in small bowl, then rub seasoning mixture all over chickens. Tuck wings behind back and tie legs together with kitchen twine. Following photo 2 at left, arrange chickens head to tail on prepared V-rack.

2. Heat all burners on high for 15 minutes. Turn all burners to low. (For charcoal grill, light 100 coals; when covered with fine gray ash, spread in even layer over grill. Set cooking grate in place and heat, covered, with lid vent halfway open, for 5 minutes.) Scrape cooking grate clean.

3. Arrange V-rack on cooking grate and grill, covered, until back of each chicken is well browned, about 30 minutes, carefully rotating V-rack 180 degrees after 15 minutes. Flip chickens and repeat until breasts

Mexican-Style Garlic Shrimp

This seemingly simple dish—just shrimp, oil, garlic, and seasonings—often features rubbery shrimp floating in a greasy, bland sauce. We set out to fix this recipe while staying true to its roots.

are well browned and thigh meat registers 155 degrees, 30 to 40 minutes longer. Brush chickens with glaze and continue grilling with lid on, flipping and glazing chicken every 5 minutes, until lightly charred in spots and thigh meat registers 170 to 175 degrees, 15 to 25 minutes.

4. Transfer chickens to cutting board, tent with foil, and let rest 10 minutes. Carve and drizzle chicken with remaining glaze. Serve.

BROWN SUGAR–BALSAMIC GLAZE

Simmer ⅓ cup packed dark brown sugar, ¼ cup balsamic vinegar, and ¼ teaspoon salt in small saucepan over medium heat until thickened, 3 to 5 minutes. (Glaze can be refrigerated in airtight container for 3 days. Gently warm glaze in small saucepan or microwave before using.)

HONEY-MUSTARD GLAZE

Simmer ⅓ cup honey, ¼ cup Dijon mustard, and ¼ teaspoon salt in small saucepan over medium heat until thickened, 3 to 5 minutes. (Glaze can be refrigerated in airtight container for 3 days. Gently warm glaze in small saucepan or microwave before using.)

SPICY MOLASSES GLAZE

Simmer ⅓ cup molasses, ¼ cup cider vinegar, ½ teaspoon red pepper flakes, and ¼ teaspoon salt in small saucepan over medium heat until thickened, 3 to 5 minutes. (Glaze can be refrigerated in airtight container for 3 days. Gently warm glaze in small saucepan or microwave before using.)

I enjoyed my first taste of Mexican-style garlic shrimp during a late lunch in a San Antonio café. The aroma of garlic filled the restaurant long before the server presented me with a bowl of tender shrimp bathed in a heady sauce of olive oil, garlic, lime, and fresh chiles. The sauce was so good that I mopped up the last bit with extra tortillas.

Back in the test kitchen, my research revealed that most recipes for this dish work the same way: Garlic is poached in oil to develop its sweet flavor, shrimp is sautéed in a few tablespoons of the flavored oil, the garlic and the rest of the oil are poured back over the shrimp, and the dish is finished with fresh jalapeños and a squeeze of lime. After preparing several of these recipes, the problems were readily apparent—most renditions were greasy or had meek garlic flavor.

The greasiness was the easier problem to address. I scaled back the olive oil in my working recipe to ¼ cup, down from the full 2 cups used in many recipes for 2 pounds of shrimp. For robust garlic flavor, I gently poached 10 cloves (halved to speed cooking) in the oil until soft, then removed the garlic and sautéed the shrimp in the infused oil. The shrimp picked up plenty of nutty garlic flavor from the oil, but it also had a dry, rubbery texture. To keep the shrimp tender and juicy, I turned down the heat to medium and put the lid on the pot to trap moisture.

Simply adding the softened garlic back to the cooked shrimp produced nice, subtle garlic flavor, but my tasters wanted something more assertive. I increased the number of cloves to 16, which bumped up the flavor but also made the chunks of garlic obtrusive in the dish. Mashing the cooked and cooled garlic into a paste with the side of my knife before adding it

back to the shrimp solved this problem with minimal effort.

Lime juice, lime zest, and fresh cilantro added at the end of cooking contributed brightness, and chopped jalapeño and four cloves of minced raw garlic gave the sauce a spicy bite—as well as another layer of garlic flavor. This was the garlic shrimp I remembered. **–Kelley Baker**

MEXICAN-STYLE GARLIC SHRIMP SERVES 4

Buy extra-large shrimp (21 to 25 per pound) for this recipe.

- 16 garlic cloves, peeled and halved, plus 4 cloves, minced
- ¼ cup olive oil
- 2 pounds extra-large shrimp, peeled and deveined
  Salt and pepper
- 1½ teaspoons grated zest and 3 tablespoons juice from 2 limes
- 2 tablespoons unsalted butter
- 2 jalapeño chiles, seeded and minced
- 2 tablespoons finely chopped fresh cilantro

1. Heat halved garlic cloves and oil in small saucepan over medium-high heat until bubbles begin to form. Reduce heat to low and cook, stirring occasionally, until garlic is softened, 12 to 15 minutes. Strain garlic, reserving oil. Use side of chef's knife to mash garlic into fine paste. (Garlic paste and oil can be refrigerated separately for up to 1 day.)

2. Pat shrimp dry with paper towels and season with salt and pepper. Heat reserved garlic oil in large skillet over medium heat until shimmering. Cook shrimp, covered, stirring occasionally, until cooked through, 3 to 5 minutes. Transfer shrimp to plate and tent with foil.

3. Reduce heat to medium-low. Add lime juice to empty skillet and whisk in butter and garlic paste until smooth. Add cooked shrimp, minced garlic, lime zest, jalapeños, and cilantro to pan and toss to coat. Season with salt and pepper. Serve.

Kitchen Know-How
BUILDING RICH GARLIC FLAVOR

For a sweet, nutty foundation of garlic flavor, poach halved garlic cloves in oil to soften them and infuse the oil. Then remove the softened cloves and mash them into a paste, which is added to the shrimp—with raw minced garlic—at the end of cooking. The infused oil is used to cook the shrimp.

We like to serve these shrimp with Mexican rice and extra lime wedges.

Rustic Peach Cake

I recently tried my hand at making a peach cake. What a waste of fresh peaches! The cake was mushy, and the peaches tasted washed out. Is there any way to make this recipe work? –Carolyn Sheahan, Baltimore, Md.

Kitchen Know-How
PREVENTING SOGGY CAKE

Ripe peaches throw off a lot of juice when they cook, and that liquid can make cakes soggy. Here's how we control the moisture in this cake.

1. Scatter chopped dried peaches or apricots over the batter before arranging the fresh peaches on top. The dried fruit soaks up the excess peach juice, eliminating a soggy cake top.

2. Arrange the peaches in a circular pattern around the edge of the cake, reserving 3 slices to fill in the center.

Easy Peach Peeling

Our preferred method for peeling peaches is to use a serrated vegetable peeler. Our favorite serrated peeler, the Messermeister Serrated Swivel Peeler, is available at most kitchen supply stores for about $6.

TOP PEELER
Messermeister Serrated Swivel Peeler

There are countless styles of cakes made with fresh peaches, but the most popular recipes for peach cake are rustic single-layer yellow cakes studded with chunks of fresh peaches. I gathered a dozen recipes for this style of cake, bought a bushel of peaches, and got baking.

These recipes had big problems. Some cakes were made mushy and wet by an excess of peach juice, while others featured chunks of bloated peaches that sank to the bottom of the pan and steamed. Since putting peaches inside the cake was causing so many problems, I decided to start with one recipe I'd tried that put the peaches on top of the cake. I found that just two peeled, pitted, and sliced peaches were enough to cover the top of my 9-inch springform pan and give the cake good peach flavor. The top portion of this cake (where the fruit met the cake) was soggy, but I could fix that problem later.

My tasters liked the fruit on top of this cake, but they didn't love the cake itself, so I shifted to using the test kitchen's recipe for yellow cake, planning to make the necessary adjustments to make it work with fresh peaches. My first move was to replace the cake flour in the yellow cake with all-purpose flour to create a sturdier crumb that could better support the fruit on top. Instead of the ¼ cup of milk in our recipe, I used a few tablespoons of sour cream for a denser, heartier texture. And because the peaches were so sweet, I cut back the sugar from ¾ cup to ½ cup, using a mixture of granulated and light brown sugars for more flavor. Two eggs and a stick of butter remained constant.

This rich, dense cake is packed with bright peach flavor.

Now that I had a rich but sturdy cake base, I could concentrate on fine-tuning the texture of the peaches. To reduce the moisture they were shedding, I tried precooking the peaches, but that muted their fresh flavor. Some recipes call for sugaring the peaches and letting them exude liquid before adding them to the cake, but the peaches continued to weep moisture into the cake no matter how long I let them sit. Tossing the peaches with thickeners like flour, cornstarch, and tapioca only made the peaches gluey.

Since I needed something dry to absorb excess moisture from the peaches, I wondered if dried peaches might work. I chopped a handful of dried peaches and scattered them on top of the cake batter before layering on the sliced fresh peaches. The dried peaches softened beautifully in the oven as they soaked up the flavorful juices from the fresh fruit, resulting in a moist—but not soggy—cake bursting with two layers of peach flavor. As dried peaches aren't always available, I tried using dried apricots and got the same great flavor and results.

–Erika Bruce

RUSTIC PEACH CAKE
SERVES 6 TO 8

Since overly ripe peaches will make the cake soggy, look for barely ripe peaches that give slightly to the touch. Serve this cake with lightly sweetened whipped cream or a scoop of vanilla ice cream.

Peaches
- ¼ cup granulated sugar
- ¼ teaspoon ground cinnamon
- 2 medium peaches, peeled (see box at left), pitted, and each cut into 8 wedges

Cake
- 1 cup all-purpose flour
- 1 teaspoon baking powder
- ¼ teaspoon salt
- ¼ cup granulated sugar
- ¼ cup packed light brown sugar
- 8 tablespoons (1 stick) unsalted butter, softened
- 2 large eggs
- 2 tablespoons sour cream
- 1 teaspoon vanilla extract
- ⅓ cup dried peaches or apricots, chopped fine

1. For the peaches: Adjust oven rack to middle position and heat oven to 350 degrees. Grease 9-inch springform pan. Combine sugar and cinnamon in medium bowl; reserve 2 tablespoons sugar mixture. Add peaches to bowl with remaining sugar mixture and toss to coat.

2. For the cake: Whisk flour, baking powder, and salt in bowl. With electric mixer on medium-high speed, beat sugars and butter until light and fluffy, about 2 minutes. Beat in eggs, sour cream, and vanilla until incorporated. Reduce speed to medium-low. Slowly add flour mixture and mix until just combined, about 30 seconds. Scrape batter into prepared pan. Scatter dried peaches over batter, then arrange sugared peaches in circular pattern over top, reserving 3 slices to fill the middle. Sprinkle reserved sugar mixture over peaches.

3. Bake until cake is golden brown and toothpick inserted in center comes out clean, 35 to 45 minutes. Cool at least 1 hour. Serve. (Cake can be stored at room temperature, wrapped in plastic, for 2 days.)

Summer Blueberry Crumble

I've been making my grandmother's recipe for blueberry crumble for years, and I'm sorry to admit that it's not very good: The filling is soupy, and the topping is mushy. Do you have a better recipe?

–Dorothy Jack, Albany, N.Y.

Just because this dish is simple—sweetened blueberries baked under a crunchy streusel topping—doesn't mean it's foolproof. As our reader Dorothy notes, many blueberry crumbles have soupy fillings. That's because the thick layer of streusel on top of the fruit prevents the excess moisture in the berries from evaporating. This filling soaks into the topping, leaving both components compromised. I wanted to make a crumble that featured a thick, fresh-tasting blueberry filling topped with a contrasting layer of crunchy streusel.

Crumbles are so named because they were originally vehicles for using up stale cake or cookies, which were crumbled over the fruit before baking. Modern recipes typically use a streusel topping of flour, butter, sugar, and oats over a simple filling of blueberries, sugar, and spices. (A crisp is similar but contains nuts.) I wasn't impressed by any of the blueberry crumble recipes I tested, so I decided to build my own from scratch.

Five cups of fresh blueberries was an ample amount for my 8-inch square baking dish. I baked batches of untopped filling (I'd get to the streusel later) to test granulated sugar against light brown and dark brown sugars, and the results were clear: The brown sugars competed with the fresh berry flavor. To the white sugar I added cinnamon, nutmeg, and cloves in varying amounts and combinations, but I was surprised to find that tasters preferred no spice at all—sugar and a pinch of salt was all the seasoning the filling needed.

I had two choices to firm up the filling: precooking the berries or adding a thickener. Simmering the mixture on the stovetop thickened the filling, but it also reduced the blueberries to mush and cooked out their fresh flavor. Moving on to the thickeners, I tried tossing the sugared berries with flour, tapioca, and cornstarch. The flour worked but made the filling pasty. Tapioca needed at least 40 minutes in the oven to thicken, which was too much cooking time for the berries. A mere 4 teaspoons of cornstarch was enough to quickly tighten up the filling without muting the flavor of the berries.

I did due diligence by testing crumbled cookies as the topping, but the texture was never truly crunchy, and too many crumbs sank into the filling. Cake crumbs were impractical—who has an extra cake?—so I made my own streusel by combining flour, butter, sugar, and oats in the food processor. While my tasters liked an austere filling, they wanted more flavor in the streusel, so I replaced the granulated sugar with light brown sugar and added a touch of cinnamon for spice.

My tasty new topping still sank into the filling and became quite soggy. I wondered if the size of the crumble was the problem. Rather than running the processor until the mixture was fine, I pulsed the cold butter into the dry streusel ingredients just until they clumped together. Better, but not perfect. To get even bigger crumbles, I pulsed the mixture into rough dime-sized pieces and used my fingers to incorporate the last dry bits. This streusel baked up crisp and crunchy, and I finally had a foolproof blueberry crumble.

–Erika Bruce

To let fresh summer blueberries take center stage, we keep the preparation—and the ingredient list—streamlined.

BLUEBERRY CRUMBLE
SERVES 6

Avoid instant or quick oats here—they are too soft and will make the crumble mushy. In step 2, do not press the topping into the berry mixture or it may sink and become soggy. Frozen berries do not work in this recipe because they shed too much liquid. Serve with vanilla ice cream or lightly sweetened whipped cream.

- ½ cup granulated sugar
- 4 teaspoons cornstarch
- ¼ teaspoon salt
- 5 cups fresh blueberries
- ⅔ cup all-purpose flour
- ½ cup old-fashioned oats
- ⅓ cup packed light brown sugar
- ½ teaspoon ground cinnamon
- 6 tablespoons unsalted butter, cut into 6 pieces and chilled

1. Adjust oven rack to lower-middle position and heat oven to 375 degrees. Combine granulated sugar, cornstarch, and ⅛ teaspoon salt in large bowl. Add berries to bowl and toss to coat. Transfer to 8-inch square baking dish.

2. Process flour, oats, brown sugar, cinnamon, and remaining salt in food processor until combined. Add butter and pulse until dime-sized clumps form. Transfer crumble to bowl and pinch together any powdery parts. Sprinkle crumble evenly over berries.

3. Bake until filling is bubbling around edges and topping is golden brown, about 30 minutes. Cool on wire rack for at least 30 minutes. Serve. (Once fully cooled, the crumble can be wrapped with plastic and refrigerated for 1 day. Bring to room temperature before serving.)

Crumble without a Food Processor

In step 2, mix flour, oats, brown sugar, cinnamon, and ⅛ teaspoon salt in large bowl. Add chilled butter to bowl and, using pastry blender or two knives, cut butter into dry ingredients until dime-sized clumps form. Pinch together any powdery parts, then sprinkle crumble evenly over berries. Proceed with recipe as directed.

Kitchen Know-How
BIG CLUMPS MAKE THE CRUNCHIEST TOPPING

The crumble mixture is easily prepared in a food processor. Stop pulsing when dime-sized clumps form.

ON A DIME
The perfect-sized crumble.

Food Shopping

DIJON MUSTARD: Tasters Want More Heat, Less Acid

To be labeled Dijon, a mustard must adhere to the formula developed more than 150 years ago in Dijon, France. Finely ground brown or black mustard seeds are mixed with an acidic liquid (vinegar, wine, and/or grape must) and sparsely seasoned with salt and sometimes a hint of spice. Dijon should be smooth and have a clean, nose-tingling heat. To find out which Dijon mustard is best, we rounded up eight nationally available brands and tasted them plain and in a simple mustard vinaigrette. What did we find out?

Our tasters preferred spicier mustards. The three hottest mustards—Grey Poupon, Maille, and Roland—were our tasters' overall favorites. Interestingly, when we measured the pH level of each brand, this hot trio also proved to be the least acidic. (Note that a higher pH value equals lower acidity.) A peek inside the mustard-making process explains why. When mustard seeds are ground, an enzyme called myrosinase is released. The myrosinase activates the mustard's dormant heat-producing chemicals (called glucosinolates), but the addition of acid retards this reaction. So less acid produces a mustard with more heat-producing chemicals. These heat-producing chemicals, however, are volatile and will dissipate over time. For this reason, we recommend checking "use by" dates, buying fresher mustards when possible, and never storing Dijon for more than six months.

What other qualities mattered? The presence or absence of wine in these mustards did not impact results: Grey Poupon has it, but Maille and Roland do not. Country of origin didn't matter either, as Grey Poupon is made in the United States, Maille in Canada, and Roland in France. What was important was balance. Mustards that were too acidic, too salty, or muddied with other flavors were downgraded by our tasters. The mustards are listed below, with tasters' comments, in order of preference. –Scott Kathan

1.   2.   3.   4.   5.   6.   7.   8.

Highly Recommended

1. **GREY POUPON** Dijon Mustard, $3.79 for 10 ounces, pH: 3.64
   This "potent," "bold" American-made mustard was deemed the hottest by tasters. It "gets you in the nose like a Dijon should." A "nice balance of sweet, tangy, and sharp" sealed the deal for one happy taster, who declared, "I want this on my ham and cheese sandwich."

2. **MAILLE** Dijon Originale Traditional Dijon Mustard, $3.99 for 7.5 ounces, pH: 3.68
   This French brand is made in Canada, where the bulk of the mustard seeds for the French mustard industry are grown. It had a "nice balance of heat and complexity," with tasters calling out "perfume-y" flavors of "smoke," "butter," "fruit," and "pepper." It was the second hottest mustard in our lineup.

3. **ROLAND** Extra Strong Dijon Mustard, $4.79 for 13 ounces, pH: 3.80
   This French mustard features a "sharp horseradish bite" and "nasal heat" and was the third hottest mustard overall. Tasters loved the "smoky," "oaky," and "meaty" flavors. "Surprising complexity."

Recommended

4. **JACK DANIEL'S** Stone Ground Dijon Mustard, $3.49 for 9 ounces, pH: 3.58
   Tasters didn't detect much heat in this "mild and sweet" sample when tasting it plain, but its heat bloomed in the vinaigrette, where it was deemed "robust" and "salty" (it had the most salt of any sample).

Recommended with Reservations

5. **ANNIE'S NATURALS ORGANIC** Dijon Mustard, $3.49 for 9 ounces, pH: 3.45
   This sample's "warm spice flavor" hurt its overall scores: "weird sweet and spice-y notes" was a common complaint. Tasters thought this mustard was too acidic, noting its "tart" character.

6. **FRENCH'S** Dijon Mustard, $2.99 for 9 ounces, pH: 3.47
   "Highly acidic—almost tastes pickled," "way too much vinegar," and "overly tangy without balance" were common complaints. Still, some tasters thought it was passable, calling this supermarket standard "not remarkable, but not terrible" and "like ballpark mustard."

7. **WESTBRAE** Natural Dijon Style Mustard, $2.50 for 8 ounces, pH: 3.45
   This mustard tied for the most acidic and had the least amount of salt, prompting tasters to describe it as "lacking depth," "with no interesting dance of flavors." A few did like its "mellow, building heat."

Not Recommended

8. **PLOCHMAN'S** Premium Dijon Mustard, $2.99 for 9 ounces, pH: 3.46
   Tasters were disappointed that this "watery," "sour," "fruity and weak" sample had "no heat or complexity." "Sissy mustard" sums up its performance.

Taste Test Vinegars

Below are the vinegars we stock in the test kitchen, notes on how we use them, and our taste-test winners.

White Distilled Vinegar
Made from grain alcohol, white vinegar has no added flavor and is therefore the harshest—and yet most pure—vinegar. We use it to make pickles and, diluted with water, as a cleaning agent for kitchen surfaces and hard-skinned fruits and vegetables.
★TEST KITCHEN WINNER: Heinz Distilled White Vinegar

Apple Cider Vinegar
This vinegar has a tangy bite and fruity sweetness that works perfectly in bread-and-butter pickles, barbecue sauce, and coleslaw. Unfiltered varieties typically have the most apple flavor.
★TEST KITCHEN WINNER: Maille Apple Cider Vinegar

Red Wine Vinegar
Use this slightly sweet, sharp vinegar for bold vinaigrettes and rich sauces—it works particularly well with potent flavors. Our tasters prefer red wine vinegars made from a blend of wine grapes and Concord grapes (typically used in grape juice) because the latter adds a welcome hint of sweetness.
★TEST KITCHEN WINNER: Spectrum Naturals Organic Red Wine Vinegar

White Wine Vinegar
This vinegar's refined, fruity bite makes it the perfect complement to light vinaigrettes and buttery sauces. We use white wine vinegar in dishes (like potato salad and hollandaise sauce) where the color of red wine vinegar would detract from the presentation.
★TEST KITCHEN WINNER: Acetaia Bellei White Wine Vinegar "Oro"

Rice Vinegar
Also referred to as rice wine vinegar, this vinegar is made from steamed rice. Since rice vinegar has a lower acidity than other vinegars, we use it to add gentle balance to Asian-influenced marinades and dressings. Avoid cooking with seasoned rice vinegar, as it can taste overly sweet.
★TEST KITCHEN WINNER: Marukan Genuine Brewed Rice Vinegar

Balsamic Vinegar
While expensive Italian balsamic vinegars are highly concentrated and aged for years, less expensive commercial varieties are often simply young wine vinegars with sugar and coloring added. We use this vinegar in vinaigrettes and glazes and to finish soups and sauces.
★TEST KITCHEN WINNER: Lucini 10-Year Gran Riserva Balsamico

Equipment Roundup

RATINGS
Good = ★★★
Fair = ★★
Poor = ★

STOVETOP GRIDDLES: Which Models Can Take the Heat?

Nonstick skillets are perfect for smaller breakfasts, but if you need to feed a crowd (and feed them quickly), a griddle that can span two burners is the way to go. Setting goals of perfectly crisp bacon and golden-brown pancakes every time, we gathered eight models priced under $100 and headed to the stove.

BRINGING HOME THE BACON (AND PANCAKES): The capabilities of each griddle soon became clear, with the results for both bacon and pancakes nothing short of extreme: raw to incinerated. Only the Anolon and All-Clad models provided consistent, even heat across the entire griddle, with no hot spots, producing golden pancakes and crispy bacon. Why did the other models produce such extreme results?

HEAT DISTRIBUTION: To measure how quickly the heat traveled across the entire griddle surface, we recorded temperatures at 1-, 3-, and 5-minute intervals at three different spots on every griddle, with only one burner set to medium. Anodized aluminum griddles heated the most quickly and evenly over the entire surface of the griddle, which translated into more evenly cooked food. Griddles made from cast iron started slowly, but then rapidly became uncontrollably hot (reaching well over 500 degrees), causing food to burn severely. Griddles made from ceramic or cast aluminum were less able to maintain a consistent heat level and produced unevenly cooked food. Finally, we measured the time it took griddles to cool down to 100 degrees (cool enough to handle). Lighter griddles made from anodized aluminum had the fastest cool-down time, and heavy pans made from cast iron were the slowest.

TOO HOT TO HANDLE: Handles matter—a lot! Flat handles made it hard to move the griddles on and off the stove and took longer to cool down. Metal handles became too hot to hold after just a few minutes of cooking. Overall, we prefer heat-resistant loop handles, like those on the Anolon Advanced, Circulon 2, and KitchenAid models, which remained cool throughout cooking.

DESIGN MATTERS: Griddles ranged in weight from 3 to 14 pounds, and testers found the lighter models much easier to handle. We assumed that a grease well would help drain off bacon fat, but most grease wells were too shallow, and on one model grease overflowed, causing a dangerous fire. The one exception was the All-Clad, which featured a large well that safely held up to ½ cup of bacon grease. Models with pour spouts won extra points, as did those with nonstick coatings.

SUMMING UP: With its even cooking, heat-resistant handles, and low price, the Anolon griddle is hard to beat. The All-Clad was another top performer. **–Meredith Butcher**

Recommended

ANOLON Advanced Double Burner Griddle
$48.95 at amazon.com
Material: Nonstick anodized aluminum
Weight: 3.7 pounds
Cooking Surface: 17 by 9.25 inches
Bacon: ★★ **Pancakes:** ★★★ **Heat Distribution:** ★★★
Handle Heat Resistance: ★★★
Comments: This griddle cooked up golden-brown pancakes every time. Bacon crisped quickly, and a convenient pour spout made grease disposal easy. Light construction makes this griddle cool down quickly (only 14 minutes) and easy to wash—convenient enough for everyday use.

ALL-CLAD LTD Grande Griddle
$99.95 at amazon.com
Material: Nonstick anodized aluminum
Weight: 5.9 pounds
Cooking Surface: 17.5 by 9 inches (excluding well)
Bacon: ★★★ **Pancakes:** ★★ **Heat Distribution:** ★★★
Handle Heat Resistance: ★★
Comments: Pancakes were golden brown, but trying to fit six large ones on the surface was a challenge—as the batter spread into the well, the round pancakes warped into odd shapes. The bacon was crisp, and most of the fat ended up in the large well, making the strips less greasy.

Recommended with Reservations

KITCHEN ESSENTIALS from Calphalon Pro Series Double Griddle
$59.99 at amazon.com
Material: Nonstick anodized aluminum
Weight: 4.95 pounds
Cooking Surface: 17.25 by 10 inches
Bacon: ★★ **Pancakes:** ★★ **Heat Distribution:** ★★
Handle Heat Resistance: ★★
Comments: This griddle had the greatest width, letting us use a large spatula to flip the pancakes. While the bacon cooked right over the burners crisped in a short time, strips in the middle of the pan took a few extra minutes—a minor flaw.

CIRCULON 2 Double Burner Griddle

$49.99 at amazon.com
Material: Nonstick anodized aluminum
Weight: 3.7 pounds
Cooking Surface: 17.25 by 9.25 inches
Bacon: ★★ **Pancakes:** ★★ **Heat Distribution:** ★
Handle Heat Resistance: ★★★
Comments: The circular ridges on the griddle surface kept food from sticking, but tasters weren't crazy about the ringed pattern these ridges imprinted on the pancakes. The bacon, which did not pick up the circular marks, crisped quickly and evenly.

KITCHENAID Gourmet Essentials Double Burner Griddle
$39.95 at amazon.com
Material: Nonstick aluminum with enamel exterior
Weight: 3.95 pounds
Cooking Surface: 17.25 by 7.25 inches
Bacon: ★ **Pancakes:** ★★★ **Heat Distribution:** ★
Handle Heat Resistance: ★★★
Comments: This griddle cooked pancakes pretty evenly, but bacon didn't fare as well. Slices arranged across its narrow 7.25-inch width hung over the edges and didn't crisp properly. The bacon began smoking after 3 minutes, which did not happen on the other griddles.

Not Recommended

NORDICWARE Pro Cast Flat-Top Reversible Grill/Griddle
$53.85 at amazon.com
Material: Nonstick cast aluminum
Weight: 5.05 pounds
Cooking Surface: 17 by 9.14 inches (excluding well)
Bacon: ★★ **Pancakes:** ★ **Heat Distribution:** ★★
Handle Heat Resistance: N/A
Comments: The lack of lip and slippery surface made flipping pancakes almost impossible, with most of them sliding off the griddle. The bacon cooked more easily, but the prospect of cleanup scared off testers, who, given the lack of handles, feared that hot grease would splash onto their hands when they tried to pour it off.

LODGE LOGIC Pro Grid Iron Griddle
$42.99 at amazon.com
Material: Preseasoned cast iron
Weight: 14 pounds
Cooking Surface: 16.81 by 8.44 inches (excluding well)
Bacon: ★ **Pancakes:** ★ **Heat Distribution:** ★★
Handle Heat Resistance: ★
Comments: This griddle is a challenge to maneuver, clean, and store. Controlling the heat was difficult, with both pancakes and bacon scorching within seconds—even with the burner on medium-low. With a 35-minute cool-down time, this 14-pound griddle is a beast.

KITCHEN ESSENTIALS from Calphalon Cast Iron Reversible Grill/Griddle
$39.99 at amazon.com
Material: Preseasoned cast iron
Weight: 11.6 pounds
Cooking Surface: 13.25 by 8.75 inches (excluding well)
Bacon: ★ **Pancakes:** ★ **Heat Distribution:** ★★
Handle Heat Resistance: ★
Comments: This griddle should come with a warning to keep a fire extinguisher close by. So small that it barely covered both burners, it also has flat handles that let flames from the stove reach the surface of the griddle, igniting a small grease fire. Only four pancakes fit at once, and batter spilled into the hard-to-clean well.

Notes from Our Test Kitchen

TIPS, TECHNIQUES, AND TOOLS FOR BETTER COOKING

Kitchen Creations

Flavored Mayonnaises

Flavored mayonnaises come together quickly and can be used as sauces for fish or chicken, spreads for sandwiches, or cooling dips for our **Crispy Sweet Potato Fries** (page 19). Each recipe makes about 1 cup and can be refrigerated for up to 4 days.

LEMON-CAYENNE MAYONNAISE

Whisk 1 cup mayonnaise, 2 tablespoons lemon juice, 1 minced garlic clove, and ¼ teaspoon cayenne pepper in small bowl. Season with salt and refrigerate for 30 minutes.

SUN-DRIED TOMATO-CAPER MAYONNAISE

Whisk 1 cup mayonnaise, 3 tablespoons minced oil-packed sun-dried tomatoes (patted dry with paper towels), 1 tablespoon finely chopped capers, and 1 minced garlic clove in small bowl. Season with salt and refrigerate for 30 minutes.

TARRAGON-MUSTARD MAYONNAISE

Whisk 1 cup mayonnaise, 2 tablespoons Dijon mustard, 2 tablespoons finely chopped fresh tarragon, and 1 tablespoon white wine vinegar in small bowl. Season with salt and refrigerate for 30 minutes.

GARDEN HERB MAYONNAISE

Whisk 1 cup mayonnaise, 1 tablespoon lemon juice, 2 tablespoons finely chopped fresh basil, 1 tablespoon finely chopped fresh parsley, 2 teaspoons finely chopped fresh chives, and ½ teaspoon minced fresh sage in small bowl. Season with salt and refrigerate for 30 minutes.

Inside the Test Kitchen
PERFECTING PRESS-IN CRUST

For a uniformly thick crust on the bottom and sides of our Icebox Oreo Cheesecake (page 17), follow these simple steps:

1. Using your hands, press half of the cookie crumbs into an even layer on the bottom of a springform pan.
2. Tip the pan to the side and press the remaining crumbs evenly into the sides, turning the springform pan as you go to ensure an even thickness.

Cheese: Buy Big

While developing our **Wilted Spinach Salad** recipes (page 13), we undertook the messy task of crumbling dozens of cups of soft cheeses, from goat to blue to feta. Looking for a faster option, we put several precrumbled cheeses to the test. While these cheeses were convenient, tasters found their texture "dry and pasty" when compared with the "creamy" hand-crumbled samples; this is because precrumbled cheeses have more surface area exposed, and so are more prone to drying out. Larger pieces of cheese also have the advantage of being less expensive than their precrumbled counterparts.

Better Texture, and Faster, Too

We discovered some interesting information about boiling potatoes while developing our recipe for **Ranch Potato Salad** (page 15). Most recipes for boiled potatoes call for starting the spuds in cold water so that they will come up to temperature slowly and cook evenly throughout. In an attempt to shorten the cooking time, we tried letting the water boil before adding the potatoes. In a side-by-side test, we weren't surprised that tasters preferred the potatoes started in cold water for their uniformly creamy texture. We were surprised, however, to find that the total cooking time for potatoes started in cold water was less than for those started in boiling water.

Shopping for Basil

Handfuls of fresh basil give our recipe for **Garden Minestrone** (page 22) a bright and bold flavor. We bought several hundred dollars' worth of basil while developing this recipe, and in the process came up with a few purchasing and storage tips. Avoid the basil sold in plastic clamshell boxes: It is of inconsistent quality and is usually overpriced. A bunch of basil sold with

BASIL WITH ROOTS
Lasts longer, tastes better.

its roots attached is a far better option. Not only will the leaves of this basil be more flavorful, but the basil will also last longer if you store it upright in a glass at room temperature, with the roots submerged in an inch or two of water.

Homemade Bread Crumbs

The recipe for **Clams Casino Pasta Sauce** (page 5) recommends finishing the dish with homemade toasted bread crumbs, which are infinitely better than the store-bought variety. To make the crumbs, pulse 2 slices of hearty white sandwich bread in a food processor until finely ground, then toast the crumbs on a baking sheet in a 350-degree oven until golden, about 8 minutes.

Kitchen Know-How
SHOCKINGLY EASY

For our **Cool and Creamy Green Bean Salad** (page 21), we recommend blanching the beans by dunking them in boiling water and then shocking them in a bowl of ice water to set their color and preserve their crisp texture. To avoid having to fish the vegetables out of icy water, we place a fine-mesh strainer in a bowl filled with ice water and dump the hot vegetables into it. When the veggies are cool, the strainer can be lifted out, leaving the ice behind.

Gadgets & Gear V-Rack

To prevent flare-ups and charring while cooking our **Glazed Grill-Roasted Chicken** (page 24), we elevate the chickens above the grill grates on a V-shaped roasting rack. Designed to be set inside a roasting pan, on the grill the V-rack allows heat to circulate around its contents, promoting even cooking. When choosing a V-rack, look for a fixed model; we find adjustable models to be unstable and flimsy. In a recent test, the All-Clad Non-Stick Roasting Rack ($24.95) rated tops. The rack features long, conveniently located handles, an easy-to-clean surface, and enough room for two chickens.

ALL-CLAD NON-STICK ROASTING RACK
Elevate your cooking with a V-rack.

Shopping with the Test Kitchen
Chicken Broth

Store-bought chicken broth is a big timesaver in recipes like our **Garden Minestrone** (page 22), but which brand is best? While tasting nine national brands of supermarket chicken broth, we found a few clues to quality. Our winning brand, Swanson Certified Organic Chicken Broth, and our other recommended broths share two important characteristics: less than 700 milligrams of sodium per serving and a short ingredient list that includes vegetables, such as carrots, celery, and onions.

OUR FAVORITE CHICKEN BROTH
Swanson Certified Organic Chicken Broth

Chinese Five-Spice

Regardless of how much soda we poured onto our **Cola-Barbecued Ribs** (page 20), we struggled to capture the flavor of cola without overloading on sugar. After imbibing several liters of cola (see cola tasting on page 20), our tasters picked up on flavors reminiscent of warm spices such as ginger, cinnamon, and clove. Thinking that a combination of similar spices might help accentuate the cola flavor in the ribs, we scoured the supermarket until we discovered a perfect solution: Chinese five-spice

FIVE-SPICE POWDER
The secret to great cola flavor.

powder, a combination of cinnamon, clove, fennel seed, star anise, and Sichuan peppercorns that is an integral seasoning in Chinese cooking. The warm spice flavors perfectly mimicked the essence of cola, and the spicy Sichuan peppercorns lent a kick reminiscent of classic barbecue sauce.

Perfect Cookies Every Time

When cookie recipes like our **Sand Tarts** (page 7) specify the size of raw cookies and their spacing, it is imperative to get these measurements right. (Accidentally increasing the dough by only ¼ inch will reduce the yield and may cause the cookies to bake improperly or spread into one another.) We found that a convenient way to ensure proper size is to use a ruler to measure the balls of dough and to mark the parchment paper for spacing cookies evenly on the baking sheet.

How to **HALVE A CAKE ROUND**

Many layer cake recipes (like our **Red, White, and Blue Layer Cake** on the inside back cover) call for individual cake rounds to be halved through the equator. Unfortunately, it's all too easy to make crooked, off-center, sloppy-looking cuts. Here's how to get evenly cut layers every time.

1. Using a long, serrated knife, first make a shallow cut around the cake to mark the cut line. Then halve the cake round through the equator, slowly rotating the cake as you cut.

2. Carefully lift the upper cake layer and set aside. For easy maneuverability, slide each layer onto a tart pan bottom or rimless baking sheet.

Chopping Dried Fruit

Dried fruit (like the dried peaches or apricots used in our **Rustic Peach Cake** on page 26) and knives have a very sticky relationship. An easy way to avoid sticking when chopping dried fruit is to give your knife a quick spritz with cooking spray before getting started.

Seeding Summer Squash

Both yellow squash and zucchini (which we call for in our **Garden Minestrone** on page 22) are filled with small, translucent seeds that can have a bitter taste and slimy texture. To avoid slippery squash, choose small to medium specimens that weigh 8 to 10 ounces (they contain fewer seeds), halve the squash lengthwise, and use a spoon or melon baller to scoop out the seeds.

SEEDS BE GONE
Avoid soggy sautés and slimy soups by seeding summer squash.

Spicy Serranos

One of the chiles called for in the recipe for **Triple-Chile Tomato Sauce** on page 5 is a fresh serrano (jalapeños and jarred banana peppers are the others). Our tasters found this chile, which is sold in varying shades of green and red and looks like a thin jalapeño, to have a "very fresh, clean flavor" and a brazen heat that dissipates relatively quickly. We like to use serrano chiles in salsas, chilis, and curries.

LITTLE PEPPER, BIG FIRE
Not for the faint of heart.

Kitchen Know-How
GRILL SAFETY PRIMER

To make sure your grilling experiences always end happily, it is important to keep safety in mind. Here are a few safety tips for firing up the grill.

LOCATION IS EVERYTHING

Always set up your grill at least 10 feet from your home on a flame-safe surface—a driveway or patio rather than grass or a wooden deck—and away from where children and pets might wander. Pay special attention when cooking with charcoal in windy weather, as sparks can fly out of the grill (we recommend keeping a spray bottle filled with water to quell any sparks or flare-ups).

CLEANLINESS COUNTS

Always scrape and oil your grill grate (with an oil-dipped wadded paper towel held with tongs) before use to help prevent food from sticking. It is important that the interior basin of your grill, whether gas or charcoal, be cleaned a few times each season to wash away built-up food matter that can ignite or lend off flavors to whatever you're cooking. Empty drip pans and ash-catchers frequently to reduce mess.

FOOD SAFETY MATTERS

Always use separate platters for raw and cooked foods to avoid cross-contamination, and always dispose of excess marinade. Save sauces until the end of cooking to prevent them from burning and to keep your basting brush from becoming contaminated by uncooked meat.

When Things Go Wrong in the Kitchen

PEPPERMINT STEAK

One of my favorite recipes calls for soaking meat in a marinade of vermouth and other ingredients. One day while I was at work, my teenage daughters decided to prepare a surprise dinner for me. Pulling the alcohol from our stash, they selected a bottle of clear liquor and began to soak the steak. Unfortunately, the bottle they used was peppermint schnapps. Their dad, loyal to a fault, ate the steak and told them it was "most unusual" in flavor, but very tender.

Helen Fones Cheverly, Md.

HOT AND SAKE SOUP

It was a busy Sunday, and I decided to make hot-and-sour soup for my family's lunch. It got rave reviews—my husband even ate two bowls. But for the first and only time, my family jointly decided to forgo our afternoon plans and take naps. I didn't think twice about it, and they raved about this hot-and-sour soup for months. Several months later, we were having a party and I reached into the liquor cabinet for the sake, only to discover that it was vinegar, not sake. I stared at the bottle and realized that if this was vinegar, what I had poured in the hot-and-sour soup that day must have been sake! I found the sake bottle more than half gone in my pantry, confirming that on that wonderful Sunday, I fed my family hot-and-sake soup.

Silvie Goldstein Chesapeake, Va.

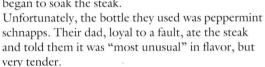

SALINE SOLUTION

Many years ago in Hawaii, a group of friends and I went to the beach for the day and had a picnic. Everyone brought a dish to share and we grilled hot dogs. With so many kids running around, it was only a matter of time before one of them bumped into the portable grill and knocked all the hot dogs into the sand. Not wanting to go without the hot dogs, we washed the sand off them in the ocean as best we could and then put them back on the grill to reheat. We didn't realize that the surf was churning up plenty of sand in our rinsing water, so our hot dogs were not only super-salty but crunchy just the same!

Theresa Nesser Apache Junction, Ariz.

SALTY TEA

We were hosting a Chinese New Year dinner party one year and had a kitchen full of friends helping with the food. I had put on a pot of salted water for blanching the long beans. Before I knew it, a friend started stir-frying the raw beans with garlic and ginger. They looked vivid green and smelled great, so I let my friend finish off the dish, thinking that perhaps I should reassess the need to blanch the beans first. We all sat down to a great meal of duck, pan-fried noodles, long beans, baby bok choy, steamed fish, rice, and tea. Soon after the meal started, I noticed a decided hush come over the table. One sip from the tea was enough to tell me that the hot water I had poured into the teapot was in fact my briny water for the long beans! The coffee was a more popular choice that day.

Susan Wing Albuquerque, N.M.

SPOONFUL OF SUGAR

As a newlywed, I wanted to make my husband a nice dinner after a hard day's work. I found a recipe for beef stew I thought he would like. Although most of the ingredients were straightforward, the addition of tapioca threw me a little. I figured there must be a reason for it, so I grabbed the box of tapioca from the cupboard and dumped in a few packages. Unfortunately, I didn't know that tapioca comes in an unsweetened version specifically used for thickening stews; it was a challenge to choke down the beef stew seasoned with tapioca pudding mix.

Carol Wright Haven, Kan.

FREEZER BURN

Once, while assembling lasagna for dinner, I spotted a brown fleck on a piece of shredded cheese. I tasted the mozzarella, thinking that it might be moldy. I realized instantly that what I had thought was shredded cheese was really the shredded frozen hash browns I had transferred to the same type of freezer bags used to store my cheese weeks before. Desperately discouraged about my hours of lost work, and finding no way to remove the layers of hash browns, I baked the lasagna. Without explaining my mistake, I served it to my husband. To my surprise, he ate every last bite, and then asked for seconds!

Rachel Spigarelli Kirkland, Wash.

FLAMING TACOS

I served tacos for a dinner party several years ago. I threw the shells into the oven to crisp up, but pressed "broil" instead of "bake" by accident! Within minutes, the shells caught fire; my husband raced into the kitchen, grabbed a kitchen towel, opened the oven, and began striking the flaming taco shells with the towel. But each time he struck one of the shells, it stuck to the towel. As he drew his arm back to prepare for another assault on the oven, flaming taco shells were catapulted all over the kitchen! The frightened guests were forced to duck behind a door, as my wannabe-fireman husband flung flaming tacos toward them.

Mardy Lane Versailles, Ky.

Send us your funniest kitchen disaster stories. E-mail us by visiting **CooksCountry.com/kitchendisasters**. Or write to us at Kitchen Disasters, Cook's Country, P.O. Box 470739, Brookline, MA 02447. If we publish your story, you'll receive a complimentary one-year subscription to *Cook's Country*.

Red, White, and Blue Layer Cake

Colorful layers of red velvet cake make the perfect foundation
for this Independence Day dessert.

To make this cake, you will need:

- 1 teaspoon unflavored powdered gelatin
- 2 tablespoons water
- 3 cups heavy cream
- ¼ cup confectioners' sugar
- 2 (8-inch) red velvet cake rounds*
  Blueberries and strawberries for garnish

For the whipped cream filling: Combine gelatin and water in medium bowl. Let stand 5 minutes to soften gelatin. Bring ¼ cup cream to simmer in small saucepan over medium heat, then whisk in gelatin mixture until no lumps remain; let cool 3 minutes. With electric mixer on medium-high speed, beat cooled gelatin mixture, sugar, and remaining cream to stiff peaks, about 2 minutes.

To assemble: Using serrated knife, cut each cake horizontally into 2 even layers (see page 31). Place 1 cake layer on serving platter. Spread one quarter of whipped cream filling over cake. Repeat, alternating layers of cake and filling. Garnish with blueberries and strawberries and refrigerate until set, about 2 hours. Serve. (Cake can be refrigerated for up to 24 hours.)

* Go to **CooksCountry.com** for our red velvet cake recipe or use your own.

Recipe Index

RC = Recipe Card

Cook's Country

AUGUST/SEPTEMBER 2008

Better Tomato Salads
Simple Method Builds Big Flavor

Grilled Pork Loin
Flavored with Smoke & Spice

Easy Skillet Pizza
10-Minute No-Yeast Dough!

GRILLED CHICKEN BREASTS
With Cheesy Herb Stuffing

SHREDDED BBQ BEEF
Secrets to Moist, Meaty 'Cue

BLUEBERRY GRUNT
Rediscovering a Lost Classic

NO-SCRATCH SCRUBBERS
Safe Enough for Nonstick?

LEMON SHEET CAKE
Big Cake, Bigger Lemon Flavor

SWEET AND SOUR RIBS
Best Slow-Cooker Recipe

SUMMER PASTA SALADS
With Fresher, Lighter Pesto

SYRACUSE SALT POTATOES
Boil Spuds with 2 Cups of Salt!

CLASSIC BEEF KEBABS
Tender, Juicy Meat Guaranteed

WOOD-GRILLED SALMON
Wood Flavor, No Plank

Watch Our New Show on Public Television!

Cook's Country from America's Test Kitchen debuts in September on public television stations across the country. Filmed in this 1806 farmhouse, our new show brings the recipes, tips, tastings, and testings of **Cook's Country** alive. Go to *CooksCountryTV.com* to watch a preview of the show.

$4.95 U.S./$6.95 CANADA

09>

0 74470 05251 7

Cook's Country

Dear Country Cook,

When I was 10 years old, I spent two weeks at a boy's camp in northern Vermont. We played capture the flag on horseback, reveille was played by a bugler who owed his syncopated style to Dizzy Gillespie, and the counselors often disappeared at night for a trip across the lake on illicit rendezvous at a neighboring girls' camp. And of course there was the endless quest for earning badges for archery, tent construction, and fire starting.

I have vivid memories of nights around the campfire: smoke in the eyes, the sound of water lapping rocks, moonlight streaking across the lake, and most of all, the sounds of the night—a yip, a breaking branch, or an otherworldly howl or hoot that was deliciously unaccountable.

A fire is so basic, so hard-wired into our experience, that it connects us directly to something forgotten. Whether it is a Dutch oven filled with baking powder biscuits nestled in burning embers or the Thanksgiving bird roasted in our wood cookstove, it is the immediacy of the experience that wakens us much the way a full breath of cold, pine-scented air brings us to our senses.

Country cooking is, at its best, basic and useful, immediate and satisfying. It gets us closer to the heart of things, to where we want to be. Cooking over a campfire is not just for kids, or teenagers looking for adventure—it is for the rest of us too. But these days, many of us are so rich in experience that we forget to rekindle those long-forgotten fires.

Christopher Kimball
Christopher Kimball
Founder and Editor, Cook's Country Magazine

Roasting Marshmallows over an open fire. 1947
Photographer: Martha Holmes/Stringer/Time Life Pictures

AUGUST/SEPTEMBER 2008

Cook's Country

departments

in every issue

features

Founder and Editor Christopher Kimball
Editorial Director Jack Bishop
Deputy Editor Bridget Lancaster
Senior Editors Scott Kathan
Jeremy Sauer
Test Kitchen Director Erin McMurrer
Associate Editors Cali Rich
Diane Unger
Test Cooks Kelley Baker
Meredith Butcher
Greg Case
Assistant Test Cook Lynn Clark
Assistant Test Kitchen Director Matthew Herron
Copy Editor Amy Graves

Online Editor Kate Mason
Online Assistant Editor Leaya Lee
Editorial Assistant Meredith Smith
Senior Kitchen Assistant Nadia Domeq
Kitchen Assistants Maria Elena Delgado
Ena Gudiel, Ben Peskin
TV Producer Melissa Baldino
Contributing Editor Eva Katz
Consulting Editor Guy Crosby

Design Director Amy Klee
Art Director, Magazines Julie Bozzo
Senior Designer Christine Vo
Designer Jay Layman
Staff Photographer Daniel J. van Ackere

Vice President New Technology Craig Morrow
Systems Administrator S. Paddi McHugh
IT Business Analyst Doug Sisko
Web Production Coordinator Evan Davis
IT Support Technician Brandon Lynch

Chief Financial Officer Sharyn Chabot
Human Resources Director Adele Shapiro
Controller Mandy Shito
Senior Accountant Aaron Goranson
Staff Accountant Connie Forbes
Accounts Payable Specialist Steven Kasha
Office Manager Danielle Pezely
Receptionist Henrietta Murray

Production Director Guy Rochford
Traffic & Projects Manager Alice Cummiskey
Production & Imaging Specialist Lauren Pettapiece
Color & Imaging Specialist Andrew Mannone

Vice President Marketing David Mack
Fulfillment & Circulation Manager Carrie Horan
Circulation Assistant Elizabeth Dayton
Partnership Marketing Manager Pamela Putprush
Direct Mail Director Adam Perry
Direct Mail Analyst Jenny Leong
Marketing Database Analyst Ariel Gilbert-Knight
Products Director Steven Browall
Product Promotions Director Randi Lawrence
E-Commerce Marketing Director Hugh Buchan
Associate Marketing Manager Laurel Zeidman
Marketing Copywriter David Goldberg
Customer Service Manager Jacqueline Valerio
Customer Service Representatives Julie Gardner
Jillian Nannicelli

Vice President Sales Demee Gambulos
Retail Sales & Marketing Manager Emily Logan
Retail Sales Associate Anthony King
Corporate Marketing Associate Bailey Vatalaro
Publicity Deborah Broide

ON THE COVER: PHOTOGRAPHY: Leight Belsch/FoodPix. ILLUSTRATION: John Burgoyne.
IN THIS ISSUE: COLOR FOOD PHOTOGRAPHY: Keller + Keller. STYLING: Mary Jane Sawyer, Marie Piraino. ILLUSTRATION: Lisa Perrett.

Cook's Country magazine (ISSN 1552-1990), number 22, is published bimonthly by Boston Common Press Limited Partnership, 17 Station Street, Brookline, MA 02445. Copyright 2008 Boston Common Press Limited Partnership. Periodicals Postage paid at Boston, Mass., and additional mailing offices. Publications Mail Agreement No. 40020778. Return undeliverable Canadian addresses to P.O. Box 875, Station A, Windsor, Ontario N9A 6P2. POSTMASTER: Send address changes to Cook's Country, P.O. Box 8382, Red Oak, IA 51591-1382. For subscription and gift subscription orders, subscription inquiries, or change-of-address notices, call 800-526-8447 in the U.S. or 515-247-7571 from outside the U.S. or write us at Cook's Country, P.O. Box 8382, Red Oak, IA 51591-1382.   PRINTED IN THE USA

America's TEST KITCHEN is a 2,500-square-foot kitchen located just outside of Boston. It is the home of *Cook's Country* and *Cook's Illustrated* magazines and is the workday destination for more than three dozen test cooks, editors, and cookware specialists. Our mission is to test recipes until we understand how and why they work and arrive at the best version. We also test kitchen equipment and supermarket ingredients in search of brands that offer the best value and performance. You can watch us work by tuning into *America's Test Kitchen* (www.americastestkitchen.com) on public television.

Watch our new show on public television!
Cook's Country from America's Test Kitchen debuts in September on public television stations across the country. The show relies on the same practical, no-nonsense food that has made *Cook's Country* magazine so successful. Watch us develop recipes, test equipment, and taste supermarket ingredients in our brand-new test kitchen. Go to CooksCountryTV.com to watch a free preview.

Kitchen Shortcuts

READERS SHARE CLEVER TIPS FOR EVERYDAY COOKING CHALLENGES

Smarter Carving

Every time I carve a roast chicken (which is frequently), I am faced with either hauling out my huge carving board with a reservoir around the edge or using a smaller, less cumbersome board that always spills juice all over my countertop. A paper towel dam creates even more of a mess. As a solution, I place my cutting board inside a large rimmed baking sheet. It is just the right size, and the tray contains all the runaway juices as I carve.

Kevin Fox Via e-mai

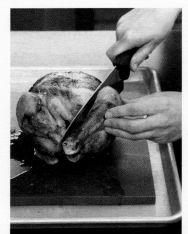

Clean Prep

Sometimes I find myself without any rubber gloves around the house, and inevitably I am preparing a dish with either raw meat or chicken. Whenever I am in this predicament, I simply place my hand inside a zipper-lock bag and continue prepping the raw food.

Dahlia Malloy
Atlanta, Ga.

Plastic Bag Storage

I save the cardboard tubes from paper towel rolls and store plastic grocery bags inside them. I am amazed by how many I can squeeze into each tube, and the tube fits in a drawer so it is tucked away out of sight.

Claudia Carrier
Sagle, Idaho

Spin It!

EVEN CAKE BATTER

Having baked and decorated over 4,500 wedding cakes over the course of more than 30 years, I discovered a sure-fire way to distribute the batter in the pan evenly without using a spatula. After pouring the cake batter into a round pan, merely give it a quick spin on the counter, being careful not to have it sail off and hit the floor. The same technique can be done with a square or rectangle, just give it a quick shake back and forth, rotating the pan once.

Marjorie Hollway Colorado Springs, Colo.

SCRUB A DUB

Instead of struggling to scrub small potatoes individually in the sink (inevitably a few potatoes go down the drain), I keep them in the mesh bag that the supermarket packages them in and use my scrub brush right through the bag. It is an easy way to quickly scrub away any caked-on dirt.

Brianne Happel
Beaverton, Ore.

NO MORE DRIPS

To keep any drips from running down the outside of bottles of olive oil, I fold a paper towel lengthwise several times until it is about an inch wide. Then, I wrap it around the neck of the bottle and secure it with a rubber band. I used to have an oily mess all over my cabinet, but now my cabinets are pristine.

Bethany Schaarschmidt
Redding, Calif.

POTATO BREAD TRICK

I make a lot of potato breads that use mashed potatoes as a main part of the ingredient list. Instead of making mashed potatoes from scratch every time, sometimes I cheat a little bit and add instant mashed potato flakes directly into the dough. It saves a lot of time.

Wendell Chapman
Dallas, Texas

SPICE SHAKER

When recipes—such as chicken tikka masala, pumpkin pie, or carrot cake—call for numerous spices, I put all the spices in a small Tupperware container. To mix the ingredients together, I simply put the lid on and shake away. This evenly mixes the spices every time.

Lucille Yip
Lahaina, Hawaii

MINI BAKING MATS

I love to use silicone baking mats, but with repeated and heavy use they become discolored and tattered. Rather than throw them away, I cut them down to fit our toaster oven pan. The "mini mats" catch crumbs and help with easy cleanup.

Bob Sabean
Barrington, N.H.

STEAM CLEANER

When cleaning my grill grate, I dip my metal grill brush in water and use it to scrape the preheated grill. The steam produced helps to clean the grates thoroughly with very little effort.

Terry Bentz
Bradenton, Fla.

DOUBLE DUTY

A water bath canner takes up a lot of space, so I use my pasta cooker for canning instead. It is easy to fill the strainer basket with jars and lower them all at once into the hot water and lift the entire basket out when the processing time is complete. I then can easily refill the basket and lower it again into the simmering water for a second processing batch, if necessary. The pasta insert allows the water to simmer around the jars and keeps them from resting on the bottom of the outer pan.

Karen Starkey
Yates Center, Kansas

CLEVER CAPPING

Whenever I open a 28-ounce can of tomatoes and don't use the whole can in a recipe, I re-use the plastic lid from an 11- to 13-ounce can of coffee as a cover for the tomatoes. This works better than covering the can with plastic wrap and is quicker than transferring the leftover tomatoes to another container. The coffee can lid also fits large cans of fruit.

Gary Hughes
West Wyoming, Pa.

If you'd like to submit a tip, please e-mail us by visiting **CooksCountry.com/kitchenshortcuts**, or send a letter to Kitchen Shortcuts, Cook's Country, P.O. Box 470739, Brookline, MA 02447. Include your name, address, and phone number. If we publish your tip, you will receive a free one-year subscription to *Cook's Country.*

NEAT TIP!

BAG THOSE RECIPES

I used to have an unorganized drawer full of recipes I'd cut out from magazines, received from friends, or printed from the Internet. To keep things organized, I simply label gallon-size storage bags with a permanent marker for each category (chicken, fish, desserts, etc.) of recipes I have and slip the recipe into the coordinating storage bag. I can neatly store these bags in a drawer in the kitchen.

Katherine Dickerson
West Yarmouth, Mass.

DUST-FREE

When I'm putting away my holiday serving bowls and platters after a party, I wrap them in plastic wrap before storing them on the shelf in my basement. This keeps them clean and dust-free for quick use the next year. I also cover my slow cooker with plastic wrap before I store it in my pantry to keep it dust-free until I use it again.

Francine Ritz
Winston-Salem, N.C.

MAKESHIFT FUNNEL

Whenever I need to pour ingredients into a small opening and can't find my funnel, I reach for a small paper plate. I simply roll the plate together and everything pours right into the opening of a jar or bottle.

Kerri Tolbert
Chambersburg, Pa.

HAVE CAKE, WILL TRAVEL

I have a trick that takes the cake! When I am transporting a frosted cake or a creamy-topped dessert on a platter, I wrap aluminum foil around a bowl or pan of the same diameter as the platter and place it on top of the dessert. Crimping the foil around the edges of both pans keeps them from pulling apart. The result is a domed protector that prevents the top of the dessert from sticking to the foil.

Mary Potter
Sterling Heights, Mich.

RECYCLED CHOCOLATE

After Easter or Halloween, we usually have several pieces of chocolate that the kids are not interested in eating. I melt the chocolate in a double boiler and spread it very thinly on a baking sheet lined with wax paper. When the chocolate is cool, I chop it up and store it to use the next time I bake cookies.

Mary Eckstein
Standish, Maine

EASY ACCESS

Searching through a drawer for cooking utensils (especially small tools like measuring spoons) can be a test of patience. To save myself from this headache, I hung a peg board in my kitchen and hang various utensils from it. Now I can quickly find the right tool without ripping apart my drawers.

Margaret Hellyer
Tacoma, Wash.

PICKLED BARBECUE

I always save the pickle brine when we finish a jar of pickles and add it to my homemade barbecue sauce. The brine gives the sauce a nice vinegary bite. Just be sure to cut down on the amount of salt in the sauce because pickle brine is very salty.

Gary Frey
Federal Way, Wash.

SINGLE-SERVE ICE CREAM

To discourage ice cream from melting as you serve it, prepare it in advance! Before your party, scoop your favorite flavor of ice cream into cupcake papers. Assemble the papers on a baking sheet and pop them into the freezer. The small portions freeze more thoroughly and melt more slowly—plus, they look festive on the table.

Martha Jack
Arlington, Mass.

CLIP IT

My husband and I entertain on our porch quite frequently in the summer, but windy weather can make a mess of paper napkins. To keep piles of napkins tidy, I use a large binder clip to hold a stack together. The clip is heavy enough to prevent the napkins from blowing away, and it's easy to grab napkins from the stack as needed.

Nancy Allen
Half Moon Bay, Calif.

A Mouse (Pad) in the Kitchen

Whenever I am using my stand mixer, it always jumps around on my countertop. To keep it stable, I place my mixer on a few computer mouse pads. It works great with minimal slippage.

Pamela Poteat
Gastonia, N.C.

Bugs Begone

During the summer, I often take my famous potato-macaroni salad to picnics. There is nothing more annoying than shooing flies and other bugs away from your picnic foods. Now, I bring my splatter screen to place on top of the bowl, which protects the salad from those pesky bugs.

Jonathan Roof
Denver, Colo.

No More Stacking

I used to stack my baking dishes and skillets (some of which are very heavy), but I got tired of lifting them all out of the cupboard to get to the one I needed, which was inevitably on the bottom of the stack. Now I use several metal bookends to hold the dishes and skillets upright, on their sides, in the cupboard. I can slide out the one I want without having to move everything around.

Elaine Darrah
Merced, Calif.

Grill Pan Cover

I use my grill pan frequently. While the pan makes great grill marks, it doesn't have a cover (like a grill does), so a lot of heat escapes and there's a lot of splatter on the stove. I don't have a domed lid that fits the pan, so instead I use large cake pans (disposable pans work, too) as makeshift covers. They fit snugly over the food, trapping heat to produce evenly cooked and juicy meat, and minimizing splatter and mess.

Donna Green
Blue Ridge, Texas

Breakfast in a Hurry!

THINKING AHEAD

I like to make baked goods for my children in the morning, but I'm often short on time. I've found two things to help me get breakfast on the table more efficiently. First, I mix the dry ingredients together the night before so I am ready to get cooking quickly. Second, I set the oven timer to come on about 30 minutes before I wake up. Using these tricks I can have hot biscuits or muffins on the table in 15 minutes! The wonderful smell also helps get the sleepyheads out of bed!

Kim Spady Hinton, Okla.

Unique Flavor Combinations Win Salad Contest

Melon shows its savory side in a refreshing salad with blue cheese, toasted pecans, and a spicy lime-basil vinaigrette.

Our $1,000 Grand-Prize Winner!

Barb Whitla
Port Charlotte, Fla.

Our grand-prize winning recipe shows that an unlikely combination of ingredients can sometimes create a memorable recipe. Barb Whitla dresses sweet cantaloupe, creamy blue cheese, and crunchy pecans with a lime-basil vinaigrette that packs some heat from black pepper. Barb found her inspiration for this unusual salad "at a posh eatery in Miami a few years ago." She tells us, "I immediately went home and re-created this dish to better suit my own tastes."

Our four runners-up also rely on a combination of unusual ingredients and fresh summer produce to put their unique touches on familiar dishes: A crisp, crunchy slaw made with broccoli and uncooked ramen noodles won points for creativity. The layering of Mexican ingredients into a flavorful salad was a surprise hit, as was a three-bean salad with Caesar flavors. The final winning entry adds sweet potatoes, arugula, and apples to potato salad.

CANTALOUPE AND BLUE CHEESE SALAD
SERVES 6 TO 8

Barb suggests using a mild blue cheese, such as Gorgonzola, in this recipe. If you don't have a melon baller, cut the melon into 1-inch pieces. Toast the pecans in a dry skillet over medium heat, shaking often, until golden, about 5 minutes.

Dressing
- 2 teaspoons grated zest and 3 tablespoons juice from 2 limes
- 1 tablespoon honey
- ¼ cup finely chopped fresh basil
- ½ teaspoon pepper
- ¼ cup extra-virgin olive oil

Salad
- 2 small cantaloupe melons, halved and seeded
- 1 cup crumbled blue cheese (see note)
- ½ cup pecans, toasted and chopped (see note)
- Salt

1. For the dressing: Combine lime zest, lime juice, honey, basil, and pepper in medium bowl. Gradually whisk in oil.

2. For the salad: Using 1-inch melon baller, scoop out cantaloupe and transfer melon balls to large bowl. Add cheese and pecans. Drizzle dressing over salad and toss until well coated. Season with salt. Serve.

Patricia Harmon
Baden, Pa.

Amber Wood
Martinsburg, W.Va.

Tracy Merriman
East Andover, N.H.

Sami Carroll
Pittsburgh, Pa.

CAESAR'S THREE-BEAN SALAD
SERVES 6 TO 8

Patricia says: "My husband, Paul, and I really enjoy Caesar salad, so I decided to try to incorporate its intense flavors into a bean salad. Paul, my official 'taster,' absolutely loves this dish." Use more or less anchovy depending on your taste.

Dressing
- 3 tablespoons lemon juice
- 2 teaspoons Dijon mustard
- 1 teaspoon Worcestershire sauce
- 1–2 anchovy fillets, minced
- 1 garlic clove, minced
- ⅓ cup extra-virgin olive oil

Salad
- 1 (16-ounce) can cannellini beans, drained and rinsed
- 1 (16-ounce) can red kidney beans, drained and rinsed
- ½ pound blanched green beans, trimmed and cut into 2-inch pieces
- 2 tablespoons sun-dried tomatoes packed in oil, rinsed, patted dry, and minced
- ½ cup drained jarred roasted red peppers, chopped
- 4 ounces fresh mozzarella cheese, cut into ½-inch chunks
- ½ cup shredded Parmesan cheese
  Salt and pepper

1. For the dressing: Combine lemon juice, mustard, Worcestershire sauce, anchovy, and garlic in medium bowl. Gradually whisk in oil.
2. For the salad: Combine beans, tomatoes, peppers, mozzarella, and Parmesan in large bowl. Drizzle dressing over salad and toss until well coated. Season with salt and pepper. Serve. (Salad can be refrigerated for several days; bring to room temperature before serving.)

LAYERED MEXICAN SALAD
SERVES 6 TO 8

Amber says: "I created this recipe with my mom's traditional layered pea salad in mind. This salad is great with fresh-from-the-garden ingredients and is always a hit at summer picnics." You will need a large (at least 2½-quart) serving bowl for this recipe. If using frozen corn, make sure to thaw and rinse it first.

Dressing
- ¼ cup mayonnaise
- ¼ cup sour cream
- ¼ cup jarred salsa
- 2 tablespoons chopped fresh cilantro
- 2 teaspoons lime juice

Salad
- 1 romaine heart, torn into bite-sized pieces (about 4 cups)
- ½ small red onion, sliced thin
- 2 cups cherry tomatoes, halved (quartered if large)
- 1 cup fresh or frozen corn kernels (see note)
- 1 (16-ounce) can black beans, drained and rinsed
- 2 ripe avocados, pitted, skinned, and chopped
- 1½ cups shredded sharp cheddar cheese
- 2 cups crushed tortilla chips

1. For the dressing: Whisk all ingredients in medium bowl.
2. For the salad: Place lettuce in large serving bowl. Spread half of dressing over lettuce, then layer with onion, tomatoes, corn, beans, avocados, and cheese. Spread remaining dressing over salad. Sprinkle with tortilla chips. Serve. (Salad can be refrigerated for 1 day; reserve tortilla chips until just before serving.)

SWEET AND RED POTATO SALAD
SERVES 6 TO 8

Tracy says: "I got the idea for this salad after a midwinter meal of roast pork with potatoes, sweet potatoes, and apples. I couldn't wait until summer to try it!" While any variety of apple will work here, we prefer the tartness and crunch of Granny Smiths in this recipe. If using baby arugula, you do not need to chop it.

Dressing
- ¼ cup cider vinegar
- 3 tablespoons whole-grain mustard
- 2 tablespoons honey
- 1 tablespoon hot sauce
- ½ cup olive oil

Salad
- 2 pounds sweet potatoes, peeled and cut into ¾-inch chunks
- 1 pound red potatoes, scrubbed and cut into ¾-inch chunks
  Salt and pepper
- 3 apples, peeled, cored, and cut into ¾-inch chunks
- 2 cups arugula, chopped rough
- 4 scallions, sliced thin

1. For the dressing: Combine vinegar, mustard, honey, and hot sauce in medium bowl. Gradually whisk in oil.
2. For the salad: Bring sweet potatoes, red potatoes, 2 tablespoons salt, and enough water to cover by 1 inch to boil in large pot over high heat. Reduce heat to medium and simmer until potatoes are just tender, about 8 minutes. Drain potatoes and cool to room temperature. Combine cooled potatoes, apples, arugula, and scallions in large bowl. Drizzle dressing over salad and toss until well coated. Season with salt and pepper. Serve.

RAMEN-BROCCOLI SLAW
SERVES 6 TO 8

Sami says: "My stepmother gave me this recipe as a way of tricking my broccoli-hating husband into eating his vegetables. He loved it!" This recipe will work with any flavor of ramen noodles, but Sami prefers the beef spice packet. Broccoli slaw is available alongside the lettuce in supermarkets.

Dressing
- ½ cup sugar
- ⅓ cup white vinegar
- ½ cup vegetable oil

Salad
- 1 (12-ounce) bag broccoli slaw mix
- 2 (3-ounce) packages ramen noodles, crushed, flavor packets reserved
- 4 scallions, sliced thin
- 1 cup shelled roasted sunflower seeds
- 1 cup slivered almonds, toasted

1. For the dressing: Whisk sugar and vinegar in medium bowl until sugar dissolves. Gradually whisk in oil.
2. For the salad: Combine broccoli slaw, ramen and flavor packets, scallions, sunflower seeds, and almonds in large bowl. Drizzle dressing over salad and toss until well coated. Refrigerate salad, covered, for at least 30 minutes or up to 2 hours. Toss salad again before serving.

We want your best holiday cookie recipes for an upcoming contest. Please submit entries by September 30, 2008. Send us your recipes by visiting **CooksCountry.com** or write to us at Recipe Contest, Cook's Country, P.O. Box 470739, Brookline, MA 02447. Include your name, address, and daytime phone number and tell us what makes your recipe special. The grand-prize winner will receive $1,000. All entries become the property of *Cook's Country*. Go to **CooksCountry.com** for more information on this and other contests.

Ask Cook's Country

WE'LL ANSWER ANY QUESTION YOU THROW AT US!

CAN A BLENDER DO IT ALL?

I'm newly married and my husband insists that if we buy a blender, we won't need a more expensive food processor. Is he right?

Josie Daraway Houston, Texas

Blenders are our first choice for handling tasks that involve liquids, including making smoothies or pureeing soups. Blenders will do a passable job of grinding small quantities of nuts or bread crumbs or making pestos. However, a food processor is much better at these tasks, and it can be used for so much more—everything from slicing vegetables to kneading bread. We recommend investing in both a food processor and blender, but if we had to choose, we'd buy a food processor first.

WHIP IT UP

My sister always refrigerates the bowl and beater before whipping cream. Is this really necessary?

Louisa Jacobs Ketchum, Idaho

To put this theory to the test, we whipped batches of cream with both chilled and room-temperature bowls and beaters and found the chilled apparatus only saved a few seconds of whipping time. Chilling the beater and bowl is not necessary for whipping cream; however, it is important that the cream itself is as cold as possible, so make sure that you don't leave the cream out on the counter before whipping.

PASTEURIZED VS. FRESH EGGS

How are eggs pasteurized? Can they be substituted for normal unpasteurized eggs?

Lorna McDaniel Roswell, Ga.

In rare cases, eating raw egg (in cookie dough, homemade mayonnaise, etc.) can result in the bacterial infection salmonella, but pasteurized eggs promise a safer alternative. Whole, in-the-shell eggs are pasteurized by going through a succession of heated water baths (warm enough to kill bacteria, but not so warm as to cook the eggs) before being chilled and waxed so that the porous shells cannot be re-contaminated.

To see how pasteurized eggs stacked up to the unpasteurized variety, we made Caesar dressing with both pasteurized and unpasteurized raw yolks, and meringues from the whites of each. We didn't notice any differences in the two dressings, but that was not the case with the meringues. We immediately noticed that the pasteurized whites were much looser and more watery than their unpasteurized counterparts. What's more, the pasteurized whites took more than twice as long to whip into a stiff and glossy meringue. Once whipped, both meringues had a similar texture and flavor. Curious how the two varieties compared when cooked, we

fried, scrambled, and baked each type of egg in a cake and found no differences in flavor or texture. Pasteurized eggs are a suitable substitute for regular eggs, but pasteurized egg whites will take more than twice as long to whip.

SAFE ALTERNATIVE
Whether in cookie dough or in Caesar dressing, pasteurized eggs provide the same flavor and texture as regular eggs—without the worry.

MEAT TENDERIZING

My sister swears that her hand-held meat tenderizer improves the texture of her pork cutlets. Are they really worth the money?

Ava Edinger Cincinnati, Ohio

Thanks to their lean nature, pork cutlets can be tough and chewy. Hand-held meat tenderizers are used to physically break down tough protein strands in the meat, presumably resulting in more tender cutlets. But do they work?

We put the two most common manual tenderizers to the test: a mallet with a jagged-toothed surface and a Jaccard meat tenderizer, which presses multiple sharp spikes into the meat. We used each tenderizer on a batch of cutlets and then compared them to cutlets that were lightly pounded with a smooth-surfaced pounder. Neither manual tenderizer improved the tenderness of the cutlets and each caused other problems. The toothed mallet gave the cutlets an unappealing pocked appearance that was especially bad around the edges. The sharp spikes on the Jaccard gave the meat a torn, "Salisbury steak" texture that we didn't like. If you want tender pork cutlets, we suggest buying tender boneless rib or loin chops and using a smooth mallet to pound them into thin ¼-inch cutlets.

TENDERIZATION AT A HEFTY COST
Neither a Jaccard meat tenderizer (top) nor a toothed mallet (bottom) improved tenderness, and both gave cutlets an unappealing torn texture.

BAKING WITH SPREADABLE BUTTER

Can packaged spreadable butter be used interchangeably for sticks of butter in baked goods?

Tanya Parish Kansas City, Kan.

Spreadable butters are simply regular butter with vegetable oil added to make them soft directly out of the refrigerator (they become liquid at room temperature). Through taste tests, we've detected slightly off, chemical flavors in these products right out of the fridge. But are they acceptable for baking? To find out, we baked a cake that called for softened butter, biscuits that called for cold butter, and cookies that called for melted butter with both spreadable and regular butter. The spreadable butter was used directly out of the refrigerator for the cake and biscuits, and it was melted as instructed for the cookies.

The spreadable butter produced a "squat and gummy" cake, compared with the tall and fluffy stick-butter version. Similarly, the biscuits made with spreadable butter were "heavy as a rock" because the mixture doesn't get firm enough to be distributed in small pieces like chilled stick butter. The cookies made with the melted spreadable butter had good texture, but all three recipes made with the spreadable butter had the same off-putting flavors we detected in their raw state. We do not recommend spreadable butter in any application.

SUITABLE SUBSTITUTE FOR BAKING?
The funky flavor of spreadable butters outweighs any convenience.

BAKING SODA AND BEANS

Why do some recipes add baking soda when cooking beans?

Jake Tallonis Buffalo, N.Y.

Dried beans can take hours of simmering to achieve a tender texture. Over years of cooking beans, we've learned that adding a little baking soda to them can speed up the cooking. Baking soda's alkaline nature is at work here: Alkalines help break down the cell structure of the beans, resulting in tender beans in less time. Baking soda also helps to set the color of some legumes, such as black beans. But use it sparingly (just ⅛ teaspoon of baking soda per pound of beans), as too much can lend a bitter, soapy flavor to the beans.

If you find yourself with a pot of beans that will not soften after the recommended cooking time—even with baking soda—your water may be the culprit. Mineral deposits in pots and green rings in porcelain sinks or tubs are signs of "hard water," which can prevent beans from softening.

To ask us a cooking question, visit **CooksCountry.com/emailus.** You can also write to Ask Cook's Country, P.O. Box 470739, Brookline, MA 02447. See if you can stump us!

Lost Recipes BLUEBERRY GRUNT

This oddly named dessert promises juicy berries topped with biscuity dumplings—and no need to turn on the oven. But the reality is more often than not a soggy, bland mess.

The blackboard specials at the diner in Maine listed something called "blueberry grunt." Was this a mistake? The waitress's description of "stewed blueberries and dumplings" didn't exactly sell the dish, nor did its sloppy appearance. But the big bowl of sweet, spiced blueberries under a dense biscuit didn't taste half-bad. Sure, the berry flavor was a bit washed out, and the biscuit dumpling was slightly soggy. But when I found out that grunt is made entirely on the stovetop, I figured this old-fashioned recipe was worth updating.

Back in the test kitchen, I learned that most grunts start with stewing fresh berries in water, sugar, and cinnamon, then topping the fruit mixture with dollops of drop-biscuit dough (flour, milk, melted butter, sugar, baking powder, and salt), covering the pot, and cooking on the stove until the dumplings cook through. The technique is attributed to Maria Rundell, who popularized the idea of cooking sweetened dumpling dough in water to make quick "puddings" in her *A New System of Domestic Cookery* (1807). Later, the dumplings were dropped into hot stewed fruit, and the dessert was given names like "slump" (for its sloppy appearance) and "grunt" (for the sound the fruit made as it bubbled beneath the dumplings). Grunt can be made with any manner of fruit, but blueberry grunt became especially popular in New England and Nova Scotia.

Dense fruit fillings for cobblers and pies are usually thickened with cornstarch or tapioca, but grunt filling is traditionally looser—it uses no thickeners (and actually adds up to ½ cup of water) to create a soupy filling that soaks into the dumplings. My tasters and I, however, felt the need to break tradition and thicken the filling, as it was bland and made the dumplings too soggy. I started by cooking down the berries (with sugar, cinnamon, lemon zest, and just 2 tablespoons of water) to a jamlike consistency. This concentrated the flavor, but my tasters missed the texture of whole berries. As a compromise, I cooked down half the berries until jammy, then stirred in the remaining berries before topping the mixture with the dumplings. I found that just a little cornstarch (1 teaspoon) further tightened the filling without making it too thick.

The dumplings were less soggy without the watery filling beneath them, but they were still a little bland and dense. Replacing the milk with buttermilk added a nice tang, and the buttermilk reacted with the baking soda to make the dumplings much lighter. My tasters noticed another problem, however: The tops of the cooked dumplings were strangely soggy. The cause was condensation dripping from the inside of the pot lid, and the solution was to place a clean kitchen towel under the lid to absorb the condensation before it could wreak havoc. I sprinkled cinnamon sugar on the cooked dumplings before serving for a final burst of flavor and crunch. At last—a grunt that can be known for more than just a funny name. –Cali Rich

BLUEBERRY GRUNT SERVES 12

Do not use frozen blueberries here, as they will make the filling watery. You will need a clean kitchen towel for this recipe.

Filling
- 8 cups fresh blueberries
- ½ cup sugar
- ½ teaspoon ground cinnamon
- 2 tablespoons water
- 1 teaspoon grated zest and 1 tablespoon juice from 1 lemon
- 1 teaspoon cornstarch

Topping
- ¾ cup buttermilk
- 6 tablespoons unsalted butter, melted and cooled slightly
- 1 teaspoon vanilla extract
- 2¼ cups all-purpose flour
- 1½ teaspoons baking powder
- ½ teaspoon baking soda
- ½ teaspoon salt
- ½ cup sugar
- ½ teaspoon ground cinnamon

1. For the filling: Cook 4 cups blueberries, sugar, cinnamon, water, and lemon zest in Dutch oven over medium-high heat, stirring occasionally, until mixture is thick and jamlike, 10 to 12 minutes. Whisk lemon juice and cornstarch in small bowl, then stir into blueberry mixture. Add remaining blueberries and cook until heated through, about 1 minute; remove pot from heat, cover, and keep warm.

2. For the topping: Combine buttermilk, butter, and vanilla in measuring cup. Whisk flour, baking powder, baking soda, salt, and 6 tablespoons sugar in large bowl. Slowly stir buttermilk mixture into flour mixture until dough forms.

3. Using small ice cream scoop or 2 large spoons, spoon golf ball–sized dumplings on top of warm berry mixture (you should have 14 dumplings). Wrap lid of Dutch oven with clean kitchen towel (keeping towel away from heat source) and cover pot. Simmer gently until dumplings have doubled in size and toothpick inserted into center comes out clean, 16 to 22 minutes.

4. Combine cinnamon and remaining sugar in small bowl. Remove lid and sprinkle dumplings with cinnamon sugar. Serve immediately.

Secrets to GREAT GRUNT

1. Use a small ice cream scoop to drop evenly sized balls of dough over the warm filling.
2. A kitchen towel beneath the lid absorbs condensation during cooking, keeping the dumplings light and fluffy.
3. A sprinkling of cinnamon sugar adds crunchy contrast to the steamed dumplings.

Grunts are distinguished from cobblers and crisps by being cooked entirely on the stovetop.

Slow Cooking SWEET AND SOUR RIBS

The best sweet and sour ribs brown in the oven while their sauce reduces to a potent, sticky glaze. How do you make this recipe work in a slow cooker, where browning and evaporation are minimal?

Test Kitchen Technique
A STAND-UP SOLUTION

We discovered the best way to evenly cook baby back ribs in the slow cooker (and even brown them a bit) was to stand them up against the sides of the insert so they're closest to the heating element. Basted with our thick, potent sweet and sour sauce, the ribs cook evenly and have a concentrated, meaty flavor.

1. Stand the rack halves up along the perimeter of the slow cooker with the wide end down and the meatier side of the ribs snug against the insert wall.
2. Spoon the sauce over the ribs, allowing it to coat the front and back of each piece.

Sweet and sour ribs have long been a favorite in Asian restaurants. The best versions coat tender ribs with a sticky sauce that balances fruity sweetness with the tang of vinegar and heat. Eager to make these at home, I was happy to find a multitude of slow cooker recipes.

The recipes were all fairly similar. Two racks of baby back ribs were cut into 3-bone segments (so they'd better fit in the cooker), placed in the insert, and covered with chopped onions, peppers, garlic, ginger, and canned pineapple chunks (all of which were strained out at the end). The sauce ingredients were added next: Ketchup, duck sauce, honey, and water (or stock) were the most common ingredients. Sadly, the results were also fairly similar: bland and bloated ribs floating in a thin, washed-out sauce. The problem was that the ribs release a lot of liquid when they cook, and in the closed environment of the slow cooker, there was no way for any liquid to evaporate.

Starting from scratch, I knew I'd have to build a sauce that was concentrated in flavor and texture, and that meant precooking on the stovetop. I started by sautéing onion, red pepper, garlic, and ginger to cook off excess moisture and intensify their flavor. My next step was to replace liquid-y sauce ingredients with more potent counterparts. As an alternative to ketchup, I added tomato paste for color and richness. Apricot jelly worked well in place

of duck sauce (which is also apricot based), and brown sugar replaced the honey. Soy sauce and red pepper flakes lent seasoning, rice vinegar provided the sour element, and frozen pineapple concentrate packed more fruit flavor than the canned chunks. I let this sauce cook down in the skillet with the sautéed vegetables and poured it over the ribs.

But submerging a stack of rib segments in the sauce meant that the ones in the very center of the pile were insulated and cooking at a slower rate. As I was wondering if I would ever get this recipe to work, it occurred to me to try partially elevating the ribs out of the liquid so they could cook more evenly. By simply halving each rack of ribs, I could stand the pieces up in a ring around the outside of the insert, where the heating coils are. This technique resulted in evenly cooked ribs with concentrated meaty flavor and even allowed the ribs to brown a little right against the heat source.

Although I was starting with a thicker sauce, the exuded liquid was still making it too thin to properly glaze the ribs. To solve the problem, I strained and defatted the sauce, reduced it again on the stovetop, and added a bit of cornstarch to thicken it further. When the tender ribs were tossed in this thick sauce, they took on a glossy, sticky sheen and were as good as any sweet and sour ribs I'd ever eaten. **–Diane Unger**

These saucy ribs aren't just sweet and sour—they're spicy too.

SLOW-COOKER SWEET AND SOUR RIBS SERVES 4 TO 6

Racks of ribs larger than 2 pounds will not properly fit in most slow cookers; ribs larger than 1½ pounds may require an extra 30 to 60 minutes of cooking time.

- 1 onion, chopped rough
- 1 red bell pepper, seeded and chopped rough
- 1 (6-inch) piece fresh ginger, peeled and chopped rough
- 6 garlic cloves, peeled
- 2 tablespoons tomato paste
- 2 tablespoons vegetable oil
- 1 (6-ounce) can frozen pineapple juice concentrate
- 1 (12-ounce) jar apricot jelly
- ¼ cup packed dark brown sugar
- ¼ cup plus 2 tablespoons soy sauce
- ¼ cup plus 1 tablespoon rice vinegar
- ¼ teaspoon red pepper flakes
- 2 racks baby back ribs (about 1½ pounds each), halved (see note)
  Salt and pepper
- 1 tablespoon cornstarch

1. Pulse onion and pepper in food processor until finely chopped; transfer to bowl. Add ginger, garlic, and tomato paste to empty processor and pulse until coarsely ground. Heat oil in large nonstick skillet over medium-high heat until shimmering. Cook onion mixture until softened, about 5 minutes. Stir in ginger mixture and cook until fragrant, about 1 minute. Stir in pineapple juice concentrate, jelly, sugar, ¼ cup soy sauce, ¼ cup vinegar, and pepper flakes and cook until slightly thickened, about 5 minutes. (Sauce can be refrigerated in airtight container for 2 days.)

2. Pat ribs dry with paper towels and season with salt and pepper. Following photos, arrange ribs with wide ends pointing down and meaty side against interior wall of slow cooker; pour sauce over ribs. Cover and cook on low until ribs are tender, 4 to 5 hours (or cook on high 2½ to 3½ hours). Transfer ribs to cutting board and tent with foil.

3. Strain and defat cooking liquid (see page 30), discard solids, and pour liquid into large skillet. Simmer over medium heat until reduced by half, about 5 minutes. Whisk cornstarch and remaining soy sauce in small bowl, then stir into skillet. Cook until sauce is glossy and thickened, about 2 minutes. Off heat, stir in remaining vinegar and season with salt and pepper. Transfer sauce to large bowl. Slice ribs between bones, add to bowl with sauce, and toss until well coated. Serve.

Recipe Makeover NEW ENGLAND CLAM CHOWDER

Heavy cream and bacon are the main sources of flavor—and fat—in this classic soup.

A full pound of potatoes—and instant potato flakes—make this rich chowder especially hearty.

Thick, creamy New England clam chowder often contains as much as 480 calories and 32 grams of fat per serving. In search of a lighter version, I first needed to understand how full-fat clam chowders are built. The test kitchen's recipe works in typical fashion. Six slices of bacon are crisped, onions are sautéed in the drippings, and flour is stirred in to make a thick roux. Clam juice and potatoes go into the pot, and the chowder is eventually finished with the clams and a cup of heavy cream.

I rounded up a handful of low-fat recipes and got busy cooking. Since I wanted this recipe to be accessible to everyone, I decided to use canned clams. Several recipes tried to replace the bacon with turkey bacon, but those chowders lacked depth and complexity; those that swapped out the cream for low-fat sour cream or cream cheese were too sour.

Eventually I realized that I couldn't eliminate the bacon altogether. I could, however, reduce the amount to just two slices if I chopped it fine so its smoky, meaty flavor was dispersed into every spoonful. After I sautéed the onion in the drippings (tasters also liked the additions of garlic, thyme, and a little white wine), it was evident that there was a problem with using so little bacon: It didn't render enough fat upon which to build a sturdy roux to thicken the chowder.

I found that I could add a pound of potatoes without tipping the scales in this recipe. To thicken the chowder, I tried pureeing half of the potatoes; this gave every drop of chowder good flavor, but tasters complained about a lack of potato chunks left in the broth. Looking for other thickeners, I tried whisking in a slurry of flour and broth (too raw) and even cooked and pureed white rice (too distinct). Rifling through the pantry, I landed on a box of instant potato flakes. Remembering the flavor from the chowder I had made with pureed potatoes, I had high hopes for potato flakes. Tasters loved the flavor of the soup, but I didn't think the flakes were fully dissolved. Microwaving the flakes with some clam broth ensured that they dissolved fully in the chowder, and a little cornstarch gave the soup a silky finish.

The chowder was flavorful and thick, but without cream it was lacking the velvety consistency of full-fat versions. Simply using less heavy cream (or light cream or milk) left the soup feeling light and thin. Half-and-half was still too fatty, but what about fat-free half-and-half? I was shocked that just ¾ cup of this product gave my low-fat clam chowder the rich texture and flavor of full-fat cream—with just a fraction of the fat and calories. This creamy, briny low-fat chowder was so good, I had no hesitation in serving myself a second bowl.

–Meredith Butcher

LOW-FAT NEW ENGLAND CLAM CHOWDER SERVES 6

Our tasters preferred the fluffy texture of russet potatoes in this chowder. While both instant potato flakes and potato buds will work here, avoid potato granules, which have a slightly metallic taste.

- 2 slices bacon, chopped fine
- 1 onion, chopped fine
- 2 garlic cloves, minced
- ¼ teaspoon dried thyme
- 1 pound russet potatoes, peeled and cut into ½-inch chunks
- ¼ cup white wine
- 2 bay leaves
- 4 (6.5-ounce) cans chopped clams, drained and juices reserved
- ¾ cup instant potato flakes (see note)
- 1 tablespoon cornstarch
- 1 (8-ounce) bottle clam juice
- ¾ cup fat-free half-and-half
- 1 tablespoon chopped fresh parsley
  Salt and pepper

1. Cook bacon in Dutch oven over medium-low heat until browned, about 10 minutes. Add onion and cook until softened, about 10 minutes. Add garlic and thyme and cook until fragrant, about 30 seconds. Add potatoes, wine, bay leaves, and reserved canned clam juice; increase heat to medium and simmer until potatoes are tender, 10 to 12 minutes.

2. Whisk potato flakes, cornstarch, and bottled clam juice in bowl. Microwave until mixture is thickened and smooth, about 1 minute. Stir potato flake mixture into pot and simmer until thickened, about 3 minutes. Add half-and-half, parsley, and chopped clams to pot and cook until heated through, about 2 minutes (do not let chowder boil or it will curdle). Discard bay leaves and season with salt and pepper. Serve.

Visit us online!
For instructions on how to make our Low-Fat New England Clam Chowder using fresh clams, visit **CooksCountry.com** and look for **Cook's Country Extras.**

And the Numbers...
All nutritional information is for one serving (about 1¼ cups of soup).

TRADITIONAL NEW ENGLAND CLAM CHOWDER
CALORIES: **480**
FAT: **32 g**
SATURATED FAT: **15 g**

COOK'S COUNTRY LOW-FAT NEW ENGLAND CLAM CHOWDER
CALORIES: **230**
FAT: **6 g**
SATURATED FAT: **2 g**

Chowder Power
For thick and creamy New England clam chowder, three ingredients were essential in this recipe makeover.

FAT-FREE HALF-AND-HALF
For rich flavor and velvety consistency without all the fat, we substituted fat-free half-and-half (which is made from fat-free milk, corn syrup, and thickeners) for the heavy cream.

POTATO FLAKES
Potato flakes thicken this chowder and lend a hearty potato flavor. Microwaving them with a little clam juice ensures that the flakes are fully dissolved in the chowder.

CORNSTARCH
Just 1 tablespoon of cornstarch lent the soup an especially silky and smooth consistency.

Easy Beef and Vegetable Kebabs

Test Kitchen Technique
CUTTING ONIONS FOR KEBABS

Cutting a single onion into 16 evenly sized pieces for kebabs isn't difficult—if you follow our instructions. We're discarding the onion's core because it is difficult to cleanly skewer.

①

②

③

④

1. Trim ¼ inch off each end of the onion and peel away the papery skin.
2. Cut the onion pole-to-pole into quarters, then remove and discard the inner core.
3. Slice each onion quarter in half lengthwise.
4. Cut each piece in half crosswise to yield rough 1½-inch pieces.

Leathery, blackened beef and bland, raw vegetables are common issues with beef and vegetable kebabs. Could we fix the problems while still keeping the recipe simple?

The best beef and vegetable kebabs are appealing because the flavors of the meat and vegetables enhance each other as they cook side by side on the grill. Unfortunately, many of us have come to accept mediocre kebabs as the norm. The recipes I tried featured beef that was incinerated on the outside but raw on the inside, or so overcooked and dry it was hard to chew. The veggies—typically onions, peppers, mushrooms, and cherry tomatoes—looked nicely charred but were under-seasoned and not cooked through (except for the tomatoes, which completely imploded). My goal was to create an easy weeknight recipe featuring deeply seasoned, perfectly cooked meat and vegetables that were done at the same time.

I needed a cut of beef that would be relatively tender, flavorful, and inexpensive. The three cuts that fit these requirements were flank steak, blade steak, and sirloin steak tips (flap meat). I bought all three kinds, cut them into cubes, threaded the meat onto skewers, and threw them on the hot grill. The flank was plenty beefy, but it was tough when not thinly sliced against the grain. Blade steaks were beefy and tender, but they contain a line of gristle that, once removed, left strips of meat too thin to be cut into decent-sized (1½-inch) cubes. The steak tips met all three criteria.

To keep steak tips juicy, even when cooked to medium-well, the test kitchen has had good luck with a marinade that uses soy sauce. The sodium in the soy sauce acts like a brine and helps the meat retain moisture when cooked. Since the steak tips had a lot of beefy flavor that I didn't want to mask, I made a simple marinade of soy sauce, olive oil, garlic, and black pepper, and poked the meat with a fork to allow the marinade to penetrate deeply. The beef tasted great, especially when I switched from the standard hot fire (which was charring the outside of the cubes too forcefully) to a medium fire that gave the meat a substantial char while it cooked through.

I had to make a tough choice with the vegetables. No matter how I handled them, I couldn't prevent cherry tomatoes from rupturing and turning to mush on the grill, so I omitted them. That left me with a mix of onions, peppers, and mushrooms that were a little bland and under-cooked by the time the meat was done. Letting the vegetables soak in extra marinade improved their flavor a bit but didn't help them cook any faster. Cooking the vegetables on skewers separate from the meat felt like cheating. The solution was to microwave the marinated vegetables—right in the bowl with the marinade—for about 5 minutes to gently precook and further infuse them with flavor. –Greg Case

With little fuss—and minimal expense—these kebabs come off the grill nicely charred, juicy, and full of flavor.

A Cut Above

Sirloin steak tips, also called flap meat, are an excellent choice for kebabs. They are relatively inexpensive

BEST CUT FOR KEBABS
For kebabs that cook evenly, buy whole sirloin steak tips and do the cutting yourself.

and well marbled so the meat is quite flavorful. Steak tips are sold as whole steaks, cubes, or strips. To ensure evenly sized pieces of meat (and therefore even cooking), we prefer to buy whole steaks and cube them ourselves.

BEEF AND VEGETABLE KEBABS SERVES 4 TO 6

Do not marinate the beef for more than 2 hours or it will be too salty. You will need six 12-inch metal skewers for this recipe. If you have pieces of meat smaller than 1½ inches, thread two small pieces together to approximate a 1½-inch cube.

- ½ cup soy sauce
- ¾ cup olive oil
- 4 garlic cloves, minced
- ¾ teaspoon pepper
- 2 pounds steak tips, poked all over with fork and cut into 1½-inch chunks
- 2 red bell peppers, seeded and cut into 1½-inch pieces
- 1 medium red onion, cut into 1½-inch pieces following photos at left
- 10 ounces white mushrooms, stemmed

1. Whisk soy sauce, oil, garlic, and pepper in bowl; transfer ⅓ cup soy mixture to large microwave-safe bowl. Place remaining soy mixture and steak tips into gallon-size zipper-lock bag. Press air out of bag, seal, and refrigerate for at least 1 hour or up to 2 hours.

2. Add bell peppers, onion, and mushrooms to bowl with reserved soy mixture and toss to coat. Wrap tightly with plastic and let marinate 30 minutes.

3. Microwave vegetables until onions are translucent at edges, 3 to 6 minutes, shaking bowl (without removing plastic) to redistribute vegetables halfway through cooking. Uncover vegetables and set aside until meat is fully marinated.

4. Thread meat and vegetables evenly onto six 12-inch metal skewers, starting and ending with meat. Grill kebabs over medium fire, covered and turning frequently, until meat is well browned and vegetables are tender, 14 to 16 minutes. Serve.

Marinated Tomato Salads

Can a lively dressing and a little time turn so-so tomatoes into a memorable salad?

A great summer tomato is best modestly dressed—salt, pepper, a good-quality olive oil, and nothing more. But most tomatoes, even in summer, need some help to become an inspired salad. Rather than mask the tomatoes' flavor by piling on the ingredients, I wanted to improve it.

Marinating sliced tomatoes in a lively vinaigrette sounds like a great idea—until the salt in the dressing coaxes liquid out of the tomatoes and waters down the salad. I wanted to create flavorful tomato salads with dressings that would enhance—not drown out—the tomatoes.

The logical first step was to try to rid the tomatoes of some of their excess moisture before adding the dressing. I sliced the tomatoes into wedges and, following test kitchen protocol, salted them and placed them on paper towels to drain (see box below). After 15 minutes, the tomatoes had purged some of their liquid and were ready to absorb a bold dressing of olive oil, vinegar, garlic, and black pepper. After letting the tomatoes sit in the vinaigrette for another 15 minutes, they were bursting with flavor, and the texture of the salad was uncompromised by excess moisture.

To complement the tomatoes, I added small amounts of potent ingredients such as arugula, fennel, jalapeño, and olives. Soft cheeses, white beans, and avocado added creamy counterpoints. Fresh herbs completed the transformation of the tomatoes from ho-hum to first-rate. –Diane Unger

MARINATED TOMATO SALAD WITH ARUGULA AND GOAT CHEESE
SERVES 4

To make the task of crumbling the goat cheese less messy, first let the cheese firm up in the freezer for 15 minutes.

- 1½ pounds ripe tomatoes, cored and sliced into ½-inch wedges
- ½ teaspoon salt
- 2 cups baby arugula
- 2 tablespoons extra-virgin olive oil
- 1 tablespoon red wine vinegar
- 1 garlic clove, minced
- ¼ cup chopped fresh basil
- ½ teaspoon pepper
- ¼ cup crumbled goat cheese (see note)

1. Toss tomatoes and salt in large bowl, then transfer to baking sheet lined with paper towels; let drain 15 minutes.
2. Return drained tomatoes to large bowl and toss with arugula, oil, vinegar, garlic, basil, and pepper. Let marinate 15 minutes. Sprinkle cheese over salad. Serve.

MARINATED TOMATO SALAD WITH FENNEL AND BLUE CHEESE
SERVES 4

We prefer mildly flavored, crumbly blue cheeses in this recipe. Stella brand blue cheese is the test kitchen's favorite supermarket blue cheese.

- 1½ pounds ripe tomatoes, cored and sliced into ½-inch wedges
- ½ fennel bulb, cored and sliced thin (see page 31)
- ½ teaspoon salt
- 2 tablespoons extra-virgin olive oil
- 1 tablespoon white wine vinegar
- 1 garlic clove, minced
- ¼ cup chopped fresh tarragon
- ½ teaspoon pepper
- ¼ cup crumbled blue cheese (see note)

1. Toss tomatoes, fennel, and salt in large bowl, then transfer to baking sheet lined with paper towels; let drain 15 minutes.
2. Return drained tomatoes and fennel to large bowl and toss with oil, vinegar, garlic, tarragon, and pepper. Let marinate 15 minutes. Sprinkle cheese over salad. Serve.

MARINATED TOMATO SALAD WITH OLIVES AND WHITE BEANS
SERVES 4

Cannellini beans are white Italian kidney beans. If you can't find them. Great Northern beans or navy beans can be substituted. Toast the pine nuts in a dry skillet over medium heat, shaking often, until golden, about 5 minutes.

- 1½ pounds ripe tomatoes, cored and sliced into ½-inch wedges
- ½ teaspoon salt
- 1 (16-ounce) can cannellini beans, drained and rinsed (see note)
- 2 tablespoons extra-virgin olive oil
- 1 tablespoon balsamic vinegar
- 1 garlic clove, minced
- 2 teaspoons minced fresh rosemary
- ½ teaspoon pepper
- ¼ cup pitted kalamata olives, finely chopped
- ¼ cup toasted pine nuts (see note)

1. Toss tomatoes and salt in large bowl, then transfer to baking sheet lined with paper towels; let drain 15 minutes.
2. Return drained tomatoes to large bowl and toss with beans, oil, vinegar, garlic, rosemary, pepper, and olives. Let marinate 15 minutes. Sprinkle pine nuts over salad. Serve.

MARINATED TOMATO SALAD WITH JALAPEÑO AND QUESO BLANCO
SERVES 4

Queso blanco, also called queso fresco, is a crumbly, slightly salty cheese commonly used in Mexican recipes. If your supermarket doesn't carry it, substitute a mild feta or farmer's cheese.

- 1½ pounds ripe tomatoes, cored and sliced into ½-inch wedges
- ½ teaspoon salt
- 2 tablespoons extra-virgin olive oil
- 1 tablespoon lime juice
- 1 garlic clove, minced
- 1 jalapeño chile, seeded and chopped fine
- 1 ripe avocado, pitted, skinned, and chopped
- ¼ cup chopped fresh cilantro
- ½ teaspoon pepper
- ¼ cup crumbled queso blanco (see note)

1. Toss tomatoes and salt in large bowl, then transfer to baking sheet lined with paper towels; let drain 15 minutes.
2. Return drained tomatoes to large bowl and toss with oil, lime juice, garlic, jalapeño, avocado, cilantro, and pepper. Let marinate 15 minutes. Sprinkle cheese over salad. Serve.

Save the cucumber and red onion for another day; these bold salads dress up tomatoes with more interesting ingredients.

Lose the Liquid

For intensely flavored tomato salads—minus the watery mess—we salt the sliced tomatoes to draw out their moisture and let them drain on paper towels (which helps to wick away more liquid than leaving the tomatoes in a colander). Once drained, the tomatoes readily absorb our flavorful dressings.

Salting and draining the tomatoes for just 15 minutes ensures that excess tomato juices won't end up in the bottom of the salad bowl.

Cornell Barbecued Chicken

I love the tangy grilled chicken they make on the elevated grills at the New York State Fair in Syracuse, but every time I try to make this recipe on my backyard grill, the meat tastes bland and the skin is charred black. Can you help? –Bud Robbins, Schenectady, N.Y.

Test Kitchen Technique
HALVING CHICKENS

Chicken halves cook more quickly than whole birds and are easier to manage on the grill than parts. You can freeze the backbone for making stock.

1. Using kitchen shears, cut along both sides of the backbone to remove it. Trim any excess fat or skin at the neck.
2. Flip the chicken over and, using a chef's knife, cut through the breastbone to separate the chicken into halves.

Cornell chicken was invented in the 1940s by the late Robert Baker, a Cornell University professor, and it has been a star attraction at the New York State Fair ever since (it is also referred to as "State Fair Chicken"). Baker's recipe and method remain unchanged at the Baker's Chicken Coop stand at the fair today: Half chickens are basted with a tangy sauce (vinegar, oil, poultry seasoning, and an egg) while they cook over a custom-made grill that elevates the birds exactly 26 inches above the coals. The combination of low heat and continual basting produces tangy, crisp-skinned chicken.

Unfortunately, recipes that try to adapt Baker's chicken to the backyard grill, where the fire is much closer to the grill grate, are problematic. The oily basting sauce inevitably drips off the chicken and into the fire, where it causes flare-ups that blacken the outside of the chicken before the inside has cooked through. I wanted to create a backyard Cornell chicken that featured crisp (but not charred) skin and meat that was deeply seasoned.

I started with the grilling method. Since Dr. Baker used low heat, I first tried grilling chicken halves over indirect heat; this method worked OK, but it meant I'd have to finish the chicken over high heat to get the crispy skin I desired. It was much easier (on either a gas or a charcoal grill) to grill two split chickens over gentle direct heat for the entire cooking time. To crisp the skin without burning it, I started the chicken skin-side up to slowly render the fat, then flipped the chicken skin-side down to brown it to a crisp.

The sauce for Cornell chicken is pretty standard: 2 parts vinegar to 1 part vegetable oil, along with poultry seasoning, salt, and a beaten egg. I discovered quickly that basting only adds flavor if the baste stays on the chicken—and in my tests, it ran off the chicken as fast as I could brush it on, causing flare-ups that led to charred chicken (this is not a problem at the Baker's Chicken Coop stand, where the distance between the coals and the chicken makes flare-ups moot). The egg was supposed to thicken the sauce; since the sauce wasn't thick enough to stay on the meat, I tried increasing the number of eggs, all the way up to four. This baste adhered to the chicken all right, creating a scrambled-egg crust that sent my tasters running for the door.

Since the eggs weren't adding desirable flavor, and I had to use too many of them to achieve any thickening power, I decided to eliminate egg from the sauce altogether (some claim that Baker included the egg in his recipe solely to aid local egg sales). I needed to find another ingredient to thicken the basting sauce so that it would adhere to the chicken.

Since the sauce is essentially a vinaigrette, I tried adding mustard (which we often use to help emulsify vinaigrettes), and it worked perfectly, contributing flavor and thickening the sauce. The sauce was now thick enough that I only had to lift the grill lid and apply it three times during cooking to match the amount of flavor achieved by continual basting with a thinner sauce; less basting also meant crispier skin.

The baste was working well, but it was only flavoring the outside of the chicken. Soaking the raw chicken in a saltwater brine helped to season the meat, and adding vinegar to the brine brought the tangy pucker all the way down to the bone. For even more flavor, I rubbed poultry seasoning (along with salt and pepper) into the skin of the meat before grilling and replaced the poultry seasoning in the sauce (where, uncooked,

it tasted a little dusty) with fresh rosemary and sage. Backyard Cornell Chicken has finally gotten an education of its own.

–Diane Unger

Cornell chicken gets its signature tangy, herby flavor from plenty of vinegar, sage, and rosemary.

CORNELL CHICKEN
SERVES 4 TO 6

Do not brine the chicken longer than 2 hours or the vinegar will make the meat mushy. Baste the chicken carefully in step 4, as any excess will drip onto the fire and flare up.

Chicken
- 2 quarts water
- 3½ cups cider vinegar
- ¼ cup salt
- 2 (3½- to 4-pound) whole chickens, halved according to photos at left

Seasoning and Sauce
- 1 tablespoon poultry seasoning
  Salt and pepper
- ½ cup cider vinegar
- 3 tablespoons Dijon mustard

The American Table:
The Chicken Man of Cornell University

Robert Baker (1921–2006) developed the recipe for Cornell chicken while employed at Pennsylvania State University, but his recipe didn't take off until he had moved on to the Animal Sciences Department at Cornell University (his alma mater) and published it in a school journal. This vinegary chicken wasn't Dr. Baker's only contribution to the culinary world: He also had a hand in developing the vacuum packaging still used by much of the poultry industry and was the inventor of chicken nuggets, turkey ham, and chicken hot dogs.

Regional Favorites: Syracuse Salt Potatoes

A little salt makes everything taste better. But in Salt City (Syracuse, New York), the only way to cook potatoes is with *a lot* of salt.

1 tablespoon chopped fresh sage

1 tablespoon chopped fresh rosemary

½ cup olive oil

1. For the chicken: Whisk water, vinegar, and salt in large bowl until salt dissolves. Add chicken and refrigerate, covered, for 1 to 2 hours.

2. For the seasoning and sauce: Combine poultry seasoning, 2 teaspoons salt, and 2 teaspoons pepper in small bowl; set aside. Process vinegar, mustard, sage, rosemary, ½ teaspoon salt, and ½ teaspoon pepper in blender until smooth, about 1 minute. With blender running, slowly add oil until incorporated. Transfer vinegar sauce to small bowl and reserve for basting chicken in step 4.

3. Heat all burners on high for 15 minutes, then turn all burners to medium-low. (For charcoal grill, light 75 coals; when covered with fine gray ash, spread evenly over bottom of grill. Set cooking grate in place and heat covered, with lid vents open completely, for 5 minutes.) Scrape and oil cooking grate.

4. Remove chicken from brine. Pat dry with paper towels and rub all over with poultry seasoning mixture. Arrange chicken skin-side up on grill and baste with vinegar sauce. Grill, covered, until chicken is well browned on bottom and meat registers 120 degrees, 25 to 30 minutes, basting with sauce halfway through cooking. Flip chicken skin-side down and baste with sauce. Continue to grill, covered, until skin is golden brown and crisp and thigh meat registers 170 to 175 degrees, 20 to 25 minutes longer. Transfer chicken to platter (do not cover) and let rest 5 minutes. Serve.

Make Ahead: Both the spice rub and the sauce can be made up to 3 days ahead. The chicken can be brined, patted dry, and rubbed with the seasoning mixture up to 8 hours ahead.

When we boil 3 pounds of potatoes in the test kitchen, we add a few teaspoons of salt to season the potatoes as they cook. But for an upstate New York recipe called salt potatoes, they're apt to use 2 cups of salt for the same amount of spuds! While this sounded preposterous to me, a co-worker from that part of the country swore I'd love salt potatoes if I just gave them a try. The recipe, I discovered, has its origins in the mid-1800s when Irish salt workers in the Syracuse area would cook unpeeled new potatoes in huge evaporation vats filled with boiling salt water. Later, area restaurateurs capitalized on that history by offering these potatoes to their customers (see box below, right).

Very curious, I found a recipe that brought 8 cups of water to a boil and then stirred in 3 pounds of golf ball–sized white potatoes and a whole, 26-ounce container of table salt. After 30 minutes of watching these potatoes bob in the brine, I removed them from the water, and as the potatoes dried, a crystallized salt crust emerged on their skins, making them resemble sugared doughnut holes. The exterior was too salty, but the potato flesh was perfectly seasoned and incredibly creamy.

How was this possible? The concentrated salt solution boils at a higher temperature than plain water (228 degrees versus 212 degrees) and thus cooks the potatoes' starch more completely, resulting in creamier, less-grainy flesh. The salt doesn't easily penetrate the skin, which is why the interior of the potato isn't overly salty.

Even this simple recipe of potatoes, salt, and water needed some refining. Recipes I found called for a range of ½ cup to over 3 cups of salt, but I found that 1¼ cups of salt to 8 cups of water was the optimum ratio for a well-seasoned (but not too salty) crust and

ultra-creamy interior. Both kosher and non-iodized table salt worked fine, but tasters rejected the mineral flavor of iodized salt outright.

Tradition dictates that salt potatoes are made with white-skinned new potatoes, but I found that small or medium red new potatoes also worked fine—as long as they were left whole (if cut or peeled, the potatoes absorb too much salt). Finally, these potatoes are typically served with plain melted butter for dipping, but adding chives and black pepper to the butter brought this dish to a new level. These Syracuse salt potatoes are ready to be shared with the rest of the country.

–Diane Unger

SYRACUSE SALT POTATOES SERVES 6 TO 8

You will need 1¼ cups of non-iodized table salt, 1½ cups of Morton kosher salt, or 2½ cups of Diamond Crystal kosher salt to equal 14 ounces.

- 8 cups water
- 14 ounces salt (see note)
- 3 pounds small white or red potatoes, scrubbed
- 8 tablespoons (1 stick) unsalted butter, cut into pieces
- 2 tablespoons minced fresh chives
- 1 teaspoon pepper

1. Bring water to boil in Dutch oven over medium-high heat. Stir in salt and potatoes and cook until potatoes are just tender, 20 to 30 minutes. Drain potatoes and transfer to wire rack set over baking sheet. Let dry until salty crust forms, about 1 minute.

2. Meanwhile, microwave butter, chives, and pepper in medium bowl until melted, about 1 minute. Transfer potatoes to serving bowl and serve, passing butter at table.

These spuds may not look like much, but they might forever change the way you boil potatoes.

Salt Magic

Just out of the salty water, the potatoes will look like any other boiled potato.

One minute after they've been drained, the characteristic salt crust will appear on the potato skins.

The high salinity means the cooking water gets hotter than normal, resulting in extra-creamy potato flesh.

The American Table: Selling Salt Potatoes

In 1914, John Hinerwadel, owner of an eponymous central New York clambake company, began offering salt potatoes on his menu. They became so popular that Mr. Hinerwadel started selling salt potato kits—complete with a sack of small white potatoes and a packet of salt—so people could make the potatoes at home. The red and white bags of potatoes with the signature red and yellow sun are still sold in the Syracuse area.

Smoked Pork Loin

Smoke and spice sound like great complements for grilled pork loin—if you can prevent them from overwhelming this mild cut.

Test Kitchen Technique
PREPARING PORK LOIN

1. To encourage the fat to render, so that it can baste the meat as it cooks, use a sharp knife to cut a shallow crosshatch pattern into the fat layer. Avoid cutting through the fat and into the meat, as this may result in moisture loss.
2. Tying the roast tightly at 1-inch intervals gives it an even shape, promoting even cooking on the grill.

Through years of grill-roasting pork loin, the test kitchen has settled on a foolproof technique. Build a fire with hot and cool sides, rub the pork loin with spices, sear the meat over high heat so that the rub ingredients caramelize and intensify in flavor, and then move the pork loin to the cool side of the grill so that it cooks gently with indirect heat and doesn't dry out. Since smoked meats are also cooked with indirect heat, smoked pork loin seemed like an easy proposition—just add a packet of soaked wood chips to the fire, rub and sear as usual, and sit back to let the smoke and low fire work their magic.

There was only one problem: the leanness of the pork loin. Fatty cuts, like those from the shoulder and ribs, take to smoke well because they have enough richness to balance the assertive smoke flavor. Pork loin isn't rich or fatty, and when I tried smoking it this way, the subtle flavor of the meat was overwhelmed by the smoke. Using fewer wood chips gave me inconsistent results. I was going to have to find ways to add more flavor to the pork loin, so that it could stand up to a healthy dose of smoke.

A basic barbecue spice rub (paprika, chili powder, cumin, oregano, cayenne, brown sugar, salt, and pepper) helped, but searing the rubbed meat at the onset meant putting it directly over the smoking wood chips on the hot side of the grill, resulting in pork that tasted sooty and ashy. Starting the meat on the cooler side and saving the searing until the end of cooking, when the wood

chips had already surrendered their smoke, proved a better way to develop flavor on the outside of the meat. But how could I build flavor on the inside?

I decided to try making a marinade with flavors that would complement the smoke. I started with one of our favorite marinade ingredients, soy sauce, which penetrates the meat (much like a saltwater brine), helping to season it and keep it moist. Garlic, Worcestershire sauce, Dijon mustard, and brown sugar lent boldness to the mild pork, but I wanted something that would specifically reinforce the smoke flavor. After rejecting liquid smoke as too one-dimensional, I settled on bourbon (a familiar ingredient in the barbecue pantry) for its smoky-sweet flavor and bold kick. **–Eva Katz**

SMOKED PORK LOIN
SERVES 6 TO 8

Look for a pork roast with about ¼ inch of fat on top. This pork is juicy and flavorful enough to stand alone, but it also goes well with any of our quick No-Cook Barbecue Sauces on page 30. While we prefer bourbon for its smoky sweetness, feel free to substitute whatever American whiskey you have on hand.

Marinade
- ¼ cup Dijon mustard
- ¼ cup whiskey, preferably bourbon (see note)
- ¼ cup soy sauce
- ¼ cup packed brown sugar
- 2 tablespoons Worcestershire sauce
- 4 garlic cloves, minced
- 1 (2½- to 3-pound) boneless pork loin roast, fat on top scored lightly and tied (see photos at left)

A potent whiskey-based marinade gives pork loin enough base flavor to stand up to this recipe's assertive smoke and spice.

Spice Rub
- 1 tablespoon brown sugar
- 1 tablespoon paprika
- 2 teaspoons chili powder
- 2 teaspoons ground cumin
- 1 teaspoon dried oregano
- 1 teaspoon salt
- 1 teaspoon pepper
- ¼ teaspoon cayenne pepper
- 2 cups wood chips, soaked for 15 minutes

1. For the marinade: Whisk mustard, whiskey, soy sauce, sugar, Worcestershire, and garlic in bowl. Place marinade and pork in gallon-size zipper-lock bag. Press air out of bag, seal, and refrigerate for 2 hours, flipping bag after 1 hour to ensure that pork marinates evenly. (Pork can marinate for up to 8 hours.)

2. For the spice rub: Combine all ingredients except wood chips in small bowl. Remove pork from marinade, pat dry with paper towels, and rub spice mixture all over roast.

3. Seal wood chips in foil packet and cut vent holes in top. Open bottom vent on grill.

Light 100 coals; when covered with fine gray ash, spread over half of grill. Arrange foil packet directly on coals. Set cooking grate in place and heat, covered, with lid vent open completely, until wood chips begin to smoke heavily, about 5 minutes. (For gas grill, place foil packet directly on primary burner. Heat all burners on high, covered, until wood chips begin to smoke heavily, about 15 minutes. Leave primary burner on high and turn other burner[s] off.) Scrape and oil cooking grate.

4. Arrange roast fat-side up on cooler side of grill. Cook, covered, until meat registers 130 to 135 degrees, about 1 hour, flipping and rotating roast once halfway through cooking. Move roast to hot side of grill and cook, covered, until pork is well browned on all sides and meat registers 140 degrees, 5 to 10 minutes. Transfer to cutting board, tent with foil, and let rest 15 minutes (temperature will rise to 150 degrees). Remove twine. Slice and serve.

Sweet Corn Spoonbread

I remember my grandmother's spoonbread as a tall, creamy custard packed with sweet corn. But all the recipes I've tried turned out squat, gritty, and bland. Can you help? –Hanna Sasso, Seattle, Wash.

To appreciate spoonbread, it helps to know its history. In the 19th century, batters of cornmeal and water were baked, fried, or griddled to make humble dishes like johnnycakes and corn dodgers. With the addition of milk and eggs, these dishes evolved into rich, "spoon-able" corn custards called spoonbreads. Some later versions elevated the dish (literally) with baking soda, but the most refined recipes folded beaten egg whites into the batter, turning spoonbread into a fluffy cornmeal soufflé with a golden crust and a silky interior.

Hoping to replicate this soufflé-style spoonbread, I rounded up half a dozen recipes and tried them out. I chose recipes that used both classic cornmeal and fresh corn kernels—a modern addition to many spoonbreads. Like Hanna, my tasters and I were disappointed by the poor texture (gritty from cornmeal, with unappealing chunks of chewy corn kernels) and weak flavor of each one. I was going to have to build my own recipe from scratch.

This style of spoonbread is made by cooking cornmeal in milk, cooling the mixture, stirring in egg yolks, and then folding in beaten egg whites and baking. After playing with the ratios, I found that 1 cup of cornmeal, 2¾ cups of milk, and 3 eggs were the right amount for my 1½-quart soufflé dish. But even though I was simmering the cornmeal in milk, it remained gritty; I tried soaking the cornmeal in milk for a few minutes before simmering, and this successfully eliminated the grit. Beating the egg whites with cream of tartar made for a more stable foam and higher rise.

The raw corn, however, was too bland and chewy. Sautéing the kernels in butter helped to intensify their flavor, as did adding a little sugar, salt, and cayenne pepper. Steeping the cooked corn in milk before adding it to the cornmeal mixture spread the deep, sweet flavor of sautéed corn throughout the spoonbread. To remedy the chewy texture, I turned to my blender and pureed the corn and milk. The silky mixture that came out of the blender tasted like cream of corn soup—good enough to eat on its own. Incorporated into the spoonbread, my "corn milk" produced a light, creamy texture and sweet corn taste that set this spoonbread far apart from its workaday ancestors. –Kelley Baker

SWEET CORN SPOONBREAD SERVES 6

You will need 3 or 4 ears of corn to yield 2 cups of kernels. See page 31 for more information about removing corn kernels from the cobs. Frozen corn can be substituted for the fresh, provided it is thawed and well drained.

- 1 cup cornmeal
- 2¾ cups whole milk
- 4 tablespoons unsalted butter
- 2 cups corn kernels (see note)
- 1 teaspoon sugar
- 1 teaspoon salt
- ⅛ teaspoon cayenne pepper
- 3 large eggs, separated
- ¼ teaspoon cream of tartar

1. Adjust oven rack to middle position and heat oven to 400 degrees. Grease 1½-quart soufflé dish or 8-inch-square baking dish. Whisk cornmeal and ¾ cup milk in bowl until combined; set aside.

2. Melt butter in Dutch oven over medium-high heat. Cook corn until beginning to brown, about 3 minutes. Stir in remaining milk, sugar, salt, and cayenne and bring to boil. Remove from heat, cover, and let mixture steep 15 minutes.

3. Transfer warm corn mixture to blender or food processor and puree until smooth. Return corn mixture to pot and bring to boil. Reduce heat to low and add cornmeal mixture, whisking constantly, until thickened, 2 to 3 minutes; transfer to large bowl and cool to room temperature, about 20 minutes. Once mixture is cool, whisk in egg yolks until combined.

4. With electric mixer on medium-low speed, beat egg whites and cream of tartar until frothy, about 1 minute.

Increase speed to medium-high and beat until stiff peaks form, about 3 minutes. Whisk one-third of whites into corn mixture, then gently fold in remaining whites until combined. Scrape mixture into prepared dish and transfer to oven. Reduce oven temperature to 350 degrees and bake until spoonbread is golden brown and risen above rim of dish, about 45 minutes. Serve immediately.

Individual Spoonbreads

To make individual spoonbreads, prepare recipe as directed and divide batter among 6 greased 7-ounce ramekins. Arrange ramekins on rimmed baking sheet and bake as directed, reducing cooking time to 30 to 35 minutes.

Egg Whites 101

Egg whites are most easily whipped in a very clean metal bowl with a pinch of cream of tartar, which promotes stabilization.

1. SOFT PEAKS
Soft peaks will droop slightly downward from the tip of the whisk or beater.

2. STIFF PEAKS
Stiff peaks will stand up tall on their own.

3. OVER-WHIPPED
Over-whipped egg whites will look curdled and separated; if you reach this point, you'll need to start over with new whites and a clean bowl.

Richer and moister than cornbread, this savory custard is packed with fresh corn flavor.

I'm Looking for a Recipe

READERS HELP READERS FIND RECIPES

We've Got Mail

Dozens of readers sent us recipes in response to the request for Spanish Pudding in our February/March 2008 issue. We really liked the recipe sent by Emily Dahlke (right). Go to **CooksCountry.com** and click **Looking for a Recipe** to find hundreds of recipes submitted by readers who responded to other recipe requests in previous issues of *Cook's Country*.

Moroccan Pie

I've been searching for this recipe for ages. The recipe called for a phyllo crust that was filled with a mixture of shredded meat and a thick, nutmeg-flavored Swiss cheese béchamel sauce and then baked. Although the recipe instructed to use pigeon, I made it with leftover chicken, duck, and turkey, and it was absolutely delicious. Thanks much!

Kit Miles
Chicago, Ill.

Butterscotch Meringue Cookies

My grandmother used to make various Christmas cookies every year for family and friends, but my all-time favorite was a layered cookie that had a cake-like cookie bottom topped with a mixture of chocolate chips and crushed walnuts, and then covered with a butterscotch meringue. My grandmother has passed and no one in my family can locate the recipe. I would love to have the recipe to carry it on in my family.

Michele Tenore
Gladstone, N.J.

Syrian Rice and Peas

When I was a child, one of my mother's friends had a Syrian husband who made a very delicious meal of Syrian rice and peas. As I recall, it consisted of tiny marble-sized meatballs (perhaps made with lamb) cooked in a mild tomato sauce and served over green peas and white rice. I don't have the recipe, and although I've tried to duplicate the dish, it never tastes quite the same. I must be leaving something out!

Deeda Stanczak
New Boston, Mich.

Sweet Potato Kuchen

One of the best food gifts we received over the holidays was a delicious sweet potato kuchen. Since the gift came from a restaurant owner, I felt I shouldn't ask for their recipe, but if anyone else has a good recipe, I would love to try it. The one we had was moist with a cheesecake-like texture and strong, not overly spiced, sweet potato flavor. Thanks for the help!

Barbara Ballard
Via e-mail

Goetta

I used to live in Cincinnati, Ohio, and could find goetta, a sliceable mixture of ground meat and oats, in many grocery stores. Can you help me locate a recipe so I can make it now that I live in Massachusetts?

Mary Ann Jablonski
Lakeville, Mass.

Turkish Pancakes

My neighbor from years ago made me unbelievably light and fluffy Turkish pancakes. When they were finished, she put them in a paper bag to toss them with powdered sugar or cinnamon. They were wonderful and I would so love to find the recipe.

Deborah Pinker
Via e-mail

Roslyn's Buttermilk Cookies

I am looking for the soft, dense buttermilk cookies that used to be sold at a bakery in Indianapolis, Indiana, called Roslyn's. Instead of being cut out, they were piped into a star shape using a ridged decorating tip. All of the buttermilk cookies I have tried (and I have tried several) are too cakey.

Claudia Choi
Los Angeles, Calif.

Rana Shrimp Grazielle

There used to be a restaurant named Rana in Bay Shore, New York, that served a dish called shrimp grazielle. It was made with shrimp, cream, butter, and mozzarella cheese, and was finished under the broiler. My friend and I particularly liked to have it over linguine. Does anyone have the recipe?

M. Fauvell
Via e-mail

Alexander Hamilton Inn's Carrot Bread

In 1965 we visited the Alexander Hamilton Inn in upstate New York. The specialty of the house was carrot bread that was served in the dining room. Unfortunately, I've since lost the recipe. Does anyone have it?

Dana DuVall
Big Bear Lake, Calif.

Pumpkin Bear Claws

During a recent move across the country, a box of my cookbooks was lost. Among them was a small booklet of Libby's pumpkin recipes, one of which, Libby's pumpkin bear claws, was part of our Christmas food tradition for years. Does anyone have this book or the recipe? Libby's website doesn't have it listed.

Janiece Bates
Selah, Wash.

German Bread with Cinnamon Gravy

My German grandmother made a steamed bread with a sweet cinnamon gravy in the 1930s. The bread dough was tied in a tea towel and then hung inside a deep covered pot of simmering water for about an hour. You would eat it by pulling off a piece of the bread (it was too soft to cut) and pouring some of the cinnamon gravy over it. I know how to make the steamed bread but can't find a recipe for the gravy.

Lesley Varwig
Via e-mail

Savory Plantain Cakes

While vacationing on Vieques Island, near Puerto Rico, we stopped at a roadside stand that offered the most delicious plantain snack. The warm, spicy, savory "cake" was flat, oval, and about five inches long and an inch thick. It was not enclosed in pastry, but the outer skin was slightly crisp. I'm guessing that unripe plantains were boiled and mashed, seasoned with a local spice blend, dredged lightly in flour, and sautéed in hot fat. Does anyone out there know of such a dish? Thank you!

Sandy Hinchman
Canton, N.Y.

Burnt Almond Chocolate Caramel

I am looking for a recipe for a candy called burnt almond chocolate caramel. I recall that the ingredients included Amaretto, unsweetened chocolate, corn syrup, sugar, and butter. I think about this candy all the time.

Marcia Rybicki
Pottawattomie Park, Ind.

Mile-High Custard Pie

Many years ago my mother told me about her famous mile-high custard pie. All I can remember about this recipe is that she made it during the 1940s and it had beaten egg whites. Her recipe might be as simple as folding stiff egg whites into a standard custard. Has anyone heard of this type of pie?

Linda Cotroneo
Burlington, Mass.

Are you looking for a special recipe? Or do you have a recipe a fellow *Cook's Country* reader is seeking? Post your requests and recipes by visiting **CooksCountry.com** and clicking on **Looking for a Recipe**. We'll share recipe requests and found recipes on CooksCountry.com and print as many as we can in the magazine. You may also write to us at Looking for a Recipe, Cook's Country, P.O. Box 470739, Brookline, MA 02447.

SPANISH PUDDING   Emily Dahlke Yermo, Calif.

SERVES 8

"Susan MacFarland's request for Spanish Pudding sounds exactly like my mother's Spanish Cream. Mother thought this was a good dessert for children at Thanksgiving, and she would serve it with nutmeg sprinkled on top." You will need eight 7-ounce ramekins or pudding cups for this recipe.

3	cups milk
1	tablespoon gelatin
½	cup sugar
3	egg yolks
¼	teaspoon salt
1	teaspoon vanilla extract
3	egg whites, beaten stiff

1. Scald milk with gelatin, about 5 minutes. Add sugar, then slowly whisk mixture into lightly beaten egg yolks. Place in double boiler and cook until mixture coats spoon, stirring constantly, about 15 minutes. Remove from heat and stir in salt and vanilla.

2. Fold in egg whites. Dip molds in cold water, then portion mixture into molds. Chill 1½ hours (mixture will separate into two distinct layers when cold) and serve with cream or orange marmalade.

Find the Rooster!

A tiny version of this rooster has been hidden somewhere in the pages of this issue. If you find it, write to us with its location (plus your name and address) and you will be entered into a random drawing. The first correct entry drawn will receive an Anolon Advanced Double Burner Griddle (the test winner from our last issue), and the next five will each receive a complimentary one-year subscription to *Cook's Country*. To enter the contest, visit **CooksCountry.com/emailus**, or write to us at Rooster, Cook's Country, P.O. Box 470739, Brookline, MA 02447. Entries are due by September 30, 2008.

Did you find the rooster in the April/May 2008 issue? It was hidden in the Creamed Spinach with Parmesan and Prosciutto photo on page 23. Pat Bell of Corona, Calif., spotted it and won a WearEver Premium Hard Anodized 12-inch Nonstick Skillet.

TEX-MEX BURGERS

CREAMY CHICKEN FETTUCCINE

PAN-SEARED COD WITH HERB BUTTER SAUCE

RUM-GLAZED GRILLED PORK TENDERLOIN

CREAMY CHICKEN FETTUCCINE SERVES 4

Either fresh or dried fettuccine can be used in this recipe.

- 2 boneless, skinless chicken breasts (about ¾ pound), cut crosswise into ¼-inch strips
  Salt and pepper
- 2 tablespoons unsalted butter
- 2 garlic cloves, minced
- 1 cup heavy cream
- 1 teaspoon grated zest and 2 tablespoons juice from 1 lemon
- 1 pound fettuccine
- 2 cups frozen peas
- 1½ cups grated Parmesan cheese
- 1 cup chopped fresh basil

1. Bring 4 quarts water to boil in large pot. Pat chicken dry with paper towels and season with salt and pepper. Melt butter in large nonstick skillet over medium-high heat. Cook chicken until no longer pink, about 3 minutes. Transfer to plate.

2. Add garlic to empty skillet and cook until fragrant, about 30 seconds. Add cream, lemon zest, and lemon juice and simmer until sauce is slightly thickened, 3 to 5 minutes. Remove from heat, cover, and keep warm.

3. Add 1 tablespoon salt and pasta to boiling water and cook until nearly al dente. Add peas to pot and cook until bright green, about 1 minute. Reserve ½ cup cooking water, drain pasta and peas, and return to pot. Add sauce, cheese, basil, and reserved chicken to pot and toss to combine, adding reserved pasta water as needed. Season with salt and pepper. Serve.

TEX-MEX BURGERS SERVES 4

Poblanos are large, blackish green chiles with a mild heat. If you can't find them, you can substitute a green bell pepper.

- 1½ pounds 85 percent lean ground beef, broken into pieces
- 2 teaspoons minced canned chipotle chiles in adobo sauce
- ½ teaspoon ground cumin
  Salt and pepper
- 1 tablespoon vegetable oil
- 4 thick slices deli pepper Jack cheese
- 1 small red onion, sliced thin
- 1 poblano chile, seeded and sliced thin (see note)
- 1 teaspoon chili powder
- 4 hamburger rolls, split

1. Using hands, gently knead beef, chipotle, cumin, ½ teaspoon salt, and ¼ teaspoon pepper in large bowl until combined. Divide mixture into 4 equal portions and lightly pack into ¾-inch-thick patties. Press a shallow divot in the center of each patty (see page 30).

2. Heat oil in large nonstick skillet over medium heat until just smoking. Add patties and cook until well browned and cooked to desired doneness, 3 to 6 minutes per side. Transfer burgers to plate, top with cheese, and tent with foil.

3. Add onion, poblano, ¼ teaspoon salt, and ¼ teaspoon pepper to empty skillet and cook until softened, about 5 minutes. Stir in chili powder and cook until fragrant, about 30 seconds. Arrange burgers on rolls and top with onion mixture. Serve.

RUM-GLAZED GRILLED PORK TENDERLOIN SERVES 4

While light, golden, and even spiced rums can be used, we prefer the deep, earthy flavor of dark rum in this recipe. Avoid blackstrap molasses—it will make the glaze unpalatably bitter.

- ½ cup packed brown sugar
- ½ cup apple jelly
- ¼ cup dark rum (see note)
- 3 tablespoons cider vinegar
- 2 tablespoons molasses (see note)
- ¼ teaspoon red pepper flakes
- 2 tablespoons Dijon mustard
- 2 tablespoons finely chopped fresh cilantro
- 2 pork tenderloins (1½ to 2 pounds total)
  Salt and pepper

1. Simmer sugar, jelly, rum, vinegar, molasses, and pepper flakes in saucepan over medium heat, stirring occasionally, until syrupy, about 5 minutes. Off heat, whisk in mustard and cilantro; cover and keep warm.

2. Season tenderloins with salt and pepper and grill over hot fire until browned on all sides and meat registers 140 degrees, about 12 minutes. Brush with half of rum glaze and cook 1 minute longer. Transfer to cutting board, tent with foil, and let rest 5 minutes. Slice pork and serve, passing remaining glaze at table.

PAN-SEARED COD WITH HERB BUTTER SAUCE SERVES 4

Use ¾- to 1-inch-thick pieces of fish, each weighing about 6 ounces. Any variety of skinless fish fillets of comparable thickness can be substituted for the cod.

- ½ cup all-purpose flour
- 4 boneless, skinless thick cod fillets (see note)
  Salt and pepper
- 3 tablespoons vegetable oil
- 1 shallot, minced
- ½ cup white wine
- 1 teaspoon grated zest and 1 tablespoon juice from 1 lemon
- 1 teaspoon minced fresh thyme
- 4 tablespoons unsalted butter, cut into 4 pieces
- 2 tablespoons finely chopped fresh parsley

1. Place flour in shallow dish. Pat fish dry with paper towels and season with salt and pepper. Coat fish lightly with flour.

2. Heat 2 tablespoons oil in large nonstick skillet over medium heat until just smoking. Cook fillets until golden and thickest part of fillets flake easily, about 3 minutes per side. Transfer to platter and tent with foil. Wipe out skillet.

3. Add remaining oil and shallot to empty pan and cook until softened, 2 to 3 minutes. Add wine, lemon zest, lemon juice, and thyme and simmer until reduced by half, about 2 minutes. Off heat, whisk in butter and parsley. Season sauce with salt and pepper and pour over cod. Serve.

30-Minute Supper

**STEAK QUESADILLAS
WITH ROASTED PEPPERS AND BOURSIN**

30-Minute Supper

MEDITERRANEAN CHICKEN BREASTS

30-Minute Supper

THAI-STYLE GRILLED CHICKEN BREASTS

30-Minute Supper

**GRILLED RIB-EYE STEAKS
WITH HOMEMADE STEAK SAUCE**

MEDITERRANEAN CHICKEN BREASTS SERVES 4

Look for pitted kalamata olives in the deli department or the salad bar of your supermarket.

    4   boneless, skinless chicken breasts (about 1½ pounds)
        Salt and pepper
    2   tablespoons olive oil
    1   onion, chopped fine
    4   garlic cloves, minced
    ¾   cup low-sodium chicken broth
    ½   cup pitted kalamata olives, chopped (see note)
    1½ cups cherry tomatoes, halved (quartered if large)
    2   tablespoons finely chopped fresh oregano
    2   tablespoons finely chopped fresh parsley

1. Pat chicken dry with paper towels and season with salt and pepper. Heat 1 tablespoon oil in large skillet over medium-high heat until just smoking. Cook chicken until golden brown, about 5 minutes per side. Transfer to plate and tent with foil.

2. Add remaining oil and onion to empty skillet and cook over medium heat until onion is lightly browned, about 5 minutes. Stir in garlic and cook until fragrant, about 30 seconds. Add broth, olives, and browned chicken along with any accumulated juices and bring to boil. Reduce heat and simmer, covered, until chicken is cooked through, 2 to 4 minutes.

3. Transfer chicken to serving platter. Add tomatoes to skillet and cook until just softened, about 1 minute. Off heat, stir in oregano and parsley and season with salt and pepper. Spoon vegetable mixture over chicken. Serve.

STEAK QUESADILLAS WITH ROASTED PEPPERS AND BOURSIN SERVES 4

Boursin cheese has a creamy, spreadable texture reminiscent of goat cheese. Though it comes in a variety of flavors, we prefer the Garlic and Fine Herbs flavor in this recipe.

    2   strip steaks, about 1 inch thick
        Salt and pepper
    1   tablespoon vegetable oil
    1   (5.2-ounce) package Boursin cheese, crumbled (see note)
    1½ cups shredded sharp cheddar cheese
    4   (12-inch) flour tortillas
    ½   cup drained jarred roasted red peppers,
        patted dry with paper towels and sliced thin
    4   scallions, sliced thin

1. Pat steaks dry with paper towels and season with salt and pepper. Heat oil in large nonstick skillet over medium-high heat until just smoking. Cook steaks until well browned, 3 to 5 minutes per side. Transfer to plate and let rest 5 minutes, then slice thin against grain. Wipe out skillet.

2. While steaks rest, combine Boursin, cheddar, ½ teaspoon salt, and 1 teaspoon pepper in bowl. Divide cheese mixture evenly over one half of each tortilla, leaving ½-inch border around edge. Top with peppers, scallions, and sliced steak. Fold tortillas over filling and press down firmly.

3. Add 2 quesadillas to empty skillet and cook over medium-high heat until golden and crisp, 1 to 2 minutes. Using spatula, flip quesadillas and cook until golden brown and cheese is melted, 1 to 2 minutes. Transfer to cutting board and repeat with remaining quesadillas. Cut into wedges and serve.

GRILLED RIB-EYE STEAKS WITH HOMEMADE STEAK SAUCE SERVES 4

The homemade steak sauce can be refrigerated in an airtight container for up to 1 week. Strip steaks or fillets of a similar thickness can also be used here.

    ½   cup water
    ⅓   cup raisins
    ¼   cup ketchup
    3   tablespoons Worcestershire sauce
    2   tablespoons Dijon mustard
    2   tablespoons white vinegar
        Salt and pepper
    4   rib-eye steaks, about 1 inch thick (see note)

1. Combine water and raisins in medium bowl. Wrap tightly with plastic and microwave until water begins to boil, 1 to 3 minutes; let stand 5 minutes until raisins are soft.

2. Process raisins, water, ketchup, Worcestershire, mustard, and vinegar in blender until smooth, about 1 minute. Season with salt and pepper.

3. Season steaks with salt and pepper and grill over hot fire until well browned and cooked to desired doneness, 4 to 8 minutes per side. Transfer to plate, tent with foil, and let rest 5 minutes. Serve, passing steak sauce at table.

THAI-STYLE GRILLED CHICKEN BREASTS SERVES 4

If you can't find fish sauce, substitute a combination of 2 minced anchovy fillets and 2 tablespoons soy sauce.

    ½   cup white vinegar
    ⅓   cup sugar
    ¼   teaspoon red pepper flakes
    ½   cup chopped fresh cilantro
    2   tablespoons fish sauce (see note)
    1   tablespoon grated fresh ginger
    3   garlic cloves, minced
    4   boneless, skinless chicken breasts (about 1½ pounds)
    1   tablespoon vegetable oil
        Salt and pepper

1. Heat vinegar, sugar, and pepper flakes in small saucepan over medium-high heat until sugar dissolves, about 1 minute. Off heat, stir in cilantro, fish sauce, ginger, and garlic.

2. Rub chicken with oil and season with salt and pepper. Grill over hot fire until cooked through, about 5 minutes per side. Transfer to platter and brush with ¼ cup sauce. Tent with foil and let rest 5 minutes. Serve, passing remaining sauce at table.

Vegetable Pesto Pasta Salads

In the heat of summer, a cool pasta salad tossed with a light, fresh vegetable puree sounds like an appealing supper. Unfortunately, most such recipes turn out bland and dry.

Traditional pesto is a no-cook sauce made by pureeing pine nuts, garlic, olive oil, Parmesan cheese, and, of course, lots of fresh basil. But there is a new category of pesto that scales back on the herbs and uses pureed vegetables as the main ingredient.

I prepared a handful of recipes for my tasters, who liked the idea but not the execution. Most of the recipes I tested were quite bland, and the thick vegetable pesto made the pasta dry and sticky. Raw vegetables yielded particularly bland pesto, but I wasn't about to cook vegetables myself. After testing a dozen ready-to-use possibilities, I landed on frozen peas (which have already been cooked), jarred roasted red peppers, and sun-dried tomatoes packed in oil as three good options for the vegetable component.

Garlic and olive oil were a must for all of my pestos, as were nuts, cheese, and a small amount of fresh herbs. The traditional combination of pine nuts, Parmesan cheese, and basil worked very well with the sun-dried tomato version. For the roasted red pepper pesto, my tasters liked almonds, Asiago cheese, and parsley; for the pea-based pesto, they liked pistachios, Pecorino Romano cheese, and mint, plus lemon zest for freshness.

The flavors were right, but the texture of these pestos was still too dry and pasty. I tried adding creamy ingredients, including mayonnaise (too greasy), sour cream (too tangy), and cottage cheese (too bland), but none of them worked. Pureed ricotta cheese, however, lent a mild flavor and silky creaminess that worked to unify the other ingredients, especially when I thinned it with a little of the pasta cooking water. **–Cali Rich**

LEMONY PEA AND PISTACHIO PESTO PASTA SALAD
SERVES 8 TO 10

Toast the nuts in a dry skillet over medium heat, stirring frequently, until fragrant, about 5 minutes.

- 1   **pound penne, fusilli, or campanelle**
-     **Salt**
- ¼   **cup ricotta cheese**
- 1¼ **cups frozen peas, thawed**
- ½   **cup unsalted pistachios, toasted and chopped**
- ¼   **cup grated Pecorino Romano cheese**
- ¼   **cup extra-virgin olive oil**
- 1   **garlic clove, minced**
- 2   **tablespoons chopped fresh mint**
- 1   **teaspoon grated lemon zest**
- ½   **teaspoon pepper**

1. Bring 4 quarts water to boil in large pot. Add pasta and 1 tablespoon salt to boiling water and cook until just past al dente. Reserve ¾ cup pasta water. Drain pasta in colander, rinse with cold water until cool, drain once more, and transfer to large bowl.

2. Puree ricotta and 2 tablespoons hot pasta water in food processor until smooth. Add ¾ cup peas, ¼ cup pistachios, Pecorino Romano, oil, garlic, mint, zest, pepper, and ½ teaspoon salt and puree until smooth. Stir pesto into pasta until well coated, adding reserved pasta water as needed to adjust consistency. Fold in remaining peas and pistachios. Season with salt. Serve.

SPICY ROASTED RED PEPPER PESTO PASTA SALAD
SERVES 8 TO 10

Divina is the test kitchen's top-rated brand of jarred roasted red peppers. Discard any pepper seeds before chopping.

- 1   **pound penne, fusilli, or campanelle**
-     **Salt**
- ¼   **cup ricotta cheese**
- 1¼ **cups drained jarred roasted red peppers, chopped**
- ½   **cup slivered almonds, toasted**
- ¼   **cup grated Asiago cheese**
- ¼   **cup extra-virgin olive oil**
- 1   **garlic clove, minced**
- 2   **tablespoons chopped fresh parsley**
- ¼   **teaspoon red pepper flakes**

1. Bring 4 quarts water to boil in large pot. Add pasta and 1 tablespoon salt to boiling water and cook until just past al dente. Reserve ¾ cup pasta water. Drain pasta in colander, rinse with cold water until cool, drain once more, and transfer to large bowl.

2. Puree ricotta and 2 tablespoons hot pasta water in food processor until smooth. Add ¾ cup roasted peppers, ¼ cup almonds, Asiago, oil, garlic, parsley, pepper flakes, and ½ teaspoon salt and puree until smooth. Stir pesto into pasta until well coated, adding reserved pasta water as needed to adjust consistency. Fold in remaining roasted peppers and almonds. Season with salt. Serve.

Potent ingredients like garlic, cheese, roasted peppers, and sun-dried tomatoes elevate these pasta salads out of the realm of the ordinary.

SUN-DRIED TOMATO BASIL PESTO PASTA SALAD
SERVES 8 TO 10

You will need one 8-ounce jar of oil-packed sun-dried tomatoes for this recipe. Toast the pine nuts in a dry skillet over medium heat, stirring frequently, until golden, about 5 minutes.

- 1   **pound penne, fusilli, or campanelle**
-     **Salt**
- ¼   **cup ricotta cheese**
- ¾   **cup sun-dried tomatoes packed in oil, rinsed and patted dry**
- ½   **cup pine nuts, toasted**
- ¼   **cup grated Parmesan cheese**
- ¼   **cup extra-virgin olive oil**
- 1   **garlic clove, minced**
- ¼   **cup chopped fresh basil**
- ½   **teaspoon pepper**

1. Bring 4 quarts water to boil in large pot. Add pasta and 1 tablespoon salt to boiling water and cook until just past al dente. Reserve ¾ cup pasta water. Drain pasta in colander, rinse with cold water until cool, drain once more, and transfer to large bowl.

2. Puree ricotta and 2 tablespoons hot pasta water in food processor until smooth. Add sun-dried tomatoes, ¼ cup pine nuts, Parmesan, oil, garlic, basil, pepper, and ½ teaspoon salt and puree until smooth. Stir pesto into pasta until well coated, adding reserved pasta water as needed to adjust consistency. Fold in remaining pine nuts. Season with salt. Serve.

Make-Ahead: These salads can be refrigerated for 3 days. Bring to room temperature before serving and thin salads with a few tablespoons of warm water if needed.

Silky Smooth

Pureeing ricotta cheese with hot pasta water makes a creamy, silky base for our pesto pasta salads. Either whole milk or part skim ricotta cheese will work in any of these recipes.

SECRET INGREDIENT
Ricotta cheese

Thin-Crust Skillet Pizza

Homemade pizza in just 30 minutes sounds like an impossibility.
Could we develop a recipe that delivers?

How to
COOK THIN-CRUST SKILLET PIZZA

1. While the first side of the dough cooks, use a fork to gently pop any bubbles that form so that the dough will stay flat and brown evenly.
2. Using tongs, flip the dough over so that the second side can brown in the oil.
3. Sprinkle the dough with toppings and cheese, cover the skillet, and lower the heat. The heat captured in the pan helps to melt the cheese and warm up the other toppings before the bottom crust burns.

Seeding and draining the tomatoes before topping the pizza prevents our thin crust from becoming soggy.

A crisp, thin-yet-sturdy crust unburdened by sauce and simply topped with melted cheese and fresh tomatoes is pizza stripped down to its finest. But making thin-crust pizza at home requires a lengthy rise for the dough and plenty of time for a pizza stone (and oven) to get ripping hot. The intense heat makes for a crisp crust, but it also turns the kitchen into a sauna. I challenged myself to make the same crisp crust pizza without the hot kitchen.

Making pizza in a skillet is not a new idea. Following the most common method, I made a traditional pizza dough (flour, water, olive oil, salt, sugar, and yeast), let the dough rise for an hour, patted it into a round, and fried it on both sides in a hot oiled skillet. After sprinkling on the toppings and cheese, I covered the pan for a few minutes while the cheese melted. The result definitely wasn't the thin, crisp crust I was striving for (it was more like a thick pan pizza), but the technique did have some promise, as the hot oil gave the crust a golden brown exterior in less than 10 minutes.

An attempt at streamlining the process led me to store-bought pizza dough, but even when rolled paper thin, the yeast in the premade dough produced a crust that was always too thick and chewy. Returning to the homemade dough, I thought that simply omitting the yeast might create a thinner crust. The crust was thin but it was also tough and tasteless. Adding baking powder to the dough was a step in the right direction, as this dough came together quickly, rolled out easily, and would have cooked up light and crisp if there hadn't been a problem with the dough bubbling. To eliminate the bubbles I used a simple tool—a fork—to pop the bubbles as the first side cooked in the skillet (poking before cooking impeded the rise). The bubbling was minimized, and the crust was now evenly browned and incredibly crisp.

But not everything was perfect, as my tasters were missing the traditional yeast flavor in the dough. The test kitchen sometimes uses mild American lager to amplify or mimic the flavor of yeast in breads, but after replacing the water in the dough with lager, the yeast flavor was still negligible in the finished pizza. Bolder, darker brown ales, which have a strong yeasty and malty flavor, were a better stand-in for yeast (see box, page 19).

In order to keep the process quick and easy (and to avoid soggy pies), I topped the pizzas with potent no-cook ingredients. Fresh tomatoes (salted and drained to eliminate excess moisture) and basil were the base flavors, and I dressed them up with black olives, roasted red peppers, and prosciutto. Semisoft mozzarella, fontina, and provolone cheeses melted best in the covered skillet, especially when I turned the heat to low after adding the cheeses to allow them to melt without the bottom crust burning. Judging by the constant stream of test cooks asking for another slice of this crisp thin-crust pizza, I had met my challenge. **–Lynn Clark**

Yeasty Flavor Without the Wait

Yeast gives traditional pizza dough its complex flavor but requires several hours to work its magic. We found that beer adds a yeasty flavor to our quick and easy pizza dough, which is leavened with baking powder. Although any beer will work here, we prefer full-flavored ales to bitter stouts or mild lagers. Our favorite, Newcastle Brown Ale, won praise for its rich, malty flavor that gave our pizza crust just the right yeast flavor. If you're looking a non-alcoholic option, our tasters liked O'Doul's Amber.

FLAVOR ENHANCER
Beer, preferably a rich brown ale, adds a yeasty flavor to our pizza dough.

SKILLET PIZZA

SERVES 2

To save time, combine the cheeses and prepare the dough while the salted tomatoes are draining. When popping the bubbles in the dough in step 3, do so gently to avoid scratching the nonstick pan.

Toppings

- 4 medium plum tomatoes, cored, seeded, and chopped
- ½ teaspoon salt
- 1 cup shredded mozzarella cheese
- ½ cup grated Parmesan cheese
- ½ cup finely chopped fresh basil

Dough

- 1 cup all-purpose flour
- ½ teaspoon baking powder
- ½ teaspoon sugar
- ½ teaspoon salt
- ⅓ cup beer (see box above)
- 7 tablespoons olive oil

1. For the toppings: Toss tomatoes and salt in large bowl, then transfer to paper towel–lined plate; let drain 15 minutes. Combine cheeses and basil in medium bowl; refrigerate while preparing dough.

2. For the dough: Combine flour, baking powder, sugar, and salt in food processor.

With processor running, slowly add beer and 1 tablespoon oil and process until dough pulls away from sides and forms shaggy ball, about 1 minute. Using floured hands, form dough into tight ball and cover loosely with plastic wrap; let rest 10 minutes. (Dough can be wrapped tightly in plastic and frozen for up to 1 week.)

3. Divide dough in half. On lightly floured surface, roll each half into very thin 9-inch round. Heat 3 tablespoons oil in large nonstick skillet over medium heat until just smoking. Following photos 1 to 3 on page 18, transfer one dough round to skillet and cook, poking any bubbles that form with fork, until bottom is deep golden brown and crisp, 3 to 4 minutes. Flip dough and sprinkle with half of drained tomatoes and half of cheese mixture. Reduce heat to low and cook, covered, until second side is crisp and cheeses have melted, about 5 minutes. Transfer pizza to cutting board. Wipe out pan and repeat with remaining oil, dough, and toppings. Slice into wedges. Serve.

FONTINA, GOAT CHEESE, AND PROSCIUTTO TOPPING

- 4 medium plum tomatoes, cored, seeded, and chopped
- ½ teaspoon salt
- 1 cup shredded fontina cheese
- ½ cup crumbled goat cheese
- 2 ounces sliced deli prosciutto, chopped
- ½ cup finely chopped fresh basil

Toss tomatoes and salt in large bowl, then transfer to paper towel-lined plate; let drain 15 minutes. Combine cheeses, prosciutto, and basil in medium bowl; refrigerate until ready to use as directed in step 3.

PROVOLONE, OLIVE, AND SPICY PEPPER TOPPING

- 4 medium plum tomatoes, cored, seeded, and chopped
- ½ teaspoon salt
- 1 cup shredded provolone cheese
- ¼ cup drained jarred roasted red peppers, chopped
- ¼ cup pitted kalamata olives, chopped
- 2 large jarred pepperoncini, stemmed, seeded, and chopped
- ½ cup finely chopped fresh basil

Toss tomatoes and salt in large bowl, then transfer to paper towel-lined plate; let drain 15 minutes. Combine provolone, roasted peppers, olives, pepperoncini, and basil in medium bowl; refrigerate until ready to use as directed in step 3.

BARBECUED CHICKEN TOPPING

- 1 cup cooked chicken, cubed
- ¼ cup barbecue sauce
- 2 scallions, sliced thin
- 2 tablespoons chopped cilantro
- 1 cup shredded mild cheddar cheese

Toss chicken and barbecue sauce in medium bowl until chicken is coated. Add scallions, cilantro, and cheese; refrigerate until ready to use as directed in step 3.

On The Side: Creamy Peppercorn Dressing

How do you make a dressing that actually tastes like pepper—but without the burn?

Stroll up and down a salad bar and you'll notice the many options for creamy dressings. While ranch is probably the most popular, I reach for creamy peppercorn. But more often than not my salad ends up covered with a gloppy dressing that either tastes nothing like pepper or makes my eyes burn. I headed into the test kitchen to make a creamy peppercorn dressing that tastes like pepper, but without any pain.

Many creamy dressing recipes start with a blend of mayonnaise and sour cream. While this combination is rich and tangy, it's pretty thick and reminds me more of a dip. Thinning the creamy base with buttermilk gave it the right consistency and added tang. Red wine vinegar, garlic, and Dijon mustard rounded out the flavors.

Adding a ton of pepper directly to the dressing left me with a mouthful of chewy, strong pepper bits. Sure, I could add less (and grind it fine), but then my dressing would lack personality. Somehow I needed to tame the fiery intensity of the pepper.

Thinking of the test kitchen recipe for pepper-crusted filet mignon, it dawned on me that I could bloom the pepper to temper its heat. As I expected, slowly simmering the pepper in oil mellowed its harshness, and when added to the dressing, each spoonful tasted deeply of pepper. Rather than discarding the oil, which also had developed a nice peppery flavor, I simply added it to my dressing and cut back a bit on the sour cream and mayonnaise.

–Meredith Butcher

CREAMY PEPPERCORN DRESSING

MAKES ABOUT 1 CUP, ENOUGH TO DRESS 16 CUPS OF LETTUCE

If you don't have buttermilk, substitute 2 tablespoons milk and increase the vinegar to 2½ teaspoons. Hearty, crisp iceberg and romaine work well with this creamy dressing.

- 1 tablespoon coarsely ground black pepper
- ¼ cup extra-virgin olive oil
- ¼ cup sour cream
- ¼ cup mayonnaise
- 2 tablespoons buttermilk (see note)
- 2 teaspoons Dijon mustard
- 2 teaspoons red wine vinegar
- 1 garlic clove, minced
  Salt

1. Heat pepper and oil in small saucepan over low heat until faint bubbles

appear. Gently simmer, swirling pan occasionally, until pepper is fragrant, about 8 minutes. Remove from heat and cool to room temperature.

2. Whisk sour cream, mayonnaise, buttermilk, mustard, vinegar, and garlic in bowl. Gradually whisk in pepper mixture until incorporated. Season with salt. (Dressing can be refrigerated in airtight container for up to 4 days.)

Shredded Barbecued Beef

Barbecuing a big beef roast until it's smoky and pull-apart tender sounds like a great idea, but dry, bland meat isn't much reward for a day's worth of cooking. Could we find a better—and faster—way?

Secrets to PERFECT BBQ BEEF

With just a few simple steps, it's easy to turn a chuck roast into smoky, tender shredded barbecued beef.

1. To speed cooking and allow the meat to absorb more smoke, cut the chuck roast into quarters, removing and discarding excess fat and gristle.

2. Place the disposable roasting pan with the spice-rubbed meat on the grill opposite the coals and packet of soaked wood chips.

3. Before wrapping the pan with foil and transferring it to the oven to finish cooking, flip the pieces of meat to maximize contact with the pan juices.

Barbecued beef brisket is great for slicing, but when you want shredded barbecued beef, most experts rely on a fatty, flavorful chuck roast. Long, slow cooking is supposed to melt the fat and connective tissue in this large shoulder roast and yield moist, tender meat.

I rounded up several recipes for shredded beef barbecue (all calling for chuck roast) and fired up the grills. The savory smoke that filled the air outside the test kitchen had my tasters eager with anticipation. Their enthusiasm turned to disappointment as they chewed their way through beef that was dry and stringy on the outside and lacked smoke flavor. Given the work involved, these recipes were true failures.

For my next test, I decided to try cooking a chuck roast the same way the test kitchen cooks a pork shoulder for pulled pork: I rubbed the outside with salt, pepper, and cayenne (a classic Texas-style rub for beef) and set the roast to smoke on the cooler side of the grill. After two hours, the meat was sufficiently crusty, so I transferred it to a baking pan, wrapped the pan in foil, and placed the roast in the oven to finish cooking to fall-apart tenderness. (This grill-to-oven method is much quicker than cooking the meat entirely on the grill and avoids the need to rebuild the fire with freshly lit coals.)

It took four hours in the oven to tenderize the tough chuck, but by that time the meat was dried out—except for where the bottom of the roast had been sitting in the exuded juices. I cooked the next roast in a disposable aluminum pan from the outset to catch those juices, which helped keep more—but not all—of the meat moist. Cutting the roast into four pieces solved the problem, as the smaller pieces of meat sat lower in the pan and thus deeper in the juices. Flipping the pieces before transferring them to the oven ensured that more of meat was "basted" and moist (by the end of cooking, the juices were coming about halfway up the sides of the pieces). What's more, the smaller pieces of beef absorbed more smoke flavor, and they cooked at least an hour faster than a single large roast.

Meat this good demanded a homemade sauce. Many recipes start by sautéing onions in vegetable oil, but for richer flavor I used some beef fat from the pan instead. Chili powder and black pepper added bite, while ketchup, vinegar, coffee, Worcestershire sauce, brown sugar, and some of the rendered beef juices rounded out the flavors. This beef was tender, juicy, smoky, and ready to be piled on a sandwich.

–Meredith Butcher

SHREDDED BARBECUED BEEF SERVES 8 TO 10

If you prefer a smooth barbecue sauce, strain the sauce before tossing it with the beef in step 4. You will need a disposable aluminum roasting pan for this recipe. We like to serve this beef on white bread with plenty of pickle chips.

Spice Rub and Beef
- 1 tablespoon salt
- 1 tablespoon pepper
- 1 teaspoon cayenne pepper
- 1 (5- to 6-pound) boneless beef chuck-eye roast
- 3 cups wood chips, soaked for 15 minutes

Barbecue Sauce
- 1 onion, chopped fine
- 4 garlic cloves, minced
- ½ teaspoon chili powder
- 1¼ cups ketchup
- ¾ cup brewed coffee
- ½ cup cider vinegar
- ½ cup packed brown sugar
- 3 tablespoons Worcestershire sauce
- ½ teaspoon pepper

Chopping the smoked beef results in a more uniform texture, but we like the meaty chunks created by shredding the meat with forks.

1. **For the spice rub and beef:** Combine salt, pepper, and cayenne in small bowl. Following photo 1, quarter roast and remove excess fat and gristle. Rub meat all over with salt mixture and transfer to large disposable aluminum roasting pan. (Salt-rubbed meat can be wrapped tightly in plastic and refrigerated for 24 hours.)

2. Seal soaked wood chips in foil packet and cut vent holes in top. Open bottom vent on grill. Light 50 coals; when covered with fine gray ash, pour in pile on one side of grill. Arrange foil packet directly on coals. Set cooking grate in place and heat, covered, with lid vent open halfway, until wood chips begin to smoke heavily, about 5 minutes. (For gas grill, place foil packet directly on primary burner. Heat all burners on high, covered, until wood chips begin to smoke heavily, about 15 minutes. Leave primary burner on high and shut other burner[s] off.) Arrange roasting pan with beef on cooler side of grill and barbecue, covered, until meat is deep red and smoky, about 2 hours.

3. Adjust oven rack to lower-middle position and heat oven to 300 degrees. Following photo 3, flip meat over, cover pan tightly with foil, and bake until fork inserted into meat can be removed with no resistance, 2 to 3 hours. Transfer meat to large bowl, tent with foil, and let rest 30 minutes. While meat rests, skim fat from accumulated juices in pan; reserve 2 tablespoons fat. Strain defatted juices; reserve ½ cup juice.

4. **For the barbecue sauce and to finish:** Combine onion and reserved fat in saucepan and cook over medium heat until onion has softened, about 10 minutes. Add garlic and chili powder and cook until fragrant, about 30 seconds. Stir in remaining ingredients and reserved meat juices and simmer until thickened, about 15 minutes. Using 2 forks, pull meat into shreds, discarding any excess fat or gristle. Toss meat with ½ cup barbecue sauce. Serve, passing remaining sauce at table.

On the Side: Drunken Beans

Beans cooked with smoky pork, spices, and beer should be flavorful, but many recipes are surprisingly bland.

Frijoles borrachos, or "drunken beans," are pinto beans cooked with smoky pork (salt pork in traditional recipes and bacon in modern adaptations), onion, garlic, spices, and, of course, beer. Unfortunately, the recipes I tested produced bland beans.

I started rebuilding this recipe with the bacon. Although my tasters liked bacon's flavor, they craved something meatier, and spicy chorizo sausage fit the bill perfectly. To preserve the chorizo's texture, I pulled it from the pot after browning and then sautéed onion, garlic, oregano, and chili powder in the sausage fat to build a rich flavor base. Smoky chipotle chiles in adobo sauce lent a welcome bite.

Most recipes soak the beans overnight to ensure even cooking, then simmer the drained beans in a mixture of water and beer. My tasters liked dark, malty Mexican beer (such as Negro Modelo). Finished with a little lime juice and cilantro, these beans are as good as any I've had in the Southwest. **–Meredith Butcher**

DRUNKEN BEANS SERVES 4 TO 6

We prefer a dark Mexican beer, such as Negro Modelo, but any lager or ale will work in this recipe. Andouille sausage may be substituted for the chorizo. Make sure to soak the beans overnight in water to cover.

- 8   ounces chorizo sausage, cut into ½-inch pieces
- 1   onion, chopped fine
- 4   garlic cloves, minced
- 1   teaspoon dried oregano
- 1   teaspoon chili powder
- 1   pound pinto beans, soaked overnight and drained
- 1   (12-ounce) bottle dark Mexican beer (see note)
- 5   cups water
- 1   tablespoon brown sugar
- 2   teaspoons minced canned chipotle chiles in adobo sauce
     Salt
- 2   tablespoons chopped fresh cilantro
- 1   tablespoon lime juice

1. Cook sausage in Dutch oven over medium heat until browned, about 8 minutes; transfer to paper towel–lined plate. Cook onion in sausage fat until softened, about 5 minutes. Stir in garlic, oregano, and chili powder and cook until fragrant, about 30 seconds. Add beans, beer, and water and bring to simmer. Reduce heat to medium-low, cover, and cook until beans are just soft, about 1 hour.

2. Stir in sugar, chipotle, and 1 teaspoon salt. Continue to simmer, uncovered, until beans are completely tender and sauce is slightly thickened, about 50 minutes. Return sausage to pot and simmer until sausage is tender, about 10 minutes. (If mixture becomes too thick, add water.) Stir in cilantro and lime juice and season with salt. Serve. (Beans can be refrigerated in an airtight container for 4 days.)

Party Favorites: Frozen Strawberry Margaritas

Great strawberry margaritas start with real strawberries—and lots of them.

The best frozen strawberry margaritas balance the sweet, tart flavor of strawberries and citrus with orange liqueur and plenty of tequila, and then blend the lot with ice to create a slushy, smooth elixir. But most versions I've had featured bland berries beaten into a washed-out mess.

For a smooth consistency, I found that equal amounts of ice and frozen berries worked best. For more strawberry flavor, I tried adding bottled mixes and juices, but they were too watery. Cooking down additional frozen berries into an intensely flavored syrup was the best way to add rich strawberry flavor to the frozen base.

I hoped fresh lime juice would brighten the strawberry flavor, but it only steamrolled it. Sweet and sour limeade enhanced the strawberry flavor perfectly. The only problem was that the limeade made the margaritas too watery. Luckily, just 3 tablespoons of frozen limeade concentrate packed plenty of flavor and kept the smooth, frosty texture intact. **–Jeremy Sauer**

FROZEN STRAWBERRY MARGARITAS

MAKES ABOUT 4 CUPS, SERVING 4 TO 6

If you don't have kosher salt, substitute ½ teaspoon table salt in step 1 and 2 tablespoons table salt in step 2. You will need roughly 16 ounces of frozen strawberries for this recipe.

- 4   cups frozen strawberries (see note)
- ¾   cup sugar
- ¼   cup kosher salt
- 3   tablespoons frozen limeade concentrate
- 2   cups ice
- ⅔   cup silver tequila
- ⅔   cup triple sec

1. Heat 2 cups strawberries, ¼ cup sugar, and ¾ teaspoon salt in medium saucepan over medium heat until berries begin to release their juices, about 5 minutes. Mash with potato masher until fruit breaks down, then simmer until mixture is syrupy and reduced to ¾ cup, about 5 minutes. Stir in limeade concentrate and transfer to large bowl. Cover with plastic wrap and refrigerate until well chilled, about 1 hour. (Mixture can be made 1 day in advance.)

2. Combine remaining sugar and salt in pie plate. Remove strawberry mixture from refrigerator and dip rims of serving glasses in liquid. Press rims of glasses into salt mixture and set aside. Transfer chilled strawberry mixture to blender. Add remaining frozen strawberries, ice, tequila, and triple sec and blend until smooth. Pour into salted glasses.

Grilled Stuffed Chicken Breasts

How to
STUFF BONELESS CHICKEN BREASTS

The key to tidy, well-distributed stuffing is to create a large pocket with a small opening.

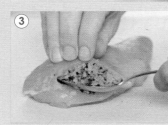

1. Use a sharp paring knife to cut a pocket in the thickest part of the chicken breast.
2. Gently work the knife back and forth until the pocket extends deep into the breast.
3. Use a small spoon to scoop the filling into each chicken breast. Gently press down to distribute the stuffing evenly.
4. Seal in the filling by threading a toothpick through the center of the pocket about ¼ inch from the edge.

Stuffing chicken breasts and grilling them over a smoky fire sounds like a great way to dress up this mild cut, but only if the meat stays juicy and the filling packs a flavorful punch.

Because they're so lean, boneless, skinless chicken breasts can be pretty bland and are prone to drying out when cooked. Two promising ways to add flavor are with the smoke and char from grilling and with a savory stuffing. I started my testing by adopting the test kitchen's easy stuffing technique, in which we cut a pocket in the chicken breast, pack it with stuffing, and seal it with a toothpick.

After a few tries, I ruled out bread-based stuffings—they held together well but were inevitably pasty. Vegetable fillings required precooking—more work than I wanted to do for a simple weeknight recipe. Herb purees (made with garlic and olive oil) packed the most flavor and came together quickly, but oozed out of the chicken as it cooked. I tried to bind the herb puree with some Parmesan, but this failed to keep the filling inside the chicken. Creamy and strong-flavored fontina, pepper Jack, and feta worked a bit better, especially when combined with just 3 tablespoons of bread crumbs (or crushed corn chips for a variation).

We sometimes grill chicken over direct heat, but with the added bulk from the stuffing, these chicken breasts had to spend extra time on the grill and became dry on the exterior. Gently grilling the chicken with indirect heat worked better, and for even more protection against drying out, I decided to employ an olive oil–based marinade. A 30-minute soak in oil, lemon juice, and garlic gave the chicken the protection it needed, plus an extra boost of flavor to complement the stuffing. Reserving a little of the marinade to brush on the cooked chicken while it rested added a final hit of bright flavor. **–Kelley Baker**

GRILLED STUFFED CHICKEN BREASTS
SERVES 4

You will need 4 sturdy, uncolored toothpicks for this recipe. We prefer the taste and texture of homemade bread crumbs (simply tear 1 slice of white sandwich bread into pieces, grind in a food processor, and toast in a dry skillet until golden), but store-bought bread crumbs are acceptable here.

- 6 tablespoons extra-virgin olive oil
- ½ teaspoon grated zest and 1 tablespoon juice from 1 lemon
- 3 garlic cloves, minced
- 1 teaspoon sugar
- ¾ teaspoon salt
- ½ teaspoon pepper
- 1 cup chopped fresh basil
- ½ cup shredded fontina cheese
- 3 tablespoons toasted bread crumbs (see note)
- 4 boneless, skinless chicken breasts (about 1½ pounds)

1. Whisk oil, zest, juice, garlic, sugar, salt, and pepper in small bowl. Pulse 2 tablespoons oil mixture, basil, cheese, and bread crumbs in food processor until coarsely ground.

2. Following photos at left, cut pocket in thick part of each chicken breast, spoon in filling, and secure with toothpick. Transfer stuffed chicken to large plate or baking dish and toss with additional ¼ cup oil mixture. Cover with plastic wrap and refrigerate for 30 minutes or up to 1 hour.

3. Heat all burners on high for 15 minutes. Leave primary burner on high and shut other burner(s) off. (For charcoal grill, light 100 coals; when covered with fine gray ash, spread over half of grill. Set cooking grate in place and heat covered, with lid vent open completely, for 5 minutes.) Scrape and oil cooking grate.

4. Arrange chicken, smooth-side down, on cooler side of grill with thicker side facing hot side of grill. Cook, covered, until chicken is beginning to brown and meat registers 140 degrees, 16 to 20 minutes, flipping and rotating breasts halfway through cooking time.

Move chicken to hot side of grill and cook covered, flipping every few minutes, until meat registers 160 degrees, 4 to 8 minutes. Transfer chicken to platter and brush with remaining oil mixture. Tent with foil and let rest 5 minutes. Remove toothpicks. Serve.

TEX-MEX GRILLED STUFFED CHICKEN BREASTS

Substitute ½ teaspoon grated lime zest and 1 tablespoon lime juice for lemon zest and juice, 1 cup chopped fresh cilantro for basil, ½ cup shredded pepper Jack cheese for fontina, and ¼ cup crushed corn tortilla chips for bread crumbs.

GREEK-STYLE GRILLED STUFFED CHICKEN BREASTS

Substitute ¾ cup chopped fresh parsley plus ¼ cup chopped fresh oregano for basil and ⅓ cup crumbled feta cheese for fontina.

Marinating these chicken breasts in oil seasoned with garlic and lemon both before and after grilling helps ensure moist and flavorful meat.

Getting to Know Dried Chiles

Used in spice rubs, salsas, and stews—and, of course, in chilis—dried chiles add heat and a concentrated, earthy flavor to any number of dishes. Below are 12 varieties, our tasting notes, and a heat rating of 1 to 5 peppers (with 5 being the hottest) for each chile. For more information on cooking with dried chiles, see page 31.

Habanero
FRUITY FIRE

These wrinkled, orange-red chiles are some of the most potent in the world. Although oppressively hot, the habanero is also one of the most flavorful members of the chile family. Tasters found them "intensely floral and fruity," with a "peachy" taste that balances the "intense burn." Whether fresh or dried, habaneros should be handled carefully and used sparingly.

Heat rating:

Arbol
DUSTY AND HARSH

With their thin, tapered shape, these chiles are called cola de rata (Spanish for "rat tail") when fresh. Because they hold their color after drying, these scarlet red chiles are often used for decorative purposes and, based on our tasting notes, their appearance may be their strongest attribute: We found the "assertively spicy" arbol to be "dusty, unbalanced, harsh, and acidic."

Heat rating:

Piquin
BIG HEAT, LITTLE PACKAGE

No more than ¾ inch long, these tiny chiles—also called bird peppers—pack a big punch. As for flavor, an initial hint of sweetness quickly turns to a "smoky," "fiery burn." Because they are so small, it's nearly impossible to rid piquins of all their seeds and stems, which leaves these chiles with an unpleasant "muddy, dusty" aftertaste. We do not recommend using this chile.

Heat rating:

Chipotle
SMOKY AND SPICY

To make chipotles, jalapeño chiles are slow-smoked and then either canned with adobo sauce (a seasoned tomato puree) or left to dry into the wrinkled, cocoa-colored chile seen above. Both the dried and canned versions are "intensely smoky" and much hotter than fresh jalapeños. Unless you plan to grind these chiles for a spice rub, we suggest using the canned variety.

Heat rating:

Pulla
TANGY AND FRUITY

Although pullas (sometimes called puyas) resemble arbol chiles in shape and color, they are only "moderately hot" and possess a "pleasantly fruity" flavor with a noticeable acidity that tasters equated with both "vinegar" and "fresh lemon juice." Because pullas are thin skinned, they can be simply crumbled and added to salsas.

Heat rating:

New Mexico
RIGHT FOR RISTRAS

Also known as the Colorado chile, this is the dried version of the red Anaheim chile. The classic shape and brick-red color of the New Mexico chile are two reasons why this variety is often tied into a chile ristra, or ornamental wreath. Its flavor is "sweet, fruity, and fresh," with a "mild citrusy" aftertaste. The thin flesh of the New Mexico chile makes it a good addition to fresh salsas.

Heat rating:

Guajillo
HEAVY METAL

This large, tapered chile is commonly used (along with anchos and pasillas) to make the classic Mexican sauce mole. Guajillos are "piney and grassy," with a "subtle smoky character" that borders on "ashy." Tasters found them to be more sweet than hot, with a distinct "metallic" flavor. Because they have a leathery skin, guajillos may require more soaking than other chiles and should be finely ground.

Heat rating:

Pasilla
BITTER, NEEDS BALANCE

The inky color of these elongated chiles earned them the nickname chile negro. They have a "bitter, grassy" flavor that some tasters equated with "coffee" or "licorice." Because pasillas are so bitter, they are best when used in conjunction with sweeter chiles or in sauces with a hint of sweetness, such as mole.

Heat rating:

Cascabel
ROUND RATTLER

The name cascabel (which in Spanish means "rattle" or "little round bell") refers to the sound the seeds make when the dried chile pod is shaken. Slightly wrinkled and purplish brown, these golf ball–sized chiles are "moderately hot," with a "balanced sweet and tangy" flavor that makes them a welcome addition to soups, stews, and sauces.

Heat rating:

Ñora
CHARRED AND MUSTY

This small, reddish-purple chile is native to Spain and is recognizable for its bell shape and smooth skin. When dried, it tastes "earthy and very mild," with a "charred-wood" flavor and a "musty" finish. These chiles are often ground into paprika or used in romesco, a tomato and chile sauce similar to pesto.

Heat rating:

Ancho
CHOCOLATY AND RICH

When fresh, these broad, blackish-green chiles are called poblanos. Anchos have a "rich, earthy" flavor reminiscent of "dark chocolate." Naturally smoky and fruity, anchos are available both whole and ground. Their complex flavor and mild heat make them an excellent option for grinding into powder for use in spice rubs or chili.

Heat rating:

Mulato
RAISINY AND MILD

Though slightly larger and darker in color than the ancho chile, the mulato is also a dried version of the poblano. The difference is that mulatos are made from poblanos that have been allowed to ripen until dark brown, giving the dried chile a "sweet, raisiny" flavor with a distinct "tobacco-like quality." Mulatos can be used ground in spice rubs, soups, or stews.

Heat rating:

Wood-Grilled Salmon

Salmon grilled directly on a cedar plank is a Northwest favorite. But can you enjoy wood-perfumed grilled salmon without the hard-to-find plank?

Kitchen Know-How
THANKS, BUT NO PLANKS

Cooking salmon on a cedar plank infuses it with gentle wood flavor rather than overwhelming smokiness. Here's how to get the same great taste, minus the mail-order plank.

1. Cut out four rectangles of heavy-duty aluminum foil and crimp edges until each tray measures 7 by 5 inches. Using a paring knife, poke small slits in the bottom of the trays. (These vents will help to heat the chips.)

2. Place soaked wood chips in the foil trays and arrange the salmon skin-side down directly on top of the wood chips.

3. Once the salmon is cooked, slide a metal spatula between the flesh and the skin; the fish should release easily.

Grilled cedar-planked salmon has its roots in Native American cultures of the Pacific Northwest, and to this day it is a popular dish in Seattle restaurants. The premise is simple: Salmon fillets are set on a soaked plank of aromatic cedar, and the plank is placed on the grill to cook. Soaking the plank keeps the fish moist during cooking and prevents the soft, resinous cedar from combusting. What makes this dish unique is that the fish is perfumed with subtle wood flavor but doesn't taste heavily smoked.

To put this recipe to the test, I mail-ordered cedar planks from a specialty grilling store and got to work. Following standard procedure, I soaked the planks for an hour, loaded them with salmon, and threw them onto the grate over moderate heat. With a bit of fiddling (and yes, I did ignite the plank during one memorable failed test), I was able to produce moist salmon tinged with a nice wood flavor. Now that I knew what I wanted, could I create the same flavor without mail-ordering cedar planks?

Wood chips, available in almost every hardware store, seemed like my best hope. I knew that I couldn't simply swap the plank for chips (the small chips would fall through the grate), so I made individual aluminum foil trays to hold the chips and salmon. I tossed a handful of soaked chips into each tray, laid my fillets on top, and set them on a hot grill to cook.

The soaked chips did lend some wood flavor to the fish, but they adhered to the salmon flesh, making for mangled fillets coming off the grill. To remedy this, I left the skin on (it prevented the chips from sticking and was easily separated from the cooked fish). The resulting moist, fully intact fillets had a bit of wood flavor, but I wanted more. Poking a few slits in the bottom of the foil allowed even more heat to reach the wood chips, causing them to release more of their woodsy—but not overly smoky—flavor.

Though the flavor and texture were great, the fish was unappealingly pale. Following the lead of a few recipes I had come across, I tried packing the fillets in a heavy coating of brown sugar; the sugar caramelized into an appealing golden hue but made the fish candy-sweet. A better solution was to coat each fillet with a thin layer of olive oil and a light sprinkling of granulated sugar for a golden, mildly sweet exterior that tasted as good as it looked.

–Greg Case

Skin-on salmon fillets are essential here; the skin keeps the fish moist and prevents it from sticking.

WOOD-GRILLED SALMON

SERVES 4

Aromatic woods such as cedar and alder give the most authentic flavor.

- 1½ teaspoons sugar
- ½ teaspoon salt
- ¼ teaspoon pepper
- 4 skin-on salmon fillets (each 6 to 8 ounces and 1¼ inches thick)
- 1 tablespoon olive oil
- 2 cups wood chips, soaked for 15 minutes

1. Combine sugar, salt, and pepper in small bowl. Pat salmon dry with paper towels. Brush flesh side of salmon with oil and sprinkle with sugar mixture. Following photos 1 and 2 on page 24, use heavy-duty aluminum foil to make four 7- by 5-inch trays. Using tip of knife, perforate bottom of each tray. Divide wood chips among trays and place salmon skin-side down on top of wood chips.

2. Place trays with salmon over hot fire and grill, covered, until center of each fillet is still just translucent, about 10 minutes. Remove trays from grill. Following photo 3, slide metal spatula between skin and flesh of fish and transfer to platter. Serve.

CHINESE-STYLE WOOD-GRILLED SALMON

In step 1, add ½ teaspoon five-spice powder and ¼ teaspoon cayenne pepper to sugar mixture. Omit oil and brush salmon with 2 tablespoons hoisin sauce before sprinkling with sugar mixture.

BBQ WOOD-GRILLED SALMON

In step 1, add ¾ teaspoon chili powder and ¼ teaspoon cayenne pepper to sugar mixture. Omit oil and brush salmon with mixture of 1 tablespoon Dijon mustard and 1 tablespoon maple syrup before sprinkling with sugar mixture.

LEMON-THYME WOOD-GRILLED SALMON

In step 1, add 2 teaspoons minced fresh thyme and 1½ teaspoons grated lemon zest to sugar mixture. Omit oil and brush salmon with 2 tablespoons Dijon mustard before sprinkling with sugar mixture.

On the Side: Grilled Sesame Asparagus

When it comes to grilled asparagus, don't get burned by a sugary glaze with very little sesame flavor.

A salty-sweet Asian glaze and crunchy sesame seeds sound like a great way to dress up smoky grilled asparagus. Most recipes toss the spears with a mixture of sesame oil, soy sauce, honey, and sesame seeds. But I found that, once on the grill, the seeds quickly burned and the sweet glaze turned into sticky, black tar. And the asparagus wasn't seasoned inside.

Instead of watching a sweet, thick glaze burn on the grate, I decided to marinate the asparagus in a thinner version of the glaze (minus the sesame seeds). I supplemented the sesame oil and soy sauce with ginger, garlic, and red pepper flakes. Instead of honey, my tasters preferred brown sugar for its deeper, caramelized flavor. On the grill the veneer of marinade browned—not burned—and the cooked asparagus was now flavored to its core.

Unfortunately, the sesame flavor was dissipating on the grill. So rather than use sesame oil in the marinade, I reserved some of the marinade and added sesame oil to it. I tossed the hot-off-the-grill asparagus in this mixture and sprinkled on toasted sesame seeds, and the asparagus was now loaded with sesame flavor. **–Lynn Clark**

GRILLED SESAME ASPARAGUS

SERVES 4

Toast the sesame seeds in a dry skillet over medium heat, stirring frequently, until golden, about 5 minutes.

- 2 tablespoons soy sauce
- 2 tablespoons vegetable oil
- 2 teaspoons light brown sugar
- 1 garlic clove, minced
- ½ teaspoon grated fresh ginger
- ⅛ teaspoon red pepper flakes
- 1 pound asparagus, trimmed
- 1 tablespoon toasted sesame oil
  Salt and pepper
- 1 tablespoon sesame seeds, toasted

1. Whisk soy sauce, vegetable oil, sugar, garlic, ginger, and pepper flakes in shallow dish. Add asparagus and toss until well coated. Let marinate at room temperature for at least 15 minutes or up to 1 hour.

2. Remove asparagus from dish (do not discard marinade) and grill over hot fire, turning frequently, until tender and lightly charred, 4 to 8 minutes.

3. Add grilled asparagus to dish with reserved marinade. Add sesame oil and

toss until asparagus is well coated. Season with salt and pepper and sprinkle with sesame seeds. Serve.

On the Side: Curried Rice Salad

Adding bold flavors to a rice salad won't camouflage mushy or starchy grains.

Curried rice salad should be an easy side dish with light, fluffy grains and balanced flavors. Unfortunately, most recipes yield sticky clumps of rice coated with a dressing that's surprisingly bland.

Since rice salad demands fluffy grains, some sort of long-grain rice is a must. Aromatic basmati rice edged out regular long-grain rice in my tests, but neither was particularly light. Once cooled, rice cooked by the absorption method (simmered in a covered pot with just enough water) solidified into a sticky mess. Rinsing the rice before cooking didn't really help. I had much better luck by treating the rice like pasta and boiling it in a large pot of salted water to wash away excess starch. Spreading the drained rice out on a baking sheet promoted less clumping and quick cooling.

Many basic recipes simply toss the cooled rice with a curry vinaigrette, and the results are predictably dull and dusty. In the test kitchen, we've found blooming curry powder in some oil unlocks its flavor. To add depth to the dish, I first sautéed some onion and jalapeño, then added the curry powder along with some ginger and garlic.

Lime juice delivered the right fruity, tart notes, while raisins (which I plumped in the lime juice with some sugar) added chewy sweetness. Chopped cilantro provided a fresh finish to this summery salad. **–Cali Rich**

CURRIED RICE SALAD SERVES 4 TO 6

- ⅔ cup raisins or currants
- ¼ cup juice from 2 to 3 limes
- ¾ teaspoon sugar
  Salt
- 1½ cups basmati or long-grain rice
- 3 tablespoons unsalted butter
- 1 onion, chopped fine
- 1 jalapeño chile, seeded and minced
- 1 tablespoon grated fresh ginger
- 1 garlic clove, minced
- 1½ teaspoons curry power
- 3 tablespoons finely chopped fresh cilantro

1. Combine raisins, lime juice, and sugar in small bowl; set aside. Bring 4 quarts water to boil in large pot. Add 1 tablespoon salt and rice to boiling water and cook until just tender, 12 to 14 minutes. Drain rice, spread on rimmed baking sheet, and cool completely, at least 20 minutes.

2. Melt butter in empty pot over medium heat. Cook onion and jalapeño until soft, about 5 minutes. Add ginger, garlic, and curry and cook until fragrant, about 30 seconds. Off heat, stir in raisin mixture.

3. Toss rice, raisin mixture, and cilantro in large bowl until combined. Season with salt. Serve. (Salad can be refrigerated for 1 day. Bring to room temperature before serving.)

Lemon Sheet Cake

A sweet-tart lemon sheet cake holds a lot of promise as a light summer dessert—but sheet cakes are hard to bake evenly, and what's the best way to get bright, not sour, lemon flavor?

Tangy buttermilk reinforces the lemon flavor in both the cake and glaze.

Test Kitchen Secret
MAKING LEMON SUGAR

Our easy homemade lemon sugar provides a flavorful base for the cake and an eye-catching, crunchy, lemony topping.

1. Beating the sugar with the lemon zest releases the flavorful oils in the zest.

2. Sprinkle extra lemon sugar over the glazed cake for added flavor and crunch.

When cookouts demand an easy bake-and-take dessert, nothing smacks of summer more than lemon sheet cake. A single bite should offer a punch of bright and sweet lemon flavor—like a gulp of great lemonade. But most recipes I tried missed the mark. The lemon flavor was either too fleeting or overpowering.

Before I addressed flavor issues, I needed a solid foundation. I started by preparing batches of the test kitchen's white and yellow sheet cakes (white cakes use only egg whites, while yellow cakes employ whole eggs), replacing a few tablespoons of the milk in each recipe with lemon juice. Tasters much preferred the denser yellow cake, as the richness of the whole eggs balanced the acidity of the lemon. This recipe uses cake flour for a fine, velvety crumb and utilizes the traditional creaming method (beating butter and sugar before adding the wet and dry ingredients) to develop structure and height in the cake.

Tasters liked the flavor of this cake, but I wasn't pleased with the domed top and sloping sides. Adding the lemon juice had changed the chemistry of this recipe. Replacing some of the baking powder with baking soda helped, as did reducing the baking temperature from 350 to 325 degrees—the slower baking meant that the edges and interior of the cake set at the same time, resulting in a perfectly flat top.

The best way to bright, clean lemon flavor was on the path I had already started down—swapping out some of the milk for freshly squeezed lemon juice. But I could only go up to ¼ cup before the cake started tasting medicinal. I added the grated zest from 3 lemons to round out the lemon flavor and used a test kitchen trick of beating the zest with sugar to create a homemade lemon sugar that lent a wallop of lemony richness to the cake. Replacing the remaining milk with buttermilk (and once again adjusting the ratios of baking powder to baking soda) added extra tang that reinforced the lemon flavor.

Other recipes weigh down this light and tender cake with heavy buttercream or cream cheese frostings, but I found nothing was easier—or better—than glazing the warm cake with a simple mixture of confectioners' sugar, buttermilk, and lemon juice. A sprinkle of some reserved lemon sugar added crunch and a final flourish of lemon flavor and color. **–Erika Bruce**

LEMON BUTTERMILK SHEET CAKE SERVES 16

You will need a total of 7 tablespoons lemon juice (from 3 or 4 lemons) for this recipe. We recommend using an offset spatula to easily and neatly glaze the warm cake.

Cake

- 2½ cups cake flour
- 1 teaspoon baking powder
- ½ teaspoon baking soda
- ½ teaspoon salt
- ¾ cup buttermilk, room temperature
- 3 tablespoons grated zest and ¼ cup juice from 3 lemons
- 1 teaspoon vanilla extract
- 1¾ cups granulated sugar
- 12 tablespoons (1½ sticks) unsalted butter, softened
- 3 large eggs plus 1 egg yolk, room temperature

Glaze

- 3 cups confectioners' sugar
- 3 tablespoons lemon juice
- 2 tablespoons buttermilk

1. For the cake: Adjust oven rack to middle position and heat oven to 325 degrees. Grease and flour 13- by 9-inch baking pan. Combine flour, baking powder, baking soda, and salt in medium bowl. Combine buttermilk, lemon juice, and vanilla in liquid measuring cup.

2. With electric mixer on medium speed, beat granulated sugar and lemon zest until moist and fragrant, about 1 minute. Transfer ¼ cup sugar mixture to small bowl, cover, and reserve. Add butter to remaining sugar mixture and beat until light and fluffy, about 2 minutes. Beat in eggs and yolk, one at a time, until incorporated. Reduce speed to low. Add flour mixture in 3 additions, alternating with 2 additions of buttermilk mixture, and mix until smooth, about 30 seconds.

3. Scrape batter into prepared pan and smooth top. Bake until cake is golden brown and toothpick inserted into center comes out clean, 25 to 35 minutes. Transfer cake to wire rack and let cool 10 minutes.

4. For the glaze: Meanwhile, whisk confectioners' sugar, lemon juice, and buttermilk until smooth. Gently spread glaze over warm cake and sprinkle evenly with reserved sugar mixture. Cool completely, at least 2 hours. Serve.

Cake Flour Substitute

Our Lemon Buttermilk Sheet Cake benefits from the use of cake flour—a low-protein flour that lends a fine texture and tender crumb to many baked goods. However, if you do not have cake flour on hand, there is an alternative. For every cup of cake flour, substitute ⅞ cup all-purpose flour and 2 tablespoons cornstarch. For this recipe you would use 2 cups plus 3 tablespoons all-purpose flour and 5 tablespoons cornstarch.

Millionaire Pie

I recently tried a recipe for this creamy, no-bake pineapple chiffon pie, but it turned out so pasty and bland I wanted my money back. Can you give this millionaire a makeover? –Beth Miller, Austin, Texas

Millionaire pie has been a staple at Furr's, a Southwestern chain of cafeterias, since 1946. The pie is so named because it's rich (from eggs and cream), it's gold (from lots of crushed pineapple), and it's supposed to taste "like a million bucks." The original recipe tops a no-cook filling (raw eggs, confectioner's sugar, and butter) with sweetened whipped cream studded with nuts and bits of pineapple. Most modern recipes avoid the raw eggs by filling a graham-cracker pie crust with a mixture of cream cheese, whipped topping (such as Cool Whip), canned pineapple, and nuts.

I knew I didn't want to make this pie with raw eggs, so I gathered a handful of the recipes based on cream cheese and whipped topping and got to work. These pies did not taste like a million bucks: They were more like pasty, cloyingly sweet frosting. Even worse, my tasters hated the soggy nuts and fibrous pineapple dispersed throughout the otherwise creamy filling.

My first decision was to abandon the cream cheese and whipped topping and instead create a pineapple chiffon filling from scratch. I started with the test kitchen's recipe for homemade pudding (sugar, cornstarch, half-and-half, and egg yolks), replacing the dairy with pineapple juice, folding in homemade whipped cream at the end, and pouring the mixture into a simple homemade graham cracker crust (ground crackers and melted butter). This filling was so loose that it was hard to cut a neat slice and was sorely lacking in pineapple flavor. Replacing the juice with pineapple juice concentrate was a step in the right direction, but for intense, complex pineapple flavor, I found that nothing worked better than cooking down a can of crushed pineapple until it was lightly browned and incredibly fragrant. I could then process the cooked pineapple into a smooth texture that my tasters loved.

This filling tasted great, but it still wasn't slicing well, and my tasters still didn't like chunks of nuts in the smooth filling. I tried adding more cornstarch to the filling to stabilize it, but that made the mixture too slippery. Plain gelatin firmed up the filling perfectly and when I switched to pineapple-flavored gelatin I finally had a sliceable filling with plenty of pineapple punch.

Since I was already grinding up graham crackers for the crust, I tried adding the pecans to the food processor. Maybe I could move the nut flavor to the crust and eliminate those soggy nuts in the filling? This worked so well that I wondered if something other than graham crackers might work better as a foundation for this pie. Animal crackers and shortbread cookies were both OK, but not as flavorful as pecan sandies, which added another layer of sweet, rich pecan flavor to the crust. With one bite, I knew I'd created a pie that really did taste like a million bucks. –Cali Rich

Moving the pecans from the filling to the cookie crust produces a smooth, fluffy filling free from distracting chunks.

The American Table: Furr's Cafeteria

Brothers Roy and Key Furr started their namesake cafeteria chain in Hobbs, New Mexico, in 1946 with the promise of wholesome food "that you'd make every day if you could." There are now 54 Furr's Cafeterias scattered throughout New Mexico, Texas, Arizona, Colorado, Kansas, and Oklahoma. Their millionaire pie remains a best-seller to this day.

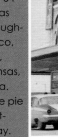

MILLIONAIRE PIE SERVES 8

Pecan Sandies are the brand name of a cookie made by Keebler; any pecan shortbread cookie will work in this recipe. If desired, top the finished pie with ¼ cup toasted and chopped pecans or ½ cup toasted sweetened flaked coconut.

Crust

- 12 pecan sandies, broken into rough pieces (about 2½ cups)
- ½ cup pecans, chopped
- 2 tablespoons unsalted butter, melted

Pie

- 1 (20-ounce) can crushed pineapple packed in juice
- ½ cup plus 1 tablespoon sugar Salt
- 3 large egg yolks
- 1 (3-ounce) box pineapple-flavored gelatin
- 1 cup frozen pineapple juice concentrate, thawed
- 2 cups heavy cream, chilled

1. For the crust: Adjust oven rack to middle position and heat oven to 350 degrees. Grind cookies and pecans in food processor to fine crumbs. Add butter and pulse until combined. Press crumbs into bottom and sides of 9-inch pie plate and refrigerate until firm, about 20 minutes. Bake until lightly browned and set, about 15 minutes. Cool completely.

2. For the pie: Cook crushed pineapple, ¼ cup sugar, and pinch salt in large nonstick skillet over medium-high heat, stirring occasionally, until liquid evaporates and pineapple is lightly browned, about 15 minutes. Scrape mixture into food processor and process until very smooth, about 1 minute; set aside.

3. Whisk yolks, additional ¼ cup sugar, and ¼ teaspoon salt in medium bowl. Combine gelatin and ½ cup pineapple juice concentrate in medium saucepan and let sit until gelatin softens, about 5 minutes. Cook over medium heat until gelatin dissolves and mixture is very hot but not boiling, about 2 minutes. Whisking vigorously, slowly add gelatin mixture to egg yolks. Return mixture to saucepan and cook, stirring constantly, until slightly thickened, about 2 minutes. Off heat, stir in remaining pineapple juice concentrate and processed pineapple mixture. Pour into clean large bowl and refrigerate until set, about 1½ hours.

4. With electric mixer on medium-high speed, whip cream and remaining sugar to stiff peaks, about 3 minutes. Whisk 1 cup whipped cream into gelatin mixture until completely incorporated. Using rubber spatula, fold additional 1 cup whipped cream into gelatin mixture until no streaks of white remain. Scrape mixture into cooled pie shell and smooth top. Spread remaining whipped cream evenly over filling and refrigerate until firm, at least 4 hours. Serve.

Food Shopping

ELBOW MACARONI: Which Brands Nudge Out the Competition?

Elbow macaroni is much more popular in the United States than it is in Italy, where it's known variously as *chifferi* or *gomiti*. This pasta has become a staple in such distinctly American recipes as macaroni salad and macaroni and cheese. But with so many brands of elbow macaroni on the market, which one should you buy? Are they all the same? To find out, we rounded up eight contenders and tasted them simply dressed with vegetable oil and in our recipe for classic macaroni and cheese. What did we discover?

Barilla, an Italian brand that makes pasta for the American market at their plant in Ames, Iowa, won our tasting by a large margin. Our tasters praised this pasta for its "wheaty," "buttery" flavor and "firm texture," and they especially liked that these elbows have small ridges and a slight twist that "holds sauce well." (Barilla, the top-selling brand in both America and Italy, does not make elbow macaroni for the Italian market.) After Barilla, our tasters didn't notice much difference among Mueller's, Ronzoni, DeCecco, DaVinci, or Prince elbows, all of which were deemed acceptable.

We did, however, throw our tasters two curveballs: we included two new products, Barilla Plus and Ronzoni Smart Taste, in our blind tasting. The tasters actually preferred (albeit only slightly) the Ronzoni Smart Taste to the traditional Ronzoni elbows; this product is simply traditional pasta enriched with extra fiber and calcium. The Barilla Plus elbows were another story. This multigrain pasta, made with wheat, lentil, chickpea, barley, and flaxseed (among other) flours, has a dark appearance and "health food" flavor that were real turn-offs. The elbow macaronis are listed below in order of preference, with tasters' comments. –Scott Kathan

Highly Recommended

1. **BARILLA Elbows** $1.33 for 16 ounces
   Comments: Tasters were nearly unanimous in praising this pasta's "hearty texture" and "rich," "wheaty" flavor. The ridged surface and slight twist in shape were big hits, especially in the macaroni and cheese portion of the tasting, where this pasta held the sauce particularly well.

Recommended

2. **MUELLER'S Elbow Macaroni** $1.19 for 16 ounces
   Comments: The "mild wheaty" flavor and "buttery aftertaste" of this pasta brought several tasters back to their childhood: "Just like Ma's" was one happy observation. The "firm and toothsome" texture held up well in the heavy cheese sauce. A few tasters complained about the "thick walls" and "chewy, dense" texture of these elbows.

3. **RONZONI Smart Taste Elbows** $2 for 14.5 ounces
   Comments: "Simple and straightforward," "neutral," and "bland but decent" were common sentiments concerning this product, which is enriched with fiber and calcium. Several tasters commented on the noodles being "blown out" and "mushy."

4. **RONZONI Elbows** $1.35 for 16 ounces
   Comments: This product scored especially well in the macaroni and cheese tasting, with tasters lauding its "creamy," "substantive" texture. A few tasters perceived a "slightly stale," "grassy" flavor that led to slightly lower scores in plain tasting.

5. **DECECCO No. 81 Elbows** $2.29 for 16 ounces
   Comments: This Italian import received mixed comments, with some tasters calling it "classic" while others deemed it "generic." The "tender" texture was stressed under the weight of the cheese sauce, making the elbows "squishy" and "mushy."

6. **DAVINCI Elbows Macaroni** $1.30 for 16 ounces
   Comments: This "simple but pleasant" brand (also from Italy) was commended for its "good springy texture;" but a few tasters were put off by its "dinky," "thin," and "wimpy" size. It had average scores for flavor and texture across the board.

7. **PRINCE Elbow Macaroni** $1.29 for 16 ounces
   Comments: "Just average," "nothing special," "unremarkable," and "a bit bland but okay" were common refrains for these elbows. While some tasters found these elbows "mushy," others liked the "soft" texture.

Not Recommended

8. **BARILLA Plus Elbows** $2.29 for 14.5 ounces
   Comments: This "dusty," "cardboard-y" brand was found by one panelist to "taste like it was fortified with sawdust." If the other samples prove that average noodles are just fine, this one makes the emphatic point that you shouldn't mess too much with a proven entity. "Scary looking," "gross," and "weird."

Taste Test Seasoning Mixes

Many seasoning mixes contain too much salt and not enough flavor. These five really do offer big flavor in a small bottle.

Chili Powder

Most chili powders are a hearty mix of ground red chile peppers, cumin, oregano, garlic, and salt; some include cloves or allspice. To bloom the spice flavors, add chili powder to the pan with the sautéed aromatics so it can cook directly in the fat for about a minute. Chili powders labeled "pure" are just one kind of ground dried pepper (usually ancho or chipotle) and can be assertively hot and smoky. Our taste test–winning brand of chili powder is Spice Islands.

Chinese Five-Spice Powder

This blend (cinnamon, cloves, fennel seed, star anise, and Sichuan peppercorn) lends a fiery, warm-spice flavor to Chinese-inspired dishes. Its use isn't relegated to just Asian cuisine, as we like to include it in sauces and rubs for sticky ribs, roasts, and barbecue. Be judicial in using this blend, as a little goes a long way.

Curry Powder

Most curry powders are made up of some combination of the following: turmeric (which lends its signature yellow hue), coriander, cumin, red pepper, black pepper, cinnamon, cloves, fennel, cardamom, ginger, and fenugreek. This blend can be used to add flavor to soups, dressings, mayonnaise, seafood, and vegetable dishes. The test kitchen's favorite supermarket brand is Durkee. Toasting curry powder in a dry skillet over medium-high heat for about a minute (stirring constantly) greatly intensifies its flavor.

Herbes de Provence

Herbes de Provence mostly commonly contains rosemary, marjoram, thyme, lavender, sage, and fennel; basil and summer savory are sometimes included. This blend works well with roasted meats and poultry, in salad dressings, and in sauces and gravies. The unique floral aroma and flavor of this blend comes from lavender, an herb not commonly used for culinary purposes in this country.

Old Bay Seasoning

This spice mix is an essential seasoning for crab boils (and crab cakes); it is also commonly used to flavor shrimp dishes. The predominant flavors in Old Bay are celery, mustard, and paprika. We use Old Bay for steamed or boiled crustaceans and bivalves, in coatings for fried chicken and seafood, and in gumbos and seafood stews.

Equipment Roundup

RATINGS
Good = ★★★
Fair = ★★
Poor = ★

NONSCRATCH SCRUBBERS: Scouring the Market for the Best

When we tested pot scrubbers in 2003, heavy-duty copper (Chore Boy Copper Scouring Pads) and steel wool pads (S.O.S Steel Wool Soap Pads) were the best at cutting through messes on stainless steel pans. Could we find a scrubber that was just as effective on delicate nonstick surfaces? To find out, we rounded up eight brands of nonscratch scrubbers, rolled up our sleeves, and got scrubbing. Our two most important criteria for these scrubbers were their effectiveness in cleaning and whether they truly lived up to the "nonscratch" name. Of secondary importance were durability and comfort.

EFFECTIVE: We sprayed nonstick loaf pans with cooking spray and baked them at 475 degrees until they were sticky and brown, and then counted how many strokes it took to get the pans clean with each scrubber. There were noticeable differences. It took the Chore Boy Soap-Filled pad and Chore Boy Scratch-Free LongLast Scrubber as few as 65 and 67 strokes, respectively, to get the job done; conversely, it took the Chore Boy All-Purpose Scrubbing Sponge more than 300 strokes.

BUT GENTLE: To test "nonscratch" claims, we scrubbed the same area on a clean, brand-new nonstick skillet 500 times using moderate pressure. Every scrubber—minus the Scotch-Brite No-Scratch scrubber—passed this test.

DESIGN MATTERS: Why did some pads scrub more effectively than others? The ribbonlike nylon strands of our two winners, the Chore Boy Scratch-Free LongLast Scrubber and the Chore Boy Soap-Filled sponge, formed a mesh of sharp, raised edges—much like a cheese grater—but with the gentleness of nylon. The nylon mesh covering of the Scotch-Brite Dobie created similar sharp pockets with which to chisel off grime. Conversely, models with thicker abrasive scrubbing surfaces, like the Scotch-Brite No-Scratch scrubber, didn't dig as deeply into grime, and thus weren't nearly as effective.

SHAPE AND SIZE: Testers agreed that curved, hourglass-shaped sponges—such as the Scotch-Brite Delicate Duty and the Chore Boy All-Purpose Sponge—became uncomfortable and less effective after prolonged scrubbing. For heavy-duty scrubbing, rectangular sponges—such as the Chore Boy mesh scrubbers and the Scotch-Brite Dobie—were more favorable, as they molded to the shape of the hand and fingers—and the corners of pans where grime likes to hide. Testers had to fight more with stiffer, thicker sponges, such as the S.O.S All-Purpose Scrub Sponge, which was too bulky to reach into tight corners.

DURABILITY: Our top three scrubbers showed slight to significant wear and tear after days of scrubbing, while our two losing scrubbers looked the most pristine at the end of testing. It makes sense that the scrubbers that worked harder to get pans clean would be a little worse for wear after extended use.

SUMMING UP: Our top three scrubbers were rectangular and employed a scrubbing surface of raised, ribbonlike nylon strands that gently but efficiently removed residue. We recommend avoiding scrubbers with curved edges (which can't reach into tough corners) and those with thick, abrasive scouring surfaces, which aren't comfortable or as effective. **–Peggy Chung**

Highly Recommended

CHORE BOY Scratch-Free LongLast Scrubber
Price: $1.19 each
Performance: ★★★
No-Scratch Test: ★★★
Comments: The raised, ribbonlike nylon strands made for an effective yet gentle scrubber. The bonus: This winning scrubber has a smooth sponge side, making it a great all-purpose sponge. The thin, pliable design made it easy to maneuver into tight corners. A few threads came loose after repeated use, but the scrubber continued to perform well.

CHORE BOY Soap-Filled Scrubber
Price: $1.69 for 2
Performance: ★★★
No-Scratch Test: ★★★
Comments: This scrubber employs the same raised, ribbonlike nylon strand technology as the Chore Boy Scratch-Free LongLast scrubber, but lacks the smooth sponge side. The extra soapiness of this scrubber helped take grime off quickly and easily. Small size and nice flexibility made for easier scrubbing.

Recommended

SCOTCH-BRITE Dobie Cleaning Pad
Price: $2.39 for 3
Performance: ★★★
No-Scratch Test: ★★★
Comments: The Dobie's nylon mesh covering removed sticky gunk in just 73 strokes. Thin and flexible, it was easy to maneuver, especially into tight corners. However, the lack of durability—the scrubber had dime-sized tears in its mesh covering after 500 strokes—and mildly uncomfortable design (some testers thought it was rough on the skin) put it just slightly below our winners.

Recommended with Reservations

SCOTCH-BRITE Delicate Duty Scrub Sponge
Price: $4.79 for 3
Performance: ★★
No-Scratch Test: ★★★
Comments: This sponge performed fairly well (120 strokes to get the pan clean), but the thickness made it harder to maneuver into corners. The scouring side of the sponge wore down significantly after 500 strokes. Testers found the "wave-like" shape awkward with repeated scrubbing.

Recommended with Reservations

O-CEL-O No-Scratch Scrub Sponge
Price: $2.29 for 2
Performance: ★★
No-Scratch Test: ★★★
Comments: At 150 strokes to get the pan clean, this sponge performed fairly well, but the colorful designs that were printed onto the scouring surface almost completely wore off after 500 strokes, revealing this scrubber's lack of durability. Some testers commented that it felt "too wide" and "not long enough," and its curved sides made it difficult to clean edges and corners.

CLOROX S.O.S All-Purpose Scrub Sponge
Price: $2.67 for 3
Performance: ★★
No-Scratch Test: ★★★
Comments: Though this scrubber achieved a fair performance rating, tiny nylon fibers from the scouring material peppered the foam of the soapy water after just a few strokes. The large, thick, and bulky sponge made this scrubber feel "heavy" and "tedious to work with."

Not Recommended

CHORE BOY All-Purpose Scrubbing Sponge
Price: $2.99 for 3
Performance: ★
No-Scratch Test: ★★★
Comments: For all of its durability—it emerged from a battery of tests looking completely untouched—this scrubber was the poorest performer. Although the tightly woven nylon fibers of the scouring material may have increased the scrubber's durability, we suspect they also created too smooth a scouring surface to be effective. The thickness of the sponge made it hard to grasp comfortably.

SCOTCH-BRITE No-Scratch Scrub Sponge
Price: $4.79 for 3
Performance: ★★
No-Scratch Test: ★
Comments: Though this scrubber cleaned fairly well (145 strokes to get the pan clean) and looked fresh after multiple scrubbings, it was the only sponge to fail the no-scratch test outright, leaving gray marks on the nonstick skillet after repeated scrubbing. We would not trust this scrubber on our good nonstick pans.

Notes from Our Test Kitchen

Kitchen Creations
No-Cook Barbecue Sauces

Here are four great-tasting, no-cook barbecue sauces that can be used to baste barbecued chicken, as a condiment for grilled hamburgers, or as a finishing sauce for our **Smoked Pork Loin** (page 14). Each sauce makes about 1¼ cups and can be refrigerated for up to 4 days.

BASIC PANTRY BBQ SAUCE

Whisk 1 cup ketchup, 3 tablespoons molasses, 1 tablespoon cider vinegar, 1 teaspoon hot sauce, and ⅛ teaspoon liquid smoke (if desired) in small bowl.

FIVE-ALARM BBQ SAUCE

Whisk 1 cup ketchup, 3 tablespoons molasses, 1 tablespoon cider vinegar, 1 tablespoon minced canned chipotle chiles in adobo sauce, 1 jalapeño chile (stemmed, seeded, and minced), and ¼ teaspoon cayenne pepper in small bowl.

CHINESE-STYLE BBQ SAUCE

Whisk 1 cup ketchup, 3 tablespoons hoisin sauce, 1 tablespoon rice vinegar, 1 tablespoon chili-garlic sauce, 1 tablespoon finely chopped cilantro, and 1 teaspoon grated fresh ginger in small bowl.

HONEY-SCALLION BBQ SAUCE

Whisk 1 cup ketchup, 3 tablespoons honey, 1 tablespoon cider vinegar, 2 teaspoons Dijon mustard, 2 finely chopped scallions, and ¾ teaspoon pepper in small bowl.

Inside the Test Kitchen
KEYS TO PERFECT TIRAMISÙ ICE CREAM CAKE

Our Tiramisù Ice Cream Cake (inside back cover) is easy to make—if you follow these simple steps.

1. Quickly dip each ladyfinger into the coffee, espresso powder, and rum mixture and transfer to a wire cooling rack. Too long a soak in the liquid will cause the ladyfingers to break down and adversely affect the appearance of the cake.
2. Let the soaked ladyfingers rest on the rack for a full 5 minutes. The resting allows the liquid mixture to permeate the entire ladyfinger.
3. Arrange the soaked ladyfingers with their short sides flush against the interior of the tube pan lined with parchment (see page 31). Gently press on the cookies to ensure that there are no gaps between them before freezing and filling with ice cream.

Building Better Burgers

Regardless of how they're cooked, hand-formed hamburgers often end up with a misshapen, bulging center that encourages condiments to slide off. This happens because the collagen in the meat shrinks as it cooks; when the sides of the burger shrink, it acts like a belt tightening around the burger, forcing the meat in the center of the patty out into the tell-tale bulging shape. To combat this phenomenon (as in our recipe card for **Tex-Mex Burgers**), we press a divot in the center of each patty before cooking. This way the burgers plateau into a perfectly flat, condiment-friendly shape every time.

Ensure perfectly flat burgers by pressing a divot in the center of the raw hamburger patties.

Cooking with Soft Woods

When the test kitchen grills with wood chips, we always use hardwoods (like oak, hickory, maple, fruit, or nut woods) to produce a clean, flavorful smoke. Soft woods like pine and cedar produce smoke that is dense, resinous, and harsh, so we don't cook with them. Or at least we didn't until we developed our unique method for **Wood-Grilled Salmon** (page 24), where we don't burn the wood chips, but rather set the salmon directly on the chips so the fish can absorb some woody—not smoky—flavor. This recipe works with any variety of wood chips, but cedar chips are most authentic to the dish's origins in the Pacific Northwest.

Salt of the Earth (and Sea)

A variety of salts are available in supermarkets today: table, iodized, kosher, and sea salt. What's the difference? Table and iodized salt (simply table salt with iodine added) have fine grains and contain anti-caking agents that help them flow freely. Kosher salt, so named because it is used in the koshering process, has larger crystals and typically contains no additives. Both table and kosher salts are considered "refined salts" because they are mined from rock salt deposits and then purified. Sea salt is harvested by evaporating seawater and therefore has a full, slightly mineral flavor. Though we use table salt in the vast majority of our recipes, the choice is a matter of preference—except when it comes to our **Syracuse Salt Potatoes** (page 13). While table, kosher, and sea salts all performed equally well in this recipe, we advise against using iodized salt as it gives the potatoes a noticeably chemical flavor.

Gadgets & Gear
Fat Separators

Although you can also use a wide, shallow spoon, a fat separator is an easier way to remove the fat from the surface of the sauce for our **Slow-Cooker Sweet and Sour Ribs** (page 8). Once the fat settles to the top of the separator, the remaining liquid can be poured off easily. Our favorite fat separator is the 4-cup Trudeau Gravy Separator, which costs about $10. We like this separator's wide mouth and built-in strainer, which is especially helpful when you're defatting pan drippings that are still mixed with chunks of aromatic vegetables, herb sprigs, or other flavorings.

TEST KITCHEN FAVORITE
Trudeau Gravy Separator

Kitchen Know-How
CUTTING CORN-ERS

Cutting the kernels off ears of corn can be tricky, as the cobs can roll around on the cutting board. Here's how we remove the kernels from the cobs for our **Sweet Corn Spoonbread** (page 15).

Use a chef's knife to cut the cobs in half. Stabilize the cobs by standing them on their cut ends, then slice the kernels from the cob.

Preparing Dried Chiles

Using whole dried chiles can add a new depth of flavor to your favorite dishes. But how do you prepare them? First, especially if you're working with spicy chiles, put on a pair of rubber gloves—even when dried, the capsaicin (the compound responsible for a chile's heat) in the chiles can irritate the skin. Now that you're suited up, just follow these simple steps:

TO USE DRIED CHILES IN SPICE RUBS: Toast the dry chile pods in a 350-degree oven for about 6 minutes until they become fragrant and puffed. When cool enough to handle, remove the stems and seeds, rip the pods into pieces, and process them in a food processor until powdery. From here,

---

Kitchen Know-How FRESH FENNEL PRIMER

Thinly sliced fennel adds crunch and flavor to our **Marinated Tomato Salads** (page 11). When shopping, look for fennel with its long, thin stalks still attached and be sure that the fennel bulb is creamy white and not bruised or discolored. Here's how we prepare fennel in the test kitchen.

1. Cut off the tough stalks and trim a thin slice from the base of the bulb.

2. Slice the bulb in half lengthwise from top to bottom.

3. Cut out and discard the triangular-shaped piece of core in each half. Slice as desired.

Shopping with the Test Kitchen Queso Fresco

We love the tangy, creamy counterpoint that soft cheeses provide in our recipes for **Marinated Tomato Salads** (page 11). In addition to blue cheese and goat cheese, we found that queso fresco was an excellent option. Popular in Mexico, queso fresco (also called queso blanco) is a fresh, mild cheese made from either cow's or goat's milk. Although it's not a great melting cheese, its crumbly-soft texture makes it an excellent option for topping enchiladas or tacos, sprinkling over bean soups, or tossing into a salad. If you can't find queso fresco, fresh farmer's cheese or a mild feta is a suitable substitute.

QUESO FRESCO
Tangy, crumbly, and creamy.

the chile powder can be added to spice rubs or used in place of jarred chili powder (typically a combination of ground chiles and other spices).

TO USE DRIED CHILES IN SALSAS: Place the chile pods in a large bowl and add enough boiling water to cover by 1 inch. Let soak until pods are soft and pliable, 5 to 10 minutes. Once softened, carefully remove chiles from water, pat dry with paper towels, and remove the stem and seeds. Finely chop the softened chiles and use as desired.

TO PUREE DRIED CHILES INTO A PASTE: Soak the chile pods as directed above. Once softened, remove chiles from water, pat dry with paper towels, and remove the stem and seeds. Transfer to food processor or blender and puree, adding enough of the chile-infused soaking water to reach the desired consistency. The resulting paste can be sautéed with onions and garlic as a base for dishes such as chile con carne or it can be thinned with a bit of white vinegar and used as a homemade hot sauce.

Choosing Chorizo

After testing different pork products in our recipe for **Drunken Beans** (page 21), we preferred the rich, meaty flavor of chorizo sausage to the comparatively bland ham hocks, salt pork, and bacon. Two kinds of chorizo are available in American supermarkets: the more common Mexican (which has a meaty texture similar to kielbasa and is seasoned with garlic, chili powder, and paprika) and the drier, cured Spanish chorizo (which has a texture similar to pepperoni and is aggressively seasoned with smoked paprika). Although we enjoy both versions of chorizo, the meaty Mexican-style sausage is most appropriate in this recipe.

We prefer the meaty flavor and texture of Mexican chorizo (top) to the dry-cured and assertively spiced Spanish variety (below) in soups, stews, and saucy dishes like our Drunken Beans.

It's about Twine

Tying roasts helps them keep their shape and cook evenly, but it's important to pick the right type of twine. After researching and testing a variety of tying materials, we found that unconventional options like unwaxed dental floss (singed on the grill and cut into the meat) and nylon twine from the hardware store (the yellow colorant leached into the roast) were not viable. Tested on our **Smoked Pork Loin** (page 14), regular kitchen twine, particularly the linen variety (cotton is also available), held a nice over-

---

How to
MAKE A PARCHMENT "DONUT" FOR A TUBE PAN

Our recipe for **Tiramisù Ice Cream Cake** (inside back cover) uses a tube pan that needs to be lined with parchment to ensure the cake turns out cleanly. While there are many ways to cut a piece of parchment paper into a properly sized "donut," we've found this one to be the easiest.

1. Starting with a square of parchment larger than the tube pan, place the pan right-side up on the paper and trace around the outside with a pencil.
2. Cut the circle out of the parchment, then rest the circle on the bottom of the inverted pan to trace the proper size of the hole.
3. Cut the hole out of the middle of the parchment (this is easily done by folding the circle in half). Then place the parchment "donut" in the greased tube pan and spray with more cooking spray.

hand knot and pulled away from the cooked meat easily, taking a minimum of seared crust with it. Cotton twine, especially a midweight, 16-ply string, works nearly as well and is more economical.

When Things Go Wrong in the Kitchen

READERS SHARE FUNNY STORIES ABOUT COOKING MISHAPS

A PAINFUL IDEA
When I was newly married and living in a tiny basement apartment, my dad gave me several bunches of extremely hot Thai peppers from his garden. I knew that I would never use them all in my cooking, so I decided to dry them and make some sort of decoration with them. I carefully arranged them on cookie sheets and put them in my warm oven. A few hours later, I went into my tiny kitchen to check on them. When I opened the oven, a puff of steam escaped and my eyes immediately started to burn and water. Next I started coughing and my throat started to sting. I slammed the oven door and ran outside with my bewildered and coughing husband behind me. I explained rather sheepishly and with lots of pauses to gasp for air that I meant to make dried peppers, but instead I had created homemade pepper spray!

Taudine Andrew Fair Oaks, Calif.

BOMBS AWAY
Twenty-three years ago, when I was about eight months pregnant with my first child, I was developing a sourdough starter and bread recipes for a newsletter I was writing. After successfully cultivating a variety of homemade versions, I had stashed my latest effort in a screw-top canning jar and left it in the refrigerator for about five days. Now, sourdough starter gets along just fine in the fridge, but perhaps the screwed-on lid was not the wisest choice. Baking day arrived and I removed my nicely grown starter from the refrigerator and started to loosen the lid. With a boom worthy of a minor Molotov cocktail, the starter exploded out of the jar, blowing the lid out of my hand and spewing starter all over the kitchen, spattering the sink, cabinets, floor and, yes, the ceiling, with gobs of dough. Fortunately my husband was at hand to help clean up the mess, and to this day we often laugh about the "famous dough bomb."

Patricia Fisher Madison, Wis.

SWEET REVENGE
My husband and I had only been married for about three months when we moved to a new town. One night while he was out with some new office friends, I decided to surprise him by making homemade molasses cookies. I had never made them before but had a recipe that came from my grandmother. I mixed the dough and baked the cookies, which smelled wonderful. I wasn't really feeling well that night, so I put them on a plate for when he came home. His quick night out turned into a late night extravaganza, but once he did finally make it home, he was pleased to see that I had baked cookies for him. However, the next morning he cautiously asked me if I was mad at him for staying out so late. I told him no, I was glad he'd enjoyed himself and made some new friends. Curious, I asked him why? He said the cookies were so awful that he thought I was trying to get back at him for getting home so late. I promptly tried the cookies myself and quickly realized the potency of blackstrap molasses. Oops!!

Roxanne Kaspar Olathe, Kan.

GET YOUR EYES CHECKED
When my son was 10 years old, he decided to make cookies from scratch. I promised to stay out of the kitchen, as he loved to cook and wanted to make them on his own. I could hear him mixing away in the kitchen, but when he called out, "Do you have any more flour?" his question struck me as odd. I knew I had plenty of flour in the house and went into the kitchen to find him struggling to stir the mixture. I asked him, "Why do you need MORE flour?" He showed me the recipe and said, "See, I need 12½ cups of flour!" That's how I found out he needed glasses, since the recipe called for only 2½ cups of flour.

Barbara Stalling via e-mail

FIRE STARTER
One afternoon I was boiling some chicken for chicken soup. My husband was sitting at the kitchen table watching the Bears football game, and I was standing at the counter next to the stove. All of a sudden I started to smell something burning but could not see anything on fire. After a moment, I asked my husband if he smelled anything too. He muttered "no" in his best "don't bother me" voice. The smell became stronger and since I still couldn't see anything on fire, I asked my husband again if he smelled anything. I finally repeated the question more forcefully and he turned around (probably only because it was halftime). He shouted that my hair was on fire and pulled my sweater over my head to smother the fire. Apparently the fire traveled from the gas range up the sleeve of my sweater and finally reached my hair, which had recently been permed. Once everything was extinguished, I sat down at the table to collect myself, and my husband asked if I could sit somewhere else since my hair smelled so bad!

Carol Murphy Chicago, Ill.

A TREACHEROUS KITCHEN
One day when I was growing up, I decided to make a lemon meringue pie. After filling and topping the pie with the meringue, I put it in the oven, set the timer, and left the kitchen for a few minutes. Unbeknownst to me, my little brother, who was a big fan of the TV show *MacGyver* and would rig "traps" around the house for me, snuck into the kitchen and tied fishing line between the cabinet knobs, making an invisible web. I returned to the kitchen, removed the pie from the oven, and made it only two steps when I tripped over the fishing line and the pie went up in the air. I watched in what seemed like slow motion as the pie landed only inches from my leg, with just a small spattering of lemon filling hitting the cuff of my jeans. I spent the rest of the afternoon chasing my little brother, and finally making him clean up the mess he'd made (including the trap).

Katrina Maple Beckley, W.Va.

Send us your funniest kitchen disaster stories. E-mail us by visiting **CooksCountry.com/kitchendisasters.** Or write to us at Kitchen Disasters, Cook's Country, P.O. Box 470739, Brookline, MA 02447. If we publish your story, you'll receive a complimentary one-year subscription to *Cook's Country.*

Tiramisù Ice Cream Cake

Our version of the classic Italian trifle fills a ring of coffee-soaked ladyfingers with coffee-chip ice cream and crowns it with whipped cream enriched by mascarpone cheese. Topped with a light dusting of cocoa, this frozen cake is as elegant as it is easy to assemble.

To make this cake, you will need:

- 2½ **cups black coffee, room temperature**
- 1½ **tablespoons instant espresso powder**
- 6 **tablespoons dark rum**
- 14 **ounces ladyfingers (42 to 60 cookies)**
- 1 **gallon coffee ice cream**
- ¼ **cup mini chocolate chips**
- 1 **(8-ounce) container mascarpone cheese**
- ¾ **cup heavy cream, chilled**
- ¼ **cup sugar**
  Cocoa powder, for garnish

For the soaked ladyfingers: Stir coffee, espresso powder, and 5 tablespoons rum in large bowl until espresso dissolves; set aside. Working with 1 cookie at a time, quickly dunk ladyfingers

in coffee mixture and transfer to wire rack set inside rimmed baking sheet; let sit 5 minutes.

To assemble: Grease tube pan with cooking spray and line with parchment paper (see page 31). Lightly coat parchment with cooking spray. Line prepared pan with soaked ladyfingers, packing gently to ensure there are no spaces between cookies; freeze until firm, about 1 hour (see page 30). When cookies are firm, scoop ice cream into large bowl and mash with wooden spoon until softened; fold in chocolate chips. Transfer softened ice cream to cookie-lined pan, smooth top, and wrap with plastic. Freeze until ice cream is firm, at least 4 hours or up to 4 days.

To serve: With electric mixer on medium speed, beat mascarpone, cream, sugar, and remaining tablespoon rum until stiff peaks form, about 2 minutes. Gently invert pan to turn cake out onto serving platter and discard parchment.* Using a rubber spatula, top cake with 1 cup mascarpone mixture and dust lightly and evenly with cocoa. Serve with remaining mascarpone mixture.

* A large tube pan with a removable bottom works best here. If your tube pan doesn't have a removable bottom, it may be necessary to soak the bottom of the pan in a large bowl of hot water for 30 seconds to help the frozen cake release from the pan.

Recipe Index

RC = Recipe Card

Cook's Country

Watch Our New Show on Public Television!
Cook's Country from America's Test Kitchen debuted in September on public television stations across the country. Filmed in the *Cook's Country* farmhouse, it features the best recipes, testings, and tastings from *Cook's Country* magazine and is hosted by the ensemble cast from *America's Test Kitchen*. Go to **CooksCountryTV.com** to find out when the show is playing in your area.

$4.95 U.S./$6.95 CANADA

0 74470 05251 7

11>

Cook's Country

Dear Country Cook,

I have felt like crying in the kitchen even when there were no onions in sight! How about the time that my perfect peach-blueberry tart slid onto the bottom of the oven, turning into a heap of smoking ruins? Or the buttermilk pie that took three hours to cook one Christmas Eve since my oven was so far out of calibration? (Guests retired to the living room to take a nap.) Or the grilled salmon that stuck so badly that it literally fused itself to the grill grates?

I once spent an entire week casting for salmon on the Matapedia River in Quebec and never had even one nibble to show for it (except for the mosquitoes and black flies, of course). As a fisherman friend of mine once said, "That's why they call it fishing, not catching." Two years and thousands of casts later, I finally landed a 16-pounder.

Failure places us squarely at the center of life, where nothing comes easily, where hard work is our lifelong friend, and where the promise of success can be sweeter than a perfect outcome. In *Cook's Country*, the kitchen provides a community of sorts, where, at one time or another, everyone has cried over onions.

Welcome to our world—it's not about perfection, it's about doing our best even when the fish aren't biting or they stick to the grill. That's what makes it so much fun.

Christopher Kimball
Founder and Editor, *Cook's Country* Magazine

Crying girl with onions, circa 1951.
Photographer: Lisa Larsen/Time & Life Pictures/Getty Images

OCTOBER/NOVEMBER 2008

Cook's Country

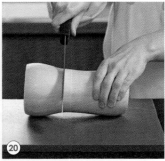

departments

in every issue

features

Founder and Editor Christopher Kimball
Editorial Director Jack Bishop
Executive Editor Peggy Grodinsky
Deputy Editor Bridget Lancaster
Senior Editors Scott Kathan
Jeremy Sauer
Test Kitchen Director Erin McMurrer
Associate Editors Cali Rich
Diane Unger
Test Cooks Kelley Baker
Lynn Clark
Kris Widican
Assistant Test Cooks Meghan Erwin
Maria del Mar Sacasa
Assistant Test Kitchen Director Matthew Herron
Copy Editor Amy Graves

Online Managing Editor David Tytell
Online Editor Kate Mason
Online Assistant Editor Leaya Lee
Executive Assistant Meredith Smith
Senior Kitchen Assistant Nadia Domeq
Kitchen Assistants Maria Elena Delgado
Ena Gudiel, Ben Peskin
TV Producer Melissa Baldino
Contributing Editor Eva Katz
Consulting Editor Guy Crosby

Design Director Amy Klee
Art Director, Magazines Julie Bozzo
Senior Designer Christine Vo
Designer Jay Layman
Staff Photographer Daniel J. van Ackere

Vice President New Technology Craig Morrow
Systems Administrator S. Paddi McHugh
Web Production Coordinator Evan Davis
IT Support Technician Brandon Lynch

Chief Financial Officer Sharyn Chabot
Human Resources Director Adele Shapiro
Controller Mandy Shito
Senior Accountant Aaron Goranson
Staff Accountant Connie Forbes
Accounts Payable Specialist Steven Kasha
Office Manager Tasha Bere
Receptionist Henrietta Murray

Production Director Guy Rochford
Traffic & Projects Manager Alice Cummiskey
Production & Imaging Specialist Lauren Pettapiece
Color & Imaging Specialist Andrew Mannone

Vice President Marketing David Mack
Circulation Director Doug Wieinski
Fulfillment & Circulation Manager Carrie Horan
Circulation Assistant Elizabeth Dayton
Partnership Marketing Manager Pamela Putprush
Direct Mail Director Adam Perry
Direct Mail Analyst Jenny Leong
Marketing Database Analyst Ariel Gilbert-Knight
Products Director Steven Browall
Product Promotions Director Randi Lawrence
E-Commerce Marketing Director Hugh Buchan
Associate Marketing Manager Laurel Zeidman
Marketing Copywriter David Goldberg
Customer Service Manager Leann Fowler
Customer Service Representative Jillian Nannicelli

Retail Sales & Marketing Manager Emily Logan
Retail Sales Associate Anthony King
Corporate Marketing Associate Bailey Vatalaro
Publicity Deborah Broide

ON THE COVER: PHOTOGRAPHY: Keller + Keller. STYLING: Mary Jane Sawyer. ILLUSTRATION: John Burgoyne.
IN THIS ISSUE: COLOR FOOD PHOTOGRAPHY: Keller + Keller. STYLING: Mary Jane Sawyer, Marie Piraino. ILLUSTRATION: Lisa Perrett.

Cook's Country magazine (ISSN 1552-1990), number 23, is published bimonthly by Boston Common Press Limited Partnership, 17 Station Street, Brookline, MA 02445. Copyright 2008 Boston Common Press Limited Partnership. Periodicals Postage paid at Boston, Mass., and additional mailing offices. Publications Mail Agreement No. 40020778. Return undeliverable Canadian addresses to P.O. Box 875, Station A, Windsor, Ontario N9A 6P2. POSTMASTER: Send address changes to Cook's Country, P.O. Box 8382, Red Oak, IA 51591-1382. **Customer Service:** It's easy to subscribe, give a gift subscription, change your address, and manage your subscription online. Visit www.americastestkitchen.com/customerservice for all of your customer service needs or write to us at Cook's Country, P.O. Box 8382, Red Oak, IA 51591-1382.

PRINTED IN THE USA

America's Test Kitchen is a 2,500-square-foot kitchen located just outside of Boston. It is the home of *Cook's Country* and *Cook's Illustrated* magazines and is the workday destination for more than three dozen test cooks, editors, and cookware specialists. Our mission is to test recipes until we understand how and why they work and arrive at the best version. We also test kitchen equipment and supermarket ingredients in search of brands that offer the best value and performance. You can watch us work by tuning in to *America's Test Kitchen* (www.americastestkitchen.com) on public television.

Watch our new show on public television!
Cook's Country from America's Test Kitchen debuted in September on public television stations across the country. The show relies on the same practical, no-nonsense food that has made *Cook's Country* magazine so successful. Watch us develop recipes, test equipment, and taste supermarket ingredients in our brand-new test kitchen. Go to **CooksCountryTV.com** to learn more.

Kitchen Shortcuts

READERS SHARE CLEVER TIPS FOR EVERYDAY COOKING CHALLENGES

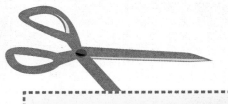

Spoon as Separator

NEAT TRICK!

An easy and tidy way to separate eggs is to crack them over a slotted spoon resting on a bowl. The white falls through the holes, leaving just the yolk in the spoon. Then you can use the spoon to easily transfer the yolks to another bowl.

Cornelius Van Gelderen
Universal City, Texas

Stack Prep Bowls

To maximize refrigerator space during the holidays, I forgo covering bowls of food with plastic wrap in favor of placing appropriately sized plates on top of the bowls (it's not an airtight seal, but it's fine for a day or two). This way I can stack several bowls on top of each other.

Eva Reed Castine, Maine

Stop the Splatter

I use a mesh splatter screen on top of the pan when frying bacon. When the bacon is almost done, I spread paper towels for draining on the top of the screen. When I'm removing the cooked bacon to the paper towels, I can shield my face and hands from splattering hot grease with the screen.

Sandy Connor
Kerrville, Texas

Gravy Saver

FOND OF FONDUE POTS

I used to get frustrated during Thanksgiving dinner when my guests went for a second helping of gravy and found it had turned into an unappetizing, congealed glob. To avoid this, I now serve the gravy in my fondue pot. The heat from the candle or burner keeps the gravy warm and at the proper consistency.

Jennifer Thompson Nashville, Tenn.

GRILLED LOBSTER

Whenever I cook lobsters for an outdoor party, I don't want to have to run in and out of the kitchen all day. Instead, I place a large disposable roasting pan on the grill, pour boiling water in the pan, and cook the lobsters right in the pan. I can fit four to six lobsters in the pan, and covered with a sheet of foil, they steam quickly. Cleanup is easy—just throw the pan right in the trash. This method also saves filling the kitchen with the mess and smell of lobster.

Elena Schjaland
Mystic, Conn.

SLOW CIDER

During the holidays, mulled cider is a popular beverage with my family. I make my own in my slow cooker. If I have family and friends over to celebrate, I can keep it on for hours with no worry or hassle.

Janice Franklin
Hartford, Conn.

GRILL-MELTED BUTTER

Whenever I am grilling corn, I keep a disposable metal pan filled with butter on the grill—as the corn chars, the butter melts. When the corn is done, I transfer it to the dish to roll each ear around in the melted butter. I can even add seasonings to the butter if I want to add flavor to the corn.

Joyce Palmer
Atlanta, Ga.

QUICK CALCULATING

I am always adding and subtracting amounts of ingredients when I am baking. Since my mind isn't as quick as it used to be, I keep a cheap calculator (one that can stand having flour thrown on it) in the kitchen at all times. That way, whenever I am trying to create a new recipe I can quickly crunch the numbers.

Gladys Turner
Bozeman, Mont.

COOKIE CATCHERS

I use round coffee filters to hold decorations for making holiday cookies. I fill them with peanuts, crushed candy, or sprinkles. This makes it a lot less messy to decorate cookies with children.

Susan Trantham
Lufkin, Texas

GUNK-BE-GONE

My wooden pizza peel has a tendency to get little bits of dough built up on it. This can wreak havoc when a pizza snags on it going into the oven. My solution is to lightly clean the peel with medium or fine sandpaper after each use. It smooths the surface of the peel, preventing future snags.

John McGlynn
San Francisco, Calif.

HOT PLATE

I like to put my morning eggs on a warm plate but hate to warm up the oven for just a single plate. So, while preparing toast, I sit my heat-proof plate on top of the toaster. This way I get toast, eggs, and a warm plate with no extra expenditure of heat or time.

Ann Grant
Fort Collins, Colo.

PLANE AND SIMPLE

To slice hard, cold butter thinly, I use a cheese planer to scrape the butter into thin slices. This works great for buttering toast, as the thin slices of butter melt quickly when the bread is warm.

Sharon Castaldo
Murrysville, Pa.

AUTOMATIC BASTING

I've tried putting butter under the skin of a turkey to keep the meat from drying out, but it always seems the butter melts too fast. Instead, I remove excess turkey skin from the bottom and legs of the bird and pound it thin. I then place that skin under the skin of the breast. It melts much more slowly and keeps the breast moist.

Dale Frohwein
Concord, Calif.

If you'd like to submit a tip, please e-mail us by visiting CooksCountry.com/kitchenshortcuts or send a letter to Kitchen Shortcuts, Cook's Country, P.O. Box 470739, Brookline, MA 02447. Include your name, address, and phone number. If we publish your tip, you will receive a free one-year subscription to Cook's Country.

PERFECTLY COOKED EGGS

When making hard-cooked eggs, it used to seem that I always had one or two eggs that would inevitably crack. That was before I found out that bringing the eggs to room temperature before cooking prevents any cracking. Just make sure to decrease your cooking time by a few minutes.

Gerald Frost
Birmingham, Ala.

SOP IT UP

When I'm done frying chicken cutlets, I'm left with hot oil that I need to dispose of. I found that the easiest, neatest way to deal with hot oil is to put the leftover bread crumbs in the skillet to sop up the oil. This tempers the heat of the oil, and your garbage will be filled with crumbs instead of an oily mess.

Danielle D'Antuono
Middletown, N.J.

CLEANER GRINDING

Rather than owning two grinders (one for coffee and one for spices), I add a few tablespoons of cornmeal to my coffee grinder, run it for a few seconds, and then store it away with the powdered corn inside. The cornmeal removes any flavors or odors, so I can use my grinder for many different ingredients.

Judy Crawford
Wilmington, Mass.

OIL YOUR OPENER

If the blade or drive wheel of my can opener is dull and hard to use, I use my mister to spray it with a little vegetable oil. It's safer for food than chemical greasers, and it gets the can opener running smoothly in a hurry.

Elise M. Maurer
Bellevue, Wash.

SINGLE-SERVE MEATBALLS

I am single, so whenever I make spaghetti and meatballs I always make too many meatballs and end up feeding them to my dog. I solved this problem by making a full batch of 15 meatballs and freezing them in increments of three (the amount I need for one meal) in individual bags. When I am ready to fix dinner, I just boil pasta, thaw a bag from the freezer, and add sauce.

Christine McCord
Topeka, Kan.

GRATE GINGER TIP

To keep fresh ginger on hand, I purchase several large pieces at a time. I grate them ahead and measure teaspoon-sized mounds onto a baking sheet. I freeze the whole sheet until the ginger is firm and toss all the pre-measured mounds into a freezer zipper-lock bag. I keep the bag in the freezer and use the pre-grated ginger as needed.

Marcia Entzel
George, Wash.

EVERYTHING IN ITS PLACE

To save time looking for recipes I make with seldom-used kitchen appliances, I store the recipes and appliances together. Bread recipes are kept in my bread machine, and ice cream recipes are kept in my ice cream machine.

Connie Pietila
Hancock, Mo.

FOOLPROOF SEASONING

To make sure my meatloaf, meatballs, stuffed cabbage, or burgers are seasoned properly before cooking, I take a teaspoon of the mixture, flatten it into a patty, and fry it. The patty cooks quickly, and after a taste of the cooked sample, I know if I've added enough seasoning and can then make any necessary adjustments before cooking all of the meat. I get perfect seasoning every time.

Geraldine Langowski
North Haledon, N.J.

NOT JUST FOR MELON

I hate kitchen tools that only have one use, so I'm always looking for new ways to use different gadgets. My melon baller pulls double-duty by serving as a spoon for jarred olives and capers. Its small size allows me to reach into the narrow neck of the jars, and the hole in the bottom allows the juice to drain out with no effort.

Arthur Augustus
Fort Monmouth, N.J.

Clean and Clever

SHOWER CAP WRAP

Instead of covering leftovers with plastic wrap, I use unused shower caps that I collect from hotels. The elastic allows the caps to fit many sized bowls, and they can be washed and reused multiple times. They are also great for covering bowls of rising bread dough.

Stefanie Bonigut
Seattle, Wash.

Bun Warmer

When boiling hot dogs, I put a cooling rack on top of the pot of simmering water. I place the hot dog buns on the cooling rack, where the steam softens and warms them. This method is especially great for refreshing stale rolls.

Bernadette O'Brien
Lacey, Wash.

SMART TIP!

Easy Washing

Instead of pulling out a colander to rinse grapes or cherries in the sink, I fill the plastic produce bag with water—with the fruit right in it—and then carefully poke holes in the bag to let the water drain. When it's drained and dry, I can throw the whole bag in the refrigerator.

Melissa Jones
Fargo, N.D.

The Big Squeeze

For an easy way to make picture-perfect pancakes every time, I fill a clean, wide-mouthed ketchup bottle with the batter. It is an easy (and fun) way to squeeze out baby-sized or plate-sized rounds of pancakes.

Suzanne McGrath
San Diego, Calif.

Fruit Soda

While some people toss cut fruit with lemon juice to prevent browning, I actually use lemon-lime or grapefruit soda. It adds a little extra flavor, and the acidity still prevents the cut fruit from browning.

Elizabeth Roberts
Cambridge, Mass.

Top Leftover Recipes Win Praise for Inventiveness

Our $1,000 Grand-Prize Winner!

Veronica Callaghan
Glastonbury, Conn.

Who says turkey leftovers have to be limited to tetrazzini and sandwiches? Veronica's Rustic Turkey Tart is an imaginative way to dress up holiday leftovers. Our judges applauded the interplay of flavors among the blue cheese, pears, pecans, and cranberries. Veronica says, "Since I often have house guests after the holidays, I wanted to create something a little more elegant than your typical turkey sandwich. This tart can be served as an appetizer or paired with a green salad for a light dinner."

Our four runners-up are similarly creative recipes. Among them are two that took inspiration from south of the border: turkey enchiladas with green sauce and plenty of cilantro, and turkey nachos spiced up with roasted poblano peppers and black beans. A sweet and savory African-inspired soup combines leftover turkey with sweet potatoes, curry powder, and peanut butter. Our final runner-up is a reimagining of Monte Cristo sandwiches in strudel form.

RUSTIC TURKEY TART

SERVES 6 TO 8
Pillsbury Just Unroll! Pie Crust is the test kitchen's favorite brand of prepared pie dough.

- 1 (9-inch) round prepared pie dough (see note)
- 1½ cups leftover turkey meat, cut into bite-sized pieces
- ¾ cup crumbled blue cheese
- 2 firm pears, peeled, cored, and diced
- ¼ cup pecans, toasted and chopped
- ¼ cup dried cranberries
- 1 cup sour cream
- 3 tablespoons heavy cream
- 1 tablespoon minced fresh thyme
  Salt and pepper

1. Adjust oven rack to middle position and heat oven to 425 degrees. Gently press pie crust into 9-inch tart pan and trim excess dough with knife. Prick bottom of dough all over with tines of fork. Bake until lightly browned, about 15 minutes; cool on wire rack.

2. Combine turkey, ½ cup cheese, pears, pecans, cranberries, sour cream, heavy cream, and thyme in large bowl; season with salt and pepper. Transfer turkey mixture to cooled pie crust, then sprinkle with remaining cheese.

3. Bake until crust is golden brown and cheese is melted, about 20 minutes. Let cool 20 minutes. Serve warm or at room temperature. (Tart can be refrigerated for 24 hours. Bring to room temperature before serving.)

This turkey tart is flavored with creamy blue cheese, pears, toasted pecans, and sweet-tart dried cranberries.

Rex Morris
Vashon, Wash.

Lila Cornello
Morton Grove, Ill.

Julie DeMatteo
Clementon, N.J.

Debbie Reid
Clearwater, Fla.

GREEN CHILE TURKEY ENCHILADAS SERVES 4 TO 6

Rex says: "I grew up in the Sonoran Desert, and hearty, spicy fare like enchiladas always reminds me of my youth. This leftover turkey version requires a minimum of ingredients, comes together quickly, and tastes great, too."

- 1 tablespoon vegetable oil
- 1 onion, sliced thin
- 3 garlic cloves, minced
- 1 tablespoon taco seasoning
- 2 cups leftover turkey meat, cut into bite-sized pieces
- ½ cup frozen corn, thawed
- 1 (16-ounce) can green enchilada sauce
- 12 corn tortillas
- 2 cups shredded pepper Jack cheese
- ½ cup sour cream
- ⅓ cup chopped fresh cilantro

1. Adjust oven rack to middle position and heat oven to 325 degrees. Heat oil in large skillet over medium heat until shimmering. Cook onion until golden brown, about 8 minutes. Add garlic and taco seasoning and cook until fragrant, about 30 seconds. Off heat, stir in turkey, corn, and ¾ cup enchilada sauce.

2. Spray tortillas on both sides with cooking spray and arrange on rimmed baking sheet. Bake until tortillas are warm and pliable, about 2 minutes. Working with 1 tortilla at a time, arrange ¼ cup turkey mixture in center of tortilla and sprinkle with 1 tablespoon cheese. Roll tortilla and transfer, seam-side down, to 13- by 9-inch baking dish. Repeat with remaining tortillas.

3. Whisk sour cream and remaining enchilada sauce in bowl. Bake enchiladas until lightly browned around edges, about 10 minutes. Spoon sour cream mixture over enchiladas and top with remaining cheese. Return to oven and bake until cheese is melted, about 10 minutes. Sprinkle with cilantro. Serve.

SPICY TURKEY NACHOS SERVES 6 TO 8

Lila says: "A few years ago, my family and I spent Thanksgiving in Mexico. My son was craving beef nachos, but my daughter wanted something lighter. To compromise, I used leftover turkey spiced up with a few fresh poblano chiles." Tostitos Natural Yellow Corn Tortilla Chips are our favorite chips for nachos.

- 3 poblano chiles
- 1 tablespoon vegetable oil
- 2 garlic cloves, minced
- 1 teaspoon chili powder
- 1 teaspoon dried oregano
- ¼ teaspoon ground cumin
- 1½ cups leftover turkey meat, cut into bite-sized pieces
- 1 (16-ounce) can black beans, drained and rinsed
- 2 teaspoons lime juice
- 8 cups tortilla chips (about 6 ounces)
- 2 scallions, sliced thin
- 4 cups shredded pepper Jack cheese

1. Adjust oven rack to the upper-middle and lower-middle positions and heat broiler. Place poblanos on rimmed baking sheet and broil on upper-middle rack until skin is charred, 3 to 5 minutes per side. Transfer poblanos to large bowl and wrap tightly with plastic. When cool enough to handle poblanos, peel, seed, and chop. Reduce oven temperature to 400 degrees.

2. Heat oil in large nonstick skillet over medium heat until shimmering. Cook garlic, chili powder, oregano, and cumin until fragrant, about 30 seconds. Off heat, stir in turkey, beans, and lime juice.

3. Arrange half of chips evenly in 13- by 9-inch baking dish. Top with half of turkey mixture, half of scallions, half of chopped poblanos, and half of cheese. Repeat. Transfer nachos to lower-middle rack and bake until cheese is melted, about 10 minutes. Serve.

CURRIED TURKEY-PEANUT SOUP SERVES 6

Julie says: "I first made this recipe 10 years ago after coming across a similar Senegalese-influenced soup in an old cookbook (minus the leftover turkey, of course). After a decade of modifying and streamlining, I've finally perfected it." For an extra spicy soup, add 1 or 2 stemmed, seeded, and minced jalapeño or serrano chiles to the pot along with the garlic in step 1. Cooking the curry powder and cumin in the hot oil greatly intensifies their flavor.

- 2 tablespoons vegetable oil
- 1 onion, chopped fine
- 1 sweet potato, peeled and cut into ½-inch chunks
- 2 garlic cloves, minced
- 1 tablespoon curry powder
- ½ teaspoon ground cumin
- 4 cups low-sodium chicken broth
- 1 (14.5-ounce) can diced tomatoes with green chiles
- ½ cup long-grain rice
- ⅓ cup creamy peanut butter
- 3 cups leftover turkey meat, cut into bite-sized pieces
- 2 tablespoons lime juice
  Salt and pepper

1. Heat oil in large Dutch oven over medium-high heat until shimmering. Cook onion and sweet potato until lightly browned, stirring frequently, about 5 minutes. Stir in garlic, curry powder, and cumin and cook until fragrant, about 30 seconds.

2. Whisk in broth, tomatoes, and rice and bring to boil. Reduce heat to medium-low and simmer, covered, until rice and potatoes are tender, about 15 minutes.

3. Stir in peanut butter until incorporated, about 1 minute, then stir in turkey and lime juice. Season with salt and pepper. Serve.

MINI MONTE CRISTO STRUDELS SERVES 6

Debbie says: "This recipe makes an elegant and impressive entrée." Defrost the phyllo at room temperature for 3 to 4 hours.

- 2 cups leftover turkey meat, cut into bite-sized pieces
- 6 ounces sliced deli ham, chopped
- 1 cup shredded Havarti cheese
- 3 tablespoons Dijon mustard
- 2 tablespoons mayonnaise
- 2 tablespoons minced fresh chives
  Salt and pepper
- 15 (13- by 9-inch) sheets phyllo dough, defrosted (see note)
- 6 tablespoons unsalted butter, melted
  Confectioners' sugar, for serving
  Raspberry preserves, for serving

1. Adjust oven rack to middle position and heat oven to 425 degrees. Line rimmed baking sheet with parchment paper. Combine turkey, ham, cheese, mustard, mayonnaise, and chives in large bowl. Season with salt and pepper.

2. Place sheet of parchment paper slightly larger than phyllo on work surface with long side toward you. Place one phyllo sheet on parchment and brush lightly with butter. Repeat with four more sheets. Cut buttered phyllo sheets in half to form two 9- by 6½-inch rectangles. With long ends facing you, place heaping ½ cup turkey mixture in 3-inch-wide strip about 1 inch from bottom of each phyllo rectangle. Fold short ends of phyllo over filling, then fold end closest to you over filling. Roll tightly, then arrange, seam-side down, on baking sheet and brush with butter. Repeat two more times with remaining phyllo, butter, and filling.

3. Cut two 1-inch vents into top of each strudel. Bake until golden and crisp, 15 to 20 minutes. Cool on wire rack 5 minutes. Dust with confectioners' sugar and serve with preserves.

Ask Cook's Country

WE'LL ANSWER ANY QUESTION YOU THROW AT US!

BUTTERMILK ALTERNATIVES

I don't consume dairy, but there are a lot of baking recipes that call for buttermilk that I want to make. Is it possible to manipulate soy or rice milk to mimic buttermilk?

Melinda Fletcher
Providence, R.I.

Tangy, thick cultured buttermilk is made by adding lactic-acid bacteria to low-fat or skim cow's milk. In the test kitchen we often make a quick facsimile of buttermilk by adding a tablespoon of fresh lemon juice (or white vinegar) to 1 cup of milk and then letting it sit for a few minutes while the milk proteins thicken. Following the same method, we stirred up samples using soy, rice, and cow's milk; after five minutes the soy and cow's milk thickened similarly, while the rice milk did not. That's because soy milk has nearly the same protein content as cow's milk, while rice milk has very little protein.

To see how each acidulated milk would fare in cooking, we prepared batches of buttermilk biscuits and pancakes using the acidulated cow's, soy, and rice milks. The biscuits made with soy milk baked up as brown and tender as the acidulated cow's milk biscuits, but they were slightly sweeter. The biscuit dough made with rice milk, however, mixed up wet and sticky (even with an additional ¼ cup flour), yielding squat and unacceptably sweet biscuits. Similarly, the soy milk pancakes mirrored the light fluffiness of the acidulated cow's milk pancakes, but the runny rice milk

DAIRY-FREE "BUTTERMILK"
Say "yes" to acidulated soy milk, and "no" to acidulated rice milk as buttermilk substitutes.

batter made thin, crêpe-like pancakes. Our conclusion: Acidulated soy milk can be substituted for buttermilk in most baked goods, but acidulated rice milk cannot.

YEAST 101

I am so confused! I've seen yeast labeled as cake, active dry, rapid rise, and instant. What's the difference?

Carolyn Myers
Waltham, Mass.

Yeast is a living organism that is grown in liquid, where it feeds on sugar and starch until it reaches the desired volume and maturity. Fresh active yeast (also called cake yeast) is drained yeast that has been pressed into a crumbly cake; it has a very short shelf life (one week or less) and must be refrigerated. For these reasons, it is not a sensible choice for most home cooks. Active dry yeast and rapid-rise (or instant) yeast, however, have been dehydrated and have much longer shelf lives (up to two years

unopened, according to the "best if used by" dates on the package), and technically do not require refrigeration. However, we found that both rapid-rise and active dry yeast benefit from being stored in a cool, dry place; a pantry, refrigerator, or, best of all, the freezer.

Active dry yeast must be activated (or proofed) in warm liquid before using; rapid-rise yeast can be added directly to the dough and does not require proofing, but the test kitchen has found that doing so does help to speed up its rise. Rapid-rise and active dry yeast may be substituted for each other if you follow this formula: 1 teaspoon active dry yeast equals ¾ teaspoon rapid-rise yeast.

PICK-A-PEPPER

I've heard that red bell peppers with three bumps on the bottom are sweeter than those with four bumps. Is this true?

Adam Vickens
Sausalito, Calif.

There's a bit of folklore concerning the number of bumps (or lobes) on the bottom of red bell peppers: that the number is determined by the sex of the fruit (false), or that peppers with three bumps are sweeter, and those with four are more firm (both also false). With a little research, we learned red bell peppers with three bumps are a slightly different variety than the peppers with four. Our taste tests confirmed that there is no flavor or textural difference between the two kinds of red peppers. When shopping for red bell peppers, look for a deep red color with taut, blemish-free skin—and pay no heed to the number of bumps on the bottom of the fruit.

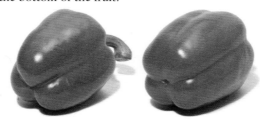

HOW MANY BUMPS ARE BEST?
These bell peppers have slightly different shapes, but they taste exactly the same.

PUMPKIN PIE SPICE SUBSTITUTION

I was recently given a pumpkin pie recipe that calls for pumpkin pie spice. Can I make the blend myself?

Janice Delgado
Buffalo, N.Y.

Pumpkin pie recipes often call for a variety of warm spices like cinnamon, nutmeg, ginger, mace, cloves, and allspice, but for a reliable benchmark on making our own blend we contacted McCormick, the industry leader in spice production. Although the company's representative would not divulge their secret formula, she suggested using ½ teaspoon

cinnamon, ¼ teaspoon ginger, ⅛ teaspoon nutmeg, and ⅛ teaspoon cloves as an equivalent to 1 teaspoon pumpkin pie spice. Interestingly, the ingredients list on the jar lists allspice, not cloves, along with the cinnamon, ginger, and nutmeg.

Curious as to which combination tasted best, we whipped up three pies: one with the premixed blend, one with the suggested ratios from McCormick, and one substituting ⅛ teaspoon allspice for the cloves. Our tasters preferred both of the homemade blends to the premixed stuff, with the allspice version edging out its clove-y competition.

MIX YOUR OWN
If your spice cabinet is well stocked with baking spices, you probably have all you need to make pumpkin pie spice superior to the premixed variety.

CAKE PAN EXCHANGE

Can I use tube pans and Bundt pans interchangeably?

Beth Anne Cacka
Canby, Ore.

Tube and Bundt pans both have hollow centers to encourage even cooking and stable structure, especially for heavier batters, but their design is different. Tube pans have flat bottoms and straight sides that flare out slightly. Two-piece tube pans, which feature a removable bottom, are specifically called angel food pans—the removable bottom helps release this sticky cake from the pan. Bundt pans, descendents of Central European kugelhopf bread pans, have fluted, gently curving walls. All three types of pans are available with nonstick finishes.

To test if nonstick tube, angel food, and Bundt pans could be used interchangeably, we made a dense pound cake, a lighter orange Bundt cake, and an angel food cake in each one. All three pans passed the pound and orange cake tests with similar cooking times and even browning, but

CHICAGO METALLIC ANGEL FOOD CAKE PAN
Our favorite tube pan.

the angel food cake was a different story. There was no problem removing the tall and fluffy cake from the angel food pan, but the cake made in the Bundt and solid tube pans (both nonstick) remained glued to the bottom. So while a Bundt or tube pan is fine for most recipes, a two-piece angel food pan performs any task at hand. We prefer heavier-gauge metal for angel food pans, as lighter models are prone to leaking. If forced to use an inferior quality pan, lay a piece of aluminum foil under it to collect any drips.

To ask us a cooking question, visit CooksCountry.com/emailus. You can also write to Ask Cook's Country, P.O. Box 470739, Brookline, MA 02447. See if you can stump us!

Recipe Makeover SPAGHETTI CARBONARA

After eliminating most of the eggs, bacon, and cream, what lower-fat ingredients could we add to get our makeover to taste like full-fat carbonara?

Carbonara typically uses either Pecorino or Parmesan cheese; by using the more assertive Pecorino, we were able to save calories and fat by adding less.

Spaghetti alla carbonara, the quintessential Roman pasta dish, is typically made by crisping a lot of bacon, sautéing garlic in the drippings, adding white wine and black pepper, and reducing it down. In another bowl, beaten raw eggs and plenty of grated cheese are combined, hot drained pasta is added, the wine mixture is poured on top, and everything is tossed to create a silky, luscious sauce. Some recipes even add heavy cream. With so many rich ingredients, it's no surprise that carbonara tips the scales at over 600 calories and 28 grams of fat per serving.

I unsuccessfully tested more than a half-dozen low-fat recipes. Egg substitutes produced bland, curdled sauces, and a version made with reduced-fat cream cheese horrified my tasters with its tacky texture and sour flavor. The worst offender was the carbonara made with turkey bacon, which tasted bitter and artificial.

Starting over with the test kitchen's favorite full-fat carbonara recipe, I cut the bacon from eight strips down to two. This pasta had decent smoky flavor but tasters complained that the pieces of crisp bacon were "hiding" in

their bowls. In order to get more meat into the finished dish, I tested leaner pork products—including ham, low-fat sausage, and even chopped hot dogs (don't ask)—before settling on a few ounces of smoky, meaty, and relatively lean Canadian bacon. I kept the two slices of bacon, which rendered enough drippings for sautéing the garlic. And bumping up the garlic, pepper, and wine brought bigger flavor without excess fat and calories.

Choosing pungent Pecorino Romano rather than milder Parmesan meant that I could get more flavor from less cheese. Most recipes use at least three eggs, but I was able to reduce the amount to just one, with an additional egg white for structure. My carbonara was getting better, but it was still dry and not creamy enough.

Many classic recipes add a splash of cream. Instead, I turned to an ingredient we've used in other recipe makeovers: fat-free evaporated milk. As I had hoped, the evaporated milk provided a silky texture similar to that of the eggs I'd lost. Unfortunately, this was a short-lived thrill, as the pasta began to soak up all the sauce after only a few minutes, making the carbonara unpalatably dry.

In traditional recipes, all that fat coats the pasta and prevents it from absorbing too much sauce. As I racked my brain for an ingredient that would coat the pasta without spiking my fat and calorie counts, a colleague half-jokingly suggested trying mayonnaise, which is made from eggs and oil. I was skeptical but out of ideas, so I gave it a try. Surprisingly, just ½ tablespoon of mayonnaise created a protective coating on the pasta that prevented it from absorbing all the sauce. The mayo was so successful that I wondered if adding some to the sauce would help. Odd as it sounds, another 1½ tablespoons of mayonnaise in the sauce fooled tasters into thinking I was serving them the real deal.

Until this point I had been whisking the sauce together in a bowl before adding it to the hot pasta. In an effort to increase the volume of the sauce without adding more ingredients, I whirled everything in a food processor with some of the pasta water. This blended all of the ingredients into an emulsified creamy sauce that easily coated the pasta.

–Meredith Butcher

And the Numbers...
All nutritional information is for one serving.

TRADITIONAL SPAGHETTI CARBONARA
CALORIES: **610**
FAT: **28g**
SATURATED FAT: **11g**

COOK'S COUNTRY LOW-FAT SPAGHETTI CARBONARA
CALORIES: **400**
FAT: **10g**
SATURATED FAT: **3g**

LOW-FAT SPAGHETTI CARBONARA SERVES 6

Any long, thin pasta such as linguine or fettuccine will also work here. An equal amount of Parmesan cheese may be substituted for the Pecorino, although the cheese flavor will be less pronounced.

1	large egg plus 1 egg white
⅔	cup grated Pecorino Romano cheese (see note)
¼	cup fat-free evaporated milk
2	tablespoons mayonnaise
2	ounces Canadian bacon, chopped
2	slices bacon, chopped
3	garlic cloves, minced
1	teaspoon pepper
⅓	cup white wine
	Salt
1	pound spaghetti (see note)

1. Bring 4 quarts water to boil in large pot. Process egg, egg white, cheese, evaporated milk, and 1½ tablespoons mayonnaise in food processor until smooth; leave mixture in food processor.

2. Cook both bacons in large non-stick skillet over medium heat until fat has rendered and bacon is browned, about 7 minutes. Using slotted spoon, transfer bacon to bowl; set aside.

3. Add garlic and pepper to fat in pan and cook until fragrant, about 30 seconds. Stir in wine and simmer until slightly thickened, about 1 minute. Remove pan from heat, cover, and keep warm.

4. Meanwhile, add 1 tablespoon salt and pasta to boiling water and cook until al dente. Reserve 1 cup pasta cooking water, drain pasta, and return to pot. Toss pasta with remaining ½ tablespoon mayonnaise until coated.

5. With motor running, slowly add wine mixture and ¼ cup hot pasta cooking water to egg mixture and process until smooth and frothy, about 1 minute. Immediately pour egg mixture over hot pasta and toss to combine, adding reserved cooking water as necessary to adjust consistency. Stir in crisp bacon and season with salt. Serve.

Big Flavor without the Fat
For creamy, silky carbonara without all the fat, three ingredients were essential in this recipe makeover.

CANADIAN BACON
Most of the bacon is replaced by Canadian bacon, which is meatier and contains significantly less fat.

EVAPORATED MILK
Fat-free evaporated milk provides thick, creamy texture.

MAYONNAISE
Just 2 tablespoons of mayonnaise adds flavor and creaminess, allowing us to use less fat and fewer eggs.

Slow-cooker stroganoff recipes promise to transform a cheap, tough cut into something special, but they forget about the sauce, which ends up watery and bland.

Dried Mushrooms 101

Many supermarkets now carry several varieties of dried mushrooms in addition to porcinis: chanterelles, morels, and shiitakes among them. Here are a few tips on purchasing and handling this potent ingredient.

BIGGER IS BETTER

PURCHASING AND STORING:

When purchasing dried mushrooms, avoid packages filled with small, dusty pieces or those labeled "wild mushroom mix"—they are often older and of lesser quality. Dried mushrooms should have an earthy (not musty or stale) aroma. Store dried mushrooms in an airtight container in a cool, dry place for up to one year.

PREPARING:

Dried mushrooms are typically gritty and tough, so they should be rinsed thoroughly to remove any dirt and grit and then microwaved, covered, with at least twice the volume of water or broth (alternately, they can be soaked in hot liquid for about 5 minutes) until they become pliable enough to chop. Don't throw the soaking liquid away—once strained (we use a fine-mesh strainer lined with a single paper towel or paper coffee filter), it adds a meaty, earthy flavor to soups, stews, and rice dishes.

Traditional stroganoff features sautéed strips of beef tenderloin (or other tender, expensive steaks), chopped mushrooms, and onions in a sauce made from beef broth and sour cream. This recipe is quick to prepare but requires a big wallet and constant attention. Slow-cooker recipes attempt to solve these problems by simmering inexpensive stew meat until tender. This process takes hours but should require little hands-on work.

But the same sauce prepared in minutes in a skillet won't work in a slow cooker, where there's no evaporation and flavors dull with time. Unfortunately, most slow-cooker recipes ignore this fact and offer no solution for the sauce.

Most slow-cooker stroganoffs simply dump the beef, onions, mushrooms (and sometimes cream of mushroom soup), and broth in the slow cooker and come back eight hours later to toss in some sour cream at the end. But the test kitchen has found that browning meats on the stovetop before adding them to the slow cooker adds flavor by developing a crust on the meat and leaving concentrated brown bits behind in the pan (these bits, called fond, provide rich flavor when a sauce is built with them). But there was a big problem with browning here: I was working with 4 pounds of stew meat, so I'd have to brown it in two or three messy, time-consuming batches, washing the pan—and wasting the fond—each time to prevent scorching. There had to be an easier, faster way to deep, rich flavor.

The solution turned out to be not one thing, but a combination of three. First, I created fond more quickly by caramelizing onions and tomato paste over medium-high heat for a full 10 minutes; the fond left behind was then used as the base for the stroganoff sauce. Second, I added a good pour of soy sauce, an ingredient proven to enhance meaty, beefy flavors. Third, I augmented the classic white mushrooms in this dish with earthy, potent dried porcini mushrooms, which I rehydrated in beef broth. In a side-by-side test, my tasters thought the stroganoff made with these three "tricks" was even beefier than a version made with browned beef.

This stroganoff tasted great, but the sauce was still a bit thin, even after I added the sour cream (always stirred in just before serving to prevent curdling). I tried thickeners like tapioca and cornstarch, but neither was as effective as pulling some of the stroganoff sauce out of the pot, mixing it with flour, and stirring the slurry back in. After simmering for just 15 minutes, my flavorful sauce was now properly thickened. With a sprinkle of fresh dill, I had an easy stroganoff that didn't break the bank.

–Cali Rich

SLOW-COOKER BEEF STROGANOFF SERVES 6 TO 8

If you can't find large chunks of stew meat, buy a 4- to 5-pound chuck roast and cut it yourself, trimming away excess fat. This stroganoff can be made up to 2 days in advance, but the sour cream and dill should be added just before serving.

- 1½ cups low-sodium beef broth
- ¼ cup dried porcini mushrooms, rinsed and patted dry
- 2 tablespoons vegetable oil
- 2 onions, chopped fine
- 2 tablespoons tomato paste
- ½ cup white wine
- ⅓ cup soy sauce
- 4 pounds boneless beef chuck stew meat cut into 1½-inch pieces (see note)
- 1 pound white mushrooms, cleaned and quartered
- 6 tablespoons all-purpose flour
- 1½ cups sour cream
- 2 tablespoons chopped fresh dill Salt and pepper

1. Combine ½ cup broth and porcini in bowl and microwave until steamy and mushrooms have softened, about 1 minute. Line fine-mesh strainer with one paper towel and strain porcini, reserving liquid. Chop porcini fine and set aside.

2. Heat oil in large skillet over medium-high heat until shimmering. Cook onions and tomato paste, stirring frequently, until lightly browned, 7 to 10 minutes. Stir in wine, soy sauce, remaining broth, chopped porcini, and reserved porcini liquid, scraping up any browned bits with wooden spoon. Bring broth mixture to boil, then transfer to slow cooker. Add beef and white mushrooms to slow cooker, cover, and cook on high until meat is tender, 6 to 7 hours (or cook on low for 9 to 10 hours).

3. Set slow cooker to high, if necessary. Skim fat from surface. Transfer 2 cups sauce from slow cooker to large bowl and whisk in flour. Stir flour mixture into slow cooker and cook, covered, until sauce thickens, about 15 minutes. Stir in sour cream and dill and season with salt and pepper. Serve.

We like to serve this rich, hearty stroganoff over buttered egg noodles or rice.

Lost Recipes HERMIT COOKIES

Recipes for hermits began appearing in late 19th century New England cookbooks, such as Maria Parloa's Miss Parloa's New Cook Book *(1880) and Fannie Merritt Farmer's* The Boston Cooking-School Cook Book *(1896).*

These old-fashioned cookies should bake up soft and chewy, with a perfect balance of sugar and spice. So why are most hermits rock-hard and overly spiced?

If your only experience with hermits is eating cardboardlike store-bought versions, these chewy, spicy cookies will be a revelation.

I pride myself on being the in-house cookie expert, so I was surprised when a colleague reminisced about a favorite childhood cookie I'd never heard of: hermits. A chewy raisin spice cookie with a sweet glaze, this New England specialty (unknown where I grew up in North Carolina) sounded appealing.

Some initial reading revealed many generations of fond memories, as hermits date back to the late 1800s. But after making a handful of recipes, I wondered if nostalgia had clouded my colleague's recollections. Most baked up more hard tack than soft batch and were peppered with bland, tough raisins. As for flavor, all but one tasted like a spice rack clearing house. My colleague (he's also my boss) insisted that hermits could be better, so I set out on a month-long baking odyssey.

Hermits typically involve creaming softened butter and brown sugar, adding eggs and molasses, and then mixing in the dry ingredients (flour, spices, baking soda, and salt). But all of the recipes I made using this method produced dry, almost biscuit-y cookies. Melted butter generally makes cookies moister and chewier, and melting the butter had the desired effect in this recipe. Taking this a step further, I cooked the butter in a saucepan until it turned light brown and fragrant, which added a nutty flavor to the cookies.

It seems like no two hermit recipes use the same combination of warm spices. Most recipes I tested used too many spices, giving the cookies an unappealing dusty quality. After testing various combinations of cinnamon, cloves, nutmeg, allspice, ginger, black pepper, cardamom, and mace, my tasters settled on the simple—yet potent—combination of cinnamon, allspice, and ginger. Adding the spices to the browned butter bloomed their natural flavor and allowed me to use less, thus avoiding the dusty texture of hermits made with too much ground spice.

My tasters were starting to warm to these cookies, but the bland, tough raisins were still a problem. Steeping the raisins in melted butter softened them and greatly improved their flavor. Pureeing the raisins into a rough paste helped distribute chewy, raisin-y goodness into every bite. Spying a bag of crystallized (or candied) ginger, I wondered if I could puree the ginger with the raisins for more flavor. Sure enough, the pureed ginger lent pungent sweetness—and even more chew—to the baked cookies, and allowed me to omit the dried ginger.

Recipes are divided as to how hermits should be shaped. One camp calls for dropping balls of dough to form round cookies; the other calls for the dough to be shaped into logs, baked, and then cut into individual cookies. A side-by-side test revealed that the hermits baked in logs and then cut were much chewier and moister, as the larger mass of dough better held its moisture through baking. As a crowning touch, I made a simple glaze of orange juice and confectioner's sugar to drizzle over the just-baked cookies. These old-fashioned cookies might not look like much, but they've earned a regular spot in my cookie jar. **–Cali Rich**

HERMITS

MAKES ABOUT 1½ DOZEN COOKIES

Crystallized (or candied) ginger is available in the spice aisle of most supermarkets. For this recipe, we prefer using mild (or light) molasses instead of the robust or blackstrap varieties; see page 30 for more information about molasses.

- 1 **cup raisins**
- 2 **tablespoons finely chopped crystallized ginger (see note)**
- 8 **tablespoons (1 stick) unsalted butter**
- 1 **teaspoon ground cinnamon**
- ¼ **teaspoon ground allspice**
- 2 **cups all-purpose flour**
- ½ **teaspoon baking soda**
- ½ **teaspoon salt**
- ¾ **cup packed dark brown sugar**
- ½ **cup molasses (see note)**
- 2 **large eggs**
- 1½ **tablespoons orange juice**
- ¾ **cup confectioners' sugar**

1. Adjust oven racks to upper-middle and lower-middle positions and heat oven to 350 degrees. Line two baking sheets with parchment paper. Process raisins and ginger in bowl of food processor until mixture sticks together and only small pieces remain. Transfer to large bowl.

2. Heat butter in small saucepan over medium-low heat, swirling pan occasionally, until nutty brown in color, about 10 minutes. Stir in cinnamon and allspice and cook until fragrant, about 15 seconds. Stir butter mixture into raisin mixture until well combined; cool to room temperature.

3. Combine flour, baking soda, and salt in bowl. Stir brown sugar, molasses, and eggs into cooled butter mixture until incorporated. Fold in flour mixture (dough will be very sticky) and refrigerate, covered, until firm, at least 1½ hours or up to 24 hours.

4. Divide dough into quarters. Transfer one piece of dough to lightly floured surface, roll into 10-inch log, and transfer to prepared baking sheet. Repeat with remaining dough. Bake until only shallow indentation remains on edges when touched (center will appear slightly soft), 15 to 20 minutes, switching and rotating sheets halfway through baking. Let cool on sheet 5 minutes, then transfer parchment to wire rack and cool completely.

5. Whisk orange juice and confectioners' sugar in small bowl until smooth. Drizzle glaze onto cooled logs and let sit until glaze hardens, about 15 minutes. Cut logs into 2-inch bars. Serve. (Cookies can be stored in airtight container at room temperature for 5 days.)

Keys to PERFECT HERMITS

1. Roll each quarter of dough into a 10-inch log, transfer to baking sheet, then use a ruler to neatly square off the sides before baking.

2. Once completely cooled, drizzle the baked hermits with glaze before slicing into individual bars.

Old-Fashioned Roast Turkey with Gravy

Even with a lot of time and effort, the white meat can be dry, chalky, and flavorless. Could we find an easy, foolproof method that ensures moist, flavorful breast meat every time?

The prospect of roasting a holiday turkey can make me pull the covers up over my head on Thanksgiving morning. It's a lot of work, a huge time commitment, and the results are all too often dry and disappointing. The only thing to be thankful for is a giant ladle of gravy that can make it all palatable.

The problem is that the white and dark meat need to be cooked to different temperatures. While the white meat starts to dry out if cooked past 165 degrees, the dark meat isn't tender and fully cooked until it reaches 175 degrees. The test kitchen has addressed this issue before, but none of our solutions are particularly effortless. Brining a turkey ensures that even overcooked breast meat will be juicy, but it takes many hours and a lot of refrigerator space. Another method starts the bird breast-side down so the dark meat is exposed to more heat and then flips the turkey so the breast skin can crisp. To my mind, wrestling with a hot, heavy bird when the house is filled with guests isn't all that appealing. I wanted to find an easier way to perfectly cooked turkey.

I remembered seeing my grandmother cook a holiday turkey by covering the breast meat with cheesecloth soaked in chicken broth, the idea being that the broth would slowly drip, keeping the meat moist and helping to prevent overcooking. While the test kitchen has learned that traditional basting doesn't work (repeatedly opening the oven leads to too much heat loss, and the liquid runs off the bird as fast as you apply it), the cheesecloth technique seemed promising. It took me a few tests to discover that the soaked cheesecloth did

We borrowed from two classic turkey-cooking techniques to create a hybrid recipe that guarantees moist, flavorful meat.

The Best Birds

In a recent tasting of eight national brands of turkey, the test kitchen's favorite natural turkey was Rubashkin's Aaron's Best, a frozen kosher turkey that is hard to find in some parts of the country. Our favorite "self-basting" turkey is the frozen basted turkey from Butterball.

BEST NATURAL TURKEY
Rubashkin's Aaron's Best

BEST SELF-BASTING TURKEY
Frozen Butterball

help to slow down the cooking of the breast meat, but if you didn't baste the cheesecloth (and keep it moist), it blackened and fused to the turkey. I wasn't going to keep opening the oven to baste the cheesecloth, but I did have a few other tricks up my sleeve.

For my next test, I covered the breast meat with cheesecloth soaked in chicken broth and then covered the cheesecloth with a double layer of aluminum foil to insulate it from drying out. I stuck a temperature probe into the thickest portion of the breast and another into the thickest portion of the thigh. I connected the probes to a computer program that could chart the temperature throughout the cooking time. As I had hoped, this method caused the breast meat to lag a perfect 10 degrees behind the thigh—with very little effort. When the breast meat reached 140 degrees, I took the cheesecloth and foil off and turned the oven up (from 350 to 425 degrees), and continued to roast the turkey until the breast meat was done and the skin was nicely browned.

My insulation was working, but I wanted to add more flavor to the bird. I tried adding herbs and peppercorns to the broth I used for soaking the cheesecloth, but the added flavor was superficial at best.

Butter wasn't much better—it quickly dripped off the turkey and into the bottom of the pan. Looking for a potent ingredient that would slowly release its flavor during cooking, I thought of a technique that has been used for poultry for ages: larding, a process of inserting strips of lard (or other animal fat) into the turkey meat so it could slowly release its flavor and moisture throughout roasting. While I didn't want to cut holes in my turkey—or infuse it with lard—I decided to try covering the breast with bacon before layering on my broth-soaked cheesecloth and foil. Once the breast meat hit 140 degrees, I took off the covering and bacon slices and finished cooking the turkey as before. The meat was definitely better-seasoned, but tasters objected to the smoky flavor that the bacon had imparted to the meat and drippings.

The bacon wasn't quite right, so I tried replacing it with ¼-inch slices of salt pork, which further insulated the breast and slowly melted in the oven, basting the turkey with flavorful pork fat. Since the tops of the turkey legs were drying out during cooking, I also gave them the salt pork, soaked cheesecloth, and foil treatment. The breast meat was moist and flavorful, the dark meat tender, and the skin beautifully browned and crisp. The salt pork added so much richness that I didn't need to soak the cheesecloth in broth—plain water worked just fine. Now that I had the perfect turkey, it was time to make the perfect gravy.

I started by simmering a stock made from the turkey giblets and neck, onion, and herbs while the turkey was in the oven. I strained the stock and was ready to start building the gravy once the turkey came out of the oven. I made a roux from turkey fat (for flavor) and flour, then added my stock and defatted pan drippings and simmered my gravy until it was nicely thickened. The gravy was richly seasoned from my homemade stock, the turkey drippings, and the salt pork. I finally had a perfectly cooked, moist turkey with great gravy—and a minimum of fuss. **–Diane Unger**

Test Kitchen Technique NEW SPINS ON OLD METHODS

For foolproof roast turkey, we turned to two old techniques: soaked cheesecloth and larding. Both techniques needed serious updating—we weren't going to continually baste the cheesecloth or force lard into the turkey meat—but their core functions of adding moisture and flavor were sound. Here's how we updated these classic techniques.

1. Use a fork to pierce the skin of the turkey breast and legs all over. This will help the rendered salt pork to moisten and flavor the meat.

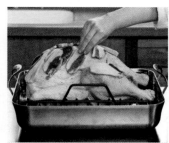

2. Cover the entirety of the breast and the tops of the legs with strips of salt pork.

3. Soak cheesecloth in cold water, then drape it over the salt pork on the breast and legs.

4. To prevent the cheesecloth from drying out and burning (and to further protect the breast), cover the cheesecloth completely with foil.

OLD-FASHIONED ROAST TURKEY WITH GRAVY
SERVES 10 TO 12

You will need one 2-yard package of cheesecloth for this recipe. Because we layer the bird with salt pork, we prefer to use a natural turkey here; self-basting turkeys may become too salty. If using a self-basting turkey, use all water in the gravy rather than a combination of water and broth. Make sure to start the gravy (step 3) as soon as the turkey goes into the oven.

Turkey
- 1 **package cheesecloth (see note)**
- 4 **cups cold water**
- 1 **(12- to 14-pound) turkey (see note), neck and giblets reserved**
- 1 **pound salt pork, cut into ¼-inch-thick slices**

Gravy
- 1 **tablespoon vegetable oil**
  Reserved turkey neck and giblets
- 1 **onion, chopped**
- 5 **cups water**
- 2 **cups low-sodium chicken broth**
- 4 **sprigs fresh thyme**
- 1 **bay leaf**
- 6 **tablespoons all-purpose flour**
  Salt and pepper

1. For the turkey: Adjust oven rack to lowest position and heat oven to 350 degrees. Remove cheesecloth from package and fold into 18-inch square. Place cheesecloth in large bowl and cover with water. Tuck wings behind back and arrange turkey, breast-up, on V-rack set inside roasting pan. Following photos 1 to 4 above, prick skin of breast and legs of turkey all over with fork, cover breast and legs of turkey with salt pork, top with soaked cheesecloth (pouring any remaining water into roasting pan), and cover cheesecloth completely with heavy-duty aluminum foil.

2. Roast turkey until breast meat registers 140 degrees, 2½ to 3 hours. Remove foil, cheesecloth, and salt pork and discard. Increase oven temperature to 425 degrees. Continue to roast until breast meat registers 165 degrees and thigh meat registers 175 degrees, 40 to 60 minutes longer. Transfer turkey to carving board and let rest 30 minutes.

3. For the gravy: While turkey is roasting, heat oil in large saucepan over medium-high heat until shimmering. Cook turkey neck and giblets until browned, about 5 minutes. Add onion and cook until softened, about 3 minutes. Stir in water, broth, thyme, and bay leaf and bring to boil. Reduce heat to low and simmer until reduced by half, about 3 hours. Strain stock into large measuring cup (you should have about 3½ cups), reserving giblets if desired.

4. Carefully strain contents of roasting pan into fat separator. Let liquid settle so that fat separates, then skim, reserving ¼ cup fat. Pour defatted pan juices into measuring cup with giblet stock to yield 4 cups stock.

5. Heat reserved fat in empty saucepan over medium heat until shimmering. Stir in flour and cook until honey colored and fragrant, about 4 minutes. Slowly whisk in giblet stock and bring to boil. Reduce heat to medium-low and simmer until slightly thickened, about 5 minutes. Chop giblets and add to gravy, if desired, and season with salt and pepper. Carve turkey and serve with gravy.

Keys to Perfect Turkey

Cheesecloth
Cheesecloth is made from finely woven, undyed cotton fabric similar in texture to gauze. Originally used to strain the curds from the whey in the cheese-making process, cheesecloth has myriad culinary uses, including draining excess moisture from yogurt or ricotta cheese, straining impurities from stock, and making a removable herb bundle, or bouquet garni, to season a simmering liquid. Cheesecloth is typically sold in 2-yard packages in most supermarkets and kitchen stores.

CHEESECLOTH
Not just for cheese makers.

Salt Pork
Covering the breast and tops of the legs of the turkey with salt pork helped to season the meat and insulate it from overcooking. Don't confuse salt pork with bacon. Although both come from the belly of the pig and are

SALT PORK
Fat equals flavor.

salt-cured, bacon is heavily smoked and is typically leaner and meatier. Salt pork is unsmoked and used primarily as a flavoring agent (traditionally in dishes like baked beans) and is rarely actually consumed. We recommend buying blocks of salt pork (precut slices can dry out) and portioning it as needed. Look for salt pork that has at least a few streaks of meat throughout. Salt pork can be refrigerated for up to one month.

Bread Stuffing Outside the Bird

Stuffing cooked inside a turkey benefits from the flavor and moisture of the drippings. We wanted to find a way to rich, moist, "meaty" stuffing cooked outside the turkey.

We always have two bowls of bread stuffing on the table during the holidays. One holds the batch saturated with flavorful drippings from being cooked inside the turkey; the other, meant to feed the rest of the large crowd, is simply baked in a dish in the oven. Sadly, without those drippings, the second batch is always dry and crumbly, and the lack of savory flavor requires an extra ladle of gravy to compensate. Is it possible to make all the stuffing outside the turkey and still have it as moist and meaty as stuffing cooked inside the bird?

Classic bread stuffing is made by combining cubed bread with sautéed aromatics and herbs, and soaking it in plenty of chicken broth before baking. Tasters liked the slightly sweet flavor of white sandwich bread, but the texture was all wrong. Toasting the bread in the oven first made it sturdy enough to absorb plenty of flavorful liquid without becoming soggy. (As an added bonus, the toasted bread tasted better.) Testing established that onion, celery, and garlic were the preferred aromatics; sage and thyme the favored herbs.

The stuffing was okay, but it still wasn't as savory as stuffing cooked inside the bird, and it was dry. I tried replacing the chicken broth with beef broth, but the beefy flavor was out of place here. Reducing the chicken broth with the sautéed onions, celery, and herbs was a good first step. Searching for even deeper flavor, I turned to soy sauce, an ingredient we've used in other recipes to mimic meatiness. Sure enough, just a tablespoon of soy sauce gave the stuffing an intense savory flavor similar to that of stuffing cooked inside a turkey.

Now that the flavors were set, it was time to determine how to create a moister stuffing. Eggs are a relatively common ingredient in bread stuffings, and I found that four eggs (most recipes call for just two or maybe three) enriched the stuffing nicely. For even more richness, I took a cue from bread pudding recipes and tested various types of dairy. Whole milk was too thin, and heavy cream was too fatty, but 1½ cups of half-and-half made my out-of-the-bird stuffing moist and rich. Drizzling the stuffing with melted butter encouraged the top to become golden and crisp in the oven. This stuffing is so savory and rich, everyone will assume it was cooked inside the turkey.

–Meredith Butcher

BREAD STUFFING

SERVES 10 TO 12

Firm sandwich breads, like Arnold Country Classics White or Pepperidge Farm Farmhouse Hearty White, work best here.

- 1 **(24-ounce) loaf hearty white sandwich bread, cut into ½-inch pieces (about 16 cups)**
- 8 **tablespoons (1 stick) unsalted butter**
- 2 **onions, chopped fine**
- 3 **celery ribs, chopped fine**
- 4 **garlic cloves, minced**
- 1½ **teaspoons dried sage**
- 1½ **teaspoons dried thyme**
- 4 **cups low-sodium chicken broth**
- 1 **tablespoon soy sauce**
- 4 **large eggs**
- 1½ **cups half-and-half**
- ¼ **cup chopped fresh parsley**
- 1 **teaspoon salt**
- 1½ **teaspoons pepper**

1. Adjust oven racks to upper-middle and lower-middle positions and heat oven to 325 degrees. Arrange bread in single layer on 2 baking sheets. Bake until golden, about 30 minutes, stirring bread and switching and rotating sheets halfway through baking. Let cool.

2. Melt 4 tablespoons butter in large skillet over medium heat. Cook onions and celery until golden, about 10 minutes. Stir in garlic, sage, and thyme and cook until fragrant, about 30 seconds. Stir in broth and soy sauce and simmer until slightly thickened and vegetables are tender, about 10 minutes. Remove from heat and let cool 5 minutes.

3. Whisk eggs, half-and-half, parsley, salt, and pepper in large bowl. Slowly whisk in warm onion mixture until incorporated. Fold in toasted bread and let sit, tossing occasionally, until bread is saturated, about 20 minutes.

4. Transfer stuffing to greased 13- by 9-inch pan. Melt remaining butter and drizzle evenly over stuffing. Bake on lower-middle rack until top is golden brown and crisp, about 50 minutes. Let cool 15 minutes. Serve.

Make Ahead: The stuffing can be prepared through step 3 and refrigerated, covered, for 1 day. When ready to bake, proceed with step 4, increasing cooking time by about 20 minutes.

Enriched with eggs and half-and-half, this stuffing resembles a savory bread pudding.

Secrets to Savory Stuffing

Without turkey drippings, it was necessary to concentrate flavors to create a rich and meaty stuffing.

MAKE IT MEATY
A combination of reduced chicken broth and soy sauce contributes a meaty flavor to the stuffing.

Skillet-Roasted Carrots and Parsnips

Is there an easy, fast way to replicate the caramelized flavor of roasted vegetables on the stovetop?

Our streamlined stovetop technique provides roasted flavor—but allows you to use your oven for other dishes.

Sweetly caramelized on the outside and tender within, roasted root vegetables are a mainstay of many holiday tables. But with so many dishes competing for oven space during this frenzied time, I wanted an alternative that could cook on the stovetop. I had no trouble finding plenty of recipes for skillet-roasted vegetables. The trouble began when I tried making them.

Many recipes cooked carrots in combination with other root vegetables such as parsnips, rutabaga, and turnips in oil over medium or high heat, covered, to simulate oven-roasting; these produced scorched exteriors and underdone centers. (Vegetables cooked this way over low heat never caramelized.) Other recipes first steamed the vegetables and then sautéed them in fat for color, but the tender vegetables fell apart when I tried to brown them at the end. Skillet in hand, I was determined to get oven-roasted results on the stovetop.

My first step was to whittle down my vegetable choices. I landed on carrots and parsnips for three reasons: Their similar shape made them easier to prep; they cook at about the same rate; and most important, their flavors work great together. I knew that I'd have to cook these vegetables in fat to caramelize them, so I tested butter

and oil side by side. The butter burned badly, even when used in conjunction with some oil.

Returning to just vegetable oil, I browned the carrots and parsnips and then turned down the heat and covered the pan so they could cook through. This gave me evenly browned, tender vegetables, but they were dry and wrinkled by the time they were tender. To rectify the moisture loss, I added ¾ cup of water to the pan before covering, which created a gentle steaming effect. I had achieved my goal of nicely browned, tender vegetables, but their flavor was a little flat.

Some recipes add sugar to enhance the natural sweetness of the vegetables, but adding sugar during the sautéing made a scorched mess of the pan. I had better results by dissolving just 1½ teaspoons of granulated sugar (and a teaspoon of salt) in the water before adding it to the pan. A few turns of the pepper mill and a sprinkle of fresh parsley rounded out the flavors.

My simple stovetop method made it easy to introduce new flavors to carrots and parsnips. I developed a variation using apple cider, maple syrup, and rosemary; another based on orange juice, honey, and thyme; and a final version featuring cilantro and lime.

–Kelley Baker

SKILLET-ROASTED CARROTS AND PARSNIPS
SERVES 6 TO 8

Parsnips wider than 1 inch may have tough, fibrous cores that are best trimmed and discarded. Using warm water helps the sugar to dissolve more readily. Any combination of carrots and parsnips with a combined weight of 3 pounds can be used in this recipe.

- 3 tablespoons vegetable oil
- 1½ pounds carrots, peeled and cut diagonally into ½-inch-thick pieces
- 1½ pounds parsnips, peeled and cut diagonally into ½-inch-thick pieces
- ¾ cup warm water
- 1½ teaspoons sugar
  Salt and pepper
- 1 tablespoon finely chopped fresh parsley

1. Heat oil in large skillet over medium-high heat until shimmering. Cook carrots and parsnips, stirring occasionally, until golden brown, 12 to 14 minutes.

2. Whisk water, sugar, and 1 teaspoon salt in small bowl until sugar dissolves. Add water mixture to skillet and cook covered, stirring occasionally, over medium-low heat until vegetables are tender and liquid has evaporated, 12 to 14 minutes. Stir in parsley and season with salt and pepper. Serve.

MAPLE-ROSEMARY SKILLET-ROASTED CARROTS AND PARSNIPS

In step 2, substitute ¾ cup apple cider for water, 1 tablespoon maple syrup for sugar, and ½ teaspoon minced fresh rosemary for parsley.

HONEY-ORANGE SKILLET-ROASTED CARROTS AND PARSNIPS

In step 2, substitute ¾ cup orange juice for water, 1 tablespoon honey for sugar, and ½ teaspoon minced fresh thyme, fresh rosemary, or fresh tarragon for parsley.

CILANTRO-LIME SKILLET-ROASTED CARROTS AND PARSNIPS

In step 2, add 1 tablespoon lime juice to water mixture. Substitute 1½ teaspoons brown sugar for the sugar, 1 tablespoon finely chopped fresh cilantro for the parsley, and ⅛ teaspoon cayenne pepper for the pepper.

Test Kitchen Technique
CUTTING TAPERED PARSNIPS

1. After cutting each parsnip in half to create thin and bulbous pieces, cut the thin piece diagonally into ½-inch pieces.

2. Quarter the bulbous part lengthwise and then diagonally cut each quarter into ½-inch pieces.

Make-Ahead Green Bean Casserole

Making this freezer-to-oven casserole with raw beans is the key to fresh flavor and texture.

Pulling a green bean casserole from the freezer sounds great around the holidays, but not if the beans are spent and the sauce is watery.

Out of desperation, I prepared a casserole using raw beans and was amazed that they came out perfectly, with a nice green color and surprisingly firm texture (not to mention brighter flavor). The long oven time required to defrost and bake the casserole gave the raw beans enough time to cook through.

But the beans were still giving up too much liquid to the sauce, which was unpalatably watery. If I couldn't prevent the beans from expelling liquid, maybe I could find something to thicken it. I tried tossing the beans with flour, but that made the casserole too pasty. Tapioca worked OK, but I had to take the extra step of pureeing the pearls in order to fully coat the beans. Cornstarch was the best option here; tossing my two pounds of beans with ¼ cup of cornstarch (before adding the sauce) thickened the liquid shed by the beans and produced a perfect sauce. I now had a green bean casserole that could be made weeks in advance and still taste like it had been made an hour before the big holiday meal.

–Meredith Butcher

MAKE-AHEAD GREEN BEAN CASSEROLE
SERVES 10 TO 12
The topping and casserole can be frozen separately for up to 2 months.

Topping
- 2 slices hearty white sandwich bread, torn into pieces
- 2 tablespoons unsalted butter, melted
- ¼ teaspoon salt
- 2 cups canned fried onions

Casserole
- 3 tablespoons unsalted butter
- 10 ounces white mushrooms, sliced thin
- 1 teaspoon salt
- ½ teaspoon pepper
- 6 garlic cloves, minced
- ½ teaspoon dried thyme
- ¼ cup all-purpose flour
- ½ cup white wine
- 1½ cups low-sodium chicken broth
- 1½ cups heavy cream
- 2 pounds green beans, trimmed and cut into 1-inch pieces
- ¼ cup cornstarch

1. For the topping: Pulse bread, butter, and salt in food processor until coarsely ground. Combine bread mixture and onions in bowl, transfer to zipper-lock freezer bag, and freeze.

2. For the casserole: Melt butter in large skillet over medium heat. Add mushrooms, salt, and pepper and cook until mushrooms release their liquid, about 5 minutes. Increase heat to medium-high and cook until liquid has evaporated, about 5 minutes. Add garlic and thyme and cook until fragrant, about 30 seconds. Stir in flour and cook until golden, about 1 minute. Slowly whisk in wine, broth, and cream and bring to boil. Reduce heat to medium and simmer, stirring occasionally, until sauce is thickened, about 10 minutes.

3. Following photo at left, toss green beans with cornstarch in large bowl and transfer to 13- by 9-inch baking dish. Pour warm mushroom mixture evenly over beans. Let cool completely, wrap with plastic, cover with foil, and freeze.

4. To serve: Adjust oven rack to middle position and heat oven to 400 degrees. Remove plastic from baking dish and replace foil. Bake until sauce is bubbling and beans are tender, about 80 minutes, stirring beans thoroughly after 50 minutes. Remove foil and spread topping mixture over beans. Bake until golden brown, about 8 minutes. Serve.

Secret Ingredient
CORNSTARCH

The raw beans in our casserole throw off a lot of liquid when thawed and baked, which adversely affects the texture of the sauce. Tossing the beans with cornstarch before assembling and freezing the casserole helps absorb the excess liquid, leaving the sauce thick and silky.

I am a big fan of green bean casserole, but with the pressure of cooking the roast, making the gravy, mashing the potatoes, and all the other preparations for a holiday dinner, having one side dish ready to go would make life much easier. But you can't just freeze and bake a regular green bean casserole: I tried it with several recipes, including the "back of the can" version, and all were bland (the freezer notoriously dulls flavor) and watery (the freezing and thawing breaks down the beans, causing them to purge liquid into the sauce). Recipes touted as "freezer-to-oven" were no different, and just as bad.

Starting over with the test kitchen's recipe for dressed-up green bean casserole, I sautéed mushrooms in melted butter, added some garlic, and then flour to thicken the sauce. Into the pan went 1½ cups each of chicken broth and cream, which are simmered for 10 minutes to reduce. I poured this mixture over blanched green beans and topped the casserole with our combination of canned fried onions and buttery bread crumbs (canned onions are too greasy on their own). After a few days in the freezer, even this version baked up lacking flavor, with spent beans and a watery sauce.

To boost the flavor of the casserole so it could stand up to freezing and baking, I doubled the amount of garlic and added white wine and fragrant thyme to the sauce. Correcting the texture of the beans and sauce was not so easy. Tackling the beans first, I wondered if the blanching was contributing to their dull color and bland flavor. I tried roasting, sautéing, steaming, and even microwaving the beans, but nothing helped.

Easy Crescent Rolls

Most recipes for crescent rolls require a lot of tedious kitchen work to layer butter into the dough before baking. Is there an easier way to make rich, buttery rolls?

Most recipes for buttery, flaky crescent rolls require repeated rolling and folding to layer softened butter into the dough. But there is an easier, faster version of crescent rolls that simply stirs melted butter together with milk, eggs, flour, sugar, yeast, and salt. The dough is briefly kneaded, allowed to rise (or proof), then rolled, cut, and shaped into rolls and proofed again before baking. The resulting rolls (sometimes called butter horn rolls) are softer and less flaky than traditional crescents, but just as rich and buttery.

Most recipes for easy crescent rolls slather extra butter on the dough before it's rolled into shape; this butter not only adds flavor but helps to prevent the rolled layers from fusing in the oven, making the rolls pull-apart tender. But the ideal easy crescent roll is elusive, and I've sampled my fair share of tough, bland versions. I was determined to create light, tender rolls that were packed with plenty of buttery goodness.

I started by taking a look at the two main ingredients: flour and butter. As I expected, recipes calling for high-protein bread flour yielded squat, tough rolls. All-purpose flour is a must for tender rolls. To make 12 decent-sized rolls, I needed 2½ cups of flour. On average, most recipes called for about 4 tablespoons of melted butter, which simply wasn't enough. I tried doubling the amount to a full stick (8 tablespoons), which gave me great butter flavor but rolls that were sticky and too soft. Using softened butter (instead of melted) resulted in rolls that were too tough and required extra mixing to fully incorporate the butter. After dozens of tests, I determined that I could use 7 tablespoons of melted butter.

Continuing along the path of enhanced richness, I tried replacing the milk in the recipe with heavy cream, but with so much fat, the cream made the rolls dense and muted the butter flavor. Half-and-half was a perfect compromise for extra-tender rolls with big buttery flavor. A generous ¼ cup of sugar added flavor and promoted tenderness in the rolls.

After the dough had proofed once and was rolled into a circle, it was time for the final smear of butter (both softened and melted butter work, but softened requires less effort) before cutting and shaping. In a second attempt to boost butter flavor, I increased the usual tablespoon here to 2, but the excess butter just oozed out of the sides of the rolls in the oven. Rather than increase the amount of butter, I found I could augment butter flavor just by sprinkling on a little salt. This seems like a minor detail, but it made a difference my tasters could easily detect.

To finish the rolls, I found that a simple wash of egg white and water brushed on just before baking gave my rolls the lustrous sheen I was after. These rich, tender, and buttery crescent rolls are so easy, you'll be putting them on the table every week.

–Kelley Baker

EASY CRESCENT ROLLS
MAKES 12 ROLLS

A pizza cutter makes quick work of cutting the dough into wedges (see box below); alternately, you can use a chef's knife or metal scraper.

- 7 tablespoons unsalted butter, melted and cooled slightly, plus 1 tablespoon unsalted butter, softened
- ½ cup half-and-half, heated to 110 degrees
- 1 teaspoon rapid-rise or instant yeast
- ¼ cup sugar
- 2 large eggs, 1 whole and 1 separated
- 2½ cups all-purpose flour
- 1¼ teaspoons salt
- 1 teaspoon water

1. Adjust oven rack to middle position and heat oven to 200 degrees. When oven reaches 200 degrees, shut oven off. Line baking sheet with parchment paper. Grease large bowl.

2. Whisk melted butter, half-and-half, yeast, and 1 teaspoon sugar in large liquid measuring cup until yeast dissolves, then whisk in 1 whole egg and 1 egg yolk. In bowl of standing mixer fitted with dough hook, mix flour, remaining sugar, and 1 teaspoon salt until combined. With mixer on low, add warm half-and-half mixture in steady stream and mix until dough comes together, about 1 minute. Increase speed to medium and mix until dough is smooth and comes away from sides of bowl, about 6 minutes. Turn dough out onto clean surface and knead to form smooth, round ball. Transfer dough to prepared bowl, cover with plastic, and place in warm oven. Let rise until doubled in size, about 1 hour.

3. Turn dough out onto lightly floured surface and roll into 12-inch circle. Spread softened butter over dough, sprinkle with remaining salt, and, following photos 1 and 2 at right, cut dough into 12 wedges, roll each wedge, and arrange (with pointed tip of dough underneath each roll) on prepared baking sheet. Cover loosely with plastic wrap and return to oven until doubled in size, about 1 hour. (At this point, rolls can be refrigerated for up to 24 hours.)

4. Remove rolls from oven and discard plastic wrap; heat oven to 350 degrees. Whisk remaining egg white and water in small bowl. Brush each roll twice with egg white mixture and bake until golden brown, about 20 minutes, rotating baking sheet halfway through cooking. Cool rolls on baking sheet 10 minutes. Serve. (Once completely cool, rolls can be stored in airtight container at room temperature for 2 days.)

How to SHAPE CRESCENT ROLLS

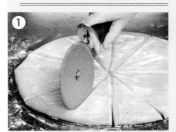

1. Using a sharp knife or a pizza cutter, cut the circle of dough into 12 wedges. The outside edge of each wedge should measure about 3 inches.

2. Starting with the wide end of each wedge, gently roll each piece into a horn shape. Space the rolls 2 inches apart with the pointed tip securely underneath the rolls.

I'm Looking for a Recipe

READERS HELP READERS FIND RECIPES

We've Got Mail

Dozens of readers sent us recipes in response to the request for Raisin Pie in our June/July 2008 issue. We really liked the recipe sent by Dorothy Trickey (right). Go to **CooksCountry.com** and click **Looking for a Recipe** to find hundreds of recipes submitted by readers who responded to other recipe requests in previous issues of *Cook's Country*.

RAISIN PIE   Dorothy Trickey   Cincinnati, Ohio

SERVES 8

"My mother always won praise—and cooking-contest ribbons—for her raisin pie. I still remember fighting with my six siblings, especially my sister Patty, over the last piece after Sunday dinners." Go to CooksCountry.com for our Double-Crust Pie Dough recipe or use one 15-ounce box of Pillsbury Just Unroll! Pie Crust. You will need one 15-ounce box of raisins for this recipe.

½	cup milk
2	tablespoons cornstarch
3	cups raisins (see note)
½	cup plus 1 tablespoon sugar
1	cup water
4	tablespoons unsalted butter
1	double-crust pie dough (see note)
1	large egg white, lightly beaten

1. Adjust oven rack to lowest position and heat oven to 350 degrees.

2. Whisk milk and cornstarch in measuring cup. Bring raisins, ½ cup sugar, and water to boil in large saucepan over medium-high heat. Remove from heat and whisk in milk mixture and butter. Pour into unbaked 9-inch pie shell. Brush edges of dough with egg white and top with remaining dough round. Seal and crimp edges. Brush top of dough with egg white and sprinkle with remaining sugar. Using paring knife, cut four vents in top of dough.

3. Bake until golden, 45 to 55 minutes. Cool on wire rack for at least 1 hour. Serve. (Pie can be wrapped in plastic and refrigerated for 2 days.)

Jelly-Filled Molasses Cookies

My favorite treat while growing up in the 1950s came in a shoe box from my grandmother. She sent me her molasses cookies for all special occasions—birthdays, confirmation, holidays, etc. The cookies were chewy and had a dollop of jelly in the center. I am now a grandmother myself and would love to find the recipe so I can share it with my grandson.

Kelley Sanderson
Cascade, Colo.

Stuffed Grape Leaves

When I was growing up, one of my mother's friends, who was of Egyptian descent, used to make the most amazing stuffed grape leaves. They were vegetarian and had a perfect balance of spices. I think about these grape leaves all the time and would love to make them. Does anyone have a great vegetarian recipe?

Maureen Lennox
Portland, Ore.

Plum Dumplings

My grandmother, who was of German-Czech-Austrian-Jewish heritage, made these dumplings at the end of the summer when small, football-shaped "prune plums" were available in New York. She wrapped them individually in dough, boiled them, and baked them with a sprinkle of sugar, cinnamon, and perhaps nutmeg. They were also served with a dollop of butter that melted on the hot blanket of dough. The dumplings were never brown and crunchy, but rather tender and just cooked through. Does anyone have a recipe?

J. Granger
Via e-mail

Fried Lunch Cake

My grandmother used to make what she called lunch cake. It was a fried sweet dough that was coated with a variety of fruit-flavored icings. Neither my mother nor my aunts have the recipe, and although they have all tried to duplicate it, no one has had success. If I know my grandmother, I would guess that there was lard in the recipe, but that has not been confirmed.

Donald R. Daily Sr.
Via e-mail

Woolworth's Cheesecake

Years ago, my husband and I used to visit the cafeteria in the old Woolworth's in Minneapolis. My husband is not usually a fan of cheesecake, but he loved the one they served because it was exceptionally light and fluffy. Is there any way to find that recipe?

Cheryl Sanocki
Maple Grove, Minn.

Williamsburg Yeast Rolls

At one time I had a recipe for rolls called Williamsburg Buns. They were very simple to make, mixed in one bowl, and not kneaded. Not to mention they were delicious! I'd really appreciate locating a recipe so I could make them again.

Janice Jones
Via e-mail

Sour Cream Cookies

I'm looking for a recipe for sour cream cookies like my grandmother used to make back in the 1960s. They were round, cakelike cookies with slightly domed chocolate- or lemon-iced tops. If anyone has a recipe, I'd love to try it.

W. Grindstaff
Columbus, Ohio

Easter Bread

When I was a child, one of my uncles, who was always traveling the world, would bring interesting recipes to test out on us. They were always delicious, but a recipe for what he called Easter bread stands out in my memory. I remember it was slightly sweet and was baked in an empty coffee can. We've been out of contact with my uncle for approximately 40 years now, but I remember his eclectic, yet kind, manner and the wonderful recipes he made in our home. If someone has a recipe that is similar to this, please let me know so that I may share it with my family.

Nancy Mossburg
Kingsland, Ga.

Catfish King's Tomato Dressing

Many years ago, there was a restaurant in the Birmingham, Alabama, area called Catfish King. They had the most delicious tomato-based salad dressing and I have never been able to duplicate it. Does anyone know someone who worked there and knows how to make this dressing?

Dale-Denise Blackston
Via e-mail

Raisin-Iced Chocolate Cake

When I was a child, my grandmother used to make a moist, layered devil's food cake with raisin icing for Thanksgiving and Christmas. Being the picky eater that I was, I would never try it, but as an adult it sounds wonderful. Of course now I can't find a recipe that is even similar! I remember watching her cook the raisin mixture on the stovetop, stirring it patiently until it reached the proper consistency. After it cooled a bit, she put the icing between the layers and around the outside. Everything my grandmother did was from memory so after she died we had nothing to help us replicate her wonderful recipes. I would love to surprise my mother with this cake on her birthday.

Joyce Leonard
Leeds, Ala.

Pickled Apples

As a little girl growing up in Romania, I had the most delicious pickled apples that were made in big wooden barrels. Even though it was a very long time ago, I can still taste them, but no one I ask seems to be familiar with such a recipe. If you could find one, I would really appreciate it.

Penny Hassan
Via e-mail

Grand Marnier Sweet Potato Casserole

About 30 years ago, I found a recipe in a magazine that covered sliced oranges and sweet potatoes with a concoction of orange juice, butter, and Grand Marnier liqueur. My family loved this recipe, but it did not make it to our new home when we moved. I hope that someone out there has the same recipe!

Joan Paal-Fridley
Big Lake, Alaska

Are you looking for a special recipe? Or do you have a recipe a fellow *Cook's Country* reader is seeking? Post your requests and recipes by visiting **CooksCountry.com** and clicking on **Looking for a Recipe.** We'll share recipe requests and found recipes on CooksCountry.com and print as many as we can in the magazine. You may also write to us at Looking for a Recipe, Cook's Country, P.O. Box 470739, Brookline, MA 02447.

Find the Rooster!

A tiny version of this rooster has been hidden somewhere in the pages of this issue. If you find it, write to us with its location (plus your name and address) and you will be entered into a random drawing. The first correct entry drawn will receive an OXO Good Grips i-Series Can Opener (our test winner—see page 29), and the next five will each receive a complimentary one-year subscription to *Cook's Country*. To enter the contest, visit **CooksCountry.com/emailus** or write to us at Rooster, Cook's Country, P.O. Box 470739, Brookline, MA 02447. Entries are due by November 30, 2008.

Did you find the rooster in the June/July 2008 issue? It was hidden in the Clams Casino Sauce photo on page 5. Patrice Adderton of Raleigh, N.C., spotted it and won an Anolon Advanced Double Burner Griddle.

30-Minute Supper

QUICK BEEF AND BEAN CHILI

30-Minute Supper

MAPLE-ORANGE GLAZED CHICKEN

30-Minute Supper

SKILLET BARBECUED PORK CHOPS

30-Minute Supper

BAKED GNOCCHI WITH TOMATO AND BASIL

MAPLE-ORANGE GLAZED CHICKEN SERVES 4

Be sure to use 100 percent pure maple syrup, not pancake syrup, for this recipe. Take care when simmering the glaze in step 3, as the skillet handle will be hot.

- ½ cup maple syrup
- 2 teaspoons Dijon mustard
- 1 teaspoon grated orange zest
- 1 tablespoon white vinegar
- 1 teaspoon minced fresh thyme
- 4 bone-in, skin-on chicken breasts (about 3 pounds), halved crosswise
  Salt and pepper
- 1 tablespoon vegetable oil

1. Adjust oven rack to middle position and heat oven to 475 degrees. Whisk maple syrup, mustard, zest, vinegar, and thyme in bowl. Pat chicken dry with paper towels and season with salt and pepper.

2. Heat oil in large ovensafe skillet over medium-high heat until just smoking. Cook chicken, skin-side down, until well browned, about 5 minutes. Turn chicken skin-side up and transfer skillet to oven. Cook until chicken is deep golden brown and cooked through, about 15 minutes. Transfer chicken to plate and tent with foil.

3. Wearing oven mitt (pan handle will be very hot), pour off any fat in skillet. Add maple mixture to empty pan and cook over medium heat, scraping up any browned bits with wooden spoon, until thick and syrupy, about 3 minutes. Season with salt and pepper. Off heat, return chicken to skillet and turn until well coated with glaze. Serve.

QUICK BEEF AND BEAN CHILI SERVES 4 TO 6

Serve with pickled jalapeños, shredded cheese, sour cream, and diced avocado.

- 2 (16-ounce) cans kidney beans, drained and rinsed
- 2 (14.5-ounce) cans diced tomatoes
- 1½ pounds 85 percent lean ground beef
- 1 onion, chopped fine
- 4 garlic cloves, minced
- 3 tablespoons chili powder
- 2 teaspoons ground cumin
- 2 teaspoons sugar
- ¼ cup chopped fresh cilantro
  Salt and pepper

1. Process half of beans and half of tomatoes in food processor to coarse paste; set aside. Cook beef and onion in Dutch oven over medium heat until meat is no longer pink, about 5 minutes. Stir in garlic, chili powder, cumin, and sugar and cook until fragrant, about 1 minute. Stir in pureed bean-tomato mixture and remaining beans and tomatoes.

2. Bring chili to boil, then reduce heat to low, and simmer, covered and stirring occasionally, until thickened, about 15 minutes. Off heat, stir in cilantro and season with salt and pepper. Serve.

BAKED GNOCCHI WITH TOMATO AND BASIL SERVES 4

The partially cooked, vacuum-packed gnocchi found in the pasta aisle work best here, but refrigerated or frozen gnocchi can also be used. If you do not have an ovensafe skillet, in step 3 transfer the gnocchi to a casserole dish before baking.

- 3 tablespoons extra-virgin olive oil
- 1 pound vacuum-packed gnocchi (see note)
- 1 onion, chopped fine
- 6 garlic cloves, minced
- ⅛ teaspoon red pepper flakes
- 1 (28-ounce) can crushed tomatoes
- 1 cup water
- ½ cup chopped fresh basil
- 2 cups shredded mozzarella cheese

1. Adjust oven rack to upper-middle position and heat oven to 475 degrees. Heat 2 tablespoons oil in large ovensafe nonstick skillet over medium-high heat until shimmering. Cook gnocchi, stirring occasionally, until lightly browned, about 4 minutes; transfer to plate.

2. Add remaining oil and onion to empty skillet and cook until onion is softened, about 3 minutes. Stir in garlic and pepper flakes and cook until fragrant, about 30 seconds. Stir in tomatoes and water and cook until slightly thickened, about 5 minutes.

3. Add basil and browned gnocchi to pan. Reduce heat to low and simmer, stirring occasionally, until gnocchi is tender, 5 to 7 minutes. Sprinkle with mozzarella and bake until cheese is well browned, about 8 minutes. Serve.

SKILLET BARBECUED PORK CHOPS SERVES 4

Bull's-Eye brand barbecue sauce is the test kitchen favorite. To prevent the chops from curling as they cook, cut 2 slits about two inches apart through the fat and connective tissue on 1 side of each chop.

- ¾ cup barbecue sauce
- 2 tablespoons cider vinegar
- 3 tablespoons brown sugar
- 1 tablespoon paprika
- ½ teaspoon ground cumin
- ½ teaspoon salt
- ½ teaspoon pepper
- ¼ teaspoon cayenne pepper
- 4 bone-in rib or center-cut pork chops, ¾ to 1 inch thick (see note)
- 1 tablespoon vegetable oil

1. Whisk barbecue sauce and vinegar in small bowl. Combine sugar, paprika, cumin, salt, pepper, and cayenne in separate bowl. Whisk 1 teaspoon spice mixture into barbecue sauce mixture.

2. Pat chops dry with paper towels and rub all over with remaining spice mixture. Heat oil in large nonstick skillet over medium-high heat until just smoking. Cook chops until well browned, about 4 minutes per side.

3. Reduce heat to medium-low. Brush chops with barbecue sauce mixture, flip, and cook until sauce is caramelized, about 1 minute. Brush once more with sauce, flip, and cook until second side is caramelized and meat registers 145 degrees, about 1 minute longer. Serve, passing remaining sauce at table.

FILET MIGNON WITH PEPPERCORN CREAM

CHICKEN PROVENÇAL

RISOTTO WITH CHICKEN, LEMON, AND BASIL

BROILED SALMON WITH POTATO CRUST

CHICKEN PROVENÇAL SERVES 4

Zest the orange before peeling and segmenting it. See page 31 for more information about segmenting oranges.

- 4 boneless, skinless chicken breasts (about 1½ pounds)
  Salt and pepper
- 2 tablespoons olive oil
- 10 ounces cremini or white mushrooms, quartered
- 1 shallot, halved and sliced thin
- ½ cup white wine
- 1 teaspoon grated zest plus segmented fruit from 1 orange (see note)
- 2 tablespoons unsalted butter
- ¼ cup pitted kalamata olives, chopped rough
- 1 teaspoon minced fresh rosemary

1. Pat chicken dry with paper towels and season with salt and pepper. Heat 1 tablespoon oil in large skillet over medium-high heat until just smoking. Cook chicken until golden brown, about 4 minutes per side. Transfer to plate.

2. Add remaining oil, mushrooms, and shallot to empty skillet and cook over medium heat until lightly browned, about 3 minutes. Add wine and simmer, scraping up any browned bits with wooden spoon, until slightly thickened, about 3 minutes. Add orange zest and browned chicken, along with any accumulated juices, and simmer, covered, until chicken is cooked through, 2 to 4 minutes; transfer chicken to serving platter.

3. Off heat, whisk butter into pan, then stir in orange segments, olives, and rosemary. Season sauce with salt and pepper and pour over chicken. Serve.

FILET MIGNON WITH PEPPERCORN CREAM SERVES 4

To ensure even cooking, choose center-cut tenderloin steaks of a consistent size and shape and avoid pieces from the tapered end of the tenderloin.

- 4 center-cut tenderloin steaks, about 1 inch thick
  Salt
- 4 teaspoons coarsely ground pepper
- 2 tablespoons vegetable oil
- 1 shallot, minced
- ¾ cup white wine
- ½ cup low-sodium chicken broth
- ½ cup heavy cream
- 1 tablespoon chopped fresh tarragon

1. Pat steaks dry with paper towels and season with salt. Rub top and bottom of steaks evenly with 3 teaspoons pepper. Heat 1 tablespoon oil in large skillet over medium-high heat until just smoking. Cook steaks until well browned and meat registers 125 degrees for medium-rare, 3 to 5 minutes per side. Transfer to serving platter and tent with foil.

2. Add remaining oil and shallot to empty skillet and cook over medium heat until softened, about 2 minutes. Stir in wine, broth, and cream and simmer, scraping up any browned bits with wooden spoon, until slightly thickened, about 5 minutes. Off heat, whisk in tarragon, remaining pepper, and any accumulated steak juices. Season with salt. Pour sauce over steaks. Serve.

BROILED SALMON WITH POTATO CRUST SERVES 4

Lay's Kettle Cooked Original potato chips are the test kitchen favorite, but any brand of kettle-cooked chips will work. Watch the fish as it cooks in step 2; the potato crust can burn in just seconds.

- 4 skin-on salmon fillets (each 6 to 8 ounces and 1¼ inches thick)
- 1 tablespoon olive oil
  Salt and pepper
- 2½ cups kettle-cooked potato chips (see note)
- 1 slice hearty white sandwich bread, torn into pieces
- 2 tablespoons chopped fresh dill
- 1 teaspoon grated lemon zest
- 2 tablespoons Dijon mustard

1. Adjust oven racks to upper-middle and lower-middle positions and heat broiler. Line rimmed baking sheet with aluminum foil. Pat fish dry with paper towels, rub all over with oil, and season with salt and pepper. Arrange salmon, skin-side down, on prepared baking sheet and broil on upper-middle rack until fish is lightly browned and edges flake when gently pressed, about 8 minutes.

2. Pulse chips, bread, dill, and lemon zest in food processor until coarsely ground. Remove salmon from oven and brush evenly with mustard. Sprinkle chip mixture evenly over fillets, pressing gently to adhere. Transfer salmon to lower-middle rack and broil until crust is golden brown and crisp, about 2 minutes. Serve.

RISOTTO WITH CHICKEN, LEMON, AND BASIL SERVES 4

If the finished risotto is too thick, stir in hot water, a few tablespoons at a time, to adjust the consistency.

- 1 cup Arborio rice
- 4 cups low-sodium chicken broth
- 6 tablespoons unsalted butter
- 1 onion, chopped fine
- 2 garlic cloves, minced
- 1 rotisserie chicken, skin discarded, meat shredded into bite-sized pieces (about 3 cups)
- ½ cup chopped fresh basil
- 2 teaspoons grated zest and 2 tablespoons juice from 1 lemon
- 1 cup grated Parmesan cheese, plus extra for serving
  Salt and pepper

1. Combine rice, 3 cups broth, and 2 tablespoons butter in large bowl. Wrap tightly with plastic wrap and microwave until rice is softened and most of liquid is absorbed, 10 to 16 minutes.

2. Meanwhile, melt additional 2 tablespoons butter in medium saucepan over medium heat. Stir in onion and cook until softened, about 3 minutes. Stir in garlic and cook until fragrant, about 30 seconds. Stir in hot rice mixture and remaining broth and simmer, stirring constantly, until rice is tender, 5 to 7 minutes. Stir in chicken and cook until heated through, about 1 minute.

3. Off heat, stir in basil, lemon zest, lemon juice, Parmesan, and remaining butter. Season with salt and pepper. Serve, passing additional Parmesan at table.

Chicken à la King

An elaborate dish once served in the finest restaurants, chicken à la king has been simplified into a bland, pasty sauce for rubbery chicken. Could we capture the essence of the old version in a streamlined weeknight recipe?

Leave the canned soup in the pantry—our simplified recipe uses fresh cream and canned broth to create a creamy, flavorful base.

Chicken à la king was created for kings, or, more correctly, for the Kings—Mr. and Mrs. Clark King, the owners of the Brighton Beach Hotel in Brooklyn, New York, sometime around the turn of the century (or so the story goes). The chef at the restaurant there tossed cubes of poached chicken in a rich, Madeira-laced cream sauce studded with mushrooms and bell peppers and served it over toast points. The cream sauce was flour-based and finished with egg yolks for the ultimate silky texture.

Recipes similar to the original have fallen out of favor because they're labor-intensive and the fussy yolks can easily scramble with overheating. Modern recipes attempt to shortcut the cream sauce by using convenience items (like canned soup or, even worse, cream cheese) that produce stodgy, bland sauces masking chicken that has been boiled to oblivion. My goal was to restore this dish to its original status as a sophisticated meal—without the fuss.

Starting with the sauce, I sautéed a chopped onion in oil, added the mushrooms and red pepper, then stirred in flour to make a roux before adding the cream and egg yolks. Hoping to eliminate the finicky egg yolks, I was relieved that my tasters preferred the lighter, cleaner version made without them. In fact, my tasters wanted me to cut back on the fat even more, so I replaced some of the cream with chicken broth. Along with the Madeira, a little parsley and lemon juice rounded out the flavors of the sauce.

Old recipes for chicken à la king ensured tenderness by using meat from a whole poached chicken. Almost every modern recipe, however, calls for poaching cubes of boneless, skinless breasts in water or broth. My tasters found the plain poached chicken bland. Dark meat thighs tasted better, but looked wrong in the white sauce. Simmering the raw cubes directly in the sauce solved the flavor problem, but the small pieces were prone to overcooking and drying out.

We often marinate chicken to keep it moist and tender, but oil-based marinades made the sauce greasy. Since I was already adding cream and lemon juice to the sauce, I decided to combine them with a little salt to mimic the buttermilk marinade we use for fried chicken. The salt acted as a brine and helped keep the breast meat moist, while the cream and lemon juice added flavor. And now I could just add the chicken and marinade to the pan all at once. Slightly overreducing the sauce before adding the chicken mixture ensured that the finished sauce was the proper consistency. I knew this dish was once again fit for a (Mr. or Mrs.) King.

–Lynn Clark

CHICKEN À LA KING
SERVES 4

An equal amount of brandy or dry Marsala can be substituted for the Madeira. For more information on Madeira, see page 30.

- ¾ cup heavy cream
- 2 tablespoons lemon juice
  Salt
- 4 boneless, skinless chicken breasts (about 1½ pounds), cut into 1-inch pieces
- 1 tablespoon vegetable oil
- 1 onion, chopped fine
- 8 ounces white mushrooms, sliced thin
- 1 red bell pepper, seeded and chopped fine
- ¼ teaspoon pepper
- 3 tablespoons all-purpose flour
- ½ cup Madeira wine (see note)
- 1½ cups low-sodium chicken broth
- 2 tablespoons finely chopped fresh parsley
- 8 slices Italian bread, buttered and toasted (see box below)

1. Whisk ½ cup cream, 1 tablespoon lemon juice, and 1 teaspoon salt in bowl. Combine chicken and cream mixture in large zipper-lock bag; refrigerate 30 minutes.

2. Heat oil in large skillet over medium-high heat until shimmering. Cook onion until golden, about 3 minutes. Add mushrooms, bell pepper, ¼ teaspoon salt, and pepper and cook until vegetables have softened, about 5 minutes. Stir in flour and cook 1 minute. Add Madeira, scraping up any browned bits with wooden spoon, and cook until thickened, about 1 minute. Add broth and remaining cream and cook until sauce is very thick and spatula leaves trail when dragged through sauce, about 5 minutes.

3. Stir in chicken mixture and reduce heat to medium-low. Simmer, stirring frequently, until chicken is no longer pink, about 10 minutes. Off heat, stir in remaining lemon juice and parsley. Serve with toasted bread.

Marinade for Tender Chicken

Our streamlined recipe marinates boneless, skinless chicken breasts in unlikely ingredients to achieve tender texture and rich flavor.

HEAVY CREAM
Rich heavy cream serves as the liquid base for both the marinade and sauce.

LEMON JUICE
Fresh lemon juice adds brightness.

SALT
The salt transforms the marinade into a brine, which ensures deeply seasoned, juicy meat.

Toast of the Town

Chicken à la king is typically served over toast. But what type of bread is best? After trying baguettes (too tough), sandwich bread (too mushy), and even puff pastry (too delicate), we found the perfect match with supermarket Italian bread, whose soft texture toasted up into a crunchy, but still fork-friendly, slice. Here's how to do it:

1. Adjust oven rack to middle position and heat oven to 400 degrees. Arrange eight 1-inch-thick slices of Italian bread on baking sheet. Brush 2 tablespoons of melted butter over both sides of bread slices.

2. Toast bread until golden brown, about 10 minutes, flipping slices halfway through cooking. Spoon chicken à la king over toast and serve.

Cider-Braised Pork Chops

Apple flavor can be fleeting. So what's the secret to infusing pork chops with deep, rich cider flavor?

Using 1-inch-thick pork chops allows for more braising time, which results in richer-flavored meat and sauce.

Pan-fried pork chops are a weeknight staple, but they can't hold a candle to fall-off-the-bone-tender, slow-braised chops. Cider is a classic choice for the braising liquid, but this pairing isn't always successful. Many of the cider-braised pork chop recipes I've tried produce watery sauces, washed-out apple flavor, and chewy meat. These problem recipes skimp on time—an essential ingredient for braised meats to become truly tender.

My first goal was to find the right chops, so I tested bone-in blade, loin, and rib chops of varying thickness. For these tests, I simply seared the chops in oil, covered them with cider, and braised them, covered, in a 300-degree oven until tender. (Most cooks keep braises on the stovetop, but in the test kitchen we prefer the all-around heat of the oven, which ensures even cooking and eliminates the risk of scorching the bottom of the pot.) At each thickness, well-marbled blade chops were preferred to the leaner loin and rib chops for their tender texture and meaty flavor. Thin blade chops buckled; my tasters much preferred 1-inch blade chops for their heft, silky meat, and rich flavor. It took a little longer for these chops to become tender, but the wait was well worth it.

Now I had to determine how to infuse these big chops with big flavor. After searing the chops and removing them from the pan, I sautéed onions and garlic in the drippings and oil left behind. Since cider alone didn't seem to be providing enough apple flavor, I added chopped apples to the pan as well as a little thyme for a heady herbal component. At the end of cooking, the sauce was still watery (these big chops shed a lot of liquid) and bland. Worse, the sauce was studded with chunks of grainy apples and stringy onions.

The apples weren't adding much, so I lost them, and a quick strain of the sauce rid it of the lifeless pieces of onion. Stirring in flour with the onion and garlic worked to thicken the sauce a bit, but too much flour made it pasty. Still searching for a way to boost cider flavor, I recalled apple season back home in upstate New York. Mom would spend autumn afternoons cooking down bushels of apples, along with cider and spices, into homemade apple butter. With nothing to lose, I tried adding jarred apple butter during cooking to infuse the braising liquid with the flavor.

As I had hoped, the apple butter added tons of flavor, and its natural pectin gave my sauce a thick, glossy consistency. With a finishing splash of cider vinegar to brighten the apple flavor, these tender, meaty chops were finally deeply infused with the sweet richness of cider. **–Kelley Baker**

CIDER-BRAISED PORK CHOPS SERVES 6

Do not use chops thinner than 1 inch. In step 3, a fat separator makes quick work of defatting the sauce.

- 6 **bone-in blade-cut pork chops, about 1 inch thick**
   Salt and pepper
- 2 **tablespoons vegetable oil**
- 1 **onion, chopped**
- 3 **garlic cloves, minced**
- 2 **tablespoons all-purpose flour**
- ¼ **cup apple butter**
- 1 **cup apple cider**
- 1 **sprig fresh thyme**
- 1 **teaspoon cider vinegar**
- 1 **tablespoon finely chopped fresh parsley**

1. Adjust oven rack to lower-middle position and heat oven to 300 degrees. Pat chops dry with paper towels and season with salt and pepper. Heat oil in large Dutch oven over medium-high heat until just smoking. Brown chops in two batches, about 4 minutes per side; transfer to plate.

2. Pour off all but 1 tablespoon fat from pot and cook onion over medium heat until softened, about 5 minutes. Stir in garlic, flour, and 2 tablespoons apple butter and cook until onions are coated and mixture is fragrant, about 1 minute. Stir in cider and thyme, scraping up any browned bits with wooden spoon, and bring to boil. Add browned chops and any accumulated juices to pot, cover, and transfer to oven. Braise until chops are completely tender, about 1½ hours.

3. Transfer chops to serving platter. Strain sauce, then use a shallow spoon to skim off fat. Whisk in vinegar, parsley, and remaining apple butter. Season with salt and pepper. Serve, passing sauce at table.

Make Ahead: Chops and sauce can be refrigerated separately for up to 2 days. To serve, heat sauce and chops together over medium heat until chops are warmed through.

---

3 Keys to Better Apple Flavor

Cider alone won't provide much apple flavor. To pack the taste of apples into our pork chops, we settled on a triple helping of apple products.

APPLE BUTTER
Apple butter provides intense apple and warm spice flavor. It also helps thicken the sauce.

CIDER VINEGAR
Finishing with a splash of cider vinegar adds brightness and complexity to the sauce.

CIDER
Sweet-tart cider provides most of the liquid for the braising mixture and sauce.

Garlic Mashed Potatoes

Infusing mashed potatoes with the flavor of roasted garlic is easy—if you have an extra hour to roast a head of garlic. Is there a faster way?

Regular mashed potatoes are great, but flavor them with sweet, nutty-tasting roasted garlic and you might make me forget the entrée is even on the plate. But mashed potatoes with roasted garlic do not have the makings of a quick side dish. First you have to roast a head of garlic for an hour and wait for it to cool so you can squeeze the garlic out of its skins, and then you have to puree the roasted garlic—all before making the mashed potatoes. I wanted to find a faster, easier way to infuse mashed potatoes with the addictive flavor of roasted garlic.

For fluffy mashed potatoes, the test kitchen has determined that russet potatoes (a high-starch spud) mashed with butter and half-and-half are best. As for "quick" roasted garlic substitutes, I tested recipes that called for pan-roasting unpeeled cloves and microwaving peeled cloves in oil. The pan-roasted garlic took almost as long as actual roasting and required much more attention. The cloves quickly microwaved in oil had pleasantly mellow garlic flavor. But when pureed and added to my mashed potatoes, the microwaved garlic and the boiled potatoes tasted like separate elements—you could taste that they hadn't been cooked together. Minced garlic sautéed in butter and added to the cooked potatoes had the same problem.

If the garlic and potatoes needed to be cooked together to integrate their flavors, I needed to re-examine my cooking method. The test kitchen has a recipe for mashed sweet potatoes where the cut potatoes aren't cooked in a big pot of boiling water; instead they're simmered, covered, on the stovetop with butter and a small amount of cream. This technique avoids the "washing away" of flavor that can come from boiling. I decided to give it a shot.

I began by mincing 12 cloves of garlic and sautéing them in plenty of butter to mellow their bite. Sprinkling in just a teaspoon of sugar helped to mimic the sweet flavor of roasted garlic. I cut the potatoes in small pieces to allow more surface area to soak up garlic flavor and promote even cooking and then tossed them in the pot to coat them with the garlic butter. My tests revealed that I needed about 1¼ cups of liquid to prevent the potatoes from scorching. Using only half-and-half muted the garlic flavor, so I replaced some of it with water.

After 25 minutes of occasional stirring, the potatoes were perfectly tender and infused with plenty of garlic flavor. I mashed them right in the pot, adding more butter and half-and-half to give the mash a smoother consistency, and they tasted great, but they were a bit on the gluey side.

The problem was the russets' excess starch, which is usually rinsed away by traditional boiling. The fix was a matter of giving the raw, cut russets a good rinse under running water before adding them to the pot. This quick recipe for roasted-garlic mashed potatoes is so easy and satisfying, you may never go back to the old method again. –Diane Unger

GARLIC MASHED POTATOES SERVES 8 TO 10

Cutting the potatoes into ½-inch pieces ensures that maximum surface area is exposed to soak up garlicky flavor.

- 4 pounds russet potatoes, peeled, quartered, and cut into ½-inch pieces
- 12 tablespoons (1½ sticks) unsalted butter, cut into pieces
- 12 garlic cloves, minced
- 1 teaspoon sugar
- 1½ cups half-and-half
- ½ cup water
  Salt and pepper

1. Place cut potatoes in colander. Rinse under cold running water until water runs clear. Drain thoroughly.

2. Melt 4 tablespoons butter in Dutch oven over medium heat. Cook garlic and sugar, stirring often, until sticky and straw colored, 3 to 4 minutes. Add rinsed potatoes, 1¼ cups half-and-half, water, and 1 teaspoon salt to pot and stir to combine. Bring to boil, then reduce heat to low and simmer, covered and stirring occasionally, until potatoes are tender and most of the liquid is absorbed, 25 to 30 minutes.

3. Off heat, add remaining butter to pot and mash with potato masher until smooth. Using rubber spatula, fold in remaining half-and-half until liquid is absorbed and potatoes are creamy. Season with salt and pepper. Serve.

Cooking the potatoes in cream and garlic infuses the flavors deep into the potatoes.

Secrets to GREAT ROASTED GARLIC FLAVOR

1. Cook the minced garlic (and a little sugar) in butter until the garlic is sticky and straw-colored; this blooms the garlic's sweet flavor and tempers its harshness.
2. For deeply integrated garlic flavor, toss the raw potatoes with the garlic-butter mixture, add the half-and-half and water directly to the pot, cover, and gently cook until tender.

Gadgets & Gear: Potato Mashers

Flimsy or poorly designed potato mashers can make an easy task overly arduous. Our favorite potato masher, the WMF Profi Plus 11¼-inch Masher (about $20), features sturdy construction and an oval mashing disk that produces soft and silky spuds with a minimum of effort.

TOP MASHER
WMF Profi Plus Potato Masher

Roasted Butternut Squash Soup

What's the best way to make a soup with sweet, caramelized roasted butternut squash?

Cutting up a whole squash may seem intimidating, but if you follow these simple steps, it's actually quite easy.

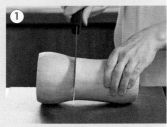

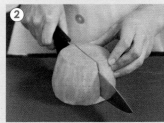

1. After removing the stem and root end, cut the squash in half crosswise where the thinner neck meets the thicker base.
2. Use a vegetable peeler or paring knife to peel the skin from the squash, then cut the base in half to expose the seeds.
3. Use a large spoon to scrape the seeds and stringy pulp from the base of the squash. Chop each piece of squash as desired.

We eat a lot of sweet, nutty, roasted butternut squash at my house, and the leftovers usually end up pureed with broth and cream in my soup pot. This makeshift soup is satisfying, but it could use some improving—the flavor of the soup is thin and underdeveloped. Determined to create a superior roasted butternut squash soup, I gathered a handful of recipes and was disappointed that they were no better than my improvised leftover version.

Not only were these recipes mediocre, but none could agree on how to best prepare the squash for roasting; some simply halved a whole squash, others peeled and halved it, while still others peeled and cubed the flesh before roasting it with a little oil. I tried roasting squash prepared each way at 425 degrees (to promote caramelization and quick cooking) and vastly preferred the peeled, cubed squash, which cooked faster than the large halves and developed more flavorful browning. Boosting the oven temperature to 450 degrees guaranteed consistently good caramelization as well as thorough cooking.

While the squash chunks roasted, I started the soup base on the stovetop by adding chicken broth to sautéed onions—I was happy to be saving time by cooking both the squash and the broth at the same time. But then it occurred to me that I might be able to cook both elements not only at the same time, but in the same roasting pan in the oven. I started by tossing chopped onion with the oil and squash. Once the vegetables had browned, I added a little broth to deglaze the roasting pan and

popped it back in the oven so the broth could reduce and concentrate in flavor. I then pureed the soup in a blender, and only when I was ready to serve the soup did I turn on the stove, add the cream, and heat everything through.

The silky texture and deep flavor of the soup won approval from my tasters, but they also noticed a sharp onion flavor that stole a little thunder from the main ingredient. A switch to shallot, which has a sweeter, milder flavor than onion, fixed this problem. I finished the soup with a pinch of nutmeg (a classic squash seasoning), a tablespoon of maple syrup to draw out even more of the squash's sweetness, and a little apple cider vinegar to brighten everything up. Now I had an easy version of roasted butternut squash soup that was so good, I'm going to have to find another way to use up my leftover squash. **–Kelley Baker**

ROASTED BUTTERNUT SQUASH SOUP SERVES 4

Because the bulbous end of butternut squash contains the seeds and stringy fibers, purchase squash with a relatively long neck—they have more usable flesh. You can replace the chicken broth with vegetable broth for a vegetarian version of this soup.

1	medium butternut squash (about 3 pounds), peeled, seeded, and cut into 1½-inch chunks (see photos at left)
3	medium shallots, peeled and quartered
¼	cup vegetable oil
	Salt and pepper
4	cups low-sodium chicken broth (see note)
1	tablespoon maple syrup
1	teaspoon cider vinegar
⅛	teaspoon ground nutmeg
¼	cup heavy cream

This satisfying soup is finished on the stovetop, but the flavor is built in the oven.

1. Adjust oven rack to middle position and heat oven to 450 degrees. Toss squash, shallots, oil, 1 teaspoon salt, and ½ teaspoon pepper in large bowl, then arrange in single layer in large roasting pan. Roast, stirring occasionally, until vegetables are golden brown and softened, about 45 minutes. Add ½ cup broth to pan and scrape up any browned bits with wooden spoon. Return to oven and cook until liquid has reduced and vegetables are glazed, about 5 minutes.

2. Working in 2 batches, puree squash mixture and remaining broth in blender until smooth. Transfer pureed squash mixture to large saucepan and stir in syrup, vinegar, nutmeg, and cream. Bring soup to simmer over medium-low heat, adding ¼ cup water at a time as necessary to adjust consistency. Serve.

(Soup can be refrigerated in airtight container for 3 days.)

CURRIED BUTTERNUT SQUASH AND APPLE SOUP

In step 1, substitute 1½ pounds Golden Delicious apples, peeled, cored, and chopped, for half of squash. In step 2, omit vinegar and substitute ½ teaspoon curry powder for nutmeg.

SOUTHWESTERN BUTTERNUT SQUASH SOUP

In step 2, substitute 1 tablespoon honey for maple syrup, 1 teaspoon lime juice for vinegar, and ½ teaspoon ground cumin for nutmeg. Just prior to serving, stir in 2 tablespoons finely chopped fresh cilantro and 1 tablespoon minced canned chipotle chiles in adobo sauce. Serve with dollop of sour cream, if desired.

Getting to Know Nuts

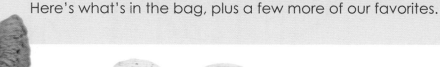

With the holiday season comes the ubiquitous bag of mixed nuts. Here's what's in the bag, plus a few more of our favorites.

Peanut
SOUTHERN LEGUME

Peanuts are not nuts but rather legumes that grow underground. Though typically sold roasted (either in the shell or shelled), fresh peanuts are a popular treat in the South, where they are boiled until tender, salted, and eaten out of hand. In the test kitchen, we sprinkle shelled, dry-roasted peanuts over stir-fries and salads or use a food processor to finely grind them for cookies.

Brazil Nut
AMAZONIAN COCONUT

Brazil nuts are neither nuts (botanically, they are seeds) nor from Brazil (most are cultivated in Bolivia). Their texture and flavor are "eerily similar to coconut" with a "musty," "vanilla-y" finish. These high-fat nuts become rancid very quickly and should be stored in the refrigerator or freezer. To make quick work of shelling Brazil nuts, boil them in their shell for 3 minutes, then let them cool to room temperature before cracking.

Almond
PEACHY KEEN

Almonds are closely related to stone fruit, which is why the shells look so much like peach pits. We like shelled whole nuts for eating out of hand, but because the teardrop shape makes them difficult to prep, we prefer sliced and slivered almonds for cooking. Thin-sliced almonds are best in cookies or cakes, salads, and pilafs, while the substantial crunch of slivered almonds works well sprinkled over stir-fries and ice cream sundaes.

Marcona Almond
SPANISH QUEEN

Also called the "Queen of Almonds," these flat, stubby (and expensive) almonds grow primarily on the Mediterranean coast of Spain. They are prized for their rich flavor and smooth texture. The "milky sweet" flavor and "complex floral aroma" of Marcona almonds are best enjoyed simply—they are traditionally fried in olive oil, salted, and eaten out of hand. Look for these almonds at gourmet markets and health food stores.

Cashew
AVOID THE SHELL

Cashew nuts grow at the base of the cashew apple; although the fruit is edible, the shell of the cashew nut is toxic (the reason they are almost always sold shelled). Whenever possible, purchase whole cashews rather than cashew "halves" or "halves and pieces," which tend to be of lower quality. When cooking with cashews, toast the nuts to enhance their flavor and crunchy texture.

Pistachio
STICK WITH GREEN

Most pistachios sold in the U.S. are cultivated in California. These mottled purple and green nuts are concealed in very hard, hinged shells. Though most often eaten out of hand, their "crunchy" texture and "fruity, citrus-y" flavor also work well in both savory and sweet dishes. Look for pistachios that are partially open—a sign that the nut is fully mature (they're also easier to shell). Avoid red pistachios, which are dyed.

Hazelnut
LOSE THE SKIN

Also called filberts or cobnuts, these sweet, heart-shaped nuts have a "soft crunch" and a "sweet-smoky" flavor. The easiest way to remove the bitter skins is to toast the nuts in a 350-degree oven for 10 to 15 minutes until fragrant. When the nuts are cool enough to handle, place them in a clean kitchen towel and rub the nuts back and forth to loosen and remove the skins.

Macadamia Nut
TOUGH TO CRACK

The macadamia tree is native to Australia. Because their shells are so strong, harvesting the nuts is an arduous—and expensive—process. Macadamia nuts have a "crunchy-chalky" texture and a "meaty," "slightly bitter" flavor. Once opened, the nuts should be refrigerated or frozen to prevent rancidity.

Pecan
SOUTHERN NUT

A member of the hickory family, pecans are native to the south-central U.S. Pecans have relatively thin shells, making them easy to crack and eat out of hand. Their nut meat is "soft, slightly oily," and "maple-y sweet" with a "pleasantly bitter" balance. With a fat content of roughly 70 percent, shelled pecans spoil easily; they should be frozen until ready to use. To check whole nuts for freshness, give them a shake. If the nut rattles in the shell, they are not fresh and should be discarded.

Pine Nut
WHEATY AND WAXY

Also called piñons (Spanish) or pignoli (Italian), these diminutive nuts are harvested from pine cones. There are two main types of pine nuts: the delicately flavored, torpedo-shaped Mediterranean pine nuts and the more assertive corn kernel–shaped Chinese pine nuts (pictured). The less-expensive Chinese variety is more widely available, but both can be used interchangeably. Pine nuts have a "mild, wheaty" taste and a "slightly waxy" texture.

Chestnut
TREE POTATO

Fresh chestnuts are available in the fall and winter, but vacuum-sealed jars of shelled chestnuts can be purchased throughout the year (though they pale in comparison to the fresh nuts). When roasted, chestnuts become "fluffy and starchy" and take on a "sweet, potato-y" flavor. To prepare fresh chestnuts, slice across the equator of the shell (without cutting into the nutmeat), roast at 425 degrees for 30 minutes, let cool, and then peel away the shell and papery skin.

Walnut
BIG AND BITTER

Although the wrinkled shells of these nuts are so hard that they are used as an industrial abrasive, a distinct seam that runs the perimeter of the shell makes them fairly easy to crack. There are two main varieties of walnuts: English (or Persian) and black. The English (pictured) is more common in the U.S. Walnuts have a "crunchy, slightly oily" texture and an "earthy bitterness" with a strong "tannic" aftertaste.

One of the keys to keeping cabbage rolls intact is to roll them as tightly as possible—which can be a challenge with tough, fibrous cabbage leaves. Here's how we solved the problem:

1. Remove the thick rib from the base of the cabbage leaves by cutting along both sides of the rib to form a narrow triangle. Continue cutting up the center about 1 inch above the triangle.
2. Overlap the cut ends of the cabbage to prevent any filling from spilling out.
3. Place 2 tablespoons of the filling ½ inch from the bottom of the leaf where the cut ends overlap. Fold the bottom of the leaf over the filling and fold in the sides. Roll the leaf tightly around the filling to create a tidy roll.

Bratwurst Blast

Cabbage rolls stuffed with the traditional filling of ground beef and rice were bland, so we lost the rice and supplemented the beef with bratwurst. Not only did this German-style pork and veal–based sausage add flavor (it's seasoned with ginger, nutmeg, and caraway seeds), but it also kept the filling tender and moist.

GERMAN ENGINEERING
Equal amounts of beef and bratwurst boosted the flavor of our filling.

Stuffed Cabbage Rolls

When my great-grandmother made stuffed cabbage, it was a sublime dish of savory ground meat, spices, rice, and tomato sauce. But when I make it, the filling is tough and bland, and the cabbage is mush. Can I make tender stuffed cabbage that tastes good and stays intact?

–Trish Rego, Red Lion, Pa.

My own grandmother always said her recipe for stuffed cabbage required some patsying, or "playing around," because it was so fussy—but it was well worth the trouble. She would boil a head of cabbage and wrap the softened leaves around a filling of seasoned ground meat and white rice, then simmer the rolls in a smooth tomato sauce flavored with warm spices, sugar, and vinegar. But after hours of testing recipes, I was left with pots of blown-out rolls filled with chewy, flavorless meat and bland rice swimming in a sugary sauce. This wasn't the dish I remembered.

I started with the easiest fix: the tomatoes. Crushed tomatoes were too watery, and diced tomatoes were distractingly chunky. Tasters liked the smooth texture of tomato puree, but it was too thick and pasty. Canned tomato sauce had the same smooth texture and was thin enough to properly coat the rolls without becoming pasty. Sautéed onions and garlic provided a savory foundation, and ground ginger, cinnamon, and nutmeg provided the requisite warm spice flavor to the sauce. Brown sugar was preferred to white for its more complex flavor, and red wine vinegar was chosen

Gently cooking the stuffed rolls in the oven (instead of on the stovetop) reduces the risk of "roll blowout."

over white for its bite.

Tasters found the traditional filling of ground beef and white rice bland and tough. Since I was already sautéing onions and garlic for the sauce, I upped the amount and added some to the filling for more flavor. In search of more meaty flavor, I tried adding Italian sausage, but the Italian seasonings were off-putting here. Kielbasa was too smoky, but bratwurst, a mild German sausage, boosted the meaty flavor perfectly. My tasters had never been fans of the rice in the filling—they found it distracting and bland. Since the rice's main function is as filler, I decided to omit it.

In its place, I added a panade of milk and bread to help keep the filling soft and moist. A quick whirl in the food processor ensured that the filling was evenly combined.

Cooking the stuffed rolls on the stovetop, even over low heat, caused the cabbage to blow apart. Instead I tried cooking them in the oven; this allowed the rolls to cook more evenly and gently, thus keeping them intact. But the cabbage itself was still a little mushy. I had been precooking the cabbage in the traditional way by blanching the head in boiling water and peeling off the hot leaves with tongs. But the inner

leaves were overcooked and soggy by the time they were released. Freezing the head of cabbage, which softened the leaves and allowed them to peel off one at a time, required a day of advance planning. Instead I turned to the microwave. After a quick turn (in a bowl covered with plastic wrap), all of the leaves were easily removed from the cabbage head and, best of all, were soft enough for filling and rolling—and not waterlogged at all.

To be sure, these aren't the cabbage rolls my grandmother made, but I'd like to think they might even be better.

–Lynn Clark

STUFFED CABBAGE ROLLS SERVES 6

If the tops of the cabbage rolls appear dry after the foil is removed in step 4, spoon some of the sauce over them before returning to the oven.

- 1 medium head green cabbage, cored
- 1 tablespoon vegetable oil
- 1 onion, chopped fine
- 3 garlic cloves, minced
- 1 teaspoon ground ginger
- ½ teaspoon ground cinnamon
- ¼ teaspoon ground nutmeg
- 1 (28-ounce) can tomato sauce
- ¼ cup packed light brown sugar
- 3 tablespoons red wine vinegar
  Salt and pepper
- 2 slices hearty white sandwich bread, torn into pieces
- ½ cup milk
- ¾ pound 85 percent lean ground beef
- ¾ pound uncooked bratwurst, casings removed

1. Adjust oven rack to middle position and heat oven to 375 degrees. Place cabbage in large bowl, wrap tightly with plastic, and microwave until outer leaves of cabbage are pliable and translucent, 3 to 6 minutes. Using tongs, carefully remove wilted outer leaves; set aside. Replace plastic and repeat until you have 15 to 17 large, intact leaves.

2. Heat oil in Dutch oven over medium-high heat until shimmering. Cook onion until golden, about 5 minutes. Add garlic, ginger, cinnamon, and nutmeg and cook until fragrant, about 30 seconds. Transfer half of onion mixture to small bowl and reserve. Off heat, stir tomato sauce, sugar, vinegar, ½ teaspoon salt, and ¼ teaspoon pepper into pot with remaining onion mixture until sugar dissolves.

3. Pulse bread and milk in food processor to smooth paste. Add reserved onion mixture, beef, bratwurst, ½ teaspoon salt, and ¼ teaspoon pepper and pulse until well combined, about ten 1-second pulses.

4. Following photos 1 to 3 on page 22, trim tough ribs from cabbage leaves, roll 2 heaping tablespoons of meat mixture into each leaf, and arrange rolls, seam-side down, in 13- by 9-inch baking dish. Pour sauce over cabbage rolls, cover with foil, and bake until sauce is bubbling and rolls are heated through, about 45 minutes. Remove foil and bake, uncovered, until sauce is slightly thickened and cabbage is tender, about 15 minutes. Serve.

Make Ahead: In step 4, after spooning meat into cabbage and arranging rolls, wrap dish with plastic and refrigerate for 1 day. Wrap and refrigerate sauce separately. Proceed with recipe as directed.

Microwave Magic

Removing leaves from a tightly packed head of cabbage is no easy feat. The most common method is to float the whole head in a vat of boiling water—a messy, cumbersome project with mixed results at best. We found the microwave a much better tool. Microwaving makes the cabbage leaves soft and pliable, not soggy and overcooked. To prepare the cabbage, cut out the core, place the head in a large, microwave-safe bowl, cover with plastic, and cook on high power until the leaves become pliable and can be easily removed.

MICROWAVE, DON'T BOIL
Microwaving the cored head of cabbage wilts the outer leaves, allowing them to be easily removed.

On the Side:

Herbed Rice Pilaf

What is the best method to get a light and fluffy—not gummy—pilaf with big herb flavor?

Rice pilaf begins by toasting long-grain rice in butter or oil to develop a rich, nutty flavor. Liquid is then added, the pot is covered, and the rice is cooked over low heat until tender. This technique lends itself to additional flavorings—typically aromatics, spices, and herbs—that can be sautéed with the rice at the beginning or stirred into cooked rice just before serving. My goal was to develop a foolproof recipe for perfectly cooked rice pilaf that was deeply flavored with fragrant herbs.

Over the years, we've found that most pilaf recipes call for too much liquid and the result is soggy, bland rice. Rather than the standard ratio of two parts water to one part rice, the test kitchen has found that 2¼ cups of water and 1½ cups of rice produce a perfect pilaf with fluffy grains.

I found that sautéing the rice in a little butter added more flavor than oil, and replacing water with chicken broth predictably made the pilaf taste more savory. Finally, I followed the lead of many classic recipes, sautéing a small chopped onion and then several garlic cloves in the butter before adding the broth.

Most recipes for herb pilaf simply toss in a handful of fresh herbs just before serving, but I wanted deep, layered herb flavor. Adding an aromatic bay leaf with the garlic provided a nice base of herb flavor. I added parsley, rosemary, sage, and thyme (alone and in combination) to the pot at various stages, and my tasters were unanimous in preferring the potent simplicity of a teaspoon of fresh thyme quickly sautéed with the garlic and bay leaf, and a handful of chopped fresh parsley mixed in just before serving. With toasted sliced almonds added for crunch, this pilaf has the perfect balance of flavors and textures.
–**Cali Rich**

HERBED RICE PILAF
SERVES 4 TO 6

If you don't have fresh thyme on hand, ½ teaspoon dried thyme can be substituted.

- 3 tablespoons unsalted butter
- 1 small onion, chopped fine
  Salt
- 1½ cups long-grain rice
- 2 garlic cloves, minced
- 1 teaspoon minced fresh thyme (see note)
- 1 bay leaf
- 2¼ cups low-sodium chicken broth
- ½ cup sliced almonds, toasted
- ¼ cup chopped fresh parsley

1. Melt butter in large saucepan over medium-high heat. Cook onion and ½ teaspoon salt until just softened, about 3 minutes. Add rice and cook, stirring frequently, until edges begin to turn translucent, about 2 minutes. Add garlic, thyme, and bay leaf and cook, stirring constantly, until fragrant, about 30 seconds.

2. Stir in broth and bring to boil. Cover, reduce heat to low, and cook until liquid is absorbed and rice is tender, about 20 minutes. Remove from heat and let stand, covered, for 10 minutes. Discard bay leaf and fluff rice with fork. Stir in almonds and parsley. Season with salt. Serve. (Rice can be refrigerated in an airtight container for 1 day.)

Skillet Supper:

Chicken Vesuvio

Could we make this Chicago restaurant classic at home and, better yet, in one skillet?

Stop anyone on the streets of Chicago and ask them where to find the best chicken Vesuvio and you'll be hit with a long list. Harry Caray's Italian Steakhouse is probably the most well known, serving bone-in chicken and potato wedges smothered in a garlicky white wine sauce and garnished with peas. Typically, this dish requires multiple pots and pans and trips back and forth to the oven. Could I develop a recipe for chicken Vesuvio that stays true to its Italian-American roots but restricts the work to just one skillet on the stovetop?

Classic chicken Vesuvio starts by browning chicken parts in a hot skillet. The browned chicken parts are set aside and the potato wedges are browned in the rendered chicken fat. The potatoes come out of the pan and it's time to build the sauce. Garlic is sautéed, oregano is added next, and the pan is deglazed with white wine. This mixture is combined with the browned chicken and potatoes in a roasting pan, and the whole thing bakes until cooked through. The sauce is then poured off and further reduced on the stovetop before being ladled over individual servings of chicken and potatoes.

Streamlining this dish meant starting with boneless, skinless chicken breasts. Bone-in, skin-on chicken parts were difficult to cook through on the stovetop without being covered with the skillet lid, which turned the skin flabby and defeated the whole reason for using skin-on parts. To get the most flavor from lean boneless breasts, I made sure to brown the breasts well (adding some oil to help the process along) before

removing them from the skillet.

Getting good browning on the potatoes was also important to flavor development. But I couldn't just grab any potato, as fluffy russets broke apart in the skillet. Yukon Gold potatoes were a little firmer, but waxy baby red potatoes were the best choice, as they held their shape and texture through cooking. And while Chicago recipes cut the potatoes into wedges, these small potatoes worked better halved and browned on the cut side, and then removed from the pan while I built the sauce.

To stay true to this dish's Italian-American roots, I needed plenty of garlic, oregano, and white wine. For more assertive flavor, I added a teaspoon of potent fresh rosemary, and to augment the chicken flavor I added chicken broth to the pan. A good knob of butter and a squeeze of fresh lemon juice brought all the flavors together.

My skillet Vesuvio was almost there, but my tasters thought the potatoes were a little bland. By leaving the potatoes in the pan while I made the sauce, I got them to absorb much more flavor (and it was less work than removing them and adding them back later). This Chicago restaurant favorite was now easy enough to prepare on a weeknight—and the kitchen didn't require an army of dishwashers.

–Meredith Butcher

SKILLET CHICKEN VESUVIO SERVES 4

If you cannot find baby red potatoes, substitute larger red potatoes that have been quartered. For a spicier Vesuvio, stir in ¼ teaspoon red pepper flakes with the garlic in step 2.

The Right Potato

Fluffy, starchy russet potato wedges are the traditional choice for Vesuvio, but we found that they became mushy and broke apart in the skillet. Halved baby red potatoes held their shape much better.

BAD POTATO
Starchy russets broke down in this recipe.

GOOD POTATO
Waxy baby red potatoes held their shape through browning and braising.

Traditional Vesuvio features braised bone-in chicken parts, but boneless breasts make more sense for our streamlined, quick-cooking skillet recipe.

4 boneless, skinless chicken breasts (about 1½ pounds)
   Salt and pepper
2 tablespoons olive oil
1½ pounds baby red potatoes, scrubbed and halved
2 garlic cloves, minced
1 teaspoon minced fresh rosemary
½ teaspoon dried oregano
½ cup white wine
1½ cups low-sodium chicken broth
1 cup frozen peas, thawed
2 tablespoons unsalted butter
2 teaspoons lemon juice

1. Pat chicken dry with paper towels and season with salt and pepper. Heat 1 tablespoon oil in large nonstick skillet over medium-high heat until just smoking. Cook chicken until golden, about 3 minutes per side. Transfer to plate.

2. Add remaining oil to pan and heat until shimmering. Cook potatoes, cut-side down, until golden brown, about 7 minutes. Stir in garlic, rosemary, oregano, and ½ teaspoon salt and cook until fragrant, about 30 seconds. Add wine and broth, scraping up any browned bits with wooden spoon, and bring to boil. Return browned chicken to skillet on top of potatoes. Reduce heat to medium-low and simmer, covered, until chicken is cooked through and potatoes are tender, about 12 minutes. Using slotted spoon, transfer chicken and potatoes to serving platter; tent with foil.

3. Increase heat to medium-high and cook, uncovered, until sauce is reduced to 1 cup, about 5 minutes. Stir in peas and cook until heated through, about 1 minute. Off heat, whisk in butter and lemon juice and season with salt and pepper. Pour sauce over chicken and potatoes. Serve.

Steak Pizzaiola

Don't be confused by the "pizza" in its name—this bold, saucy steak dish is definitely not pizza parlor fare.

As legend has it, Italian pizza makers used to slow-simmer cheap cuts of beef in their extra pizza sauce to create a hearty, satisfying lunch. Once their customers got a look and demanded some, the dish known as steak pizzaiola was born. Italian-American restaurants have modernized this recipe by ladling slow-simmered marinara sauce enriched with sautéed onions, peppers, and mushrooms over tender seared steaks. I liked the speed of searing in this latter method, so my goal was to create a quick sauce with the same complexity as a long-cooked marinara in the time it took to cook the steaks.

For maximum flavor, I wanted to build the sauce from the brown bits (called fond) left in the pan from searing the steaks. I seared the steaks for three to five minutes per side, then removed them to a plate (tented with foil) while I started the sauce in the unwashed pan. I sautéed chopped onion, green pepper, and white mushrooms before adding a splash of red wine to deglaze the fond. When the wine had reduced, I poured in a can of crushed tomatoes. After 10 minutes of cooking, the sauce reduced to the right consistency but lacked the long-simmered flavor I was after.

A favorite tomato sauce in the test kitchen calls for draining a can of diced tomatoes and caramelizing the tomato chunks before adding the juice. In my recipe, I found that just three minutes in a hot pan deepened the flavor of the drained diced tomatoes. Two keys to long-simmered flavor were replacing the button mushrooms with earthier creminis, and using smoky roasted red peppers instead of the bell peppers. Swapping out the wine for balsamic vinegar as the deglazing liquid added another dimension of richness, and plenty of garlic and oregano helped to round out the sauce.

I was getting close but wanted to add even more depth to my quick sauce. I tried adding tomato paste, but with such a short cooking time it tasted raw and bitter. Searching for another tomato product to lend depth to the sauce, it occurred to me to try chopped sun-dried tomatoes. Just a tablespoon lent bright, complex flavor. Off heat, a sprinkle of fresh basil contributed a welcome freshness.

Although the sauce was ready in just 20 minutes, the steaks were no longer hot by the time they got to the table. Holding the seared steaks in a 200-degree oven only dried them out. Instead, I found that if I seared the steaks more quickly (just three minutes per side), I could then finish them in a 350-degree oven while I prepared the sauce. This potent combination of tomatoes, onions, mushrooms, and peppers truly tasted long-cooked and was a perfect complement to the steaks. **–Lynn Clark**

STEAK PIZZAIOLA

SERVES 4

To cook 4 steaks simultaneously you will need a skillet that is at least 12 inches in diameter and steaks that are no more than 3 inches wide. If your steaks are too large to fit comfortably in the skillet, they can be browned in 2 batches.

- 4 strip steaks, about 1 inch thick (see note)
  Salt and pepper
- 2 tablespoons vegetable oil
- 8 ounces cremini mushrooms, quartered
- 1 onion, chopped fine
- 3 garlic cloves, minced
- ½ teaspoon dried oregano
- 1 tablespoon sun-dried tomatoes packed in oil, rinsed, patted dry, and minced
- ¼ cup balsamic vinegar
- 1 (14.5-ounce) can diced tomatoes, drained, juices reserved
- 1 cup drained jarred roasted red peppers, chopped
- 2 tablespoons chopped fresh basil

1. Adjust oven rack to middle position and heat oven to 350 degrees. Pat steaks dry with paper towels and season with salt and pepper. Heat 1 tablespoon oil in large skillet over medium-high heat just until smoking. Brown steaks, about 3 minutes per side, then transfer to wire rack set inside rimmed baking sheet. Roast steaks until meat registers 125 degrees (for medium-rare), about 10 minutes. Transfer steaks to serving platter, tent with foil, and let rest while preparing sauce.

2. While steaks are in oven, add mushrooms, onion, ¼ teaspoon salt, and remaining oil to empty pan and cook until softened, about 8 minutes. Add garlic, oregano, and sun-dried tomatoes and cook until fragrant, about 30 seconds. Add vinegar and cook, scraping up any browned bits with wooden spoon, until thick and syrupy, about 1 minute. Transfer mushroom mixture to bowl; set aside.

3. Add drained diced tomatoes to empty pan and cook until deep red and dry, about 3 minutes. Stir in roasted peppers, reserved tomato juices, and mushroom mixture. Reduce heat to medium-low and simmer until sauce is no longer watery, about 5 minutes. Off heat, stir in basil and season with salt and pepper. Spoon sauce over steaks. Serve.

To ensure perfectly cooked steaks, use an instant-read thermometer to gauge their temperature rather than relying solely on the recommended cooking time.

Roasted Red Pepper Tasting

To determine which brand of jarred roasted red peppers was best, we rounded up eight nationally available brands and tasted them plain and in a simple roasted red pepper soup. Peppers that were packed with flavorful ingredients like garlic, herbs, and vinegar tasted good plain, but those flavors weren't always appreciated in the soup. In the end, our tasters' favorite roasted red peppers was Dunbars Sweet Roasted Peppers ($2.19 for 12 ounces), which lists only red bell peppers, water, salt, and citric acid in its ingredient list. These peppers were great on their own, and their sweet, earthy, unmarred essence made for terrific soup.

OUR FAVORITE ROASTED RED PEPPERS
Dunbars Sweet Roasted Peppers

Big Flavor in a Little Package

Sweet, tangy sun-dried tomatoes add depth and another layer of tomato flavor to our sauce for Steak Pizzaiola.

SUN-DRIED TOMATOES
Concentrated tomato flavor

Easiest Apple Pie

Homemade apple pie can take several hours to prepare. Can this crustless apple pie—which involves no fussy rolling of dough—give new meaning to the phrase "easy as pie"?

How to ASSEMBLE EASY APPLE PIE

With no sticky dough to roll out, Easy Apple Pie lives up to its name.

1. Sprinkle half of the bread crumbs into the bottom of a buttered springform pan. Then tip the pan on its side and evenly press the remaining crumbs halfway up the sides, turning the pan as you go.

2. Gently arrange the apples in the prepared pan, taking care to not press down too heavily. (You want the batter to seep between the apple slices.) Make sure the apples go all the way to the edge of the pan.

3. Slowly and evenly pour the batter over the apples.

Anyone who has ever made an apple pie from scratch knows there's nothing easy about it. Dough rips as you roll it, perfect rounds are nearly impossible to achieve, and the edging rarely resembles anything pictured in cookbooks. That's why I was so intrigued when I came across a no-crust apple pie at a bake sale at my son's school. The texture was unlike any pie I'd ever had—a hybrid of light cake and dense pie, with an apple-studded filling that crisped on the top and bottom to resemble the crusts of a traditional pie. The woman working the bake sale told me I "wouldn't believe how easy it was to make," and I was determined to put her claim to the test.

My research turned up several different styles of crustless apple pies (which are sometimes called Swedish apple pies), but recipes for the custard-y version I'd sampled all worked the same way. Melted butter was combined with flour, sugar, eggs, and cinnamon and then poured over thinly sliced apples before baking in a 350-degree oven. I tried several recipes and the pies tasted pretty good, but they were disappointingly soggy, with no crisping of either the top or bottom crusts.

Working from the bottom up, I turned to an ingredient we often use to build structure and crispness: bread crumbs. I toasted fresh bread crumbs in butter until they were golden brown (¾ cup was all I needed), buttered my pie plate, and coated the plate with a thin layer of crumbs. I then filled the plate with apples as usual and poured in my working batter. This gave me a well-defined bottom crust, but the interior of the pie was still soggy.

To thicken the batter, I increased the amount of flour and added baking powder to give it some lift. Just two tablespoons of sour cream added a welcome tang to the batter. But there was another issue with the filling: The apples weren't cooking through in the time it took the batter to set up. To solve the problem, I reduced the oven temperature to 325 degrees and cooked the pie longer to allow the apples to gently soften as the batter set. The test kitchen has found that a mixture of tart and sweet apples makes for a nicely balanced pie filling. Tasters like a combination of tart Granny Smiths, which have the added advantage of retaining their texture and shape through baking, and sweet Braeburn apples (Golden Delicious and Gala also work well).

Up to this point, I'd been making my pie in a deep-dish pie plate, but occasionally the batter would spill over the edge and make a mess in the oven. Also, the pie plate made it difficult to serve without wrecking the thin bottom crust of bread crumbs. Switching to a deeper springform pan solved both issues. I might still break out the rolling pin to make a traditional apple pie for the holidays, but this easy apple pie is my new go-to weeknight dessert.

–Diane Unger

EASY APPLE PIE
SERVES 8

To make the bread crumbs, grind 1 slice of hearty white sandwich bread in a food processor to fine crumbs. In step 3, be sure that the melted butter is still slightly warm when whisked into the dry ingredients. Golden Delicious or Gala apples can be substituted for the Braeburn.

- 2 tablespoons unsalted butter plus 8 tablespoons (1 stick) unsalted butter, melted
- ¾ cup finely ground fresh bread crumbs (see note)
- 3 Granny Smith apples, peeled, cored, quartered, and cut crosswise into thin slices
- 2 Braeburn apples (see note), peeled, cored, quartered, and cut crosswise into thin slices
- 1¼ cups sugar
- 1 cup plus 1 tablespoon all-purpose flour
- 1½ teaspoons ground cinnamon
- ¼ teaspoon ground nutmeg
- ½ teaspoon baking powder
- ½ teaspoon salt
- 2 large eggs, lightly beaten
- 2 tablespoons sour cream

1. Adjust oven rack to middle position and heat oven to 325 degrees. Grease bottom and sides of 9-inch spring-form pan with 1 tablespoon butter. Melt remaining softened butter in large nonstick skillet over medium heat. Add bread crumbs and toast, stirring occasionally, until golden brown, about 3 minutes. Transfer crumbs to bowl and let cool.

2. Toss apples, 2 tablespoons sugar, and 1 tablespoon flour in large bowl. Following photos 1 and 2 at left, coat bottom and sides of prepared pan with toasted crumbs, then arrange apples in pan.

3. Combine 1 cup sugar, remaining flour, cinnamon, nutmeg, baking powder, and salt in large bowl. Whisk in eggs, sour cream, and melted butter until smooth. Following photo 3, pour batter evenly over apples. Sprinkle remaining sugar evenly over batter and bake until deep golden brown and crisp, 70 to 80 minutes. Transfer to wire and cool completely, at least 1 hour. Remove ring, slice, and serve.

Toasted bread crumbs bond with the batter to form a crust on the bottom of this apple pie.

St. Louis Gooey Butter Cake

My mom was born in St. Louis and would always bring home a gooey butter cake from her occasional visits. It was similar to a yeasted coffee cake, but it had a creamy, pudding-like topping. Have you heard of this recipe?

–Janice Wallerin, St. Petersburg, Fla.

As any St. Louis native will tell you, there are actually two distinct styles of gooey butter cake—and everyone I talked to during a recent two-day visit had a favorite. Many bakeries and coffee shops sell squares of gooey butter cake that are more like a chewy (and messy) bar cookie than a cake. The base is cake batter and the topping is like cheesecake. The second style is more like an old-fashioned coffee cake, with a rich yeast dough and custardy topping. Janice grew up with this style of gooey butter cake and I can see why it's so memorable. The combination of tender yeast cake and silky custard literally melts in your mouth.

My initial recipe tests were pretty far from the mark. The bases were dry and tough (more like pizza dough than coffee cake) and the toppings were runny and soupy. The cake portion of the best of these early recipes mixed 1½ cups of flour, 1 egg, and 4 tablespoons of butter with yeast, water, sugar, and salt in a mixer, then kneaded the dough and let it rise before pressing it into the pan. The topping was made by creaming butter and sugar, then mixing in corn syrup, an egg, vanilla, and flour. Once assembled, the cake was baked in a 350-degree oven.

I knew I needed to enrich, tenderize, and sweeten the cake base. Taking inspiration from rich yeasted doughs like brioche and Danish, I doubled the number of eggs. Doubling the butter to a full stick made the dough a little greasy; 6 tablespoons was the right compromise. Switching from water to milk gave the cake even more substance. Doubling the sugar (from 2 tablespoons to 4) lent more than the obvious sweetness; it also helped tenderize the cake. With a richer, more tender foundation in place, I moved on to the topping.

Bakers in St. Louis told me that by the time the cake base is cooked through, the topping should still jiggle slightly. As the gooey butter cake cools, the topping will set up into a velvety, custard-like consistency. Unfortunately, my experience with the topping was quite different. It was much too runny and puddled liked melted ice cream when the cake was sliced.

My first thought was to add more flour, but the filling became pasty. I had better luck when I beat some cream cheese in with the butter and sugar. The cream cheese partially firmed up the filling without making it pasty, but using any more than 2 ounces made the topping too tangy

and cheesecakelike. Cornstarch gave the filling an unpleasant slippery texture, but spurred the idea of trying instant pudding (which contains cornstarch as a thickener). Sure enough, a few tablespoons of vanilla pudding mix added flavor and provided the creamy, gooey-yet-sliceable texture I'd been looking for. With a dusting of confectioners' sugar, I had finally created a recipe that can compete with the best St. Louis bakeries.

–Cali Rich

ST. LOUIS GOOEY BUTTER CAKE SERVES 9

Remove the cake from the oven when the perimeter is golden brown and the center is still slightly loose; the topping will continue to set as the cake cools.

Dough
- ¼ cup whole milk, heated to 110 degrees
- 1½ teaspoons rapid-rise or instant yeast
- ¼ cup granulated sugar
- 2 large eggs, room temperature
- ½ teaspoon vanilla extract
- ½ teaspoon salt
- 1½ cups all-purpose flour
- 6 tablespoons unsalted butter, cut into 6 pieces and softened

Topping
- ½ cup granulated sugar
- 4 tablespoons unsalted butter, softened
- 2 ounces cream cheese, softened
- 2 tablespoons light corn syrup
- 1 large egg, room temperature
- 1 teaspoon vanilla extract
- ⅓ cup all-purpose flour
- 3 tablespoons instant vanilla pudding mix
- 2 tablespoons confectioners' sugar

1. For the dough: Adjust oven rack to lower-middle position and heat oven to 200 degrees. When oven reaches 200 degrees, shut oven off. Line 8-inch square baking pan with foil sling. Grease foil and medium bowl.

2. In bowl of standing mixer fitted with paddle attachment,

This coffee cake features the signature sweet and gooey topping over a sturdy, yeast-dough base. A dusting of confectioners' sugar puts it over the top.

mix milk and yeast on low speed until yeast dissolves. Add sugar, eggs, vanilla, salt, and flour and mix until combined, about 30 seconds. Increase speed to medium-low and add butter, one piece at a time, until incorporated, then continue mixing for 5 minutes. Transfer batter to prepared bowl, cover with plastic, and place in warm oven. Let rise until doubled in size, about 30 minutes. Spread batter in prepared pan. Heat oven to 350 degrees.

3. For the topping: In bowl of standing mixer fitted with paddle attachment, beat granulated sugar, butter, and cream cheese on medium speed until light and fluffy, about 2 minutes. Reduce speed to low and add corn syrup, egg, and vanilla until combined. Add flour and pudding mix and mix until just incorporated. Portion dollops of topping evenly over batter, then spread into even layer.

4. Once oven is fully heated, bake until exterior is golden

and center of topping is just beginning to color (center should jiggle slightly when pan is shaken), about 25 minutes. Cool in pan at least 3 hours. Use foil overhang to lift cake from pan. Dust cake with confectioners' sugar. Serve. (Cake can be refrigerated for 2 days.)

BUTTERSCOTCH GOOEY BUTTER CAKE

For dough, substitute ¼ cup packed light brown sugar for granulated sugar in step 2. For topping, substitute 3 tablespoons instant butterscotch pudding mix for vanilla pudding mix in step 3.

CHOCOLATE GOOEY BUTTER CAKE

For dough, replace 3 tablespoons flour with equal amount of Dutch-processed cocoa in step 2. For topping, substitute 3 tablespoons instant chocolate pudding mix for vanilla pudding mix in step 3.

Secret Ingredients

INSTANT PUDDING
Adds flavor, sweetness, and structure.

LIGHT CORN SYRUP
The secret to a gooey topping.

Food Shopping

MICROWAVE POPCORN: The Problem with Prepackaged Brands

Americans spend over $1 billion annually on unpopped popcorn kernels. Corn producers large and small develop as many as 30,000 hybrids (which have varying flavor, textural, and volume characteristics) a year in search of better products.

To find out which supermarket microwave popcorn we liked best, we popped up seven national brands in their basic butter flavor and called our tasting panel to the table for a blind sampling. As a baseline, we also tasted plain popcorn kernels popped in our favorite microwave popper (see box below) and dressed with a modest amount of melted butter and salt.

The homemade popcorn won by a landslide. Out of the seven store-bought brands, only two received acceptable grades—the almost underseasoned Orville Redenbacher's Natural ("just a hint of butter") and the highly seasoned Pop Secret ("tastes like movie theater popcorn"). The biggest problem with the prepackaged popcorns was "artificial tasting" flavors from the "natural and/or artificial butter flavor" and preservatives. It wasn't surprising that popcorns with "artificial butter flavor" would taste artificial (this flavor is typically a blend of chemicals designed to mimic real butter, with one eye squarely on the bottom line).

We were, however, very surprised that brands with "natural butter flavor," like ACT II and both popcorns from Newman's Own, weren't better. Since butter is perishable, it needs heavy processing (butter's flavor molecules are typically extracted by enzyme reaction, solvent extraction, or steam distillation) and/or added preservatives to be shelf-stabilized for these packages—and both of those roads lead to unnatural or weak butter flavor. Our overall rankings are a reflection of how closely each microwave popcorn came to replicating the clean, rich flavor of fresh butter: Obviously, none of them did a very good job. We recommend buying a microwave popper and kernels and adding the butter yourself. –Scott Kathan

Highly Recommended

Freshly popped kernels with butter and salt
About $.54 for 3.3 ounces, or $1.62 for the equivalent of one box
Comments: Tasters sang the praises of this popcorn's "clean butter flavor" and "pleasant balance of corn and butter." It stood out for having "no artificial aftertaste."

Recommended with Reservations

ORVILLE REDENBACHER'S Gourmet Popping Corn Natural Butter Flavor
$2.79 for three 3.3-ounce bags
Comments: Tasters viewed this popcorn's "muted," "neutral" flavor as a positive, as it had "only a touch of butter" and a "mellow corn aftertaste." While this popcorn didn't knock tasters' socks off, it was our overall favorite.

POP-SECRET Premium Popcorn Butter Flavor
$2.29 for three 3.5-ounce bags
Comments: "Oh my, a butter bomb!" said one happy taster. While many tasters commented on this popcorn's "fake butter flavor" that a few compared to "butter buds," others liked the "sweet aftertaste" and its resemblance to "movie theater popcorn."

Not Recommended

ACT II Butter Microwave Popcorn
$2.49 for three 3.3-ounce bags
Comments: Tasters noted the "less overt fake (butter) flavor" and "natural tasting" flavor. A few dissenters likened this brand's "squishy," "soft" texture to "Styrofoam."

JOLLY TIME Better Butter Butter Flavor
$2.59 for three 3.35-ounce bags
Comments: "Buttery in that awesome artificial way," said one taster. "Bland but okay" and "chewy" were common themes. Some tasters thought this popcorn was too salty.

NEWMAN'S OWN Organics Pop's Corn Butter Organic Microwave Popcorn
$3.29 for three 3.5-ounce bags
Comments: This sample scored very high for its "natural, toasty" corn flavor, but its butter flavor was deemed "bland and boring" and "flat."

ORVILLE REDENBACHER'S Gourmet Popping Corn Butter
$2.79 for three 3.3-ounce bags
Comments: One taster felt this brand resembled popcorn with "golden topping." Tasters didn't mince words, calling this sample "awful," "gross," and "truly inedible."

NEWMAN'S OWN Oldstyle Picture Show Microwave Popcorn Butter Flavor
$2.59 for three 3.5-ounce bags
Comments: This brand had the lowest sodium, fat, and scores of our lineup. A few tasters likened its "fishy," "chemical" flavors to "buttered popcorn jelly beans."

Taste Test Bottled Asian Seasonings

Most supermarkets carry a wealth of Asian seasonings. Here are four of our favorites, along with notes on usage and the brands we stock in the test kitchen.

Soy Sauce

Real soy sauce is made from fermented soybeans and wheat (cheaper brands are often "imitation" soy sauces). We use this product not only in Asian dishes, but also to enhance meaty flavor in sauces, stews, soups, and braises. We've found that soy sauce acts like a brine in beef and poultry marinades, helping to keep the meat juicy and adding seasoning.
★ **TASTE TEST WINNER: Lee Kum Kee Tabletop Soy Sauce**

Hoisin Sauce

This thick sauce is a blend of ground soybeans, sugar, vinegar, garlic, chiles, and spices. The spiciness, flavor, consistency, and color of hoisin sauce vary widely among brands. We like to use hoisin sauce in stir-fry sauces, Asian-inspired dips and salad dressings, and in glazes for roasted or grilled meats.
★ **TASTE TEST WINNER: Kikkoman Hoisin Sauce**

Oyster Sauce

Thick, dark, briny, and pungent, oyster sauce is made from oysters, salt, soy sauce, and assorted seasonings. It is used to add salty richness to stir-fry sauces, fried rice, and sauces for Kung Pao and General Tso's dishes. Use judiciously, as a little goes a long way.
★ **TASTE TEST WINNER: Lee Kum Kee Premium Oyster Flavored Sauce**

Fish Sauce

Fish sauce is a pungent, concentrated condiment made from salted fermented fish. Used in moderation, this sauce lends a unique salty complexity to many Southeast Asian dishes; we've found that the darker the color, the stronger the flavor. We add a few drops to sauces for stir-fries and dumplings, noodle dishes (like pad Thai), and soups. You can approximate the flavor of fish sauce by substituting 1 minced anchovy fillet and 1 tablespoon of soy sauce per tablespoon of fish sauce.
★ **TASTE TEST WINNER: Thai Kitchen Fish Sauce**

The Best Way to Make Popcorn

With a relatively inexpensive microwave popping bowl and a handful of unadulterated kernels, you can make better-tasting, healthier, less-expensive popcorn in the same amount of time it takes to make the prepackaged stuff—and you can season it any way you want. In a testing of microwave popping bowls, we preferred the simple design and fool-proof results of the Back to Basics Microwave Popping Bowl ($12.99).

OUR FAVORITE MICROWAVE POPPER
Back to Basics Microwave Popping Bowl

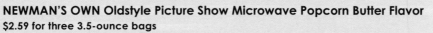

Equipment Roundup

SAFETY CAN OPENERS: Which Model Blows the Lid Off the Competition?

Traditional can openers cut through can lids from the top, leaving sharp edges on the lids (which sit atop the contents and must be fished out). Safety can openers, on the other hand, cut from the side and remove the entire top part of the can (lid and all), leaving dull "safe" edges behind. In a previous testing featuring both types, our favorite was a $35 safety can opener by Rösle. Hoping to find a less-expensive alternative, we rounded up six safety openers as well as two traditional openers boasting "safer" operation; all models are priced under $20.

ATTACHMENT ISSUES: Efficiency starts with locking onto the cans. Safety can openers come in two basic designs: top mounting and side mounting. Side-mounting can openers proved to be much less intuitive for first-time users; testers had particular difficulty getting the CIA opener to attach. Top-mounting can openers (their turning cranks are parallel to the counter) all attach by scissor action; the Kuhn Rikon and Progressive models were especially easy to attach.

The two traditional can openers have locking mechanisms with push-button releases; this worked great on the OXO, but several testers had trouble disengaging the Chef'n opener from the cans.

EASE OF OPERATION: Our testers preferred openers with easy, smooth-turning motions—opening a can shouldn't induce a sweat. The biggest loser here was a safety opener by CIA, which required too much muscle to operate comfortably. The handles on the Zyliss and Chef'n openers were angled so that short tuna cans tilted and spilled liquid when not opened with the handle hanging over the counter: a major flaw. Left-handed and right-handed testers had similar experiences with all models tested.

SAFETY MATTERS: Whether a can lid is sharp (from a traditional opener) or dull-edged (from a safety opener), the danger lies in having to handle it; the best openers allow no-touch lid disposal. The Kuhn Rikon and Progressive safety openers both had metal pincers that gripped the lid for safe—if not perfectly easy—disposal. The side-mounting safety openers were downgraded for lacking mechanisms for no-touch lid disposal. The two traditional openers we included featured magnets designed for no-touch lid disposal. The OXO's magnet received good marks for easy lid-grabbing, but the Chef'n opener's magnet was so weak, it dropped many lids on the counter.

SUMMING UP: In opening over 120 cans, we discovered that there isn't a single style of opener that works best. Our surprise winner, the traditional-style OXO Good Grips ($19.95), did leave sharp edges on the lid, but its lid-catching magnet made disposing of the lid easy and safe. This opener was intuitive and comfortable to use and very efficient. The runner-up was a safety opener by Kuhn Rikon ($11.95), which featured a comfortable, oversized crank and won extra points for being dishwasher safe. The openers are listed, with comments, in order of preference. **–Charlotte Weigel**

Recommended

OXO Good Grips i-Series Can Opener
Type: Traditional opener with magnet for lid removal
Price: $19.95 at Cooking.com
Performance: ★★★
Comfort: ★★★
Safety: ★★
Comments: This can opener was intuitive to use and easy to attach and detach from cans. It was "comfortable," "very smooth," and very efficient in operation. Because it is a traditional opener, this model leaves a lid with sharp edges (its only downfall), but minimizes potential danger with a magnet that allows "neat and safe" lid disposal.

KUHN RIKON Slim Safety LidLifter
Type: Top-mounting safety opener with pincers for lid removal
Price: $11.95 at Amazon.com
Performance: ★★
Comfort: ★★★
Safety: ★★★
Comments: Testers praised the handy "change in feeling" once the can was completely open. The "dishwasher-safe" claim was spot-on: There were no changes in performance or appearance after several wash cycles. A few testers had mild complaints about the "awkward position" of the oversized turning knob, resulting in a slight demerit in the performance rating.

PROGRESSIVE International Safety I-Can Opener
Type: Top-mounting safety opener with pincers for lid removal
Price: $12.79 at Theglasswarestore.com
Performance: ★★
Comfort: ★★★
Safety: ★★★
Comments: The unique ratchet cutting wheel mechanism was "easy to operate" and comfortable, but was "hard to know when finished." Pincers disposed of the cut lid safely. For some testers, the instructions for this opener were "not obvious," even with visuals on the packaging.

GOOD COOK 4-1WHT Safe Can Opener
Type: Side-mounting safety opener
Price: $9.99 at Amazon.com
Performance: ★★★
Comfort: ★★
Safety: ★★
Comments: "Clearly written instructions" and "smooth gears" made this opener easy and efficient at first use. Also, testers appreciated the "perceptible change in feeling" when the can opener had rounded the entire can. This model lost a few points for not having a lid-gripper.

Recommended with Reservations

ZYLISS Safe Edge Can Opener
Type: Top-mounting safety opener
Price: $14.95 at Amazon.com
Performance: ★★
Comfort: ★★★
Safety: ★★
Comments: Testers appreciated the "good visuals" in the instructions for this opener. Although the handle was "very comfortable," its angle made opening short cans of tuna awkward and messy. Additionally, testers could not operate the lid lifter and had to dispose of the cut lid by hand.

MIU CanDo Safety Can Opener
Type: Side-mounting safety opener
Price: $9.99 at Amazon.com
Performance: ★★
Comfort: ★★
Safety: ★★
Comments: Downgraded for its lack of instructions, this opener operated smoothly once testers figured out how to use it. This model claimed to be dishwasher-safe, but the cutting wheel rusted after several washes—a serious flaw that affects both performance and longevity.

Not Recommended

CHEF'N EZ Squeeze 1-Handed Can Opener
Type: Traditional opener with magnet for lid removal
Price: $14.99 at Amazon.com
Performance: ★★
Comfort: ★★
Safety: ★
Comments: Testers found the instructions for attaching and detaching this opener from the can unclear. The gripper handle was "easy to squeeze," but was angled such that opening short cans of tuna was "messy and awkward." Also, the release button struggled to disengage the opener from the can. The magnet designed for lid removal failed to pick the lids out of most cans.

CIA Masters Collections Side Can Opener
Type: Side-mounting safety opener
Price: $14.95 at Chefsresource.com
Performance: ★
Comfort: ★
Safety: ★★
Comments: This opener left testers tired and confused. Most testers found the instructions to be "a little vague." The opener was tricky to attach to the kcan, and the handle was remarkably difficult to turn, once attached.

Notes from Our Test Kitchen

TIPS, TECHNIQUES, AND TOOLS FOR BETTER COOKING

Kitchen Creations
Doctored Cranberry Sauces

With just a few pantry items, plain old canned cranberry sauce can be turned into a star side dish. Each of these quick cranberry sauces yields about 2 cups (though they can be doubled or even tripled) and can be refrigerated in an airtight container for up to one week.

BROWN SUGAR AND WALNUT CRANBERRY SAUCE

Pulse one 16-ounce can cranberry sauce, ¼ cup chopped toasted walnuts, 2 tablespoons brown sugar, and 1 tablespoon lemon juice in food processor until combined. Refrigerate, covered, for 30 minutes. Serve chilled or at room temperature.

SPICED HONEY CRANBERRY SAUCE

Pulse one 16-ounce can cranberry sauce, 2 tablespoons honey, 1 tablespoon lemon juice, ¼ teaspoon ground cinnamon, and ¼ teaspoon ground allspice in food processor until combined. Refrigerate, covered, for 30 minutes. Serve chilled or at room temperature.

PICKLED GINGER CRANBERRY SAUCE

Pulse one 16-ounce can cranberry sauce, 2 tablespoons drained pickled ginger, and 1 teaspoon wasabi powder or dry mustard in food processor until combined. Refrigerate, covered, for 30 minutes. Serve chilled or at room temperature.

Squashed for Time?

While testing our recipe for **Roasted Butternut Squash Soup** (page 20), we noticed that, in addition to whole squash, there were two other options in the produce department: precut chunks of peeled butternut squash and peeled, halved butternut squash. Though both options promised to streamline the prep time, we were concerned that what we saved in time would be offset by dry texture and stale flavor. After trying the squash chunks and halved squash in our soup, we weren't surprised that tasters preferred the "creamy" texture and "earthy sweetness" of the soup made with fresh, whole squash that you peel and cube yourself. Still, tasters found the peeled, halved squash to be an acceptable substitute in the soup, lauding it as "balanced and nutty" though "not as squashy" as the whole squash. The precut chunks, however, were "dry and stringy" with "barely any squash flavor."

PEELED AND CHOPPED
Dry and flavorless.

PEELED AND HALVED
Acceptable in a pinch.

Molasses Primer

Thick, sticky-sweet molasses is a byproduct of the sugar-refining process—it is the liquid that is drawn off after the cane juice has been boiled and undergone crystallization. Once the sugar crystals are removed, the remaining liquid is packaged and sold as mild (or light) molasses, or it is boiled again and marketed as robust or full-flavored molasses. If the molasses is reduced a third time, it is labeled blackstrap. With each boil, the molasses becomes darker, more concentrated in flavor, and more bitter. Though we prefer mild molasses in our **Hermit Cookies** (page 9)—its subtle flavor allows the spice flavor to shine through—robust molasses is an acceptable substitute. Although some people swear by it, we've never warmed to the assertive, overpowering bitterness of blackstrap molasses; it should be avoided when baking.

Madeira Wine

Madeira, a key ingredient in our recipe for **Chicken à la King** (page 17), is fortified wine, which is made from both red and white grapes and additional alcohol (usually brandy; originally added to extend shelf life). Madeira gained favor in the 17th century when it was first shipped from the Portuguese island of Madeira to the New World. The cargo ships carrying

MADEIRA
Complex flavor, subtle sweetness.

Madeira passed through the tropics, where warm temperatures lent soft, caramel-y flavors to the wine; today, the fortified wine is heated to mimic the effects of those long sea travels. Madeira is made from several different grapes, but the most common variety is the dark, complex, and mildly sweet Malmsey. While connoisseurs may enjoy Madeira as an aperitif, it is most commonly used in cooking.

Inside the Test Kitchen
TAKING TURKEY'S TEMPERATURE

To ensure perfectly cooked turkey (as for our Old-Fashioned Roast Turkey with Gravy recipe on page 11), it's important to know where to insert the thermometer for the most accurate and useful readings. Here's how to do it.

1. To take the temperature of the breast, insert the thermometer into the deepest part of the breast, holding it parallel to the bird at the neck end. Confirm the temperature by inserting the thermometer in both sides of the breast, being careful to not go so deep as to hit the bone (which can compromise the reading).
2. To take the temperature of the thigh, insert the thermometer into the thickest portion of the thigh away from the bone. Confirm the temperature by inserting the thermometer in both thighs.

Rice: The Long and Short of It

Every variety of rice on the market can be categorized in one of three ways: long grain, medium grain, and short grain. A good rule is the shorter the grain, the starchier and stickier the rice. Long-grain varieties, from plain old supermarket rice to more exotic basmati and jasmine, cook up dry, fluffy, and light, making them perfect for our **Herbed Rice Pilaf** (page 23), as well as in rice salads. Medium grains like Arborio and Valencia have a creamy, starchy texture suited for risotto, paella, and rice pudding. Short-grain rices, also known as pearl or glutinous rice, are nearly round, very starchy, and moist. They are best suited for sushi.

Shopping with the Test Kitchen Canadian Bacon

To reduce the fat and calories in our **Low-Fat Spaghetti Carbonara** (page 7) without skimping on the bacon, we looked to the Great White North. Cut from the loin rather than the belly, Canadian bacon, aka "back bacon," packs a lot of savory, smoky flavor with less than half the fat of regular bacon. After tasting five major brands, our tasters unanimously chose Applegate Farms Canadian bacon as their favorite. While other brands were panned for their "dry, tough" texture and "cheap deli ham" flavor, Applegate Farms was praised for its "salty, smoky balance" and "meaty, bacon-y chew."

**APPLEGATE FARMS
CANADIAN BACON**
Our favorite brand

Apples to Apples

Apple butter was the perfect ingredient to add another layer of apple flavor to our **Cider-Braised Pork Chops** (page 18). Believed to have originated in Pennsylvania Dutch communities as a way to preserve apples for the winter months, apple butter is made by stewing apples with cider (or water) and warm spices until they break down into a thick paste. This intensely flavored preserve is used primarily as a condiment; we especially like it spread on toast or dolloped on warm pancakes. Although apple butter brands vary regionally, after tasting five brands we found that the best apple butters have a short ingredient list that includes only apples, water or cider, spices—and no added sugar.

Crystallized Ginger

We found an unlikely ingredient to add a chewy-spicy kick to our **Hermit Cookies** (page 9): crystallized ginger. This product, also called "candied ginger," is simply peeled young ginger root that has been boiled in sugar syrup and then sprinkled with coarse sugar. Crystallized ginger has a pleasantly chewy texture and sweet, floral flavor with just a hint of raw ginger's nasal heat. It is often sold in bulk in health food stores, but small spice jars of crystallized ginger can be found in the spice aisle of most supermarkets. Crystallized ginger can be eaten out of hand or used to lend a spicy-sweet kick to any number of confections. When purchasing, look for large, unbroken pieces of ginger that are slightly pliable. Store crystallized ginger in an airtight container at room temperature for up to three months.

CRYSTALLIZED GINGER
Chewy, sweet, and spicy.

Choosing Chops

In our recipe for **Cider-Braised Pork Chops** (page 18), we use bone-in blade chops. Cut from the shoulder end of the loin, these tough—but flavorful—chops are perfect for braising, as the moist, slow cooking helps tenderize the meat. But not all pork chops work well for all applications. Here's how to choose the right chop.

BLADE
Though flavorful, these chops can be tough and are best suited to low-and-slow cooking methods that break down their connective tissue. Braise, barbecue, or smoke.

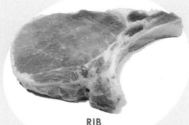

RIB
Tender and flavorful, but relatively lean, these chops are best suited to quick cooking techniques such as grilling and sautéing.

CENTER CUT
A T-shaped bone separates the loin and tenderloin muscles in this lean chop. Although tender and flavorful, the dual muscles make these chops a challenge to cook. Grill or sauté.

Meat-Probe Thermometers

Repeatedly opening the oven door to monitor the internal temperature of a turkey or roast can throw cooking times off. Luckily, there's another option: a meat probe thermometer. The probe is attached to a thin cord that snakes out of the oven and into a base that includes a digital readout. We tested 11 models, and while none were flawless, the best of the bunch was an easy-to-use thermometer from ThermoWorks (it costs about $20). Check your probe thermometer for accuracy by taking a reading in boiling water before trying it with a roast: The probe should read within a few degrees of 212 degrees when submerged in the boiling water.

**THERMOWORKS ORIGINAL
COOKING THERMOMETER/TIMER**
The best tool for monitoring the temperature of roasts.

Potato Chips

Our recipe card for **Broiled Salmon with Potato Crust** uses kettle-cooked potato chips to help create a crisp, flavorful crust on the fillets. In a recent tasting of potato chips (both kettle cooked and regular), Lay's Kettle Cooked Original were our favorite chips. Tasters love their thick cut, which contributed to the big potato flavor of these chips.

**OUR FAVORITE
POTATO CHIP**
Lay's Kettle Cooked Original

How to SEGMENT CITRUS

To produce perfect orange segments for our recipe card for **Chicken Provençal**, it was important to cut each one free from the membranes, which are fibrous and bitter. Here's how we segment oranges (or any other citrus fruit) in the test kitchen.

1. Using a sharp knife, cut off the ends of the fruit. Following the fruit's natural contour, cut away the peel and white pith to expose the flesh.
2. Insert the blade of the knife between the membrane and the segment and slice toward the center to separate one side of the segment.
3. Slice along the membrane on the other side of the segment until it falls out. Repeat with the remaining segments.

Gadgets & Gear Apple Corers

Armed with nothing more than a paring knife, coring and seeding even a few apples can be a tedious process. That's why an apple corer can be so handy for prepping recipes like our **Easy Apple Pie** (page 26). In a recent testing of five models, we preferred the OXO Good Grip Corer ($7.95). With its wide mouth, sharp teeth, and no-slip handle, the OXO corer makes coring an apple as easy as pie.

THE OXO GOOD GRIP CORER
Sharp teeth and plenty of length allow this corer to make short work of the largest apples.

When Things Go Wrong in the Kitchen

READERS SHARE FUNNY STORIES ABOUT COOKING MISHAPS

NOW THAT'S CLEAN

When I was a young bride, I wanted to prepare a nice Thanksgiving dinner for my husband. It was just the two of us, so I wanted to make sure that every part of the dinner was perfect. Since I'd never cooked a turkey before, I called my mother for directions. The last thing she said to me was, "Don't forget to clean the bird before you stuff it." Well, she had never used anything but Tide detergent, so I figured that would do the best job. Needless to say, when my husband came into the kitchen and saw me washing out the bird with bubbles going everywhere, his eyes almost popped out of his head!

Linda Breschini Lakewood, Ohio

A FIRM FROSTING

Before I went to cooking school, I volunteered to make a chocolate birthday cake for my friend's birthday party. Without knowing what I was doing, I melted a ton of dark chocolate and poured it all over the baked and cooled cake and took the cake to the party. What a surprise when my friend tried to stick in the candles—it was impossible to poke them through my "frosting"!

Anastasia Simpson Marina, Calif.

DON'T WOK AWAY FROM THE STOVE

One afternoon I decided to delegate the cooking of dinner to my very responsible 10-year-old son, Daniel, so I could catch a quick nap. I gave him careful verbal instructions on how to simply boil hot dogs in a pan filled with plenty of water. My sleep was quickly disrupted by the smell of smoke and the sound of kids playing outside. I ran downstairs, smelling something like burned electronics in the air. Daniel had gone out to play, and there on the electric burner sat my red electric wok (thankfully, without the power cord attached) with its support legs smoking and smoldering, and the hot dogs happily cooking away in plenty of water!

Rhonda Wilkinson Levittown, Pa.

A THANKFUL KITTY

Our turkey is always hard to fit in the refrigerator at the holidays. One year, I put the bird into my roasting pan, covered it with foil, and set it in my cold garage to keep until morning. When I went out to bring the turkey back into the house the next day, I immediately saw that the foil had been knocked off, but I didn't see the full extent of the damage until I got the bird in the house. Something had chewed the turkey's tail off! I was hysterical and my husband came running to see what was wrong. He tried to calm me down, but I kept wondering where I was going to get another turkey to feed the crowd we had coming. He gave the bird a good scrubbing and cut off the pieces we thought had been chewed on. I then stuffed and cooked the turkey, and no one even noticed the trim job throughout a very nice dinner. When we told our family what had happened that evening, they all laughed and didn't think anything of it. And later that night we found our neighbor's cat sitting in our garage, hoping for another big feast.

Gail Ahrens Lockport, Ill.

ONE PLAIN HAM

Many years ago, when I was throwing my first dinner party, I wanted to serve ham. I had forgotten the brand of ham my mother usually bought, and I didn't really have a clue how to make her candied ham, but I decided to improvise. I took the large ham out of the can, scraped off the jelly, spread mustard and brown sugar on the top, and then covered the top with pineapple rings. After baking it a few hours, I took the ham out to serve to my hungry guests. It looked a little strange because all the toppings had fallen off the ham into the pan. My husband soon found out why when he went to carve the ham. The ham was still encased in plastic! Our guests politely ate my very bland ham anyway.

Lynn Molzen Holmes, N.Y.

BLUEBERRY BOLT PIE

At the age of 4, I was proudly standing on a chair to assist my mother in preparing a blueberry pie for my new stepfather. I suspect that the baking of the pie had something to do with the fact that he was working hard at the kitchen table trying to repair the windshield wipers for our car. In any case, the two events soon became intertwined, and I accidentally incorporated a windshield wiper bolt into the filling! Guess whose piece it ended up in? Fortunately, my new stepfather didn't break any teeth, and our family still jokes that I did it on purpose. But I think the years of metal-free goodies I've baked for him since have hopefully proven otherwise.

Rachel Billings Holland, Mich.

PIE ON FIRE

When I was 18, I was in Germany staying with some friends for several weeks, and I learned that they were big fans of apple pie. I offered to make my signature pie, which is baked in a paper grocery bag. They were leery of the idea of putting a paper bag in their oven, but I assured my friends that I had made the pie dozens of times with no problems. I proceeded and placed it in the oven, but that was the only part that went according to plan. The bag caught on fire, filling their kitchen with smoke and charring the top of my pie. Only after the smoke was cleared (and the pie partially saved) did they inform me that their oven ran 50 degrees too hot!

Katie Campos Grants Pass, Ore.

Chocolate Shadow Cake

Its name invokes the spirit of Halloween, but what could be scary about a rich chocolate butter cake layered with fluffy seven-minute icing and topped with a drippy chocolate glaze?

To make this cake, you will need:

- **4 large egg whites**
- **3 tablespoons water**
- **1¼ cups sugar**
- **1 teaspoon cream of tartar**
- **Pinch salt**
- **1 teaspoon vanilla extract**
- **3 (8-inch) chocolate cake rounds***
- **4 ounces bittersweet chocolate, chopped**
- **4 tablespoons unsalted butter**
- **2 tablespoons light corn syrup**

For the icing: Whisk egg whites, water, sugar, cream of tartar, and salt in large heat-resistant bowl set over medium saucepan filled with ½ inch of barely simmering water (don't let bowl touch water). With hand-held mixer on medium-high speed, carefully beat egg white mixture to stiff peaks, 6 to 8 minutes. Remove bowl from heat, add vanilla, and continue to beat until icing is very thick and stiff and cooled to room temperature, about 8 minutes.

To assemble: Spread 1 cup icing on bottom cake layer. Repeat with second cake layer and additional 1 cup icing. Top with final cake layer and spread top and sides with remaining icing.

To decorate: Place chocolate, butter, and corn syrup in large heat-resistant bowl set over medium saucepan filled with ½ inch of barely simmering water (don't let bowl touch water). Stir until melted and smooth, then remove bowl from heat and let cool 5 minutes. Spoon ¼ cup chocolate mixture over top of cake and then drizzle remaining glaze along top edge of cake, allowing it to drip about halfway down the sides.

*Go to CooksCountry.com for our Chocolate Layer Cake recipe or use your own.

Recipe Index

RC = Recipe Card

Cook's Country

DECEMBER/JANUARY 2009

Best Holiday Cookies
5 Prize-Winning Reader Recipes

Classic Roast Beef and Gravy
Juicy Meat, Perfect Gravy

Delmonico Potatoes
Cheesy, Creamy, and Crispy!

BACON-Y GREEN BEANS
Simplified Southern Classic

BETTER CASHEW CHICKEN
Marinade Keeps Meat Tender

RATING TOASTERS
Which Brown, Not Burn?

HOLIDAY PORK ROAST
Dressing Up an Inexpensive Cut

GINGERBREAD CAKE
With Fresher, Bolder Flavor

OVEN-FRIED SHRIMP
Secrets to "Fried" Crunch

ULTIMATE CINNAMON BUNS
Buttery and Iced Twice

FOOLPROOF POPOVERS
Unique, Sure-Fire Recipe

SOUTHERN CARAMEL CAKE
Never-Fail Caramel Frosting

Watch Our New Show on Public Television!

Cook's Country from America's Test Kitchen debuted in September on public television stations across the country. Filmed in the *Cook's Country* farmhouse, it features the best recipes, testings, and tastings from *Cook's Country* magazine and is hosted by the ensemble cast from *America's Test Kitchen*. Go to **CooksCountryTV.com** to find out when the show is on in your area.

$4.95 U.S./$6.95 CANADA

0 1>

0 74470 05251 7

Cook's Country

Dear Country Cook,

My strongest memories are built on taste. Drinking grape soda in the front seat of a green Ford pickup, headed home, the afternoon milking finished, and Charlie Bentley's collie, Daisy, crowded between us, the cab scented with hay and filled with the sound of Daisy's hot, sloppy breaths. Or the taste of penny candies purchased at the Weston Country Store. Watermelon slices. Root beer barrels. Long strings of red and black licorice. Chewy turtles made from caramel, chocolate, and nuts. Mallo Cups with a stretchy marshmallow filling and a crispy milk chocolate coating.

As kids, we didn't have to describe the experience, didn't need adjectives to tell our story. We just gulped down the Nehi or started at one end of the chocolate bar and kept on going until it had slid home. We didn't share. We didn't compare notes. We didn't have to tell the story of how something tasted.

And that, I think, is the difference between pure, unadulterated joy and pleasure. One is ecstatic; the other is controlled. One is pure out-of-body happiness; the other is self-observed. In joy, one is overwhelmed by the senses, not merely tempted. It is what food promises but rarely delivers.

That is why good cooks are often children at heart, easily swayed by a finger dipped into chocolate batter, their hearts open to the unexpected. We know that at any moment, we may once again fall in love with the juiciness of a peach, the flakiness of a pie pastry. We are like old lovers who continually rediscover the beauty of each other in a glance, in a thought, in a happenstance.

That's why country cooks are my favorite people. They are open to the childlike pleasures of food and the joyous temptations of the family table.

Christopher Kimball

Christopher Kimball
Founder and Editor, *Cook's Country Magazine*

A child fully engrossed in her bounty of holiday sweets (1948).
Bettmann/CORBIS

DECEMBER/JANUARY 2009

Cook's Country

(5)

(9)

(15)

Founder and Editor Christopher Kimball
Editorial Director Jack Bishop
Executive Editor Peggy Grodinsky
Deputy Editor Bridget Lancaster
Senior Editors Scott Kathan
Jeremy Sauer
Test Kitchen Director Erin McMurrer
Associate Editors Cali Rich
Diane Unger
Test Cooks Kelley Baker
Lynn Clark
Kris Widican
Assistant Test Cooks Maria del Mar Sacasa
Meghan Erwin
Assistant Test Kitchen Director Matthew Herron
Copy Editor Amy Graves

Online Managing Editor David Tytell
Online Editor Kate Mason
Online Assistant Editor Leaya Lee
Executive Assistant Meredith Smith
Senior Kitchen Assistant Nadia Domeq
Kitchen Assistants Maria Elena Delgado
Ena Gudiel, Ben Peskin
TV Producer Melissa Baldino
Contributing Editor Eva Katz
Consulting Editor Guy Crosby

Design Director Amy Klee
Art Director, Magazines Julie Bozzo
Senior Designer Christine Vo
Designers Jay Layman
Lindsey Timko
Staff Photographer Daniel J. van Ackere

Systems Administrator S. Paddi McHugh
Web Production Coordinator Evan Davis
IT Support Technician Brandon Lynch

Chief Financial Officer Sharyn Chabot
Human Resources Director Adele Shapiro
Controller Mandy Shito
Senior Accountant Aaron Goranson
Staff Accountant Connie Forbes
Accounts Payable Specialist Steven Kasha
Office Manager Tasha Bere
Receptionist Henrietta Murray

Production Director Guy Rochford
Traffic & Projects Manager Alice Cummiskey
Production & Imaging Specialists
Lauren Pettapiece
Judy Blomquist
Color & Imaging Specialist Andrew Mannone

Vice President Marketing David Mack
Circulation Director Doug Wicinski
Fulfillment & Circulation Manager Carrie Horan
Partnership Marketing Manager Pamela Putprush
Direct Mail Director Adam Perry
Marketing Database Analyst Ariel Gilbert-Knight
Products Director Steven Browall
Product Promotions Director Randi Lawrence
E-Commerce Marketing Director Hugh Buchan
Associate Marketing Manager Laurel Zeidman
Marketing Copywriter David Goldberg
Customer Service Manager Jacqueline Valerio
Customer Service Representatives
Jillian Nannicelli
Kate Sokol

Sponsorship Sales Director Marcy McCreary
Retail Sales & Marketing Manager Emily Logan
Corporate Marketing Associate Bailey Vatalaro
Publicity Deborah Broide

ON THE COVER: PHOTOGRAPHY: Yamada Taro. ILLUSTRATION: John Burgoyne.
IN THIS ISSUE: COLOR FOOD PHOTOGRAPHY: Keller + Keller. STYLING: Mary Jane Sawyer, Marie Piraino. ILLUSTRATION: Lisa Perrett.

Cook's Country magazine (ISSN 1552-1990), number 24, is published bimonthly by Boston Common Press Limited Partnership, 17 Station Street, Brookline, MA 02445. Copyright 2008 Boston Common Press Limited Partnership. Periodicals Postage paid at Boston, Mass., and additional mailing offices. Publications Mail Agreement No. 40020778. Return undeliverable Canadian addresses to P.O. Box 875, Station A, Windsor, Ontario N9A 6P2. POSTMASTER: Send address changes to Cook's Country, P.O. Box 8382, Red Oak, IA 51591-1382. **Customer Service:** It's easy to subscribe, give a gift subscription, change your address, and manage your subscription online. Visit www.americastestkitchen.com/customerservice for all of your customer service needs or write to us at Cook's Country, P.O. Box 8382, Red Oak, IA 51591-1382.
PRINTED IN THE USA

America's TEST KITCHEN

America's Test Kitchen is a 2,500-square-foot kitchen located just outside of Boston. It is the home of *Cook's Country* and *Cook's Illustrated* magazines and is the workday destination for more than three dozen test cooks, editors, and cookware specialists. Our mission is to test recipes until we understand how and why they work and arrive at the best version. We also test kitchen equipment and supermarket ingredients in search of brands that offer the best value and performance. You can watch us work by tuning in to *America's Test Kitchen* (www.americastestkitchen.com) on public television.

Watch our new show on public television!
Cook's Country from America's Test Kitchen debuted in September on public television stations across the country. The show relies on the same practical, no-nonsense food that has made *Cook's Country* magazine so successful. Watch us develop recipes, test equipment, and taste supermarket ingredients in our brand-new test kitchen. Go to **CooksCountryTV.com** to learn more.

Kitchen Shortcuts

Extra-Large Trivet

When roasts, casseroles, and cookies are parading out of my oven during the holidays, I always run out of places to put hot pans. In a pinch, I use an inverted, rimmed baking sheet as a makeshift trivet. Not only does it give me an extra landing zone for hot pans, it works especially well for large roasting pans or Dutch ovens.

Adele Wilde
Las Vegas, Nev.

Better Batter Vessel

Whenever I make muffins or oil-based cakes, I mix the batter right in my large (8-cup) glass measuring cup. There are

three great advantages: Holding the handle is much easier than trying to hold on to a bowl when mixing, the spout makes it easier to pour the batter (especially for muffins), and you can measure how much batter you have, making it easy to portion out the batter.

Elayne Liggieri
West Milford, N.J.

KEEP IT FRESH!

Storing Vanilla Beans

Vanilla beans are expensive and I try to buy them in bulk if I find a good price. To keep them from drying out, I store them in a tall bottle of vanilla extract. The beans stay moist, fresh, and flavorful. Your extract will get an extra boost of vanilla flavor, too!

Cameron Wilding
Bedford, N.H.

Arm Extender

DOUBLE-DUTY TONGS

Being height-challenged, it's hard for me to reach to the top shelf. My pair of tongs is perfect to grab a box or jar—I can squeeze tight and bring it down to the counter. Even better, I recently thought to wrap rubber bands around each tip, creating a no-slip grip!

Dale McCarthy Needham, Mass.

NO-FUSS FRENCH TOAST

After a holiday party, I always have some leftover eggnog, which is delicious but very rich. Fortunately, it works perfectly for making French toast—just dip sliced bread in the eggnog instead of batter and fry as usual.

Rachel Billings
Holland, Mich.

STUFFING, WITH A PLAN

Store-bought bread cubes for stuffing are convenient, but they are not nearly as tasty as homemade. Whenever I have a few slices left in a loaf of bread (any kind), I cube them up, let them dry on a plate overnight, and put them in a zipper-lock bag in the freezer. By holiday time, I end up with a variety of cubes—hearty white sandwich, whole grain, etc.—that are ready to use.

Carol Britt
Thibodaux, La.

FAST CHICKEN NOODLE SOUP

We like homemade noodles with our homemade chicken soup, but who has time to make them? Instead, I purchase packages of 3-inch by 3-inch Asian wonton wrappers (the dough is nice and light). I stack them about five high and cut them into strips or squares. They can be dropped right into the simmering soup just before serving.

Angela Oliva
Chicago, Ill.

GREAT GRILLED CHEESE

When my kids make grilled cheese sandwiches or quesadillas, they often get frustrated with flipping: If the cheese isn't melted, the sandwich comes apart or bits of grated cheese come out in the pan. Now, they microwave the sandwich or quesadilla just long enough to soften the cheese and then finish cooking them in the pan. They come out perfectly toasted and intact.

Holly Grieve
Seattle, Wash.

BETTER BAKING SODA STORAGE

For the 20-plus years that I have been cooking, I've always found the baking soda box annoying: The box never stays closed, the box top is cumbersome to use for leveling off measuring spoons, and I never know if the soda has stayed fresh. I thought of using a small canister, but wanted something with a lip. What I did was save an empty baking powder can, remove the label, and re-label it for baking soda—the can has a lip for leveling and the baking soda stays fresher for longer.

Emilie Harlow
Mechanicsville, Va.

KITCHEN ASSISTANT

To keep everything from family recipes to appliance instruction manuals organized, I purchased a three-ring binder, see-through page protectors, and some dividers from an office supply store. I created a custom recipe book that I can add to as I collect recipes and I can remove one protected recipe at a time to use in the kitchen as needed! The page protectors keep them mess-free and are easily wiped down.

Lee Pantuso
Hillsborough, Calif.

QUICK PASTA AND VEGETABLES

Boiling pasta on a weeknight is an easy way to get dinner on the table. I found a way to add vegetables to the meal without getting another pot or bowl dirty. I get out some frozen vegetables and add them to the cooking water along with the pasta according to how long they need to cook—a minute or two before the pasta is done for peas or corn, a few minutes longer for carrots or asparagus. I drain everything together and just add sauce.

Dave Nahum
Franktown, Colo.

If you'd like to submit a tip, please e-mail us by visiting CooksCountry.com/kitchenshortcuts, or send a letter to Kitchen Shortcuts, Cook's Country, P.O. Box 470739, Brookline, MA 02447. Include your name, address, and phone number. If we publish your tip, you will receive a free one-year subscription to Cook's Country.

PIES BY THE DOZEN

Around the holidays, I bake dozens of pies. To streamline the work, I make a large batch of pie dough a few months in advance. I roll each crust out, wrap it in wax paper, and then pack them up in freezer zipper-lock bags according to what the pie requires—a bag labeled "apple" gets two crusts (one top and one bottom), a bag labeled "pumpkin" gets one crust. The bags stack up nice and flat in the freezer for easy storage. The night before I am going to bake a pie, I defrost the appropriate bag in the refrigerator overnight.

Dana Ross
Maylene, Ala.

NEATER BREAD CUBES

When I make stuffing, croutons, or bread pudding, I freeze my bread before I cut it into cubes. The bread firms up, making it much easier to cut into pieces with clean, not shaggy, edges.

Kati Gallagher
Charlestown, Mass.

NO TOOTHPASTE REQUIRED

I use the small holes on my box grater whenever a recipe calls for lemon zest or ginger. I used to have a problem with the bits of zest and stringy ginger that get caught up in the grater—they fused onto the grater after a turn in the hot dishwasher. Now I make quick work of grater cleanup by using a toothbrush dedicated to this task. It works like a charm.

Eileen Baione
Jensen Beach, Fla.

STEADIER ROLLING

When I am rolling out biscuit or pie dough between two sheets of parchment or wax paper, the bottom has a tendency to slide around. To prevent this, I wet the bottom sheet with a little bit of water—it sticks to the counter and keeps everything in place.

Meg Gallagher
Santa Monica, Calif.

KITCHEN RULES

I purchased a plastic ruler just for the kitchen and keep it in my utensil jar. It's handy for everyday kitchen tasks like measuring pie dough diameter, making sure you have the right size pan or cookie cutter, or preparing to cut ingredients to a certain size. It cleans up easily—I've even thrown it in my dishwasher!

Danielle Beauchesne
Southborough, Mass.

PARCHMENT PAPER TRICK

Cookie recipes often call for parchment paper to line the baking sheet. Recently, I was about to discard a used piece of parchment—and line the pan with a new sheet for my second batch of cookies—when I discovered that the cookies had left clear "spots" behind on the paper. I flipped the sheet over and, not only did I have a fresh surface of parchment to bake on, but the "spots" were visible on the other side, showing me exactly where to place the dough for a perfectly spaced second batch.

Dave Stebbins
Charlottesville, Va.

SOUPER TIP

Holiday crowds get me thinking about creative ways to serve meals family-style. I like to make soup for special occasions (mostly because it's quick and easy), but it's hard for people to manage their drinks and a bowl of soup when standing or sitting without a table. Instead, I pre-ladle soup into mugs and serve the mugs on a buffet tray—each guest can take one to sip from. Easy to make, serve, and eat!

Jennifer Lebo
Milton, Mass.

EXPRESS FUNNEL

To make a quick funnel for dry ingredients, I use an envelope and cut diagonally across a corner (1 inch or more, depending upon how big you want the funnel hole to be). Cut straight across the opposite end of the envelope to create an opening into which ingredients can be poured—this works great when you are adding dry ingredients into a stand mixer.

Julie Pecoraro
El Paso, Texas

TONG-TIED

I have several different sizes of tongs, most of which don't have locks to keep the tips together for neat, easy storage. To remedy the problem, I put each pair of tongs in an appropriately sized empty cardboard roll from paper towels or food wrap. It keeps the tongs together and from getting tangled up with each other and other tools in the kitchen drawer.

Jenny Kuenzi
Uniontown, Ohio

Brush It Clean!

A VERSATILE TOOL

While I usually use my pastry brush for brushing crusts with egg or biscuits with melted butter, I discovered that I can use it in another way. The dry brush comes in handy to clean flour and dough out of the nooks and crannies of a stand mixer after mixer "explosions"—which I never have, of course!

Deborah Davidson Watertown, N.Y.

Toasted (Not Burnt) Coconut

Instead of toasting coconut in the oven (where it can easily burn), use your microwave instead. Just spread the coconut in an even layer on a large microwave-safe plate and cook it on high power until it's golden brown. It takes a couple of minutes and you need to stir it a few times (at about 30-second intervals), but there's no more worrying about leaving coconut in the oven to burn!

Jessica Christenson Boston, Mass.

String Storage

NEAT TRICK!

To keep your kitchen twine clean (it's used during messy holiday tasks like tying turkeys or roasts), keep the ball in a sealed, plastic pint-sized container—deli containers or clean cottage cheese tubs are perfect. I cut a small "X" in the lid and thread the twine through, pulling out however much twine I need for the job at hand. The container is easily wiped down and neatly stored.

Deborah Tanaka
Richwood, Ohio

Grease Be Gone

I am always looking for an easy way to get grease off the surface of stews and sauces. A friend recently suggested I try using an uncoated paper plate to do the job. For my next batch of beef stew, I pressed the bottom of a paper plate to the greasy surface of the stew, and voilà! The grease came away with the plate and was less messy than blotting with paper towels—and it was much less tedious than skimming with a spoon.

Lisa Washburn
Wellesley Hills, Mass.

Underwater Cherry Pitting

For neater cherry pitting, I place a large bowl of water in the sink. I add the cherries and then pit them at the bottom of the bowl. The pits float to the surface for easy removal, the cherries are rinsed in the process, and my hands (and the kitchen walls) aren't bright red from the juice.

Anne Cross
New Canaan, Conn.

Our $1,000 Grand-Prize Winner!

Susan Bazan
Sequim, Wash.

Prize-Winning Cookies Taste as Great as They Look

When you can't find the perfect holiday cookie to suit your tastes, you might have to do what Susan did—invent it. She explains, "I wanted a cookie that combined my two favorite things: peanut butter and chocolate. My Fudgy Peanut Butter Mousse Cups have been a huge success at cookie exchanges." Our judges were similarly impressed with Susan's pretty cookies, which call for baking a pecan sugar-cookie crust in a mini-muffin tin and then filling the shells with melted chocolate and peanut butter mousse.

Our runners-up are just as flavorful and attractive. A simple sandwich cookie made with almonds and raspberry jam is the picture of elegance. A fresh spin on chocolate-caramel-pecan turtles simplifies the classic recipe by using melted caramel candies. Another runner-up packs a moist and chewy bar cookie with dried cranberries, pistachios, white chocolate, and coconut. Finally, our panel praised Italian-inspired chocolate-hazelnut cookies made with instant espresso powder and Nutella.

FUDGY PEANUT BUTTER MOUSSE CUPS

MAKES ABOUT 3 DOZEN COOKIES
You will need a mini-muffin tin for this recipe. For neat assembly, use a piping bag to fill the cups with the peanut butter mixture. Sugar cookie mix is sold in the baking aisle alongside boxed cake mixes.

- 1 (17.5-ounce) package sugar cookie mix (see note)
- 1 cup pecans, toasted and chopped fine
- 2 tablespoons all-purpose flour
- 8 tablespoons (1 stick) unsalted butter, melted
- 1¼ cups heavy cream
- 1 cup chunky peanut butter
- 1 (8-ounce) package cream cheese, softened
- 1 cup confectioners' sugar
- 1 teaspoon vanilla extract
- 1 cup semisweet chocolate chips

1. Adjust oven rack to middle position and heat oven to 350 degrees. Grease 12-cup mini-muffin tin. Combine cookie mix, pecans, and flour in bowl. Slowly stir in butter until mixture resembles wet sand. Press 1 tablespoon cookie mixture into bottom and sides of each muffin cup. Bake until golden, about 10 minutes. Cool 20 minutes in tin, then turn out cookies. Repeat with remaining dough.

2. With electric mixer on medium-high speed, beat 1 cup cream to stiff peaks, about 2 minutes. In another bowl, beat peanut butter, cream cheese, sugar, and vanilla on medium speed until smooth, about 1 minute. Fold in whipped cream.

3. Microwave chocolate and remaining cream in small bowl, stirring occasionally, until smooth, about 1 minute. Pour ½ teaspoon chocolate mixture into each cookie cup, then fill cups with 1 tablespoon peanut butter mixture. Drizzle remaining chocolate evenly over cookies and refrigerate until firm, about 1 hour.

These crisp cookie shells are filled with a mixture of whipped cream, peanut butter, and cream cheese—with chocolate both below and above.

Robin Evans
Evergreen, Colo.

Jennifer Parks
Tucson, Ariz.

Mike Hendricks
St. Joseph, Mo.

Bridget Peterson
Manly, Iowa

CHOCOLATE TURTLE COOKIES

MAKES ABOUT 2 DOZEN COOKIES

Robin says: "I pride myself on making beautiful cookies for family and friends as far away as Australia, Spain, and Japan."

- 1 cup all-purpose flour
- ⅓ cup cocoa powder
- ¼ teaspoon salt
- 8 tablespoons (1 stick) unsalted butter, softened
- ⅔ cup sugar
- 1 large egg, separated, plus 1 egg white
- 2 tablespoons milk
- 1 teaspoon vanilla extract
- 1 cup pecans, chopped fine
- 14 soft caramel candies
- 3 tablespoons heavy cream

1. Adjust oven rack to upper-middle and lower-middle positions and heat oven to 350 degrees. Line 2 baking sheets with parchment paper. Combine flour, cocoa, and salt in bowl. With electric mixer on medium-high speed, beat butter and sugar until fluffy, about 2 minutes. Add egg yolk, milk, and vanilla and mix until incorporated. Reduce speed to low and add flour mixture until just combined. Refrigerate dough until firm, at least 1 hour.

2. Whisk egg whites in bowl until frothy. Place pecans in another bowl. One at a time, roll dough into 1-inch balls, dip in egg whites, then roll in pecans. Place balls 2 inches apart on prepared baking sheets. Using teaspoon measure, make indentation in center of each ball. Bake until set, 10 to 12 minutes, switching and rotating sheets halfway through baking.

3. Meanwhile, microwave caramels and cream in bowl, stirring occasionally, until smooth, 1 to 2 minutes. Once cookies are removed from oven, gently press existing indentations with teaspoon measure. Fill each with ½ teaspoon caramel mixture. Cool 5 minutes, then transfer to wire rack and cool completely.

HAZELNUT CHEWIES

MAKES ABOUT 3½ DOZEN COOKIES

Jennifer says: "For my birthday I finally got a mixer and have been experimenting with different cookies ever since. This recipe combines elements of three different recipes." Nutella is a chocolate-hazelnut spread that can be found near the peanut butter in most grocery stores; you will need one 13-ounce jar for this recipe.

- 3 cups all-purpose flour
- 2 teaspoons baking powder
- ½ teaspoon salt
- 1¼ cups Nutella spread (see note)
- 4 tablespoons unsalted butter, softened
- 1⅓ cups granulated sugar
- 1 teaspoon vanilla extract
- 1 teaspoon instant espresso powder
- 2 large eggs
- ⅓ cup milk
- 1½ cups hazelnuts, toasted and chopped fine
- 1 cup confectioners' sugar

1. Adjust oven racks to upper-middle and lower-middle positions and heat oven to 375 degrees. Line 2 baking sheets with parchment paper. Combine flour, baking powder, and salt in bowl. With electric mixer on medium-high speed, beat Nutella, butter, and granulated sugar until light and fluffy, about 2 minutes. Add vanilla, espresso, and eggs and mix until incorporated. Reduce speed to low, add flour mixture and milk, and mix until just combined. Fold in ½ cup hazelnuts and refrigerate dough until firm, about 1 hour.

2. Place remaining hazelnuts in bowl. Add confectioners' sugar to another bowl. One at a time, roll dough into 1-inch balls, roll in hazelnuts, then roll in confectioners' sugar. Place balls 2 inches apart on prepared baking sheets. Bake until set, about 8 minutes, switching and rotating sheets halfway through baking. Cool 5 minutes on sheets, then transfer to wire rack and cool completely. Repeat with remaining dough.

CRANBERRY PISTACHIO COCONUT TRIANGLES

MAKES ABOUT 1½ DOZEN COOKIES

Mike says: "I came up with this recipe for my wife, who absolutely loves pistachios and dried cranberries."

- 1 cup plus 2 tablespoons all-purpose flour
- 1 cup plus 2 tablespoons packed light brown sugar
- 5 tablespoons unsalted butter, cut into 5 pieces and chilled
- 1 large egg
- 2 tablespoons maple syrup
- ¾ teaspoon vanilla extract
- ½ teaspoon almond extract
- ½ teaspoon salt
- 1 cup pistachios, toasted and chopped
- 1 cup dried cranberries
- ¾ cup sweetened, shredded coconut
- 2 ounces white chocolate, chopped

1. Adjust oven rack to middle position and heat oven to 375 degrees. Line 8-inch square baking pan with foil, allowing excess foil to hang over pan edges. Grease foil. Process 1 cup flour and 2 tablespoons sugar in food processor until combined. Add butter, 1 piece at a time, and pulse until only pea-sized pieces remain. Press mixture into prepared pan and bake until light golden, about 15 minutes. Cool completely.

2. Whisk egg, syrup, extracts, salt, remaining flour, and remaining sugar in large bowl. Fold in pistachios, cranberries, and coconut, then spread mixture evenly over cooled crust. Bake until topping is golden and begins to pull away from sides of pan, 15 to 20 minutes. Cool completely.

3. Using foil overhang, lift cookies out of pan. Cut into 2½-inch squares and cut each square diagonally into 2 triangles. Microwave white chocolate in small bowl, stirring occasionally, until melted, 30 to 60 seconds. Dip cookie corners in melted chocolate and place on wire rack until chocolate sets, about 30 minutes.

RASPBERRY ALMOND COOKIES

MAKES ABOUT 2 DOZEN COOKIES

Bridget says: "My mother-in-law makes these cookies for us every Christmas. They are our family's favorite." If you don't have slivered almonds on hand, 1½ cups sliced almonds can be substituted.

- 2 cups all-purpose flour
- 1¼ cups slivered almonds (see note)
- 1 cup sugar
- 16 tablespoons unsalted butter (2 sticks), cut into ½-inch pieces and chilled
- 1 teaspoon vanilla extract
- ½ cup raspberry jam

1. Adjust oven racks to upper-middle and lower-middle positions and heat oven to 350 degrees. Line 2 baking sheets with parchment paper. Process 1 cup flour and almonds in food processor until finely ground. Add ½ cup sugar and remaining flour and process until combined. Add butter and vanilla to food processor and pulse until dough forms.

2. On lightly floured surface, roll dough to ¼ inch thickness. Using 2-inch round cookie cutter, cut out cookies, gathering and rerolling dough as necessary. Place cookies 2 inches apart on prepared baking sheets and bake until light brown around edges, about 15 minutes, switching and rotating sheets halfway through baking. Cool 5 minutes on sheets, then transfer to wire rack.

3. Transfer remaining sugar to bowl. Working quickly, spread 1 teaspoon jam on bottom of half of warm cookies, then press remaining cookies onto jam to form sandwiches. Roll cookies in sugar to coat. Cool completely on wire rack. Repeat with remaining dough.

Cookie Storage

The Fudgy Peanut Butter Mousse Cups can be refrigerated in an airtight container for 3 days; the other cookies can be stored in an airtight container at room temperature for 3 days.

Ask Cook's Country

WE'LL ANSWER ANY QUESTION YOU THROW AT US!

ALL EGGS AREN'T EQUAL

Is there really a difference between the different grades of eggs? Will it affect my cooking if I don't use the specified size?

Les Myers
Jackson, Miss.

The USDA labels eggs either AA, A, or B according to their shell appearance and the quality of the egg inside. A misshapen or thin shell typically merits the lowest B grade, and such eggs are usually used commercially. To distinguish AA from A, graders use a method called candling: Each egg is held up to a bright light in a dark room to check the interior quality. Grade AA eggs have whites that are so thick that the firm yolk is hard to see; grade AA eggs are rare (and more expensive) in supermarkets. Grade A eggs have slightly looser whites and softer yolks; this grade accounts for most of the eggs sold in supermarkets across the country. Both are acceptable in any application.

Depending on the chicken's size, eggs can vary from about one to three ounces (see chart below). In the test kitchen, we typically use large eggs, but other sizes can be substituted according to weight.

Egg Weight Chart

SIZE	WEIGHT (in ounces)
Medium	1.75
Large	2.00
Extra-Large	2.25
Jumbo	2.50

PACKAGED BROTH ALTERNATIVES

I've always used cartons of chicken broth, but I have run out several times and wonder if the chicken bouillon sitting in my pantry is a passable emergency substitute.

Wanda Vincent
San Diego, Calif.

Chicken bouillon cubes are compact and affordable, but are they any good? To find out, we reconstituted a popular supermarket chicken bouillon brand, Knorr, according to package directions and tasted it plain and in a quick chicken soup against our favorite packaged broth, Swanson's Certified Organic Free Range Chicken Broth. We also tried broth made from Better Than Bouillon refrigerated chicken base; this concentrated paste will last over a year in the refrigerator and, like cubes, is simply rehydrated with hot water.

Tasters disliked the broth made from the Knorr bouillon cubes both on its own and in the soup—it was overwhelmingly salty. The Swanson broth came out on top again. And the broth made from Better Than Bouillon base? Though milder, it lived up to its name and was deemed acceptable in a pinch.

COOKIE SHEETS: NECESSARY OR NOT?

My sister swears by her cookie sheets, but I've always relied on rimmed baking sheets for all of my baking needs. Is a pan for cookies worth the extra investment?

Diane Esher
Buffalo, N.Y.

In our recent testing of cookie sheets, the Vollrath cookie sheet beat out all contenders for its thickness, durability, and substantial weight (all of which promote even cooking) and light color (which staves off overbrowning). But we have never tested it against our winning rimmed baking sheet, the Lincoln Foodservice Half-Size Heavy Duty Sheet Pan, which gets heavy use in the test kitchen for everything from roasting vegetables to toasting nuts.

We lined each pan with parchment and baked up batches of traditional butter cookies (to compare browning) and ultrathin lace cookies (to compare heat conductivity). Both cookies cooked evenly on both pans, but the cookies on the baking sheet were done a few minutes earlier. And although some claim that the rimless design of cookie sheets encourages air flow and thus more even browning on top of the cookies, we found that the rimmed sheet consistently produced beautifully browned cookies. So, although cookie sheets provide easier access to hot cookies, a hefty rimmed baking sheet bakes cookies just as well.

SUN-DRIED TOMATO PASTE

I've recently noticed sun-dried tomato paste in the grocery store. Can this be substituted for regular tomato paste?

Jeannie Watchlen
Denver, Colo.

Tomato paste, a concentrated, cooked puree of ripened tomatoes that have been skinned and seeded, is often used to add flavor and body to pasta sauces, soup, stews, and sauces, but its sun-dried counterpart was new to us. In addition to sun-dried tomatoes, this version is pureed with oils, vinegar, and spices.

To see how the sun-dried version compared to regular Amore tomato paste (a previous test kitchen winner), we whipped up a cooked pasta sauce and a flavored mayonnaise with each. Tasters favored the "bold, sharp" flavor of the regular tomato paste in both applications, faulting the sun-dried version as "just salty" with little tomato flavor. Curious how the sun-dried paste might measure up to jarred

NOT RECOMMENDED
Though we love Amore's regular tomato paste, the sun-dried tomato version was a miss.

sun-dried tomatoes themselves, we tested an equal amount of each pureed in another round of pasta sauce and mayonnaise. Once again, tasters noted the paste's meek flavor in comparison to the freshly pureed sun-dried tomatoes. We do not recommend Amore sun-dried tomato paste.

SILICONE ROLLING PIN

I've heard that dough doesn't stick to silicone rolling pins like it does to wooden ones. Is this true?

Mary Evans
Tampa, Fla.

We've put marble, glass, nylon, aluminum, and Teflon-coated rolling pins to the test, but nothing has compared to wooden pins. Eager to test silicone's nonstick property in a rolling pin, we whipped up two batches of basic pie dough and notoriously sticky sugar cookie dough, and rolled them out with our favorite wooden pin and a new silicone pin.

While the silicone was not completely stick-free, it didn't require as much additional flour (which can toughen baked goods) on the pin and work surface as its wooden counterpart. Also, unlike porous wood, the silicone provides an easy-to-clean, germ-free surface. And as for the shape, the Sil-Pin brand offers a handled pin, a barrel-shaped baker's pin, and the test kitchen's favorite shape, the French-style pin with tapered ends. The silicone pins, however, did have one drawback: Depending on the shape and size, they cost $30 to $40. Our favorite wooden French-style tapered pin, made by Fante, costs about $8.

WORKS WELL, COSTS A LOT
Unless the price of silicone rolling pins comes down, the test kitchen won't be throwing out our wooden rolling pins.

SMOKE WITHOUT FIRE

I recently saw a recipe that called for cold-smoked salmon. What is cold smoking?

María Argüello
Clermont, Fla.

Cold smoking is accomplished by separating the heat source from the food to be smoked; the smoke is often pumped into the smoking chamber through a cooled pipe to chill it. Common examples of cold-smoked foods include artisanal bacon, smoked salmon, and smoked cheddar and Gouda cheeses.

To ask us a cooking question, visit CooksCountry.com/emailus. You can also write to Ask Cook's Country, P.O. Box 470739, Brookline, MA 02447. See if you can stump us!

It takes days of cooking to produce traditional cassoulet, a rustic, flavorful stew with creamy beans and a host of tender meats. Could we simplify it for the slow cooker?

Classic cassoulet is a project recipe. There's the overnight soaking and long cooking of the white beans, the half-week needed to make confit (goose or duck cooked in its own fat), and the slow simmering of pork and sausages—and that's before all the ingredients are simmered together so that their flavors can meld. Most recipes I found for slow-cooker cassoulet dump canned white beans, cubed pork loin, sausage, chicken parts (in lieu of confit), broth, wine, and tomatoes into the cooker; six hours later, you're left with a washed-out mess of gray meats and blown-out beans. There had to be a better way.

I wanted to replace the lean pork loin with something that wouldn't dry out during long cooking. Cubes of well-marbled pork shoulder worked, but a big shoulder roast provided more meat than I needed. Boneless country-style ribs gave me more control over how much I bought. To enhance their meatiness, I browned the ribs before adding them to the slow cooker.

Chicken breasts became dry and stringy with long cooking; my tasters preferred the moist texture and richer flavor of bone-in thighs. Unfortunately, six hours of cooking (the time the pork needed, even when cut into small chunks) was too much for the thighs. To slow down their cooking, I wrapped the thighs in a foil packet and cooked them on top of (rather than in) the stew; after six hours, the thigh meat was moist and ready to be shredded. Pork sausages are traditional for cassoulet, but my tasters found andouille and chorizo (common additions to slow-cooker recipes) too distinctly flavored. They preferred garlicky kielbasa, especially when I browned it first and added it to the stew just before serving (to prevent it from drying out).

I knew that I wanted to use dried white beans; great Northern beans are similar to traditional French flageolets yet easier to find. Added raw, however, the beans didn't soften fully in six hours of slow cooking. Hoping to avoid an overnight soak, I tried a common trick of boiling the beans and then letting them sit for an hour off-heat. This worked, but not fast enough for me. Simmering the beans for 20 minutes before adding them to the cooker gave them just enough of a head start so that they were tender and creamy by the time the stew was done.

For the broth base, I sautéed chopped onion in the flavorful drippings left from browning the meats, then added plenty of garlic and thyme, as well as tomato paste for richness and body. Next, I stirred in chicken broth and brandy (this had a complexity my tasters preferred to the more traditional white wine) along with canned tomatoes and added this mixture to the cooker. To thicken the stew, I removed a cup of the cooked beans, mashed them to a paste, and returned them to the broth. A buttery bread-crumb topping provided the classic crowning touch to this rich, meaty cassoulet. –Cali Rich

SLOW-COOKER CASSOULET

SERVES 6 TO 8

An equal amount of boneless pork shoulder roast can be substituted for country-style ribs. We prefer great Northern beans here.

- 1 **pound dried medium-sized white beans, rinsed and picked over**
- 2 **pounds boneless country-style pork ribs, cut into 1-inch chunks**
  Salt and pepper
- 1 **tablespoon vegetable oil**
- 8 **ounces kielbasa sausage, halved lengthwise and sliced thin**
- 2 **onions, chopped fine**
- 6 **garlic cloves, minced**
- 1 **tablespoon minced fresh thyme**
- 1 **tablespoon tomato paste**
- 3½ **cups low-sodium chicken broth**
- ½ **cup brandy**
- 1 **(14.5-ounce) can diced tomatoes, drained**
- 4 **bone-in, skin-on chicken thighs (about 2 pounds), excess fat trimmed**
- 2 **slices hearty white sandwich bread, torn into pieces**
- 2 **tablespoons unsalted butter, melted**

1. Bring beans and 8 cups water to boil in medium saucepan over medium-high heat. Reduce heat to low and simmer, covered, until just beginning to soften, about 20 minutes. Drain beans and transfer to slow cooker.

2. Pat pork dry with paper towels and season with salt and pepper. Heat oil in Dutch oven over medium-high heat until just smoking. Cook pork until well browned, about 10 minutes; transfer to slow cooker. Brown kielbasa in empty pan, about 5 minutes; using slotted spoon, transfer to paper towel–lined plate and reserve in refrigerator. Add onions to fat in pan and cook until softened, about 5 minutes. Stir in garlic, thyme, and tomato paste and cook until fragrant, about 30 seconds. Add broth, brandy, and tomatoes, scraping up any browned bits with wooden spoon. Bring broth mixture to boil, then transfer to slow cooker.

3. Season chicken with salt and pepper and wrap in foil according to photo 1 at right. Place foil packet atop stew in slow cooker. Cover and cook on low until pork and chicken are tender, 6 to 7 hours.

4. Remove foil packet from slow cooker and transfer to plate. When chicken is cool enough to handle, pull meat from bones in large chunks, discarding skin, bones, and excess fat. Transfer 1 cup beans from slow cooker to bowl and mash until smooth. Stir mashed beans, chicken meat, and reserved kielbasa into slow cooker. Cook, covered, until heated through, about 10 minutes.

5. Meanwhile, pulse bread, butter, and ¼ teaspoon salt in food processor until coarsely ground. Toast crumbs in large skillet over medium-high heat until golden, about 5 minutes. Season cassoulet with salt and pepper. Serve, passing bread crumbs at table.

Make Ahead: The finished cassoulet can be refrigerated in an airtight container for 3 days. When ready to serve, bring cassoulet to simmer over medium heat, thinning broth with water as necessary. The crispy bread crumbs can be stored in an airtight container for 1 day.

Despite its French name, this hearty stew is built on the familiar flavors of pork, chicken, and beans.

Secrets to
SLOW-COOKER CASSOULET

Here's how we ensured everything was done at the same time.

1. SLOW DOWN: Place chicken on one side of a large piece of aluminum foil. Fold over the foil, shaping it into a packet that will fit into your slow cooker, then crimp the edges to seal. The foil packet helps to protect the chicken from overcooking.

2. SPEED UP: Simmering the dried beans for 20 minutes before adding them to the slow cooker gives them the head start they need.

Recipe Makeover CRÈME BRÛLÉE

Are heavy cream and egg yolks the only ways to create the signature creaminess and richness of this classic baked custard?

And the Numbers...
All nutritional information is for one serving.

TRADITIONAL CRÈME BRÛLÉE
CALORIES: 570
FAT: 51g
SATURATED FAT: 30g

COOK'S COUNTRY LOW-FAT CRÈME BRÛLÉE
CALORIES: 240
FAT: 14g
SATURATED FAT: 8g

Kitchen Know-How
CREAMY CUSTARD, LIGHTER ON FAT AND CALORIES

The rich, silky-smooth texture of traditional crème brûlée comes from large quantities of egg yolks and heavy cream. Early attempts to reduce the amount of either left us with lean, soupy custards. Here's how we kept the silky texture and rich flavor while slashing the fat and calories.

1. By adding cornstarch and cooking until the mixture is thick enough to coat the back of a spoon, we were able to reduce the number of yolks from 12 to 5 and replace the cream with a combination of half-and-half and milk.

2. The hot dairy mixture is strained over chopped white chocolate, which lends sweetness and body.

Crème brûlée is all about excess. The test kitchen's favorite recipe stirs together a dozen egg yolks, 4 cups of heavy cream, and ⅔ cup of sugar. This high-fat mixture is divided into individual portions and gently baked in a water bath (to ensure even cooking) before being chilled and brûléed (a torch is used to caramelize extra sugar sprinkled on top). At 570 calories and 51 grams of fat per serving, this recipe is an obvious candidate for a makeover.

I gathered several recipes for "light" crème brûlée, headed to the test kitchen, and lined up the ramekins. Custards that replaced the heavy cream with 2 percent or low-fat milk tasted and felt lean, while those made with soy or rice milk were thin and flavorless. A few versions replaced the eggs with egg substitutes or tofu; even worse than their artificial flavor was their rubbery texture. Since not a single "healthy" recipe was worth eating, my approach would have to start with the real thing and work backward.

Swapping the heavy cream for a combination of whole milk and half-and-half and reducing the yolks to 5 made great strides in limiting the overall fat and calorie count—at the expense of texture and flavor. The custard didn't firm up properly, and it tasted thin.

The protein in egg yolks is what helps traditional crème brûlée set up into a velvety consistency. To replace their setting power, I first tested egg whites, which have even more protein, but augmenting the yolks with even a single white resulted in a springy, overset texture. I turned to other thickeners, all of which required gentle cooking on the stovetop to activate them before baking in the water bath. Gelatin set well initially, but dissolved into a liquidy mess under the heat of the torch. Flour made the custard too pasty, but 3 tablespoons of cornstarch (any more and it became slippery) made for a thicker custard impervious to the torch's fury.

My custard was now setting up nicely, but tasters complained that without the cream it lacked the proper velvety feel. I tried adding dry milk powder and evaporated milk, but neither added the right creamy quality. Remembering that the test kitchen has used white chocolate to help fortify baked goods like cheesecake, I won-

dered if just a little could help enrich the texture without bumping up the nutritional numbers too much. Sure enough, just 2 ounces brought a luxurious feel without a significant increase in fat.

As a bonus, the white chocolate added enough sweetness that I could reduce the amount of sugar in the custard by half. My crème brûlée now had fewer than half the calories and 70 percent less fat than the original—and my tasters were none the wiser.

–Kelley Baker

LOW-FAT CRÈME BRÛLÉE
SERVES 8
You will need eight 4-ounce ramekins and a kitchen torch (see page 31) for this recipe. For a more substantial crust, turbinado or Demerara sugar can be substituted for the granulated sugar.

- 2 cups half-and-half
- 1½ cups whole milk
- ⅓ cup plus 8 teaspoons sugar
- 1 vanilla bean, split lengthwise and seeds removed
- ¼ teaspoon salt
- 5 large egg yolks
- 3 tablespoons cornstarch
- 2 ounces white chocolate, chopped

1. Adjust oven rack to middle position and heat oven to 300 degrees. Combine half-and-half, milk, ⅓ cup sugar, vanilla seeds and pod, and salt in large saucepan. Whisk egg yolks and cornstarch in bowl until combined, then whisk into half-and-half mixture. Bring half-and-half mixture to boil over medium heat, stirring constantly, then reduce heat to medium-low and simmer until thickened, about 1 minute. Place chopped white chocolate in large liquid measuring cup and strain half-and-half mixture through fine-mesh strainer on top of chocolate. Whisk until completely smooth.

2. Bring 2 quarts water to boil. Place kitchen towel in bottom of roasting pan and arrange eight 4- to 5-ounce ramekins (or shallow fluted dishes) on towel. Divide custard mixture evenly among ramekins. Carefully place pan on oven rack and pour boiling water into pan until water comes halfway up sides of ramekins. Bake until custard is just set and center registers 170 degrees, about 30 minutes (about 20 minutes if using shallow fluted dishes).

3. Carefully transfer ramekins to wire rack and cool to room temperature, about 2 hours. Refrigerate, covered, until cold, at least 4 hours or up to 2 days.

4. Uncover ramekins; if condensation has collected on surface, blot gently with paper towel. Sprinkle 1 teaspoon sugar evenly over surface of each custard. Caramelize sugar with torch until deep golden brown (see instructions on page 30). Let stand 5 minutes. Serve.

Our low-fat version boasts a silky-smooth, vanilla-infused custard and crunchy burnt sugar topping—but with less than half the calories and 70 percent less fat than traditional recipes.

This little-known Dixie dessert—a rich, caramel-y custard pie dressed up with dried fruit and nuts— deserves a national introduction.

The South remains sweet on its Civil War leaders: Robert E. Lee has a lemon curd–filled cake, while Confederate President Jefferson Davis ("Jeff" to some recipe writers) has a pie named after him. Despite my Southern upbringing (in North Carolina), I wasn't acquainted with Jefferson Davis pie, which research revealed to be a simple brown-sugar chess pie studded with dried fruit and nuts. Most recipes make a no-cook filling by combining brown sugar, egg yolks, butter, milk, warm spices, dried fruit, pecans, and a few tablespoons of flour; the mixture is poured into a raw pie shell and the pie is baked until the custard sets. This sounded like a pie worth getting to know!

But when I baked off a handful of recipes, I wasn't sure Mr. Davis and I were going to be friends. Most of my test pies baked up with saccharine, loose fillings and soggy crusts. And while my tasters appreciated the flavor of the fruit and nuts, they didn't like the distraction of having them suspended in the otherwise smooth custard.

My first goal was sliceable custard with a good balance of sweetness and spice. Most recipes started out with 2 (or more) cups of brown sugar, but I found that 1 cup was just fine, as less sugar let the flavors of the cinnamon and allspice (favored over common but imposing additions like cloves, nutmeg, and mace) shine through. Using heavy cream instead of milk gave the pie a silkier, thicker texture and much richer flavor.

Most custard pies are made with whole eggs, which set faster than just the yolks used in Jefferson Davis pie, so custard pies bake faster (in a half hour or less) and require a parbaked pie shell to ensure even cooking. Because yolks take longer to set, Jeff Davis pie usually bakes in a raw pie shell for about 45 minutes. The pies are typically started at a high temperature (about 425) to firm up the crust and finished at a moderate 350 degrees. But without fail, this method resulted in custards that dried out around the edges before they were fully set in the center. After several tests,

I found a slightly longer bake (about an hour) in a gentle 325-degree oven allowed the crust to brown in the same time it took for the custard to set to the requisite firmness.

Some recipes saddle this pie with 2 cups of raisins and dates and more than a cup of pecans. I started by halving those amounts and finely grinding them in the food processor for a more homogenous filling. But my tasters still balked at the bits of fruit and nuts in the custard. So instead of folding them in, I tried pressing them into the bottom of the raw crust and gently pouring the custard over. This pie baked up with a thin, distinct layer of fruit and nuts on the bottom and a creamy, smooth custard layer on top. A dollop of bourbon-fortified whipped cream was all I needed to make this pie worthy of a national introduction. –Cali Rich

JEFFERSON DAVIS PIE SERVES 8

Use your favorite pie dough or go to CooksCountry.com for our recipe. For a convenient option, use one sheet of Pillsbury Just Unroll! Pie Crusts, available in the refrigerator section of your supermarket. Serve with our Bourbon Whipped Cream or vanilla ice cream. We prefer the mild flavor of golden raisins in this recipe, but regular raisins will work.

½	cup raisins (see page 31)
½	cup chopped dates
½	cup pecans, toasted and chopped
1	(9-inch) pie shell, chilled in pie plate for 30 minutes (see note)
3	tablespoons all-purpose flour
1	teaspoon ground cinnamon
¼	teaspoon ground allspice
½	teaspoon salt
1	cup packed light brown sugar
8	tablespoons (1 stick) unsalted butter, softened
5	large egg yolks
1¼	cups heavy cream

1. Adjust oven rack to lowest position and heat oven to 325 degrees. Pulse raisins, dates, and pecans in food processor until finely ground. Transfer mixture to chilled pie shell and gently press into even layer.

The dense bottom layer of pureed nuts and dried fruit provides a flavorful base for the spiced brown-sugar custard layer above.

2. Combine flour, cinnamon, allspice, and salt in small bowl. With electric mixer on medium-low speed, beat sugar and butter until just combined, about 1 minute. Mix in yolks, one at a time, until incorporated. Add flour mixture and cream and mix, scraping down sides of bowl as necessary, until just combined.

3. Pour filling over fruit and nuts in prepared crust and bake until surface is deep brown and center jiggles slightly when pie is shaken, 55 to 65 minutes. Cool completely on wire rack, about 4 hours. Serve. (Pie can be refrigerated, covered in plastic wrap, for 2 days.)

BOURBON WHIPPED CREAM
MAKES ABOUT 2 CUPS

Though any style of whiskey will work here, we prefer the smoky sweetness of bourbon. For the most efficient whipping, make sure your heavy cream is as cold as possible.

1	cup heavy cream
2	tablespoons bourbon
1½	tablespoons light brown sugar
½	teaspoon vanilla extract

With electric mixer on medium speed, beat cream, bourbon, sugar, and vanilla until stiff peaks form, about 2 minutes. (Whipped cream can be refrigerated for 4 hours.)

Topping Jeff Davis Pie

Some mid-century recipes for Jefferson Davis Pie, like the one published in the 1950 *Romantic Recipes of the Old South* pamphlet from Imperial Pure Cane Sugar (pictured), called for a baked meringue topping. We tried these recipes and didn't think the meringue added anything to the pie—except a lot of extra work and bland sweetness. Most modern recipes instead top the pie with whipped cream. Our Bourbon Whipped Cream takes just 2 minutes to prepare and is the perfect finish for this pie.

Wisconsin Cheddar Beer Soup

Rich, creamy cheddar beer soup helps take the chill off long Wisconsin winters; unfortunately, most recipes cook up greasy and gritty. We needed to find cheese that could take the heat.

To make it the way they do in Wisconsin, use sharp orange cheddar cheese and top the soup with popcorn.

Secrets to Smoothness

Because cheddar—and especially sharp cheddar—is a poor melting cheese, most recipes for cheddar beer soup end up grainy. Here's how we made a smooth soup with intense cheddar flavor.

AMERICAN CHEESE
Adding 1 cup of shredded American cheese (which contains emulsifiers that promote even melting) to the flavorful cheddar resulted in a smooth texture.

CORNSTARCH
A few tablespoons of cornstarch tossed in with the shredded cheese ensured thorough, efficient melting, which kept the soup silky and free from clumps.

Which Beer Is Best?

Although any domestic lager will work in this soup, Wisconsin Cheddar Beer Soup just didn't seem authentic without a Wisconsin beer. We tasted five widely available Wisconsin brands—Miller, Miller High Life, Miller Genuine Draft, Schlitz, and Pabst Blue Ribbon—both in soup and on their own. After some heated debate, tasters selected Miller High Life for its hoppy character and balanced flavor, praising it as the "perfect complement to the tanginess of the cheddar."

THE CHAMPAGNE OF BEERS
For honest beer flavor minus the bitterness, reach for the High Life.

Wisconsin is known for its cheese and its beer, so it's no surprise that cheddar beer soup—complete with the traditional popcorn garnish—is a standard item on local menus. This hearty soup is simple to make: Carrots, onion, and celery are sautéed in butter, flour is added to make a roux, and then chicken broth, dairy, and beer are whisked in. Shredded sharp cheddar cheese is added at the end and melts to a velvety smooth consistency. Or at least that's the idea. But just as often the cheese clumps together or breaks, leaving the soup streaked with pools of fat.

I started according to custom by sautéing onion, carrot, and celery, but my tasters found the celery bitter, so I omitted it. Cream and half-and-half were both too heavy, even when cut with the chicken broth—milk worked better. Thinking I'd want an intensely flavored beer, I tested robust ales like Bass and Samuel Adams (and even a few Wisconsin microbrews), but my tasters were keen on the milder, less bitter flavor of American lagers (see box, below). Some recipes keep the soup chunky, but my tasters preferred the texture of a pureed soup.

It was time to focus on the big problem—the cheese. All that aging gives sharp cheddar plenty of flavor, but an aged cheese has very little moisture. (That's why aged cheddars crumble.) It turns out that low-moisture cheeses are much more likely to break when melted. The result is a grainy, greasy soup. Milder cheddar (which is aged less) wasn't much of an improvement. Even colby—a mild Wisconsin cheese similar to Monterey Jack—was grainy in the soup. Knowing that American cheese is made with emulsifiers to promote melting, I tried a 50-50 ratio of sharp cheddar and American, which melted smoothly but was bland. One cup of American to three cups of sharp cheddar was the best mix for non-grainy melting and rich flavor.

While most of the soup was melting smoothly, it was studded with hard little clumps of cheese. I was adding the shredded cheese off heat, but it still clumped when I tried stirring in the cheese over low heat—and using high heat caused the soup to separate.

Some research helped me understand that while shredded cheese melts faster than larger pieces, the surface of the shredded cheese melts so quickly that pieces can fuse together, creating a mass that becomes harder to melt. To keep the shredded cheese from fusing, I tried packaged shredded cheese, which includes cornstarch to prevent clumping. Finally the soup was smooth! Adding my own cornstarch to hand-shredded block cheese worked just as well and let me use any good sharp cheddar. –Lynn Clark

WISCONSIN CHEDDAR BEER SOUP SERVES 6

You will need one 4-ounce chunk of American cheese from the deli counter for this recipe; do not use presliced or packaged shredded cheese here. Freeze the American cheese for 15 minutes to make shredding easier.

- 4 tablespoons unsalted butter
- 1 onion, chopped fine
- 2 carrots, peeled and chopped fine
- 2 garlic cloves, minced
- ⅓ cup all-purpose flour
- 1¾ cups low-sodium chicken broth
- 1 (12-ounce) beer (see box at left)
- 2 cups whole or low-fat milk
- 3 cups shredded sharp cheddar cheese
- 1 cup shredded American cheese (see note)
- 2 teaspoons cornstarch
  Salt and pepper

1. Melt butter in large pot over medium heat. Cook onion and carrots until lightly browned, about 10 minutes. Add garlic and cook until fragrant, about 30 seconds. Stir in flour and cook until golden, about 1 minute. Slowly whisk in broth, beer, and milk. Bring mixture to simmer, then reduce heat to low and simmer gently (do not boil) until carrots are very soft, 20 to 25 minutes.

2. Meanwhile, toss shredded cheeses and cornstarch in large bowl until well combined. Puree soup in blender in two batches until completely smooth, return to pot, and simmer over medium-low heat. Whisk in cheese mixture, one handful at a time, until smooth. Season with salt and pepper. Serve. (Soup can be refrigerated in an airtight container for 3 days.)

The Best Reuben Sandwiches

My husband and I always argue about our Reubens—he insists his are better, but both of ours turn out soggy, and we can never find flavorful sauerkraut or dressing in the supermarket. I hope to use your recipe as my secret weapon in our Reuben war. –Melissa K., via e-mail

The grilled Reuben—sliced corned beef, tangy sauerkraut, creamy Russian or Thousand Island dressing, and melted Swiss cheese on rye—is the epitome of a New York deli sandwich. But even *The New York Times* reports that the Reuben was created in the 1920s at the Blackstone Hotel in Omaha, Nebraska, when a local grocer, Reuben Kulakofsky, concocted it for his poker buddies, then convinced the hotel owner to put it on the menu. A waitress there won a national contest with the sandwich in the 1950s, and it soon swept the country. Today, Reubens are everywhere, but most recipes I tried produced sandwiches with chilly centers, unmelted cheese, soggy rye, watery sauerkraut, and sugary supermarket dressing.

Bottled Russian and Thousand Island dressings are nearly identical: Both are made from mayonnaise, ketchup, pickle relish, vinegar, and sugar, and both were unacceptably sweet here. A homemade dressing using the same ingredients—minus the sugar—was much better, but my tasters wanted more punch. Hot peppers tasted out of place, but horseradish (an ingredient sometimes found in Russian dressings) provided welcome heat. To streamline ingredients, I tried replacing the ketchup and horseradish with prepared cocktail sauce, and my tasters couldn't tell the difference. While most recipes use pickle relish, tasters preferred the fresher flavor and crunch of hand-chopped pickles. Finally, replacing the vinegar with pickle juice balanced tang with sweetness.

I spread the dressing on rye bread, and to combat soggy sandwich syndrome, I drained the sauerkraut before layering it with the meat and cheese. The sauerkraut still exuded enough moisture to saturate the bread. Even worse, since the meat and cheese had come straight from the refrigerator, the contents of the sandwich were cold (and the cheese unmelted) by the time the bread was sufficiently browned. I tried cooking the sauerkraut in a skillet before assembling the sandwiches. This allowed the excess moisture to evaporate, plus the hot sauerkraut helped warm the meat. Cooking the sauerkraut also presented an opportunity to add flavor, and I found that adding 2 tablespoons of cider vinegar and a little brown sugar improved the sauerkraut considerably.

The interior of my Reubens was warmer, but the cheese still wasn't melting fully. The test kitchen uses shredded cheese to make grilled cheese sandwiches, and switching to shredded Swiss helped a little. A colleague suggested covering the skillet, which is how her mother taught her to make grilled cheese. I always thought covering made for soggy sandwiches, but condensation never developed in the short cooking time, and the higher temperature under the lid melted the cheese perfectly. With this recipe as your secret weapon, I think you'll win your Reuben war. **–Lynn Clark**

REUBEN SANDWICHES
SERVES 4

Corned beef is typically made from either the brisket or the round. We prefer the corned beef brisket. We prefer pouched sauerkraut (see page 31), sold near the pickles in most supermarkets, to jarred or canned varieties.

- ¼ cup mayonnaise
- ¼ cup finely chopped sweet pickles plus 1 teaspoon sweet pickle juice
- 2 tablespoons cocktail sauce
- 1 cup sauerkraut, drained and rinsed (see note)
- 2 tablespoons cider vinegar
- 1 teaspoon brown sugar
- 8 slices rye bread
- 1 cup shredded Swiss cheese
- 12 ounces thinly sliced deli corned beef (see note)
- 4 tablespoons unsalted butter

1. Whisk mayonnaise, pickles, pickle juice, and cocktail sauce in small bowl; set aside. Cook sauerkraut, vinegar, and sugar in large skillet over medium-high heat, stirring occasionally, until liquid evaporates, about 3 minutes. Transfer sauerkraut to bowl and wipe out skillet.

2. Spread dressing evenly on 1 side of each slice of bread. Layer half of cheese on 4 slices bread, then top with half of corned beef. Divide sauerkraut evenly over meat, then top with remaining corned beef and remaining cheese. Arrange remaining bread, dressing-side down, over cheese.

3. Melt 2 tablespoons butter in empty skillet over medium heat. Place 2 sandwiches in pan and cook until golden brown on first side, 2 to 3 minutes. Flip sandwiches and cook, covered, over medium-low heat until second side is golden brown and cheese is melted, about 2 minutes longer. Transfer to wire rack and repeat with remaining butter and sandwiches. Serve.

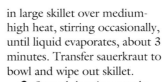

Our flavorful homemade sauce is a hybrid of Russian and Thousand Island dressings—and it's worlds better than anything you can buy in a supermarket.

The American Table:
From Haute Cuisine to Fast Food

Back in 1912, after a day of leading fishing trips in the upstate New York Thousand Islands region, guide George LaLonde, Jr., and his wife, Sophia, would serve guests "shore dinners." One guest, actress May Irwin, was so taken with Mrs. LaLonde's creamy dressing (a derivative of Russian dressing that contained hard-cooked eggs and chives) she coined its name and brought the recipe back to New York City. There, it gained widespread acclaim on the menu of the elegant Waldorf-Astoria Hotel (pictured). It's since gone downmarket; even a certain fast food chain's "special sauce" is a version of Thousand Island.

Test Kitchen Secret
REINVENTING REUBEN

Soggy bread and a cold interior are common problems for Reuben sandwiches. Here's the secret to a better Reuben.

Quickly cooking the sauerkraut evaporates the excess moisture that can cause a soggy sandwich; it also provides an opportunity to build flavor by adding sugar and vinegar. The cooked sauerkraut also helps to warm the meat and melt the cheese in the middle of the sandwich.

Classic Roast Beef and Gravy

Great Gravy

A combination of sautéed mushrooms, tomato paste, beef broth, and Worcestershire sauce mimicked the roasted, beefy flavor of traditional gravy made with pan drippings.

FLAVOR BUILDERS
Keys to rich, meaty gravy made without juices from the roast

The Right Cut

Through extensive testing of every cut of beef, the test kitchen has settled on top sirloin as our favorite inexpensive roast. Look for a roast with at least a ¼-inch fat cap on top; the fat renders in the oven, basting the roast and helping to keep it moist.

TOP SIRLOIN
The best balance of beefy flavor, tender texture, and value

The best roast beef is cooked gently to keep all its juices inside. But without enough pan drippings, how do you make rich, beefy gravy?

The worst roasts produce the best gravy. That's because when roast beef is cooked at too high a temperature, the fibers in the meat contract, forcing out the flavorful juices. These juices are the foundation of great gravy, but if you find a lot in the roasting pan, it means the meat will be dry and tough. For beef roasts that cook evenly and retain their flavorful juices, we've learned that a low-to-moderate oven is best. But how do you make rich, meaty gravy from a roast that doesn't throw off much liquid?

I began with top sirloin roast, the test kitchen's choice for a beef roast that balances flavor, tenderness, and economy. To determine the ideal roasting temperature, I seasoned five top sirloin roasts with salt and pepper (letting the salted roast sit for an hour or more promoted well-seasoned, even juicier meat) and browned each roast on the stovetop to develop a flavorful crust. I roasted each one at a different oven temperature until the meat registered 125 degrees (for medium-rare). The roast cooked at 375 degrees threw off a plethora of juice, leaving the meat dry and with an overcooked gray ring around the exterior. The roast improved with each step down in roasting temperature. The best temperature was 275, which produced juicy meat (having expelled very little liquid), a uniformly rosy interior (no gray ring from too much heat) in under two hours—and precious little liquid in the roasting pan.

This rich, savory gravy is built from the flavorful brown bits left in the pot after searing the roast.

Gravy is usually made by pouring these liquid contents into a fat separator. The fat is heated in a pan (sometimes the empty roasting pan), and flour is stirred in to make a roux. Then the flavorful juices are whisked in and reduced into rich, viscous gravy. I didn't have any meat juices to work with, but I did have some rendered fat (and fond, the flavorful browned bits that form on the pan bottom) in my Dutch oven from searing the roast. I started my gravy by sautéing onion, carrot, and celery in the rendered fat. Once the vegetables were soft, I stirred in the flour, then store-bought beef broth, scraping up the flavor-rich fond. I reduced and strained the gravy, but without the meat juices it was missing richness. For the next batch, I added garlic to the vegetables and red wine to the broth. Both additions helped, but the gravy still lacked complexity and roasted flavor.

We often use sautéed mushrooms and tomato paste to add depth of flavor reminiscent of roasted meats. These two ingredients greatly improved the "meaty" flavor of the gravy (with the tomato paste also contributing body), but something was still missing. That something turned out to be Worcestershire sauce, whose salty, sweet, and acidic essence made the gravy taste truly rich and meaty. After dozens of tests, I'd finally made a gravy—without pan drippings—that was worthy of my perfectly cooked roast beef.

–Kelley Baker

CLASSIC ROAST BEEF AND GRAVY SERVES 6 TO 8

For the best flavor and texture, refrigerate the roast overnight after salting. If you don't have a V-rack, cook the roast on a wire rack set inside a rimmed baking sheet.

- 1 (4-pound) top sirloin roast, fat trimmed to ¼ inch thick
  Salt and pepper
- 1 tablespoon vegetable oil
- 8 ounces white mushrooms, chopped
- 2 onions, chopped fine
- 1 carrot, peeled and chopped
- 1 celery rib, chopped
- 1 tablespoon tomato paste
- 4 garlic cloves, minced
- ¼ cup all-purpose flour
- 1 cup red wine
- 4 cups low-sodium beef broth
- 1 teaspoon Worcestershire sauce

1. Pat roast dry with paper towels. Rub 2 teaspoons salt evenly over surface of meat. Cover with plastic wrap and refrigerate for at least 1 hour or up to 24 hours.

2. Adjust oven rack to lower-middle position and heat oven to 275 degrees. Pat roast dry with paper towels and rub with 1 teaspoon pepper. Heat oil in large Dutch oven over medium-high heat until just smoking. Brown roast all over, 8 to 12 minutes, then transfer to V-rack set inside roasting pan (do not wipe out Dutch oven). Transfer to oven and cook until meat registers 125 degrees (for medium-rare), 1½ to 2 hours.

3. Meanwhile, add mushrooms to fat in Dutch oven and cook until golden, about 5 minutes. Stir in onions, carrot, and celery and cook until browned, 5 to 7 minutes. Stir in tomato paste, garlic, and flour and cook until fragrant, about 2 minutes. Stir in wine and broth, scraping up any browned bits with wooden spoon. Bring to boil, then reduce heat to medium and simmer until thickened, about 10 minutes. Strain gravy, then stir in Worcestershire and season with salt and pepper; cover and keep warm.

4. Transfer roast to cutting board, tent with foil, and let rest 20 minutes. Slice roast crosswise against grain into ½-inch-thick slices. Serve with gravy.

Delmonico Potatoes

Originally made to order in restaurants, this creamy potato dish turns heavy and gluey when cooked for a crowd at home. We set out to rethink this American classic.

Look up a modern recipe for Delmonico potatoes and you'll most likely find a casserole made of cubed, overboiled potatoes baked in a creamy cheddar sauce and topped with more cheese. I baked up a half-dozen of these recipes and found them soggy, heavy, and bland—more like institutional fare than the elegant side dish I'd envisioned.

But it wasn't always this way. Flash back to 1837 and the lavish dining room of Delmonico's Restaurant in New York City. Their signature side dish featured boiled, finely shredded potatoes cooked with milk and heavy cream. When an order came in, a serving of potatoes was sprinkled with Parmesan cheese and "gratinéed" under the broiler. The result was a potato gratin with a creamy interior and a crusty, cheesy topping. I wanted to bring back the simplicity and elegance of the original dish, but make it more practical to feed a crowd.

Reinventing the original dish as a casserole in a 13- by 9-inch baking pan was problematic. Pounds of potatoes had to be partially boiled, cooled, and shredded before adding the dairy. By the time the middle of the casserole was cooked, the potatoes on the outside resembled paste. It was clear that I'd have to take a cue from modern recipes and lose the shredded potatoes in favor of more manageable cubes, which would hold their texture better in the casserole.

I started by sautéing onions and garlic, adding cream, and, using a test kitchen trick, cooking the cubed potatoes until nearly tender right in that mixture. Exchanging some of the cream for chicken broth helped to lighten the dish and add savory flavor, and lemon juice and zest brought a welcome brightness. I folded in 2 cups of cheddar and baked

the casserole, but my tasters thought it was too heavy. I systematically cut back on the cheddar until I wasn't using any, and my tasters approved.

To create the crusty topping, I tried going back to the shredded potatoes of the original recipe, but shredded raw potatoes took too long to cook, and boiled shredded potatoes turned to mush. I was starting to give up hope when I spotted a bag of frozen shredded hash browns (which are partially cooked) in a test kitchen freezer.

To ensure a flavorful topping, I sautéed the thawed hash browns in butter, then added some of the cream and chicken broth I was using for the base. Fresh chives added bite and color, and in a final nod to the original recipe, I added Parmesan cheese to the topping before layering it on the partially cooked casserole and baking until it was golden brown and crusty. With these creamy, deeply-seasoned cubed potatoes topped with a Parmesan-laced crust, I had a casserole recipe sure to stand the test of time. –Diane Unger

DELMONICO POTATO CASSEROLE SERVES 8 TO 10

We prefer the buttery flavor of Yukon Gold potatoes here, but all-purpose and red potatoes also work; do not use russets—their high starch content will make the casserole gluey. We had good results with Ore-Ida Country Style shredded hash brown potatoes, available in the freezer section of most supermarkets.

- 3 tablespoons unsalted butter
- 1 onion, chopped fine
- 2 garlic cloves, minced
- 2½ cups heavy cream
- 1½ cups low-sodium chicken broth
- 2½ pounds Yukon Gold potatoes, peeled and cut into ½-inch cubes (see note)

For an appealing contrast of textures, tender cubes of potatoes are crowned with a crusty hash brown topping.

- ⅛ teaspoon freshly grated nutmeg
  Salt and pepper
- 1 teaspoon grated zest and 2 teaspoons juice from 1 lemon
- 5 cups frozen shredded hash brown potatoes, thawed and patted dry with paper towels (see note)
- ¾ cup grated Parmesan cheese
- ¼ cup finely chopped fresh chives

1. Adjust oven rack to upper-middle position and heat oven to 450 degrees. Melt 1 table-spoon butter in Dutch oven over medium-high heat. Cook onion until softened, about 3 minutes. Stir in garlic and cook until fragrant, about 30 seconds. Stir in 2 cups cream, 1 cup broth, Yukon Golds, nutmeg, 2 teaspoons salt, and 1 teaspoon pepper. Bring to boil, then reduce heat to medium and simmer until potatoes are translucent at edges and mixture is slightly thickened, about 10 minutes. Off heat, stir in lemon zest and juice.

2. Transfer potato mixture to 13- by 9-inch baking dish

and bake until bubbling around edges and surface is just golden, about 20 minutes. Meanwhile, melt remaining butter in large nonstick skillet over medium-high heat. Cook shredded potatoes until beginning to brown, about 2 minutes. Add remaining cream, remaining broth, and ½ teaspoon pepper to skillet and cook, stirring occasionally, until liquid has evaporated, about 3 minutes. Off heat, stir in ½ cup cheese and 2 tablespoons chives.

3. Remove baking dish from oven and top with shredded potato mixture. Sprinkle with remaining cheese and continue to bake until top is golden brown, about 20 minutes. Let cool 15 minutes. Sprinkle with remaining chives. Serve.

Make Ahead: The recipe can be made through step 1, cooled completely, transferred to the baking dish, and refrigerated, covered with plastic wrap, for 1 day. To serve, proceed as directed in step 2, increasing baking time to 25 to 30 minutes.

Perfecting Popovers

The perfect popover soars to towering heights, but only if you get the baking magic just right. Could we create a foolproof recipe that would produce tall popovers with a crisp exterior and custardy interior every single time?

To keep these towering popovers from collapsing, poke a small hole in the top of each when they're almost done baking to allow steam to escape.

Nothing exemplifies the magic of baking more than the popover. The classic recipe is quite simple: A pancake-like batter of milk, eggs, flour, melted butter, and salt is poured into the deep cups of a popover pan and baked in a very hot oven. Even without leaveners or whipped egg whites for lift, the batter somehow climbs the pan until it pops over the top into a sky-high balloon. Crack into the hot popover and you'll be met with a shattering crust and a hollow, custardy interior ready for butter or jam.

I've chased the perfect popover for years, but cookbook recipes only led me to squat, tough, or sunken versions. I wanted to develop a recipe that guaranteed a high rise every time. I had no idea that it would take over 100 batches—yes, I made more than 600 popovers—and some debunking of popover mythology to get the job done.

The most common formula for popover batter is 1 cup each of flour and whole milk, 2 eggs, and 1 tablespoon of melted butter; since these amounts made for skimpy popovers, my first move was to double the recipe to fill the same 6-cup popover pan. Tasters wanted more butter flavor, so I increased the amount to 4 tablespoons. As for the flour, I tested my working recipe using cake flour (a favorite of modern recipes), all-purpose flour, and bread flour. The bread flour has the highest protein content of the three, so it built the strongest structure—the highest rise and crispest crust—in the popovers. The bread flour proved so sturdy that it sometimes set up too quickly, impeding the initial rise. Resting the batter for an hour before baking gave the proteins in the flour time to relax and prevented the popovers from setting up too quickly, promoting a consistently better rise. But I wanted the popovers to rise even higher.

The 2 cups of whole milk, 4 eggs, and 4 tablespoons of melted butter I was using were making for flavorful popovers, but at a cost: The fat in these ingredients was weighing down the batter and inhibiting the popovers' rise. Reducing the amount of milk made them dry; switching to low-fat milk made for a higher-rising, moist finished product. Heating the milk allowed the batter to come together with less mixing, which was key to avoiding an overworked batter (which makes for tough popovers). I found I could cut the eggs from four to three, and the butter from 4 to 3 tablespoons to help the popovers

Popover Pans

Popover pans are composed of six tall, heavyweight steel cups affixed to one another with thick steel wire. The open design maximizes heat transfer, which is crucial to high-rising popovers. Very few companies manufacture popover pans these days; in fact, most cookware stores carry only one brand—Chicago Metallic Professional Nonstick Popover Pans. We found that these pans, which cost about $20, brown popovers well and release them easily.

PERFECT POPOVER PAN
Made of nonstick, heavyweight steel, the Chicago Metallic popover pan is designed for maximum heat transfer.

The Truth about Baking Popovers

After baking over 100 batches of popovers, we learned what causes the most common problems with other recipes.

THE PROBLEM
POP NEVER: Short, squat popovers

THE CAUSES
- Using cake flour, which doesn't provide enough structure.
- Using too little batter. Traditional recipes skimp.
- Not starting in a hot oven. A big initial burst of steam and rise is essential.

THE PROBLEM
POP UNDER:
Deflated popovers

THE CAUSES
- Popovers weren't baked long enough to set up properly.
- Popovers weren't poked to release steam, which can compromise structure.

THE PROBLEM
POP UGLY: Huge, misshapen top and tiny bottom

THE CAUSE
- Using a preheated, oiled pan; the batter that first hits the pan immediately rises up through the wet batter, resulting in an ugly shape and uneven baking.

maximize their rising potential; further reductions made the popovers taste too lean. A pinch of salt and sugar helped more with flavor.

Popovers baked at 450 degrees were too crusty on the outside by the time they were fully cooked, but reducing the starting temperature meant the popovers didn't rise as high. I had the best results baking the popovers for 20 minutes at 450 to initiate the rise and then turning the oven down to 300 degrees so the interior would be done at the same time as the crust.

These popovers were showstoppers in the oven, but they collapsed like leaking tires as they cooled. The problem was steam trapped inside the popover; this moisture slowly dissolved the lofty, crusty structure I'd worked so hard to build. I solved the problem by poking a hole in the top of the popovers when they were almost done cooking, and then again as they cooled. This allowed the steam to escape and kept the crisp structure intact. After more than 100 tests, I finally had the perfect popover. **–Diane Unger**

PERFECT POPOVERS
MAKES 6 POPOVERS

Greasing the pans with shortening ensures the best release, but cooking spray may be substituted; do not use butter. To gauge the popovers' progress without opening the oven door, use the oven light during baking. Bread flour makes for the highest and sturdiest popovers, but an equal amount of all-purpose flour may be substituted.

    Vegetable shortening
    (see note)
3   large eggs
2   cups low-fat milk, heated to
    110 degrees
3   tablespoons unsalted butter,
    melted and cooled slightly
2   cups bread flour (see note)
1   teaspoon salt
1   teaspoon sugar

1. Adjust oven rack to lower-middle position and heat oven to 450 degrees. Grease interior of 6-cup popover pan with shortening, then dust lightly with flour. Whisk eggs until light and foamy in medium bowl. Slowly whisk in milk and butter until incorporated.

2. Combine flour, salt, and sugar in large bowl. Whisk three-quarters of milk mixture into flour mixture until no lumps remain, then whisk in remaining milk mixture. Transfer batter to large measuring cup, cover with plastic, and let rest at room temperature for 1 hour. (Alternatively, batter can be refrigerated for 1 day. Bring to room temperature before proceeding with recipe.)

3. Whisk batter to recombine, then pour into prepared popover pan (batter will not quite reach top of cups). Bake until just beginning to brown, about 20 minutes. Without opening oven door, decrease oven temperature to 300 degrees and continue to bake until popovers are golden brown all over, 35 to 40 minutes longer. Poke small hole in top of each popover with skewer and continue to bake until deep golden brown, about 10 minutes longer. Transfer popover pan to wire rack. Poke again with skewer and let cool 2 minutes. Turn out popovers. Serve.

Make Ahead: Once popovers have cooled completely, they can be stored at room temperature in zipper-lock bag for 2 days. To serve, adjust oven rack to middle position and heat oven to 400 degrees. Heat popovers on rimmed baking sheet until crisp and heated through, 5 to 8 minutes.

Making Popovers in a Muffin Tin

If you don't have a popover pan, you can bake the popovers in a nonstick 12-cup muffin tin—with a sacrifice in stature. To ensure even cooking, fill only the 10 outer cups to ¼ inch from the top (you may have some batter left over). Reduce initial baking time in step 3 to 15 minutes, and reduce secondary baking time to 20 to 25 minutes after oven temperature has been lowered. Poke popovers as directed and continue to bake for another 10 minutes.

On the Side:
Southern-Style Green Beans

What's the fastest way to infuse green beans with rich pork flavor?

For crisp texture and bright color, cooking green beans quickly is the way to go. But in the South, green beans are often simmered for hours in a deep pot with water, ham hock, sugar, and vinegar—much the same way collard greens are cooked. Although these beans are more soft than crisp and their color is muted, they offer something that quick-cooked beans never can: deep, sweet, smoky pork flavor. I wanted to develop the same rich flavor in minutes, not hours, so I turned to my trusty skillet.

I knew immediately that the ham hock would have to go, as it wouldn't give up its flavor in the shorter cooking time. Wondering if smoky bacon might work as a substitute, I crisped bacon slices, removed them from the skillet, sautéed onion in the drippings before adding the beans and water, and crumbled the bacon back in at the end. While the bites with bacon were good, the bacon flavor wasn't permeating the beans. Leaving a few slices of bacon in the skillet while the beans cooked infused them with meaty flavor, and returning the crumbled bacon to the beans before serving made certain there was bacon in every bite.

Switching from water to chicken broth boosted the meaty flavor, and adding cider vinegar twice—once to season the broth, and at the end of cooking for brightness—lent a nice tart element. A little brown sugar, minced thyme, salt, and plenty of pepper rounded out the flavors. **–Lynn Clark**

BACON-BRAISED GREEN BEANS SERVES 8
Large, thick green beans hold up best in this preparation.

6   slices thick-cut bacon
1   onion, chopped fine
2   pounds green beans, trimmed and halved (see note)
1   cup low-sodium chicken broth
2   tablespoons cider vinegar
1   tablespoon brown sugar
1   teaspoon minced fresh thyme
    Salt and pepper

1. Cook bacon in large skillet over medium heat until crisp, about 8 minutes. Transfer 4 slices bacon to paper towel–lined plate; when cool enough to handle, crumble bacon and reserve.

2. Add onion to pan with remaining slices bacon and cook, stirring frequently, until golden brown, about 8 minutes. Add beans, broth, 1 tablespoon vinegar,

sugar, thyme, ¼ teaspoon salt, and ¼ teaspoon pepper. Bring to boil, then reduce heat to medium-low and cook, covered, until beans are tender, about 12 minutes.

3. Uncover skillet and discard bacon slices. Increase heat to medium-high and cook until liquid evaporates, 3 to 5 minutes. Off heat, stir in remaining vinegar and crumbled bacon. Season with salt and pepper. Serve.

I'm Looking for a Recipe

READERS HELP READERS FIND RECIPES

We've Got Mail

Dozens of readers sent us recipes in response to the request for Gilchrist Macaroons in our February/March 2008 issue. We really liked the recipe sent by Gale Dayton (right). Go to **CooksCountry.com** and click **Looking for a Recipe** to find hundreds of recipes submitted by readers who responded to other recipe requests in previous issues of *Cook's Country*.

Frederick and Nelson's Coconut Cake

Every year for my birthday, my mom would go to the Frederick & Nelson department store in Seattle, Wash., and pick up a coconut cake. It was light, moist, and just plain delicious. Nothing can compare to it in my mind. Even after 35 years, just thinking about it brings a smile to my face. Does anyone have their secret recipe? I would be forever grateful!

Jill Bohan
Via e-mail

Holiday Fruit and Nut Roll

My mother used to make this rolled confection around the holidays. First she would take a flour-sack dish towel and cover it with powdered sugar. Next she would cook a sugar syrup to softball stage and mix in chopped dates, nuts, and maraschino cherries. The candy mixture was cooled and poured onto the sugared towel, shaped into a roll, and refrigerated. Once firm, it was ready to be sliced for her holiday cookie trays. Does anyone have any clues about the specific measurements and directions for this recipe?

Carol Odenweller
Salem, Ore.

Alfajores

Many years ago I was friends with an Argentinean girl whose mother made alfajores, sandwich cookies filled with dulce de leche and rolled in coconut. The cookie itself was pale and had a very fine, crumbly texture like shortbread, though not as buttery. Her mother has never given the recipe to anyone, but I would love to make them for myself.

Diana Singer
New York, N.Y.

Blackberry Doobie

I have found several recipes for this old-fashioned steamed cobbler, but I'm specifically looking for one with a sugar topping. A friend of mine is dying to try this, and I would love to make it for her.

Nedra Lyman
Via e-mail

Fried Ralston

My grandmother used to warm us on cold winter mornings with fried Ralston, or wheat mush, served with warm maple syrup. Does anyone have a recipe for making fried Ralston cakes? Also, unfortunately I can't find Ralston cereal in my town so I would love a recommendation for a substitution for it. Any help would be appreciated. I want to share this tummy-warming breakfast with my son.

Caroline Woodward
Pittsburgh, Pa.

Henkel Flour Scones

When I was a teenager, I used to make scones for my family from a recipe in an old 1940s Henkel Flour cookbook. That particular book was not among my mom's things when she passed away, and I've since looked for it at flea markets, old bookstores, etc., but have not been successful. Sure hope you can help!

Elizabeth J. Streebeck
Somerville, Tenn.

Refrigerator Bran Muffins

In the early 1980s there was a recipe for bran muffins using All-Bran cereal. The recipe made a huge amount of batter and could be stored in the refrigerator for several weeks. I sure would love to find this recipe again.

Lucie Doty
Carl Junction, Mo.

Thousand Island Eggs

This recipe was a favorite of ours as newlyweds in the early 1970s. It is basically baked shirred eggs served with a sauce similar to Thousand Island dressing. I don't remember the exact amounts, baking temperature, or baking time, but I do recall that the sauce was made with sour cream, ketchup, chopped olives, and a dash of Tabasco. I am almost positive that this is the name of the recipe, but an online search just led to a multitude of recipes for Thousand Island dressing and thousand-year-old eggs!

Margaret Sharp
Ithaca, N.Y.

Pineapple Cottage Cheese Cheesecake

As a newlywed in the early 1960s, I found a recipe for cheesecake using crushed pineapple and cottage cheese in our local newspaper. It made a large cheesecake and was wonderful to take to luncheons and potlucks. I would love to be able to make this for my friends and neighbors again.

Lynda Lowman
Bonners Ferry, Idaho

Droste Chocolate Pie

My wife of 53 years loved the chocolate pie recipe that was printed on Droste cocoa tin cans in the 1970s. We made that pie a hundred times and had the recipe on a note card. My wife recently died and our children asked me to make Mom's chocolate pie, but for the life of me I can't find the recipe card and have not been able to locate it on the Internet. If you could provide me with the recipe I would be eternally grateful.

Robert L. Brewer
Via e-mail

Jack Robinson Cake

There was an old recipe for Jack Robinson Cake that I would love to have again. It was a fairly simple yellow cake that was covered with a pecan meringue-like topping. The unique aspect of the recipe was that the topping was spread over the cake batter in a 13- by 9-inch baking pan and baked together! How the cake and meringue turned out perfectly at the same time I have no idea. I hope that someone can help.

Judy Coombs
Via e-mail

Carrot Pudding Cake

My mother-in-law used to make a carrot pudding cake, but she has since misplaced the recipe. Though she can find recipes for carrot pudding, they are nothing like this steamed cake.

Christina Solley
Odessa, Texas

Dutch Meatballs

In the 1960s in Brookline, Mass., I met some college students of Dutch ancestry. One of their parents served us Dutch meatballs, made with corned beef, I think, and topped with a mustard sauce. I can't find a recipe that compares to the version I was served.

Pam Hindley
East Falmouth, Mass.

> **Are you looking for a special recipe?** Or do you have a recipe a fellow *Cook's Country* reader is seeking? Post your requests and recipes by visiting **CooksCountry.com** and clicking on **Looking for a Recipe.** We'll share recipe requests and found recipes on CooksCountry.com and print as many as we can in the magazine. You may also write to us at Looking for a Recipe, Cook's Country, P.O. Box 470739, Brookline, MA 02447.

GILCHRIST MACAROONS Gale Dayton Weston, Mass.

MAKES 18 COOKIES

"My mother was obsessed with Gilchrist Macaroons, an extra-chewy almond variety, and tried for years to replicate them. She finally settled on this recipe and claimed her secret to a super chewy texture was using granulated sugar instead of the confectioners' sugar that most recipes call for." To ensure a clean release from the parchment, briefly rest the cookie-topped parchment on a damp kitchen towel before removing the macaroons.

1	(7-ounce) tube almond paste
3	large egg whites
1¼	cups plus 1 tablespoon sugar
¼	cup all-purpose flour

1. Adjust oven racks to upper-middle and lower-middle positions and heat oven to 325 degrees. Line two baking sheets with parchment paper.

2. Process almond paste and egg whites in food processor until smooth. Add 1¼ cups sugar and flour and process until mixture is thickened and no lumps remain, about 1 minute. Transfer mixture to pastry bag with plain tip and refrigerate until slightly firm, about 30 minutes.

3. Pipe 2½-inch rounds on prepared baking sheets. Sprinkle remaining sugar evenly over rounds and bake until light golden, about 25 minutes, switching and rotating sheets halfway through baking.

4. Transfer parchment to wire rack and cool completely. Serve. (Cookies can be stored in airtight container for up to 3 days.)

Find the Rooster!

A tiny version of this rooster has been hidden somewhere in the pages of this issue. If you find it, write to us with its location (plus your name and address) and you will be entered into a random drawing. The first correct entry drawn will receive a Michael Graves Design Hamilton Beach 4-Slice Toaster (our test winner—see page 29), and the next five will each receive a complimentary one-year subscription to *Cook's Country*. To enter the contest, visit **CooksCountry.com/emailus,** or write to us at Rooster, Cook's Country, P.O. Box 470739, Brookline, MA 02447. Entries are due by January 31, 2009.

Did you find the rooster in the August/September 2008 issue? It was hidden in the Beef and Vegetable Kebabs photo on page 10. Diane Tyler of Kirby, Texas, spotted it and won an Anolon Advanced Double Burner Griddle.

STEAK TIPS WITH MUSHROOMS
AND SOUR CREAM SAUCE

LEMON CHICKEN WITH ARTICHOKES AND POTATOES

CRISPY PARMESAN CHICKEN CUTLETS

SKILLET GOULASH

LEMON CHICKEN WITH ARTICHOKES AND POTATOES
SERVES 4

Though we prefer the flavor and texture of frozen artichoke hearts, one 14-ounce can of artichoke hearts (drained and patted dry with paper towels) may be substituted.

 1 pound small red potatoes, quartered
 2 tablespoons vegetable oil
 4 boneless, skinless chicken breasts (about 1½ pounds)
   Salt and pepper
 1 (9-ounce) box frozen artichoke hearts, thawed
 4 garlic cloves, minced
 1 teaspoon grated zest and 1 tablespoon juice from 1 lemon
 2 tablespoons finely chopped fresh oregano

1. Toss potatoes and 1 tablespoon oil in large bowl. Wrap tightly with plastic wrap and microwave until edges of potatoes begin to soften, 4 to 7 minutes, shaking bowl (without removing plastic) to redistribute potatoes halfway through cooking.

2. Pat chicken dry with paper towels and season with salt and pepper. Heat remaining oil in large nonstick skillet over medium-high heat until just smoking. Add chicken and cook until golden brown and cooked through, about 5 minutes per side. Transfer to serving platter and tent with foil.

3. Add potatoes to empty skillet and cook until well browned, about 4 minutes. Stir in artichoke hearts and cook until heated through, about 2 minutes. Add garlic, lemon zest, lemon juice, and oregano and cook until fragrant, about 30 seconds. Season with salt and pepper and transfer to platter with chicken. Serve.

STEAK TIPS WITH MUSHROOMS AND SOUR CREAM SAUCE **SERVES 4**

Steak tips, also known as flap meat, are sold as whole steaks, cubes, and strips. To ensure evenly sized chunks, we prefer to purchase whole steak tips and cut them ourselves. Serve over rice or buttered egg noodles.

 1½ pounds sirloin steak tips, cut into 2-inch chunks
    Salt and pepper
  2 tablespoons vegetable oil
 10 ounces white mushrooms, sliced
  2 shallots, halved and sliced thin
  ¾ cup low-sodium beef broth
  ½ cup brandy
 1½ teaspoons minced fresh thyme
  ½ cup sour cream
  2 tablespoons coarse-grain mustard

1. Pat steak tips dry with paper towels and season with salt and pepper. Heat 1 tablespoon oil in large skillet over medium-high heat until just smoking. Add meat and cook until well browned all over, 6 to 8 minutes. Transfer to serving platter and tent with foil.

2. Heat remaining oil in empty skillet until shimmering. Cook mushrooms, shallots, and ¼ teaspoon salt, covered, until vegetables have softened, about 3 minutes. Stir in broth, brandy, and thyme and simmer until reduced by half, about 7 minutes. Off heat, stir in sour cream, mustard, and any accumulated steak juices. Season with salt and pepper. Pour sauce over meat. Serve.

SKILLET GOULASH **SERVES 4**

Be sure to trim the steaks of all visible fat before cooking. Use sweet paprika, not the hot or smoked varieties, in this recipe.

 2 strip steaks, about 1 inch thick, trimmed of fat
   Salt and pepper
 3 tablespoons vegetable oil
 1 onion, halved and sliced thin
 1 red bell pepper, seeded and chopped fine
 ¼ cup paprika (see note)
 1 tablespoon tomato paste
 4 cups low-sodium beef broth
 ½ pound wide egg noodles (about 4 cups)
 ⅔ cup sour cream

1. Pat steaks dry with paper towels and season with salt and pepper. Heat 1 tablespoon oil in large nonstick skillet until just smoking. Cook steaks until well browned, 3 to 5 minutes per side. Transfer to plate and tent with foil.

2. Heat remaining oil in empty skillet over medium heat until shimmering. Cook onion and bell pepper until softened, about 5 minutes. Stir in paprika and tomato paste and cook until fragrant, about 30 seconds. Stir in broth and noodles and cook covered, stirring occasionally, until noodles are tender, about 8 minutes. Remove from heat, cover, and keep warm.

3. Cut steaks in half lengthwise, then cut into thin slices. Stir sour cream and sliced steak, along with any accumulated juices, into pan. Season with salt and pepper. Serve.

CRISPY PARMESAN CHICKEN CUTLETS **SERVES 4**

For the best texture, shred the Parmesan on the large holes of a box grater. This recipe works best with chicken cutlets that are no more than ¼ inch thick. If your cutlets are thicker, pound them to ¼-inch thickness before cooking.

 ½ cup plus 1 tablespoon all-purpose flour
 3 large eggs
 2¼ cups shredded Parmesan cheese
 2 teaspoons pepper
 6 thin-cut boneless, skinless chicken cutlets (about 1¼ pounds; see note)
 ¼ cup vegetable oil

1. Adjust oven rack to middle position and heat oven to 200 degrees. Place ½ cup flour in shallow dish. Beat eggs in second shallow dish. Combine Parmesan, pepper, and remaining flour in third shallow dish.

2. Pat chicken dry with paper towels. One at a time, coat cutlets lightly with flour, dip in egg mixture, dredge in Parmesan mixture, and return to flour, pressing to adhere.

3. Heat 2 tablespoons oil in large nonstick skillet over medium heat until just smoking. Cook half of cutlets until golden brown, 2 to 3 minutes per side. Drain on paper towel–lined plate and transfer to oven to keep warm. Wipe out skillet and repeat with remaining oil and cutlets. Serve.

DINER-STYLE PORK CHOPS AND GRAVY

SICHUAN ORANGE CHICKEN

SKILLET SHEPHERD'S PIE

PENNE WITH SPICY SHRIMP AND TOMATO SAUCE

SICHUAN ORANGE CHICKEN SERVES 4

Serve over steamed rice or noodles.

- 3 tablespoons hoisin sauce
- 2 teaspoons zest and ¾ cup juice from 3 oranges
- 4 boneless, skinless chicken breasts (about 1½ pounds), cut crosswise into ¼-inch-thick pieces
  Salt and pepper
- 3 tablespoons vegetable oil
- 1 red bell pepper, seeded and sliced thin
- 3 garlic cloves, minced
- 2 teaspoons grated fresh ginger
- ½ teaspoon red pepper flakes
- 2 scallions, sliced thin

1. Whisk hoisin, orange zest, and orange juice in bowl; set aside. Pat chicken dry with paper towels and season with salt and pepper. Heat 1 tablespoon oil in large nonstick skillet over medium-high heat until just smoking. Add half of chicken and cook until lightly browned, 1 to 2 minutes per side; transfer to plate. Repeat with another tablespoon oil and remaining chicken.

2. Add remaining tablespoon oil and bell pepper to skillet and cook over medium heat until just softened, about 3 minutes. Stir in garlic, ginger, and pepper flakes and cook until fragrant, about 30 seconds. Add hoisin mixture and simmer until sauce has thickened, 3 to 5 minutes. Add scallions and cooked chicken, along with any accumulated chicken juices, to pan and toss to combine. Season with salt and pepper. Serve.

DINER-STYLE PORK CHOPS AND GRAVY SERVES 4

If you can't find ground fennel, use a coffee grinder to process 1½ teaspoons of whole fennel seeds to a fine powder.

- 8 slices bacon, chopped
- 4 bone-in rib or center-cut pork chops, about 1 inch thick
  Salt and pepper
- 1 onion, halved and sliced thin
- 2 tablespoons all-purpose flour
- 1½ teaspoons ground fennel (see note)
- 1½ teaspoons ground sage
- ½ cup low-sodium chicken broth
- 2 cups whole milk

1. Cook bacon in large nonstick skillet over medium-high heat until crisp, about 5 minutes; transfer to paper towel–lined plate. Pour off all but 2 tablespoons bacon fat from skillet. Pat chops dry with paper towels and season with salt and pepper. Cook chops in skillet until well browned and meat registers 145 degrees, about 5 minutes per side. Transfer to serving platter and tent with foil.

2. Add onion to fat in skillet and cook, covered, until softened and browned, about 4 minutes. Stir in flour, fennel, and sage and cook until flour is absorbed, about 1 minute. Whisk in broth and milk, then reduce heat to medium and simmer until sauce is thickened, about 8 minutes. Stir in reserved bacon and any accumulated pork juices and season with salt and pepper. Pour gravy over chops. Serve.

PENNE WITH SPICY SHRIMP AND TOMATO SAUCE
SERVES 4

Jars of sliced cherry peppers can be found in the condiment aisle of most supermarkets, near the pickles. This sauce also works well with strand pastas such as spaghetti and linguine.

- 1½ pounds extra-large shrimp, peeled and deveined
- ¼ cup extra-virgin olive oil
- 3 tablespoons finely chopped jarred cherry peppers, plus 2 tablespoons cherry pepper brine (see note)
  Salt and pepper
- 3 garlic cloves, minced
- ¼ teaspoon red pepper flakes
- 2 (14.5-ounce) cans diced tomatoes
- 1 pound penne pasta (see note)
- 3 tablespoons finely chopped fresh oregano

1. Bring 4 quarts water to boil in large pot. Combine shrimp, 2 tablespoons oil, cherry peppers, cherry pepper brine, ½ teaspoon salt, and ¼ teaspoon pepper in bowl; set aside.

2. Heat remaining oil, garlic, and pepper flakes in large nonstick skillet over medium-high heat until fragrant, about 1 minute. Add tomatoes and simmer until slightly thickened, about 8 minutes. Add shrimp mixture and simmer covered, stirring occasionally, until shrimp are just cooked through, about 3 minutes.

3. While sauce simmers, add 1 tablespoon salt and pasta to boiling water and cook until al dente. Reserve ½ cup cooking water. Drain pasta and return to pot. Add tomato-shrimp mixture and oregano to pot and toss to combine, adding reserved pasta water as needed. Season with salt and pepper. Serve.

SKILLET SHEPHERD'S PIE SERVES 4

Be sure to purchase shredded hash brown potatoes (sometimes labeled "country style") rather than the cubed variety. Ground lamb can be substituted for the beef.

- 8 cups frozen shredded hash brown potatoes (see note)
- 4 tablespoons unsalted butter, melted
  Salt and pepper
- 1½ pounds 85 percent lean ground beef
- 1 onion, chopped fine
- 1½ teaspoons minced fresh thyme
- ¼ cup all-purpose flour
- 2 cups low-sodium beef broth
- 2 teaspoons Worcestershire sauce
- 2 cups frozen pea and carrot medley, thawed

1. Adjust oven rack to upper-middle position and heat broiler. Toss potatoes with 2 tablespoons butter, 1 teaspoon salt, and ¼ teaspoon pepper in large bowl. Wrap tightly with plastic and microwave until potatoes are tender, 7 to 10 minutes.

2. While potatoes are cooking, cook beef and onion in large heatproof skillet over medium-high heat until beef is no longer pink, about 5 minutes. Drain beef mixture in colander.

3. Return drained beef mixture to pan. Stir in thyme and flour and cook until incorporated, about 1 minute. Stir in broth and Worcestershire and cook until sauce is thickened, 6 to 8 minutes. Stir in pea and carrot medley and simmer until heated through, about 1 minute. Season with salt and pepper.

4. Scatter cooked potatoes over beef mixture and brush with remaining butter. Broil until potatoes are golden brown, 3 to 5 minutes. Serve.

Cashew Chicken

Most recipes for cashew chicken dish out syrupy sauces and tough chicken—and sorely lack cashew flavor and crunch.

The best cashew chicken features tender, juicy cubes of chicken breast and crisp vegetables in a sweet and savory soy-based sauce, with the crunch of cashews accenting every bite. I thought this seemingly straightforward stir-fry would be easy to re-create, but most recipes featured dry, overcooked chicken, a befuddling array of bland and limp vegetables, and candy-sweet sauces. Worst of all were the meager amounts of cashews, which were left to simmer in the sauce until soggy and bland.

To remedy the dry and flavorless chicken, I marinated the breasts in a little soy sauce. The salt in the soy penetrates the meat much like a brine, promoting juiciness and deep seasoning. While the cooked chicken was moister, the exterior was a little tough. I turned to a technique called velveting, where raw chicken is tossed with cornstarch and oil. This forms a thin coating around the chicken and protects it from the heat. Velveting worked great, but I wondered if I could save a step by adding those ingredients right to the marinade. Sure enough it worked, producing juicy chicken that was tender inside and out. Now I could start working on the vegetables and sauce.

Many recipes for cashew chicken are packed with onion, carrot, and celery, which don't add much flavor, so I omitted them and increased the amount of chicken. My tasters appreciated the freshness of snow peas and the crunch of water chestnuts added toward the end of cooking to preserve their texture.

Most American recipes combine soy sauce, rice wine vinegar, and sugar for the sauce, while more authentic recipes sometimes include Chinese black vinegar, which has an intense savory flavor. After testing various combinations, I went with soy sauce (cut with chicken broth to mitigate its saltiness), and replaced the rice wine vinegar and sugar with mirin, a sweet rice wine available in most supermarkets. My tasters liked the richness of the Chinese black vinegar, but it can be hard to find, so I turned to a potent ingredient most people have on hand, Worcestershire sauce, to give the sauce the perfect complex richness.

It was obvious that the half cup of cashews most recipes call for wouldn't be enough. I doubled the amount and then tried grinding them into a homemade cashew butter to better distribute their flavor; unfortunately, this gave the sauce an unappealing chalky texture. I had better results toasting the cashews for a few minutes in a 350-degree oven to intensify their flavor and crunch. Chopping half of the nuts to better incorporate them into the sauce and adding them at the last minute meant that there was plenty of nutty crunch in every bite. **–Kris Widican**

Velveting 101

When meat is coated with cornstarch before cooking, the cornstarch forms a protective barrier that helps prevent overcooking: this technique is called velveting. In this recipe, we add the cornstarch to the marinade for more efficient preparation.

PROTECTIVE COATING

Using toasted sesame oil in the marinade and sauce reinforces the nutty flavor of the cashews.

CASHEW CHICKEN
SERVES 4 TO 6

Toast the cashews on a baking sheet in a 350-degree oven until lightly browned, about 5 minutes, stirring frequently. Presliced water chestnuts can be waterlogged; for the crunchiest texture, use canned whole water chestnuts and slice them yourself. It is imperative to use low-sodium chicken broth in this recipe.

Marinade and Sauce
- ½ cup mirin
- 6 tablespoons soy sauce
- 2 tablespoons plus 2 teaspoons toasted sesame oil
- 2 tablespoons plus 4 teaspoons cornstarch
- 4 boneless, skinless chicken breasts (about 1½ pounds), cut into ¾-inch pieces
- 1 cup low-sodium chicken broth (see note)
- 3 tablespoons Worcestershire sauce

Stir-Fry
- 2 tablespoons vegetable oil
- 8 ounces snow peas, stems snapped off and strings removed, halved crosswise
- 1 tablespoon grated fresh ginger
- 6 garlic cloves, minced
- ¼ teaspoon red pepper flakes
- 1 (8-ounce) can whole water chestnuts, drained and sliced thin (see note)
- 1 cup toasted cashews (see note); half roughly chopped, half left whole

1. For the marinade and sauce: Whisk 3 tablespoons mirin, 2 tablespoons soy sauce, 2 tablespoons sesame oil, and 2 tablespoons cornstarch in large bowl. Add chicken and toss to coat. Refrigerate, covered, for at least 30 minutes or up to 2 hours.

2. Whisk broth, Worcestershire, remaining mirin, remaining soy sauce, remaining sesame oil, and remaining cornstarch in separate bowl; set aside.

3. For the stir-fry: Remove chicken from marinade and pat dry with paper towels. Heat 2 teaspoons vegetable oil in large nonstick skillet over medium-high heat until just smoking. Brown half of chicken, stirring occasionally, until no longer pink, about 4 minutes. Transfer chicken to plate and tent with foil; repeat with additional 2 teaspoons vegetable oil and remaining chicken.

4. Add remaining vegetable oil to empty skillet and heat over medium-high heat until shimmering. Cook snow peas until bright green, about 1 minute. Add ginger, garlic, and pepper flakes to pan and cook until fragrant, about 30 seconds. Stir in water chestnuts and reserved broth mixture and cook, stirring constantly, until sauce is thickened, about 2 minutes. Return chicken, along with any accumulated juices, to skillet and cook until heated through, about 1 minute. Off heat, stir in cashews. Serve.

Holiday Stuffed Pork Roast

Could we transform an inexpensive cut of meat usually destined for pulled pork into a roast worthy of the holiday table?

Test Kitchen Technique
BUTTERFLYING A BOSTON BUTT

Boston butt roasts have great meaty flavor, but because they're made of several different muscles, they can be tricky to butterfly. Here's how we do it:

1. Insert a chef's knife into the opening where the bone has been removed. Cut horizontally, stopping at least 1 inch before the edge, and open the meat like a book.

2. Make another cut diagonally into the thicker portion of the roast. Open this flap, smoothing out the butterflied rectangle of meat.

3. Cover the pork with plastic wrap and, using a meat pounder, pound the meat to an even ¾-inch thickness. The pork is now ready to be cut in half, stuffed, rolled, and tied.

Halving the butterflied, pounded meat creates two roasts that are easier to stuff and roll—and that cook much faster than one big roast.

I'm a longtime fan of the test kitchen recipe for pork roast, which slowly cooks a well-marbled, tough Boston butt to meltingly tender effect. The recipe is always such a hit that I wondered if I could dress up the same cut for the holidays. To elevate this big workaday roast to holiday status, I decided to try stuffing it.

I cut a pocket in the roast, crammed in the test kitchen's recipe for poultry bread stuffing, and tied and roasted it. Unfortunately, not much stuffing fit into my roast, and what did was too bland to stand up to the pork. Clearly, I'd need a more potent stuffing, one that would deliver flavor in every bite.

I'd come across a promising pork roast recipe from northern Minnesota called porketta (or porchetta), introduced by Italian immigrant miners to the state's Iron Range region. It calls for opening up a pork butt like a book, lavishing it with gutsy seasonings, and then rolling and roasting. I decided to borrow the seasoning mix but aim for a more substantial filling.

In a side-by-side tasting of six variations, a stuffing made with garlic, fennel seeds, red pepper flakes, plenty of onion, and ground pork stood out. (Old recipes call for minced lard, prosciutto, or pancetta, so ground pork wasn't much of a stretch.)

Although I'd nailed the flavor, my job was far from done: The stuffing was baking up dry. I'd been using cooked ground pork; now I tried adding it raw. Bingo. It made for moister stuffing, especially when bound with fresh bread crumbs and egg, which also helped to hold the stuffing in place.

Tasters liked the stuffing so much that they wanted more. To increase the surface area of the pork so that I could pile it high with stuffing, I butterflied it as before and then pounded it to an even ¾-inch thickness. This increased the stuffing-to-meat ratio as I'd intended, but my rolled and tied meat was too long for most roasting pans. Cutting the large butterflied meat into two smaller roasts neatly solved this problem. As a bonus, the smaller roasts cooked in less than half the time.

I'd been covering the pork with foil as it roasted to ensure that it stayed moist, but this method prevented flavorful browning. Searing the meat in a skillet before roasting fixed that, but the technique was cumbersome. What if I simply rubbed the raw roast with salt, pepper, and brown sugar (the last to promote browning)? For the final half hour of cooking, I uncovered the roast and upped the heat. Success! My stuffed roast, with its crisp crust, juicy meat, and assertive stuffing, could fittingly grace any holiday table. –Meghan Erwin

HOLIDAY PORK ROAST
SERVES 8

Boneless pork shoulder, often labeled Boston butt, is usually wrapped in netting. If all you can find is a bone-in roast, have the butcher remove the bone. To make the bread crumbs, pulse 1 or 2 pieces of hearty white sandwich bread in a food processor until coarsely ground.

Stuffing

- 2 tablespoons vegetable oil
- 1 onion, chopped fine
- 10 garlic cloves, minced
- 8 ounces ground pork
- 1 cup fresh bread crumbs (see note)
- 3 tablespoons finely chopped fresh parsley
- 1 teaspoon fennel seeds
- ½ teaspoon red pepper flakes
- 1 teaspoon salt
- 1 large egg, lightly beaten

Pork

- 2 tablespoons brown sugar
- 1 tablespoon salt
- 1 tablespoon pepper
- 1 (4- to 5-pound) boneless pork shoulder roast (see note)

1. For the stuffing: Heat oil in large nonstick skillet over medium heat until shimmering. Cook onion until golden, about 8 minutes. Stir in garlic and cook until fragrant, about 30 seconds; transfer to large bowl and let cool. Add ground pork, bread crumbs, parsley, fennel seeds, pepper flakes, salt, and egg to bowl with onion mixture and knead with hands until well combined.

2. For the pork: Adjust oven rack to middle position and heat oven to 300 degrees. Combine sugar, salt, and pepper in small bowl. Following photos 1 to 3 at left, butterfly pork and pound to ¾-inch thickness; you should have rectangle measuring about 15 by 8 inches. With long side facing you, cut pounded pork in half crosswise. Spread stuffing in even layer over each half of pork, leaving a 1-inch border around edges. Roll and tie each half securely with kitchen twine at 1-inch intervals. Rub roasts evenly with sugar mixture and transfer to rimmed baking sheet. Cover baking sheet tightly with foil and roast until meat registers 170 degrees, about 2 hours.

3. Remove foil and increase oven temperature to 400 degrees. Cook until roasts are well browned and meat registers 190 degrees, about 30 minutes. Transfer roasts to cutting board, tent with foil, and let rest 20 minutes. Remove kitchen twine. Slice and serve.

HOLIDAY PORK ROAST WITH CHERRY STUFFING

In step 1, substitute 1 cup crumbled cornbread for fresh bread crumbs, 2 tablespoons minced fresh thyme for parsley, and 1 teaspoon black pepper for red pepper flakes; omit fennel seeds; and add 1 cup chopped dried cherries.

Baked Goat Cheese Salads

Warm, crisp goat cheese rounds on a bed of greens are good. We came up with three ways to make a good thing better.

The test kitchen has a recipe for baked goat cheese salad in which the cheese is rolled in herbs, eggs, then Melba toast crumbs. The rounds are chilled, then baked and served on a bed of greens. The warm, slightly gooey cheese rounds beautifully dress up the greens. For the holiday season, I wanted to go further and add a variety of flavors to the cheese.

A nut coating seemed apt for a holiday first course, and it was easy to replace the Melba toast crumbs with nuts ground in the food processor. Since I already had the machine out, I experimented with giving the cheese a whirl in the bowl, which allowed me to incorporate herbs throughout the cheese.

The technique was easy to vary: I could add dried fruit and honey or sun-dried tomatoes to the food processor instead of the herbs. I paired my dolled-up rounds with greens and a classic red wine vinaigrette. Now I had three salads worthy of any holiday table. –Kris Widican

HERBED BAKED GOAT CHEESE SALAD SERVES 6
For a sweet counterpoint to the herb flavor, add 1 cup dried cherries, golden raisins, or dried cranberries to the salad just before tossing it.

- 1½ cups pecans
- 12 ounces goat cheese, softened
- 2 tablespoons chopped fresh chives
- 1 teaspoon minced fresh thyme
- 2 large eggs
- 12 cups hearty salad greens
- 1 recipe Basic Vinaigrette (see box above)

1. Pulse pecans in food processor until finely chopped; transfer to medium bowl. Add cheese, chives, and thyme to food processor and process until smooth. Refrigerate cheese mixture in covered bowl until firm, at least 1 hour or up to 2 days.

2. Using hands, roll 2 tablespoons chilled cheese mixture into twelve 1½-inch balls. Beat eggs in medium bowl. One at a time, dip balls in egg, then roll in nuts, pressing gently to adhere. Place balls 2 inches apart on rimmed baking sheet. Press balls into 2-inch disks with greased measuring cup. Cover with plastic wrap and freeze until completely firm, at least 2 hours or up to 1 week.

3. Adjust oven rack to upper position and heat oven to 475 degrees. Remove plastic and spray cheese lightly with cooking spray. Bake until nuts are golden brown and cheese is warmed through, 7 to 10 minutes. Let cool 3 minutes. Toss greens with vinaigrette. Serve warm cheese rounds over dressed salad.

HONEY-RAISIN BAKED GOAT CHEESE SALAD
SERVES 6
For crunch, add 2 thinly sliced apples or firm pears.

- 1½ cups almonds
- 12 ounces goat cheese, softened
- 1 tablespoon golden raisins
- 1 teaspoon honey
- 2 large eggs
- 12 cups hearty salad greens
- 1 recipe Basic Vinaigrette (see box above)

1. Pulse almonds in food processor until finely chopped; transfer to medium bowl. Add cheese, raisins, and honey to food processor and process until smooth. Refrigerate cheese mixture in covered bowl until firm, at least 1 hour or up to 2 days.

2. Using hands, roll 2 tablespoons chilled cheese mixture into twelve 1½-inch balls. Beat eggs in medium bowl. One at a time, dip balls in egg, then roll in nuts, pressing gently to adhere. Place balls 2 inches apart on rimmed baking sheet. Press balls into 2-inch disks with greased measuring cup. Cover with plastic wrap and freeze until completely firm, at least 2 hours or up to 1 week.

3. Adjust oven rack to upper position and heat oven to 475 degrees. Remove plastic and spray cheese lightly with cooking spray. Bake until nuts are golden brown and cheese is warmed through, 7 to 10 minutes. Let cool 3 minutes. Toss greens with vinaigrette. Serve warm cheese rounds over dressed salad.

SUN-DRIED TOMATO BAKED GOAT CHEESE SALAD SERVES 6
To bring out the brightness of the tomatoes, toss a cup or so of roughly torn basil leaves in with the salad greens.

- 1½ cups walnuts
- 12 ounces goat cheese, softened
- 1 tablespoon sun-dried tomatoes packed in oil, rinsed and patted dry
- 1 tablespoon chopped fresh basil
- 2 large eggs
- 12 cups hearty salad greens
- 1 recipe Basic Vinaigrette (see box above)

1. Pulse walnuts in food processor until finely chopped; transfer to medium bowl. Add cheese, tomatoes, and basil to food processor and process until smooth. Refrigerate cheese mixture in covered bowl until firm, at least 1 hour or up to 2 days.

2. Using hands, roll 2 tablespoons chilled cheese mixture into twelve 1½-inch balls. Beat eggs in medium bowl. One at a time, dip balls in egg, then roll in nuts, pressing gently to adhere. Place balls 2 inches apart on rimmed baking sheet. Press balls into 2-inch disks with greased measuring cup. Cover with plastic wrap and freeze until completely firm, at least 2 hours or up to 1 week.

3. Adjust oven rack to upper position and heat oven to 475 degrees. Remove plastic and spray cheese lightly with cooking spray. Bake until nuts are golden brown and cheese is warmed through, 7 to 10 minutes. Let cool 3 minutes. Toss greens with vinaigrette. Serve warm cheese rounds over dressed salad.

> ### BASIC VINAIGRETTE
> MAKES ABOUT ⅓ CUP DRESSING, ENOUGH TO DRESS 12 CUPS SALAD GREENS
>
> - ¼ cup extra-virgin olive oil
> - 1½ tablespoons red wine vinegar
> - 2 teaspoons Dijon mustard
> - 1 small shallot, minced
> - ⅛ teaspoon salt
>
> Combine all ingredients in jar, seal lid, and shake vigorously until emulsified.

Coating the cheese rounds in ground nuts (instead of bread crumbs) adds another layer of flavor to these salads.

Perils of Temperature
Cheese rounds that aren't frozen lose their shape when baked.

NOT FROZEN
A Runny Mess

Visit us online!
For a Kalamata Olive Baked Goat Cheese Salad variation, visit **CooksCountry.com** and look for **Cook's Country Extras.**

Ultimate Cinnamon Buns

Ultimate cinnamon buns should be tender, gooey, and unapologetically large. Tragically, most recipes yield lean buns—and ultimate disappointment.

Test Kitchen Technique
ASSEMBLING CINNAMON BUNS

1. Roll the dough into an 18-inch square on a lightly floured work surface.
2. Leaving a ½-inch border around edges, spread the softened butter over the dough, sprinkle with the sugar mixture, and lightly press the sugar mixture into the dough.
3. Use a knife (or metal dough scraper) to cut the rolled log in half and then into 8 equal pieces.

Whether they're from a neighborhood bakery or the food court at the mall, sweet, gooey, softball-sized cinnamon buns are worth every last calorie. This mammoth breed of cinnamon bun is distinguished from its leaner, punier cousins by its size, yes, but also by the richness of the soft, buttery yeasted dough, the abundance of cinnamon-sugar filling, and the thickness of the sticky cream cheese glaze.

My research turned up recipes based on various types of dough. After trying several iterations of each, my tasters rejected recipes based on sweet bread dough (too lean), Danish dough (too buttery, flaky, and labor intensive), and challah (not rich or soft enough). Buttery, tender brioche proved the best base for rich cinnamon buns.

Most recipes use 2 or 3 cups of all-purpose flour to make eight buns. To bump them up to "ultimate" status, I started this recipe with 4½ cups of flour. To this I added sugar and salt, then slowly stirred in the wet ingredients: 3 beaten eggs, ¾ cup whole milk, and yeast. I tested various amounts of butter that I softened and slowly added to the mixer, and my tasters liked the richness brought by 12 tablespoons. The dough is kneaded and left to rise until doubled in size. It's then rolled out, sprinkled with filling, rolled up, cut into buns, and baked. These buns tasted fabulous, but they were a little tough.

I hoped I could tenderize the buns by replacing the all-purpose flour with lower-protein cake flour, which makes for especially tender cakes and other baked goods. But in this case the cake flour worked too well, producing buns that baked up so soft that they never rose properly. In the test kitchen, we sometimes approximate cake flour by cutting all-purpose flour with a little cornstarch (the ratio is ⅞ cup flour to 2 tablespoons cornstarch). I found that if I manipulated that formula (I ended up at 4¼ cups of all-purpose flour and ½ cup cornstarch), I got the benefit of good structure and height from the flour, and tenderness from the cornstarch.

My tasters found granulated sugar too bland for the filling and dark brown sugar too bold. Light brown sugar worked best and I doubled the amount of sugar most recipes use to 1½ cups. For big cinnamon pop, I blended 1½ table-

Adding cornstarch to the dough makes these rich, gooey buns especially tender.

spoons of cinnamon—and no other distracting spices—with the sugar. To keep this thick filling from spilling out as the dough was rolled up, I needed more than a simple brushing of butter, and instead slathered 4 tablespoons of softened butter all over the dough. Baked together, the butter and cinnamon sugar turned into a truly rich, gooey filling.

Many recipes cover the buns with a frosting made of butter, cream cheese, and confectioners' sugar—which pushed these already rich buns over the edge. I wondered if a thick glaze made with just cream cheese, confectioners' sugar, and milk would do. I spread this mixture over the warm buns. Everything seemed

fine—until I came back 30 minutes later to find that the glaze had soaked into the buns. For the next batch, I reserved a little of the glaze to apply again after the buns cooled. Now my "ultimate buns" truly looked the part. –Erika Bruce

ULTIMATE CINNAMON BUNS MAKES 8 BUNS

In step 2, if after mixing for 10 minutes the dough is still wet and sticky, add up to ¼ cup flour (a tablespoon at a time) until the dough releases from the bowl. For smaller cinnamon buns, cut the dough into 12 pieces in step 3.

Dough
- ¾ cup whole milk, heated to 110 degrees
- 1 envelope (2¼ teaspoons) rapid-rise or instant yeast
- 3 large eggs, room temperature
- 4¼ cups all-purpose flour
- ½ cup cornstarch
- ½ cup granulated sugar
- 1½ teaspoons salt
- 12 tablespoons (1½ sticks) unsalted butter, cut into 12 pieces and softened

Filling
- 1½ cups packed light brown sugar
- 1½ tablespoons ground cinnamon
- ¼ teaspoon salt
- 4 tablespoons unsalted butter, softened

Glaze
- 4 ounces cream cheese, softened
- 1 tablespoon whole milk
- 1 teaspoon vanilla extract
- 1½ cups confectioners' sugar

1. For the dough: Adjust oven rack to middle position and heat oven to 200 degrees. When oven reaches 200 degrees, shut off. Line 13- by 9-inch baking pan with foil, allowing excess foil to hang over pan edges. Grease foil and medium bowl.

2. Whisk milk and yeast in liquid measuring cup until yeast dissolves, then whisk in eggs. In bowl of stand mixer fitted with dough hook, mix flour, cornstarch, sugar, and salt until combined. With mixer on low, add warm milk mixture in steady stream and mix until dough comes together, about 1 minute. Increase speed to medium and add butter, one piece at a time, until incorporated. Continue to mix until dough is smooth and comes away from sides of bowl, about 10 minutes. Turn dough out onto clean surface and knead to form a smooth, round ball. Transfer dough to prepared bowl, cover with plastic wrap, and place in warm oven. Let rise until doubled in size, about 2 hours.

3. For the filling: Combine brown sugar, cinnamon, and salt in small bowl. Turn dough out onto lightly floured surface. Following photos 1 and 2 on page 20, roll dough into 18-inch square, spread with butter, and sprinkle evenly with filling. Starting with the edge nearest you, roll dough into tight cylinder, pinch lightly to seal seam, and, following photo 3, cut into 8 pieces. Transfer pieces, cut-side up, to prepared pan. Cover with plastic wrap and let rise in warm spot until doubled in size, about 1 hour.

4. For the glaze and to bake: Heat oven to 350 degrees. Whisk cream cheese, milk, vanilla, and confectioners' sugar in medium bowl until smooth. Discard plastic wrap and bake buns until deep golden brown and filling is melted, 35 to 40 minutes. Transfer to wire rack and top buns with ½ cup glaze; cool 30 minutes. Using foil overhang, lift buns from pan and top with remaining glaze. Serve.

Make Ahead: After transferring pieces to prepared pan in step 3, buns can be covered with plastic wrap and refrigerated for 24 hours. When ready to bake, let sit at room temperature for 1 hour. Remove plastic wrap and continue with step 4 as directed.

Homemade Pancake Mix

The convenience of boxed pancake mix comes at a cost—fake-tasting, even bitter pancakes. We set out to create our own homemade mix, one that delivers store-bought ease and from-scratch taste.

On busy mornings I can barely make a cup of coffee, much less follow a recipe for pancakes. That's why boxed pancake mix is so handy. Throw a scoop of mix into a bowl, add eggs and milk, ladle the batter into a hot pan, and soft, fluffy pancakes are on the table in no time. But boxed mixes, designed to last for months, often taste of the preservatives that ensure their long shelf life. Also, manufacturers include extra baking powder to guarantee high-rising pancakes, with the unintended consequence of bitter flavor.

Plenty of recipes for homemade pancake mix exist. Most use a food processor to cut vegetable shortening into a blend of flour (4 cups makes a manageable amount of mix), baking powder, baking soda, sugar, and salt. When you're ready to get cooking, you add eggs and milk and grab your skillet. But the homemade mixes I tried produced heavy, bland pancakes.

My first discovery was that all-purpose flour made pancakes that were too tough. It turns out that the preservatives in a boxed mix also promote tenderness. A switch to lower-protein cake flour didn't fix the problem; I got flat, dry pancakes. But replacing half the all-purpose flour with cake flour yielded the sturdy yet tender cakes I was after.

Some recipes fortify the dry mix with powdered milk or powdered buttermilk; since my tasters couldn't tell much difference, I opted for the powdered milk, which is easier to find. Beyond salt and sugar, I attempted to build flavor with vanilla, cinnamon, even ground oatmeal; none impressed my tasters. Then I tried an unusual ingredient I had spied in the supermarket near the powdered milk: malt powder (see box at right). My tasters loved the sweet, nutty flavor it brought to the pancakes.

Not surprisingly, they also preferred the flavor of butter to the vegetable shortening that the homemade mixes typically call for. While many recipes use only 8 tablespoons of fat (for 4 cups of flour), I found that 12 tablespoons delivered moister, more flavorful pancakes. Using butter meant that the mix needed to be stored in the refrigerator or freezer (for up to 2 months), but this seemed like a minor inconvenience for such a big improvement in flavor. For the leavener, my tasters stopped me at 2 tablespoons of baking powder—any more and they could taste its bitter, chemical flavor.

Now my pancakes tasted good and were plenty soft, but they lacked stature. Dried buttermilk powder hadn't made the grade in the mix, but I wondered if I could get higher-rising pancakes by using fresh buttermilk instead of milk when I mixed up the batter. For that to work, I'd need to add some baking soda to my mix—one teaspoon was plenty. Sure enough, the acid in the buttermilk reacted with the baking soda right away, causing the batter to bubble and the pancakes to rise higher in the skillet. With a mile-high stack of pancakes on my plate, I had finally beaten the box.

–Diane Unger

A container of our easy-to-make homemade mix in the freezer means that tender, high-rising pancakes are just minutes away.

BETTER-THAN-THE-BOX PANCAKE MIX

MAKES ABOUT 6 CUPS OF MIX, ENOUGH FOR 3 BATCHES OF 8 PANCAKES EACH

- 2 cups all-purpose flour
- 2 cups cake flour
- 1 cup nonfat dry milk powder
- ¾ cup malted milk powder (see sidebar)
- ⅓ cup sugar
- 2 tablespoons baking powder
- 1 teaspoon baking soda
- 1 tablespoon salt
- 12 tablespoons (1½ sticks) unsalted butter, cut into ½-inch pieces

Process all ingredients in food processor until no lumps remain and mixture is texture of wet sand, about 2 minutes. Freeze in airtight container for up to 2 months.

To make 8 pancakes:
Whisk 2 cups mix, 2 lightly beaten large eggs, and ½ cup buttermilk in large bowl until smooth. Pour ¼-cup portions of pancake batter onto lightly oiled large nonstick skillet or griddle and cook over medium-low heat until golden brown, about 2 minutes per side. Repeat with remaining batter as desired. Serve. (If you don't have buttermilk, make clabbered milk by whisking ½ tablespoon white vinegar or lemon juice into ½ cup whole or low-fat milk and letting the mixture thicken for 10 minutes.)

Secret Ingredient

To give our pancakes complexity and depth, we added malted milk powder to the mix. This product is made from malted barley that has been evaporated and pulverized, and sometimes includes flour or evaporated milk powder. It is commonly used to make milkshakes.

MALTED MILK POWDER
Not just for milkshakes

Updating Gingerbread Cake

Most gingerbread cake is dull and dry. We set out to infuse this old-fashioned dessert with enough "oomph" to make it count.

Traditional gingerbread cake is easy to make. Most recipes combine butter, sugar, eggs, flour, leavener, warm spices, molasses, and water; pour the batter into a square pan; and bake. But what's the point of making gingerbread if no one wants to eat it? The recipes I tried produced cakes that were dry and far too sweet, with unbalanced spicing dominated by the dusty burn of powdered ginger. Without unduly complicating the recipe, I wanted to turn this neglected cake into a moist, boldly flavored yet balanced cake.

The first thing to go was the square baking pan; for more substantial slices, I decided to bake my gingerbread in a Bundt pan. I found that 2½ cups of all-purpose flour, 16 tablespoons butter, and 4 eggs filled the pan nicely. Creaming the butter and sugar in a mixer made the cake a little too light and fluffy. Searching for a denser, moister texture, I tried a dump-and-stir mixing method that replaced the butter with an equal volume of vegetable oil, but that made the cake greasy and lacking in richness. I tried the same method using melted butter, which proved the best path to a moist, dense, richer cake.

The standard liquid combination of mild molasses and water seemed lackluster, so I switched to robust molasses. In place of water, I tried milk and buttermilk; both were fine but didn't add much. I tested unexpected liquids like coffee (too bitter) and orange juice (too sour) before I remembered a recipe I'd seen that used stout. Willing to try anything, I stirred the beer in and was shocked that it gave the cake a deep malty tang that my tasters loved.

Powdered ginger gave the cake some bite, and a little cinnamon and allspice supported the ginger flavor nicely (tasters nixed nutmeg, cloves, and cardamom). A surprising ingredient, black pepper, helped draw out even more of the ginger's pleasing burn.

Ground spices used in large quantities gave the cake a dusty texture. Rather than increasing amounts to promote flavor, I tried cooking the spices in melted butter, a technique we use in the test kitchen for savory spiced dishes like curry and chili. The flavors bloomed (and any dusty feel was gone), but tasters still wanted more ginger. Maybe old-fashioned recipes were stuck with powdered ginger; I went to the real McCoy and found that four teaspoons of grated fresh ginger added an unmistakable element that the dried spices couldn't muster.

With a glaze of confectioners' sugar and ginger ale, I'd finally managed to put the "ginger" back in gingerbread.

–Erika Bruce

Robust molasses, stout, and three sources of ginger turn an old-fashioned recipe into something special.

BOLD AND SPICY GINGERBREAD SERVES 12

Guinness is the test kitchen's favorite brand of stout. An equal amount of orange or lemon juice can be substituted for the ginger ale in the glaze. Be sure to use finely ground black pepper here.

Cake

- 2½ cups all-purpose flour
- 2 teaspoons baking powder
- ¾ teaspoon baking soda
- ¾ teaspoon salt
- 16 tablespoons (2 sticks) unsalted butter
- 2 tablespoons ground ginger
- 2 teaspoons ground cinnamon
- 1 teaspoon ground allspice
- ¼ teaspoon pepper (see note)
- 4 large eggs, room temperature
- 1½ cups sugar
- 4 teaspoons grated fresh ginger
- ¾ cup robust or dark molasses
- ¾ cup stout beer (see note)

Glaze

- 1¾ cups confectioners' sugar
- 3 tablespoons ginger ale (see note)
- 1 teaspoon ground ginger

1. For the cake: Adjust oven rack to middle position and heat oven to 375 degrees. Grease and flour 12-cup nonstick Bundt pan. Whisk flour, baking powder, baking soda, and salt in large bowl. Melt butter in saucepan over medium heat until bubbling. Stir in ground ginger, cinnamon, allspice, and pepper and cook until fragrant, about 30 seconds. Remove from heat and let cool slightly.

2. Whisk eggs, sugar, and fresh ginger in large bowl until light and frothy. Stir in melted butter mixture, molasses, and stout until incorporated. Whisk flour mixture into egg mixture until no lumps remain.

3. Pour batter into prepared pan and gently tap pan on countertop to release any trapped air bubbles. Bake until toothpick inserted into center comes out clean, about 45 minutes. Cool cake in pan 20 minutes, then turn out onto wire rack set inside rimmed baking sheet; let cool completely.

4. For the glaze: Whisk confectioners' sugar, ginger ale, and ginger in bowl until smooth. Pour glaze over cooled cake. Let glaze set 15 minutes. Serve. (Cake can be stored at room temperature, covered in plastic wrap, for 2 days.)

Gingerbread with a Kick

Once spicy and bold, gingerbread has become sweet and bland over time. Here's how we breathed new life into a tired recipe.

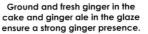

Ground and fresh ginger in the cake and ginger ale in the glaze ensure a strong ginger presence.

Robust molasses and stout add richness and a bitter edge that balance the spicy ginger.

Getting to Know Pears

Their crisp cousins—apples—may be more popular, but juicy, tender pears have a character and complexity all their own. Here are 12 varieties along with our tasting notes. See page 31 for more information about pears.

Anjou
JUICY BUT GRAINY

The most widely available variety in the U.S., this medium-sized, egg-shaped pear can be either green or red and does not change color as it ripens. The flesh of an Anjou is "juicy and very soft," albeit slightly grainy, with a "delicate, lemony" finish. Eat them out of hand, roast or bake, but avoid poaching these pears—their slightly granular flesh becomes shaggy and soggy.

Asian
APPLE LOOK-ALIKE

There are many varieties of Asian pear, but the most common is the Hosui. At first glance, it resembles an off-colored Granny Smith apple. A closer look reveals tough skin flecked with small white dots. Its flesh is "super-crunchy," much like an apple, but its flavor is closer to a "crisp, but perfectly ripe, honeydew melon." Eat out of hand or slice and add to salads, but do not cook—heat destroys its crisp texture.

20th Century
CRISP AND JUICY

This variety of Asian pear originated in Japan in the early 1900s. It is highly prized there and often conferred as a gift to celebrate successful business relationships. It has thin, yellow skin and "firm, slightly porous" flesh that is "very juicy, yet crisp—like jicama." Its mildly sweet flavor reminded tasters of watermelon. More delicate than other Asian pears, this variety is often sold individually wrapped in a Styrofoam sock.

Seckel
TINY SUGAR PEAR

Don't be fooled by these tiny green and red fruits (the smallest commercially grown pears). They pack a "super-sweet punch," hence their nickname: sugar pears. Seckel pears have a distinct floral flavor with hints of rose and lavender. Their firm flesh makes them a good option for eating raw or poaching, but avoid roasting—their dry texture will turn leathery in the oven.

Prickly
HANDLE WITH CARE

Also called "cactus pear" or, in Spanish, "tuna," these are not true pears: They are berries of the prickly pear cactus. Dotted with hard seeds, the flesh is mashed and strained to collect an "earthy, melon-y" juice. Peel the pears and push them through a sieve to remove the seeds. Alternatively, buy bottled or canned juice—it adds a bold flavor to smoothies, margaritas, and sorbets.

Bosc
FIRM AND CRISP

This popular wintertime pear is easily identified by its slender shape and russet color. Bosc pears are firm and have a thick, slightly bitter skin. Their flesh boasts a "crisp, apple-y acidity" that reminded more than one taster of kiwi. While Bosc pears are fine for eating out of hand, their firm flesh holds its shape well, making them equally well suited for poaching, roasting, or baking into pies and crisps.

Forelle
"TROUT" PEAR

This handsome pear's name means "trout" in German, a nod to its reddish-gold speckling, which is said to resemble the fish. We found its beauty only skin-deep. Although juicy, these small pears are "surprisingly bland" and have a "mealy, cottony" texture. Luckily, roasting or poaching improves their texture and unlocks a "buttery, grape-y" flavor.

Comice
BIG BOTTOM

The full name of this French varietal is Doyenné du Comice. It is a large, bottom-heavy pear with green skin that sometimes blushes to reddish-brown. Its "highly aromatic," ivory-colored flesh is "smooth and creamy" with a "sweet, but distinctly peppery" finish. Its juiciness and complex flavor make it a favorite dessert pear and one that also pairs well with cheese—particularly Brie and blue cheeses. Comice pears exhibit almost no color change as they ripen.

Taylor's Gold
KIWI SPECIALTY

A natural mutation of the Comice, the Taylor Gold pear was discovered in a New Zealand orchard in the 1980s. Some tasters described it as "sweet, perfume-y, and exceptionally juicy"; others found its thick, coarse skin reminiscent of "fine-textured sandpaper." The "dense, smooth" flesh makes it an excellent all-purpose pear. Eat out of hand, peel and add to salads, or use in cooked applications.

Bartlett
CANNING PEAR

Plump and bell-shaped, this archetypical pear is a favorite on both sides of the Atlantic (in England, it's known as the Williams pear). Although some Bartletts are red-skinned, most ripen to a bright yellowish-green with a reddish blush. The juiciness of the Bartlett is unmatched. Often referred to as "canning" pears, they have a "soft, slightly grainy" and "honey-sweet, musky" flavor also suitable for eating out of hand, poaching, or roasting.

Packham's Triumph
NOT SO TRIUMPHANT

This bottom-heavy Australian pear was first produced by Charles Packham in 1896. The name "Packham's Triumph" was bestowed upon this pear by the Australian Department of Agriculture, which claimed it was the finest of its sort. We beg to differ. They are considered "dessert" pears for their supposed sweetness, but we found them "watery and mealy," "one-dimensional," "boring," and "musky."

Quince
PERFUMED "PEAR"

The quince is only a distant relative of the pear family. Popular in Europe and the Middle East, it is rarely eaten raw, as its flesh is "dry as cardboard" and "bitter as lemon pith." Happily, cooking unlocks its exotic flavor, which tasters likened to guava and apricot. Because of their high pectin content, quinces are typically stewed into jams or confections such as dulce de membrillo, a Spanish favorite eaten with cheese.

Chicken Piccata

I love chicken piccata but have trouble making it. It either has overcooked chicken or the sauce is so tart from the lemons that my mouth puckers! Any suggestions on how to get tender chicken and make a sauce with balanced flavor? –Heather Read, Norman, Okla.

Secrets to PERFECT PICCATA

Thin cutlets are easy to over-cook, and the traditional flouring doesn't have time to brown (especially on the second side, which only cooks for about a minute). Here's how we solved the problems:

1. Soaking the thin-cut chicken breasts for just 15 minutes in a mixture of salt, sugar, and water allowed the chicken to remain moist while it browned.

2. Flouring the chicken cutlets on only one side helped thicken the sauce without making the chicken slippery.

Although originally a veal preparation, most recipes for piccata are now made with thin chicken cutlets that are floured, sautéed, and then removed from the pan so a lemony, caper-studded pan sauce can be quickly assembled. It's a dish my friends who rarely cook make to impress company—it looks and sounds impressive but is very simple to make.

I started my testing by dredging thin-cut boneless, skinless cutlets in flour and browning them over high heat before removing them from the pan; this gave the cutlets good color, but the high heat dried out the lean breast meat. Moderate heat (and a slightly shorter cooking time for the second side) worked much better, but the cutlets were still a little dry by the time they were cooked through. I knew a saltwater brine would help keep the meat moist and juicy, but I was reluctant to wait an hour for the brining. After dozens of tests, I was happy to discover that if I increased the salinity of a normal brine (to ½ cup of salt for 4 cups of water), these thin cutlets reaped all the benefits of brining in a mere 15 minutes.

Most recipes remove the chicken and deglaze the pan with lemon juice, but my tasters thought this muted the lemon's bright complexity. Directly deglazing with white wine and broth—and adding a full 2 tablespoons of lemon juice at the end of cooking to preserve its flavor—worked much better. Looking to deepen the lemon flavor, I tried simmering lemon slices in the sauce as it reduced, but the pith (the white part between the peel and flesh) made the sauce too bitter. Grated zest added the right flavor, but tasters didn't like the chewy bits. Strips of zest were the answer here; they released their flavorful oils while the sauce cooked, and I could easily discard them before serving. Adding sugar to the saltwater brine mellowed any sourness from my two-part lemon punch.

Salty, vinegary capers are an integral part of this dish, and my tasters didn't allow me to skimp, demanding a full 2 tablespoons. But at this volume, the capers were making the sauce taste a little too pickle-y. Quickly sautéing them (with a little garlic for added flavor) before deglazing the pan tempered the capers' harshness.

This piccata was almost perfect, but since I was only cooking the second side of the cutlets for about a minute, the flour on that side wasn't cooking and was becoming gluey. Omitting the flour altogether meant the first side didn't brown as well. A simple compromise was to flour only the first side of each cutlet, which still gave me good browning on the presenta-tion side and a nicer texture on the more quickly cooked (and unfloured) second side. My piccata is still quick and easy—but now it's really good, too. –Lynn Clark

For potent-yet-balanced lemon flavor, we use strips of lemon zest as well as fresh lemon juice in the sauce.

CHICKEN PICCATA
SERVES 4

In step 1, do not soak the chicken for more than 30 min-utes or it may become too salty.

- ½ cup salt
- ½ cup sugar
- 8 thin-cut boneless, skinless chicken cutlets (about 1½ pounds)
  Pepper
- ¼ cup all-purpose flour
- 4 tablespoons unsalted butter
- 2 garlic cloves, minced
- 2 tablespoons drained capers
- 1 cup low-sodium chicken broth
- ½ cup white wine
- 4 strips zest (each about 2 inches long) and 2 tablespoons juice from 1 lemon

1. Whisk 4 cups cold water, salt, and sugar in large bowl until salt and sugar dissolve. Add chicken and refrigerate, covered, for at least 15 minutes but no longer than 30 minutes.

2. Pat cutlets dry with paper towels and season with pepper. Spread flour in shallow dish. Dredge one side of each cutlet lightly in flour; transfer to large plate. Heat 1 tablespoon butter in large nonstick skillet over medium heat until foaming subsides. Cook 4 cutlets, floured-side down, until golden brown, about 2 minutes. Flip and cook until just cooked through, about 1 minute on second side. Transfer to clean platter and tent with foil. Repeat with additional table-spoon butter and remaining cutlets.

3. Add garlic and capers to empty pan and cook over high heat until fragrant, about 30 seconds. Add broth, wine, and lemon zest and simmer until reduced to ½ cup, 8 to 10 minutes. Return chicken and any accumulated juices to pan to heat through, about 30 seconds. Off heat, stir in remaining butter and lemon juice. Serve.

Oven-Fried Shrimp

Oven-frying means fewer batches and less mess than deep-frying. But can you get a "fried" crust in the oven before the shrimp turn to rubber?

The best deep-fried shrimp have a crisp, golden crust that complements the firm, sweet, and juicy shrimp. Oven-fried recipes promise the same results but with less fuss. Too bad most don't deliver. Most use a classic "fish-fry" coating based on seasoned cornmeal and "fry" the shrimp on a preheated baking sheet in the oven. I tried this method, but the coating baked up gritty and bland, and the shrimp were like jerky (with a steamed, wet underside) by the time any significant browning had occurred on the top.

My first challenge was achieving browning in the relatively short time it takes for shrimp to cook. With that in mind, I started with large shrimp, which take longer to cook and thus give the exterior more time to brown. Using the fish-fry coating as my working recipe, I quickly learned that a relatively short spin in a super-hot, 500-degree oven was my best hope for a crust that resembled deep-fried. To avoid the soggy-bottom problem, I elevated the shrimp on a flat rack set in a baking sheet, which promoted better air circulation and meant no flipping was required. Baking the shrimp on the top oven rack produced maximum color.

I was making progress, but the coating wasn't sticking to the shrimp. While a dry fish-fry coating will fuse to shrimp once they hit a pot of hot oil, my cornmeal mixture tended to fall off in the oven. I found that a traditional breading—made by dredging the shrimp in flour, dipping them in egg, and then coating the shrimp with corn-meal—was much sturdier.

Since the cornmeal in the coating was too tough and pebbly, I tested ground tortilla chips and Fritos, products I hoped would give me corn flavor and a crisp texture—but both were gritty and dry. Instant polenta (which is softened via precooking) provided the rich corn flavor I was after, and it was neither tough nor gritty. But it wasn't exactly crisp.

I tried adding toasted fresh bread crumbs to the instant polenta without success. I had better luck with store-bought panko bread crumbs, as their chunky texture added some serious crunch to the coating. Toasting the coating mixture in the microwave (see box at right) made it even more crisp.

With a crisp coating under my belt, I could concentrate on building "fried" flavor. I stole a trick the test kitchen uses for oven-fried onion rings and added crunchy ground potato chips to the coating. Once the shrimp were breaded, I discovered that a good 30 minutes' rest in the refrigerator let the breading set up and really adhere. These flavorful, crisp yet tender shrimp rivaled deep-fried—without all the hassle.

–Diane Unger

OVEN-FRIED SHRIMP
SERVES 4

Large shrimp (26 to 30 shrimp per pound) are essential here. Lay's Kettle Cooked Original is our favorite brand of potato chips. Panko is a Japanese-style bread crumb available in most grocery stores (see page 30 for more information). Instant polenta is available in the international section of most supermarkets.

- 2 cups panko bread crumbs (see note)
- ¼ cup instant polenta (see note)
- 1½ teaspoons paprika
- ¼ teaspoon cayenne pepper
  Salt
- ¼ cup vegetable oil
- 2 cups potato chips (about 2 ounces), crushed to fine crumbs
- ¾ cup all-purpose flour
- 2 large eggs
- 1½ pounds large shrimp, peeled and deveined

1. Adjust oven rack to upper position and heat oven to 500 degrees. Toss bread crumbs, polenta, paprika, cayenne, 1 teaspoon salt, and oil in microwave-safe bowl until well coated. Microwave crumb mixture until golden brown and crisp, 1 to 3 minutes, stirring halfway through cooking time. Stir potato chips into crumb mixture, then transfer to shallow dish. Spread flour in second shallow dish. In third shallow dish, whisk eggs until evenly combined.

2. Pat shrimp dry with paper towels and season with salt. One at a time, coat shrimp lightly in flour, dip in egg mixture, then dredge in crumbs, pressing gently to adhere. Arrange breaded shrimp ½ inch apart on wire rack set inside rimmed baking sheet. Refrigerate for at least 30 minutes or up to 2 hours.

3. Spray shrimp with cooking spray and bake until crumbs are deep golden brown and shrimp are just cooked through, 5 to 7 minutes. Serve.

We like to serve these crunchy, spicy shrimp with lemon wedges and tartar sauce.

Test Kitchen Technique
MICROWAVE TOASTING

The five minutes (or so) it takes to cook these shrimp isn't enough time for the breading to turn brown and crisp in the oven. We discovered that toasting the instant polenta and panko in the microwave gave them a head start and ensured a crisp coating on the shrimp.

Building a Better Breading

Three unlikely ingredients combine to make the perfect coating for our Oven-Fried Shrimp.

PANKO CRUMBS
Light, crisp Japanese-style bread crumbs act as a foundation for the crunchy coating.

INSTANT POLENTA
Instant polenta adds corn flavor without being too chewy.

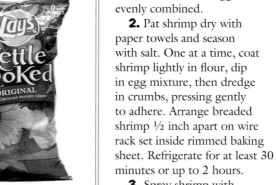

POTATO CHIPS
Crushed potato chips add even more crunch and give the coating a great "deep-fried" flavor.

Easy Caramel Cake

The tangy buttermilk in the cake helps to balance the intense sweetness of the caramel frosting.

My grandmother's caramel cake is my favorite cake on earth, but the best part—the caramel frosting—is troublesome to make. I would love an easier recipe. –Susie Rendle, Alpharetta, Ga.

Kitchen Know-How
GOOF-PROOF CARAMEL

Traditional caramel made with granulated sugar requires a candy thermometer to pinpoint timing. Our easy, foolproof caramel uses dark brown sugar and a simple visual cue—a ring of bubbles around the perimeter of the pan—to signal when it's time to add the cream and, later, to remove the mixture from the heat.

I too love the rich, toffee-flavored frosting on a caramel cake. Spread over yellow cake layers, this unique frosting starts out creamy but quickly firms up to a fudgelike consistency. The exterior of the frosting develops a thin, crystalline crust while the frosting closest to the cake remains silky and smooth.

While the appeal of this Southern specialty is clear, it's easy to understand why few bakers make it, even in the South. Caramel frosting is notoriously tricky. Traditional recipes call for cooking granulated sugar (sometimes with water) in a saucepan until dark amber, carefully adding cream while it violently sputters, then beating in butter and confectioners' sugar. Some recipes shortcut the process by starting with brown sugar, but you generally still need a candy thermometer to recognize when the caramel

has reached the "soft ball" stage. If these challenges aren't enough, the frosting can harden at lightning speed. My goal was an easier, foolproof caramel icing that would stay creamy long enough to frost a two-layer cake—without racing the clock.

I first needed a sturdy cake with enough flavor to stand up to the sweet frosting. I started with the test kitchen's recipe for classic yellow cake, which relies on the "reverse creaming" mixing method. Standard creaming beats butter and sugar until fluffy, then alternately adds the wet and dry ingredients. The result is a tender, fluffy cake. Reverse creaming beats the butter (followed by dairy) into the dry ingredients. Less air is beaten into the batter, and the crumb is finer and less fluffy.

Tests confirmed that reverse creaming produced a somewhat sturdier cake better suited to caramel frosting. Switching from cake flour to higher-protein all-purpose flour gave the cake yet more structure to handle the heavy frosting. To temper the cake's sweetness, I tried cutting back on the 1½ cups of sugar, but even a slight reduction made the cake dry. I had better luck replacing the milk with tangy buttermilk.

I researched "easy" caramel frostings made with brown sugar. The most promising recipe cooked 2 cups of brown sugar, 12 tablespoons of butter, and ½ cup of heavy cream over medium heat; when bubbles formed around the perimeter of the saucepan, the mixture was transferred to a mixer to beat in confectioners' sugar. This method was easy, but because the brown sugar was cooking in so much liquid, it never developed enough caramelized flavor. For my next test I simmered just the sugar and butter before adding the cream; now the flavor of caramel was unmistakable.

But the icing still stiffened before I finished frosting the cake. Upping the amount of butter kept the mixture soft for longer, but it also made the frosting greasy. Thinking of how creamy buttercream frostings whip softened butter with confectioners' sugar, I tried beating a little softened butter into the finished frosting. This frosting was rich and silky, and the fat from the butter kept the frosting soft and spreadable for a few precious extra minutes. The best part? The signature of a Southern caramel cake, the crystalline crust, formed in about 30 minutes. –Cali Rich

EASY CARAMEL CAKE
SERVES 8

In step 5, the cooled frosting stays soft and spreadable longer than other recipes, but it will harden over time. If the frosting does begin to stiffen, you can microwave it for about 10 seconds (or until it returns to a spreadable consistency).

Cake
- ½ cup buttermilk, room temperature
- 4 large eggs, room temperature
- 2 teaspoons vanilla extract
- 2¼ cups all-purpose flour
- 1½ cups granulated sugar
- 1½ teaspoons baking powder
- ½ teaspoon baking soda
- ¾ teaspoon salt
- 16 tablespoons (2 sticks) unsalted butter, cut into 16 pieces and softened

Frosting
- 12 tablespoons (1½ sticks) unsalted butter, cut into 12 pieces and softened
- 2 cups packed dark brown sugar
- ½ teaspoon salt
- ½ cup heavy cream
- 1 teaspoon vanilla extract
- 2½ cups confectioners' sugar, sifted

1. For the cake layers: Adjust oven rack to middle position and heat oven to 350 degrees. Grease and flour two 9-inch cake pans. Whisk buttermilk, eggs, and vanilla in large measuring cup. With electric mixer on low speed, mix flour, granulated sugar, baking powder, baking soda, and salt until combined. Beat in butter, 1 piece at a time, until only pea-sized pieces remain. Pour in half of buttermilk mixture and beat over medium-high speed until light and fluffy, about 1 minute. Slowly add remaining buttermilk mixture to bowl and beat until incorporated, about 15 seconds.

2. Scrape equal amounts of batter into prepared pans and bake until golden and toothpick inserted in center comes out clean, 20 to 25 minutes. Cool cakes in pans 10 minutes, then turn out onto wire racks. Cool completely, at least 1 hour.

3. For the frosting: Heat 8 tablespoons butter, brown sugar, and salt in large saucepan over medium heat until small bubbles appear around perimeter of pan (see photo at left), 4 to 8 minutes. Whisk in cream and cook until ring of bubbles reappears, about 1 minute. Off heat, whisk in vanilla.

4. Transfer hot frosting mixture to bowl and, with electric mixer on low speed, gradually mix in confectioners' sugar until incorporated. Increase speed to medium and beat until frosting is pale brown and just warm, about 5 minutes. Add remaining butter, 1 piece at a time, and beat until light and fluffy, about 2 minutes.

5. To assemble: Place 1 cake round on serving platter. Spread ¾ cup frosting over cake, then top with second cake round. Spread remaining frosting evenly over top and sides of cake. Serve.

Chocolate Bread Pudding

Chocolate and bread pudding sound like a match made in heaven. So why do most versions turn out treacly and dull, packing no chocolate punch?

Creamy, custardy bread pudding has humble origins as a way to use up stale bread, and its rustic nature—and ease of preparation—make it all the more appealing. The simplest versions soak stale or toasted bread in a mixture of eggs, sugar, and dairy (cream or milk) and bake. Adding chocolate to the mix sounds like a winning proposition, but the reality isn't so rosy.

I tested eight published recipes from reputable sources and had a hard time convincing my colleagues that adding chocolate to bread pudding was even a good idea. Recipes that simply stirred cocoa powder into the custard base were pale and lacking chocolate punch. Recipes that added melted chocolate tasted better, but the dense chocolate thickened the base so it never fully permeated the bread, making for bland, dry bread cubes suspended in chocolate custard.

I started over with a test kitchen recipe for bread pudding that soaks cubed, toasted white sandwich bread in a custard base of egg yolks, heavy cream, milk, and sugar. For round chocolate flavor, I knew a combination of cocoa powder and melted chocolate would be key. Dutch-processed cocoa gave the mixture a good foundation of chocolate flavor, and my tasters much preferred the richness of melted semisweet chocolate to milk chocolate (too sweet and bland) or unsweetened (sour and grainy). Just a tablespoon of instant espresso powder enhanced the chocolate flavor without being identifiable on

its own. Since the sandwich bread was a little light for my chocolaty custard, I made a batch using toasted challah, a richer bread that suited the chocolate base better.

The base tasted chocolaty, but it was so thick that it still wasn't fully soaking into the bread. To thin it, I made a batch that omitted the melted chocolate (which I would add back later) and was happy to find that it soaked through the toasted challah more efficiently. To further loosen the liquid, I removed the egg yolks (again, I'd add them back later) from the soaking mixture, which was now just cream, milk, cocoa, espresso powder, and sugar. Without the yolks, I could heat the mixture to better dissolve the cocoa and sugar and to promote a deeper soak.

Now that the bread cubes were fully saturated with my "hot cocoa" mixture, I could combine the egg yolks and melted chocolate with more cream and sugar to make a rich chocolate custard for the bread pudding. I poured this thick mixture over the soaked bread and baked the pudding in a gentle 325-degree oven for 45 minutes. When it came out of the oven, the tantalizing smell lured a horde of hungry test cooks to my work station. To tempt them further, I drizzled a little reserved chocolate sauce (just melted chocolate and cream) over the warm bread pudding. Judging from the way my colleagues enthusiastically crowded around for seconds, I knew that this chocolate bread pudding recipe was finally a winner. **–Kelley Baker**

CHOCOLATE BREAD PUDDING SERVES 12

Challah can be found in most bakeries and many supermarkets. It is important to use Dutch-processed cocoa in this recipe. Natural cocoa powder will make the bread pudding too bitter.

- 1 (12-inch) loaf challah, cut into ½-inch cubes (about 12 cups) (see note)
- 4 cups heavy cream
- 2 cups whole milk
- ½ cup Dutch-processed cocoa powder
- 1 tablespoon instant espresso powder
- 1 cup sugar
- 8 ounces semisweet chocolate, chopped
- 10 large egg yolks

1. Adjust oven rack to middle position and heat oven to 300 degrees. Toast bread on rimmed baking sheet, stirring occasionally, until golden and crisp, about 30 minutes. Transfer to large bowl.

2. Increase oven temperature to 325 degrees. Grease 13- by 9-inch baking pan. Heat 1½ cups cream, milk, cocoa, espresso, and ½ cup sugar in saucepan over medium-high heat, stirring occasionally, until steaming and sugar dissolves. Pour warm cream mixture over toasted bread and let stand, tossing occasionally, until liquid has been absorbed, about 10 minutes.

3. Meanwhile, bring additional 1 cup cream to simmer in saucepan over medium-high heat. Remove from heat and stir in chocolate until smooth. Transfer 1 cup chocolate mixture to medium bowl and

let cool 5 minutes (cover pan and reserve remaining chocolate mixture for serving). Add egg yolks, remaining cream, and remaining sugar to bowl with chocolate mixture and whisk to combine.

4. Transfer soaked bread mixture to prepared pan and pour chocolate custard mixture evenly over bread. Bake until pudding is just set and surface is slightly crisp, about 45 minutes. Let cool 30 minutes. Warm reserved chocolate mixture over low heat, then pour over bread pudding. Serve. (Leftover bread pudding should be refrigerated; reheat individual portions in microwave.)

Make Ahead: In step 4, once soaked bread mixture has been transferred to prepared pan, the pan can be covered with plastic wrap and refrigerated overnight. When ready to bake, remove plastic and proceed with recipe as directed, increasing baking time to 55 to 60 minutes. Let reserved chocolate serving sauce cool, then cover with plastic wrap and refrigerate. Heat sauce in microwave when needed.

Our chocolate bread pudding is enriched with a ganache sauce made of melted chocolate and cream.

Secret to a Proper Soak

Melted semisweet chocolate adds big flavor to our chocolate bread pudding, but it's so thick that it doesn't soak into the bread. We soak our toasted bread in a warm mixture of heavy cream, milk, cocoa powder, and sugar to infuse each piece with chocolate flavor before adding the rich custard made with melted chocolate.

SOAKED IN DAIRY, COCOA, AND SUGAR
Bread is fully saturated.

SOAKED IN CUSTARD MADE WITH MELTED CHOCOLATE
Bread remains dry in spots.

Food Shopping

BOXED BROWNIE MIXES: Do Any Come Close to Homemade?

There are times, such as a last-minute bake sale or Cub Scout troop meeting, when the convenience of a boxed brownie mix is appealing. To find out just how good these mixes are, we rounded up seven national brands of boxed brownie mixes, did extensive pretasting to determine a sole contender from brands that offer different styles (as do Betty Crocker, Duncan Hines, and Ghirardelli), baked them according to package instructions, and called our tasters to the table.

As expected, the majority of the brownies were awful, featuring "chemical" flavors, cloying sweetness, and a distinct lack of chocolate flavor. There were,

however, two bright spots. The brownies from chocolate manufacturer Ghirardelli and gourmet brand Barefoot Contessa were actually pretty good—not as good as homemade (check out our favorite recipe at CooksCountry.com), but surprisingly close.

What separated these brands from the pack? For one, they were the only mixes to include additional sources of chocolate (other than chips). The Ghirardelli mix comes with a packet of chocolate syrup; the Barefoot Contessa mix has both semi-sweet chocolate chunks and mini chocolate chips. Tasters also praised the "rich," "balanced" chocolate flavor of these mixes, which comes in part from

their inclusion of both natural and Dutch-processed cocoa powder. (Third-place Pillsbury also contains both types of cocoa.) We often find natural cocoa powder bitter, but used in conjunction with milder Dutch-processed cocoa, plenty of sugar, and another source of chocolate, it can make for richer, more chocolaty brownies.

Most mixes, including the winning Ghirardelli, call for vegetable oil; the Barefoot Contessa mix calls for butter, which contributes richness and flavor and gave this brand a significant leg up in our tasting. The brownie mixes are listed below in order of preference. –Scott Kathan

① ② ③ ④ ⑤ ⑥ ⑦

Recommended

1. GHIRARDELLI Chocolate Syrup Brownie Mix $3.69 for 18.75 ounces
Requires: ⅓ cup vegetable oil, 1 egg, and ¼ cup water for 8- by 8-inch pan of brownies (can also bake in 9- by 9-inch pan)
Comments: "Balanced chocolate (flavor) and sweetness" was tasters' assessment of these "moist, chewy" brownies, which were also praised for their "perfect texture." One taster gushed, "Just like Mom used to make."

2. BAREFOOT CONTESSA Outrageous Brownie Mix $8.99 for 20.8 ounces
Requires: 8 tablespoons (1 stick) unsalted butter, 2 eggs, and ¾ cup chopped walnuts (optional; we did not use them) for 8- by 8-inch pan of brownies
Comments: Most tasters lauded the "very rich," "real," and "natural" chocolate flavor of this upscale brand from television personality and cookbook author Ina Garten. The "dense and chewy," "moist and fudgy" texture was also a hit. A few naysayers complained about "burnt" or "acrid" notes.

Recommended with Reservations

3. PILLSBURY Brownie Classics Traditional Fudge Premium Brownie Mix $2.59 for 19.5 ounces
Requires: ½ cup oil, 2 eggs, and ¼ cup water for 13- by 9-inch pan of brownies
Comments: "Sweeter than most and not as chocolaty" and "pretty sweet but good" sum up tasters' opinions of this brand's middle-of-the-road flavor. Comments on texture were not as kind: "spongy," "extremely oily," and "weird chewy clumps."

4. BETTY CROCKER Hershey's Ultimate Fudge Supreme Brownie Mix $2.99 for 21 ounces
Requires: ½ cup vegetable oil, 2 eggs, and 2 tablespoons water for 8- by 8-inch pan of brownies (can also bake in 9- by 9-inch or 13- by 9-inch pan)
Comments: With the longest ingredient list in our lineup, it wasn't surprising that tasters found these "very chewy" brownies to have a "fake" chocolate flavor and an "off aftertaste." "More sweet than chocolaty."

Not Recommended

5. DUNCAN HINES Family-Style Chewy Fudge Brownies $1.69 for 21 ounces
Requires: ½ cup vegetable oil, 2 eggs, and ¼ cup water for 8- by 8-inch pan of brownies (can also bake in 9- by 9-inch or 13- by 9-inch pan)
Comments: Cries of "too sweet," "all sugar and no chocolate," and "lacks flavor" dominated the comment sheets. "Looks awesome, but [tastes like] crud" and "tastes like microwave brownies" were other complaints.

6. KING ARTHUR FLOUR All-American Fudge Brownie Mix $3.83 for 18 ounces
Requires: ⅓ cup vegetable oil, 2 eggs, and 3 tablespoons water for 8- by 8-inch pan of brownies
Comments: Our tasters clamored over strange flavors: "offensive molasses," "rank artificial chocolate," "strange cinnamon aftertaste," "prune-y," and "tastes sort of dirty" were among the telling remarks.

7. CHERRYBROOK KITCHEN Fudge Brownie Mix with Chocolate Chips $5.29 for 16 ounces
Requires: ⅓ cup melted margarine, 2 teaspoons vegetable oil, and ¾ cup water for 9- by 9-inch pan of brownies
Comments: The "stale and sour," "murky" flavors didn't come from the margarine—these eggless brownies were still last across the board when made with butter. The non-dairy chocolate chips in the mix didn't seem to boost chocolate flavor. Tasters detected hints of "carob," "fruit juice," and "banana"—not chocolate.

Taste Test Potatoes

Potatoes come in all shapes, sizes, and colors, but the most important thing to know when cooking them is their relative starch and moisture content. In the test kitchen, we sort potatoes into the following three categories.

Starchy Potatoes
(20 to 22 percent starch)
Also known as baking potatoes, these are also our first choice for French fries because their interiors are so fluffy. Because of their dry texture, they readily absorb butter and cream to make for especially creamy mashed or scalloped potatoes. Starchy potatoes break down in moist environments, which makes them a poor choice when you want distinct chunks of potato in soups or stews.
COMMON VARIETIES: Russet, Idaho

Medium-Starch Potatoes
(18 to 20 percent starch)
These potatoes are slightly mealy, a little closer to starchy potatoes than to waxy. These versatile potatoes can be mashed or baked, but they won't be as fluffy as dry, starchy spuds; likewise, they can be used in soups and stews, but don't hold their shape quite as well as firmer waxy potatoes. Many varieties of medium-starch potatoes, such as Yukon Gold and Yellow Finn, are very flavorful.
COMMON VARIETIES: Yukon Gold, Katahdin, Yellow Finn, Kennebec

Low-Starch Potatoes
(16 to 18 percent starch)
Low-starch (or waxy) potatoes hold their shape and texture through moist cooking, and so are a good choice for soups, stews, potato salads, or any boiled application. Freshly dug young potatoes (often called new potatoes) are in this group; their sugars do not convert into starch until the potatoes are older.
COMMON VARIETIES: Red Bliss, French Fingerling, Red Creamer, White Rose

Equipment Roundup

RATINGS
Good = ★★★
Fair = ★★
Poor = ★

INEXPENSIVE 4-SLICE TOASTERS: Is Good Toast Too Much to Expect?

You can spend over $300 on a showpiece toaster that makes impeccable toast every time. But is great toast too much to ask if your budget is $50 (or under)? To find out, we bought eight 4-slot toasters priced under $50 and put them through their paces in the test kitchen, toasting bread, frozen waffles, bagels, and Pop-Tarts.

BASIC TOAST: All toasters included a mechanism to control the degree of toasting. Our first test was to make sure that each machine could produce distinctly light, medium, and dark toast at the corresponding setting; every toaster passed this test.

However, some (including the Sunbeam and Toastmaster) weren't toasting evenly on both sides of the bread. A look inside the toasters revealed the source of the problem. The models that toasted the most evenly, the Michael Graves and the Oster, had a similar number (between nine and 10) of evenly spaced heating elements on each side of the slot. In contrast, the Sunbeam and Toast-master had three extra elements on one side. We wondered if the extra elements were there to toast bagels more on one side, but found that they were of no benefit in any toasting.

CONTINUITY COUNTS: To see how the toasters performed with heavy use, we did a rapid-fire test, making three consecutive rounds of toast on the medium setting. As the toasters heated up, the toasting times got shorter—and the toast progressively lighter. Only the Michael Graves toaster showed minimal differences between the rounds. Rapid-fire toasting also exposed a problem with the Toastmaster—its surface became dangerously hot (approaching 130 degrees); the other models averaged about 90 degrees after three rounds.

ALL-AROUND CHAMPS: In addition to bread, toasters should be able to handle frozen waffles, bagels, and pastries such as Pop-Tarts with ease. All of the toasters came with extra-wide slots that easily accommodated bagels, and all save one (the last-place Toastmaster) had bagel settings that either adjusted the toasting time for a bagel's thickness or toasted only the cut side of the bagel. Three models that toasted only on one side, the Cuisinart, Farberware, and Sunbeam, gave unclear instructions on which way to orient the bagel. The one toaster with a setting for Pop-Tarts, the Toastmaster, actually did the worst job with them; a few good pastries were mangled in the slots of this model.

DESIGN ISSUES: Neatness counts with toasters, and our testers downgraded models with poorly designed crumb trays. Our top three models all featured deep trays that easily slid in and out of the toasters. Our testers preferred toasters with clear and intuitive controls; while the Farberware toaster's controls were intuitive, we downgraded it because the function buttons and carriage levers were split between the side and front of the toaster, making operation more complicated than necessary. Two toasters, the Oster and Sunbeam, lost points because their slots were too short to accommodate our favorite (albeit slightly oversized) sandwich bread from Pepperidge Farm. –Emma Christensen

Highly Recommended
MICHAEL GRAVES DESIGN HAMILTON BEACH 4-Slice Toaster, Model 24301
Price: $34.99 at target.com
Features: Browning control, Bagel, Defrost, Reheat, Cancel
Toast: ★★★
Bagels/Pastries: ★★★
Design: ★★★
Comments: This toaster simply out-performed the others, producing evenly golden toast in test after test. The toaster's carriage held all foods securely and prevented any possibility of items falling through or getting caught. Our sole complaint: This bulky toaster took up more counter space than we'd prefer.

Recommended
KENMORE 4-Slice Toaster, Model 81004
Price: $49.99 at sears.com
Features: Browning control, Bagel, Defrost, Reheat, Cancel
Toast: ★★
Bagels/Pastries: ★★★
Design: ★★★
Comments: The controls on this toaster were well marked and intuitive, and we liked the light-up display around the dial and the backlighting for the "cancel" button. There was minor inconsistency in the color between the two sides of the toast, but not enough for a serious downgrade.

OSTER Inspire 4-Slice Brushed Stainless Steel Toaster, Model 6330
Price: $49.99 at shoposter.com
Features: Browning control, Toast, Bagel, Frozen, Warm, Cancel
Toast: ★★★
Bagels/Pastries: ★★
Design: ★★
Comments: This toaster produced some of the best toast with minimal consistency issues. Its drawbacks were in the design. Billed as a four-slice toaster, we found the two slots just a touch too short to fit four pieces of large sandwich bread, and there were no visual cues for which way to orient a cut bagel (the cut side should face inward). A few testers marked this model down because it lacked separate controls for the two slots.

CUISINART Electronic Cool-Touch 4-Slice Toaster, Model CPT-140
Price: $49.99 at amazon.com
Features: Browning control, Bagel, Defrost, Reheat, Cancel
Toast: ★★
Bagels/Pastries: ★★
Design: ★★★
Comments: This toaster performed admirably in the rapid-fire test, but there was some minor inconsistency between the sides of the toast. Testers loved the intuitiveness of operation and ease of cleaning (the crumb trays were great). There was no visual cue for which way to orient a cut bagel.

Recommended (continued)
BLACK & DECKER 4-Slice Toaster, Model T4560B
Price: $24.88 at walmart.com
Features: Browning control, Bagel, Frozen, Cancel
Toast: ★★
Bagels/Pastries: ★★★
Design: ★★
Comments: This toaster had minor problems toasting both sides of bread evenly, especially at the higher settings, and toast was not consistent in our rapid-fire test. On the bagel setting, however, this model was a champ, nicely browning the cut side while gently warming the exterior. The crumb trays slid in and out easily, but were too shallow and thus messy to empty.

Not Recommended
SUNBEAM 4-Slice Toaster, Model 3823-100
Price: $22.99 at shopsunbeam.com
Features: Browning control, Bagel, Stop
Toast: ★★
Bagels/Pastries: ★★
Design: ★★
Comments: The slots on this toaster were too short for our large sandwich bread. With 11 wires on one side and 14 on the other, the toaster produced inconsistent (but acceptable) toast. Several testers didn't notice the "cancel" button, which blended into the plastic face below the carriage lever. This toaster's crumb tray was too shallow.

FARBERWARE Millennium 4-Slice Toaster, Model FACT450T
Price: $49.99 at amazon.com
Features: Browning control, Cancel, Bagel, Defrost; switch for 2- or 4-slice toasting
Toast: ★★
Bagels/Pastries: ★★
Design: ★
Comments: Because it has controls on both the front and side, we constantly needed to shift the toaster to access the different features. Top-heavy pastries tipped over and toasted unevenly in the angled slots. Even with bread, toasting was spotty and almost the same at light and medium settings. The crumb tray was well designed, but crumbs accumulated in the lower corner of the angled slots and never fell down into the trays.

TOASTMASTER Dual Control 4-Slice Toaster, Model T2040W
Price: $27.00 at amazon.com
Features: Browning control
Toast: ★
Bagels/Pastries: ★★
Design: ★
Comments: Bread had to be run through this toaster a few times before it was adequately toasted; the exterior of the toaster became dangerously hot. The bread guides inside the toaster didn't hold any of the food securely and actually tilted one side of the item closer to the heating element. A trap door released crumbs from the bottom, making "cleaning" messy and awkward.

Notes from Our Test Kitchen

TIPS, TECHNIQUES, AND TOOLS FOR BETTER COOKING

Kitchen Creations
Flavored Butters for Popcorn

Here are three flavored butters that can jazz up a bowl of plain popcorn (they are also great on baked potatoes and steamed vegetables). Each of these flavored butters makes enough to coat about 2 quarts of popcorn (from about ¼ cup raw corn kernels). The recipes can be doubled.

GARLIC AND HERB BUTTER

Melt 2 tablespoons unsalted butter in small skillet over medium heat. Add 1 minced garlic clove and 1 teaspoon minced fresh rosemary, thyme, or dill to pan and cook until fragrant, about 30 seconds. Drizzle butter over popcorn and toss to coat. Season with salt. Serve.

PARMESAN-PEPPER BUTTER

Melt 2 tablespoons unsalted butter in small skillet over medium heat. Add ¼ teaspoon pepper and 1 minced garlic clove to pan and cook until fragrant, about 30 seconds. Drizzle butter over popcorn, then sprinkle with ½ cup grated Parmesan cheese and toss to coat. Season with salt. Serve.

SWEET CURRY BUTTER

Melt 2 tablespoons unsalted butter in small skillet over medium heat. Add 1 tablespoon sugar, ½ teaspoon curry powder, ½ teaspoon garam masala, and ⅛ teaspoon cayenne pepper and cook until fragrant, about 30 seconds. Drizzle butter over popcorn and toss to coat. Season with salt. Serve.

Inside the Test Kitchen
BRÛLÉEING THE CRÈME

To ensure an evenly browned caramelized sugar crust for crème brûlée (such as our Low-Fat Crème Brûlée on page 8), blot the surface of the custard with paper towels to remove excess moisture before brûléeing as instructed below.

1. Sprinkle each custard with sugar, tilting and tapping the ramekins to ensure the sugar is evenly distributed.
2. Use torch to caramelize the sugar by continually sweeping the flame about 2 inches above the ramekin until the sugar turns deep golden brown, keeping a watchful eye to avoid burning.

Kielbasa Tasting

Our **Slow-Cooker Cassoulet** (page 7) calls for a half pound of kielbasa sausage to beef up the flavor of the stew. But with so many brands of kielbasa on the market, which is best? We tested five national supermarket brands and found two that nearly tied for first place. Smithfield Naturally Hickory Smoked Polska Kielbasa ranked slightly higher than Wellshire Farms Polska Kielbasa in our tasting. Both possessed smoky, complex flavor profiles, and tasters preferred their heartier texture to the springy, hot dog–like textures of the other kielbasas. Smithfield kielbasa can be found in national supermarket chains; Wellshire Farms kielbasa is available nationwide at Whole Foods Markets.

OUR FAVORITE KIELBASA
Smithfield Naturally Hickory Smoked Polska Kielbasa

How to MAKE YOUR OWN CHICKEN CUTLETS

Our recipe for **Chicken Piccata** (page 24) calls for thin-cut, boneless, skinless chicken cutlets. As our two favorite brands of chicken, Empire Kosher and Bell & Evans, don't sell thin cutlets, we often make our own in the test kitchen using boneless, skinless breasts. Here's how:

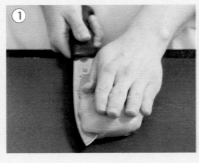 

1. After removing the tenderloin, place each chicken breast, smooth-side up, on a cutting board. Holding one hand on top of the breast, carefully slice the breast in half horizontally to yield two pieces, each about ½ inch thick.

2. For thinner cutlets, cover the halved breasts with plastic and, using a meat pounder, pound them to the desired thickness.

Vanilla Beans 101

In our **Low-Fat Crème Brûlée** (page 8), we prefer the complex flavor of vanilla bean (simmered in dairy) to vanilla extract. Vanilla beans start out as the green seedpod of an orchid that blooms for only one day per year; the blossoms must be hand-pollinated for the pods to form. Once picked, the pods are painstakingly cured and dried for months to develop their intoxicating flavor. When buying vanilla beans, look for plump, pliable pods and avoid those that are dry or shriveled. Wrapped in plastic and refrigerated in an airtight container, vanilla beans will hold their flavor for months. Both the seeds and the pod pack a lot of flavor; removing the seeds from the pod—and then using both elements together—maximizes the vanilla flavor.

To remove vanilla seeds, halve the pod lengthwise and, in one smooth motion, gently scrape seeds from the interior using the flat side of a paring knife.

Panko Primer

To give our **Oven-Fried Shrimp** (page 25) an extra-crispy coating, we turned to panko bread crumbs. These light, flaky crumbs (which originated in Japan) add big crunch and a neutral flavor to fried foods. Once the domain of specialty shops and Asian markets, panko bread crumbs are now available in most supermarkets. But if you can't find them, you can use the following recipe to create a reasonable facsimile at home.

HOMEMADE PANKO

Adjust oven rack to middle position and heat oven to 300 degrees. Remove crust from 5 slices of hearty white sandwich bread, then cut bread into quarters. Process bread through shredding disk of food processor, using the weight of the feed tube to press bread against disk. Transfer crumbs to rimmed baking sheet and bake, stirring occasionally, until crumbs are dry and crisp but not toasted, about 6 minutes. Cool completely. (Crumbs can be stored in airtight container at room temperature for 2 weeks.)

Salad Green Yields

When we develop salad recipes like our **Baked Goat Cheese Salads** (page 19), we typically call for a specific cup-measure of greens. But if you're buying whole heads of lettuce, how do you know how many cups each head will yield? Check the chart below for estimates of lettuce yields and plan on serving 2 to 4 cups of greens per person.

Type	Amount	Yield (cups)
Iceberg	1-pound head	12
Romaine	14-ounce head	10
	6-ounce heart	4
Spinach	11-ounce bunch	6
	5-ounce bag	6
Radicchio	9-ounce head	4
Red or Green Leaf	13-ounce head	12
Mesclun	4-ounce bag	6
Escarole	15-ounce head	15
Bibb	8-ounce head	8
Arugula	6-ounce bunch	4
	5-ounce bag	6

Fresh Lemon Juice Substitutes

When making **Chicken Piccata** (page 24), a fresh lemon with both juice and zest is essential. But when squeezed for time, will anything else do? To find out, we tested six packaged lemon juice products both in lemonade and in a lemon curd. Not surprisingly, none came close to beating the tart, clean, bright flavor of fresh-squeezed lemon juice when tasted in lemonade. But when cooked in the lemon curd, ReaLemon lemon juice from concentrate and True Lemon crystallized lemon juice both capably mimicked the tart acidity of fresh-squeezed lemon juice and were deemed acceptable in a pinch. Both can be found at grocery stores nationwide—ReaLemon in the bottled juice aisle, and True Lemon in the baking aisle.

ACCEPTABLE IN A PINCH
Not for lemonade but okay for some cooked applications

Rating Raisins

Although their color is strikingly different from that of the common purple-black raisin, golden raisins come from the same fruit: green Thompson seedless (also called sultana) grapes. How the fruit is processed accounts for the color variation. While common raisins are dried in the sun for several weeks, golden raisins are mechanically dehydrated and treated with sulfur dioxide to preserve their light color. Setting looks aside, we wondered if there were flavor and textural differences between the two. When we tasted both out of hand and baked into our **Jefferson Davis Pie** (page 9), we found that golden raisins had a "fresher, fruitier" flavor and a moister chew than the tougher, "slightly bitter" common raisins.

Pear Pointers

After purchasing and tasting more than 100 pears for **Getting to Know Pears** (page 23), we learned a few tips about selecting the fruit. First, pears are a climacteric fruit, meaning that they will continue to ripen after they have been harvested. To ensure the best quality fruit, purchase firm pears and let them ripen at room temperature for a few days. (You can speed the ripening process by placing the pears in a closed paper bag.) To check for ripeness, gently press the pear near the stem end; if it gives slightly, the pear is ripe. Because pears ripen from the inside out, don't wait for the round middle section to become soft; by then, the inside will be overripe.

Selecting Sauerkraut

Briny, salty sauerkraut is an essential component of our **Reuben Sandwiches** (page 11). To see which brand of sauerkraut is best, we tasted eight national contenders—in jars, cans, and vacuum-sealed bags—both plain and in a Reuben. Right off the bat, tasters panned the heavily processed (and long-cooked) canned brands as "flaccid and flavorless," "flat." Jarred and bagged brands are cooked less; these generally had more crunch and flavor. Our winning sauerkraut, Boar's Head, is a bagged variety that was praised for its "chewy-crisp" texture and "fresh, vinegary kick." Another bagged brand of sauerkraut, Great Lakes Kraut Co. Krrrrisp Kraut, was our runner-up.

KING OF KRAUT
We liked Boar's Head sauerkraut on Reubens, hot dogs, or served alone as a simple side dish.

Shopping with the Test Kitchen Goat Cheese

Goat cheese (sometimes labeled chèvre) is the principal ingredient in our **Baked Goat Cheese Salads** (page 19). Just like cow's or sheep's milk cheeses, goat cheese can be aged or fresh, soft or firm, domestic or imported, musky or mild, etc. That said, most of what you can buy in supermarkets (and the variety we favor in our salad) is relatively young cheese packaged in a log shape; it has a creamy, slightly grainy texture and a tangy, milky flavor. When shopping for goat cheese, avoid precrumbled cheeses—they tend to be dry and chalky—and be sure to take a close look at the label, as many supermarket goat cheeses include herbs and spices that could affect how you use them. Once opened, goat cheese should be wrapped in parchment or wax paper and can be stored in the refrigerator for up to 2 weeks.

TASTE TEST WINNER
Vermont Butter & Cheese Chèvre has a distinct—but not overpowering—tang that works well in recipes or on its own.

Our **Gingerbread-Pear Trifle** (inside back cover) looks festive and extravagant, but assembling it is really just a matter of simple layering. Working one tier at a time, line the outside of the dish by alternating decorative half-moons of gingerbread with pear fans (photo 1). After the outside elements are in place, fill the interior of the trifle with a single layer of gingerbread scraps, a layer of chopped pears, and then finally a layer of custard (photo 2) spread evenly to the outside of the dish. The finished trifle should have a total of three layers, with whipped cream replacing the custard on the very top.

Kitchen Torches

To get an authentically caramelized crust on **Crème Brûlée** (like our low-fat version on page 8), you need to use a torch. While a regular propane "plumbers' torch" will do the job (its powerful flame requires a gentle touch and watchful eye), we like the pinpoint control offered by mini kitchen torches. To find out which mini kitchen torch was best, we purchased four models and started brûlée-ing. Our favorite was the Bernzomatic ST2200T ($28.99). Compact and easy to use, it has a flame adjuster that allows for precise brûléeing and stays cool to the touch during operation.

OUR FAVORITE TORCH
The Bernzomatic mini torch

When Things Go Wrong in the Kitchen

READERS SHARE FUNNY STORIES ABOUT COOKING MISHAPS

ALMOST A CANDLELIGHT DINNER

For my very first dinner party years ago, I made homemade macaroni and cheese. Everyone dished out healthy helpings of the creamy pasta, but I noticed that as we chatted my guests were eating less and less. I hadn't taken a bite of mine (I was busy keeping the conversation going), but finally sunk my fork into the mound on my own plate. The macaroni and cheese was stiff! I broke off a piece and couldn't believe how solid it was—my guests had fused lumps of pasta on their plates, too. I was embarrassed and went to the kitchen to check the white porcelain pot of mac and cheese. That's when I remembered that the last time I had used that pot, a week before, was to melt paraffin wax to seal the tops of jelly jars. There had been about an inch of leftover wax in the pot that I'd forgotten about and hadn't noticed when I mixed and baked the mac and cheese. With the addition of a wick, that pasta would have made a fine candle.

Bonnie Arendt Sedgwick, Maine

A PEPPER PROBLEM

About 20 years ago I got my first microwave oven. One afternoon, as I was hanging hot cayenne peppers outside to dry in the sun, I had a brainstorm and thought that I could dry them faster in my microwave. Within 5 minutes the whole house filled up with horrid fumes that were burning my family's eyes and noses. The kids upstairs started yelling and running for the front door, and my husband, who had been taking a bath, was screaming for a towel and choking from the burning fumes. He ended up wrapping a shirt around himself and running outside, where we all stood with burning eyes and gasping for breath. I learned not to dry peppers in a microwave—unless you're trying to get rid of unwanted company.

Deborah Suleski Belfast, N.Y.

BURNED AT THE STEAK

It was late in the day and I was in the kitchen teaching my younger sister to pan-fry steak. "Get a couple cups of flour and put in a little salt and pepper," I said. I put the steaks to soak in buttermilk and went to sit down for a bit. A while later, I heard her shouting, "It's burning! It's burning!" I rushed to the kitchen to discover my sister amid a mess of smoky, black steaks. She hadn't cooked the whole batch, so I dipped a couple more in the flour mixture and flopped them into a clean, hot pan with a little oil. Strangely, the steaks seemed to be seeping out a burbling brown liquid. I couldn't figure out what was going wrong. Was the buttermilk old? Too much oil in the pan? It was only after we tasted one of the strangely sweet, burnt steaks that it hit me. "Sis, are you sure you used flour for the steaks?" She showed me the container she'd taken the "flour" out of, and I discovered the reason for her mess: It was powdered sugar.

C. Beer Brookings, Ore.

A VERY LOUD EGG TIMER

After dinner one evening, I decided to make tuna salad for my lunch the next day. I put two eggs on to boil and then started to watch TV. Two hours later there was this tremendous "BANG!" from the kitchen, followed by another "BANG!" five seconds later—it sounded like someone had fired a gun through my back door. I ran to the kitchen to find that I'd forgotten the eggs, which exploded after the pan had boiled dry. There were bits of egg all over the kitchen, even the ceiling, and the stench of burnt sulphur was everywhere. Needless to say, now I always set a timer when I put eggs on to boil.

Beth Rognerud Breckenridge, Colo.

READ THE LABEL

I thought I would impress my husband-to-be by re-creating an amazing rigatoni with vodka-tomato sauce that we'd had at an Italian restaurant. As I was making the sauce, I tasted it periodically to make sure everything was fine. But something was off—I just couldn't put my finger on it. As we sat down to eat, I didn't say anything and neither did he. Finally I asked, "Does this taste strange?" and he said it did. "What did you use?" he asked. "Vodka," I said. "What vodka?" he asked. "The one in the blue bottle." "Oh," he said, "you mean the gin." And then he went in for seconds to prove that he loved me despite my lack of liquor knowledge. Note: Though both are clear, gin and vodka are NOT interchangeable in cooking.

Laura Young Chicago, Ill.

ROLLING IN THE DOUGH

Every year the women of our church raise money by selling yeasted dinner rolls we call "Granny's Hot Buns." Last fall, my friend Julie and I got together at her home in the early morning for the mixing and rising portion of the process. We mixed the yeasty dough by hand and put it to rest in Julie's laundry room. Then we turned on the washer and dryer to provide moist warmth so the dough could rise, closed the door, and began to clean up the kitchen. About 30 minutes later, Julie peeked into the laundry room and shouted, "Holy Schnikees!" The dough had risen over the bowls, spilled off the tables and onto the concrete floor, and was still rising and puffing with a life of its own! We dissolved into laughter at the sight. We were able to salvage enough dough to make over 550 rolls for the church fundraiser, so it wasn't a total loss, but the story lives in church legend even today.

Gwenn Lasswell Spring, Texas

U.S. POSTAL SERVICE STATEMENT OF OWNERSHIP, MANAGEMENT AND CIRCULATION

1. Publication Title: Cook's Country; 2. Publication No. 1552-1990; 3. Filing Date: 9/28/08; 4. Issue Frequency: Dec/Jan, Feb/Mar, Apr/May, Jun/Jul, Aug/Sep, Oct/Nov; 5. No. of Issues Published Annually: 6; 6. Annual Subscription Price: $29.70; 7. Complete Mailing Address of Known Office of Publication: 17 Station Street, Brookline, MA 02445; 8. Complete Mailing Address of Headquarters or General Business Office of Publisher: 17 Station Street, Brookline, MA 02445; 9. Full Names and Complete Mailing Address of Publisher, Editor and Managing Editor: Publisher: Christopher Kimball, 17 Station Street, Brookline, MA 02445; Editor: Christopher Kimball, 17 Station Street, Brookline, MA 02445; Managing Editor: Jack Bishop, 17 Station Street, Brookline, MA 02445; 10. Owner: Boston Common Press Limited Partnership, Christopher Kimball, 17 Station Street, Brookline, MA 02445; 11. Known Bondholders, Mortgagees, and Other Securities: None; 12. Tax Status: Has Not Changed During Preceding 12 Months; 13. Publication Title: Cook's Country; 14. Issue Date for Circulation Data Below: October/November 2008; 15a. Total Number of Copies: 369,129 (Oct/Nov 2008: 387,083); b. Paid Circulation: (1) Mailed Outside-County Paid Subscriptions Stated on PS Form 3541: 286,076 (Oct/Nov 2008: 292,538); (2) Mailed In-County Paid Subscriptions Stated on PS Form 3541: 0 (Oct/Nov 2008: 0); (3) Paid Distribution Outside the Mails Including Sales Through Dealers and Carriers, Street Vendors, Counter Sales, and Other Paid Distribution Outside the USPS: 29,909 (Oct/Nov 2008: 31,319); (4) Paid Distribution by Other Classes of Mail through the USPS: 0 (Oct/Nov 2008: 0); c. Total Paid Distribution: 315,985 (Oct/Nov 2008: 323,857); d. Free or Nominal Rate Distribution: (1) Free or Nominal Rate Outside-County Copies Included on PS Form 3541: 1,016 (Oct/Nov 2008: 1,572); (2) Free or Nominal Rate In-County Copies Included on Form PS 3541: 0 (Oct/Nov 2008: 0); (3) Free or Nominal Rate Copies Mailed at Other Classes Through the USPS: 0 (Oct/Nov 2008: 0); (4) Free or Nominal Rate Distribution Outside the Mail: 65 (Oct/Nov 2008: 65); e. Total Free or Nominal Rate Distribution: 1,081 (Oct/Nov 2008: 1,637); f. Total Distribution: 317,066 (Oct/Nov 2008: 325,494); g. Copies Not Distributed: 52,063 (Oct/Nov 2008: 61,589); h. Total: 369,129 (Oct/Nov 2008: 387,083); i. Percent Paid: 99.66% (Oct/Nov 2008: 99.50%).

Gingerbread-Pear Trifle

Spicy gingerbread is the basis for this fancy holiday trifle made with pears poached in red wine, creamy vanilla custard, and whipped cream.

To make this trifle, you will need:

- 3 cups red wine
- 1 cup sugar
- 1 cinnamon stick
- 1 tablespoon black peppercorns
- 4 pounds firm pears, such as Bosc or Bartlett, peeled, halved lengthwise, and cored
- 1 recipe Bold and Spicy Gingerbread (see page 22)
- 3 cups vanilla custard*, chilled
- 2 cups lightly sweetened whipped cream

For the pears: Bring wine, sugar, cinnamon, and peppercorns to boil in large pot, stirring occasionally, until sugar dissolves. Reduce heat to low, add pears, and simmer, covered, until pears are nearly tender, about 10 minutes.

Remove from heat and let cool to room temperature, about 30 minutes. Refrigerate until chilled, at least 2 hours or up to 3 days. Using slotted spoon, remove pears from liquid and slice thinly crosswise; discard liquid (or reserve for another use). Reserve one 5-slice section from large part of each pear and cut remaining pear into ½-inch pieces.

For the cake: Slice gingerbread into ½-inch-thick pieces. Cut each piece in half horizontally. Reserve top halves for decorating and cut remaining scraps into ½-inch chunks.

To assemble: Place reserved pear slices on clean surface and press gently with palm of hand to spread pears into fan shape. Following photos 1 and 2 on page 31, arrange reserved cake halves and pear fans around base of 3-quart trifle dish. Place single layer of gingerbread scraps in center of dish and top with single layer of chopped pear pieces. Spread 1½ cups custard over pear pieces. Repeat layering once more, then top with final layer of gingerbread halves, pear fans, gingerbread scraps, and pear pieces. Spoon whipped cream over trifle. Serve. (Trifle can be refrigerated for 6 hours.)

*Go to CooksCountry.com for our vanilla custard recipe or use your own.

Recipe Index